北京外国语大学"奋进之举"项目成果

当代西方中国学研究英文书目选粹
（1949—2019）

学苑出版社

图书在版编目（CIP）数据

当代西方中国学研究英文书目选粹：1949-2019 / 管永前编 . -- 北京：学苑出版社，2021.8
ISBN 978-7-5077-6236-5

Ⅰ.①当… Ⅱ.①管… Ⅲ.①中国学—研究—英文—图书目录—汇编—西方国家— 1949-2019 Ⅳ. ① Z88：K207.8

中国版本图书馆 CIP 数据核字（2021）第 162380 号

责任编辑：	潘占伟　李　媛
出版发行：	学苑出版社
社　　址：	北京市丰台区南方庄 2 号院 1 号楼
邮政编码：	100079
网　　址：	www.book001.com
电子信箱：	xueyuanpress@163.com
联系电话：	010-67601101（销售部）、010-67603091（总编室）
印 刷 厂：	北京建宏印刷有限公司
开本尺寸：	787×1092　1/16
印　　张：	34
字　　数：	825 千字
版　　次：	2021 年 9 月第 1 版
印　　次：	2021 年 9 月第 1 次印刷
定　　价：	188.00 元

目 录

前 言 001

1. 中国总论 001
    1.1 总论 001
    1.2 中国形象 006
2. 中国历史与地理 009
    2.1 历史 009
        2.1.1 通史 009
        2.1.2 古代中国 011
            2.1.2.1 总论 011
            2.1.2.2 商、周、秦、汉、隋、唐 012
            2.1.2.3 宋、辽、元、明 015
        2.1.3 清代 018
        2.1.4 近现代 023
        2.1.5 史学 027
        2.1.6 考古 030
        2.1.7 哈佛中国史系列 031
        2.1.8 剑桥中国史系列 031
    2.2 游记与地方史 032
        2.2.1 北京 032
        2.2.2 上海 035
        2.2.3 广东/广州 041
        2.2.4 旅游及其他 041
        2.2.5 何伟游记系列 046
        2.2.6 地理 047
    2.3 中国边疆 047
        2.3.1 西藏 047
        2.3.2 新疆 052

2.3.3	南海/东海	053
2.3.4	边疆	054
2.4	台、港、澳	056
2.4.1	中国台湾	056
2.4.2	中国香港	058
2.4.3	中国澳门	061

3. 中国哲学与宗教 062

- 3.1 哲学 062
  - 3.1.1 美学 068
- 3.2 宗教 068
  - 3.2.1 中国宗教 068
  - 3.2.2 基督教 072
    - 3.2.2.1 天主教 077
    - 3.2.2.2 传教士 078
  - 3.2.3 伊斯兰教 081
  - 3.2.4 佛教 083
  - 3.2.5 道教 088

4. 中国文学与艺术 092

- 4.1 文学 092
- 4.2 诗歌 105
- 4.3 戏剧 108
- 4.4 神话/传说 112
- 4.5 艺术、创意、收藏 113
- 4.6 绘画、书法、摄影、服饰 120
- 4.7 音乐、舞蹈 123

5. 中国语言与文字 126

- 5.1 语言 126
- 5.2 文字、词典 137
- 5.3 翻译学 140

6. 中国文化与文明 143

- 6.1 文化总论 143
- 6.2 儒学与经典 152
  - 6.2.1 儒学 152

		6.2.2	孔子	160

- 6.2.2 孔子 … 160
- 6.2.3 《论语》 … 163
- 6.2.4 老子、庄子与《道德经》 … 165
- 6.2.5 《易经》 … 167
- 6.2.6 传统经典与诸子百家 … 168

6.3 思想与文明 … 171
- 6.3.1 思想传统 … 171
- 6.3.2 中外思维 … 173
- 6.3.3 现代主义 … 173
- 6.3.4 左派与后现代 … 174
- 6.3.5 乌托邦 … 175
- 6.3.6 东方主义 … 176
- 6.3.7 人类文明 … 176
  - 6.3.7.1 长城 … 179
  - 6.3.7.2 瓷器 … 179

6.4 教育 … 180
- 6.4.1 孔子学院 … 190
- 6.4.2 心理学 … 191

6.5 知识分子 … 192

6.6 传媒与网络 … 195
- 6.6.1 新闻媒体 … 195
- 6.6.2 电影 … 198
- 6.6.3 互联网 … 202
- 6.6.4 出版印刷 … 203
- 6.6.5 传播学 … 204

6.7 医学 … 205
- 6.7.1 医学与医疗 … 205
- 6.7.2 中医与中药 … 208
- 6.7.3 疾病与防控 … 215
- 6.7.4 气功 … 217

6.8 园林建筑 … 218

6.9 食品与饮食 … 220

6.10 武术 … 225

7. 中国社会与族群 … 227

7.1 儿童 … 227

7.2 婚姻家庭 … 229

7.3	女性	232
7.4	男性	240
7.5	性别	241
7.6	性文化	242
7.7	人口	244
7.8	老龄、保健	246
7.9	就业、阶层与移民	247
7.10	贫困	249
7.11	社会生活/社会学	250
7.12	仪式、丧葬、巫术与民俗	254
	7.12.1 仪式与丧葬	254
	7.12.2 巫术、鬼神	255
	7.12.3 秘密会社、民俗	256
7.13	人类学	256
7.14	族群与宗族	257
	7.14.1 族群	257
	7.14.2 宗族	260
	7.14.3 犹太人	261

8. 中国政治与外交 … 263

8.1	政治	263
	8.1.1 研究总论	263
	8.1.2 中国共产党	264
	8.1.3 毛泽东	270
	8.1.4 中国道路/中国梦	279
	8.1.5 中国崛起	283
	8.1.6 改革与转型	288
	8.1.7 中国革命	291
	8.1.8 中国治理	297
	8.1.9 政治体制	300
	8.1.10 民主建设/劳工关系	302
	8.1.11 公民社会/非政府组织	304
	8.1.12 公民权利	304
	8.1.13 政治思想	305
	8.1.14 政治文化	306
	8.1.15 政治精英	307
	8.1.16 话语建设	307

	8.1.17	软实力	308
	8.1.18	民族主义/民族国家	309
	8.1.19	国家建设	311
	8.1.20	长征	313
	8.1.21	国际共运	313
	8.1.22	马克思主义	313
	8.1.23	中国与资本主义	316
	8.1.24	智库	317
8.2	外交		317
8.3	国际关系		322
	8.3.1	中国与美国	322
	8.3.2	中国与苏联/俄罗斯	338
	8.3.3	中国与日本	341
	8.3.4	中国与英国	346
	8.3.5	中国与印度	349
	8.3.6	中国与欧洲	354
	8.3.7	中国与非洲	357
	8.3.8	中国与越南	360
	8.3.9	中国与东盟	361
	8.3.10	中国与亚洲	361
		8.3.10.1 亚洲研究	365
	8.3.11	中国与世界/其他国家和地区	368

9. 中国法律与军事 373

9.1	法律与法治		373
9.2	军事与战争		382
	9.2.1	抗日战争	382
	9.2.2	南京大屠杀	384
	9.2.3	朝鲜战争	385
	9.2.4	冷战	386
	9.2.5	鸦片战争	389
	9.2.6	中外战争	390
	9.2.7	战争文化与生态	393
	9.2.8	内战与军史	394
	9.2.9	军事与军力	395
	9.2.10	核力量	399
	9.2.11	美军在中国	399

10. 中国经济与自然 ······ 401

    10.1 经济增长与发展 ······ 401

    10.2 经济管理与改革 ······ 409

    10.3 财政与金融、投资 ······ 415

    10.4 工业与产业 ······ 422

        10.4.1 物流运输 ······ 426

    10.5 商业与贸易 ······ 427

    10.6 企业与创业 ······ 433

    10.7 城市 ······ 439

    10.8 农业与农村 ······ 443

    10.9 科技与自然 ······ 451

        10.9.1 科学技术 ······ 451

        10.9.2 创新 ······ 455

        10.9.3 动植物 ······ 456

        10.9.4 天文太空 ······ 458

        10.9.5 数理化 ······ 459

    10.10 水利、环保、能源 ······ 460

        10.10.1 气候水利 ······ 460

        10.10.2 环保生态 ······ 464

        10.10.3 能源 ······ 468

    10.11 人力资源 ······ 471

11. 中西交通 ······ 473

    11.1 总论 ······ 473

    11.2 丝绸之路/一带一路 ······ 482

    11.3 全球化 ······ 486

    11.4 华侨与移民 ······ 491

12. 中国研究参考 ······ 504

    12.1 中国学研究 ······ 504

        12.1.1 汉学家与中国学家 ······ 508

        12.1.2 区域研究 ······ 509

    12.2 工具书 ······ 509

        12.2.1 传记回忆录 ······ 512

        12.2.2 皇后传略 ······ 516

致　谢 ······ 518

前　言

目录学是开启人类智慧之门的钥匙，它教会人们在浩瀚的文献和知识的海洋中，迅速、准确地找到自己所需要的知识。清代史学家王鸣盛在《十七史商榷》第一卷中说："目录之学，学中第一要紧事。必从此问途，方能得其门而入。然此事非苦学精究，质之良师，未易明也。"又说："凡读书最切要者，目录之学。目录明，方可读书，不明，终是乱读。"[1]清末洋务派代表人物张之洞在《书目答问》中开卷就说："诸生好学者来问应读何书，书以何本为善。偏举既嫌絓漏，志趣学业亦各不同，因录此告初学。"[2]张之洞分别从经、史、子、集、丛书五个方面，列出了2200余种图书，每本书皆注明作者、版本、卷数的异同。为了指引初学者选读，又择要略加按语。近代目录学家余嘉锡在其所著《目录学发微》一书中说道："目录学为读书引导之资。凡承学之士，皆不可不涉其藩篱。"[3]1926年10月26日，法国著名汉学家伯希和（Paul Pelliot, 1878—1945）在一场演讲中曾明确指出："治'中国学'须有三方面的预备：（1）目录学与藏书；（2）实物的收集；（3）与中国学者的接近。"[4]当代海外汉学研究大家张西平先生则多次呼吁"海外汉学文献学亟待建立"，"加强海外汉学目录学的研究"。[5]这些中外学人都以切身体会，强调目录学是读书治学的入门之学。可见，读书治学，宜得门径，得门而入，事半功倍。做学问要从研究书目入手，这是治学的常识，也是经验之谈。做中国的学问如此，做海外汉学（中国学）研究也是如此。

长期以来，国外有关中国问题的研究被称为"汉学"。张西平先生认为，西方汉学的发展历史大体经历了"游记汉学""传教士汉学""专业汉学"三个阶段。"游记汉学"的代表人物是马可·波罗（Marco Polo, 1254—1324），"传教士汉学"的开启者是

---

[1]（清）王鸣盛：《十七史商榷》，上海：上海书店出版社，2005年版。
[2]（清）张之洞：《书目答问》，上海：商务印书馆，1925年版。
[3] 余嘉锡：《目录学发微》，北京：中国人民大学出版社，2004年版，第17页。
[4] 胡适：《胡适全集》（第30卷），安徽教育出版社，2003年版，第396页。
[5] 张西平：《加强海外汉学目录学的研究》，《国际汉学》2019年增刊，第123页。

罗明坚（Michele Ruggleri, 1543—1607）和利玛窦（Matteo Ricci, 1552—1610），"专业汉学"的首位汉学家是雷慕沙（Jean Pierre Abel-Rémusat, 1788—1832）。[1]西方汉学（Sinology）始于欧洲，其中西班牙、意大利、荷兰、法国、德国、瑞典等国是汉学开展较早的国家，传教士曾发挥了重要作用。1814年，法兰西学院开设了欧洲第一个汉学讲座，雷慕沙任讲座教授，这是汉学作为一门学科在西方诞生的标志。此后，汉学开始进入西方各国大学，确立了独立的学科地位，法国的儒莲（Stanislas Julien, 1797—1873）、沙畹（Edouard Chavannes, 1865—1918）、伯希和（Paul Pelliot, 1878—1945）、马伯乐（Henri Maspero, 1883—1945），德国的福兰阁（Otto Franke, 1863—1946）和傅吾康（Wolfgang Franke, 1912—2007）父子，瑞典的高本汉（Klas Bernhard Johannes Karlgren, 1889—1978）等都对汉学（中国学）研究有重大贡献。

如果从"游记汉学"算起，西方汉学至今已有700多年历史；如果从"传教士汉学"算起，至今有400多年历史；如果从"专业汉学"算起，至今也有200多年历史。其特点是以研究中国的哲学、宗教、艺术、历史、文学、语言等人文学科为主，对政治、经济、军事、教育等社会科学领域的研究涉猎较少。第二次世界大战后，特别是中华人民共和国成立以来，以美国为代表的西方汉学开始转向专注于对中国当代事务的研究，"它完全打破了传统汉学的狭隘的学科界限，将社会科学的各种理论、方法、手段融入汉学研究和中国历史研究之中，从而大大开阔了研究者的研究视野，丰富了中国研究的内容"[2]，在国际上成为具有现代意识、更多地具有社会科学内容的汉学——"中国学"（chinese studies）。"中国学"所关心的不完全是中国的传统文化，更多的是中国的政治、经济、军事、教育和社会生活、社会心理等各个层面的问题。"中国学"以现实为中心，以实用为原则，以国家战略利益为考量，以非文化或者泛文化为特征，极大地影响了传统汉学的研究方向和内容，其影响力甚至超过了传统汉学。

与欧洲的汉学研究传统不同，美国的中国研究诞生于区域研究（regional studies或area studies）的框架之下。它强调现实性，认为历史研究不是象牙塔式的学问，不是只有少数学术大师才能够理解和精通的书斋式的学问，研究历史的目的是为了更好地了解现实，是为了将研究成果介绍给广大读者群体，其中包括学生、政策制定者、政策咨询机构以及广大读者。美国的中国研究，因基于美国人寻求了解中国现状的急切需求，媒体人员与学者纷纷报道有关中国的讯息，媒体的注意重点在政治与战争，学者的研究课题则超越了传统的"汉学"，不再局限于文史语文为主的范围。卜凯（John L. Buck,

---

[1] 张西平：《欧洲早期汉学史》，北京：中华书局，2009年版。
[2] 侯且岸：《当代美国的"显学"——美国现代中国学研究》，北京：人民出版社，1995年版，第12页。

1890—1975）、[1]葛德石（George B. Cressey, 1895—1953）、[2]德效赛（Homer H. Dubs, 1892—1969）、施坚雅（G. William Skinner, 1925—2008）、莫顿·弗莱德（Morton H. Fried, 1923—1986）[3]等人的研究广泛包含了社会结构、地理条件、劳动力、自然资源等课题。他们的著作至今还有相当的价值。在中国抗战前及战时，有不少美国文史哲学者来华，例如顾立雅（Herrlee G. Creel, 1905—1994）、费正清（John K. Fairbank, 1907—1991）、德克·卜德（Derk Bodde, 1909—2003）等。在中国抗战及内战期间，也有许多中国学者到美国执教，如赵元任（Chao Yuen Ren, 1892—1982）、李方桂（Li Fang-Kuei, 1902—1987）、萧公权（Hsiao Kung-chuan, 1897—1931）、洪业（William Hung, 1893—1980）、邓嗣禹（Teng Ssu-yu, 1905—1988）、杨联升（Yang Lien-Sheng, 1914—1990）、刘子健（James T. C. Liu, 1919—1993）、杨庆堃（Yang C. K., 1911—1999）、许烺光（Francis L. K. Hsu, 1909—1999）、刘大中（Liu Ta-Chung, 1914—1975）、周舜莘（Chou Hsun-hsin, 1915—2001）、何炳棣（Ho Ping-ti, 1917—2012）、袁同礼（Yuan Tung-li, 1895—1965）等。他们谙熟中文资料，又能掌握当代的研究方法，对于美国的中国研究发挥了关键作用。同时，美国学者傅路德（Luther G. Goodrich, 1894—1986）、恒慕义（Arthur W. Hummel, 1884—1975）、狄百瑞（William Theodore De Bary, 1919—2017）等人与中国学术圈也有颇多切磋。他们吸收了当代中国学者的研究成果，辅以西方的研究方法，很多人成为中国研究的一代宗师。

二战后，美国成为西方世界的中心。美国《退伍军人权利法案》（*Servicemen's Readjustment Act of 1944*）资助复员军人深造，公私基金会设立研究资助计划，战后大学进行扩张等，都使美国的"区域研究"有了空前发展，其中尤以"中国研究"为重点。美国高等教育和科研机构广泛参与中国研究的国际学术交流活动，美国出版的各种学术期刊为中国研究领域的建立提供发表成果、开展争鸣的论坛，特别是一批研究资助机构成为推动中国研究的重要力量，其中包括美国国家人文基金会（National Endowment for the Humanities）、美国学术团体联合会（American Council of Learned Societies）、美国社会科学研究理事会（Social Science Research Council）、美国亚洲研究协会（Association

---

[1] 卜凯（John Lossing Buck, 1890年11月27日—1975年9月27日），美国农业经济学家，专精中国农村经济，中国金陵大学农业经济系首任系主任（1925—？），1931年江淮水灾后走访灾区写成*The 1931 Flood in China: An Economic Survey*，被誉为该水灾里唯一可靠的用现代方法计算死亡的文献。1914—1944年留华。与赛珍珠（Pearl S. Buck）结婚，1935年离婚。

[2] 葛德石（George Babcock Cressey, 1896年12月5日—1963年10月21日），美国地理学家，作家，学者。出生于俄亥俄州的蒂芬，先后就读于丹尼森大学和芝加哥大学，并在芝加哥大学取得地质学博士学位。后来到了中国，在上海沪江大学任教，并在中国广泛游历。1929年回到美国，1934完成关于中国的著作——《中国的地理基础》（*China's Geographic Foundations*）。

[3] 莫顿·弗莱德（Morton H. Fried, 1923年3月21日—1986年12月18日），美国人类学家，著有《中国社会的结构——一个中国县城的社会生活》（*Fabric of Chinese Society: A Study of the Social Life of a Chinese County Seat.* New York: Octagon Books, 1953, 1969）。该书为关于中国东部楚县的人类学研究著作，研究家庭、世系和非世系关系，以及对中国人生活的影响。

of Asian Studies）、福特基金会（Ford Foundation）、梅隆基金会（Andrew W. Mellon Foundation）、亨利·卢斯基金会（Henry Luce Foundation）等。这些机构设立中国研究基金，资助有关中国研究项目，组织中国研究专题学术会议，出版了大量中国研究成果。

根据许倬云的观察，20世纪60年代以来，美国各处公私大学设立中国研究专业者，不下百余所。其中大型中心有十余处，中型中心有十余处。大多院校中会有三五位中国研究人员，分别在人文社会学科执教。20世纪50至60年代培养的学者，早期有贺凯（Charles O. Hucker, 1919—1994）、芮沃寿（Arthur Wright, 1913—1976）、芮玛丽（Mary C. Wright, 1917—1970）、史华慈（Benjamin I. Schwartz, 1916—1999）、列文森（Joseph R. Levenson, 1920—1969）、傅礼初（Joseph Fletcher, 1934—1984）等人，后期有魏斐德（Frederic Wakeman, Jr, 1937—2006）、史景迁（Jonathan D. Spence, 1936— ）、伊佩霞（Patricia Buckley Ebrey, 1947— ）、白威廉（William L. Parish）、罗斯基（Thomas G. Rawski, 1943— ）和罗友枝（Evelyn S. Rawski, 1939— ）夫妇、孔飞力（Philip A. Kuhn, 1933—2016）、保罗·柯文（Paul A. Cohen, 1934— ）、马若德（Roderick MacFarquhar, 1930—2019）、傅高义（Ezra F. Vogel, 1930—2020）等人，都卓然有成。美国的中国研究规模已颇为宏大，美国亚洲研究协会（Association of Asian Studies，简称AAS）的年会会员人数，也有三五千人之多。[1]

20世纪50至80年代，美国的中国研究范围几乎涵盖了人文社会学科的各个领域：文化传统、社会结构与变动、经济形态的变化、族群关系、国家权力、中央与地方、城乡关系、宗教与民俗、经典文学、艺术、音乐等。20世纪80年代后，中国逐渐崛起，研究中国成为世界热门。一些年轻学者感受时代风气，选择研究课题时逐渐改变了趋向：平民生活与心态、地方与边陲、妇女、劳工、农民与弱者地位、生态环境等种种问题成为学者关心之所在，一改过去以帝王将相、国家制度、战争与外交、思想大师等为研究重点的传统。从最近二三十年的变化，可以看到一些趋势：无论是人文社会学科，抑或是中国研究的范围，研究课题逐渐由国家转向社会，由精英思想转向平民心态，由典章制度转向日常生活，由使用文献转向访谈与计量，由关心主流转向关心弱势，由宗教研究转向信仰与仪式，由个别人物转向一般民众，由静态结构转向动态运动，由单一现象转向多项的整体讨论，经济之外还注意生态与天人关系等。[2]不过，议题分散也可能造成无法聚焦的后果，以致虽有陈述却不易分析，数量增加却难有累计增长。虽然学术探索领域开拓了，却可能蔓延而难以阐释其义。任何学术研究人员，尤其是"地区研究"的学

---

[1] 许倬云：《序》，载张海惠主编《北美中国学：研究概述与文献资源》，北京：中华书局，2010年版，第4页。

[2] 同上，第5—6页。

者,都必须具备能出能入的反省功夫,既能从情境外做客观的观察,又能进入情境,领悟、体会其不着言诠之处,如此回还映照,方能得到适当分寸的表运陈述。再进一步阐释解读,终于建构理论,以抽绎其普遍性的意义。[1]这是一个拓荒的时代,如何整合,有待学术界的共同努力。

随着中西交通的不断拓展,数百年来西方各种语言的汉学研究成果可谓层出不穷、汗牛充栋。对于世界各地的中国关注者来说,要想掌握有关中国的基础知识,研究中国的某一方面,了解谁做过相同的研究或者出版过多少相关文献,需要一本全面、权威且最新的中国研究书目。这样不仅可以节省许多搜集、整理的精力,获取最直接、最实用的参考,也可尽量避免重复前人已经充分研究或涉及的主题。事实上,随着中国研究文献数量的迅猛增长,西方研究中国问题的各种书目相继出现,从精而细的专题书目到大而全的综合性书目陆续出版。其中,具有代表性的研究书目主要有以下几种:

一是法国汉学家考狄(Henri Cordier, 1849—1925)主编的《西人论中国书目》(*Bibliotheca Sinica*)。[2]这是西方第一部综合性汉学(中国学)书目,为西方自16世纪中叶至1924年关于中国文献的总目,包括用各种欧洲语言写成的有关中国的专著和文章,甚至小启事和书评,不论在何地出版,都几乎尽数囊括。它对于早期西方的中国研究有不可替代的指南作用,至今仍是欧美研究中国问题学者的必读书,可谓是迄今为止内容最为全面、最为丰富的一部法文汉学书目。

考狄又译高第,1849年8月8日出生于美国新奥尔良,1852年随全家移居法国巴黎,本人先后在巴黎和英国接受教育。1869年进入中国,两年后成为"皇家亚洲协会"中国北方分部的图书管理员,由此开始了他的汉学生涯。1876年他离开中国,1880年获法兰西学院儒莲奖(Stanislas Julien Prize),1925年3月16日去世。考狄治学广泛,一生共计撰写了1000多部(篇)著述,主要以远东历史、地理,尤其是西方在中国的事业(探险、商业、政治)史为中心。他是重要的东方学刊物《通报》(*T'oung Pao*)杂志创办人,在汉学和东方学文献方面的成就非常大,但其一生影响最大的还是编写《西人论中国书目》和创办《通报》这两件事。《西人论中国书目》第一版共3卷,1878年在巴黎首次出版第1卷第1分册,其余卷册于1879—1885年相继出版。第二版共5卷,1904—1908年出版前4卷,1922—1924年又增补1卷。全部5卷收录总篇目近7万条。此后国内外以第二版为底本多次再版。2016年,中华书局出版了此书的中译本,该版本扩展为6卷,增加德国汉学家、目录学家魏汉茂(Hartmut Walravens)编制的人名索引。

---

[1] 许倬云:《序》,载张海惠主编《北美中国学:研究概述与文献资源》,北京:中华书局,2010年版,第7页。
[2] 该书全称为:*Bibliotheca Sinica: Dictionnaire Bibliographique des Ouvrages Relatives à l'Empire Chinois*,直译为《中国书目:有关中华帝国著述的书目词典》。

《西人论中国书目》虽以法文为出版语言，但所收文献语言不拘，涉及英语、法语、拉丁语、德语、意大利语、西班牙语、葡萄牙语、俄语等欧洲主要语种。与此前面世的少则数十条、多不过数千条的相关书目相比，不管是以收录规模论，还是以文献语种论，该书都可称得上是前所未有的恢宏巨制。作为一部力求"合理编排"的综合性书目，《西人论中国书目》在编纂时极尽网罗之能，除了确证无从判断的信息外，几乎不做主观的取舍，基本做到了对所有重要书目对象的收录登记。[1]

　　二是中国学者袁同礼（1895—1965）主编的《西方文献里的中国——续考狄之〈汉学书目〉》（*China in Western Literature: A Continuation of Cordier's Bibliotheca Sinica*）。这本书1958年出版，是继考狄后西方汉学界当时最全的汉学研究著作目录。全书收录1921—1957年以英、法、德文（包含部分研究澳门的葡萄牙文）出版的18000种有关中国的著述，不包括期刊论文（论文以专题文章形式单独出版的除外）。按主题编排，包含28个大类，分别是"书目与参考书""总论性著作""地理与游记""历史""传记""政治与政府""陆海空军""法律法规""外交关系""经济与工商业""社会状况与问题""哲学""宗教""教育""语言""文学""考古与美术""音乐与运动""自然科学""农业与林业""医药与公共卫生""东北各省（满洲）""蒙古与蒙古人（包括唐努-图瓦）""西藏""新疆""台湾""香港""澳门"。各大类下再按一定标准分为若干二级类目。书目正文还有更详细的分类，但未能在分类目次中体现。每类下的条目按责任者名称升序排列。书前有缩略语解释，书中设有"互见"（see also），书后有附录（连续出版物和补遗）和索引（人名索引和中文书名索引）。[2]

　　此外，袁同礼还编制了一系列汉学书目，分别是：

　　《俄文汉学书目》（*Russian Works on China 1918—1958: A Selected Bibliography*, 1959）：收录1918—1958年间出版的研究中国（不包括边疆地区如蒙古、西藏、新疆）的俄文专著318种，主要集中在历史文化领域。

　　《美国图书馆藏俄文汉学书目》（*Russian Works on China, 1918—1960 in American Libraries*, 1961）：收录1918—1960年间出版的研究中国的俄文专著1348种。

　　《中国音乐书谱目录》（*Bibliography on Chinese Music*）：收录古今中外有关中国音乐的论著。袁同礼原编有343种（中文290种、英法德文53种），梁在平增订了138种（中文133种、英法德日文5种），又收入Waterman等人编录的中国西文音乐目录378种，共计859种。

　　《现代中国经济社会发展目录》（*Economic and Social Development of Modern China:*

---

[1] 王兴：《纲纪簿属　遗泽流风——法国汉学家考狄埃编〈中国书目〉刍探》，《国家图书馆学刊》，2014年第6期，第108-113页。

[2] 潘梅：《袁同礼晚年的目录著作及其价值》，《大学图书馆学报》，2011年第4期，第101-110页。

A Bibliographical Guide, 1956）：收录20世纪初—1955年底用英、法、德文出版的关于现代中国社会经济发展的专著和小册子。在书目后编制了中国学者的中外文名字对照表。

《新疆研究文献目录：1886—1962》（日文本，*Classified Bibliography of Japanese Books and Articles concerning SINKIANG*）：由袁同礼、渡边宏合编，收录1886—1962年间在日本刊行的日本学者有关新疆之著作、论文、翻译作品等1166种。

《现代中国数学研究目录：1918—1960》（*Bibliography of Chinese Mathematics 1918—1960*, 1963）：收录1918—1960年间用西方语言发表的数学专著和论文，并选录数学家在相关领域的部分论文，如弹性力学、液体力学、量子力学、流体动力学、热力学、计算力学、应用统计学等。目录既包含西方学者的研究，也包含中国学者的研究，对中国科技史的研究具有重要价值。

《中国艺术考古西文目录》（*The T. L. Yuan Bibliography of Western Writings on Chinese Art and Archaeology*, 1975）：袁同礼去世后，由美国芝加哥大学范德本（Harrie A. Vanderstappen）教授进行整理编辑，1975年伦敦Mansell出版社出版。收录1920—1965年间（也包括1920年前的一些主要成果）用英语、德语、荷兰语、斯堪的纳维亚语、斯拉夫语、法语及其他罗马语言出版的有关中国艺术及考古（也包括蒙古、中亚、韩国和日本出版的与中国有关的材料）的15000条文献，包含图书、评论、展览目录、期刊文章等类型。

《中国留美同学博士论文目录：1905—1960》（*A Guide to Doctoral Dissertations by Chinese Students in America 1905—1960*）：收录1905—1960年间中国留美同学博士论文2789篇，并附中国留学加拿大同学博士论文28篇。

《中国留英同学博士论文目录：1916—1961》（*Doctroral Dissertations by Chinese Students in Great Britain and North Ireland 1916—1961*）：收录1916—1961年间中国留英学生博士论文346篇。

《中国留学欧洲大陆各国博士论文目录：1907—1962》（*A Guide to Doctoral Dissertations by Chinese Students in Continental Europe 1907—1962*）：收录1907—1962年间中国留学法国、比利时、瑞士、德国、奥地利、荷兰、意大利、西班牙8国同学博士论文1574篇。

《美国国会图书馆藏中国善本书目》（*A Descriptive Catalog of Rare Chinese Books in the Library of Congress*）：王重民辑录，袁同礼重校，共收录1777部国会图书馆藏中国善本书籍。其中善本宋代11部，金代1部，元代14部，明代1518部，清代70部；手稿140部；在韩国出版者11部，在日本出版者11部；拓本1部。

《胡适先生西文著作目录》（*Bibliography of Dr. Hu Shih's Writings in Western Languages*）：由袁同礼与尤金·德拉菲尔德（Eugene L. Delafield）合编，收录胡适先生西文著作目录237种。

通过以上基本目录我们可以看出，袁同礼书目在西方汉学史上具有重要的学术价值。袁同礼作为中国近代图书馆事业的奠基人，不仅在中国图书馆事业的发展上呕心沥血，做出了巨大的贡献，而且在西方汉学文献学、目录学上也有着重大的贡献，无论是在汉学目录收集的范围上还是数量上都已经大大超越了他的前辈考狄。如果说考狄书目主要反映的是以法国为代表的西方汉学的早期研究进展，那么袁同礼书目则反映了以美国为代表的西方汉学的研究进展。这两部书目都以其完整性和准确性受到西方汉学界的一致好评，成为西方汉学研究的必备的重要参考书。[1]

三是英国学者约翰·鲁斯特（John Lust）主编的《外文期刊有关中国论文索引》（Index Sinicus: A Catalogue of Articles Relating to China in Periodicals and Other Collective Publications, 1920—1955, 1964）。该索引1964年出版，为袁同礼先生所编书目的姊妹篇。它专收1920—1955年间用西方语言出版的期刊论文、纪念文集、会议录和学术讨论集，共2万余篇文章，同时还兼收重要的评论和讣告，但不收专著，与《西方文献里的中国——续考狄之〈汉学书目〉》一起，完整地反映了20世纪20年代到50年代西方中国学研究的实际水平，同时又弥补了袁氏书目的不足。该书目有著者索引和主题索引，使用非常方便。

四是美国中国学家施坚雅（G. William Skinner）主编的《近代中国社会研究论著类目索引》（Modern Chinese Society: An Analytical Bibliography, Publications in Western Languages, 1644—1972）。[2]该书目共3卷，1973年由斯坦福大学出版社出版，是中国学领域里第一部利用电子计算机的代表作。这部书目规模巨大，著录与注释文献31441种，是从9万余种文献中精选出来的，对1970年以前中国（包括港、澳、台）、日本和欧美地区出版的中国社会史研究成果进行了比较全面的分类整理。该书共设6种索引，即综合性索引、历史索引、地理索引、地方索引、编著者姓名索引和编著者机关索引。除综合性索引外，其他5种索引全部由电子计算机编制，是一部大型的分类与注释性索引，它不仅可以起一般索引的作用，而且起指导与启发研究的作用。该书目分成三个独立的部分，即西文、中文与日文。遗憾的是用俄文写的出版物和俄文目录没有收录。[3]

除上述四种外，西方综合性中国研究书目还有：美国亚洲学会（Association for Asian Studies）主编的分作者索引和主题索引的14卷本的《亚洲研究书目集成（1941—1970）》（Cumulative Bibliography of Asian Studies, 1941—1970, 1969—1970），金鹏程

---

[1] 张西平：《袁同礼：中国西方汉学文献学的奠基人》，《甘肃社会科学》，2020年第3期，第115-122页。

[2] G. William Skinner (ed.), *Modern Chinese Society: An Analytical Bibliography, Publications in Western Languages, 1644—1972*, 3 Vols. Stanford: Stanford University Press, 1973.

[3] 张锡高、李迁：《西文中国学书目简评——兼论我们的任务》，《大学图书馆学报》，1990年第5期，第35-37页。

（Paul R. Goldin）主编的《西方中国学研究文献总目》（在线更新，最近一次更新到2020年8月1日），[1]马利克（Lubna Malik）和白霖（Lynn White）主编的《普林斯顿中国书目》（在线，2007—2008），[2]那宗训（Zongxun Na）主编的《英语世界的中国研究：精选参考书目》（1991），[3]钱存训（Tsuen-hsuin Tsien）编著的《中国书目解题汇编》（1978），[4]大卫·威兹曼（David Weitzman）编著的《中国学平装书目》（1967）等。

其他专题性书目主要有：

1.关于文化、历史、哲学和语言：鲁惟一（Michael Loewe）主编的《中国古代文献书目指南》（1993），[5]诺尔曼·坦尼斯（Norman E. Tanis）等人主编的《书里的中国：西方语言基本参考书目》（1979），[6]阿尔伯托·桑切斯（Alberto R. Sanchez）主编的《中国文化在美国：附注释书目》（1977），[7]陈荣捷（Wing-Tsit Chan）编著的《中国哲学大纲与参考书目》（1955），[8]钱存训（Tsuen-hsuin Tsien）的硕士论文《通过翻译看西方对中国的影响：书目研究》（1952）。[9]

2.关于华人与华侨：格里贝尔（Rosemary Griebel）编著的《中国人：现代中国注释书目》（1986），[10]唐德刚（T. K. Tong）和Robert Wu主编的《亚洲人在美国：精选参考文献注释书目》（1975），[11]藤本三郎（Isao Fujimoto）等人主编的《美国的亚洲人：精选书目》（1971），[12]哈里·基塔诺的《美国的亚洲人：社会工作教育中使用的精选书目》（1971），[13]刘广京（Kwang-Ching Liu）主编的《美国人和中国人：历史论文与参

---

[1] Paul R. Goldin, *Ancient Chinese Civilization: Bibliography of Materials in Western Languages*. https://www.academia.edu/37490636/Ancient Chinese Civilization Bibliography of Materials in Western Languages.

[2] Lubna Malik and Lynn White, *Princeton China Bibliography*. Winter 2007—2008 Edition. http://www.princeton.edu/~lynn/chinabib.pdf

[3] Zongxun Na, *Chinese Studies in English: A Selected Bibliography of Books* (AICS Bibliographical Series; No. 1). American Institute of Chinese Studies, 1991.

[4] Tsuen-hsuin Tsien, *China: An Annotated Bibliography of Bibliographies*. Boston: G. K. Hall, 1978.

[5] Michael Loewe, *Early Chinese Texts: A Bibliographical Guide*. The society for the study of early China, 1993.

[6] Norman E. Tanis, David Perkins, Justine Pinto, *China in Books: A Basic Bibliography in Western Language* (Foundation in library and information science; v. 4). Greenwich, Conn.: Jai Press, 1979.

[7] Alberto R. Sanchez, *Chinese Culture in the United States of Amreica: An Annotated Bibliography*. Cross Cultural Resource Center, California State University, 1977.

[8] Wing-Tsit Chan, *An Outline and a Bibliography of Chinese Philosophy*. Hanover, New Hampshire, 1955.

[9] Tsien Tsuen-Hsuin, *Western Impact on China through Translation: A Bibliographical Study*. Thesis for the Degree of Master of Arts, University of Chicago, 1952.

[10] Rosemary Griebel, Alberta Educational Communications Corporation; Cultural Development Division, *The Chinese: An Annotated Bibliography on Modern China*. Alberta Library Services Branch, 1986.

[11] T. K. Tong, Robert Wu, *Asians in America: An Annotated Bibliography of Selected Reference Works* (Bibliography prepared by the Curriculum Development Program in Comparative Ethnicity Project). City Coll. Research Foundation, New York, NY, 1975.

[12] Isao Fujimoto, Michiyo Yamaguchi Swift and Rosalie Zucker, *Asians in America: A Selected Annotated Bibliography*. University of California, Davis. Asian American Research Project. Working Publication; No. 5., 1971.

[13] Harry H. L. Kitano, *Asians in America: A Selected Bibliography for Use in Social Work Education*. New York: Council on Social Work Education, 1971.

考书目》（1963），[1]罗伯特·厄内斯特·考恩（Robert Ernest Cowan）等人主编的《美国之华人问题参考书目》（1909）。[2]

3.关于中美关系：艾文博（Robert L. Irick）、余英时、刘广京合编的《中美关系史书目》（1960）。[3]

4.关于"文革"与毛泽东：吴一兴（Yiching Wu）编著的《中国"文化大革命"：英文学术研究书目》（2014），[4]张东华（Tony H. Chang）编著的《中国"文化大革命"（1966—1976）：英文参考书目精选》（1999），[5]艾伦（Alan Lawrance）编著的《毛泽东参考书目》（1991）。[6]

5.关于神话与电影：李福清（B. Riftin, 1932—2012）主编的《中国各民族神话研究外文论著目录（1839—1990）》[7]，程健（Jim Cheng）主编的《中国电影研究注释书目》（2004）。[8]

6.关于中西交通：Ying Liu等人主编的《郑和海上航行（1405—1433）与中国和印度洋世界的关系：多语种书目》（2014），[9]罗闻达（Björn Löwendahl, 1941—2013）主编的《从西文印本书籍看中西关系、中国观、文化影响与汉学发展（1477—1877）》。[10]

7.关于传教士：香港大学图书馆主编的《马礼逊藏书目录》（2010）。[11]

8.关于女性研究：叶山（Robin D. S. Yates）的《从远古时代至今的中国女性：西文书目研究》（2009）。[12]

9.关于战争：尤金·拉索的（Eugene L. Rasor）编著的《中国—缅甸—印度战役

---

[1] Kwang-Ching Liu, *Americans and Chinese: A Historical Essay and a Bibliography*. Cambridge: Harvard University Press, 1963.

[2] Robert Ernest Cowan, Boutwell Dunlap, *Bibliography of the Chinese Question in the United States*. A. M. Robertson, San Francisco, 1909.

[3] Robert L. Irick, Ying-Shih Yu, Kwang-Ching Liu, *American-Chinese Relations, 1784—1941: A Survey of Chinese-language Materials at Harvard* = Chung Mei kuan hsi shih shu mu. Harvard University Press, 1960.

[4] Compiled by Yiching Wu, *China's Cultural Revolution: A Bibliography of English-Language Scholarship*. University of Toronto, 2014.

[5] Tony H. Chang, *China during the Cultural Revolution, 1966—1976: A Selected Bibliography of English Language Works*. Greenwood Press, 1999.

[6] Alan Lawrance, *Mao Zedong: A Bibliography* (Bibliographies of World Leaders).Greenwood, 1991.

[7] B. Riftin（李福清），*A Bibliography of Foreign-Language Studies of the Mythology of All the Nations of China*（1839—1990）. Beijing Library Press（2007）.

[8] Jim Cheng, *An Annotated Bibliography of Chinese Film Studies*. Hong Kong University Press, 2004.

[9] Ying Liu, Zhongping Chen, Gregory Blue, *Zheng He's Maritime Voyages (1405—1433) and China's Relations with the Indian Ocean World: A Multilingual Bibliography*. Brill Academic Publishers, 2014.

[10] Björn Löwendahl, *Sino-Western Relations, Conceptions of China, Cultural Influences and the Development of Sinology: Disclosed in western Printed Books, 1477—1877*. Hua Hin, Elephant Press, 2008.

[11] The University of Hong Kong Libraries, *Catalogue of the Morrison Collection*. The University of Hong Kong Libraries, 2010.

[12] Robin D.S. Yates, *Women in China from Earliest Times to the Present: A Bibliography of Studies in Western Languages*. Brill, 2009.

（1931—1945）：史学和注释书目》（1998）。[1]

需要说明的是，以上书目仅是笔者在学习和研究中所亲见和收集到的，其他重要书目如有遗漏实为在所难免。无论如何，这些汉学（中国学）研究书目，或是对考狄书目和袁同礼书目的延续，或是对其补遗，或是对相关专业领域研究的统整，均为了解西方汉学（中国学）史提供了极为重要的参考资料，不同程度地推动了汉学（中国学）的发展。然而非常可惜的是，至今上述英文书目著述大部分没有中译本，只能静静地躺在国外图书馆里。

回顾国内，自20世纪80年代以来，中国学术界对海外当代中国研究的再研究逐步展开，先后翻译出版了大量海外中国学著作，并出现一批关于海外中国研究的专著、重要学术文章和书目。其中，书目部分主要有（不完全统计）：中国社会科学院情报研究所编《国外研究中国问题书目索引：1977—1978》（书目文献出版社，1981），中国社会科学院近代史研究所图书馆按年度编辑的《国外出版中国近代史论著目录》，中共中央党史研究室科研局编译处编《国外中共党史中国革命史论著目录大全（1919—1989）》（中央党史出版社，1993），李学勤主编《国际汉学著作提要》（江西教育出版社，1996），马钊主编《1971—2006年美国清史论著目录》（人民出版社，2007），赵晓阳编译《北京研究外文文献题录》（北京图书馆出版社，2007），印永清等主编《海外上海研究书目（1845—2005）》（上海辞书出版社，2009），上海社会科学院世界中国学研究所、复旦大学中华文明国际研究中心编《2013年海外中国研究书目提要》（未正式出版，2014）等。

通过上述对国内外中国研究书目情况的简要梳理不难看到，国外已出版的书目比较全面地收录了从16世纪到21世纪初的中国学文献，所收文献种类比较齐全，在时间和内容上有连续性，涉及中国社会的各个方面，文种也较多，无论从编制技巧还是从书目内容上看都有较高的水平。反观国内，虽然有一些专门性的书目，但到目前为止还没有一部能综合反映1949年中华人民共和国成立以来海外当代中国研究（1949—2019）发展全貌的多学科、综合性中国学书目。国内对海外当代中国研究的关注还远远不够，对海外当代中国研究的认识基本上还局限在一个个点上，或者一条条线上，对于中国整体研究而言，这些点和线都是零散的，不成系统的。这对我们研究国外的中国学现状，借鉴国外好的研究成果很不利，也与我国的经济文化发展水平不相适应。如何在这些已描画出的点和线的基础上，绘制出海外关于当代中国研究的整体地图，形成对中国更全面、更完整的看法，是一项亟待完成的研究工作。

2017—2018年，笔者受国家留学基金委资助在美国丹佛大学访学，为完成所主持

---

[1] Eugene L. Rasor, *The China-Burma-India Campaign, 1931—1945: Historiography and Annotated Bibliography*. Greenwood, 1998.

的国家社科基金课题，先后走访了美国国会图书馆、哈佛大学、普林斯顿大学、耶鲁大学、斯坦福大学、哥伦比亚大学、华盛顿大学（西雅图）、密歇根大学、加州大学洛杉矶分校等机构的东亚图书馆负责人，对美国收藏、出版的当代中国研究文献进行了初步考察和收集整理。当我奔走于美国各大学图书馆，置身于中国研究文献资料的海洋之中时，萦绕在脑际并久久挥之不去的一段话是考狄1878年6月的"自述"：

> 差不多10年前，当我抵达中国时，当我开始对这一庞大的帝国进行历史、科学、道德与风俗方面的研究时，我发现自己面对所有最初进入一个无限深广的研究领域的人所面临的困境。置身于这数量极为巨大、以各种语言完成、处理主题极尽繁复的有关中国的出版物之间，谁能给我指点迷津？我的第一个反应是求助于合理编排的书目，而这种书目并不存在；这迫使我自己动手对所能得到的这类著作进行某种挑选，某种分类整理。希望能够使其他人免除我自己正不得不做的这种无益而烦琐的工作，我产生了这个想法：一部精心编排的与这个中央帝国有关的著作目录的出版，将能够对那些研究远东方面的学者和对远东问题感兴趣的人有所裨益。[1]

所幸我们是站在前人研究的坚实基础上，才能够"接着说"和"接着做"。我用了两年多时间，参照《中国图书馆分类法》（第五版），以著者、书名、出版单位、出版年为基本内容，对收集到的美国各大学图书馆收藏的当代中国研究英文著作进行了初步分类、编目、整理和翻译。目前已整理完成海外当代中国研究英文文献（主要为图书和部分硕博论文，不含学术期刊论文）书目7090种，共计31万余字。通过这些代表性著作目录，我们大致可以了解海外当代中国研究的基本内容、主要观点和发展概貌。

本书主要收集当代海外关于中国研究的英文著作书目，[2]时间上以1949年后特别是改革开放以来的著作为主，兼顾中华人民共和国成立前的经典著述；[3]内容上以中国哲学社会科学诸学科（政、经、法、文、史、哲）为主，兼顾科技、环保等自然学科；国别来源以英美国家为主，兼顾法、德、俄、日等。因本书为英文书目选粹，故收录的书目作者多为海外学者，其中有些作者是著名的汉学家或者中国学家，他们大多拥有比较地道的中文名字，如费正清、傅高义、史景迁等。在本书中，如果作者有中文名，一般在其

---

[1] ［法］亨利·考狄著，韩一宇译：《我与"汉学"书目之缘——〈中国书目〉第一版序》，《国际汉学》2009年第1期，第256-267页。

[2] 这些书目绝大多数是外国学者的著作；少数中国学者在海外出版的著作也被收录其中；中国学者的著作被译为外文，出版地在海外的也收录；国内出版的英文书目不被收录；中国台湾、香港、澳门地区出版的英文书目也不收录。

[3] 具体到每一类书目，总的顺序是按照出版时间由近及远；如果为同一年的出版物，首先按月份先后排序，如无月份，则按作者姓氏字母顺序排列。

外文名后以括号标注。本书主要内容包括：总论，历史与地理，哲学与宗教，文学与艺术，语言与文学，文化与文明，社会与族群，政治与外交，法律与军事，经济与自然，中西交通以及研究参考12部分。全书结构安排方面，在参照国图分类法的基础上，主要根据海外中国学研究的实际情况，重新进行结构调整，与国内编排有所不同。

本书目分为12个子目录，具体类别和内容如下：

一、中国总论（119种）：其中含中国形象书目33种。

二、中国历史与地理（803种）：包括历史、游记与地方史、边疆和台港澳共4大类。

其中：（一）历史类书目，含通史41种，古代史101种，清代史84种，近现代史59种，史学39种，考古19种，哈佛中国史系列6种，剑桥中国史系列13种；（二）游记与地方史类书目，含北京53种，上海78种，广东/广州9种，旅游及其他87种，地理11种；（三）边疆类书目，含西藏67种，新疆20种，南海/东海13种，其他31种；（四）台港澳类书目，含台湾27种，香港39种，澳门6种。

三、中国哲学与宗教（452种）：包括哲学和宗教共2大类。

其中：（一）哲学类（含美学）书目111种；（二）宗教类书目，含中国宗教57种，基督教（含天主教和传教士）129种，伊斯兰教24种，佛教90种，道教41种。

四、中国文学与艺术（530种）：包括文学、诗歌、戏剧、神话/传说、艺术/创意/收藏、绘画/书法/摄影/服饰、音乐/舞蹈共7大类。

其中：（一）文学类（含鲁迅研究）书目197种；（二）诗歌类书目64种；（三）戏剧类书目51种；（四）神话/传说类书目24种；（五）艺术/创意/收藏类书目111种；（六）绘画/书法/摄影/服饰类书目57种；（七）音乐/舞蹈类书目26种。

五、中国语言与文字（246种）：包括语言、文字/词典和翻译学共3大类。

其中：（一）语言类书目169种；（二）文字/词典类书目47种；（三）翻译学类书目30种。

六、中国文化与文明（1212种）：包括文化总论、儒学与经典、思想与文明、教育、知识分子、传媒与网络、医学、园林建筑、食品与饮食、武术共10大类。

其中：（一）文化总论类目146种；（二）儒学与经典类书目，含儒学132种，孔子49种，《论语》21种，老子、庄子与《道德经》37种，《易经》20种，传统经典与诸子百家41种；（三）思想与文明类书目，含传统思想32种，中外思维7种，现代主义14种，左派与后现代17种，乌托邦3种，东方主义10种，人类文明（含长城、瓷器）60种；（四）教育类（含孔子学院、心理学）书目163种；（五）知识分子类书目42种；（六）传媒与网络类书目，含新闻媒体48种，电影64种，互联网23种，出版印刷15种，传播学12种；（七）医学类书目，含医学与医疗30种，中医与中药112种，疾病与防控26种，气功14种；（八）园林建筑类书目40种；（九）食品与饮食类书目59种；（十）武术类书目17种。

七、中国社会与族群（526种）：包括儿童、婚姻家庭、女性、男性、性别、性文化、人口、老龄/保健、就业/阶层与移民、贫困、社会生活/社会学、仪式/丧葬/巫术与民俗、人类学、族群与宗族共14大类。

其中：（一）儿童类书目32种；（二）婚姻家庭类书目48种；（三）女性类书目129种；（四）男性类书目9种；（五）性别类书目11种；（六）性文化类书目35种；（七）人口类书目23种；（八）老龄、保健类书目15种；（九）就业、阶层与移民类书目26种；（十）贫困类书目24种；（十一）社会生活/社会学类书目52种；（十二）仪式、丧葬、巫术与民俗类书目30种；（十三）人类学类书目11种；（十四）族群与宗族类（含犹太人）书目81种。

八、中国政治与外交（1654种）：包括政治、外交和国际关系共3大类。

其中：（一）政治类书目，含研究总论15种，中国共产党107种，毛泽东145种，中国道路/中国梦54种，中国崛起71种，中国改革与转型55种，中国革命98种，中国治理50种，政治体制23种，民主建设/劳工关系36种，公民社会/非政府组织10种，公民权利6种，政治思想15种，政治文化14种，政治精英6种，话语建设20种，软实力6种，民族主义/民族国家36种，国家建设19种，长征4种，国际共运2种，马克思主义52种，中国与资本主义14种，智库2种；（二）外交类书目77种；（三）国际关系类书目，含中国与美国219种，中国与苏联/俄罗斯46种，中国与日本82种，中国与英国42种，中国与印度72种，中国与欧洲38种，中国与非洲40种，中国与越南10种，中国与东盟5种，中国与亚洲61种，中国与世界/其他国家和地区51种，亚洲研究51种。

九、中国法律与军事（399种）：包括法律与法治、军事与战争共2大类。

其中：（一）法律与法治类书目141种；（二）军事与战争类书目，含抗日战争36种，南京大屠杀9种，朝鲜战争13种，冷战41种，鸦片战争14种，中外战争44种，战争文化与生态12种，内战与军史26种，军事与军力53种，核力量7种，美军在中国6种。

十、中国经济与自然（1055种）：包括经济增长与发展、经济管理与改革、财政与金融/投资、工业与产业、商业与贸易、企业与创业、城市、农业与农村、科技与自然、水利/环保/能源、人力资源共11大类。

其中：（一）经济增长与发展类书目129种；（二）经济管理与改革类书目76种；（三）财政与金融、投资类书目117种；（四）工业与产业类（含物流运输）书目64种；（五）商业与贸易类书目104种；（六）企业与创业类书目75种；（七）城市类书目71种；（八）农业与农村类书目111种；（九）科技与自然类书目，含科学技术58种，创新21种，动植物22种，天文太空15种，数理化21种；（十）水利、环保、能源类书目，含气候水利44种，环保生态67种，能源36种；（十一）人力资源类书目24种。

十一、中西交通（420种）：包括总论、丝绸之路/"一带一路"、全球化、华侨与移民4大类。

其中：（一）总论类书目125种；（二）丝绸之路/一带一路类书目59种；（三）全球化类书目69种；（四）华侨与移民类书目167种。

十二、中国研究参考（204种）：包括中国学研究、工具书、传记回忆录共3大类。

其中：（一）中国学研究类书目53种，另有汉学家与中国学家书目15种，区域研究书目6种；（二）工具书类书目45种；（三）传记回忆录类书目79种，另有皇后传略书目6种。

本书的特色为学术性、综合性及咨政性。

首先，本书重点收录现当代（尤其是改革开放以来）海外中国研究的最新学术著作目录，以期实现国内学界对国际研究动态的及时追踪与了解，推动中国学术界主动参与国际对话交流。

其次，本书涉及历史中国的史学、哲学、宗教、文学、语言以及当代中国的政治、经济、文化等内容，几乎涵盖所有的中国研究中的人文学科乃至军事、科技、环保等自然科学学科，具有综合性、跨学科和广泛性特点，为深化全球化背景下中国对于外部世界的了解做出探索。

最后，本书旨在梳理勾勒海外学者对于当代中国研究的历程与进展，研究历史的目的是为了更好地服务现实，通过分析海外学者关于当代中国政治、经济、文化等方面的基本认知，为中国对外政策的制定及战略布局提供咨政性借鉴。

管永前
2020年8月25日于北京

1. 中国总论

海外中国研究，通称汉学（Sinology）或中国学（China Studies），又称国际汉学/中国学、海外汉学/中国学、域外汉学/中国学、世界汉学/中国学等，是指中国以外的学者（中国国内学者纯粹研究本土的学问不在此列，但中国学者在海外发表的或被翻译发表的有关中国的成果包括在内）对有关中国的各种学问进行研究的综合性学科，包括中国政治、经济、社会、历史、哲学、宗教、语言、文字、文学、艺术、天文、地理、工艺、科技等各种学问。

1.1 总论

1. 《大国：中国与世界》Timothy Brook（卜正民），*Great State: China and the World*. Profile Books Ltd. (2019)
2. 《何为中国：疆域、民族、文化与历史》Zhaoguang Ge（葛兆光），Michael Gibbs Hill (translator), *What Is China: Territory, Ethnicity, Culture, and History*. Belknap Press (2018)
3. 《了解今日中国：关于政治、经济、社会和国际关系的探索》Silvio Beretta, Axel Berkofsky, Lihong Zhang (eds.), *Understanding China Today: An Exploration of Politics, Economics, Society, and International Relations* (Understanding China). Springer International (2017)
4. 《比较视野下的中国》Hans Steinmüller, Stephan Feuchtwang, *China in Comparative Perspective*. World Scientific (2017)
5. 《中国》Coll., *China* (Berlitz Pocket Guides). Berlitz Publishing (2016)
6. 《中国》Mark Rosenfelder, *China* (Construction Kit). Yonagu Books (2015)
7. 《中国之道》Min Ding, Jie Xu, *The Chinese Way*. Routledge (2014)
8. 《中国》Earle Rice, *China*. Mitchell Lane Publishers (2014)
9. 《不安的中国》Perry Link（林培瑞）, Richard P. Madsen, Paul G. Pickowicz（毕克伟）, *Restless China*. Rowman & Littlefield Publishers (2013)
10. 《论中国》Henry Kissinger（基辛格），*On China*. Penguin Press (2011)
11. 《中国简介》Andrea Pelleschi, *China* (Countries of the World). Essential Library (2011)
12. 《中国》（第2版）Gary T. Whiteford, Christopher L. Salter, *China*. 2nd Edition (Modern World Nations). Infobase Publishing (2010)
13. 《这就是中国：第一个5000年》Haiwang Yuan（袁海旺），Ronald G. Knapp, Margot E. Landman, Gregory Veeck, *This Is China: The First 5,000 Years*. Berkshire Publishing (2010)

14. 《21世纪的中国：每个人都需要知道》Jeffrey N. Wasserstrom（华志坚）, *China in the 21st Century: What Everyone Needs to Know*. Oxford University Press (2010)
15. 《中国兴衰》Richard Baum（包瑞嘉）, *Fall and Rise of China*. The Teaching Company (2010)
16. 《中国》（引入对立观点介绍问题）Lauri S. Friedman, *China* (Introducing Issues with Opposing Viewpoints). Greenhaven (2009)
17. 《中国》Robert Andre LaFleur, *China* (Asia in Focus). ABC-CLIO Press (2009)
18. 《现代中国》Rana Mitter（米德）, *Modern China* (A Brief Insight). Sterling (2009)
19. 《现代中国简介》Rana Mitter（米德）, *Modern China: A Very Short Introduction*. Oxford University Press, USA (2008)
20. 《当代中国简介》Michael Dillon, *Contemporary China: An Introduction*. Routledge (2008)
21. 《真实的中国：共和国的人民》Sang Ye（桑晔）(author), Edited by Geremie Randall Barmé（白洁明）with Miriam Lang, *China Candid: The People on the People's Republic*. University of California Press (2006)
22. 《中国概况》Country Information and Policy Unit, Immigration and Nationality Directorate, Home Office, United Kingdom（英国内政部移民和国籍局国家信息和政策股）, *China: Country Report*. (2005)
23. 《中国》Gary T. Whiteford, *China*. Chelsea House Publishing (2003, 2005)
24. 《中华人民共和国版图》Tara Boland-Crewe, David Lea, *The Territories of the People's Republic of China*. Europa Publications Limited (2002)
25. 《中国》Susan Sinnott, *China*. Compass Point Books (2000)
26. 《当代中国》Alan Hunter, John Sexton, *Contemporary China*. Macmillan Education UK (1999)
27. 《中国简介：关于中国社会、商业和政治的基本事实》Barry Turner (eds.), *China Profiled: Essential Facts on Society, Business and Politics in China* (SYB Factbook series). Palgrave Macmillan UK (1999)
28. 《中国》Charles Wishart Hayford, Peter Cheng, *China* (World Bibliographical Series; V. 35). ABC-CLIO Press (1997)
29. 《解构中国：政治、贸易和区域主义》David S.G. Goodman, Gerald Segal, *China Deconstructs: Politics, Trade and Regionalism* (Routledge in Asia). Routledge (1995)
30. 《追寻现代中国》Jonathan D. Spence（史景迁）, *The Search for Modern China*. W. W. Norton & Company (1990)
31. 《中国：国家研究》Robert L. Worden, Andrea Matles Savada, and Ronald E. Dolan, *China: A Country Study*. United States Government as represented by the Secretary of the Army (1988)
32. 《2001年的中国》Han Suyin（韩素音）, *China in the Year 2001*. New York: Basic Books (1967)
33. 《中国》A. G. Wenley, John Alexander Pope, *China*. Smithsonian Institute Press, Washington (1944)
34. 《中国》Y. L. Liang, Neville Whymant, *China*. Macdonald and Co. Ltd, London (1946)

35. 《爆竹之乡：面向年轻读者的中国世界图片》Florence Ayscough（艾思柯）, *Firecracker Land: Pictures of the Chinese World for Younger Reader*. Boston and New York, Houghton Mifflin Co. (1932)

36. 《中国分析》Frank Johnson Goodnow, *China: An Analysis*. Baltimore: Johns Hopkins Press (1926)

37. 《关于中国的重要事实》Julean Herbert Arnold（安立德）, *Salient Facts about China*. The China Sociaty of America (1926)

38. 《中国的昨天和今天》Edward Thomas Williams（卫理）, *China Yesterday and Today*. George G. Harrap And Co. Ltd. (1923)

39. 《中国述论》James W. Bashford, *China: An Interpretation*. The Abingdon Press (1916)

40. 《中国总论》（第一、二卷）Samuel Wells Williams（卫三畏）, *The Middle Kingdom: A Survey of the Geography, Government, Education, Social Life, Arts, Religion, etc. of the Chinese*. Vols.1, 2. New York: Charles Scribner's Sons (1913)

41. 《中国》（第4版）Robert K. Douglas, Ian C. Hannah, *China*. Fourth Edition. London: T. Fisher Unwin (1912)

42. 《如花如画的帝国》Chester R. Stratton, *Picturesque China, or The Flowery Kingdom*. Geo. W. Bertron (1910)

43. 《中国》Mortimer Menpes, Henry Arthur Blake, *China*. Adam and Charles Black (1909)

44. 《基督王：关于中国的概括性研究》Arthur H. Smith（明恩溥）, *Rex Christus: An Outline Study of China*. London: Macmillan Company (1904)

45. 《中国》（第4版）Robert Kennaway Douglas, *China*. Revised and Enlarged. The Saalfield Publishing Company (1903, 1895)

46. 《中国与中国家园掠影》Edward Sylvester Morse, *Glimpses of China and Chinese Homes*. Little, Brown and Company (1902)

47. 《中国历史、艺术和文学》Frank Brinkley, *China: Its History, Arts, and Literature*. J. B. Millet Company (1902)

48. 《汉学菁华》William Alexander Parsons Martin（丁韪良）, *The Lore of Cathay: or, The Intellect of China*. Edinburgh and London: Oliphant, Anderson & Ferrier (1901)

49. 《中国概貌与中国女人》J. T. (John Talbot) Gracey, *China in Outline, and Woman in China*. 177 Pearl Street, Rochester, N. Y. (1900)

50. 《中国简史》Demetrius Charles Boulger（包罗杰）, *China*. With a Supplementary Chapter of Recent Events by Mayo W. Hazeltine. New York and London: The Co-opertative Publication Society (1900)

51. 《中国》Harold E. Gorst, *China*. London: Sands and Company (1899)

52. 《中国》Robert K. Douglas, *China*. Second Edition. London: T. Fisher Unwin (1899)

53. 《中国》Demetrius Charles Boulger, Mayo W. Hazeltine, *China*. Peter Fenelon Collier (1898)

54. 《中国和中国人：包含中国宗教哲学、语言文学、历史地理的教科书》John Fryer, *China*

and the Chinese: A Text-book Comprising the Religions and Philosophies, the Language and Literature, the History and Geography of China. Shanghai: Printed by Kelly & Walsh, Limited (1897)

55. 《中国》John L. Stoddard, *China*. Belford, Middlebrook & Company (1897)

56. 《中国今昔：对外交往、进步和资源；传教问题等》R. S.Gundry, *China Present and Past: Foreign Intercourse, Progress and Resources; the Missionary Question, etc.* London, Chapman and Hall (1895)

57. 《中国》J. T. (John Talbot) Gracey, *China*. Rochester, N. Y. (1895)

58. 《中国及其人民》William Henry Withrow (ed.), *China and Its People*. William Briggs (1894)

59. 《中国》Robert K. Douglas, *China*. Second Edition, Revised. London: Society for Promoting Christian Knowledge (1887)

60. 《旧中国杂记》William C. Hunter, *Bits of Old China*. London: Kegan Paul, Trench (1885)

61. 《中国》Robert K. Douglas, *China*. London: Society for Promoting Christian Knowledge (1882)

62. 《中国和中国人》（修订版）John Livingston Nevius（倪维思）, *China and the Chinese: A General Description of the Country and Its Inhabitants; Its Civilization and Form of Government; Its Religious and Social Institutions; Its Intercourse with Other Nations, and Its Present Condition and Prospects*. Philadelphia: Presbyterian Board of Publication (1882 Revised edition)

63. 《中国人：其教育、哲学和文字》William Alexander Parsons Martin（丁韪良）, *The Chinese: Their Education, Philosophy, and Letters*. New York: Harper & Brothers (1881)

64. 《中国：法律、风貌及习惯之历史》William Gow Gregor, *China: A History of the Laws, Manners and Customs of the People*. Vol. 1. Macmillan Company, London, UK (1878)

65. 《中国辞汇》William Frederick Mayers（梅辉立）, *The Chinese Reader's Manual: A Handbook of Biographical, Historical, Mythological, and General Literary Reference*. Shanghai: American Presbyterian Mission Press (1874)

66. 《中国与中国人影像》（全四卷）John Thomson, *Illustrations of China and Its People: A Series of Two Hundred Photographs, With Letterpress Description of the Places and People Represented*. 4 vols. London: Sampson, Low (1874)

67. 《中国和中国人》John L.Nevius（倪维思）, *China and The Chinese: A General Description of the Country and Its Inhabitants; Its Civilization and Form of Government; Its Religious and Social Institutions; Its Intercourse with other Nations; and Its Present Condition and Prospects*. New York: Harper & Brothers (1869)

68. 《中国和中国人：他们的宗教、性格、习俗和制造业；鸦片贸易引发的邪恶；与我国的宗教、道德、政治和商业交往一瞥》（第一、二卷）Henry Charles Sirr, *China and the Chinese: Their Religion, Character, Customs, and Manufactures; The Evils Arising from the Opium Trade, with a Glance at our Religions, Moral, Political and Commercial Intercourse with the Country*. Vols. 1, 2. London: Wm. S. Orr & Co. (1849)

1. 中国总论　　005

69. 《中国政治、商业和社会：向女王陛下政府提交的官方报告》Robert Montgomery Martin, *China: Political, Commercial, and Social; In an Official Report to Her Majesty's Government.* James Madden (1847)

70. 《中华大观》John R. Peters, *Miscellaneous Remarks upon the Government, History, Religions, Literature, Agriculture, Arts, Trades, Manners, and Customs of the Chinese.* Boston: Eastburn's Press (1845)

71. 《中国人：中国历史概述》*The People of China: or, A Summary of Chinese History.* Philadelphia: American Sunday-School Union (1844)

72. 《万唐人物》Nathan Dunn, William B. Langdon, *Ten Thousand Chinese Things: A Descriptive Catalogue of the Chinese Collection, with Condensed Accounts of the Genius, Government, History, Literature, ... of the Celestial Empire.* Now Exhibiting at St. George's Place, Hyde Park Corner. London: Printed for the Proprietor (1842，压缩版)

73. 《万唐人物》William B. Langdon, *Ten Thousand Things Relating to China and the Chinese: An Epitome of the Genius, Government, History, Literature, ... of the Celestial Empire.* London: Hyde Park Corner (1842)

74. 《中国及其资源和特质：物质、政治、社会和商业》Robert Mudie, *China and Its Resources, and Peculiarities: Physical, Political, Social, and Commercial; With a View of the Opium Question, and a Notice of Assam.* Grattan and Gilbert (1840)

75. 《中国打开大门：展示中华帝国的地形、历史、风俗、礼仪、艺术、制造、商业等》（二卷本）Karl Friedrich August Gützlaff, Andrew Reed, *China Opened: Or, a Display of The Topography, History, Customs, Manners, Arts, Manufactures, Commerce, etc. of the Chinese Empire.* In two volumes. Smith, Elder and Co. (1838)

76. 《中国：现状与前景》W. H. Medhurst（麦都思）, *China: Its State and Prospects.* London: John Snow, 26, Paternoster Row (1838)

77. 《中国历史与分类记述：古今历史、语言、文学、宗教、政府、工业、礼仪和社会状况……》（第一、二、三卷）Hugh Murray, John Crawfurd, Peter Gordon, Captain Thomas Lynn; William Wallace... and Gilbert Burnett...with a Map, and Thirty-Six Engravings by Jackson, *An Historical and Descriptive Account of China: Its Ancient and Modern History, Language, Literature, Religion, Government, Industry, Manners, and Social State; Intercourse with Europe from the Earliest Ages; Missions and Embassies to the Imperial Court; British and Foreign Commerce; Directions to Navigators; State of Mathematics and Astronomy; Survey of Its Geography, Geology, Botany, and Zoology.* Vols. 1, 2, 3. Edinburgh Oliver & Boyd; [etc., etc.] (1836)

78. 《中国：中华帝国及其居民概述》（第一、二卷）John Francis Davis, *The Chinese: A General Description of the Empire of China and Its Inhabitants.* Vols. 1, 2. New-York: Harper (1836)

79. 《中国：其政府、法律和策略，以及英国在华的大使、与华的交往》Peter Auber,

China: An Outline of Its Government, Laws, and Policy; And of the British and Foreign Embassies to, and Intercourse with that Empire. London: Parbury, Allen and Co. (1834)

80.《中国梗概：附原始插图》William W. Wood, *Sketches of China: With Illustrations from Original Drawings*. Philadelphia: Carey and Lea (1830)

81.《与中国有关的杂记以及我们与该国的商业往来》George Thomas Staunton, Alexander Pearson, *Miscellaneous Notices Relating to China, and Our Commercial Intercourse with That Country*. Havant I. Skelton (1828)

82.《中国人：其历史、宫廷、宗教、政府、立法、机构、法庭、农业、语言、文学、制造、艺术、科学、法律和习俗》Anon, *The People of China: Their History, Court, Religion, Government, Legislation, Institutions, Tribunals, Agriculture, Language, Literature, Manufactures, Arts, Sciences, Manners and Customs*. London: The Religious Tract Society (1799)

83.《有关中华帝国的历史、地理及哲学介绍》William Winterbotham, *An Historical, Geographical, and Philosophical View of the Chinese Empire*. London: J. Ridcwat, and W. Button (1795)

84.《中华帝国全志：中华帝国及其所属鞑靼地区的地理、历史、编年纪、政治和博物》（第一至四卷）Jean Baptiste Du Halde（杜赫德）, *The General History of China: Containing a Geographical, Historical, Chronological, Political and Physical Description of the Empire of China, Chinese-Tartary, Corea and Thibet*. Vols.1-4.Watts (1741)

85.《中华帝国全志》（第一、二卷）Jean Baptiste Du Halde（杜赫德）, *A Description of the Empire of China and Chinese-Tartary, together with the Kingdoms of Korea and Tibet*. Vols.1, 2. London: Printed by Edward Cave, at St. John's Gate (1738)

86.《回忆与观察（中国近事报道）》Louis Le Comte（李明）, *Memoirs and Observations: Topographical, Physical, Mathematical, Mechanical, Natural, Civil, and Ecclesiastical, Made in a Late Journey through the Empire of China, and Published in Several Letters; Particularly upon the Chinese Pottery and Varnishing, the Silk and Other Manufactures [sic], the Pearl Fishing, the History of Plants and Animals, with a Description of Their Cities and Publick Works, Number of People, Their Language, Manners and Commerce, Their Habits, Economy, and Government; the Philosophy of Confucius; the State of Christianity, and Many Other Curious and Useful Remarks*. London: Benjamin Tooke and Sam Buckley (1697)

1.2 中国形象

1.《美丽中国》Lina Unali, *Beautiful China*. Newcastle upon Tyne: Cambridge Scholars Publishing (2016)

2.《西方对中华人民共和国的看法：政治、经济和社会》Colin Mackerras（马克林）, *Western Perspectives on the People's Republic of China: Politics, Economy and Society*. Singapore; Hackensack, New Jersey, World Scientific Publishing Co. Pte. Ltd. (2015)

3.《美国的中国形象：身份、权力、政策》Oliver Turner, *American Images of China:*

Identity, Power, Policy. New York: Routledge (2014)

4. 《从傅满洲到功夫熊猫：美国电影中的中国形象》Naomi Greene Sheldon H. Lu, *From Fu Manchu to Kung Fu Panda: Images of China in American Film*. University of Hawaii Press (2014)

5. 《东方是黑色的：黑人激进派想象中的冷战中国》Robeson Taj Frazier, *The East Is Black: Cold War China in the Black Radical Imagination*. Duke University Press Books (2014)

6. 《"黄祸"：傅满洲博士与中国恐惧症的兴起》Christopher Frayling, *The Yellow Peril: Dr. Fu Manchu and the Rise of Chinaphobia*. Thames Hudson (2014)

7. 《美国之东方：从殖民时代到20世纪想象中的东方》David Weir, *American Orient: Imagining the East from the Colonial Era through the Twentieth Century*. Massachusetts: University of Massachusetts Press (2011)

8. 《中国与国际关系：中国观与王赓武的贡献》Zheng Yongnian（郑永年）, *China and International Relations: The Chinese View and the Contribution of Wang Gungwu* (China Policy Series).Taylor & Francis (2010)

9. 《对镜猜谜：美国的中国革命观》William Hinton（韩丁）, *Through a Glass Darkly: American Views of the Chinese Revolution*. Monthly Review Press (2006)

10. 《中国的美国形象》Carola McGiffert, *Chinese Images of the United States*. Washington, D.C.: CSIS Press, Center for Strategic and International Studies (2005)

11. 《中国神秘：赛珍珠、黄柳霜、宋美龄与美国东方主义的转型》Karen J. Leong, *The China Mystique: Pearl S. Buck, Anna May Wong, Mayling Soong, and the Transformation of American Orientalism*. Berkeley University of California Press (2005)

12. 《中华无限：制造中国和中国属性的意象》Gregory B. Lee（利大英）, *Chinas Unlimited: Making the Imaginaries of China and Chineseness*. Honolulu: University of Hawai'i Press (2003)

13. 《黑暗王国：美帝国崛起中的中国形象（1784—1844）》（博士论文）Min Wu, *The Kingdom of Darkness: China in the Rise of the American Empire, 1784—1844*. Ph. D. Dissertation, Duke University (2003)

14. 《西方社会与政治思想中的中国形象》David Martin Jones, *The Image of China in Western Social and Political Thought*. Palgrave (2001)

15. 《美国华裔男子气概：从傅满洲到李小龙》(Studies in Asian Americans) Jachinson Chan, *Chinese American Masculinities: From Fu Manchu to Bruce Lee*. Routledge (2001)

16. 《傅满洲博士归来》(New Millennium Library) Sax Rohmer, *The Return of Dr. Fu-Manchu*. iUniverse (2001)

17. 《中国形象：中国人在西方思想中的自我认知》Rupert Hodder, *In China's Image: Chinese Self-perception in Western Thought*. Palgrave Macmillan UK (2000)

18. 《审美的形成与现代中国形象：蔡仪的哲学美学》（博士论文）Peter Randolph Button, *Aesthetic Formation and the Image of Modern China: The Philosophical Aesthetics of Cai Yi*. Ph. D. Dissertation, Cornell University (2000)

19. 《有限对手：冷战后中美相互影像》Jianwei Wang, *Limited Adversaries: Post-Cold War Sino-American Mutual Images*. Oxford, UK; New York: Oxford University (2000)

20. 《大汗之国：西方眼中的中国》Jonathan D. Spence（史景迁）, *The Chan's Great Continent: China in Western Minds*. W. W. Norton & Company (1999)

21. 《中土：17、18世纪欧洲文学中的中国建构》Adrian Hsia, *Chinesia: The European Construction of China in the Literature of the 17th and 18th Centuries*. Max Niemeyer Verlag Tübingen (1998)

22. 《美国的中国观：过去与现在的美国中国形象》Jonathan Goldstein, Jerry Israel, Hilary Conroy, *America Views China: American Images of China Then and Now*. Lehigh University Press (1991)

23. 《美国的中国形象》Benson Lee Grayson, *The American Image of China*. New York: Ungar (1979)

24. 《中国认知：中美关系中的形象与政策》John King Fairbank（费正清）, *China Perceived: Images and Policies in Chinese-American Relations*. New York: Knopf; distributed by Random House (1974)

25. 《中国变色龙：欧洲对中华文明的认知分析》Raymond Stanley Dawson, *The Chinese Chameleon: An Analysis of European Conceptions of Chinese Civilization*. London; New York: Oxford University Press (1967)

26. 《中国与中国人在〈内陆月刊〉杂志中的形象（1868—1875，1883—1935）》（博士论文）Limin Chu, *The Images of China and the Chinese in "Overland Monthly," 1868—1875, 1883—1935*. Ph. D. Dissertation, Duke University (1966)

27. 《1885—1915年美国华人形象》（博士论文）John Berdan Gardner, *The Image of the Chinese in the United States, 1885—1915*. Ph. D. Dissertation, University of Pennsylvania (1961)

28. 《思想遗痕：美国的中国和印度形象》Harold R. Isaacs（伊罗生）, *Scratches on Our Minds: American Images of China and India*. The John Day Company (1958)

29. 《Sangley[1]：菲律宾反华情绪的形成——偏见刻板印象的文化研究》Margaret Wyant Horsley, *Sangley: The Formation of Anti-Chinese Feeling in the Philippines: A Cultural Study of the Stereotypes of Prejudice*. Columbia University (1950)

30. 《傅满洲的阴影》Sax Rohmer, *Shadow of Fu Manchu*. Crime Club (1948)

31. 《另眼看中国》Elise McCormick, *Audacious Angles of China*. New York: D. Appleton and Company (1923)

32. 《来自中国内部：印象与经验》Charles Ernest Scott, *China from Within: Impressions and Experiences*. New York: Fleming H. Revell (1917)

33. 《中国之心》Oliver Bainbridge（潘伯礼）, *The Heart of China*. London: African Times and Orient Review (1912)

---

[1] Sangley：从16世纪到18世纪，西班牙人一直称在菲律宾做生意的中国人为"Sangley"，是对中国人的一种蔑称。

2. 中国历史与地理

2.1 历史

2.1.1 通史

1. 《中国简史：王朝、革命与转型，从中央王国到中华人民共和国》Jonathan Clements, *A Brief History of China: Dynasty, Revolution and Transformation: From the Middle Kingdom to the People's Republic*. Tuttle Publishing (2019)
2. 《中国历史指南》Michael Szonyi（宋怡明）(ed.), *A Companion to Chinese History*. Wiley-Blackwell (2017)
3. 《中国（1839—1997）》Michael Lynch, *China 1839—1997*. Hodder Education Publishers (2016)
4. 《中国历史与文化：17世纪至20世纪》Ying-shih Yu（余英时）, Josephine Chiu-Duke, Michael Duke, *Chinese History and Culture: Seventeenth Century Through Twentieth Century* (Masters of Chinese Studies). Columbia University Press (2016)
5. 《中国历史与文化：公元前6世纪至公元17世纪》Ying-shih Yu（余英时）, Josephine Chiu-Duke, Michael Duke, *Chinese History and Culture: Sixth Century B.C.E. to Seventeenth Century* (Masters of Chinese Studies). Columbia University Press (2016)
6. 《从元到近代中国和蒙古：罗茂锐著作》Morris Rossabi（罗茂锐）, *From Yuan to Modern China and Mongolia: The Writings of Morris Rossabi*. Brill Academic Pub. (2014)
7. 《中国简史：从古代到经济强国》Gordon Kerr, *A Short History of China: From Ancient Dynasties to Economic Powerhouse*. Oldcastle Books (2013)
8. 《中国历史》Morris Rossabi（罗茂锐）, *A History of China*. Wiley-Blackwell (2013)
9. 《中国历史》Cao Dawei and Sun Yanjing, *China's History* (The Sinopedia Series). Cengage Learning Asia Pte Ltd (2011)
10. 《中国历史》Kenneth Pletcher, *The History of China* (Understanding China). Britannica Educational Publishing (2011)
11. 《中国历史》David Curtis Wright, *The History of China*. 2nd Edition. Greenwood, ABC-CLIO (2011)
12. 《中国历史：从新石器时代文化到大清帝国（公元前10,000年至公元1799年）》（第一卷）Harold M. Tanner, *China: A History. Volume 1: From Neolithic Cultures through the Great Qing Empire, 10,000 BCE: 1799 CE*. Hackett Publishing Company, Inc. (2010)
13. 《世界历史中的中国》Paul S. Ropp, *China in World History*. Oxford University Press (2010)
14. 《中国5000年简明史》Ong Siew Chey, *China Condensed: 5,000 Years of History &*

15. 《中国历史读本》Sun Xiaoyu, *A Chinese History Reader*. Cengage Learning (2009)
16. 《中国历史》John Keay, *China: A History*. Basic Books (2009)
17. 《中国历史高级读本》（第2版）Wallace Johnson (ed.), *Advanced Reader in Chinese History* (2nd rev).The University of Kansas (2009)
18. 《中国新史》John King Fairbank（费正清）, Merle Goldman（梅谷）, *China: A New History*. Belknap Press of Harvard University Press (2006)
19. 《从尧到毛泽东：中国5000年史》（三卷本）Kenneth J. Hammond, *From Yao to Mao: 5000 Years of Chinese History*. 3 vols. The Teaching Company (2004)
20. 《中国历史手册》（修订和扩大版）Endymion Wilkinson, *Chinese History: A Manual, Revised and Enlarged*.Harvard University Asia Center (2000)
21. 《中国2000年简介：持续转型》Tyrene White, *China Briefing 2000: The Continuing Transformation*. M.E. Sharpe (2000)
22. 《中国历史》J. A. G. Roberts, *A History of China*. Macmillan Education UK (1999)
23. 《剑桥插图中国史》Patricia Buckley Ebrey（伊沛霞）, Kwang-ching Liu（刘广京）, *The Cambridge Illustrated History of China*. Cambridge University Press (1999)
24. 《中国大历史》Ray Huang（黄仁宇）, *China: A Macro History*. M.E. Sharpe (1997)
25. 《中国：理解其过去》Eileen H. Tamura [et al.], *China: Understanding Its Past*. Includes bibliographical references and index. University of Hawai'i Press (1997)
26. 《经济视角下的中国历史》Thomas G. Rawski（罗斯基）, Lillian M. Li (eds.), *Chinese History in Economic Perspective* (Studies on China). University of California Press (1992)
27. 《中国》David Wingrove, *Chung Kuo: The Middle Kingdom*. Dell (1989, 2004)
28. 《中国图说》Athanasius Kircher（基歇尔）, Translated by Dr. Charles D. Van Tuyl from the 1677 original Latin edition, *China Illustrata*.Indiana University Research Institute (1987)
29. 《中国历史》Wolfram Eberhard（艾伯华）, *A History of China*. Routledge And Kegan Paul, London (1948, 1950)
30. 《中华民族简史》L. Carrington Goodrich（傅路德）, *A Short History of Chinese People*. Third Edition. Harper and Brothers (1943) ; Allen & Unwin (1948, 1957)
31. 《四万万人：中国简史》Mary A. Nourse, *The Four Hundred Million: A Short History of the Chinese*. The Bobbs-Merrill Company (1935)
32. 《中国的发展》Kenneth Scott Latourette（赖德烈）, *The Development of China*. Houghton Mifflin (1917)
33. 《中国人的起源》John Ross, *The Origin of the Chinese People*. Edinburgh; London: Oliphants Ltd (1916)
34. 《大清国》Marshall Broomhall（海思波）, *The Chinese Empire: A General & Missionary Survey*. London, Morgan & Scott; Philadelphia, China Inland Mission (1907)

35. 《中华帝国史：中国历史学家编纂的帝国史》John Macgowan, *The Imperial History of China: Being a History of the Empire as Compiled by the Chinese Historians*. American Presbyterian Mission Press (1906)
36. 《中华开门：唐人录记书》Rounsevelle Wildman, *China's Open Door: A Sketch of Chinese Life and History*. Boston, Lothrop Publishing Company (1900)
37. 《"黄祸"：中国对抗世界》J. Martin Miller, *China, the Yellow Peril at War with the World: A History of the Chinese Empire from the Dawn of Civilization to the Present Time*. J. Martin (1900)
38. 《中国历史》Demetrius Charles Boulger（包罗杰）, *The History of China*. In 2 volumes. Vol. 1. New and rev. ed. London, W. Thacker & Co.; Calcutta, Thacker, Spink & Co. (1898)
39. 《青年人的中国历史》W. G. E. (William George Etler) Cunnyngham, *A Young People's History of the Chinese*. Publishing House of the Methodist Episcopal Church, South (1896)
40. 《中国简史与中国故事》Alexander Brebner, *A little History of China, and a Chinese Story*. London: T. F. Unwin (1895)
41. 《中国历史与札记》Herbert A. Giles（翟理斯）, *Historic China and Other Sketches*. London: Thos. de la Rue & Co. (1882)

2.1.2 古代中国

2.1.2.1 总论

1. 《认识中华帝国：朝代、生活与文化》Andrew R. Wilson, *Understanding Imperial China: Dynasties, Life, and Culture* (The Great Courses). The Teaching Company (2017)
2. 《中国古代史》John S. Major, Constance A. Cook, *Ancient China: A History*. Routledge (2016)
3. 《中华帝国（1350—1900）》Jonathan Porter, *Imperial China 1350—1900*. Rowman & Littlefield Publishers (2016)
4. 《中国古代王朝》Cindy Jenson-Elliott, *Ancient Chinese Dynasties*. ReferencePoint Press (2014)
5. 《发现古代中国》Neil D. Bramwell, *Discover Ancient China*. Erslow Pub Inc (2014)
6. 《中国早期社会文化史》Li Feng, *Early China: A Social and Cultural History*. Cambridge University Press (2013)
7. 《中华帝国如何衰落》Joseph W. Esherick, C. X. George Wei, *China: How the Empire Fell*. Routledge (2013)
8. 《世界历史中的中国》Paul S. Ropp, *China in World History*. Oxford University Press, USA (2010)
9. 《东域纪程录丛：古代中国闻见录》（第一、二卷）Henry Yule editor, *Cathay and the Way Thither, Volume 1-2, Being a Collection of Medieval Notices of China*. (Cambridge Library Collection-Hakluyt First Series). Cambridge University Press (2010)
10. 《古代中国》Arthur Cotterell, *Ancient China* (DK Eyewitness Books). DK Publishing, Inc. (2005)
11. 《剑桥中国古代史：从文明起源到公元前221年》Michael Loewe（鲁惟一）, Edward L. Shaughnessy（夏含夷）, *Cambridge History of Ancient China: From the Origins of*

Civilization to 221 BC. Cambridge University Press (1999)

12. 《古代巴蜀与中国之统一》Steven F. Sage, *Ancient Sichuan and the Unification of China*. State University of New York Press (1992)

13. 《中国古代之旅：从新石器时代到明代》Han Zhongmin and Hubert Delahaye (author), Wang Fangzi and Nebojsa Tomasevic (Editor), *A Journey Through Ancient China: From the Neolithic to the Ming*. Gallery Books (1985)

14. 《中国过去的模式》Mark Elvin, *The Pattern of the Chinese Past*. Stanford University Press (1973)

15. 《关于远东的好书：中国历史概要》Florence Ayscough（艾思柯）, *Friendly Books on Far Cathay: Being a Bibliography for the Student, and a Synopsis of Chinese History*. Shanghai: Commercial Press, Ltd. (1921)

16. 《愿尔中兴：中国的过去和现在》Edward Harper Parker（庄延龄）, *China: Past and Present*. London, Chapman and Hall, London (1903)

17. 《诸夏原来》Edward Harper Parker（庄延龄）, *Ancient China Simplified*. Chapman & Hall, London (1908)；Kessinger Publishing, LLC (2010)

18. 《中国简史：古代帝国和人民读本》Demetrius Charles Boulger, *A Short History of China: Being an Account for the General Reader of an Ancient Empire and People*. Allen (1893, 1900)

19. 《中华帝国（插图本铜版画）》Thomas Allom, *The Chinese Empire, Illustrated*. The London Printing and Publishing Company (1858)

2.1.2.2　商、周、秦、汉、隋、唐

1. 《兵马俑：探索中国历史上最有趣的谜》Edward Burman, *The Terracotta Warriors: Exploring the Most Intriguing Puzzle in Chinese History*. Pegasus Books (2018)

2. 《中国汉代的危机与冲突：公元前104年至公元9年》(Routledge Library Editions: History of China (Book 5)) Michael Loewe（鲁惟一）, *Crisis and Conflict in Han China, 104 BC to AD 9*. Routledge (2018)

3. 《洛阳大火：东汉史（公元23至220年）》(Sinica Leidensia) Rafe De Crespigny（张磊夫）, *Fire over Luoyang: A History of the Later Han Dynasty, 23-220 AD*. Brill Academic Pub. (2016)

4. 《汉代行政问题：宗法仪式、赋权与抗争手段》Michael Loewe（鲁惟一）, *Problems of Han Administration: Ancestral Rites, Weights and Measures, and the Means of Protest (China Studies)*. Brill (2016)

5. 《奇迹城市与转型：中国唐代长安及叙事经验》Linda Rui Feng, *City of Marvel and Transformation: Changan and Narratives of Experience in Tang Dynasty China*. University of Hawai'i Press (2015)

6. 《第一个公元千年期间中国东南地区的汉化》Hugh R. Clark, *The Sinitic Encounter in Southeast China Through the First Millennium CE*. University of Hawai'i Press (2015)

7. 《帝国的诞生：秦国再审视》Yuri Pines, Gideon Shelach, Lothar von Falkenhausen, Robin D. S.

Yates (eds.), *Birth of an Empire: The State of Qin Revisited*. University of California Press (2014)

8. 《中古中国门阀大族的消亡》Nicolas Tackett（谭凯）, *The Destruction of the Medieval Chinese Aristocracy*. Harvard University Asia Center (2014)

9. 《帝制早期中国的交通与合作：展示秦朝》Charles Sanft, *Communication and Cooperation in Early Imperial China: Publicizing the Qin Dynasty*. State University of New York Press (2014)

10. 《野蛮的交流：汉代帝国主义、中国文学风格与经济想象力》Tamara T. Chin, *Savage Exchange: Han Imperialism, Chinese Literary Style, and the Economic Imagination*. Harvard University Asia Center (2014)

11. 《唐代中国在多极化的亚洲：外交和战争史》Wang Zhenping, *Tang China in Multi-Polar Asia: A History of Diplomacy and War*. University of Hawai'i Press (2013)

12. 《中国五代时期画像：王仁裕回忆录（880—956）》Glen Dudbridge（杜德桥）, *A Portrait of Five Dynasties China: From the Memoirs of Wang Renyu (880—956)* (Oxford Oriental Monographs). Oxford University Press (2013)

13. 《隋唐中国及其吐蕃—蒙古邻国：文化、权力和联系（580—800）》Jonathan Karam Skaff, *Sui-Tang China and its Turko-Mongol Neighbors: Culture, Power and Connections, 580—800*. Oxford University Press (2012)

14. 《中国南唐（937—976）》Johannes L. Kurz, *China's Southern Tang Dynasty, 937—976* (Asian States and Empires). Routledge (2011)

15. 《王位之路：刘邦如何创立中国汉朝》Hing Ming Hung, *The Road to the Throne: How Liu Bang Founded China's Han Dynasty*. Algora Pub. (2011)

16. 《十世纪中国的权力与政治：前蜀政权》Hongjie Wang（王宏杰）, *Power and Politics in Tenth-Century China: The Former Shu Regime*. Cambria Press (2011)

17. 《与历史对话：20世纪中国对越王勾践的叙述》Paul A. Cohen（柯文）, *Speaking to History: The Story of King Goujian in Twentieth-Century China* (Asia Local Studies Global Themes 16). University of California Press (2010)

18. 《兵马俑：中国第一位皇帝与一个国家的诞生》John Man, *The Terra Cotta Army: China's First Emperor and the Birth of a Nation*. Da Capo Press (2009)

19. 《帝国之间：中国南北朝》Mark Edward Lewis, *China between Empires: The Northern and Southern Dynasties*. Belknap Press of Harvard University Press (2009)

20. 《中国唐代女皇武则天》X. L. Woo, *Empress Wu the Great: Tang Dynasty China*. Algora Publishing (2008)

21. 《中世纪早期中国的王权》Andrew Eisenberg, *Kingship in Early Medieval China* (Sinica Leidensia). Brill Academic Pub (2008)

22. 《班固的中国古代史》Anthony E. Clark, *Ban Gu's History of Early China*. Cambria Press (2008)

23. 《古代中华民族与帝国之形成》（第一卷）Chun-shu Chang（张春树）, *The Rise of the*

Chinese Empire, Vol. One: Nation, State, and Imperialism in Early China, ca. 1600 B.C.-A.D. 8. University of Michigan Press (2007)

24. 《汉代之边疆与帝国》（第二卷）Chun-shu Chang（张春树）, The Rise of the Chinese Empire, Vol. Two: Frontier, Immigration, and Empire in Han China, 130 B.C.–A.D.157. University of Michigan Press (2007)

25. 《第一位皇帝：〈史记〉选编》Sima Qian, K. E. Brashier, Raymond Dawson, The First Emperor: Selections from the Historical Records (Oxford World's Classics). Oxford University Press, USA (2007)

26. 《分裂的中国：为统一做准备（883—947）》Wang Gungwu（王赓武）, Divided China: Preparing for Reunification, 883—947. World Scientific Publishing (2007)

27. 《中国青铜时代早期：殷商文明》Robert L. Thorp, China in the Early Bronze Age: Shang Civilization. University of Pennsylvania Press (2006)

28. 《古代中国的景观与权力：西周的危机与衰落（公元前1045—前771年）》Li Feng, Landscape and Power in Early China: The Crisis and Fall of the Western Zhou, 1045—771 BC. Cambridge University Press (2006)

29. 《隋炀帝的生平、时代及遗产》Victor Cunrui Xiong, Emperor Yang of the Sui Dynasty: His Life, Times, and Legacy. State University of New York Press (2006)

30. 《汉帝国与中华帝国的建立》Grant Hardy, Anne Kinney, The Establishment of the Han Empire and Imperial China. Greenwood (2005)

31. 《唐代中国：世界历史上的东方崛起》Samuel Adrian M. Adshead, T'ang China: The Rise of the East in World History. Palgrave Macmillan (2004)

32. 《中国汉代的统治阶层：秦、汉、新朝历代人物传记辞典读本》(Handbook of Oriental Studies, Section 4 China) Michael Loewe（鲁惟一）, The Men Who Governed Han China: Companion to a Biographical Dictionary of the Qin, Former Han and Xin Periods. No. 17. Brill (2004)

33. 《传统中国的日常生活：唐代》Charles Benn, Daily Life in Traditional China: The Tang Dynasty. Greenwood (2001)

34. 《隋唐长安：中国中世纪后期城市史研究》Victor Xiong, Sui-Tang Changan: A Study in the Urban History of Late Medieval China (Michigan Monographs in Chinese Studies). The University of Michigan (2000)

35. 《祖先的景观：中国商代后期的时间、空间和社区（约公元前1200—前1045）》David N. Keightley, The Ancestral Landscape: Time, Space, and Community in Late Shang China (ca. 1200—1045 B.C.) (China Research Monograph, 53). Institute of East Asian Studies, University of California (2000)

36. 《曹丕登仙：汉代末年中国王朝建立的政治文化》Howard L. Goodman, Tsao Pi Transcendent: The Political Culture of Dynasty-founding in China at the End of the Han. Scripta Serica,

Seattle, Washington (1998)

37. 《唐代官史撰写》Denis Twitchett（崔瑞德）, *The Writing of Official History under the Tang* (Cambridge Studies in Chinese History, Literature and Institutions). Cambridge University Press (1992)
38. 《西周史料：青铜器铭文》Edward L. Shaughnessy（夏含夷）, *Sources of Western Zhou History: Inscribed Bronze Vessels*. Berkeley: University of California Press (1992)
39. 《〈后汉书〉诸志研究：其作者、来源、内容及在中国史学中的地位》B. J. Mansvelt Beck, *The Treatises of Later Han: Their Author, Sources, Contents and Place in Chinese Historiography*. E. J. Brill (1990)
40. 《唐代国家与学者》David Mcmullen, *State and Scholars in Tang China*. Cambridge University Press (1988)
41. 《汉代官僚体制》Hans Bielenstein（毕汉斯）, *The Bureaucracy of Han Times*. Cambridge University Press (1980)
42. 《商代史料：中国青铜时代的甲骨文铭文》David M. Keightley, *Sources of Shang History: The Oracle-bone Inscriptions of Bronze Age China*. University of California Press (1978)
43. 《中国治国之源：西周帝国》（第一卷）Herrlee Glessner Creel（顾立雅）, *Origins of Statecraft in China: The Western Chou Empire*. Vol. 1. University of Chicago Press (1970)
44. 《征服者与统治者：中世纪中国社会的力量》Wolfram Eberhard（艾伯华）, *Conquerors and Rulers: Social Forces in Medieval China*. Brill (1970)
45. 《汉代贸易与扩张：汉胡经济关系结构研究》Yingshi Yu（余英时）, *Trade and Expansion in Han China: A Study in the Structure of Sino-barbarian Economic Relations*. University of California Press (1967)
46. 《汉代行政记录》（两卷本）Michael Loewe（鲁惟一）, *Records of Han Administration*. 2 vols. Cambridge University Press (1967)
47. 《汉代以前的中国》William Watson, *China Before the Han Dynasty*. Frederick A. Praeger (1966)
48. 《先秦社会史论（公元前722—前222）》Cho-yun Hsu（许倬云）, *Ancient China in Transition: An Analysis of Social Mobility, 722—222 B. C*. Stanford University Press, Stanford, California (1965)
49. 《中国西汉奴隶制（公元前206—公元25年）》C. Martin Wilbur（韦慕庭）, *Slavery in China during the Former Han Dynasty, 206 B.C.—A.D. 25*. Chicago (1943)
50. 《中国第一个统一者：从李斯的一生研究秦代》Derk Bodde（卜德）, *China's First Unifier: A Study of the Ch'in Dynasty As Seen in the Life of Li Ssu (280？—208 B.C.)*. Brill (1938)

2.1.2.3 宋、辽、元、明

1. 《马背上的帝国：第一个游牧文明与中国的形成》John Man, *Empire of Horses: The First*

Nomadic Civilization and the Making of China. Pegasus Books (2020)

2. 《墙上的野蛮人：第一个游牧帝国与中国的建立》John Man, *Barbarians at the Wall: The First Nomadic Empire and the Making of China.* Bantam Press (2019)

3. 《从蒙元到明朝：乞讨僧人朱元璋如何成为中国皇帝》Hung Hing Ming, *From the Mongols to the Ming Dynasty: How a Begging Monk Became Emperor of China, Zhu Yuan Zhang.* Algora Publishing (2016)

4. 《四季：16世纪的中国明朝皇帝与其大学士》John W. Dardess, *Four Seasons: A Ming Emperor and His Grand Secretaries in Sixteenth-Century China.* Rowman & Littlefield Publishers (2016)

5. 《蒙古世纪：中国元代视觉文化（1271—1368）》Shane McCausland, *The Mongol Century: Visual Cultures of Yuan China, 1271—1368.* Reaktion Books (2015)

6. 《五代十国一大帝：宋太祖如何统一中国》Hung Hing Ming, *Ten States, Five Dynasties, One Great Emperor: How Emperor Taizu Unified China in the Song Dynasty.* Algora Publishing (2014)

7. 《宋徽宗》Patricia Buckley Ebrey（伊沛霞）, *Emperor Huizong.* Harvard University Press (2014)

8. 《欧亚（文化）对元朝的影响》Morris Rossabi（罗茂锐）, *Eurasian Influences on Yuan China.* Institute for Southeast Asian Studies (2013)

9. 《16世纪明代中国的税收与财政》Ray Huang（黄仁宇）, *Taxation and Governmental Finance in Sixteenth-Century Ming China* (Cambridge Studies in Chinese History, Literature and Institutions). Cambridge University Press (2009)

10. 《剑桥内亚史：元朝》Nicola Di Cosmo, Allen J. Frank, Peter B. Golden, *The Cambridge History of Inner Asia: The Chinggisid Age.* Cambridge University Press (2009)

11. 《行善的艺术：晚明中国的慈善事业》Joanna Handlin Smith（韩德玲）, *The Art of Doing Good: Charity in Late Ming China.* University of California Press (2009)

12. 《文化、朝臣和竞争：明代宫廷（1368—1644）》David M. Robinson, Dora C. Y. Ching, Chu Hung-lam, *Culture, Courtiers, and Competition: The Ming Court (1368—1644).* Harvard University Press (2008)

13. 《以共同语言划分：北宋后期的派系冲突》Ari Daniel Levine, *Divided by a Common Language: Factional Conflict in Late Northern Song China.* University of Hawai'i Press (2008)

14. 《宋徽宗与北宋末年中国：文化的政治与政治文化》Patricia Buckley Ebrey（伊佩霞）, Maggie Bickford（毕嘉珍）, Peter K. Bol（包弼德）, John W. Chaffee（贾志扬）, *Emperor Huizong and Late Northern Song China: The Politics of Culture and the Culture of Politics* (Harvard East Asian Monographs 266). Harvard University Asia Center (2006)

15. 《化干戈为玉帛：宋与契丹、辽的外交关系》David Curtis Wright, *From War to Diplomatic Parity in Eleventh-century China: Sung's Foreign Relations with Kitan Liao.* Brill (2005)

16. 《明代社会中的国家》Timothy Brook（卜正民）, *The Chinese State in Ming Society* (Critical Asian Scholarship). RoutledgeCurzon (2005)

17. 《中国历史中的宋、元、明转型》Paul Jakov Smith（史乐民），Richard von Glahn（万志英），Bettine Birge（柏清韵），Peter K. Bol（包弼德），*The Song-Yuan-Ming Transition in Chinese History* (Harvard East Asian Monographs). Harvard University Asia Center (2003)

18. 《流血与中国历史：东林党及其镇压》John W. Dardess, *Blood and History in China: The Donglin Faction and Its Repression, 1620—1627*. University of Hawai'i Press (2002)

19. 《土匪、太监和天子：中国明代中期的反叛与暴力经济》David M. Robinson, *Bandits, Eunuchs and the Son of Heaven: Rebellion and the Economy of Violence in Mid-Ming China*. University of Hawai'i Press (2001)

20. 《纵乐的困惑：明代的商业与文化》Timothy Brook（卜正民），*The Confusions of Pleasure: Commerce and Culture in Ming China*. University of California Press (1999)

21. 《明代社会：14至17世纪的江西泰和县》John W. Dardess, *A Ming Society: T'ai-ho County, Kiangsi, in the Fourteenth to Seventeenth Centuries*. University of California Press (1996)

22. 《号令世界：宋代国家与社会的进路》Robert Hymes, Conrad Schirokauer, *Ordering the World: Approaches to State and Society in Sung Dynasty China* (Studies on China). University of California Press (1993)

23. 《中国在蒙古西部的统治：元代地方行政》Elizabeth Endicott, *West Mongolian Rule in China: Local Administration in the Yuan Dynasty*. Harvard (1989)

24. 《忽必烈的生平与时代》Morris Rossabi（罗茂锐），*Khubilai Khan: His Life and Times*. University of California Press (1989)

25. 《蒙古帝国：蒙哥汗在汉地、俄罗斯和伊斯兰国家的政策（1251—1259）》Thomas T. Allsen, *Mongol Imperialism: The Policies of the Grand Qan Möngke in China, Russia, and the Islamic Lands, 1251—1259*. University of California Press (1987)

26. 《蒙古帝国主义：1251—1259年蒙哥大汗对中国、俄国和伊斯兰地区的政策》Thomas T. Allsen, *Mongol Imperialism: The Policies of the Grand Qan Möngke in China, Russia, and the Islamic Lands, 1251—1259*. University of California Press (1987)

27. 《宋代的朝廷与家庭：明州史氏的政治成就与家族命运（960—1279）》Richard L. Davis（戴仁柱），*Court and Family in Sung China 960—1279: Bureaucratic Success and Kinship Fortunes for the Shih of Ming-Chou*. Duke University Press (1986)

28. 《棋逢对手：10—14世纪的中国及其邻国》Morris Rossabi（罗茂锐），*China Among Equals: The Middle Kingdom and Its Neighbors, 10th—14th Centuries*. University of California Press (1983)

29. 《南宋的村庄与官僚机构》Brian E. McKnight（马伯良），*Village and Bureaucracy in Southern Sung China*. University Of Chicago Press (1971)

30. 《蒙古入侵前夜的中国日常生活（1250—1276）》Jacques Gernet（谢和耐）; Translated from the French by H. M. Wright, *Daily life in China: On the Eve of the Mongol Invasion, 1250—1276*. Stanford University Press (1962)

31. 《宋代中国的改革：王安石（1021—1086）及其新政》James T. C. Liu（刘子健），*Reform in Sung China: Wang An-shih (1021—1086) and His New Policies*. Harvard University Press (1959, 1968)

32. 《辽代社会史（907—1125）》Karl August Wittfogel（魏特夫），Feng Chia-sheng（冯家升）et al., *History of Chinese Society, Liao, 907—1125* (American Philosophical Society, Transactions). Macmillan Company (1949)

2.1.3 清代

1. 《白莲战争：中华帝国晚期的叛乱与镇压》Yingcong Dai, The White Lotus War: Rebellion and Suppression in Late Imperial China. University of Washington Press (2019)

2. 《太监的内心世界：清代帝王仆从的社会史》Melissa S. Dale, Inside the World of the Eunuch: A Social History of the Emperor's Servants in Qing China. Hong Kong University Press (2019)

3. 《清代西游者：晚清外交与信息秩序》Jenny Huangfu Day, Qing Travelers to the Far West: Diplomacy and the Information Order in Late Imperial China. Cambridge University Press (2018)

4. 《重塑中华帝国：满—朝关系（1616—1911）》Yuanchong Wang, Remaking the Chinese Empire: Manchu-Korean Relations, 1616—1911. Cornell University Press (2018)

5. 《言说利益：包世臣与19世纪中国改革》William T. Rowe（罗威廉），Speaking of Profit: Bao Shichen and Reform in Nineteenth-Century China (Harvard-Yenching Institute Monograph Series). Harvard University Asia Center (2018)

6. 《帝国的匪徒：中越边界的不法分子和叛乱分子》Bradley Camp Davis, Imperial Bandits: Outlaws and Rebels in the China-Vietnam Borderlands. University of Washington Press (2017)

7. 《国家支持的不平等：中国东北的八旗制度与社会分层》Shuang Chen, State-Sponsored Inequality: The Banner System and Social Stratification in Northeast China. Stanford University Press (2017)

8. 《人参与边疆：1636—1912年清代中国与朝鲜的疆界和政治关系》Seonmin Kim（金宣旼），Ginseng and Borderland: Territorial Boundaries and Political Relations Between Qing China and Choson Korea, 1636—1912. University of California Press (2017)

9. 《奢华的网络：18世纪中国盐商、地位与治国方略》Yulian Wu（吴玉廉），Luxurious Networks: Salt Merchants, Status, and Statecraft in Eighteenth-Century China. Stanford University Press (2017)

10. 《中国清代流行骗术》Mark P. McNicholas, *Forgery and Impersonation in Imperial China: Popular Deceptions and the High Qing State*. University of Washington Press (2016)

11. 《贸易与社会：中国海岸的厦门人际网（1638—1735）》Ng Chin-keong, *Trade and Society: The Amoy Network on the China Coast, 1638—1735*. NUS Press (2015)

12. 《地方秩序：中华帝国晚期惠州商人的跨区域实践》Yongtao Du, *The Order of Places: Translocal Practices of the Huizhou Merchants in Late Imperial China*. Brill Academic Pub (2015)

13. 《晚清政治、诗学与性别：薛绍徽与改革时代》Nanxiu Qian（钱南秀），*Politics,*

Poetics, and Gender in Late Qing China: Xue Shaohui and the Era of Reform. Stanford University Press (2015)

14. 《对中国清朝衰落的再思考：19世纪之际的帝国主义激进主义与边疆管理》Daniel McMahon, *Rethinking the Decline of China's Qing Dynasty: Imperial Activism and Borderland Management at the Turn of the Nineteenth Century* (Asian States and Empires). Routledge (2014)

15. 《清朝开放海洋：中国海洋政策（1684—1757）》Gang Zhao, *The Qing Opening to the Ocean: Chinese Maritime Policies, 1684—1757*. University of Hawaii Press (2013)

16. 《清代总督及其省区：中国领土管理的演变（1644—1796）》（新版）R. Kent Guy, *Qing Governors and Their Provinces: The Evolution of Territorial Administration in China, 1644—1796* (A China Program Book). New Edition. University of Washington Press (2013)

17. 《中华帝国晚期的科举考试和任人唯贤》Benjamin A. Elman（艾尔曼）, *Civil Examinations and Meritocracy in Late Imperial China*. Harvard University Press (2013)

18. 《微虫世界：一部关于太平天国的回忆录》Zhang Daye, translated with an introduction by Xiaofei Tian（田晓菲）, *The World of a Tiny Insect: A Memoir of the Taiping Rebellion and Its Aftermath*. University of Washington Press (2013)

19. 《天国之秋：中国、西方和太平天国内战史诗故事》Stephen R. Platt（裴士锋）, *Autumn in the Heavenly Kingdom: China, the West, and the Epic Story of the Taiping Civil War*. Knopf (2012)

20. 《义和团运动与中国大博弈》David J. Silbey, *The Boxer Rebellion and the Great Game in China*. Hill and Wang (2012)

21. 《躁动的帝国：1750年以来的中国与世界》Odd Arne Westad（文安立）, *Restless Empire: China and the World Since 1750*. Basic Books (2012)

22. 《太平天国运动（1851—66）》(Men-at-Arms) Ian Heath, Michael Perry, *The Taiping Rebellion 1851—66*. Osprey Publishing (2010)

23. 《最后的中华帝国：大清》William T. Rowe（罗威廉）, *China's Last Empire: The Great Qing*. Belknap Press of Harvard University Press (2009)

24. 《乾隆帝：上天之子，宇内之主》Mark Elliott（欧立德）, *Emperor Qianlong: Son of Heaven, Man of the World*. Longman (2008)

25. 《铁泪图：19世纪中国对于饥馑的文化反应》Kathryn Edgerton-Tarpley（艾志端）, *Tears from Iron: Cultural Responses to Famine in Nineteenth-Century China*. Berkeley: University of California Press (2008)

26. 《晚清与民国时期历史生产的政治学》Tze-ki Hon and Robert J. Culp (ed.), *The Politics of Historical Production in Late Qing and Republican China*. Brill (2007)

27. 《拳匪、中国和世界》Robert Bickers（毕可思）, R. G. Tiedemann, *The Boxers, China, and the World*. Rowman & Littlefield Publishers (2007)

28. 《清：蒙古、佛教和帝制晚期的中国》Johan Elverskog, *Our Great Qing: The Mongols, Buddhism, And the State in Late Imperial China*. University of Hawai'i Press (2006)

29. 《一位17世纪中国满族士兵的日记》Nicola Di Cosmo（狄宇宙）, *Diary of a Manchu Soldier in Seventeenth-Century China*. Routledge (2006)

30. 《太平天国：帝国的反叛与亵渎》Thomas H. Reilly（赖利）, *The Taiping Heavenly Kingdom: Rebellion and the Blasphemy of Empire*. University of Washington Press (2004)

31. 《新清史：承德山庄的中亚帝国》James A. Millward, Mark C. Elliott（欧立德）, Philippe Forêt, Ruth W. Dunnell, *New Qing Imperial History: The Making of the Inner Asian Empire at Qing Chengde*. RoutledgeCurzon (2004)

32. 《清朝征服前夕的满族—蒙古关系文献史》(Brill's Inner Asian Library) Nicola Di Cosmo（狄宇宙）, Dalizhabu Bao, *Manchu-Mongol Relations on the Eve of the Qing Conquest: A Documentary History*. Brill Academic Publing (2003)

33. 《1900年的北京：义和团运动》Peter Harrington, *Peking 1900: The Boxer Rebellion*. Osprey (2001)

34. 《满族之道：清朝的八旗与民族认同》Mark C. Elliott（欧立德）, *The Manchu Way: The Eight Banners and Ethnic Identity in Late Imperial China*. Stanford University Press (2001)

35. 《天津盐商：中华帝国晚期的国家权力和市民社会》Man Bun Kwan, *The Salt Merchants of Tianjin: State-Making and Civil Society in Late Imperial China*. University of Hawaii Press (2001)

36. 《爪牙：清代县衙的书办差役》Bradly Reed（白瑞德）, *Talons and Teeth: County Clerks and Runners in the Qing Dynasty* (Law, Society, and Culture in China). Stanford University Press (2000)

37. 《半透明镜：清代帝国思想中的历史和认同》Pamela Kyle Crossley（柯娇燕）, *A Translucent Mirror: History and Identity in Qing Imperial Ideology*. University of California Press (1999)

38. 《骆驼王的故事及其他：清末农民反现代化的抗争运动》Roxann Prazniak, *Of Camel Kings and Other Things: Rural Rebels Against Modernity in Late Imperial China*. Rowman & Littlefield Publishers (1999)

39. 《最后的皇帝：清代宫廷社会史》Evelyn S. Rawski（罗友枝）, *The Last Emperors: A Social History of Qing Imperial Institutions*. Berkeley: University of California Press (1998)

40. 《历史三调：作为事件、经历和神话的义和团》Paul A. Cohen（柯文）, *History in Three Keys: The Boxers as Event, Experience, and Myth*. Columbia University Press (1998)

41. 《中国：糖与社会——农民、技术和世界市场》Sucheta Mazumdar（穆素洁）, *Sugar and Society in China: Peasants, Technology, and the World Market*. Harvard University Asia Center (1998)

42. 《大门口的陌生人：1839—1861年间华南的社会动乱》Frederic Wakeman, Jr.（魏斐德）, *Strangers at the Gate: Social Disorder in South China, 1839—1861*. University of California Press (1997)

43. 《光荣的商家：晚清的商业与自修》Richard John Lufrano, *Honorable Merchants: Commerce and Self-Cultivation in Late Imperial China*.University of Hawaii Press (1997)

44. 《天国之子和他的世俗王朝：洪秀全与太平天国》Jonathan D. Spence（史景迁）, *God's Chinese Son: The Taiping Heavenly Kingdom of Hong Xiuquan*. W. W. Norton & Company (1996)

45. 《女真统治下的中国：清代知识分子与文化史论文集》Hoyt Cleveland Tillman, Stephen H. West, *China under Jurchen Rule: Essays on Chin Intellectual and Cultural History* (SUNY series in Chinese philosophy and culture). State University of New York Press (1995)

46. 《沈葆桢与中国19世纪的现代化》David Pong（庞百腾）, *Shen Pao-chen and China's Modernization in the Nineteenth Century*. Cambridge University Press (1994)

47. 《君主与大臣：清中期的军机处（1723—1820）》Beatrice S. Bartlett（白彬菊）, *Monarchs and Ministers: The Grand Council in Mid-Ch'ing China, 1723—1820*. University of California Press (1994)

48. 《功过格：晚清中国的社会变迁与道德秩序》Cynthia Joanne Brokaw, *The Ledgers of Merit and Demerit: Social Change and Moral Order in Late Imperial China*. Princeton University Press (1991)

49. 《君主与大臣：清中期的军机处（1723—1820）》Beatrice S. Bartlett（白彬菊）, *Monarchs and Ministers: The Grand Council in Mid-Ch'ing China, 1723—1820*. University of California Press (1990)

50. 《经学、政治和宗族：中华帝国晚期常州今文学派研究》Benjamin A. Elman（艾尔曼）, *Classicism, Politics, and Kinship: The Ch'ang-chou School of New Text Confucianism in Late Imperial China*. Berkeley: University of California Press (1990)

51. 《四库全书：乾隆晚期的学者与国家》R. Kent Guy（盖博坚）, *The Emperor's Four Treasuries Scholars and the State in the Late Ch'ien-lung Era*. Council on East Asian Studies, Harvard University (1987)

52. 《义和团运动的起源》Joseph W. Esherick（周锡瑞）, *The Origins of the Boxer Uprising*. University of California Press (1987)

53. 《洪业：清朝开国史》Frederic Wakeman, Jr.（魏斐德）, *The Great Enterprise: The Manchu Reconstruction of Imperial Order in Seventeenth-Century China*. University of California Press (1986)

54. 《州县官的银两：18世纪中国的合理化财政改革》Madeleine Zelin（曾小萍）, *The Magistrate's Tael: Rationalizing Fiscal Reform in Eighteenth Century Ch'ing China*. Berkeley: University of California Press (1984)

55. 《义和团运动》Lynn Bodin, Chris Warner, *The Boxer Rebellion*. Osprey (1979)

56. 《中华民国简史（1919—1949）》George F. Botjer, *A Short History of Nationalist China, 1919—1949*. Putnam (1979)

57. 《千年末世之乱：1813年八卦教起义》Susan Naquin（韩书瑞）, *Millenarian Rebellion in China: Eight Trigrams Uprising of 1813* (Historical Publications). Yale University Press (1977)

58. 《中华帝国晚期的冲突与控制》Frederic Wakeman Jr.（魏斐德）, Carolyn Grant (eds.), *Conflict and Control in Late Imperial China*. University of California Press (1975)

59. 《在传统与现代性之间：王韬与晚清革命》Paul A. Cohen（柯文）, *Between Tradition*

and Modernity: Wang T'ao and Reform in Late Ch'ing China. Cambridge: Harvard University Press (1974)

60. 《清代田赋刍论》Yeh-Chien Wang（王业键）, Land Taxation in Imperial China, 1750—1911. Harvard University Press (1974)

61. 《曾国藩的私人官僚机构》Jonathan Porter, Tsêng Kuo-fan's Private Bureaucracy. Berkeley, Center for Chinese Studies, University of California (1972)

62. 《中华帝国晚期的叛乱及其敌人：1796—1864年的军事化与社会结构》Philip A. Kuhn（孔飞力）, Rebellion and Its Enemies in Late Imperial China: Militarization and Social Structure, 1796—1864 (East Asian). Harvard University Press (1971)

63. 《中国早期工业化：盛宣怀（1844—1916）和官督商办企业》Albert Feuerwerker（费维恺）, China's Early Industrialization: Sheng Hsuan-huai (1844—1916) and Mandarin Enterprise. Scribner (1970)

64. 《太平叛乱：历史和文献》（第一卷：历史）Franz Michael, Chung-li Chang（张仲礼）, The Taiping Rebellion: History and Documents. Volume 1: History. University of Washington Press (1966)

65. 《明清社会史论》Ping-ti Ho（何炳棣）, The Ladder of Success in Imperial China: Aspects of Social Mobility, 1368—1911 (Studies of the East Asian Institute, Columbia University). John Wiley & Sons (1964)

66. 《中国和西方（1858—1861）：总理衙门的起源》Masataka Banno, China and the West, 1858—1861: The Origins of the Tsungli Yamen. Harvard University Press (1964)

67. 《中国清代地方政府》T'ung-tsu Ch'u（瞿同祖）, Local Government in China under the Ch'ing (Harvard East Asian Monographs). Harvard University Asia Center (1962)

68. 《中国十八省府》William Edgar Geil, Eighteen Capitals of China. Philadelphia & London: J. B. Lippincott Company (1911)

69. 《中国之将来》Joseph King Goodrich, The Coming China. Chicago A. C. McClurg & Co. (1911)

70. 《中国各省：连同宣统第一年的历史，以及中国政府的记述》Clarence Dalrymple Bruce, The Provinces of China, together with a history of the first year of H.I.M. Hsuan Tung, and an account of the government of China. Shanghai, The National Review Office (1910)

71. 《中国公行考：附公行商人或广州公行的描述》Hosea Ballou Morse（马士）, The Gilds of China, With an Account of the Gild Merchant or Co-hong of Canton. London, New York: Longmans, Green (1909)

72. 《中华帝国的贸易和管理》Hosea Ballou Morse（马士）, The Trade and Administration of the Chinese Empire. Longmans, Green, And Co. (1908, 1920)

73. 《中国觉醒》William Alexander Parsons Martin（丁韪良）, The Awakening of China. London: Hodder & Stoughton (1907)

74. 《清国及其臣民：一位美国外交人员的观察、回忆与结论》（两卷本）Charles Denby

（田贝）, *China and Her People: Being the Observations, Reminiscences, and Conclusions of an American Diplomat*. In 2 Vols. Boston L. C. Page & Company (1906)

75. 《中国内幕：中国危机的真相》Stanley P. Smith（司米德）, *China From Within: Or the Story of the Chinese Crisis*. Marshall Brothers (1901)

76. 《北京围攻：中国对抗世界》William Alexander Parsons Martin（丁韪良）, *The Siege in Peking: China against the World*. New York: Fleming H. Revell Company (1900)

77. 《中国危机》George B. Smyth, etc., *The Crisis in China*. Harper & Brothers Publishers (1900)

78. 《中国对抗世界》George B. Smyth, Charles Johnston, Poultney Bigelow, Charles Frederick Holder, John Barrett, *China against the World*. New York: The North American Review Publishing Co. (1900)

79. 《中国在转型》Archibald R. Colquhoun, *China in Transformation*. New York and London: Harper & Brothers Publishers (1898)

80. 《在华四十年：转变中的中国》Rosewell Hobart Graves（纪好弼）, *Forty Years in China, or, China in Transition*. Baltimore, R. H. Woodward Company (1895)

81. 《中国问题》James MacDonald, *The China Question*. London: Effingham Wilson, Royal Exchange (1870)

82. 《戈登常胜军纪实及镇压太平天国运动始末》Andrew Wilson, *The "Ever-Victorious Army": A History of the Chinese Campaign Under Lt.-Col. C.G. Gordon, and of the Suppression of the Tai-Ping Rebellion*. Edinburgh and London: William Blackwood and Sons (1868)

83. 《太平天国革命史》（两卷本）Augustus F. Lindley, *Ti-ping Tien-kwoh: The History of the Ti-ping Revolution*. 2 vols. London: Day & Son (limited) (1866)

84. 《1860年华北战役叙事：包含中国人性格的个人经验，以及国家道德和社会状况》Robert Swinhoe, *Narrative of the North China Campaign of 1860: Containing Personal Experiences of Chinese Character, and of the Moral and Social Condition of the Country*. London, Smith, Elder and Company (1861)

2.1.4 近现代

1. 《中国近代史：1850年至今的大国兴衰》Jonathan Fenby, *The Penguin History of Modern China: The Fall and Rise of a Great Power, 1850 to the Present*. Penguin Books Ltd (2019)

2. 《未完成的革命：孙中山与近代中国的斗争》Kayloe Tjio, *The Unfinished Revolution: Sun Yat-Sen and the Struggle for Modern China*. Marshall Cavendish International (Asia) Pte Ltd (2018)

3. 《构建中国：关于人民共和国的冲突性看法》Mobo Gao（高默波）, *Constructing China: Clashing Views of the People's Republic*. Pluto Press (2018)

4. 《没有长城：民国时期的贸易、关税和民族主义（1927—1945）》Felix Boecking, *No Great Wall: Trade, Tariffs, and Nationalism in Republican China, 1927—1945* (Harvard East Asian Monographs 397). Harvard University Asia Center (2017)

5. 《近代早期与现代东亚的"全球"与"地方"》Benjamin A. Elman（艾尔曼）, Chao-Hui

Jenny Liu（刘昭慧）(eds.), The "Global" and the "Local" in Early Modern and Modern East Asia (Leiden Series in Comparative Historiography). Brill (2017)

6. 《二十世纪中国：革命、倒退与平等之路》Wang Hui, Saul Thomas, China's Twentieth Century: Revolution, Retreat, and the Road to Equality. Verso Books (2016)

7. 《牛津图解中国现代史》Jeffrey N. Wasserstrom（华志坚）, Ian Johnson（张彦）, The Oxford Illustrated History of Modern China. Oxford University Press, USA (2016)

8. 《想象现代中国：形象、历史和记忆（1750年至今）》James A. Cook, Joshua Goldstein, Matthew D. Johnson, Visualizing Modern China: Image, History, and Memory, 1750-Present. Lexington Books (2014)

9. 《1978年以来的当代中国史》Yongnian Zheng（郑永年）, Contemporary China: A History since 1978 (Blackwell History of the Contemporary World). Wiley-Blackwell (2013)

10. 《重构近代中国：中国历史写作中的想象与真实》Huaiyin Li（李怀印）, Reinventing Modern China: Imagination and Authenticity in Chinese Historical Writing. University of Hawai'i Press (2013)

11. 《今日中华人民共和国：内部和外部挑战》Zhiqun Zhu（朱志群）, The People's Republic of China Today: Internal and External Challenges. World Scientific Publishing Company (2010)

12. 《摆动的支点：1800年以来的中国历史阐释》Pamela Kyle Crossley（柯娇燕）, The Wobbling Pivot, China since 1800: An Interpretive History. Wiley-Blackwell (2010)

13. 《中华人民共和国（1949—1976）》Michael Lynch, The People's Republic of China 1949—1976 (Access to History). Hodder Education (2010)

14. 《开放时代：毛泽东时代前的中国》Frank Dikotter（冯客）, The Age of Openness: China before Mao. Hong Kong University Press (2008)

15. 《"中华民国"》Diana Lary（戴安娜·拉里）, China's Republic. Cambridge University Press (2007)

16. 《胜利的困境：中华人民共和国的最初岁月》Jeremy Brown, Paul G. Pickowicz（毕克伟）, Dilemmas of Victory: The Early Years of the People's Republic of China. Harvard University Press (2007)

17. 《阐明公民身份：1912—1940年中国东南部的公民教育和学生政治》Robert Culp, Articulating Citizenship: Civic Education and Student Politics in Southeastern China, 1912—1940 (Harvard East Asian Monographs). Harvard University Asia Center (2007)

18. 《中国（1900—1976）》Geoff Stewart, China 1900—1976. Heinemann Secondary Education (2006)

19. 《历史与怪兽：二十世纪中国的历史、暴力与叙事》David Der-Wei Wang（王德威）, The Monster That Is History: History, Violence, and Fictional Writing in Twentieth-Century China. University of California Press (2004)

20. 《20世纪中国：档案中的历史》R. Keith Schoppa（萧邦奇），*Twentieth Century China: A History in Documents*. Oxford University Press (2004)

21. 《20世纪中国：研究新视角》Jeffrey N. Wasserstrom（华志坚），*Twentieth Century China: New Approaches*. Routledge (2002)

22. 《鸦片、国家与社会：中国毒品经济与国民党（1924—1937）》Edward R. Slack, *Opium, State, and Society: China's Narco-Economy and the Guomindang, 1924—1937*. University of Hawai'i Press (2001)

23. 《国民党在欧洲：文献资料手册》Marilyn A. Levine and Chen San-ching (eds.), *The Guomindang in Europe: A Sourcebook of Documents*. Institute of East Asian Studies, University of California, Berkeley, Center for Chinese Studies (2000)

24. 《哥伦比亚中国近代史指南》R. Keith Schoppa（萧邦奇），*The Columbia Guide to Modern Chinese History*. Columbia University Press (2000)

25. 《被设计的权力：民国时期的宪政构建》Suisheng Zhao（赵穗生），*Power by Design: Constitution-Making in Nationalist China*. University of Hawai'i Press (1996)

26. 《1911年以来的中国》Richard T. Phillips, *China Since 1911*. Macmillan Education UK (1996)

27. 《中国近代史》（第6版）Immanuel C. Y. Hsu（徐中约），*The Rise of Modern China*. Sixth Edition. Oxford University Press (1995)

28. 《从战争到民族主义：1924—1925年中国的转折点》Arthur Waldron, *From War to Nationalism: China's Turning Point, 1924—1925* (Cambridge Studies in Chinese History, Literature and Institutions). Cambridge University Press (1995)

29. 《腹地的形成：华北内陆的国家、社会和经济（1853—1937）》Kenneth Pomeranz（彭慕兰），*The Making of a Hinterland: State, Society, and Economy in Inland North China, 1853—1937*. Berkeley: University of California Press (1993)

30. 《长江下游地区的租金、税收和农民反抗（1840—1950）》Kathryn Bernhardt, *Rents, Taxes, and Peasant Resistance: The Lower Yangzi Region, 1840—1950*. Stanford University Press (1992)

31. 《国民党时代的中国（1927—1949）》Lloyd E. Eastman, Jerome Ch'en（陈志让），Suzanne Pepper, Lyman P. Van Slyke, *The Nationalist Era in China, 1927—1949*. Cambridge University Press (1991)

32. 《1900年以来的中国》Josh Brooman, *China Since 1900*. Addison-Wesley Pub (Sd) (1990)

33. 《中国的蓝衣社：法西斯主义与民族主义的发展》Maria Hsia Chang, *The Chinese Blue Shirt Society: Fascism and Developmental Nationalism*. Institute of East Asian Studies (and) Center for Chinese Studies, University of California, Berkeley (1985)

34. 《现代中国专辑》Frederick King Poole, *An Album of Modern China*. F. Watts (1981)

35. 《孙中山与法国人（1900—1908）》Jeffrey G. Barlow, *Sun Yat-sen and the French, 1900—1908*. Berkeley: Center for Chinese Studies, Institute of East Asian Studies,

University of California (1979)

36. 《孙中山：壮志未酬的爱国者》C. Martin Wilbur（韦慕庭）, *Sun Yat-Sen: Frustrated Patriot*. Columbia University Press (1976)

37. 《"中华民国"：1911—1949年的民族主义、战争与共产主义的兴起》Franz Schurmann（舒尔曼）, Orville Schell（夏伟）, *Republican China: Nationalism, War, and the Rise of Communism 1911—1949* (China Reader, Vol 2). Random House Trade Paperbacks (1967)

38. 《近日中国：一个世纪的变迁（1850—1950）》Emily Hahn（项美丽）, *China Only Yesterday, 1850—1950: A Century of Change*. Garden City, N. Y., Doubleday (1963)；Open Road Media (2015)

39. 《五四运动史：现代中国的知识革命》Tse-tsung Chow（周策纵）, *May Fourth Movement: Intellectual Revolution in Modern China*. Harvard University Press. Tokyo, Japan, Yishuweibian Company (1960)

40. 《中国没有狗：今日中国报道》William Kinmond, *No Dogs in China: A Report on China Today*. Thomas Nelson (1957)

41. 《中国的危机》Lawrence K. Rosinger（罗辛格）, *China's Crisis*. Alfred A. Knopf (1945)

42. 《直面中国》Harold B. Rattenbury, *Face to Face with China*. George G Harrap & Co. (1945)

43. 《中国取得应有地位》Carl Crow, *China Takes Her Place*. Harper & Brothers, New York (1944)

44. 《新中国的诞生：1842—1942百年概述》Arthur Clegg, *The Birth of New China: A Sketch of One Hundred Years, 1842—1942*. India Publishers, Allahabad (1944)

45. 《蒋介石的中国：一项政治研究》Paul M. A. Linebarger, *The China of Chiang Kai-shek: A Political Study*. World Peace Foundation (1941)

46. 《中国将重新站起》May-ling Soong Chaing（宋美龄）, *China Shall Rise Again*. Harper & Brothers (1940)

47. 《中国为统一而奋斗》J. M. D. Pringle, *China Struggles For Unity*. Penguin Books Limited, England (1939)

48. 《中国事务："中华民国"近代历史与现状调查》Sir Eric Teichman（台克满）, *Affairs of China: A Survey of the Recent History and Present Circumstances of the Republic of China*. Methuen (1938)

49. 《中国人就是这样》Carl Crow, *The Chinese Are Like That*. Harper & Brothers (1938)

50. 《现代中国：政治、经济和社会简史》Yun Shan Tan（谭云山）, *Modern China: A Short History, Political, Economic and Social*. Kitabistan, Allahabad (1938)

51. 《苦难的中国》Hallett Abend, *Tortured China*. Ives Washburn (1930)

52. 《建立新中国》No Yong Park, *Making A New China*. Boston: The Stratford Company (1929)

53. 《中国局势》Stanley K. Hornbeck, *The Situation in China*. The China Society of America (1927)

54. 《英文中国近代历史文选》Harley Farnsworth Macnair（宓亨利）, *Modern Chinese History: Selected Readings*. Commercial Press, Shanghai (1923)

55. 《日新䔳议》Min-Ch'ien T. Z. Tyau, *China Awakened*. Macmillan (1922)
56. 《关于中国的真相》*The Truth about China*. Being a Series of Articles, Reprinted from the "Peking and Tientsin Times". (1921)
57. 《中国的重塑》Adolf S. Waley, *The Remaking of China*. London: Constable and Co., Ltd. (1914)
58. 《中国最新发展：克拉克大学讲演集》George H. Blakeslee (ed.) *Recent Developments in China: Clark University Addresses*. New York: G. E. Stechert (1913)
59. 《转变的中国》William Gascoyne-Cecil, Florence Cecil, *Changing China*. New York: D. Appleton and Company (1912)

2.1.5 史学

1. 《边疆记忆：寻找后毛泽东时代的中国历史认同》Martin Thomas Fromm, Borderland Memories: Searching for Historical Identity in Post-Mao China. Cambridge University Press (2019)
2. 《后冷战之后：中国历史的未来》Jinhua Dai（戴锦华）, Lisa Rofel, After the Post-Cold War: The Future of Chinese History. Duke University Press Books (2018)
3. 《中国史学史纲要》Huaiqi Wu, An Historical Sketch of Chinese Historiography (China Academic Library). Springer-Verlag Berlin Heidelberg (2018)
4. 《观念的魔力：20世纪中国历史与经济》Rebecca E. Karl（柯瑞佳）, The Magic of Concepts: History and the Economic in Twentieth-Century China. Duke University Press Books (2017)
5. 《〈报任安书〉与司马迁的遗产》Stephen Durrant, The Letter to Ren An and Sima Qian's Legacy. University of Washington Press (2016)
6. 《中国中世纪早期资料手册》Wendy Swartz（田菱）, Robert Ford Campany（康儒博）, Yang Lu and Jessey J. C. Choo, Early Medieval China: A Sourcebook. Columbia University Press (2014)
7. 《历史与大众记忆：危机时刻的故事力量》Paul A. Cohen（柯文）, History and Popular Memory: The Power of Story in Moments of Crisis. Columbia University Press (2014)
8. 《展示过去：后社会主义中国的历史记忆与博物馆政治》Kirk A. Denton（邓腾克）, Exhibiting the Past: Historical Memory and the Politics of Museums in Postsocialist China. University of Hawai'i Press (2014)
9. 《可疑的事实：中国早期史学的证据》Garret P. S. Olberding, *Dubious Facts: The Evidence of Early Chinese Historiography*. State University of New York Press (2012)
10. 《近代中国记忆的位置：历史、政治与身份》Marc Andre Matten, *Places of Memory in Modern China: History, Politics, and Identity* (Leiden Series in Comparative Historiography). Brill (2011)
11. 《淮南子：汉初政府理论与实践指南》John S. Major, An Liu, *The Huainanzi: A Guide to the Theory and Practice of Government in Early Han China*. Columbia University Press (2010)
12. 《现代史学的全球史》George G. Iggers, Q. Edward Wang（王晴佳）, Supriya Mukherjee,

A Global History of Modern Historiography. Pearson Education (2008)

13. 《〈史记〉：汉代回忆录》（第八卷，第一部分）Ssu-ma Ch'ien, Edited by William H. Nienhauser, Jr.（倪豪士）, *The Grand Scribe's Records: Volume VIII. The Memoirs of Han China, Part I.* Indiana University Press (2008)

14. 《晚清和民国时期历史生产的政治学》Tze-ki Hon, Robert J. Culp (eds.), *The Politics of Historical Production in Late Qing and Republican China* (Leiden Series in Comparative Historiography). Brill (2007)

15. 《〈史记〉：汉代以前的世家》（第一卷，第一部分）Ssu-ma Ch'ien, Edited by William H. Nienhauser, Jr.（倪豪士）, *The Grand Scribe's Records: Volume I. The Hereditary Houses of Pre-Han China, Part I.* Indiana University Press (2006)

16. 《历史真相、历史批判与意识形态：新比较视角下的中国史学与历史文化》Helwig Schmidt-Glintzer, Achim Mittag, Jorn Rusen, *Historical Truth, Historical Criticism, And Ideology: Chinese Historiography And Historical Culture From A New Comparative Perspective*. Brill (2005)

17. 《世鉴：中国帝制时代的历史书写与运用》On Cho Ng（伍安祖）, Q. Edward Wang（王晴佳）, *Mirroring the Past: The Writing and Use of History in Imperial China*. University of Hawai'i Press (2005)

18. 《解缚的中国：变动中的中国历史研究视角》Paul A. Cohen（柯文）, *China Unbound: Evolving Perspectives on the Chinese Past* (Asia's Transformations: Critical Asian Scholarship). Routledge (2003)

19. 《史学转折点：一种跨文化的角度》Q. Edward Wang（王晴佳）, Georg G. Iggers (eds.), *Turning Points in Historiography: A Cross-Cultural Perspective* (Rochester Studies in Historiography). University of Rochester Press (2002)

20. 《〈吕氏春秋〉研究》James D. Sellmann, *Timing and rulership in Master Lü's Spring and Autumn Annals- (Lüshi chunqiu).* State University of New York Press (2002)

21. 《过去的模式：中国早期史学的形式与思想》David Schaberg, *A Patterned Past: Form and Thought in Early Chinese Historiography*. Harvard University Asia Center (2001)

22. 《吕氏春秋》Jokn KnoLlock and Jeffrey Riegel, *The Annals of Lu Buwei*.Translated, Annotated, and with an Introduction. Stanford University Press (2000)

23. 《透过历史发明中国：历史学的五四取向》Q. Edward Wang（王晴佳）, *Inventing China Through History: The May Fourth Approach to Historiography* (SUNY Series in Chinese Philosophy and Culture). State University of New York Press (2000)

24. 《中国早期历史的新来源：碑文和手稿阅读导论》Edward Shaughnessy（夏含夷）(ed.), *New Sources of Early Chinese History: An Introduction to the Reading of Inscriptions and Manuscripts*. Brill (1997)

25. 《从"历史"到"经典"：董仲舒关于〈春秋繁露〉的解释学》Sarah A. Queen, *From Chronicle to Canon: The Hermeneutics of the Spring and Autumn, According to Tung Chung-shu*.

Cambridge University Press (1996)

26. 《中国档案入门指南》Ye Wa and Joseph W. Esherick（周锡瑞）, *Chinese Archives: An Introductory Guide*. Institute of East Asian Studies, University of California, Center for Chinese Studies (1996)

27. 《〈史记〉：汉代以前的回忆录》（第七卷）Ssu-ma Ch'ien, Edited by William H. Nienhauser, Jr.（倪豪士）, *The Grand Scribe's Records: Volume VII. The Memoirs of Pre-Han China*. Indiana University Press (1995)

28. 《〈史记〉：汉代以前的基础编年史》（第一卷）Ssu-ma Ch'ien, Edited by William H. Nienhauser, Jr.（倪豪士）, *The Grand Scribe's Records: Volume I. The Basic Annals of Pre-Han China*. Indiana University Press (1994)

29. 《史记：译自司马迁著〈史记〉》（两卷本）Burton Watson, Chien Ssu-Ma, *Records of the Grand Historian: Translated from the Shih chi of Ssu-Ma Ch'ien* (Records of civilization sources and studies no. 65.: UNESCO collection of representative works. Chinese series), in two volumes. Columbia University Press (1993)

30. 《在中国发现历史：中国中心观在美国的兴起》Paul A. Cohen（柯文）, *Discovering History in China: American Historical Writing on the Recent Chinese Past* (Studies of the Weatherhead East Asian Institute). Columbia University Press (1984)

31. 《中华人民共和国明清史研究》Frederic Wakeman, Jr.（魏斐德）(ed), *Ming and Qing Historical Studies in the People's Republic of China*. Institute of East Asian Studies, University of California, Berkeley, Center for Chinese Studies (1980)

32. 《中华帝制的衰落》Frederic Wakeman, Jr.（魏斐德）, *The Fall of Imperial China* (The Transformation of Modern China Series). New York: Free Press (1975)

33. 《史记：译自司马迁著〈史记〉》（第一卷：汉代初年，公元前209年至公元前141年）Burton Watson, *Records of the Grand Historian of China: Translated from the Shih chi of Ssu-ma Ch'ien. Volume 1, Early Years of the Han Dynasty, 209 to 141 B.C.* Columbia University Press (1971)

34. 《史记：译自司马迁著〈史记〉》（第二卷：汉代，修订版）Burton Watson, *Records of the Grand Historian of China: Translated from the Shih chi of Ssu-ma Ch'ien. Volume 2, Han Dynasty. Revised Edition*. Columbia University Press (1971)

35. 《顾颉刚与中国新史学：民族主义与替代传统的寻求》(Center for Chinese Studies, University of Michigan) Laurence A. Schneider, *Ku Chieh-Kang and China's New History: Nationalism and the Quest for Alternative Traditions*. University of California Press (1971)

36. 《中国传统与现代化的新视角》John King Fairbank（费正清）, *New Views of China's Tradition and Modernization*. Washington: Service Center for Teachers of History (1968)

37. 《中国伟大史家司马迁》Burton Watson, *Ssu-ma Ch'ien: Grand Historian of China*. Columbia University Press (1963)

38. 《东方专制主义：对于极权力量的比较研究》Karl August Wittfogel（魏特夫）, *Oriental*

Despotism: A Comparative Study of Total Power. Yale University Press (1957)

39. 《一位中国历史学家的自传："古史辨"专题研讨会序言》Arthur William Hummel（恒慕义）, *The Autobiography of a Chinese Historian: Being the Preface to a Symposium on Ancient Chinese History (Ku shih pien).* Taipei: Reprinted by Ch'eng Wen Pub. Co. (1931; 1966)

2.1.6　考古

1. 《东亚考古学：中国、韩国和日本文明的兴起》Gina L. Barnes, *Archaeology of East Asia: The Rise of Civilisation in China, Korea and Japan.* Oxbow Books (2015)

2. 《兵马俑的秘密：一位中国古代皇帝的陵墓》(Archaeological Mysteries) Michael Capek, *Secrets of the Terracotta Army: Tomb of an Ancient Chinese Emperor.* Capstone Press (21 Dec 2015)

3. 《中国古墓宝藏：女性墓葬的考古学》Wolfram Grajetzki, *Tomb Treasures of the Late Middle Kingdom: The Archaeology of Female Burials.* University of Pennsylvania Press (2014)

4. 《中国考古手册》Anne P. Underhill (ed.), *A Companion to Chinese Archaeology.* Wiley-Blackwell (2013)

5. 《蒙古人中国与丝绸之路：丝绸之路考古和历史》Hans van Roon, *Mongols China and the Silk Road: Archeology and History of the Silk Road.* (2013)

6. 《伟大的中国青铜时代：中华人民共和国展览》Wen Fong (edit.), *The Great Bronze Age of China: An Exhibition from The People's Republic of China.* Metropolitan Museum of Art (2013; 1980)

7. 《中国考古：从旧石器时代晚期到青铜器时代早期》Li Liu, Xingcan Chen, *The Archaeology of China: From the Late Paleolithic to the Early Bronze Age.* Cambridge University Press (2012)

8. 《匈奴考古：内亚第一个草原帝国的多学科视角》Ursula Brosseder, Bryan K. Miller, *Xiongnu Archaeology: Multidisciplinary Perspectives of the First Steppe Empire in Inner Asia.* Vor-und Fruhgeschichtliche Archaologie (2011)

9. 《中国古代盐业生产与社会等级：中国三峡专业考古调查》Rowan K. Flad, *Salt Production and Social Hierarchy in Ancient China: An Archaeological Investigation of Specialization in China's Three Gorges.* Cambridge University Press (2011)

10. 《中国新石器时代：早期轨迹》Li Liu, *The Chinese Neolithic: Trajectories to Early States.* Cambridge University Press (2005)

11. 《领导战略、经济活动以及区域互动：中国东北社会的复杂性》（中国考古）Gideon Shelach, *Leadership Strategies, Economic Activity, and Interregional Interaction: Social Complexity in Northeast China.* Kluwer Academic Publishers (2002)

12. 《探索中国之过去：考古学、艺术的新发现和新研究》Roderick Whitfield, Wang Tao, *Exploring China's Past: New Discoveries and Studies in Archeology and Art* (International Series in Chinese Art and Archaeology, 1). Saffron (2000)

13. 《东北考古：长城以外》Sarah Milledge Nelson, *The Archaeology of Northeast China-Beyond the Great Wall.* Routledge (1995)

14. 《中国之地下王国》Editors of Time Life Books, *China's Buried Kingdoms*.Time Life (1993)
15. 《人类、猿和中国化石：人类进化的新启示》Charles E. Oxnard, *Humans, Apes, and Chinese Fossils: New Implications for Human Evolution* (Occasional papers' series: Hong Kong University Press, No. 4.). HongKong University Press (1985)
16. 《中国考古新发现："文化大革命"中的发现》Hsia Nai, Ku Yen-wen, Lu Wen-kao, *New Archaeological Finds in China: Discoveries During the Cultural Revolution*.Foreign Language Press (1972; 1974)
17. 《中国宝藏》Michael Ridley, *Treasures of China*.The Dolphin Press (1973)
18. 《内蒙古锡林郭勒地区考古研究》Bo Sommarstrom, *Archaeological Researches in the Edsen-gol Region Inner Mongolia*. Statens Etnografiska Museum (1956)
19. 《中国沙漠中的遗址》（总2卷）Aurel Stein（斯坦因）, *Ruins of Desert Cathay: Personal Narrative of Explorations in Central Asia and Westernmost China*. 2 Vols. London: Macmillan and Co. (1912)

2.1.7 哈佛中国史系列

1. 《最后的中华帝国：大清》（第六卷）William T. Rowe（罗威廉）, *China's Last Empire: The Great Qing*. Vol. 6. Belknap Press of Harvard University Press (2009)
2. 《挣扎的帝国：元与明》（第五卷）Timothy Brook（卜正民）, *The Troubled Empire: China in the Yuan and Ming Dynasties*. Vol. 5. Belknap Press of Harvard University Press (2010)
3. 《儒家统治的时代：宋的转型》（第四卷）Dieter Kuhn（迪特·库恩）, *The Age of Confucian Rule: The Song Transformation of China*. Vol. 4. Belknap Press of Harvard University Press (2009)
4. 《世界性的帝国：唐朝》（第三卷）Mark Edward Lewis（陆威仪）, *China's Cosmopolitan Empire: The Tang Dynasty*. Vol. 3. The Belknap Press of Harvard University Press (2012)
5. 《分裂的帝国：南北朝》（第二卷）Mark Edward Lewis（陆威仪）, *China Between Empires: The Northern and Southern Dynasties*. Vol. 2. The Belknap Press of Harvard University Press (2008)
6. 《早期中华帝国：秦与汉》（第一卷）Mark Edward Lewis（陆威仪）, *The Early Chinese Empires: Qin and Han*. Vol. 1.The Belknap Press of Harvard University Press (2007)

2.1.8 剑桥中国史系列

1. 《剑桥中华人民共和国史·中国革命内部的革命（1966—1982）》（第十五卷）Roderick MacFarquhar（马若德）and John K. Fairbank（费正清）, *Cambridge History of China vol. 15: People's Republic Part 2, 1966—1982*. Cambridge University Press (1991)
2. 《剑桥中华人民共和国史—革命的中国的兴起（1949—1965）》（第十四卷）Roderick MacFarquhar（马若德）and John K. Fairbank（费正清）, *Cambridge History of China vol. 14: People's Republic Part 1, 1949—1965*. Cambridge University Press (1987)
3. 《剑桥"中华民国"史1912—1949年（下卷）》（第十三卷）John K. Fairbank（费正

清）and Albert Feuerwerker（费维恺）, *Cambridge History of China vol. 13: Republican China 1912—1949 Part 2*. Cambridge University Press (1986)

4. 《剑桥"中华民国"史1912—1949年（上卷）》（第十二卷）John K. Fairbank（费正清）, DenisTwitchett（崔瑞德）, *Cambridge History of China vol. 12: Republican China 1912—1949 Part 1*. Cambridge University Press (1983)

5. 《剑桥中国晚清史1800—1911年（下卷）》（第十一卷）John K. Fairbank（费正清）and Kwang-Ching Liu（刘广京）, *Cambridge History of China vol. 11: Late Ching 1800—1911 Part 2*. Cambridge University Press (1980)

6. 《剑桥中国晚清史1800—1911年（上卷）》（第十卷）John K. Fairbank（费正清）, *Cambridge History of China vol. 10: Late Ching 1800—1911 Part 1*. Cambridge University Press (1978)

7. 《剑桥中国清代史（至1800年）》（第九卷）Willard J. Peterson, *Cambridge History of China v 09 The Ching Empire to 1800 Part 1*. Cambridge University Press (2002)

8. 《剑桥中国明代史（1368—1644年）（下卷）》（第八卷）DenisTwitchett（崔瑞德）, Frederick W. Mote（牟复礼）, *Cambridge History of China vol. 08: The Ming Dynasty 1368—1644 Pt 2*. Cambridge University Press (1998)

9. 《剑桥中国明代史（1368—1644年）（上卷）》（第七卷）Frederick W. Mote（牟复礼）and DenisTwitchett（崔瑞德）, *Cambridge History of China vol. 07: The Ming Dynasty 1368—1644 Pt 1*. Cambridge University Press (1988)

10. 《剑桥中国辽西夏金元史（907—1368年）》（第六卷）DenisTwitchett（崔瑞德）and Herbert Franke（傅海波）, *Cambridge History of China vol. 06: Alien Regimes and Border States 907—1368*. Cambridge University Press (1995)

11. 《剑桥中国五代、宋及其前史（907—1279年）》（第五卷）DenisTwitchett（崔瑞德）and Paul Jakov Smith, *Cambridge History of China vol. 05: Five Dynasties and Sung and Its Precursors 907—1279 AD*. Cambridge University Press (2009)

12. 《剑桥中国隋唐史（589—906年）》（第三卷）DenisTwitchett（崔瑞德）, *Cambridge History of China vol. 03: Sui and T'ang 589-906 AD Part 1*. Cambridge University Press (1979)

13. 《剑桥中国秦汉史（公元前221—公元220年）》（第一卷）DenisTwitchett（崔瑞德）, Michael Loewe（鲁惟一）, *Cambridge History of China vol. 01: Chin and Han Empires 221 BC-AD 220*. Cambridge University Press (1987)

2.2 游记与地方史

2.2.1 北京

1. 《京报：19世纪中国历史读本》Lane J Harris, *The Peking Gazette: A Reader in Nineteenth-Century Chinese History*. Brill (2018)

2. 《老北京：皇城明信片》Felicitas Titus, Susan Naquin（韩书瑞）, *Old Beijing: Postcards*

from the Imperial City. Tuttle Publishing (2018)

3. 《拼图现代北京：空间、情感与文学形态》Weijie Song, *Mapping Modern Beijing: Space, Emotion, Literary Topography*. Oxford University Press (2017)

4. 《北京城市记忆：历史建筑和历史街区、中轴线和城墙》Fang Wang（汪芳）, *Beijing Urban Memory: Historic Buildings and Historic Areas, Central Axes and City Walls*. Springer Singapore (2016)

5. 《北京争夺战（1858—1860）：法英冲突在中国》Harry Gelber, *Battle for Beijing, 1858—1860: Franco-British Conflict in China*. Palgrave Macmillan (2016)

6. 《地下北京：地铁的现代性、美学与技术》Shiye Fu, *Beijing Underground: Modernity, Aesthetics and Technology in the Subway*. Columbia University (2016)

7. 《污泥处理的环境和社会经济影响：北京案证》Guofeng Zhang, *Environmental and Social-economic Impacts of Sewage Sludge Treatment: The Evidence of Beijing*. Springer Singapore (2016)

8. 《百年变迁：20世纪北京的城市结构》Yi Wang, *A Century of Change: Beijing's Urban Structure in the 20th Century*. Springer International Publishing (2016)

9. 《书写北京　中国当代文学与电影中的城市空间与文化想象》Yiran Zheng, *Writing Beijing: Urban Spaces and Cultural Imaginations in Contemporary Chinese Literature and Films*. Lexington Books (2016)

10. 《北京的死者：民国时期中国的谋杀案和法医学》Daniel Asen, *Death in Beijing: Murder and Forensic Science in Republican China*. Cambridge University Press (2016)

11. 《支持北京城市规划的地理空间分析》Ying Long, Zhenjiang Shen, *Geospatial Analysis to Support Urban Planning in Beijing*. Springer International Publishing (2015)

12. 《北京、天津、河北发展报告（2013）：衡量承载力和对策》Kui Wen, Erjuan Zhu (eds.), *Report on Development of Beijing, Tianjin, and Hebei Province (2013) : Measurement of Carrying Capacity and Countermeasures* (Current Chinese Economic Report Series). Springer (2015)

13. 《从乡巴佬到红色中国》Anne Depaulis, *From Rednecks to Red China*. CreateSpace Independent Publishing Platform (2015)

14. 《北京农民工的空间流动》Ran Liu, *Spatial Mobility of Migrant Workers in Beijing, China*. Springer International Publishing (2015)

15. 《北平历史地理》Renzhi Hou（侯仁之）, *An Historical Geography of Peiping* (China Academic Library). Springer Berlin Heidelberg (2014)

16. 《20世纪初中国的法律移植：民国时期的北京执法》Michael H. K. Ng, *Legal Transplantation in Early Twentieth-Century China: Practicing law in Republican Beijing*. Routledge (2014)

17. 《北京》(Cityscopes) Linda Jaivin, *Beijing*. Reaktion Books (2014)

18. 《中国的沉默大军：北京形象中的开拓者、商人、毒贩和工人重塑世界》Juan Pablo Cardenal, Heriberto Araujo, *China's Silent Army: The Pioneers, Traders, Fixers and Workers Who Are Remaking the World in Beijing's Image*. Crown Publishers (2013)

19. 《北京旅游奇遇》Lorien Holland, Steve Vidler, *China: A Travel Adventure*. Periplus Editions (2013)

20. 《北京欢迎你：揭秘首都的未来》Tom Scocca, *Beijing Welcomes You: Unveiling the Capital City of the Future*. Riverhead Books; Reprint Edition (2012)

21. 《万物·生命：当代北京的养生》Judith Farquhar（冯珠娣）, Qicheng Zhang（张其成）, *Ten Thousand Things: Nurturing Life in Contemporary Beijing*. Zone Books (2012)

22. 《北京护照：毛泽东时代的英国代表团》Patrick Wright, *Passport to Peking: A Very British Mission to Mao's China*. Oord University Press (2010)

23. 《北京记录：现代北京规划的自然和政治史》Jun Wang, *Beijing Record: A Physical and Political History of Planning Modern Beijing*. World Scientific (2010)

24. 《老北京的最后时光：在一个城市改造正在消失的小巷的生活》Michael Meyer, *The Last Days of Old Beijing: Life in the Vanishing Backstreets of a City Transformed*. Bloomsbury Publishing Plc: Walker & Company (2010)

25. 《亚当·斯密在北京：21世纪谱系》Giovanni Arrighi, *Adam Smith in Beijing: Lineages of the Twenty-First Century*. Verso (2007)

26. 《北京与上海》(Eyewitness Travel Guides) DK Publishing, *Beijing & Shanghai*. Dorling Kindersley Publishing (2007)

27. 《北京简史》Stephen G. Haw, *Beijing: A Concise History*. Routledge (2006)

28. 《寻找消逝的北京：中国首都历史指南》M. A. Aldrich, *The Search for a Vanishing Beijing: A Guide to China's Capital Through the Ages*. Hong Kong University Press (2006)

29. 《重建北京：天安门广场与一个政治空间的开创》Wu Hung（巫鸿）, *Remaking Beijing: Tiananmen Square and the Creation of a Political Space*. University of Chicago Press (2005)

30. 《后毛泽东时代北京的形成与出售》Anne-Marie Broudehoux, *The Making and Selling of Post-Mao Beijing* (Planning, History and Environment Series). Routledge (2004)

31. 《北京：附长城和其他旅行》Graeme Smith, Josh Chin & Peter Neville-Hadley, *Frommer's Beijing, with the Great Wall and Other Side Trips*. 3rd Edition. Wiley Publishing, Inc. (2004)

32. 《中国空间战略：帝制时代北京（1420—1911）》Jianfei Zhu, *Chinese Spatial Strategies: Imperial Beijing, 1420—1911*. RoutledgeCurzon (2004)

33. 《骑自行车从孟买到北京》Russell McGilton, *Bombay to Beijing by Bicycle*. Momentum (2004)

34. 《民国时代的北京：一部城市史》Madeleine Yue Dong（董玥）, *Republican Beijing: The City and Its Histories*. University of California Press (2003)

35. 《北京》Philip Gambone, *Beijing* (A novel). The University of Wisconsin Press (2003)

36. 《鸟类爱好者：北京之旅》Alastair Morrison, Robert Hefner, *The Bird Fancier: A Journey to Peking*. Pandanus Books (2001)

37. 《北京人的故事》Penny Van Oosterzee, *The story of Peking Man*. Allen & Unwin (2001)

38. 《北京的庙宇和城市生活（1400—1900）》Susan Naquin（韩书瑞）, *Peking Temples*

and City Life, 1400—1900. Universit of California Press (2000)

39. 《紫禁城的秘密世界：中华帝国的辉煌（1644—1911）》（展览）Secret World of the Forbidden City: Splendors from Imperial China, 1644—1911. And Change and Continuity: Chinese Americans in California. Exhibition Information and Curriculum Guide for Teachers Grades 2-11. Oakland Museum of California (2000)

40. 《北京老城区改造：菊儿胡同邻里项目》Liang-Yung Wu, Rehabilitating the Old City of Beijing: A Project in the Ju'er Hutong Neighbourhood. University of British Columbia Press (1999)

41. 《中国皇城规划》Nancy Shatzman Steinhardt, Chinese Imperial City Planning. University of Hawai'i Press (1990)

42. 《北京的人力车夫：20世纪20年代的市民与政治》David Strand（史谦德）, Rickshaw Beijing: City People and Politics in the 1920s. University of California Press (1989)

43. 《北京故事：旧中国的最后时光》（纪念司徒雷登）David Kidd, Peking Story: The Last Days of Old China. New York Review Books, (1988, 2003)

44. 《北京目标》Adam Hall (Elleston Trevor), The Peking Target. Playboy Press (1981)

45. 《京华烟云》Yutang Lin（林语堂）, Moment in Peking.The John Day Company (1939, 1980)

46. 《燕京胜迹》Herbert C. White, Introduction by Hu Shih, Peking the Beautiful. The Commercial Press, Shanghai, China (1927)

47. 《普林斯顿在北京》Annual Report of the Board of Trustees for 1923, Princeton in Peking. (Volume 3) (1924)

48. 《北京的城墙和城门》Osvald Siren（喜仁龙）, The Walls and Gates of Peking.London: John Lane the Bodley Head Limited (1924)

49. 《北京美观》（限量本）Donald Mennie, Putnam Weale, The Pageant of Peking: Comprising Sixty-Six Vandyck Photogravures of Peking and Environment. Shanghai: A. S. Watson & Co. (1920)

50. 《北京照相》（德文版）Wang Marine-Stabsarzt, In und um Peking. Wahrend der kriegswirren 1900—1901. (1902)

51. 《从阿穆尔到北京到紫禁城》（第九册）(Burton Holmes Travelogues) Burton Holmes, Down the Amur; Peking; The Forbidden City. Book Nine. The Travelogue Bureau, Chicago, New York (1917)

52. 《北京儿歌》Baron Guido Vital（威达雷）, Chinese folklore. Pekinese Rhymes, First Collected and Edited with Notes and Translation. Peking: Pei-Tang Press (1896)

53. 《中国旅行：说明、观察和比较》（含圆明园的记录）John Barrow, Travels in China: Containing Descriptions, Observations and Comparisons. Cambridge University Press (1804, 2010)

2.2.2 上海

1. 《上海免费出租车：新中国骗子和叛徒的旅程》Frank Langfitt, The Shanghai Free Taxi: Journeys with the Hustlers and Rebels of the New China. Public Affairs (2019)

2. 《离开上海的最后一艘船：逃离毛泽东革命的中国人的史诗故事》Helen Zia（谢汉

兰）, *Last Boat out of Shanghai: The Epic Story of the Chinese Who Fled Mao's Revolution*. Ballantine Books (2019)

3. 《危难时刻的关怀：上海单身女性从事创意工作研究》(Palgrave Studies in Globalization, Culture and Society) Chow Yiu Fai, *Caring in Times of Precarity: A Study of Single Women Doing Creative Work in Shanghai*. Springer International Publishing, Palgrave (2019)

4. 《都市饮食文化：20世纪的悉尼、上海和新加坡》Cecilia Leong-Salobir, *Urban Food Culture: Sydney, Shanghai and Singapore in the Twentieth Century*. Palgrave Macmillan US (2019)

5. 《上海及无锡方言连读变调之变异性研究》(Frontiers in Chinese Linguistics 4) Hanbo Yan, *The Nature of Variation in Tone Sandhi Patterns of Shanghai and Wuxi Wu*. Springer Singapore (2018)

6. 《上海圣城：世界城市的宗教景观》Benoît Vermander, *Shanghai Sacred: The Religious Landscape of a Global City*. University of Washington Press (2018)

7. 《上海忆旧：名流、学者与恶棍的故事》Claire Chao（赵芝洁）, Isabel Sun Chao（孙树莹）, *Remembering Shanghai: A Memoir of Socialites, Scholars and Scoundrels*. Plum Brook (1 May 2018)

8. 《魔鬼之城：统治旧上海黑社会的两个人》Paul French, *City of Devils: The Two Men Who Ruled the Underworld of Old Shanghai*. Picador (2018)

9. 《身体、社会、民族：上海公共卫生与城市文化的创立》(Harvard East Asian monographs 414) Chieko Nakajima, *Body, Society, and Nation: The Creation of Public Health and Urban Culture in Shanghai*. Harvard University Asia Center (2018)

10. 《上海的澳大利亚人：中国条约口岸的种族、权利和民族》Sophie Loy-Wilson, *Australians in Shanghai: Race, Rights and Nation in Treaty Port China*. Routledge (2017)

11. 《1937年上海和南京：长江大屠杀》Benjamin Lai, *Shanghai and Nanjing 1937: Massacre on the Yangtze* (Osprey Campaign 309). Osprey Publishing (2017)

12. 《影子现代主义：1925—1937年的上海摄影、写作和空间》William Schaefer, *Shadow Modernism: Photography, Writing, and Space in Shanghai, 1925—1937*. Duke University Press Books (2017)

13. 《现代艺术世界的形成：民国时期上海国画的制度化与合法化》Pedith Pui Chan, *The Making of a Modern Art World: Institutionalisation and Legitimisation of Guohua in Republican Shanghai*. Brill (2017)

14. 《城市漏洞：上海城市中心的空间生产创意联盟》Ying Zhou, *Urban Loopholes: Creative Alliances of Spatial Production in Shanghai's City Center*. Birkhauser (2017)

15. 《镰刀与城市：上海的死亡社会史》Christian Henriot（安克强）, *Scythe and the City: A Social History of Death in Shanghai*. Stanford University Press (2016)

16. 《永恒的幸福街：上海路上的大城市梦》Rob Schmitz, *Street of Eternal Happiness: Big City Dreams Along a Shanghai Road*. Crown (2016)

17. 《上海夜景：一个全球城市的夜间传记》James Farrer, Andrew David Field, *Shanghai*

Nightscapes: A Nocturnal Biography of a Global City. University of Chicago Press (2015)

18. 《上海家园：私人生活的梦想》Jie Li, *Shanghai Homes: Palimpsests of Private Life*. Columbia University Press (2015)

19. 《上海文学想象：转型中的城市》(Asian Cities) Lena Scheen, *Shanghai Literary Imaginings: A City in Transformation*. Amsterdam University Press (2015)

20. 《〈时代〉画报：上海漫画家邵洵美的艺术圈和陈伊范的游记（1926—1938）》Paul Bevan, *A Modern Miscellany: Shanghai Cartoon Artists, Shao Xunmei's Circle and the Travels of Jack Chen, 1926—1938*. Brill (2015)

21. 《创意产业区：上海创意集群的动态、网络及影响分析》(Advances in Asian Human-Environmental Research) Jinliao He, *Creative Industry Districts: An Analysis of Dynamics, Networks and Implications on Creative Clusters in Shanghai*. Springer Internat (2014)

22. 《上海的未来：重塑现代性》Anna Greenspan, *Shanghai Future: Modernity Remade*. Oxford University Press (2014)

23. 《穿越上海时光的无序循环》Nick Land, *Templexity: Disordered Loops through Shanghai Time*. Urbanatomy Electronic (2014)

24. 《逃离上海》Paul C.Huang, *Escape from Shanghai*. PCH Publishing, LLC (2014)

25. 《上海刘氏家族》Sherman Cochran（高家龙）, Andrew Hsieh, *The Lius of Shanghai*. Harvard University Press (2013)

26. 《学习上海教育成功经验》(Education in the Asia-Pacific Region: Issues, Concerns and Prospects 21) Charlene Tan, *Learning from Shanghai: Lessons on Achieving Educational Success*. Springer-Verlag Singapur (2013)

27. 《上海街头时尚》Toni Johnson-Woods, Vicki Karaminas, *Shanghai Street Style*. Intellect Ltd (2013)

28. 《新上海的媒介与记忆》(Palgrave Macmillan Memory Studies) Amanda Lagerkvist, *Media and Memory in New Shanghai: Western Performances of Futures Past*. Palgrave Macmillan UK (2013)

29. 《上海逃生》（犹太难民）Kathy Kacer, *Shanghai Escape*. Canada: Second Story Press (2013)

30. 《长江三角洲：上海地区商业指南》(China Briefing) Dezan Shira, Chris Devonshire-Ellis, Samantha L. Jones (auth.), Chris Devonshire-Ellis, Samantha L. Jones, Eunice Ku (eds.), *The Yangtze River Delta: Business Guide to the Shanghai Region*. Springer-Verlag Berlin Heidelberg (2012)

31. 《战时上海与中欧犹太难民：多民族城市的生存、共存与认同》(New Perspectives on Modern Jewish History) Irene Eber, *Wartime Shanghai and the Jewish Refugees from Central Europe: Survival, Co-Existence, and Identity in a Multi-Ethnic City*. de Gruyter (2012)

32. 《流亡上海：逃离第三帝国的故事》(Palgrave Studies in Oral History) Steve Hochstadt, *Exodus to Shanghai: Stories of Escape from the Third Reich*. Palgrave Macmillan US (2012)

33. 《教会的斗士：龚品梅主教与天主教在共产主义上海的抵抗》Paul P. Mariani, *Church Militant: Bishop Kung and Catholic Resistance in Communist Shanghai*. Harvard University Press (2011)
34. 《晚清上海现代性：寓居城市的建筑空间、性别和视觉文化（1853—1898）》(Asia's transformations) Samuel Y. Liang（梁允翔）, *Mapping Modernity in Shanghai: Space, Gender, and Visual Culture in the Sojourners' City, 1853—1898*. Routledge (2010)
35. 《追逐同样的信号：黑箱交易如何影响从华尔街到上海的股市》(Wiley trading) Brian R. Brown, *Chasing the Same Signals: How Black-Box Trading Influences Stock Markets from Wall Street to Shanghai*. John Wiley (2010)
36. 《徒步大中国：从上海步行到西藏》Graham Earnshaw, *The Great Walk of China: Travels on Foot from Shanghai to Tibet*. Blacksmith Books (2010)
37. 《上海女孩》Mina Hanbury-Tension, Lan Lan, *Shanghai Girls: Uncensored & Unsentimental*. Make Do Publishing (2010)
38. 《上海星条旗：向和平过渡的见证（1945—1946）》Alfred Emile Cornebise, *The Shanghai Stars and Stripes: Witness to the Transition to Peace, 1945—1946*. McFarland & Company, Inc., Publishers (2010)
39. 《金焰：上海巨星》Richard Meyer（马浩然）, *Jin Yan: The Rudolph Valentino of Shanghai*. Hong Kong University Press (2009)
40. 《世界性公共空间：半殖民地上海的英语印刷文化》Shuang Shen, *Cosmopolitan Publics: Anglophone Print Culture in Semi-Colonial Shanghai*. Rutgers University Press (2009)
41. 《上海女孩》Lisa See（邝丽莎）, *Shanghai Girls: A Novel*. Random House (2009)
42. 《上海长江隧道：理论、设计与建设》(Balkema: Proceedings and Monographs in Engineering, Water and Earth Sciences) R. Huang, *The Shanghai Yangtze River Tunnel: Theory, Design and Construction*. CRC Press (2008)
43. 《上海星球：中国大都市的建筑、家庭、食物、时尚和文化》Justin Guariglia, *Planet Shanghai: Architecture, Family, Food, Fashion and Culture of, China's Great Metropolis*. Chronicle Books (2008)
44. 《上海粗略指南》Kurt Pitzer, Tara Stevens, *The Rough Guide to Shanghai*. Rough Guides (2008)
45. 《美食怀旧：上海地域饮食文化与都市体验》Mark Swislocki, *Culinary Nostalgia: Regional Food Culture and the Urban Experience in Shanghai*. Stanford University Press (2008)
46. 《上海繁华：都会经济伦理与近代中国的形成（1843—1949）》Wen-hsin Yeh（叶文心）, *Shanghai Splendor: Economic Sentiments and the Making of Modern China, 1843—1949*. University of California Press (2007)
47. 《上海工业》Ji Xiaohui, *Shangai Industries* (Shanghai Series). Cengage Learning (2007)
48. 《上海媒体圈：文化生产的美学》Alexander Des Forges, *Mediasphere Shanghai: The Aesthetics of Cultural Production* (Study of the Weatherhead East Asian Institute). University of Hawai'i Press (2007)

49. 《上海浦东：全球与地方互动时代的城市发展》Yawei Chen, *Shanghai Pudong: Urban Development in an Era of Global-Local Interaction*. IOS Press (2007)
50. 《上海教育》Shen Xiaoming, *Shanghai Education* (Shanghai Series). Cengage Learning (2007)
51. 《丁先生的鸡爪：从上海到德州的慢船》Gillian Kendall, *Mr. Ding's Chicken Feet: On a Slow Boat from Shanghai to Texas*. University of Wisconsin Press (2006)
52. 《夏洛克在上海：犯罪与侦查故事》Cheng Xiaoqing, Translated by Timothy C. Wong, *Sherlock in Shanghai: Stories of Crime and Detection*. University of Hawai'i Press (2006)
53. 《建设上海：中国门户的故事》Edward Denison, Guang Yu Ren, *Building Shanghai: The Story of China's Gateway*. Wiley-Academy (2006)
54. 《上海与帝国边缘》Meng Yue, *Shanghai and the Edges of Empires*. University of Minnesota Press (2006)
55. 《水与中国发展：上海水政策的政治经济学》(Series on Contemporary China, Vol. 6) Seungho Lee, *Water and Development in China: The Political Economy of Shanghai Water Policy*. World Scientific Publishing Company (2006)
56. 《海上花列传》Han Bangqing（韩邦庆）, Eileen Chang（张爱玲）, *The Sing-song Girls of Shanghai*. Columbia University Press (2005)
57. 《全球减贫：学习与创新促进发展，来自上海全球学习倡议的发现》Blanca Moreno-dodson (ed.), *Reducing Poverty on a Global Scale: Learning and Innovating for Development: Findings from the Shanghai Global Learning Initiative*. World Bank (2005)
58. 《中国专业人士与共和：上海专业协会的兴起（1912—1937）》Xiaoqun Xu, *Chinese Professionals and the Republican State: The Rise of Professional Associations in Shanghai, 1912—1937*. Cambridge University Press (2004)
59. 《销售幸福：20世纪初上海的日历海报和视觉文化》Ellen Johnston Laing, *Selling Happiness: Calendar Posters and Visual Culture in Early Twentieth-century Shanghai*. Honolulu: University of Hawai'i Press (2004)
60. 《披着战争的尘土：从比亚利斯托克到上海再到应许之地，口述历史》（犹太难民）Samuel Iwry, L. J. H. Kelley (ed.), *To Wear the Dust of War: From Bialystok to Shanghai to the Promised Land, an Oral History* (Palgrave Studies in Oral History). London: Palgrave Macmillan (2004)
61. 《十个绿瓶子：一家人从饱受战火蹂躏的奥地利到上海贫民区的真实故事》Vivian Jeanette Kaplan, *Ten Green Bottles: The True Story of One Family's Journey from War-torn Austria to the Ghettos of Shanghai*. St. Martin's Press (2004)
62. 《转型中的上海：中国大都市变化中的视角与社会轮廓》Jos Gamble, *Shanghai in Transition: Changing Perspectives and Social Contours of a Chinese Metropolis*. RoutledgeCurzon (2003)
63. 《现代上海银行史：中国金融资本主义的兴衰》Ji Zhaojin, *A History of Modern Shanghai Banking: The Rise and Decline of China's Financial Capitalism*. Routledge (2002)

64. 《上海再思：建筑、城市和另一类现代化的寻求》Mario Gandelsonas, *Shanghai Reflections: Architecture, Urbanism, and the Search for an Alternative Modernity*. Princeton Architectural Press (2002)

65. 《做牛做马：上海的民族主义和劳工，1895—1927》S. A. Smith, *Like Cattle and Horses: Nationalism and Labor in Shanghai, 1895—1927* (Comparative and International Working-Class History). Duke University Press (2002)

66. 《霓虹灯外：20世纪初日常生活中的上海》Hanchao Lu, *Beyond the Neon Lights: Everyday Shanghai in the Early Twentieth Century*. University of California Press (1999)

67. 《上海摩登：一种新都市文化在中国（1930—1945）》Leo Ou-fan Lee（李欧梵）, *Shanghai Modern: The Flowering of a New Urban Culture in China, 1930—1945*. Harvard University Press (1999)

68. 《战时上海》Wen-hsin Yeh（叶文心）(ed.), *Wartime Shanghai*. Routledge (1998, 2005)

69. 《从上海到科雷吉多：保卫菲律宾的海军陆战队》(Marines in World War II commemorative series) J. Michael Miller; United States Marine Corps History and Museums Division, *From Shanghai to Corregidor: Marines in the Defense of the Philippines*. History and Museums Division Marine Corps Historical Center (1997)

70. 《上海歹士：战时恐怖活动与城市犯罪（1937—1941）》Wakeman Frederic, Jr.（魏斐德）, *The Shanghai Badlands: Wartime Terrorism and Urban Crime, 1937—1941* (Cambridge Studies in Chinese History, Literature and Institutions). Cambridge University Press (1996)

71. 《上海城市土地私有化》Ling Li, *Privatization of Urban Land in Shanghai*. Hong Kong University Press (1996)

72. 《上海警察：1927—1937》Wakeman Frederic, Jr.（魏斐德）, *Policing Shanghai, 1927—1937*. Berkeley: University of California Press (1995)

73. 《籍贯、城市与国家：1853—1937年上海的区域网络与身份》Bryna Goodman, *Native Place, City, and Nation: Regional Networks and Identities in Shanghai, 1853—1937*. Berkeley: University of California Press (1995)

74. 《日本和英国在上海（1925—1931）》(St Antony's Series) Harumi Goto-Shibata, *Japan and Britain in Shanghai, 1925—31*. Palgrave Macmillan UK (1995)

75. 《上海地铁：战争中的间谍、阴谋和法国人》Michael Barry Miller, *Shanghai on the Métro: Spies, Intrigue, and the French between the Wars*. University of California Press (1994)

76. 《上海：亚洲大都市的革命与发展》Christopher Howe（克里斯托弗·豪）, *Shanghai: Revolution and Development in an Asian Metropolis* (Contemporary China Institute Publications). Cambridge University Press (1981)

77. 《上海的职业生涯：中国城市发展中的个人活力社会指南》Lynn T. White（白霖）, *Careers in Shanghai: The Social Guidance of Personal Energies in a Developing Chinese City, 1949—1966* (Publications-Center for Chinese Studies). University of California Press (1978)

78. 《上海市警察自卫手册》W. E. Fairbairn, *Shanghai Municipal Police Manual of Self Defense*. China Publishing & Printing Co. (1915)

2.2.3 广东/广州

1. 《此房非家：欧洲人在广州和澳门的日常生活（1730—1830）》(Studies in global social history, 34) Lisa Hellman, *This House Is Not a Home: European Everyday Life in Canton and Macao, 1730—1830*. Brill (2019)
2. 《美国医生在广州：中国现代化（1835—1935）》Guangqiu Xu, *American Doctors in Canton: Modernization in China, 1835—1935*. Transaction Publishers (2011)
3. 《饥荒之乡的美食家：近代广州的稻米文化与政治》Seung-Joon Lee, *Gourmets in the Land of Famine: The Culture and Politics of Rice in Modern Canton*. Stanford University Press (2011)
4. 《中国珠江三角洲、广州和深圳》Simon Foster, *China's Pearl River Delta, Guangzhou & Shenzhen*. E-Pub Direct; Hunter Publishing (2010)
5. 《可见的城市：广州、长崎、巴塔维亚与美国人的来临》Leonard Blusse, *Visible Cities: Canton, Nagasaki, and Batavia and the Coming of the Americans* (Edwin O Reischauer Lectures). Harvard University Press (2008)
6. 《了解广州：民国时期的大众文化反思》Virgil Ho, *Understanding Canton: Rethinking Popular Culture in the Republican Period* (Studies on Contemporary China). Oxford University Press (2006)
7. 《国家、治理与中国现代性：广州（1900—1927）》Michael Tsin, *Nation, Governance and Modernity in China: Canton, 1900—1927*. Stanford University Press (1999)
8. 《先行一步：改革中的广东》Ezra F Vogel（傅高义）, *One Step Ahead in China: Guangdong under Reform*. Harvard University Press (1989)
9. 《共产主义下的广州：一个省会的规划与政治（1949—1968）》Ezra F Vogel（傅高义）, *Canton under Communism: Programs and Politics in a Provincial Capital, 1949—1968*. Harvard University Press (1969)

2.2.4 旅游及其他

1. 《中国旅游经济理论与实践（1978—2017）》(Research Series on the Chinese Dream and China's Development Path) Peng Zhou, *The Theory and Practice of China's Tourism Economy (1978—2017)*. Springer Singapore (2019)
2. 《中国邮轮产业发展报告（2018）：邮轮产业绿皮书》Hong Wang (ed.), *Report on the Development of Cruise Industry in China (2018)：Green Book on Cruise Industry*. Springer (2019)
3. 《中国酒店业与旅游业：新增长、趋势与发展》Jinlin Zhao, *The Hospitality and Tourism Industry in China: New Growth, Trends, and Developments* (Advances in hospitality and tourism book series). Apple Academic Press (2018)
4. 《中国邮轮产业报告》Hong Wang (eds.), *Report on China's Cruise Industry*. Springer Singapore (2018)

5. 《重建传统：中国旅游与遗产认证》Xiaoyan Su, Fan Hong, *Reconstruction of the Tradition: Tourism and Authentication of Heritage in China* (Countries and Cultures of the World). Nova Science Publishers (2017)

6. 《中国旅游指南》(Travel Guides) Damian Harper, *China Travel Guide*. Lonely Planet (2017)

7. 《中国极客：发现阿里巴巴、子弹列车和点心之地》Matthew B. Christensen, *A Geek in China: Discovering the Land of Alibaba, Bullet Trains and Dim Sum*. Tuttle Publishing (2016)

8. 《中国终极指南：如何教英语，旅游，学汉语，在中国找工作》Nick Lenczewski, *Ultimate China Guide: How to Teach English, Travel, Learn Chinese, & Find Work in China*. CreateSpace Independent Publishing Platform (2016)

9. 《孤独星球：中国（旅游指南）》Damian Harper et al., *Lonely Planet China* (Travel Guide). Lonely Planet (2015)

10. 《美德之城：乌托邦愿景时代的南京》Chuck Wooldridge, *City of Virtues: Nanjing in an Age of Utopian Visions* (China Program Books). University of Washington Press (2015)

11. 《中国与欧盟旅游与酒店业发展》Guojun Zeng (eds.), *Tourism and Hospitality Development Between China and EU*. Springer-Verlag Berlin Heidelberg (2015)

12. 《敦煌莫高窟旅游可持续发展战略》Martha Demas, Neville Agnew, Jinshi Fan, *Strategies for Sustainable Tourism at the Mogao Grottoes of Dunhuang, China*. Springer International Publishing (2015)

13. 《旅游景观：中国少数民族农村旅游工作》Jenny T. Chio, *A Landscape of Travel: The Work of Tourism in Rural Ethnic China*. University of Washington Press (2014)

14. 《中国时光：来自中国西部蛮荒之地的视觉日志》（在中国的视觉旅程）Henrik Drescher, *China Days: A Visual Journal from China's Wild West*. Chronicle Books (2014)

15. 《新中国的旅行者：中国旅游革命带来的商机》(Palgrave Pocket Consultants) Gary Bowerman, *The New Chinese Traveler: Business Opportunities from the Chinese Travel Revolution*. Palgrave Macmillan UK (2014)

16. 《中国旅游指南》DK Publishing, *DK Eyewitness Travel Guide: China*. DK Eyewitness Travel (2014)

17. 《中国旅游指南》Shawn Low, Damian Harper, *Lonely Planet China* (Travel Guide). Lonely Planet (2013)

18. 《解码中国：今日中国旅行、学习和工作手册》Matthew B. Christensen, *Decoding China: A Handbook for Traveling, Studying, and Working in Todays China*. Tuttle Publishing (2013)

19. 《中国遗产管理、旅游和治理：管理之古为今用》Robert J. Shepherd, Larry Yu, *Heritage Management, Tourism, and Governance in China: Managing the Past to Serve the Present*. Springer-Verlag New York (2013)

20. 《神游：早期中古时代与十九世纪中国的行旅写作》Xiaofei Tian（田晓菲）, *Visionary Journeys: Travel Writings from Early Medieval and Nineteenth-Century China*. Harvard

University Asia Center (2012)

21. 《中国生存指南：如何避免旅行困境和不幸事故》Larry Herzberg, Qin Herzberg, *China Survival Guide: How To Avoid Travel Troubles and Mortifying Mishaps*. Stone Bridge Press (2011)

22. 《钻石山：百年中韩之旅》Tessa Morris-Suzuki, *To the Diamond Mountains: A Hundred-Year Journey through China and Korea* (Asia: Pacific: Perspectives). Rowman & Littlefield Publishers (2010)

23. 《中国旅游手册—第四版》Simon Foster, Jen Lin-Liu, Sherisse Pham, Sharon Owyang, Beth Reiber, Lee Wing-sze, Christopher D. Winnan, *Frommer's China*, 4th Edition (Frommer's Complete). Wiley (2010)

24. 《微光中国》William Arthur Cornaby, *China Under the Secrch-Light* (Cambridge Library Collection-Travel and Exploration). Cambridge University Press (1901, 2010)

25. 《季风之北，彩云之南：云南的形成（公元前2世纪—公元20世纪）》Bin Yang（杨斌）, *Between Winds and Clouds: The Making of Yunnan* (Second Century BCE to Twentieth Century CE). New York: Columbia University Press (2009)

26. 《另一个中国的记述：亚洲冒险》Troy Parfitt, *Notes from the Other China: Adventures in Asia*. New York: Algora Publishing (2008)

27. 《中国道路：一个崛起大国的未来之路》Rob Gifford, *China Road: A Journey into the Future of a Rising Power*. Random House (2008)

28. 《中国旅游：目的地、文化和社区》Chris Ryan, *Tourism in China: Destination, Cultures and Communities*. Routledge (2008)

29. 《中国旅游手册（第三版）》Simon Foster, Jen Lin-Liu, Sharon Owyang, Sherisse Pham, Beth Reiber, Lee Wing-sze, Christoper Winnan, *Frommer's China*, 3rd Edition (Frommer's Complete).Frommers (2008)

30. 《中国探险指南》Simon Foster, *Adventure Guide: China* (Adventure Guides Series). Hunter Publishing, Inc. (2008)

31. 《帝国之眼：旅行写作与跨文化》Mary Louise Pratt, *Imperial Eyes: Travel Writing and Transculturation*. New York, N.Y.: Routledge (2008)

32. 《红色季节：中国旅游记》Kirsty Needham, *A Season in Red: My Great Leap Forward into the New China*. Allen & Unwin (2007)

33. 《徒步跨越中国：一个人不可思议的探索》Edwin John Dingle, Ding Le Mei, *Across China on Foot: One Man's Incredible Quest*. Arc Manor (2007)

34. 《中国鬼：女儿的美国之旅，我的为父之道》Jeff Gammage, *China Ghosts: My Daughter's Journey to America, My Passage to Fatherhood*. HarperCollins (2007)

35. 《中国和印度当代酒店与旅游管理问题：今日龙与虎》Stephen Ball, Susan Horner, Kevin Nield, *Contemporary Hospitality and Tourism Management Issues in China and India: Today's Dragons and Tigers*. Elsevier Ltd. (2007)

36. 《中国旅游探险》Lorien Holland, *China: A Travel Adventure*. Periplus Editions (2006)

37. 《中国出境旅游》Wolfgang Arlt, *China's Outbound Tourism* (Contemporary Geographies of Leisure, Tourism and Mobility). Routledge (2006)

38. 《中国哲学导论：从古代哲学到中国佛教》JeeLoo Liu, *An Introduction to Chinese Philosophy: From Ancient Philosophy to Chinese Buddhism*. Wiley-Blackwell (2006)

39. 《中国旅游指南》DK Publishing, *China: Eyewitness Travel Guides*. Dorling Kindersley Limited, London (2005)

40. 《说扬州：一个中国城市（1550—1850）》Antonia Finnane, *Speaking of Yangzhou: A Chinese City, 1550—1850*. Published by the Harvard University Asia Center (2004)

41. 《云南：探索中国的隐秘境界》Seth Faison, *South of the Clouds: Exploring the Hidden Realms of China*. St. Martin's Press (2004)

42. 《中国懒人》Helene Chung Martin, *Lazy Man in China*. Pandanus Books (2004)

43. 《清初扬州文化》Tobie Meyer-Fong（梅尔清）, *Building Culture in Early Qing Yangzhou*. Stanford University Press (2003)

44. 《深圳：来自中国的游记》Guy Delisle, *Shenzhen: A Travelogue from China*. Drawn & Quarterly (2003, 2006)

45. 《漂泊在中国》Simon Myers, *Adrift in China* (Summersdale Travel). Summersdale Publishers (2002)

46. 《大篷车到中国》Carol Gaskin, *Caravan to China* (# 21 Time Machine, No 21). A Byron Preiss Book (2001)

47. 《中国旅游与地方发展：桂林、苏州、北戴河个案研究》Gang Xu, *Tourism and Local Development in China: Case Studies of Guilin, Suzhou and Beidaihe*. Routledge (1999)

48. 《适应中国：实用指南，情感之旅》Kathleen Wheeler, Doug Werner, *Adopting in China: A Practical Guide, An Emotional Journey*. Tracks Publishing (1999)

49. 《中国最好的珍宝与乐趣》Ronald L. Krannich, Caryl Rae Krannich, *The Treasures and Pleasures of China: Best of the Best*. Impact Publications (1998)

50. 《中国旅游与现代性》Tim Oakes, *Tourism and Modernity in China* (Routledge Studies in China in Transition). Routledge (1998)

51. 《位于世界中心的河流：溯长江之旅，回中国时代》Simon Winchester, *The River at the Center of the World: A Journey Up the Yangtze, and Back in Chinese Time*. Penguin Books (1997)

52. 《神秘的中国》Erick Wujcik, *Mystic China*. Palladium Books (1994)

53. 《题刻山水：中华帝国的旅游书写》Richard E. Strassberg, translator, annotations, & introduction, *Inscribed Landscapes: Travel Writing from Imperial China*. Berkeley: University of California Press (1994)

54. 《中国风景：以村落为中心》Ronald G. Knapp, *Chinese Landscapes: The Village as Place*. University of Hawai'i Press (1992)

55. 《骑铁公鸡：乘火车穿越中国》Paul Theroux, *Riding the Iron Rooster: By Train through China*. Ivy Books (1989)
56. 《一位摄影师在中国的旅行（1933—1946）》Hedda Morrison, *Travels of a Photographer in China, 1933—1946*. Oxford University Press (1987)
57. 《骑乘铁公鸡：搭火车横越中国》Paul Theroux, *Riding the Iron Rooster: By Train Through China*. Mariner Books (1983)
58. 《中国旅游指南》Arne J. DeKeijzer, Fredric M. Kaplan, *The China Guidebook: A Traveler's Guide to the People's Republic of China*. Palgrave Macmillan UK (1979)
59. 《中国巡游》Richard P. Dobsons, *China Cycle*. Macmillan (1946)
60. 《进入中国》Eileen Bigland, *Into China*. Collins Clear-Type Press (1940)
61. 《乐往中国》Lucy (Farrar) Soothill（苏路熙，1858—1932）, *A Passport to China: Being the Tale of Her Long and Friendly Sojourning Amongst a Strangely Interesting People*. With a Foreword by Her Daughter, Lady Hosie; 16 Illustrations. London, Hodder and Stoughton Ltd. (1931)
62. 《中国旅游手册》（第3版）Carl Crow, *The Travelers' Handbook For China*. Ed.3.Thos. Cook and Son (1921)
63. 《一个爱尔兰女人中国见闻录》Mrs. De Burgh Daly, *An Irishwoman in China*. London, T. Werner Laurie, Ltd. (1915)
64. 《中国旅游手册》Carl Crow, *The Travelers' Hand Book for China*. Hwa-mei Book Concern (1913)
65. 《一个博物学家在华西》（照片插图）E. H. Wilson, Charles Sprague Sargent, *A Naturalist in Western China: With Vasculum, Camera and Gun. Being Some Account of Eleven Years' Travel, Exploration, and Observation in the More Remote Parts of the Flowery Kingdom*. 2 Vols. Methuen & Co., Ltd. (1913)
66. 《穿越陕甘：1908—1909年克拉克考察队华北行纪》Robert Sterling Clark, Arthur de C. Sowerby, *Through Shen-kan: The Account of the Clark Expedition in North China, 1908—9*. London: T. Fisher Unwin (1912)
67. 《在中国禁区》Vicomte D'ollone (Author), Translated from the French of the Second Edition by Barnard Miall, *In Forbidden China: The D'ollone Mission, 1906—1909, China-Tibet-Mongolia*. London, T. Fisher Unwin (1912)
68. 《中国见闻录》J. R. Chitty, *Things Seen in China*. London: Seeley, Service & Co. Limited (1912)
69. 《步行过中国》Edwin John Dingle（丁乐梅，1881—1972）, *Across China on Foot: Life in the Interior and the Reform Movement*. New York: H. Holt and Co. (1911)
70. 《帝国丽影/中华奇观》Thomas Hodgson Liddell（李通和）, *China: Its Marvel and Mystery*. London: George Allen & Sons (1910)
71. 《窥览中华》Lena E. Johnston, Norman H. Hardy, *Peeps at Many Lands: China*. Adam and Charls Black（1909, 1910）

72.《晚清中华面貌》Emily Georgiana Kemp, *The Face of China: Travels in East, North, Central and Western China, With Some Account of the New Schools, Universities, Missions, and the Old Religious Sacred Places of Confucianism, Buddhism, and Taoism, the Whole Written & Illustrated*. London: Chatto and Windus (1909)

73.《中国狩猎》T. R. Jernigan, *Shooting in China*. Methodist Publishing House (1908)

74.《一个澳大利亚人在中国：从中国至缅甸平静之旅叙事》George Ernest Morrison（莫理循），*An Australian in China: Being the Narrative of a Quiet Journey Across China to Burma*. London: Horace Cox (1902)

75.《中国图像记》Isabella Lucy Bird, *Chinese Pictures: Notes on Photographs Made in China*. Charles L. Bowman, New York (1900)

76.《跨越长江流域：中国之旅记录，主要在四川境内》Isabella Lucy Bird, *The Yangtze Valley and Beyond: An Account of Journeys in China, Chiefly in the Province of Sze Chuan and among the Man-tze of the Somo Territory*. London: John Murray (1899)

77.《中国西部三年游记：四川、贵州和云南》Alexander Hosie, *Three Years in Western China: A Narrative of Three Journeys in Ssu-ch'uan, Kuei-chow, and Yun-nan*. London: George Philip & Son (1890)

78.《中国旧公路》Isabelle Williamson, *Old Highways in China* (Cambridge Library Collection: Travel and Exploration). Cambridge University Press (1884, 2010)

79.《岭南纪行：华南及海南腹地闻见记》Benjamin Couch Henry, *Ling-Nam: Interior Views of Southern China, Including the Hitherto Untraversed Island of Hainan*. S.W. Partridge and Co., London (1886)

80.《和华人同居：内地，沿岸和海上》Robert Fortune（福钧），*A Residence among the Chinese: Inland, on the Coast, and at Sea*. John Murray, Albermarle Street (1857)

81.《两访中国茶乡和喜马拉雅山麓上的英国茶园》Robert Fortune（福钧），*Two Visits to the Tea Countries of China and the British Tea Plantations in the Himalaya*. 2 Vols. London: John Murray (1853)

82.《中国内地一瞥：在丝茶产区的一次旅行所见》Walter Henry Medhurst（麦都思），*A Glance at the Interior of China: Obtained during a Journey through the Silk and Green Tea Districts Taken in 1845*. Shanghai, Mission Press (1849)

83.《中国北方三年之旅》Robert Fortune, *Three Years' Wanderings in the Northern Provinces of China*. John Murray, London (1847)

84.《中国旅行记》John Barrow, *Travels in China*. London: T. Cadell & W. Davis (1804)

2.2.5 何伟游记系列

1.《甲骨文：流离时空里的新生中国》Peter Hessler（何伟），*Oracle Bones: A Journey between China's Past and Present*. HarperCollins (2006)

2.《消失中的江城》Peter Hessler（何伟），*River Town: Two Years on the Yangtze*. Harper

Perennial (2006)

3. 《寻路中国：从乡村到工厂的自驾之旅》Peter Hessler（何伟）, *Country Driving: A Journey Through China from Farm to Factory*. HarperCollins (2009)

2.2.6 地理

1. 《中国演化经济地理学》(Economic Geography) Canfei He（贺灿飞）, Shengjun Zhu（朱晟君）, *Evolutionary Economic Geography in China*. Springer Singapore (2019)

2. 《地质之美：百年来中国地质测绘艺术》Chenyang Li, Liqiong Jia, Xuan Wu, *The Beauty of Geology: Art of Geology Mapping in China Over a Century*. Springer Singapore (2019)

3. 《地理学伙伴：清代中国制图中的东西方合作（约1685—1735）》Mario Cams, *Companions in Geography: East-West Collaboration in the Mapping of Qing China (c.1685—1735)*. Brill (2017)

4. 《中国历史地理学研讨会》Renzhi Hou（侯仁之）, *Symposium on Chinese Historical Geography* (China Academic Library). Springer-Verlag Berlin Heidelberg (2015)

5. 《地理复仇：地图告诉我们即将到来的冲突及命运之争》（中译本《即将到来的地缘战争：无法回避的大国冲突及对地理宿命的抗争》) Robert D. Kaplan, *The Revenge of Geography. What the Map Tells Us About Coming Conflicts and the Battle Against Fate*. Random House (2012)

6. 《中国地理学：全球化与政治、经济和社会变革的动力》Gregory Veeck, Clifton W. Pannell, Christopher J. Smith, Youqin Huang, *China's Geography: Globalization and the Dynamics of Political, Economic, and Social Change* (Changing Regions in a Global Context), Second Edition. Rowman & Littlefield Publishers, Inc. (2011)

7. 《中国地理：历史名胜》Kenneth Pletcher, *The Geography of China: Sacred and Historic Places* (Understanding China). Britannica Educational Publishing (2011)

8. 《当代中国地理：邓小平十年的影响》Terry Cannon, *The Geography of Contemporary China: The Impact of Deng Xiaoping's Decade*. Routledge (1990)

9. 《中国新地图索引》Edwin John Dingle, Harold John Fruin, *Index to the New Map of China*. Shanghai: Far Eastern Geographical Establishment (1915)

10. 《中国研究：系统地质学》Bailey Willis（维理士）, *Research in China: Systematic Geology*. Vol. 2. Washington, D. C.: Carnegie Institution of Washington (1907)

11. 《中国研究：岩石和动物学；汉语音节》Eliot Blackwelder, Friedrich Hirth（夏德）, *Research in China: Petrography and Zoöology; Syllabary of Chinese Sounds*. Vol. I, Pt. II. Washington, D. C.: Carnegie Institution of Washington (1907)

2.3 中国边疆

2.3.1 西藏

1. 《在中国藏区学校和家庭中成为双语者：奋斗的故事》(Multilingual Education 34) YiXi

LaMuCuo, *Becoming Bilingual in School and Home in Tibetan Areas of China: Stories of Struggle*. Springer International Publishing (2019)

2. 《毛泽东时代后西藏的道德与寺院复兴》Jane Caple, Mark Michael Rowe, *Morality and Monastic Revival in Post-Mao Tibet*. University of Hawaii Press (2019)

3. 《中国区域发展与西藏》Rongxing Guo, *China's Regional Development and Tibet*. Springer (2016)

4. 《用心收集：藏传密宗史》Jacob P. Dalton, *The Gathering of Intentions: A History of a Tibetan Tantra*. Columbia University Press (2016)

5. 《白石圈：与藏东游牧民族穿越季节》Gillian G. Tan, Stevan Harrell, *In the Circle of White Stones: Moving through Seasons with Nomads of Eastern Tibet* (Studies on Ethnic Groups in China). University of Washington Press (2016)

6. 《达赖喇嘛和中国皇帝：西藏轮回制度政治史》Peter Schwieger, *The Dalai Lama and the Emperor of China: A Political History of the Tibetan Institution of Reincarnation*. Columbia University Press (2015)

7. 《藏医：中国古代之疗愈精神、身体和灵魂》The Healthy Reader, *Tibetan Medicine: Ancient Chinese Healing To Rejuvenate Mind, Body, And Soul* (Chinese Medicine, Chinese Herbs, Herbal Remedies, Natural Healing). Amazon.com (2014)

8. 《走出大凉山：一个纳木依藏族女孩的蜕变》Li Xiaoqiong（李小琼Drolma）, *A Namuyi Tibetan Woman's Journey from Chinese Village to Indian City to Beijing*. Asian Highlands Perspectives (2014)

9. 《西藏农村的一妻多夫制婚姻》Ben Jiao, *Polyandrous Marital In Rural Tibet*. China Tibetology Publishing House (2014)

10. 《西藏：未完的故事》Lezlee Brown Halper, Stefan Halper, *Tibet: An Unfinished Story*. Oxford University Press (2014)

11. 《西藏的崩溃：从西藏高原到亚洲三角洲中国对生态系统的鲁莽破坏》Michael Buckley, *Meltdown in Tibet: China's Reckless Destruction of Ecosystems from the Highlands of Tibet to the Deltas of Asia*. Palgrave Macmillan (2014)

12. 《在东部女王的土地上：汉藏边界的性别和种族政治》Jinba Tenzin, *In the Land of the Eastern Queendom: The Politics of Gender and Ethnicity on the Sino-Tibetan Border*. University of Washington Press (2014)

13. 《现代西藏史：风暴来临（1955—1957）》（第三卷）Melvyn C. Goldstein, *A History of Modern Tibet. Volume 3, The Storm Clouds Descend, 1955—1957* (Philip E. Lilienthal Books). University of California Press (2014)

14. 《和谐社会的边缘：社会主义中国的藏族和维吾尔族》Trine Brox, Ildiko Beller-Hann, *On the Fringes of the Harmonious Society: Tibetans and Uyghurs in Socialist China*. NIAS Press (2013)

15. 《驯服西藏：景观改造与中国发展的礼物》Emily T. Yeh, *Taming Tibet: Landscape*

Transformation and the Gift of Chinese Development. Cornell University Press (2013)

16. 《通往中国的高原之路：乔治·博格尔、班禅喇嘛和第一支英国西藏探险队》Kate Teltscher, *The High Road to China: George Bogle, the Panchen Lama and the First British Expedition to Tibet.* Bloomsbury Publishing (2013)

17. 《受威胁的"藏族"：中国青海的新一体化、少数民族教育与职业发展战略》Adrian Zenz, *"Tibetanness" Under Threat: Neo-Integrationism, Minority Education and Career Strategies in Qinghai, P.R. China* (Inner Asia Book Series). Brill Academic Publishers (2013)

18. 《藏族口传史诗〈格萨尔王〉唐卡》Zou Aiming（周爱明）, Jambian Gyamco, *Thangka Painting of the Tibetan Oral Epic King Gesar.* China Intercontinental Press（五洲传播出版社）(2013)

19. 《西方想象中的西藏》Tom Neuhaus, *Tibet in the Western Imagination.* Palgrave Macmillan UK (2012)

20. 《恶魔的驯服：藏传佛教中的暴力与解放》Jacob P Dalton, *The Taming of the Demons: Violence and Liberation in Tibetan Buddhism.* Yale University Press (2011)

21. 《西藏边界的宗教复兴》Koen Wellens, *Religious Revival in the Tibetan Borderlands: The Premi of Southwest China.* University of Washington Press (2011)

22. 《四川边防和西藏：清初帝国战略》Yingcong Dai, *The Sichuan Frontier and Tibet: Imperial Strategy in the Early Qing.* University of Washington Press (2009)

23. 《一个藏族姑娘的头饰礼仪》Tshe dpal rdo rje, with Rin chen rdo rje, G Roche, and CK Stuart, *A Tibetan Girls's Hair Changing Ritual.* Asian Highlands Perspectives (2009)

24. 《纳木依藏族民间音乐、订婚仪式念诵与笛曲》Libu Lakhi (Li Jianfu 李建富, Dawa Tenzin) with Qi Huimin（祁慧民）, Charles Kevin Stuart, and Gerald Roche, *China's Namzi Tibetan Songs, Engagement Chants, & Flute Music.* Xining City Plateau (2009)

25. 《汉藏概论》Paul K. Benedict, *Sino-Tibetan: A Conspectus* (Princeton Cambridge Studies in Chinese Linguistics No. 2). Cambridge University Press (2009)

26. 《现代西藏史：风暴前的平静（1951—1955）》（第二卷）Melvyn C. Goldstein, *A History of Modern Tibet, Volume 2: The Calm before the Storm (1951—1955).* University of California Press (2007)

27. 《旅游与西藏文化转型：一个叫"香格里拉"的地方》Ashild Kolas, *Tourism and Tibetan Culture in Transition: A place called Shangrila* (Routledge Contemporary China Series). Routledge (2007)

28. 《拥挤的山峦，空旷的城镇：西藏东部冬虫夏草收获季节的商品化与竞争》（一位喇嘛写的有关虫草的人类学硕士论文）Kunga T. Lama, *Crowded Mountains, Empty Towns: Commodification and Contestation in Cordyceps Harvesting in Eastern Tibet.* Thesis for the Degree of Master of Arts, University of Colorado (2007)

29. 《中国统治下的拉萨生活记忆》Tubten Khétsun, Matthew Akester, *Memories of Life in*

Lhasa Under Chinese Rule. Columbia University Press (2007)

30. 《西藏的故事：与达赖喇嘛对话》Thomas Laird, *The Story of Tibet: Conversations with the Dalai Lama*. Grove Press (2006)

31. 《西藏与民国边疆：阴谋和民族政治学（1928—1949）》Hsiao-ting Lin, *Tibet And Nationalist China's Frontier: Intrigues and Ethnopolitics, 1928—1949*. University of British Columbia Press (2006)

32. 《来自敦煌的西藏密宗手稿》Jacob Dalton, Sam van Schaik, *Tibetan Tantric Manuscripts from Dunhuang*. Brill (2006)

33. 《纳卡的觉醒：从西藏到中国南海导航湄公河的第一人》Mick O'shea, *In the Naga's Wake: The First Man to Navigate the Mekong, from Tibet to the South China Sea*. Allen & Unwin (2006)

34. 《拉萨街头记忆》Robert Barnett, *Lhasa: Streets with Memories* (Asia Perspectives: History, Society, and Culture). Columbia University Press (2006)

35. 《大英帝国与西藏（1900—1922）》Wendy Palace, *The British Empire and Tibet (1900—1922)*. RoutledgeCurzon (2005)

36. 《近代中国形成中的藏传佛教》Gray Tuttle, *Tibetan Buddhists in the Making of Modern China*. Columbia University Press (2005)

37. 《双掌相击之音：藏传佛教的僧侣教育》Georges B.J. Dreyfus, *The Sound of Two Hands Clapping: The Education of a Tibetan Buddhist Monk*. University of California Press (2003)

38. 《原始藏缅语手册：汉藏重建的系统与哲学》James Alan Matisoff, James Matisoff, *Handbook of Proto-Tibeto-Burman: System and Philosophy of Sino-Tibetan Reconstruction*. University of California Press (2003)

39. 《汉藏语言》G. Thurgood, *Sino-Tibetan Languages* (Routledge Language Family Series). Routledge (2003)

40. 《风的语言：喜马拉雅山区经幡研究》（博士论文）Katherine Anne Paul, *Words on the Wind: A Study of Himalayan Prayer Flags*. Ph. D. Dissertation, University of Wisconsin-Madison (2003)

41. 《现代藏语藏英新辞典》Melvyn C. Goldstein, *The New Tibetan English Dictionary of Modern Tibetan*. University of California Press (2001)

42. 《中国西藏政策》Dawa Norbu, *China's Tibet policy*. Curzon Press (2001)

43. 《汉藏英常用新词语图解词典》*Chinese-Tibetan-English Visual Dictionary of New Daily Vocabulary* (2000)

44. 《西藏问题》Mark La Porte, *The Tibet Question*. (10th Grade Lesson). Schools of California Online Resources for Education (SCORE). Connecting California's Classrooms to the World. (2000)

45. 《冷战孤儿：美国与西藏人的生存斗争》John Kenneth Knaus, *Orphans of the Cold War: America and the Tibetan Struggle for Survival*. Public Affairs Press (1999)

46. 《Śālistambha经：藏语原文，梵语重构，英语翻译，重要注释》N. Ross Reat, *The Śālistambha SŪ Tra: Tibetan Original, Sanskrit Reconstruction, English Translation,*

Critical Notes (including Pali parallels, Chinese version, and ancient Tibetan fragments). Motilal Banarsidass Publishers (1998)

47. 《当代西藏佛教：宗教复兴与文化认同》Melvyn C. Goldstein, Matthew T. Kapstein, Orville Schnell, *Buddhism in Contemporary Tibet: Religious Revival and Cultural Identity*. University of California Press (1998)

48. 《为现代西藏奋斗：扎西次仁自传》Melvyn C. Goldstein, Tashi Tsering, William Siebenschuh, *The Struggle for Modern Tibet: The Autobiography of Tashi Tsering*. East Gate Book (1997)

49. 《西藏七年》Heinrich Harrer, *Seven Years in Tibet* (1 edition). Tarcher (1997)

50. 《中亚的西藏帝国：中世纪早期西藏人、土耳其人、阿拉伯人和中国人角逐大国的历史》Christopher I. Beckwith, *The Tibetan Empire in Central Asia: A History of the Struggle for Great Power among Tibetans, Turks, Arabs, and Chinese during the Early Middle Ages*. Princeton University Press (1993)

51. 《现代藏文学精要：阅读教程与参考语法》Melvyn C. Goldstein, Gelek Rimpoche, Lobsang Phuntshog, *Essentials of Modern Literary Tibetan: A Reading Course and Reference Grammar*. University of California Press (1991)

52. 《藏西游牧民族：一种生活方式的幸存》Melvyn C. Goldstein, Cynthia M. Beall, *Nomads of Western Tibet: The Survival of a Way of Life*. University of California Press (1990)

53. 《藏—英佛教术语词典》Tsepak Rigzin, *Tibetan-English Dictionary of Buddhist Terminology*. Library of Tibetan Works and Archives (1986)

54. 《现代藏语英藏词典》Melvyn C. Goldstein, *English-Tibetan Dictionary of Modern Tibetan*. University of California Press (1984)

55. 《对藏传佛教认识论发展的贡献：11—13世纪》Leonard W. J. van der Kuijp, *Contributions to the Development of Tibetan Buddhist Epistemology: From the eleventh to the thirteenth century*. Franz Steiner Verlag GmbH Wie (1983)

56. 《开放的城市拉萨：西藏之旅》Han Suyin（韩素音）, *Lhasa, The Open City: A Journey to Tibet*. G. P. Putnam's Sons (1977)

57. 《西藏农奴站起来》(Modern China Series No. 1) Anna Louise Strong（斯特朗）, *When Serfs Stood Up in Tibet*. Red Sun Publishers (1976)

58. 《西藏政治制度的人类学研究》（博士论文）Melvyn C. Goldstein, *Anthropological Study of the Tibet Political System*. Ph. D. Dissertation, Washington University (1968)

59. 《共产主义中国和西藏：第一个十二年》George Ginsburgs, Michael Mathos, *Communist China and Tibet: The First Dozen Years*. Springer Netherlands (1964)

60. 《雍和宫：北京喇嘛大教堂图解，附喇嘛神话与崇拜注释》Gosta Montell, Ferdinand Diederich Lessing, *Yung-Ho-Kung, An Iconography of the Lamaist Cathedral in Peking. With Notes on Lamaist Mythology and Cult*. Stockholm (1942, 1993)

61. 《在鞑靼、西藏和中国旅行（1844至1846年）》（第一卷）Evariste-Regis Huc, Joseph

Gabet, *Travels in Tartary, Thibet and China, 1844—1846* (The Broadway Travellers), Volume 1. Routledge (1928, 2005)

62.《在鞑靼、西藏和中国旅行（1844至1846年）》（第二卷）Evariste-Regis Huc, Joseph Gabet, *Travels in Tartary, Thibet and China, 1844—1846* (The Broadway Travellers), Volume 2. Routledge (1928, 2005)

63.《西藏人头骨和骨骼的使用》Berthold Laufer, *Use of Human Skulls and Bones in Tibet*. Field Museum of Natural History (1923)

64.《达赖喇嘛和清朝皇帝的关系（1644—1908）》William W. Rockhill（柔克义）, *The Dalai Lamas of Lhasa and Their Relations with the Manchu Emperors of China 1644—1908*. Library of Tibetan Works and Archives (1910, 1998)

65.《喇嘛之国：Trashilhamo的故事》Edward Amundsen, *In the Land of the Lamas: The Story of Trashilhamo. A Tibetan Lassie, in which Are Described Tibetan Character, Life, Customs, and History*. Marshall Brothers, Ltd. (1910)

66.《西藏三年》Ekai Kawaguchi ([日]河口慧海), *Three Years in Tibet, with the Original Japanese Illustrations*. Theosophical publishing society (1909)

67.《西藏旅行日记》Hamilton Bower, *Diary of a Journey Across Tibet*. London: Rivington, Percival and Co., (1894)

2.3.2 新疆

1.《中国新疆援助项目的社会学分析》Yuhui Li, *China's Assistance Program in Xinjiang: A Sociological Analysis*. Lexington Books (2018)

2.《新疆与现代中国》Justin M. Jacobs, *Xinjiang and the Modern Chinese State*. University of Washington Press (2016)

3.《维吾尔族：俄中边疆的改革与革命》David Brophy, *Uyghur Nation: Reform and Revolution on the Russia-China Frontier*. Harvard University Press (2016)

4.《新疆、乌鲁木齐和中国北方》Lonely Planet, *Lonely Planet Xinjiang, Urumqi & Northern China* (Travel Guide Chapter). Lonely Planet (2016)

5.《清代新疆的起源：吐鲁番历史源流》David Brophy, Takahiro Onuma, *The Origins of Qing Xinjiang: A Set of Historical Sources on Turfan* (NIHU program Islamic area studies: TIAS central Eurasian research series). University of Tokyo (2016)

6.《笔争：维吾尔族的民族话语和国家利益（1900—1949）》Ondrej Klimeš, *Struggle by the Pen: The Uyghur Discourse of Nation and National Interest, c.1900—1949*. Koninklijke Brill NV, Leiden, The Netherlands (2015)

7.《中国的社会政策和民族冲突：来自新疆的教训》Shaoying Zhang, Derek McGhee, *Social Policies and Ethnic Conflict in China: Lessons from Xinjiang*. Palgrave Macmillan UK (2014)

8.《石油、矿石与新疆的民族构建（1893—1964）》（博士论文）Judd Creighton Kinzley- Oil, Ores and State-building in Xinjiang Province, 1893—1964. Ph. D. Dissertation, University

9. 《帝国围城：新疆的中国统治（1884—1971）》（博士论文）Justin Jacobs, Empire Besieged: The Preservation of Chinese Rule in Xinjiang, 1884—1971. Ph. D. Dissertation, University of California, San Diego (2011)

10. 《新疆与中国在中亚的崛起历史》Michael E. Clarke, Xinjiang and China's Rise in Central Asia: A History. Routledge (2011)

11. 《新疆的社区事务（1880—1949）：走向维吾尔族的历史人类学》Ildiko Beller-Hann, Community Matters in Xinjiang 1880—1949: Towards a Historical Anthropology of the Uyghur. Brill Academic Pub (2008)

12. 《位于中国和中亚之间的维吾尔人》Bellér-HannIldikó, CesàroM. Cristina, HarrisRachel and FinleyJoanne Smith (eds.), Situating the Uyghurs between China and Central Asia. Aldershot, UK Ashgate (2007)

13. 《欧亚大陆十字路口：新疆史》James A. Millward, Eurasian Crossroads: A History of Xinjiang. London: Hurst & Company (2007)

14. 《狂野的中国西部：新疆的驯服》Christian Tyler, Wild West China: The Taming of Xinjiang. Rutgers University Press (2004)

15. 《中国新疆博物馆吐火罗文〈弥勒会见记剧本〉残片译释》Ji Xianlin（季羡林）, Werner Winter, Georges-Jean Pinault, Fragments of the Tocharian A Maitreyasamiti-Nataka of the Xinjiang Museum, China (Trends in Linguistics, vol. 113). De Gruyter Mouton (1998)

16. 《中国中亚的军阀和穆斯林：民国时期新疆政治史（1911—1949）》Andrew D.W. Forbes, Warlords and Muslims in Chinese Central Asia: A Political History of Republican Sinkiang 1911—1949. Cambridge University Press (1986)

17. 《亚洲支点：新疆及中俄的内亚边疆》Owen Lattimore（拉铁摩尔）, Pivot of Asia: Sinkiang and the Inner Asian Frontiers of China and Russia. Atlantic Little Brown (1950)

18. 《新疆考古研究，尤其是罗布泊地区的民俗》Folke Bergman, Archaeological Researches in Sinkiang, Especially the Lop-Nor Region by Folke. Bokforlags Aktiebolaget Thule (1939)

19. 《古代和田：中国新疆考古发掘的详细报告》M. Aurel Stein（斯坦因）, Ancient Khotan: Detailed Report of Archaeological Explorations in Chinese Turkestan. 2 Vols. Oxford at the Clarendon Press (1907)

20. 《中国新疆地区考古和地形探测之旅初步报告》M. Aurel Stein（斯坦因）, Preliminary Report on A Journey of Archaeological and Topographical Exploration in Chinese Turkestan. London: Eyre and Spottiswoode (1901)

2.3.3 南海/东海

1. 《南海濒危物种和脆弱的生态系统：菲律宾诉中国的仲裁》Alfredo C. Robles Jr., Endangered Species and Fragile Ecosystems in the South China Sea: The Philippines v. China Arbitration. Springer Singapore: Palgrave Macmillan (2020)

2. 《南海的中国自信：动力源、国内政治和反应性外交政策》Richard Q. Turcsányi, *Chinese Assertiveness in the South China Sea: Power Sources, Domestic Politics, and Reactive Foreign Policy* (Global Power Shift). Springer International Publishing (2018)

3. 《中国南海的企业、地方、人民与政策：表面之下》Jonathan Spangler, Dean Karalekas, Moises Lopes de Souza (eds.), *Enterprises, Localities, People, and Policy in the South China Sea: Beneath the Surface*. Palgrave Macmillan (2018)

4. 《边界与超越：中国帝制晚期的东南沿海》Ng Chin-keong, *Boundaries and Beyond: China's Maritime Southeast in Late Imperial Times*. National University of Singapore Press (2017)

5. 《弥合困境：中国、日本与东海海事秩序》James Manicom, *Bridging Troubled Waters: China, Japan, and Maritime Order in the East China Sea*. Georgetown University Press (2014)

6. 《解决中国南海争端，促进区域合作与发展：中国视角》Shicun Wu, *Solving Disputes for Regional Cooperation and Development in the South China Sea: A Chinese Perspective*. Chandos Publishing (2013)

7. 《中国海的战争、贸易和海盗（1622—1683）》(TANAP Monographs on the History of Asian-European Interaction: v. 16) Cheng Wei-chung, *War, Trade and Piracy in the China Seas (1622—1683)*. Brill (2013)

8. 《南海：古海洋学与沉积学》Pinxian Wang, Qianyu Li, *The South China Sea: Paleoceanography and Sedimentology* (Developments in Paleoenvironmental Research). Springer (2009)

9. 《南海安全与国际政治：建立合作管理制度》Sam Bateman, Ralf Emmers, *Security and International Politics in the South China Sea: Towards a Co-operative Management Regime*. Routledge (2009)

10. 《南海海事安全》Shicun Wu, Keyuan Zou, *Maritime Security in the South China Sea* (Corbett Centre for Maritime Policy Studies Series). Ashgate Publishing Limited (2009)

11. 《中国海洋力量的崛起》Peter Howarth, *China's Rising Sea Power*. Routledge (2006)

12. 《转型中的海洋中国（1750—1850）》Gungwu Wang（王赓武）, Chin-Keong Ng (eds.), *Maritime China in Transition, 1750—1850*. Otto Harrassowitz (2004)

13. 《南海：碳氢化合物联合开发的潜力与可能性》Mark J. Valencia (Eds.), *The South China Sea: Hydrocarbon Potential and Possibilities of Joint Development*. Elsevier Science Publishing Company (1981)

2.3.4 边疆

1. 《区域和全球视野下的中国西南（1600—1911）：金属、交通、贸易和社会》Theobald Ulrich, *Southwest China in a Regional and Global Perspective (c.1600—1911): Metals, Transport, Trade and Society* (Monies, Markets, and Finance in East Asia, 1600—1900). Brill (2018)

2. 《自然资源与新边界：建设现代中国的边疆》Judd Kinzley, *Natural Resources and the New Frontier: Constructing Modern China's Borderlands*. University of Chicago Press (2018)

3. 《跨越森林、草原和山脉：清代中国边疆的环境、身份和帝国》David A. Bello, *Across*

Forest, Steppe, and Mountain: Environment, Identity, and Empire in Qing China's Borderlands. Cambridge University Press (2016)

4. 《古代中国与越：南方边疆的认知与认同（公元前400—公元前50年）》Erica Brindley, Ancient China and the Yue: Perceptions and Identities on the Southern Frontier, c. 400 BCE-50 CE. Cambridge University Press (2015)

5. 《皇帝在远方：行走在中国的边缘》David Eimer, The Emperor Far Away: Travels at the Edge of China. Bloomsbury Publishing PLC (2014)

6. 《映画香格里拉：汉藏边界有争议的景观》Emily T. Yeh, Christopher R. Coggins (eds.), Mapping Shangrila: Contested Landscapes in the Sino-Tibetan Borderlands. University of Washington Press (2014)

7. 《陶醉的满洲：中国东北的酒精、鸦片和文化》Norman Smith, Intoxicating Manchuria: Alcohol, Opium, and Culture in China's Northeast. University of Washington Press (2012)

8. 《边缘中国：边境省份与安全政策》Carla Freeman, China on the Edge: China's Border Provinces and Chinese Security Policy. The Center for the National Interest and Johns Hopkins SAIS (2011)

9. 《重铸天下：革命、战争、外交及二十世纪的中国边疆》Xiaoyuan Liu, Recast All under Heaven: Revolution, War, Diplomacy, and Frontier China in the 20th Century. Bloomsbury Academic (2010)

10. 《中国的边疆政策和国际影响》Bill K. P. Chou, Yufan Hao（郝雨凡）, China's Policies on Its Borderlands and the International Implications. World Scientific Publishing Company (2010)

11. 《建立和平解决中国领土和边界争端的新框架》Junwu Pan, Toward a New Framework for Peaceful Settlement of China's Territorial and Boundary Disputes. Koninklijke Brill NV, Leiden, The Netherlands (2009)

12. 《强大的边界，安全的国家：中国领土争端中的合作与冲突》M. Taylor Fravel（傅泰林）, Strong Borders, Secure Nation: Cooperation and Conflict in China's Territorial Disputes. Princeton University Press (2008)

13. 《汉代之边疆与帝国》Chun-shu Chang（张春树）, The Rise of the Chinese Empire, Vol. Two-Frontier, Immigration, and Empire in Han China. The University of Michigan Press (2007)

14. 《中国西南》Damien Harper, China's Southwest. Lonely Planet Publications (2007)

15. 《边界的中国政府》Diana Lary（戴安娜·拉里）, The Chinese state at the borders. UBC Press (2007)

16. 《云雾缭乱：中国在贵州的殖民开拓（1200—1700）》John E. Herman, Amid the Clouds and Mist: China's Colonization of Guizhou, 1200—1700. Harvard University Asia Center (2007)

17. 《无限忠诚：辽代中国边境交叉处》Naomi Standen, Unbounded Loyalty: Frontier Crossings in Liao China. University of Hawai'i Press (2007)

18. 《西征：清朝对中亚的征服》Peter C. Perdue（濮德培）, China Marches West: The Qing

Conquest of Central Eurasia. Belknap Press of Harvard University Press (2005)

19. 《欧亚历史上的卡拉·怀特帝国：在中国与伊斯兰世界之间》Michal Biran, *The Empire of the Qara Khitai in Eurasian History: Between China and the Islamic World* (Cambridge Studies in Islamic Civilization). Cambridge University Press (2005)

20. 《近代蒙古：从可汗到政委到资本家》Morris Rossabi（罗茂锐）, *Modern Mongolia: From Khans to Commissars to Capitalists*. University of California Press (2005)

21. 《国内政治、国际谈判与中国领土争端》Chien-pen Chung, *Domestic Politics, International Bargaining and China's Territorial Disputes*. RoutledgeCurzon (2004)

22. 《治理中国多民族边疆》Morris Rossabi（罗茂锐）, *Governing China's Multiethnic Frontiers* (Studies on Ethnic Groups in China). University of Washington Press (2004)

23. 《主权与本真性：满洲国与东亚现代》Prasenjit Duara（杜赞奇）, *Sovereignty and Authenticity: Manchukuo and the East Asian Modern*. Rowman & Littlefield Publishers (2003)

24. 《远离中心的中国：中央王国边缘拼图》Susan Debra Blum, Lionel M. Jensen, *China off Center: Mapping the Margins of the Middle Kingdom*. University of Hawaii Press (2002)

25. 《中国边界》John Hay, *Boundaries in China*. Reaktion Books Ltd (1994)

26. 《中国在中亚：早期（公元前125年至公元23年）》F. P. Hulsewe, *China in Central Asia: The Early Stage: 125 B.C.–A.D. 23*. Brill, Leiden (1979)

27. 《牧民与人民委员：再访蒙古》Owen Lattimore（拉铁摩尔）, *Nomads and Commissars: Mongolia Revisited*. Oxford University Press (1962)

28. 《中国西南古纳西王国》Joseph Francis Charles Rock, *The Ancient Na-khi Kingdom of Southwest China*. 2 Vol.s. Harvard University Press (1947)

29. 《中国的亚洲内陆边疆》Owen Lattimore（拉铁摩尔）, *Inner Asian Frontiers of China*. American Geographical Society (1940)

30. 《满州：冲突的摇篮》Owen Lattimore（拉铁摩尔）, *Manchuria: Cradle of Conflict*. Macmillan (1932)

31. 《跨越蒙古平原：一位自然主义者对中国"大西北"的述说》Roy C. Andrews, *Across Mongolian Plains: A Naturalist's Account of China's "Great Northwest"*. New York: D. Appleton and Company (1921, 2008)

2.4 台、港、澳

2.4.1 中国台湾

1. 《台湾与国际人权：一个转型的故事》(Economics, Law, and Institutions in Asia Pacific) Jerome A. Cohen, William P. Alford, Chang-fa Lo, *Taiwan and International Human Rights: A Story of Transformation*. Springer Singapore (2019)

2. 《台湾的政治调整和"外交"挑战》(Politics and Development of Contemporary China) Wei-chin Lee, *Taiwan's Political Re-Alignment and Diplomatic Challenges*. Springer

International Publishing: Palgrave Macmillan (2019)

3. 《巨流河：从满洲到台湾的中国回忆录》Chi Pang-yuan（齐邦媛）, John Balcom, *The Great Flowing River: A Memoir of China, from Manchuria to Taiwan* (Modern Chinese Literature from Taiwan). Columbia University Press (2018)

4. 《当台湾的教育遇到政治：博弈论视角（1994—2016）》Ka-ho Kwok, *When Education Meets Politics in Taiwan: A Game Theory Perspective (1994—2016)* (Spotlight on China). Sense Publishers (2017)

5. 《17世纪中国征服台湾：满月的胜利》Young-tsu Wong, *China's Conquest of Taiwan in the Seventeenth Century: Victory at Full Moon*. Springer Singapore (2017)

6. 《两岸关系和国际组织：对华关系语境下"台湾"参与政府间组织》Björn Alexander Lindemann, *Cross-Strait Relations and International Organizations. Taiwan's Participation in IGOs in the Context of Its Relationship with China*. Springer Fachmedien Wiesbaden (2014)

7. 《原乡、故乡：钟理和文选》Thomas Michael McClellan, Lihe Zhong, *From the Old Country Stories and Sketches of China and Taiwan*. Columbia University Press (2014)

8. 《台北：移民之城》Joseph R. Allen, *Taipei: City of Displacements*. University of Washington Press (2012)

9. 《台湾活力：政治、经济、社会与文化》Steve Tsang (eds.), *The Vitality of Taiwan: Politics, Economics, Society and Culture*. Palgrave Macmillan UK (2012)

10. 《1979年以来台湾海峡两岸关系：海峡两岸政策调整与制度变迁》Kevin G. Cai (ed.), *Cross-Taiwan Straits Relations Since 1979: Policy Adjustment and Institutional Change Across the Straits*. World Scientific Publishing Company (2011)

11. 《台湾指南大全》John F. Copper, *The A to Z of Taiwan (Republic of China)*. Rowman and Littlefield Publishing Group; Scarecrow Press (2010)

12. 《台湾历史词典（第三版）》John F. Copper, *Historical Dictionary of Taiwan* (Republic of China). The Scarecrow Press, Inc. (2007)

13. 《台湾和大陆的商业投资环境：以IT和高科技电子产业为重心》Chen-min Hsu, Wei-Guo Zhang, Leslie Lok, *Business and Investment Environment in Taiwan and Mainland China: A Focus on the IT and High-Tech Electronic Industries*. World Scientific Publishing Co. Pte. Ltd. (2007)

14. 《日本殖民统治下的"台湾"（1895—1945）：历史、文化与记忆》Ping-hui Liao（廖炳惠）, David Der-Wei Wang（王德威）, *Taiwan Under Japanese Colonial Rule, 1895—1945: History, Culture, Memory*. Columbia University Press (2006)

15. 《台湾党派政治：政党变革与台湾民主发展（1991—2004）》Dafydd Fell, *Party Politics in Taiwan: Party Change and the Democratic Evolution of Taiwan, 1991—2004*. Routledge (2005)

16. 《台湾电影导演》（李安、侯孝贤等）Emilie Yueh-yu Yeh and Darrell William Davis, *Taiwan Film Directors: A Treasure Island*. Columbia University Press (2005)

17.《当代台湾文化、种族和政治民族主义：本土化》John Makeham, A-chin Hsiau, *Cultural, Ethnic, and Political Nationalism in Contemporary Taiwan: Bentuhua*. Palgrave Macmillan (2005)

18.《台湾史》Jonathan Manthorpe, *Forbidden Nation: A History of Taiwan*. Palgrave Macmillan (2005)

19.《台湾原住民》Josiane Cauquelin, *The Aborigines of Taiwan*. RoutledgeCurzon (2004)

20.《台湾现代化：美国化与儒家表现的现代化》Wei-Bin Zhang, *Taiwan's Modernization: Americanization and Modernizing Confucian Manifestations*. Singapore World Scientific Publishing (2003)

21.《台湾化的起源与政治》George Tsai Woei, Peter Yu Kien-Hong, *Taiwanisation: Its Origin & Politics*. World Scientific Pub Co Inc (2001)

22.《国际治理、制度和全球化：来自北京和台北的案例研究》Peter Kien-hong Yu, *International Governance, Regimes, and Globalization: Case Studies from Beijing and Taipei*. Lexington Books (2001)

23.《台湾历史词典》John F. Copper, *Historical Dictionary of Taiwan* (Republic of China). Scarecrow Press (2000)

24.《台湾现代汉语诗选》Michelle Yeh, N. G. D. Malmqvist (eds.), *Frontier Taiwan: An Anthology of Modern Chinese Poetry*. Columbia University Press (2000)

25.《客厅即工厂：台湾的阶级、性别与卫星厂体系》Ping-Chun Hsiung, *Living Rooms as Factories: Class, Gender, and the Satellite Factory System in Taiwan*. Temple University Press (1996)

26.《台湾发展中的灵活性、前瞻性与命运》Steve Chan, Cal Clark, *Flexibility, Foresight and Fortuna in Taiwan's Development*. Routledge (1992)

27.《福尔摩沙（中国台湾）：中国历史研究》W. G. Goddard, *Formosa: A Study in Chinese History*. Palgrave Macmillan UK (1966)

2.4.2 中国香港

1.《法律视角下中国中央政府与港澳地方政府间关系》(China Academic Library) Zhenmin Wang, *Relationship Between the Chinese Central Authorities and Regional Governments of Hong Kong and Macao: A Legal Perspective*. Springer Singapore (2018)

2.《中国香港：政治与文化视角》Shigong Jiang, *China's Hong Kong: A Political and Cultural Perspective*. Springer Singapore (2017)

3.《中国、香港与漫长的70年代》Priscilla Roberts, Odd Arne Westad（文安立）, *China, Hong Kong, and the Long 1970s* (Cambridge imperial and post-colonial studies series). Springer International Publishing (2017)

4.《新千年的香港文化与社会：以香港为方法》(The Humanities in Asia 4) Yiu-Wai Chu（朱耀伟）(eds.), *Hong Kong Culture and Society in the New Millennium: Hong Kong as Method*. Springer Singapore (2017)

5.《香港和宝莱坞：亚洲电影的全球化》Joseph Tse-Hei Lee, Satish Kolluri (eds.), *Hong Kong* and Bollywood: Globalization of Asian Cinemas. Palgrave Macmillan US (2016)

6. 《亚洲主要金融中心的商业和政治：香港、新加坡和上海》J. J. Woo, Business and Politics in Asia's Key Financial Centres: Hong Kong, Singapore and Shanghai. Springer Singapore (2016)

7. 《冷战中的香港》Priscilla Roberts, John Carroll, Hong Kong in the Cold War. Hong Kong University Press (2016)

8. 《迷失在中国：1997年后香港的法律、文化和身份》Carol A. G. Jones, Lost in China: Law, Culture and Identity in Post-1997 Hong Kong. Cambridge University Press (2015)

9. 《香港华人青少年：家庭生活、心理健康和危险行为》Daniel T.L. Shek, Rachel C. F. Sun, Cecilia M.S. Ma (eds.), Chinese Adolescents in Hong Kong: Family Life, Psychological Well-Being and Risk Behavior. Springer (2014)

10. 《超越帝国的网络：1914—1941年香港—新加坡走廊的中国商业与民族主义》(Chinese Overseas) Huei-Ying Kuo, Networks Beyond Empires: Chinese Business and Nationalism in the Hong Kong-Singapore Corridor, 1914—1941. Brill Academic Pub (2014)

11. 《行使中国在香港和台湾的主权》Sow Keat Tok, Managing China's Sovereignty in Hong Kong and Taiwan (Critical Studies of the Asia Pacific Series). Palgrave Macmillan UK (2013)

12. 《从帝国到国际：香港圣约翰大教堂的历史》Stuart Wolfendale, Imperial to International: A History of St. John's Cathedral, Hong Kong. Hong Kong University Press (2013)

13. 《世界中心的贫民窟（香港重庆大厦）》Gordon Mathews（麦高登）, Ghetto at the Center of the World. University of Chicago Press (2011)

14. 《中国早期海岸气象学：1882—1912年香港作用》P. Kevin MacKeown, Early China Coast Meteorology: The Role of Hong Kong, 1882—1912. Hong Kong University Press (2011)

15. 《内地与香港的新自由主义和文化：倒计时》Hai Ren, Neoliberalism and Culture in China and Hong Kong: The Countdown of Time. Routledge (2010)

16. 《北京与香港关系动态：台湾的典范》Sonny Shiu-Hing Lo, The Dynamics of Beijing-Hong Kong Relations: A Model for Taiwan. Hong Kong University Press (2010)

17. 《香港特别行政区和澳门特别行政区概览》Ming K. Chan, Sonny Shiu-Hing Lo, The A to Z of the Hong Kong SAR and the Macao SAR. Rowman and Littlefield Publishing Group: Scarecrow Press (2010)

18. 《模范城市：香港的空间、文化与资本主义》Janet Ng, Paradigm City: Space, Culture, and Capitalism in Hong Kong (Global Modernity). State University of New York Press, Albany (2009)

19. 《香港政治与政府：中国主权下的危机》Ming Sing, Politics and Government in Hong Kong: Crisis under Chinese sovereignty. Routledge (2008)

20. 《生活工作在香港：在中国门户侨居生活的完整实用指南》Rachel Wright, Living and Working in Hong Kong: The Complete Practical Guide to Expatriate Life in China's Gateway. How to Books Ltd (2008)

21. 《治理香港：从19世纪到回归中国的行政官员（1862—1997）》Steve Tsang, Governing

Hong Kong: Administrative Officers from the 19th Century to the Handover to China, 1862—1997 (International Library of Colonial History).I.B.Tauris & Co Ltd (2007)

22. 《殖民地香港和现代中国：互动与融合》Pui-Tak Lee, *Colonial Hong Kong And Modern China: Interaction And Reintegration*. Hong Kong University Press (2006)

23. 《帝国边缘：香港的中国精英和英国殖民主义》John M. Carroll, *Edge of Empires: Chinese Elites and British Colonials in Hong Kong*. Harvard University Press (2005)

24. 《中国基督徒：精英、中间商与香港教会》Carl Smith, *Chinese Christians: Elites, Middlemen, and the Church in Hong Kong*. Hong Kong University Press (2005)

25. 《勉为其难的英雄：香港和广州的人力车夫（1874—1954）》Fung Chi Ming（冯志明）, *Reluctant Heroes: Richshaw Pullers in Hong Kong And Canton, 1874—1954* (Royal Asiatic Society Hong Kong Studies Series). Hong Kong University Press (2005)

26. 《香港近代史》Steve Tsang, *A Modern History of Hong Kong-Hong*. Kong University Press (2004)

27. 《香港与冷战：英美关系（1949—1957）》Chi-kwan Mark, *Hong Kong and the Cold War: Anglo-American Relations 1949—1957* (Oxford Historical Monographs). Oxford University Press (2004)

28. 《马利诺多明我外方传教女修会在香港（1921—1969）：爱上中国人》Cindy Yik-yi Chu, *The Maryknoll Sisters in Hong Kong, 1921—1969: In Love with the Chinese*. Palgrave Macmillan US (2004)

29. 《重塑香港公民身份：社区、国家与全球城市》Agnes S. Ku, Ngai Pun (eds.), *Remaking Citizenship in Hong Kong: Community, Nation and the Global City* (Asia's Transformations). RoutledgeCurzon (2004)

30. 《香港电影：殖民者、祖国与自我》Yingchi Chu, *Hong Kong Cinema: Coloniser, Motherland, and Self*. RoutledgeCurzon (2003)

31. 《中国内地和香港的牛仔工业》Li Yi, L. Yao, K.W. Yeung, *The China and Hong Kong Denim Industry* (Woodhead Publishing Series in Textiles). Woodhead Publishing, Published in Association With The Textile Institute (2003)

32. 《香港电影：历史、艺术与身份》Poshek Fu（傅葆石）, David Desser, *The Cinema of Hong Kong: History, Arts, Identity*. Cambridge University Press (2000)

33. 《香港转型：回归的岁月》Robert Ash, Peter Ferdinand, Brian Hook, Robin Porter, *Hong Kong in Transition: The Handover Years*. Macmillan Press Ltd (2000)

34. 《同志与资本家：回归以来的香港》Rowan Callick, *Comrades and Capitalists: Hong Kong Since the Handover*. UNSW Press (1998)

35. 《在香港的华人商业集团与华南政治变革（1900—1925）》Stephanie Po-Yin Chung, *Chinese Business Groups in Hong Kong and Political Change in South China, 1900—25* (St. Antonys Series).Palgrave Macmillan (1998)

36. 《香港转型（1842—1997）》Judith M. Brown, Rosemary Foot (eds.), *Hong Kong's Transitions, 1842—1997*. Palgrave Macmillan UK (1997)

37. 《香港：中国大都市的人类学》Grant Evans, Maria Tam, *Hong Kong: The Anthropology of a Chinese Metropolis*. Honolulu: University of Hawai'i Press (1997)

38. 《中国统治下的香港：回归的经济与政治意义》Warren I. Cohen（孔华润）, Li Zhao (eds.), *Hong Kong under Chinese Rule: The Economic and Political Implications of Reversion* (Cambridge Modern China Series). Cambridge University Press (1997)

39. 《香港华南贝类》Brian Morton, *The Malacofauna of Hong Kong and Southern China*. 2 vols. Hong Kong University Press (1985)

2.4.3 中国澳门

1. 《1999年以来澳门政治经济：成功的困境》Yufan Hao（郝雨凡）, Li Sheng, Guanjin Pan, *Political Economy of Macao since 1999: The Dilemma of Success*. Palgrave (2017)

2. 《广州与澳门商人：18世纪中国贸易的成败》Paul A. Van Dyke, *Merchants of Canton and Macao: Success and Failure in Eighteenth-Century Chinese Trade*. Hong Kong University Press (2016)

3. 《一个国家，两种制度，三个法律秩序：进化的视角——中国恢复主权后的澳门自治》Jorge Oliveira, Paulo Cardinal, *One Country, Two Systems, Three Legal Orders-Perspectives of Evolution: Essays on Macau's Autonomy after the Resumption of Sovereignty by China*. Springer (2009)

4. 《澳门味道：中国海岸的葡萄牙美食》Annabel Jackson, *Taste of Macau: Portuguese Cuisine on the China Coast*. Hong Kong University Press (2003)

5. 《澳门转型：从殖民地到自治区》Herbert S. Yee, *Macau in Transition: From Colony to Autonomous Region*. Palgrave Macmillan UK (2001)

6. 《澳门》Richard Louis Edmonds, *Macau* (World Bibliographical Series, 105). ABC-Clio Inc. (1989)

3. 中国哲学与宗教

3.1 哲学

1. 《在道义论与正义论之间：中西方观点》(Routledge Studies in Contemporary Chinese Philosophy) Genyou Wu, *Between Deontology and Justice: Chinese and Western Perspectives*. Routledge: Taylor & Francis Group (2020)
2. 《作为备选的和谐主义》(Key Concepts in Chinese Thought and Culture) Keping Wang, *Harmonism as an Alternative*. Springer Singapore: Palgrave Pivot (2019)
3. 《动力、不确定性与推理：第二届中国逻辑与论证大会》(Logic in Asia: Studia Logica Library) Beishui Liao, Thomas Agotnes, Yi N. Wang, *Dynamics, Uncertainty and Reasoning: The Second Chinese Conference on Logic and Argumentation*. Springer Singapore (2019)
4. 《郭店楚简指要》(Dao Companions to Chinese Philosophy 10) Shirley Chan（陈慧）, *Dao Companion to the Excavated Guodian Bamboo Manuscripts*. Springer International Publishing (2019)
5. 《中国道德教育哲学》Zhuran You, A. G. Rud, Yingzi Hu, *The Philosophy of Chinese Moral Education*. Palgrave Macmillan US (2018)
6. 《遇到中国：迈克尔·桑德尔与中国哲学》Michael J. Sandel, Paul J. D'Ambrosio (eds.), *Encountering China: Michael Sandel and Chinese Philosophy*. Harvard University Press (2018)
7. 《程颐的哲学》Yung-ch'un Ts'ai, *The Philosophy of Ch'eng I* (China Academic Library). Springer Singapore (2018)
8. 《欣赏中国差异：与安乐哲合作探讨方法、问题和角色》(SUNY series in Chinese Philosophy and Culture) Jim Behuniak (ed.), *Appreciating the Chinese Difference: Engaging Roger T. Ames on Methods, Issues, and Roles*. State University of New York Press (2018)
9. 《中国当代价值体系》(China Insights) Zhen Han（韩震）, Weiwen Zhang, *Contemporary Value Systems in China*. Springer Singapore (2018)
10. 《唐君毅：儒家哲学与现代性的挑战》Thomas Freohlich, *Tang Junyi: Confucian Philosophy and the Challenge of Modernity*. Brill (2017)
11. 《20世纪初德国思想中的中国佛教哲学》Eric S. Nelson, *Chinese and Buddhist Philosophy in early Twentieth-Century German Thought*. Bloomsbury Academic (2017)
12. 《中国早期哲学中的情感》Curie Virág, *The Emotions in Early Chinese Philosophy* (Emotions of the past). Oxford University Press (2017)
13. 《中国命运哲学》Yixia Wei, *The Chinese Philosophy of Fate*. Springer (2017)
14. 《重新认识21世纪的儒家哲学》Xinzhong Yao (eds.), *Reconceptualizing Confucian Philosophy*

in the 21st Century. Springer Singapore (2017)

15. 《成己与成物：意义世界的生成》Yang Guorong（杨国荣）, Chad Austin Meyers, Hans-Georg Moeller, *The Mutual Cultivation of Self and Things: A Contemporary Chinese Philosophy of the Meaning of Being.* Indiana University Press (2016)

16. 《比较与跨文化哲学基础》Lin Ma, Jaap van Brakel, *Fundamentals of Comparative and Intercultural Philosophy* (SUNY series in Chinese philosophy and culture). State University of New York Press (2016)

17. 《连续性与断裂：毛泽东时代的哲学》J. Moufawad-Paul, *Continuity and Rupture: Philosophy in the Maoist Terrain.* Zero Books (2016)

18. 《道路：关于美好生活中国哲学家可以教给我们什么》Michael Puett, Christine Gross-Loh, *The Path: What Chinese Philosophers Can Teach Us About the Good Life.* Simon & Schuster (2016)

19. 《中国古典哲学中人的尊严：儒家、墨家与道家》Qianfan Zhang, *Human Dignity in Classical Chinese Philosophy: Confucianism, Mohism, and Daoism.* Palgrave Macmillan US (2016)

20. 《哲学文化问题选集：前沿探索》Yijie Tang（汤一介）, *Anthology of Philosophical and Cultural Issues: An Exploration into New Frontiers* (China Academic Library). Springer Singapore (2016)

21. 《荀子哲学指南》Eric L. Hutton (eds.), *Dao Companion to the Philosophy of Xunzi.* Springer Netherlands (2016)

22. 《中国古典哲学中的人格尊严：儒、墨、道》Qianfan Zhang, *Human Dignity in Classical Chinese Philosophy: Confucianism, Mohism, and Daoism.* Palgrave MacMillan (2016)

23. 《意识独特性新论》Shili Xiong, John Makeham, *New Treatise on the Uniqueness of Consciousness.* Yale University Press (2015)

24. 《从命运到道：中国先秦哲学概观》Kejian Huang, *From Destiny to DAO: A Survey of Pre-Qin Philosophy in China.* Enrich Professional Publishing (2015)

25. 《中西哲学中的道德与智慧：向德的转向》Mi Chienkuo（米建国）, Michael Slote, Ernest Sosa, *Moral and Intellectual Virtues in Western and Chinese Philosophy: The Turn Toward Virtue.* Routledge (2015)

26. 《陌生人与中国道德想象》Haiyan Lee, *The Stranger and the Chinese Moral Imagination.* Stanford, California: Stanford University Press (2014)

27. 《天地不仁道：中国古典哲学中的恶问题》Franklin Perkins, *Heaven and Earth Are Not Humane: The Problem of Evil in Classical Chinese Philosophy.* Indiana University Press (2014)

28. 《牟宗三晚年作品：中国哲学文选》Jason Clower, *Late Works of Mou Zongsan: Selected Essays on Chinese Philosophy.* Brill (2014)

29. 《转变意识：近代中国的瑜伽思想》John Makeham（梅约翰）, *Transforming Consciousness: Yogacara Thought in Modern China.* Oxford University Press (2014)

30. 《胡适英文文存：中国哲学思想史》（第二卷）Hu Shih (auth.), Chih-P'ing Chou（周质平）(eds.), *English Writings of Hu Shih: Chinese Philosophy and Intellectual History*

(Volume 2) (China Academic Library). Springer Berlin Heidelberg (2013)

31. 《韩非哲学指南》Paul R. Goldin (auth.), Paul R. Goldin (eds.), *Dao Companion to the Philosophy of Han Fei.* Springer Netherlands (2013)

32. 《婆罗门与道：中印哲学与宗教比较研究》(Studies in Comparative Philosophy and Religion) Ithamar Theodor, Zhihua Yao, *Brahman and Dao: Comparative Studies of Indian and Chinese Philosophy and Religion.* Lexington Books (2013)

33. 《竹子哲学：中国早期文本与意义生产》Dirk Meyer（麦笛）, *Philosophy on Bamboo: Text and the Production of Meaning in Early China.* Brill (2012)

34. 《中国思想》Christopher Bollas, *China on the Mind.* Routledge (2012)

35. 《三道之师：中国先哲对知足生活的思考》Hung Ying-Ming, *Master of the Three Ways: Reflections of a Chinese Sage on Living a Satisfying Life.* Random House (2012)

36. 《中国逻辑的发现》Joachim Kurtz（顾有信）, *The Discovery of Chinese Logic.* Brill (2011)

37. 《深度中国：人的道德生活》Arthur Kleinman, Yunxiang Yan, Jing Jun, Sing Lee, Everett Zhang, Pan Tianshu, Wu Fei, Jinhua Guo, *Deep China: The Moral Life of the Person.* University of California Press (2011)

38. 《创造力与道教：中国哲学、艺术与诗歌研究》Chung-yuan Chang, *Creativity and Taoism: A Study of Chinese Philosophy, Art and Poetry.* Singing Dragon (2011)

39. 《梁漱溟的宗教哲学：隐秘的佛教徒》(Modern Chinese Philosophy 3) Thierry Meynard, *The Religious Philosophy of Liang Shuming: The Hidden Buddhist.* Brill Academic Pub. (2010)

40. 《柏拉图在现代中国：中国当代柏拉图主义研究》（博士论文）Leihua Weng, *Plato in Modern China: A Study of Contemporary Chinese Platonists.* Ph. D. Dissertation, University of South Carolina (2010)

41. 《何为启蒙：中国能回答康德的问题吗？》Wei Zhang, *What Is Enlightenment: Can China Answer Kant's Question?* State University of New York Press (2010)

42. 《哲学、宗教与玄学》Alan K. L. Chan, Yuet-keung Lo, *Philosophy and Religion in Early Medieval China.* State University of New York Press (2010)

43. 《郭店：中国宗教哲学和政治哲学新发现的起源》Kenneth Holloway, *Guodian: The Newly Discovered Seeds of Chinese Religious and Political Philosophy.* Oxford University Press, USA (2009)

44. 《列维纳斯：中国与西方观点》Chung-Ying Cheng（成中英）(eds.), *Levinas: Chinese and Western Perspectives.* Wiley-Blackwell (2009)

45. 《中国古代家庭尊严：〈孝经〉的哲学翻译》Henry Rosemont, Jr.（罗思文）, Roger T. Ames（安乐哲）, *The Chinese Classic of Family Reverence: A Philosophical Translation of the Xiaojing.* University of Hawai'i Press (2009)

46. 《东西二分法》Thorsten Pattberg（裴德思）, *The East-West Dichotomy.* LoD Press, New York (2009)

47. 《佛教哲学概论》Stephen J. Laumakis, *An Introduction to Buddhist Philosophy.* Cambridge

University Press (2008)

48. 《中国哲学史》Bo Mou, *History of Chinese Philosophy*. Routledge (2008)

49. 《仪式与尊重：比较语境中的中国哲学延伸》Robert C. Neville, *Ritual and Deference: Extending Chinese Philosophy in a Comparative Context*. Sunny Press (2008)

50. 《中国哲学概论》Karyn L. Lai, *An Introduction to Chinese Philosophy*. Cambridge University Press (2008)

51. 《拓展过程：探索中西方哲学和神学的转型》(SUNY series in Chinese philosophy and culture.) John H. Berthrong, *Expanding Process: Exploring Philosophical and Theological Transformations in China and the West*. State University of New York Pres (2008)

52. 《中国早期哲学中的德性伦理与结果论》Bryan W. Van Norden, *Virtue Ethics and Consequentialism in Early Chinese Philosophy*. Cambridge University Press (2007)

53. 《向中国哲学学习：相互依赖的伦理与情境的自我》Karyn Lai, *Learning from Chinese Philosophies: Ethics of iInterdependent and Contextualised self*. Ashgate (2006)

54. 《中国辩证法：从易经到马克思主义》Chenshan Tian（田辰山）, *Chinese Dialectics: From Yijing to Marxism*. Lexington Books (2005)

55. 《人性、仪式与历史：荀子与中国哲学研究》Antonio S. Cua, *Human Nature, Ritual, and History: Studies in Xunzi and Chinese Philosophy*. Catholic University of America Press (2005)

56. 《孔子之后：中国早期哲学研究》Paul Rakita Goldin, *After Confucius: Studies in Early Chinese Philosophy*. University of Hawai'i Press (2005)

57. 《全球化时代的中国哲学》Robin R. Wang, *Chinese Philosophy in an Era of Globalization*. State University of New York Press (2004)

58. 《物质美德：中国早期伦理与身体》Mark Csikszentmihalyi, *Material Virtue: Ethics And The Body In Early China* (Sinica Leidensia). Leiden, Boston: Brill (2004)

59. 《杜威、孔子与全球哲学》Joseph Grange, *John Dewey, Confucius, and Global Philosophy*. State University of New York Press (2004)

60. 《庄子与中国早期哲学：模糊、转化与悖论》Steve Coutinho, *Zhuangzi and Early Chinese Philosophy: Vagueness, Transformation and Paradox* (Ashgate World Philosophies Series). Ashgate (2004)

61. 《中国哲学百科全书》Antonio S. Cua (ed.), *Encyclopedia of Chinese Philosophy*. Routledge (2003)

62. 《重塑21世纪中国公共哲学》Jinghao Zhou, *Remaking China's Public Philosophy for the Twenty-first Century*. Praeger Publishers (2003)

63. 《中国哲学的比较方法》(Ashgate World Philosophies Series) Bo Mou, *Comparative Approaches to Chinese Philosophy*. Routledge (2003)

64. 《张载的思想（1020—1077）》Ira E. Kasoff, *The Thought of Chang Tsai: 1020—1077* (Cambridge Studies in Chinese History, Literature and Institutions). Cambridge University Press (2002)

65. 《当代中国哲学》Chung-Ying Cheng（成中英）, Nicholas Bunnin, *Contemporary Chinese Philosophy*. Wiley-Blackwell (2002)
66. 《中国早期思想中的意义认识论》(Monographs of the Society for Asian and Comparative Philosophy no. 19.) Jane Geaney, *On the Epistemology of the Senses in Early Chinese Thought*. University of Hawai'i Press (2002)
67. 《康德传记》Manfred Kuehn, *Kant: A Biography*. Cambridge University Press (2001)
68. 《亚洲经典哲学：精华文本指南》Joel J. Kupperman, *Classic Asian Philosophy: A Guide to the Essential Texts*. Oxford University Press (2001)
69. 《政治哲学：从柏拉图到毛泽东》Martin Cohen, *Political Philosophy From Plato to Mao*. Pluto Press (2001)
70. 《中国哲学经典读本》Philip J. Ivanhoe, Bryan W. Van Norden (eds.), *Readings in Classical Chinese Philosophy*. Seven Bridges Press (2001)
71. 《朱熹宗教思想》Julia Ching（秦家懿）, *The Religious Thought of Chu Hsi*. Oxford University Press (2000)
72. 《东方哲学关键读本》Oliver Leaman, *Eastern Philosophy: Key Readings*. Routledge (2000)
73. 《亚里士多德在中国：语言、类别和翻译》Robert Wardy, *Aristotle in China: Language, Categories and Translation* (Needham Research Institute Studies). Cambridge University Press (2000)
74. 《东方哲学关键概念》Oliver Leaman, *Key Concepts in Eastern Philosophy*. Routledge (1999)
75. 《生活的艺术》Lin Yutang（林语堂）, *The Importance of Living*. Harper Paperbacks (1998)
76. 《中国哲学与现代化》Fang-Tung Liu, Huang Songjie, George F. McLean, *Philosophy and Modernization in China* (Chinese Philosophical Studies, 13). Council for Research in Values and Philosophy (1997)
77. 《亚洲哲学百科》Brian Carr, Indira Mahalingam, *Companion Encyclopedia of Asian Philosophy*. Routledge (1997)
78. 《中国哲学新论》Hsueh-li Cheng, *New Essays in Chinese Philosophy* (Asian thought and culture 28). Peter Lang Publishing (1997)
79. 《中国哲学小史》Fung Yu-Lan（冯友兰）, Derk Bodde（卜德）, *A Short History of Chinese Philosophy*. Free Press (1997)
80. 《自我与欺骗：跨文化的哲学探究》Roger T. Ames（安乐哲）, *Self and Deception: A Cross-Cultural Philosophical Enquiry*. SUNY Press (1996)
81. 《18世纪的中国哲学、语言学和政治学：李绂与清代陆王学派》Chin-shing Huang, *Philosophy, Philology, and Politics in Eighteenth-Century China: Li Fu and Lu-Wang School under the Ch'ing*. Cambridge University Press (1995)
82. 《荣格与东方思想：与东方对话》J. J. Clarke, *Jung and Eastern Thought: A Dialogue with the Orient*. Routledge (1994)
83. 《空谷幽兰：寻访现代中国隐士》Bill Porter, Steven Johnson, *Road to Heaven: Encounters*

with Chinese Hermits. Mercury House (1993)

84. 《道与逻各斯：文学阐释、东方与西方》Longxi Zhang（张隆溪）, *The Tao and the Logos: Literary Hermeneutics, East and West* (Post-Contemporary Interventions). Duke University Press (1992)

85. 《中国哲学和哲学文学研究》(SUNY series in Chinese philosophy and culture) Angus Charles Graham（葛瑞汉）, *Studies in Chinese Philosophy and Philosophical Literature*. State University of New York Press (1990)

86. 《道之辩：中国古代的哲学论争》Angus Charles Graham（葛瑞汉）, *Disputers of the Tao: Philosophical Argument in Anciant China*. Open Court Publishing (1989)

87. 《东方哲学和宗教百科全书：佛教，印度教，道教，禅宗。亚洲智慧之名师、传统和文献的全面考察》Ingrid Fischer-Schreiber, Franz-Karl Ehrnard, Kurt Friedrichs, Michael S. Diener, *The Encyclopedia of Eastern Philosophy and Religion: Buddhism, Hinduism, Taoism, Zen. A Complete Survey of the Teachers, Traditions and Literature of Asian Wisdom*. Shambhala, Boston (1989)

88. 《阴阳与关联思想的本质》Angus Charles Graham（葛瑞汉）, *Yin-Yang and the Nature of Correlative Thinking*. Singapore: Institute of East Asian Philosophies (1986)

89. 《中国第六世纪的心灵哲学：帕拉马哈的"意识的演化"》Diana Y. Paul, *Philosophy of Mind in Sixth-Century China: Paramartha's "Evolution of Consciousness"*. Stanford University Press (1984)

90. 《中西哲学对话中的生命现象学》Anna-Teresa Tymieniecka (ed.), *Phenomenology of Life in a Dialogue between Chinese and Occidental Philosophy* (Analecta Husserliana 17). Springer Netherlands (1984)

91. 《公元3纪中国的哲学与论争》Hsi K'Ang, Robert Henricks, *Philosophy and Argumentation in Third-Century China*. Princeton University Press (1983)

92. 《当代中国哲学》Joseph P. McDermott (auth.), Frederick J. Adelmann, S. J. (eds.), *Contemporary Chinese Philosophy* (Boston College Studies in Philosophy 9). Springer Netherlands (1982)

93. 《中国哲学文献选编》Wing-Tsit Chan（陈荣捷）, *A Source Book in Chinese Philosophy*. Princeton University Press (1969)

94. 《王阳明哲学》Frederick Goodrich Henke, James H. Tufts, *The Philosophy of Wang Yang-ming* (2nd. ed.). New York: Paragon Book Reprint Corp. (1964)

95. 《〈大同书〉：康有为的大同哲学》Laurence Thompson, *Ta T'ung Shu: The One-world Philosophy of K'ang Yu-wei*. Allen & Unwin (1958)

96. 《中国哲学五十年》E. R. Hughes, translated from the French by Laurence G. Thompson, *Fifty Years of Chinese Philosophy* (1898—1950). George Allen & Unwin (1956)

97. 《中国哲学大纲与参考书目》Wing-Tsit Chan（陈荣捷）, *An Outline and a Bibliography*

of Chinese Philosophy. Hanover, New Hampshire (1955)

98.《中国哲学小史》Yu-lan Fung（冯友兰）, Derek Bodde（卜德）, *A Short History of Chinese Philosophy*. The Free Press (1948, 1966)

99.《天才的冒险》Will Durant, *Adventures in Genius*. New York, Simon and Schuster (1931)

100.《人性哲学》Chu His（朱熹）, Trans. By J. Percy Bruce, *The Philosophy of Human Nature*. London Probsthain & Co. (1922)

101.《王阳明哲学》Translated From the Chinese by Frederick Goodrich Henke, Introd. by James H. Tufts, *The Philosophy of Wang Yang-Ming*. Open Court Publing Company (1916)

102.《中国早期哲学简史》Daisetz Teitaro Suzuki, *A Brief History of Early Chinese Philosophy*. London: Probsthain (1914)

103.《武士的宗教：中国和日本禅宗哲学学科研究》Kaiten Nukariya, *Religion of the Samurai: A Study of Zen Philosophy and Discipline in China and Japan*. Luzac & Co. (1913)

3.1.1 美学

1.《美学与艺术》Jianping Gao, *Aesthetics and Art* (China Academic Library). Springer Berlin Heidelberg (2018)

2.《美学与创新》Xingjian Gao（高行健）, Mabel Lee, *Gao Xingjian: Aesthetics and Creation* (Cambria Sinophone World). Cambria Press (2012)

3.《华夏美学》Li Zehou（李泽厚）; Translated by Maija Bell Samei, *The Chinese Aesthetic Tradition*. University of Hawai'i Press (2010)

4.《中国文学与审美现代性的真实形态》Peter Button, *Configurations of the Real in Chinese Literary and Aesthetic Modernity* (Ideas, History, and Modern China). Koninklijke Brill NV, Leiden, The Netherlands (2009)

5.《赞美温和：从中国思想和美学出发》François Jullien, *In Praise of Blandness: Proceeding from Chinese Thought and Aesthetics*. Zone Books (2004)

6.《美学与马克思主义：中国美学马克思主义者与其西方同代人》Kang Liu, *Aesthetics and Marxism: Chinese Aesthetic Marxists and Their Western Contemporaries* (Post-Contemporary Interventions). Duke University Press (2000)

7.《当代中国美学》Liyuan Zhu（朱立元）, H. Gene Blocker (eds.), *Contemporary Chinese aesthetics* (Asian thought and culture 17). Peter Lang Publishing (1995)

8.《中国美学问题》Haun Saussy, *The Problem of a Chinese Aesthetic*. Stanford University Press (1993)

3.2 宗教

3.2.1 中国宗教

1.《天国是空的：中国古代"宗教"与帝国的跨文化解读》Filippo Marsili, *Heaven Is Empty: A Cross-Cultural Approach to "Religion" and Empire in Ancient China*. State

University of New York Press (2019)

2. 《中国先祖宗教中的意义与争议》Paulin Batairwa Kubuya, *Meaning and Controversy within Chinese Ancestor Religion* (Asian Christianity in the Diaspora). Palgrave Macmillan (2018)

3. 《中国人的宗教信仰》Xinping Zhuo（卓新平）, *Religious Faith of the Chinese* (China Insights). Springer Singapore (2018)

4. 《中国宗教地图集：社会地理背景》Fenggang Yang（杨凤岗）, *Atlas of Religion in China: Social and Geographical Contexts*. Brill (2018)

5. 《中国早期和现代宗教的范式转变》John Lagerwey, *Paradigm Shifts in Early and Modern Chinese Religion*. Brill (2018)

6. 《中国灵魂：毛泽东时代后的宗教回归》Ian Johnson, *The Souls of China: The Return of Religion After Mao*. Pantheon (2017)

7. 《中国的宗教认知："宗教信仰者"与"龙"》Ryan G. Hornbeck, Justin L. Barrett, Madeleine Kang (eds.), *Religious Cognition in China: "Homo Religiosus" and the Dragon*. Springer International Publishing AG (2017)

8. 《中国宗教通史》（第一部分）Mou Zhongjian（牟钟鉴）, Zhang Jian. Translated by Chi Zhen, *General History of Religions in China*. Part I. Paths International Ltd. (2017)

9. 《边疆女神：中国西南地区的宗教、种族和性别》Megan Bryson, *Goddess on the Frontier: Religion, Ethnicity, and Gender in Southwest China*. Stanford University Press (2016)

10. 《现代中国宗教II: 1850—2015》（两卷本）Vincent Goossaert, Jan Kiely, and John Lagerwey, *Modern Chinese Religion II: 1850—2015*. 2 Vols. Brill ((2015)

11. 《性别化中国宗教：主体、身份及身体》Jinhua Jia（贾晋华）, Xiaofei Kang（康笑菲）, Ping Yao（姚平）, *Gendering Chinese Religion: Subject, Identity, and Body*. SUNY Press (2014)

12. 《宗教、技术和大大小小的分歧：中国和欧洲相比（700—1800）》Karel Davids, *Religion, Technology, and the Great and Little Divergences: China and Europe Compared, c. 700—1800*. Brill (2013)

13. 《中国思想中的宗教多样性》Perry Schmidt-Leukel, Joachim Gentz (eds.), *Religious Diversity in Chinese Thought*. Palgrave Macmillan (2013)

14. 《中国早期与古希腊的占卜和预测》Lisa Ann Raphals, *Divination and Prediction in early China and Ancient Greece*. Cambridge University Press (2013)

15. 《中国宗教与哲学要旨：内圣外王之道》Chun Shan, *Major Aspects of Chinese Religion and Philosophy: Dao of Inner Saint and Outer King*. Springer-Verlag Berlin Heidelberg (2012)

16. 《威利—布莱克威尔中国宗教指南》Randall L. Nadeau, *The Wiley-Blackwell Companion to Chinese Religions*. Wiley-Blackwell (2012)

17. 《中国宗教：共产党统治下的生存与复兴》Fenggang Yang, *Religion in China: Survival and Revival under Communist Rule*. Oxford University Press (2012)

18. 《当代中国宗教：复兴与创新》Adam Yuet Chau, *Religion in Contemporary China: Revitalization and Innovation* (Routledge contemporary China series, 59). Routledge (2011)

19. 《现代中国宗教问题》Vincent Goossaert, David A Palmer, *The Religious Question in Modern China*. University of Chicago Press (2011)

20. 《中国宗教的社会科学研究：方法论、理论和研究结果》Fenggang Yang, Graeme Lang (eds.), *Social Scientific Studies of Religion in China: Methodology, Theories, and Findings* (Religion in Chinese Societies volume 1). Brill (2011)

21. 《中国宗教生活》David A. Palmer, Glenn Landes Shive, Philip L. Wickeri, *Chinese Religious Life*. Oxford University Press (2011)

22. 《纠正上帝的名字：刘智关于一神论与伊斯兰教法的儒家翻译》James D. Frankel, *Rectifying God's Name: Liu Zhi's Confucian Translation of Monotheism and Islamic Law*. University of Hawai'i Press (2011)

23. 《中国：一个宗教国家》John Lagerwey, *China: A Religious State*. Hong Kong University Press (2010)

24. 《迷信的政权：宗教与中国现代性政治》(Harvard East Asian monographs 322.) Rebecca Nedostup, *Superstitious Regimes: Religion and the Politics of Chinese Modernity*. Harvard University Asia Center (2009)

25. 《修仙：古代中国的修行与社会记忆》Robert Ford Campany（康儒博）, *Making Transcendents: Ascetics and Social Memory in Early Medieval China*. University of Hawai'i Press (2009)

26. 《20世纪华北的地方宗教》Daniel L. Overmyer, *Local Religion in North China in the Twentieth Century* (Handbook of Oriental Studies). Brill (2009)

27. 《创造宗教，创造国家：现代中国的宗教政治》Yoshiko Ashiwa, David Wank, *Making Religion, Making the State: The Politics of Religion in Modern China*. Stanford University Press (2009)

28. 《中国早期宗教：第1部分，从商至汉（公元前1250—公元220年）》John Lagerwey, Marc Kalinowski, *Early Chinese Religion. Part One: Shang through Han (1250 BC—220 AD)*. Brill (2009)

29. 《中国早期宗教：第2部分，分裂时期（公元220—589年）》John Lagerwey, Lv Pengzhi, *Early Chinese Religion. Part Two: The Period of Division (220—589 AD)*. Brill (2009)

30. 《中国宗教：电子书》Mario Poceski, *Chinese Religions: The eBook*. Journal of Buddhist Ethics Online Books, Ltd. (2009)

31. 《文明的使命：国际宗教机构在中国》Miwa Hirono, *Civilizing Missions: International Religious Agencies in China* (Culture and Religion in International Relations). Palgrave Macmillan (2008)

32. 《中国人的宗教感：现代性的痛苦与国家构建》Mayfair Mei-hui Yang, *Chinese Religiosities: Afflictions of Modernity and State Formation* (Global, Area, and International Archive). University of California Press (2008)

33. 《灵验：当代中国民间宗教》Adam Yuet Chau, *Miraculous Response: Doing Popular Religion in Contemporary China*. Stanford University Press (2006)

34. 《狐仙敬拜：帝国晚期和现代中国的权力、性别与民众宗教》Xiaofei Kang（康笑菲）, *The Cult of the Fox: Power, Gender, and Popular Religion in Late Imperial and Modern China*. Columbia University Press (2006)

35. 《中国宗教》E. R. Hughes, *Religion in China*. Routledge Taylor & Francis Group (2005)

36. 《中国的国家与宗教》Anthony C. Yu, *State and Religion in China*. Open Court Publishing Company (2005)

37. 《邪恶之道：中国宗教文化中的神性与恶魔》Richard von Glahn, *The Sinister Way: The Divine and the Demonic in Chinese Religious Culture*. University of California Press (2004)

38. 《宗教与早期现代国家：中国、俄罗斯与西方的观点》James D. Tracy, Marguerite Ragnow, *Religion and the Early Modern State: Views from China, Russia, and the West*. Cambridge University Press (2004)

39. 《中国历史上的民间宗教运动与异端教派》Hubert Michael Seiwert（苏为德）, in collaboration with Ma Xisha, *Popular Religious Movements and Heterodox Sects in Chinese History* (China Studies China Studies). Brill (2003)

40. 《成为神：中国早期的宇宙论、祭祀与自我神化》Michael J. Puett, *To Become a God: Cosmology, Sacrifice, and Self-Divinization in Early China* (Harvard-Yenching Institute Monograph Series). Harvard University Asia Center (2002)

41. 《中国民间宗教：帝国的隐喻》Stephan Feuchtwang（王斯福）, *Popular Religion in China: The Imperial Metaphor*. Curzon Press (2001)

42. 《中国社会中的宗教与仪式》Arthur P. Wolf（武雅士）, *Religion and Ritual in Chinese Society*. Stanford University Press (1999)

43. 《不守规矩的神：中国的神性与社会》Meir Shahar, Robert P. Weller, *Unruly Gods: Divinity and Society in China*. University of Hawai'i Press (1996)

44. 《唐代宗教体验与世俗社会：戴孚〈广异记〉的一种解读》Glen Dudbridge（杜德桥）, *Religious Experience and Lay Society in T'ang China: A Reading of Tai Fu's Kuang-i chi*. Cambridge University Press (1995)

45. 《中国宗教》Julia Ching, *Chinese Religions* (Themes in Comparative Religion). Palgrave Macmillan UK (1993)

46. 《唐宋时期的宗教与社会》Patricia Buckley Ebrey（伊佩霞）, Peter N. Gregory (eds.), *Religion and Society in Tang and Sung China*. University of Hawai'i Press (1993)

47. 《中国宗教的统一性与多样性》Robert P. Weller, *Unities and Diversities in Chinese Religion*. Palgrave Macmillan UK (1987)

48. 《中国社会中的宗教》C. K. Yang（杨庆堃）, *Religion in Chinese Society: A Study of Contemporary Social Functions of Religion and Some of Their Historical Factors*. University of

California Press (1961)

49. 《中国宗教：儒教与道教》Max Weber（马克思.韦伯）, *The Religion of China: Confucianism and Taoism*. The Free Press (1959)

50. 《从谚语看中国宗教/中国宗教谚语》Clifford H. Plopper, *Chinese Religion Seen Through Proverbs*. Shanghai, The China Press (1926)

51. 《儒释道三教：牛津大学讲座》William Edward Soothill（苏慧廉）, *The Three Religions of China: Lectures Delivered at Oxford*. London, New York etc.: Hodder and Stoughton (1913)

52. 《伟大的东方宗教导师》Alfred W. Martin, *Great Religious Teachers of the East*. New York: The Macmillan Co. (1911)

53. 《中国宗教研究》Edward Harper Parker（庄延龄）, *Studies in Chinese Religion*. London: Chapman and Hall, ltd. (1910)

54. 《中国古代宗教》Herbert Allen Giles（翟理斯）, *Religions of Ancient China*. Constable Co. (1905)

55. 《中国的宗教》Joseph Edkins（艾约瑟）, *Religion In China: Containing a Brief Account of the three Religions of the Chinese, with Observations on the Prospects of Christian Conversion Amongst That People*. Rev. ed. London: Kegan Paul, Trench, Trübner, & Co. Ltd. (1893)

56. 《龙、肖像与恶魔：中国三大宗教儒、释、道》Hampden C. DuBose, *The Dragon, Image, And Demon: Or, the Three Religions of China; Confucianism, Buddhism and Taoism*. New York: A. C. Armstrong & Son (1887)

57. 《在中国God是谁？"神"还是"上帝"？》S. C. Malan, *Who is God in China, Shin or Shang-te? Remarks on the Etymology of "Elohim" and of "theos", and on the Rendering of Those Terms into Chinese*. London: Samuel Bagster and Sons (1855)

3.2.2 基督教

1. 《中国与真耶稣：中国基督教教会的魅力与组织》Melissa Wei-Tsing Inouye, *China and the True Jesus: Charisma and Organization in a Chinese Christian Church*. Oxford University Press (2019)

2. 《当代中国基督教、女权主义与社会变革》(Palgrave Studies in Oral History) Li Ma, *Christianity, Femininity and Social Change in Contemporary China*. Springer International Publishing: Palgrave Macmillan (2019)

3. 《一个从未旅行者的全球纠葛：17世纪的中国基督徒及其冲突的世界》Dominic Sachsenmaier, *Global Entanglements of a Man Who Never Traveled: A Seventeenth-Century Chinese Christian and His Conflicted Worlds* (Columbia Studies in International and Global History). Columbia University Press (2018)

4. 《中国公共神学：中国基督教的代际转换与儒家想象》Alexander Chow, *Chinese Public Theology: Generational Shifts and Confucian Imagination in Chinese Christianity*. Oxford University Press, USA (2018)

5. 《华南的基督教化：近代潮汕的传教、发展与认同》Joseph Tse-Hei Lee, *Christianizing South China: Mission, Development, and Identity in Modern Chaoshan*. Palgrave Macmillan, Cham (2018)

6. 《威权遏制：中国城市公安局与新教家庭教会》Marie-Eve Reny, *Authoritarian Containment: Public Security Bureaus and Protestant House Churches in Urban China*. Oxford University Press (2018)

7. 《神圣的网络：闽南新教徒的社会生活和网络，1840年代至1920年代》Chris White, *Sacred Webs: The Social Lives and Networks of Minnan Protestants, 1840s—1920s* (Religion in Chinese Societies). Brill Academic Publishers (2017)

8. 《爱国的合作：中国基督教会的边境服务与20世纪20年代至50年代的中国教会—国家关系》Diana Junio, *Patriotic Cooperation: The Border Services of the Church of Christ in China and Chinese Church-State Relations, 1920s to 1950s* (Religion in Chinese Societies). Brill (2017)

9. 《新教圣经翻译与普通话作为中国国语》George Kam Wah Mak, *Protestant Bible Translation and Mandarin as the National Language of China* (Sinica Leidensia). Brill Academic Publishers (2017)

10. 《中国化的基督教》(Studies in Christian Mission) Yangwen Zheng, *Sinicising Christianity*. Brill (2017)

11. 《全球华人五旬宗与灵恩派基督教》(Global Pentecostal and Charismatic studies Volume 22) Allan H.Anderson, Joy Kooi-Chin Tong, Feng Gang Yang, *Global Chinese Pentecostal and Charismatic Christianity*. Brill (2017)

12. 《太平天国神学：基督教在中国的本土化（1843—64）》Carl S. Kilcourse, *Taiping Theology: The Localization of Christianity in China, 1843—64* (Christianities of the World). Palgrave Macmillan US (2016)

13. 《宝血会中国修女与天主教会的演变》Cindy Yik-yi Chu, *The Chinese Sisters of the Precious Blood and the Evolution of the Catholic Church* (Christianity in Modern China). Palgrave Macmillan (2016)

14. 《中国基督教家庭教会：从乡村传教士到城市牧师》Jie Kang, *House Church Christianity in China: From Rural Preachers to City Pastors* (Global diversities). Palgrame Macmillan (2016)

15. 《东方之星：基督教在中国的崛起》Rodney Stark, Xiuhua Wang, *A Star in the East: The Rise of Christianity in China*. Templeton Press (2015)

16. 《基督教中国与世界之光：中国大觉醒的神奇故事》David Aikman, Georgina Sam, David Wang, *Christian China and the Light of the World: Miraculous Stories from China's Great Awakening*. Baker Publishing Group; Chosen Books (2014)

17. 《天人同一：全球语境下的中国天主教见证》Bit-shing Abraham Chiu, *Heaven and Humans Are One: The Witness of the Chinese Catholic Ministry in a Global Context* (American University Studies). Peter Lang (2014)

18. 《中国、基督教和文化问题》Huilin Yang（杨慧林）, *China, Christianity, and the Question of Culture*. Baylor University Press (2014)

19. 《中国公共生活中的基督教：宗教、社会与法治》Joel A. Carpenter, Kevin R. den Dulk (eds.), *Christianity in Chinese Public Life: Religion, Society, and the Rule of Law*. Palgrave Macmillan US (2014)

20. 《共产主义中国的基督教价值观》Gerda Wielander, *Christian Values in Communist China* (Routledge Contemporary China Series). Routledge (2013)

21. 《神论、中国基督教神学与第二次中国启蒙：天人合一》Alexander Chow, *Theosis, Sino-Christian Theology and the Second Chinese Enlightenment: Heaven and Humanity in Unity*. Palgrave Macmillan US (2013)

22. 《即将到来的中国教会：中国日益增长的信仰如何跨越国界》Paul Golf, Pastor Lee, *The Coming Chinese Church: How Rising Faith in China Is Spilling Over Its Boundaries*. Monarch Books (2013)

23. 《河南：中国的加利利（火与血：中国教会的故事）》Paul Hattaway, *Henan: The Galilee of China (Fire & Blood: the Story of the Church in China)*. William Carey Library Pub. (2013)

24. 《耶稣在北京：基督教如何改变中国和全球力量的平衡》David Aikman, *Jesus in Beijing: How Christianity Is Transforming China and Changing the Global Balance of Power*. Regnery Publishing (2012)

25. 《东正教百科全书》John Anthony McGuckin, *The Encyclopedia of Eastern Orthodox Christianity*. Wiley-Blackwell (2011)

26. 《上帝是红色的：基督教在共产主义中国如何生存和繁荣的秘密故事》Liao Yiwu（廖亦武）, *God Is Red: The Secret Story of How Christianity Survived and Flourished in Communist China*. HarperOne (2011)

27. 《中国基督教新史》Daniel H. Bays, *A New History of Christianity in China* (Blackwell Guides to Global Christianity). Wiley-Blackwell (2011)

28. 《世界屋脊上的耶稣会士：18世纪西藏的Ippolito Desideri传教团》Trent Pomplun, *Jesuit on the Roof of the World: Ippolito Desideri's Mission to Eighteenth-century Tibet*. Oxford University Press (2010)

29. 《基督教差会在中国参考指南：16到20世纪》R. G. Tiedemann, *Reference Guide to Christian Missionary Societies in China: From the Sixteenth to the Twentieth Century*. M.E. Sharpe, Inc. (2009)

30. 《面对儒家理解的基督教救赎教义》Paulos Huang, *Confronting Confucian Understandings of the Christian Doctrine of Salvation*. Brill (2009)

31. 《中国基督教：美国图书档案资源学术指南》Xiaoxin Wu, Daniel Bays, *Christianity in China: A Scholars' Guide to Resources in the Libraries and Archives of the United States*. M.E. Sharpe, Inc. (East Gate Books) (2009)

32. 《中国基督教手册：1800年至今》（第三卷）R. G. Tiedemann (ed.), *Handbook of Christianity in China, Volume 2: 1800-Present* (Handbook of Oriental Studies. Section 4 China volume 15). Brill (2009)

33. 《祖先、处女与修士：晚清时期作为地方宗教的基督教》Eugenio Menegon, *Ancestors, Virgins, & Friars: Christianity as a Local Religion in Late Imperial China*. Harvard University, Asia Center for the Harvard-Yenching Institute (2009)

34. 《"权柄"与"黄祸"：1859—1967年新教对加拿大中国移民的传教》Jiwu Wang, *"His Dominion" and the "Yellow Peril": Protestant Missions to Chinese Immigrants in Canada, 1859—1967* (Editions SR). Wilfrid Laurier University Press (2006)

35. 《客家人面对新教基督教（1850—1900年）：八位客家基督徒的自传和评论》Jessie Gregory Lutz, Rolland Ray Lutz-Hakka, *Chinese Confront Protestant Christianity, 1850—1900: With the Autobiographies of Eight Hakka Christians, and Commentary*. Routledge (2005)

36. 《近代中国基督教：第一个本土新教教会的形成》David Cheung (Chen Yiqiang), *Christianity in Modern China: The Making of the First Native Protestant Church*. Brill (2004)

37. 《天上人：中国基督徒云弟兄的真实故事》Brother Yun, Paul Hattaway, *The Heavenly Man: The Remarkable True Story of Chinese Christian Brother Yun*. Monarch Books (2002)

38. 《中国基督徒在美国：转换、同化和附着身份》Fenggang Yang, *Chinese Christians in America: Conversion, Assimilation, and Adhesive Identities*. Pennsylvania State University Press (1999)

39. 《上帝与中国古代人》Samuel Wang, Ethel R. Nelson, *God and the Ancient Chinese*. Read Books Publisher (1998)

40. 《带基督教去中国：亚拉巴马州传教士在中国（1850—1950）》Wayne Flynt, Gerald W. Berkley, *Taking Christianity to China: Alabama Missionaries in the Middle Kingdom, 1850—1950*. University of Alabama Press (1997)

41. 《革命之火的洗礼：美国社会福音和基督教青年会在中国（1919—1937）》Chün Hsing, Jun Xing, *Baptized in the Fire of Revolution: The American Social Gospel and the YMCA in China, 1919—1937*. Lehigh University Press (1996)

42. 《基督教历史中的黑暗面》Helen Ellerbe, *The Dark Side of Christian History*. Morningstar and Lark (1995)

43. 《被遗忘的杭州基督徒》D. E. Mungello（孟德卫）, *The Forgotten Christians of Hangzhou*. University of Hawai'i Press (1994)

44. 《当代中国基督新教》Alan Hunter, Kim-Kwong Chan, *Protestantism in Contemporary China* (Cambridge Studies in Ideology and Religion (No. 3)). Cambridge University Press (1993)

45. 《受洗的中国人》Andrei Bely, *The Christened Chinaman*. Hermitage Publishers (1991)

46. 《创世记的发现：汉语中隐藏的创世纪真相是如何被发现的》C. H. Kang Ethel R Nelson, *The Discovery of Genesis: How the Truths of Genesis Were Found Hidden in the Chinese Language*. Concordia Pubing House (1979)

47. 《中国与基督教：传教运动与中国排外主义的成长（1860—1870）》Paul A. Cohen（柯文）, *China and Christianity: The Missionary Movement and the Growth of Chinese Antiforeignism, 1860—1870*. Harvard University Press (1963)

48.《中华》（奥古斯塔纳信义会在河南）Augusta Highland, *China = Chung Hwah*. Evangelical Lutheran Augustana Synod of North America; Woman's Missionary Society (1945)

49.《中国的基督教艺术》Berthold Laufer, *Christian Art in China*.Peking, China, Reprinted by the Licoph Service (1939)

50.《基督教在华传教史》Kenneth Scott Latourette（赖德烈）, *A History of Christian Missions in China*. New York: The Macmillan Company (1929)

51.《基督教传教与东方文明：文化接触研究》Maurice Thomas Price, *Christian Missions and Oriental Civilizations: A Study in Culture Contact.The Reactions of Non-Christian Peoples to Protestant Missions from the Standpoint of Individual and Group Behavior: Outline, Materials, Problems, and Tentative Interpretations*. Shanghai, China (1924)

52.《中国基督教教育》Chinese Educational Commission; Foreign Missions Conference of North America, Committee of Reference and Counsel, *Christian Education in China: A Study Made by An Educational Commission Representing the Mission Boards and Societies Conducting Work in China*. New York City: Committee of Reference and Counsel of the Foreign Missions Conference of North America (1922)

53.《中华归主：中国基督教宣教事业统计》Milton T. Stauffer（司德敷）, Tsinfang C. Wong, *The Christian Occupation of China: A General Survey of the Numerical Strength and Geographical Distributon of the Christian Forces in China*. Shanghai: China Continuation Committee（中华续行委办会）(1922)

54.《中国西部》*West China*, American Baptist Foreign Mission Society (1920)

55.《中国宣教手册》The Bishops in China, *The China Mission: A Manual for the Use of Volunteers and Newly Appointed Members of the Staff*. Church Missions House, New York (1918)

56.《中国最近的发展》George H. Blakeslee (ed.), *Recent Developments in China*. Clark University Addresses, November, 1912. New York: G. E. Stechert and Cmpany (1913)

57.《在华五十年：回忆与观察》Arthur Evans Moule（慕雅德）, *Half a Century in China: Recollections and Observations*. Hodder and Stoughton (1911)

58.《中国》Frank L. (Frank Lushington) Norris（鄂方智）, *(Handbook of English Church Expansion) China, with Illustrations and Map*. A. R. Mowbray & Co. Ltd. (1908)

59.《基督新教在华一百年（1807—1907）》MacGillivray Donald, *A Century of Protestant Missions in China (1807—1907): Being the Centenary Conference Historical Volume*. Shanghai: Printed at the American Presbyterian Mission Press (1907)

60.《美国圣公会在中国》Annette B. Richmond, *The American Episcopal Church in China*. The Domestic and Foreign Missionary Society of the Protestant Episcopal Church in the United States of America (1907)

61.《入华百年纪念文献集》James Whitford Bashford（柏赐福，柏思福，贝施福）, *China Centennial Documents*.Vol.1. The Board of Foreign Missions of the Methodist Episcopal

Church, New York (1907)

62. 《中国的英雄：义和团运动中本地基督徒遭受迫害的记录》Isaac Taylor Headland（何德兰），*Chinese Heroes: Being a Record of Persecutions Endured by Native Christians in the Boxer Uprising*. New York, Eaton & Mains; Cincinnati, Jennings & Pye (1902)

63. 《泉之城：泉州传教散记》Annie N. Duncan, *The City of Springs: Or, Mission Work in Chinchew*. Edinburgh and London: Oliphant Anderson and Ferrier (1902)

64. 《中国人对基督徒的恐惧和迫害》Henry Davenport Northrop, *Chinese Horrors and Persecutions of the Christians, Containing a Full Account of the Great Insurrection in China; Atrocities of the Boxers... Together with the Complete History of China Down to the Present Time*. National Pub. Co. (1900)

65. 《基督还是孔子？厦门传教团的故事》John Macgowan, *Christ or Confucius, Which? or, The Story of the Amoy Mission*. London, London Missionary Society (1889)

66. 《中国》Secretary Treat, etc., *China*. Boston: American Board of Commissioners for Foreign Missions (1867)

67. 《美国浸礼会在亚洲、非洲、欧洲和北美洲的传教史》William Gammell, *A history of American Baptist Missions in Asia, Africa, Europe and North America*. Boston: Gould, Kendall and Lincoln (1849)

68. 《美国对异教徒的传教史》JosephTracy, *History of American Missions to the Heathen, from Their Commencement to the Present Time*. Worcester: Spooner & Howland (1840)

69. 《中国的现状与传教展望》Walter Henry Medhurst（麦都思），*China: Its State and Prospects, with Special Reference to the Spread of the Gospel, Containing Allusions to the Antiquity, Extent, Population, Civilization, Literature, and Religion of the Chinese*. London: John Snow (1838)

70. 《基督教新教在华最初十年之回顾》William Milne（米怜）*A Retrospect of the First Ten Years of the Protestant Mission to China*. Malacca: Printed at the Anglo-Chinese Press (1820)

3.2.2.1 天主教

1. 《台湾天主教会：问题与前景》Francis K.H. So, Beatrice K.F. Leung, Ellen Mary Mylod (eds.), *The Catholic Church in Taiwan: Problems and Prospects* (Christianity in Modern China). Palgrave Macmillan (2018)

2. 《中国最后的耶稣会士：查尔斯·J·麦卡锡与天主教上海传教团的终结》Amanda C. R. Clark, *China's Last Jesuit: Charles J. McCarthy and the End of the Mission in Catholic Shanghai* (Christianity in Modern China). Springer Singapore (2017)

3. 《中华耶稣宝血修女会与天主教的演化》Cindy Yik-yi Chu, *The Chinese Sisters of the Precious Blood and the Evolution of the Catholic Church*. Palgrave Macmillan (2016)

4. 《1900年至今的中国天主教：中国教会的发展》Cindy Yik-yi Chu (ed.), *Catholicism in China, 1900-Present: The Development of the Chinese Church*. Palgrave Macmillan US (2014)

5. 《中国历史中的圣母玛利亚与天主教身份》Jeremy Clarke, *The Virgin Mary and Catholic Identities in Chinese History*. Hong Kong University Press (2013)

6. 《中国天主教会：1978年至今》Cindy Yik-yi Chu, *The Catholic Church in China: 1978 to the Present*. Palgrave Macmillan, New York (2012)

7. 《中国圣徒：清代的天主教殉道（1644—1911）》Anthony E. Clark, *China's Saints: Catholic Martyrdom during the Qing (1644—1911)* (Mission Work in China). Lehigh University Press (2011)

8. 《灵与肉：山东的天主教（1650—1785）》D. E. Mungello（孟德卫）, *The Spirit and the Flesh in Shandong, 1650—1785*. Rowman & Littlefield Publishers (2001)

9. 《东方观察：日本、韩国、满洲、中国、印度支那和菲律宾的天主教传教之旅》James Anthony Walsh, Charles William Wason, *Observations in the Orient: The Account of a Journey to Catholic Mission Fields in Japan, Korea, Manchuria, China, Indo-China, and the Philippines*. Ossining, New York: Catholic Foreign Mission Society of America (1919)

3.2.2.2 传教士

1. 《从基督到孔子：1860—1950年德国传教士、中国基督徒与基督教全球化》Albert Monshan Wu, *From Christ to Confucius: German Missionaries, Chinese Christians, and the Globalization of Christianity, 1860—1950*. Yale University Press (2016)

2. 《形成自己的新世界：大航海时代中国与耶稣会科学的遭遇》Qiong Zhang, *Making the New World Their Own: Chinese Encounters with Jesuit Science in the Age of Discovery*. Brill (2015)

3. 《传教士的诅咒等中国天主教村的民间故事》Henrietta Harrison（沈艾娣）, *The Missionary's Curse and Other Tales from a Chinese Catholic Village*. University of California Press (2013)

4. 《中国传教：利玛窦和耶稣会与东方的相遇》Mary Laven, *Mission to China: Matteo Ricci and the Jesuit Encounter with the East*. Faber & Faber (2012)

5. 《紫禁城中的耶稣会士：利玛窦（1552—1610）》R. Po-chia Hsia, *A Jesuit in the Forbidden City: Matteo Ricci 1552—1610*. Oxford University Press (2012)

6. 《慕拉蒂：历史与传奇中的南方浸信会传教士》Regina D. Sullivan, *Lottie Moon: A Southern Baptist Missionary to China in History and Legend* (Southern Biography Series). Louisiana State University Press (2011)

7. 《梅威良与义和团运动：英雄主义、傲慢和理想的传教士》Larry Clinton Thompson, *William Scott Ament and the Boxer Rebellion: Heroism, Hubris and the Ideal Missionary*. McFarland & Company, Inc., Publishers (2008)

8. 《东游记：耶稣会在中国（1579—1724）》Liam Matthew Brockey, *Journey to the East: The Jesuit Mission to China, 1579—1724*. Belknap Press of Harvard University Press (2007)

9. 《石拱门之外：一位美国传教士医生在中国（1892—1932）》Edward Bliss Jr., *Beyond the Stone Arches: An American Missionary Doctor in China, 1892—1932*. John Wiley & Sons (2001)

10. 《裨治文与千禧年的感召：美国第一位来华新教传教士》（博士论文）Michael C. Lazich（雷孜智）, *E. C. Bridgman and the Coming of the Millennium: America's first Missionary to*

China. Ph. D. Dissertation, State University of New York at Buffalo (1997)

11. 《神学与文化的和解：1583—1742年利玛窦与耶稣会中国传教团》（硕士论文）Louis Kam-tat Ho, *Theological and Cultural Accommodation: Matteo Ricci and the Jesuit Mission in China, 1583—1742*. St. Thesis for the Degree of Master of Theological Studies, Stephen's College (Canada) (1996)

12. 《反鸦片十字军：新教传教士在中国（1874—1917）》Kathleen L. Lodwick, *Crusaders Against Opium: Protestant Missionaries in China, 1874—1917*. University Press of Kentucky (1995)

13. 《奇异的国度：耶稣会适应政策及汉学的起源》D. E. Mungello（孟德卫）, *Curious Land: Jesuit Accommodation and the Origins of Sinology*. University of Hawaii Press (1988)

14. 《中国传教士新闻家：林乐知和他的杂志（1860—1883）》Adrian Arthur Bennett, *Missionary Journalist in China: Young J. Allen and His Magazines, 1860—1883*. Athens, Ga.: University of Georgia Press (1982)

15. 《我在那里……当它在中国发生时》Mary Culler White（白美丽）, *I Was There...When It Happened In China*. New York, Nashville: Abingdon-Cokesbury Press (1947)

16. 《传教士与清朝官吏：中国宫廷中的耶稣会士》Arnold H. Rowbotham（罗柏森）, *Missionary and Mandarin: The Jesuits at the Court of China*. Berkeley and los Angeles: University of California Press (1942)

17. 《中国弟兄》Franklin Henry Crumpacker, *Brethren in China*. Brethren Publishing House (1937)

18. 《亲历晚清四十五年：李提摩太在华回忆录》Timothy Richard（李提摩太）, *Forty-Five Years in China: Reminiscenses*. T. Fisher Unwin (1916)

19. 《传教士来华鸟瞰》Thomas John Cochrane, *Survey of the Missionary Occupation of China*. Shanghai: The Christian Literature Society for China (1913)

20. 《狄考文传：中国山东四十五年》Daniel Webster Fisher, *Calvin Wilson Mateer: A Biography. Forty-Five Years A Missionary in Shantung. China*. Philadelphia, The Westminster press (1911)

21. 《中国五十年见闻录》Archibald John Little, Mrs Archibald Little, *Gleanings from Fifty Years in China*. Philadelphia: J. B. Lippincott (1910)

22. 《在中国：美国长老会在华宣教概述》Henry F. Williams, *In China: A Sketch of the Foreign Missions of the Presbyterian Church, U.S., in China*. Executive Committee of Foreign Missions, MasKville, Tennessee (1910)

23. 《中国的上升》Arthur H. Smith（明恩溥）, *The Uplift of China*. London: Church Missionary Society (1909)

24. 《中国使命》William Edward Soothill（苏慧廉）, *A Mission in China*. Edinburgh and London: Oliphant, Anderson and Ferrier (1907, 2009)

25. 《中国传教纪事》（又译《晚清温州纪事》）William Edward Soothill（苏慧廉）, *A Typical Mission in China*. Fleming H. Revell Co. (1907)

26. 《中国的呼声/来自华夏的声音》Griffith John（杨格非/杨笃信，1831—1912.首位来湖北传教的英国基督教传教士），*A Voice from China*. James Clarke & Co. Ltd (1907)

27. 《教会的传教士先驱》Charles Cole Creegan, *Pioneer Missionaries of the Church*. New York: American Tract Society (1903)

28. 《纪念皮德金》Robert Elliott Speer, *A Memorial of Horace Tracy Pitkin*. New York, Chicago, Toronto: Fleming H. Revell Company (1903)

29. 《华南地区的传教问题和传教方法：福音派神学讲座》J. Campbell Gibson, *Mission Problems and Mission Methods in South China: Lectures on Evangelistic Theology*. Baptist Mission Work in Swatow (1902)

30. 《内地会殉道传教士及某些逃生者所受之险难》Marshall Broomhall, *Martyred Missionaries of the China Inland Mission: With a Record of the Perils and Sufferings of Some Who Escaped*. London: Morgan & Scott (1901)

31. 《三十年后中国之觉醒》Frederick Brown（宝复礼）, *China's Dayspring after Thirty Years*. London: Murry and Evenden (1900)

32. 《花甲忆记：一位美国传教士眼中的晚清帝国》William Alexander Parsons Martin（丁韪良）, *A Cycle of Cathay: or, China, South and North, with Personal Reminiscences*. New York: Fleming H. Revell (1896, 1900)

33. 《伟大的教会传教士》Charles Cole Creegan, Josephine A. B. Goodnow, *Great Missionaries of the Church*. Nashville: Publishing House of the Methodist Episcopal Church, South (1895)

34. 《倪维思传：在华传教四十年》Helen Sanford Coan Nevius, *The life of John Livingston Nevius, for Forty Years a Missionary in China*. New York, Chicago etc.: Fleming H. Revell Co. (1895)

35. 《在中国传教四十年：打马字牧师传记》John Gerardus Fagg, *Forty Years in South China: The Life of Rev. John Van Nest Talmage, D. D.* New York: Anderson D. F. Randolph & Company (1894)

36. 《华北的冬天》T. M. Morris, *A Winter in North China*. London: Religious Tract Society (1892)

37. 《中国一瞥/管窥中国》Gilbert Reid（李佳白）, *Glances at China/Peeps into China*. London: The Religious Tract Society (1892)

38. 《在华传教士》Alexander Michie (Tientsin), *Missionaries in China*. London: Edward Stanford (1891)

39. 《马礼逊：在华传教士的先驱》William John Townsend, *Robert Morrison: The Pioneer of Chinese Mission*. London: S.W. Partridge (1890)

40. 《卫三畏生平及书信：传教士、外交家与汉学家》Frederick Wells Williams（卫斐列）, *The Life and Letters of Samuel Wells Williams, LL.D.: Missionary, Diplomatist, Sinologue*. New York: G. P. Putnam's Sons (1889)

41. 《1867年以前来华基督教传教士列传及著作目录》Alexander Wylie（伟烈亚力）, William Gamble, *Memorials of Protestant Missionaries to the Chinese: Giving a List of Their Publications,*

and Obituary Notices of the Deceased. Shanghai: American Presbyterian Mission Press (1867)

42. 《美国在华传教先驱：裨治文的生活和工作》Eliza J. Gillet Bridgman, *The Pioneer of American Missions in China: The Life and Labors of Elijah Coleman Bridgman.* New York: Anson D. F. Randolph (1864)

43. 《在华一年记》Mrs. H. Dwight Williams, *A Year in China, and a Narrative of Capture and Imprisonment, when Homeward Bound, on Board...*New York: Hurd and Houghton (1864)

44. 《华夏传教事业：包括各种在华传教的差会》William Dean, *The China Mission: Embracing a History of the Various Missions of all Denominations among the Chinese, with Biographical Sketches of Deceased Missionaries.* New York: Sheldon and Company (1859)

45. 《在华岁月》William Charles Milne（美魏茶，传教士米怜之子）, *Life in China.* London: Routledge (1858)

46. 《第一位来华美国女传教士叔何显理女士回忆录》Jeremiah Bell Jeter (ed.), *A Memoir of Mrs. Henrietta Hall Shuck, the First American Female Missionary to China.* Boston: Gould, Kendall, and Lincoln (1850)

47. 《雅裨理回忆录》David Abeel, G. R. Williamson, comp., *Memoir of the Rev. David Abeel, D.D., Late Missionary to China.* New York, R. Carter (1848)

48. 《在华传教十六年：撒母耳·戴尔牧师回忆录》Evan Davies, *Memoir of the Rev. Samuel Dyer, Sixteen Years Missionary to the Chinese.* London: John Snow (1846)

49. 《马礼逊回忆录》Eliza A. Morrison, Mrs. Robert (ed.), *Memoirs of the Life and Labours Robert Morrison...* 2 Vols. London: Longman, Orme, Brown, and Longmans (1839)

50. 《在中国及周边国家居住的日志》David Abeel, *Journal of a Residence in China, and the Neighboring Countries: With a Preliminary Essay, on the Commencement and Progress of Missions in the World.* New York: J. A. Williamson (1836)

3.2.3 伊斯兰教

1. 《培养魅力型领袖：中国伊斯兰领袖的实践》Tiffany Cone, *Cultivating Charismatic Power: Islamic Leadership Practice in China.* Palgrave Macmillan (2018)

2. 《前现代中国的穆斯林商人：一个亚洲海上贸易散居地的历史（750—1400）》(New Approaches to Asian History 17) John W. Chaffee（贾志扬）, *The Muslim Merchants of Premodern China: The History of a Maritime Asian Trade Diaspora, 750—1400.* Cambridge University Press (2018)

3. 《中国和伊斯兰教：先知、党和法律》Matthew S. Erie, *China and Islam: The Prophet, the Party, and Law.* Cambridge University Press (2017)

4. 《中国穆斯林与全球穆斯林团体：青海回族的伊斯兰复兴与民族认同》(Routledge Contemporary China) Alexander Blair Stewart, *Chinese Muslims and the Global Ummah: Islamic Revival and Ethnic Identity Among the Hui of Qinghai Province.* Routledge (2017)

5. 《穆斯林三字经：中国伊斯兰教定义的转变与延续》Roberta Tontini, *Muslim Sanzijing:*

Shifts and Continuities in the Definition of Islam in China (China Studies). Brill Academic Pub. (2016)

6. 《中国与伊斯兰教：先知、政党与法律》Matthew S. Erie, *China and Islam: The Prophet, the Party, and Law.* Cambridge University Press (2016)

7. 《穆斯林、商人、游牧民族和间谍：中国冷战与西藏边疆人民》Sulmaan Wasif Khan, *Muslim, Trader, Nomad, Spy: China's Cold War and the People of the Tibetan Borderlands* (The New Cold War History). The University of North Carolina Press (2015)

8. 《香港伊斯兰教：中国世界城市的穆斯林和日常生活》Paul O'Connor, *Islam in Hong Kong: Muslims and Everyday Life in China's World City.* Hong Kong University Press (2012)

9. 《"东伊运"：中国的伊斯兰武装分子和全球恐怖主义威胁》J. Todd Reed, Diana Raschke, *The ETIM: China's Islamic Militants and the Global Terrorist Threat* (PSI Guides to Terrorists, Insurgents, and Armed Groups). Praeger (2010)

10. 《中国族群和城市生活：回族穆斯林和汉族的比较研究》Xiaowei Zang, *Ethnicity and Urban Life in China: A Comparative Study of Hui Muslims and Han Chinese.* Routledge (2007)

11. 《龙的统治下：伊斯兰教、种族歧视、犯罪和中国维吾尔族》Blaine Kaltman, *Under the Heel of the Dragon: Islam, Racism, Crime, and the Uighur in China.* Ohio University Press (2007)

12. 《中国的苏丹：伊斯兰教、种族和中国西南回民（潘泰人）起义（1856—1873）》David Atwill（龙戴维）, *The Chinese Sultanate: Islam, Ethnicity, and the Panthay Rebellion in Southwest China, 1856—1873.* Stanford University Press (2005)

13. 《穆罕默德之道：中华帝国晚期穆斯林的文化史》Zvi Ben-Dor Benite, *The Dao of Muhammad: A Cultural History of Muslims in Late Imperial China* (Harvard East Asian Monographs). Harvard University Asia Center, Harvard University Press (2005)

14. 《解构中国：对穆斯林、少数族裔和其他次级主体的思考》Dru C. Gladney, *Dislocating China: Reflections on Muslims, Minorities, and Other Subaltern Subjects.* The University of Chicago Press (2004)

15. 《中国圣战：穆斯林叛乱和中亚国家（1864—1877）》Hodong Kim, *Holy War in China: The Muslim Rebellion and State in Chinese Central Asia, 1864—1877.* Stanford University Press (2004)

16. 《中国伊斯兰教：现代化与汉化之间的回族和维吾尔族》Jean A. Berlie, *Islam in China: Hui and Uyghurs between Modernization and Sinicization.* White Lotus Press (2004)

17. 《新疆：中国穆斯林边疆》S. Frederick Starr, *Xinjiang: China's Muslim Borderland.* M. E. Sharpe Inc. (2004)

18. 《中国伊斯兰教》Mi Shoujiang, You Jia (author), translated by Min Chang, *Islam in China.* China Intercontinental Press (2004)

19. 《新疆：远在中国西北的穆斯林》Michael Dillon, *Xinjiang: China's Muslim Far Northwest.* Routledge (2003)

20. 《麦加和北京之间：中国城市穆斯林的现代化和消费》Maris Gillette, *Between Mecca and*

Beijing: Modernization and Consumption Among Urban Chinese Muslims. Stanford University Press (2002)

21. 《中国穆斯林回族社区：移民、定居和派别》Michael Dillon, *China's Muslim Hui Community: Migration, Settlement and Sects*. Curzon (1999)
22. 《熟悉的陌生人：中国西北穆斯林历史》Jonathan N. Lipman, *Familiar Strangers: A History of Muslims in Northwest China*. University of Washington Press (1998)
23. 《中国和伊斯兰教的亚洲腹地研究》Joseph F. Fletcher, *Studies on Chinese and Islam Inner Asia*. Variorum (1995)
24. 《穆斯林华人：人民共和国的种族民族主义》Dru Gladney, *Muslim Chinese: Ethnic Nationalism in the People's Republic*. Harvard University Asia Center (1991)

3.2.4 佛教

1. 《日本佛教哲学读本》(Dao Companions to Chinese Philosophy 8) Gereon Kopf, *The Dao Companion to Japanese Buddhist Philosophy*. Springer Netherlands (2019)
2. 《中国佛教哲学读本》(Dao Companions to Chinese Philosophy 9) Youru Wang（王又如）, Sandra A. Wawrytko, *Dao Companion to Chinese Buddhist Philosophy*. Springer Netherlands (2018)
3. 《无门关》David Hinton, *No-Gate Gateway: The Original Wu-Men Kuan*. Shambhala (2018)
4. 《近现代中国之得道成圣》David Ownby, Vincent Goossaert, and Ji Zhe, *Making Saints in Modern China*. Oxford University Press (2017)
5. 《净土中的无政府状态：重塑现代佛教对弥勒的崇拜》Justin Ritzinger, *Anarchy in the Pure Land: Reinventing the Cult of Maitreya in Modern Chinese Buddhism*. Oxford University Press (2017)
6. 《禅宗的历史》Yu-hsiu Ku, *History of Zen*. Springer Singapore (2016)
7. 《近代中国的佛教复兴》Jan Kiely, J. Brooks Jessup, *Recovering Buddhism in Modern China*. Columbia University Press (2016)
8. 《马祖语录和禅宗经典文学的形成》Mario Poceski, *The Records of Mazu and the Making of Classical Chan Literature*. Oxford University Press (2015)
9. 《法宝东渐：汉文佛教大藏经的形成与演变》(The Sheng Yen Series in Chinese Buddhist Studies) Jiang Wu（吴疆）, Lucille Chia（贾晋珠）(eds.), *Spreading Buddha's Word in East Asia: The Formation and Transformation of the Chinese Buddhist Canon*. Columbia University Press (2015)
10. 《身体咒语：中世纪中国佛教的法术与仪式想象》Paul Copp, *Body Incantatory: Spells and the Ritual Imagination in Medieval Chinese Buddhism* (The Sheng Yen series in Chinese Buddhist studies). Columbia University Press (2014)
11. 《狂僧济公历险记：中国最著名禅宗和尚的醉酒智慧》Guo Daoji, Xiaoting, *Adventures of the mad monk Ji Gong: the drunken wisdom of China's most famous Chan Buddhist monk*. Tuttle Publishing (2014)
12. 《亚洲佛教：物质、知识和文化交流网络》Tansen Sen, *Buddhism Across Asia: Networks*

of Material, Intellectual and Cultural Exchange. Volume 1.Institute of Southeast Asian Studies (2014)

13. 《建造圣山：中国五台山的佛教建筑》Wei-Cheng Lin, *Building a Sacred Mountain: The Buddhist Architecture of China's Mount Wutai.* University of Washington Press (2014)

14. 《超越单一性与差异性：中国佛教思想中的礼与一致性及其由来》Brook Ziporyn, *Beyond Oneness and Difference: Li and Coherence in Chinese Buddhist Thought and its Antecedents.* State University of New York Press (2013)

15. 《中国佛教：许理和论文集》Jonathan A. Silk. *Buddhism in China: Collected Papers of Erik Zürcher.* Brill Academic Publishers (2013)

16. 《禅宗本质：中国禅宗的品格与精神》Guo Jun, Kenneth Wapner (Editor), Robert A. F. Thurman (Foreword), *Essential Chan Buddhism: The Character and Spirit of Chinese Zen.* Monkfish Book Publishing (2013)

17. 《冥祥：中国中古早期的佛教灵应故事》Robert Ford Campany（康儒博）, *Signs from the Unseen Realm: Buddhist Miracle Tales from Early Medieval China* (Classics in East Asian Buddhism). University of Hawaii Press (2012)

18. 《佛教在来华路上如何获得心性》Jungnok Park, *How Buddhism Acquired a Soul on the Way to China.* Equinox Publishing Ltd (2012)

19. 《中国禅宗大师》Richard Bryan McDaniel (Author), Albert Low (Foreword), *Zen Masters of China: The First Step East.*Tuttle Publishing (2012)

20. 《佛教汉语词典》(East Asia Intercultural Studies: Interkulturelle Ostasienstudien) Konrad Meisig, Marion Meisig, *A Buddhist Chinese Glossary: Buddhistisch-Chinesisches Glossar*：佛教汉语词典. Harrassowitz Verlag (2012)

21. 《东南亚和中国的佛教丧葬文化》Paul S. Williams, Patrice Ladwig, *Buddhist Funeral Cultures of Southeast Asia and China.* Cambridge University Press (2012)

22. 《永明延寿在〈宗镜录〉中的禅观念：圣典内的一种特殊传播》Albert Welter（魏雅博）, *Yongming Yanshou's Conception of Chan in the Zongjing lu: A Special Transmission within the Scriptures.* Oxford University Press (2011)

23. 《禅宗的中国传统：大师及其教诲》Andrew Ferguson, *Zen's Chinese Heritage: The Masters and Their Teachings.*Wisdom Publications (2011)

24. 《禅行：中国朝圣》Red Pine, *Zen Baggage: A Pilgrimage to China.* Counterpoint (2010)

25. 《佛心，中国心：一个20世纪和尚倓虚的一生》（此书错误百出）James Carter（卡特）, *Heart of Buddha, Heart of China: The Life of Tanxu, a Twentieth Century Monk.* Oxford University Press, USA (2010)

26. 《佛经翻译：问题与前景》Konrad Meisig, *Translating Buddhist Chinese: Problems and Prospects.* Harrassowitz (2010)

27. 《中国佛教文化》Fang Li-tian, *China's Buddhist Culture.* Gale Asia (2009)

28. 《庞居士语录：中国禅宗经典》Yun Pang, James Green (translator), *The Sayings of Layman P'ang: A Zen Classic of China*. Shambhala (2009)
29. 《西藏与中国的佛教》Matthew Kapstein (ed.), *Buddhism between Tibet and China*. Wisdom Publications (2009)
30. 《中国佛教寺庙指南：汉族主要寺院的历史和文化遗产》Christian Cochini, *Guide to Buddhist Temples of China: History and Cultural Heritage of the Main Monasteries of the Han Nationality*. Macau Ricci Inst. (2009)
31. 《禅宗何以成为禅宗：关于开悟的争论和宋代禅宗的形成》Morten Schlütter, *How Zen Became Zen: The Dispute over Enlightenment and the Formation of Chan Buddhism in Song-dynasty China*. Kuroda institute (2008)
32. 《现代宇宙论中的禅》Chi-Sing Lam, *The Zen in Modern Cosmology*. University of British Columbia (2008)
33. 《孝道与救赎：两种观音宝卷》Wilt L. Idema（伊维德）, *Personal Salvation and Filial Piety: Two Precious Scroll Narratives of Guanyin and Her Acolytes*. Kuroda Institute (2008)
34. 《著名尼姑：17世纪中国女性禅师》Beata Grant, *Eminent Nuns: Women Chan Masters of Seventeenth-Century China*. University of Hawai'i Press (2008)
35. 《争论中的启蒙：17世纪中国禅宗的重塑》Jiang Wu, *Enlightenment in Dispute: The Reinvention of Chan Buddhism in Seventeenth-Century China*. Oxford University Press, USA (2008)
36. 《佛教与道教面对面：中世纪中国的经文、仪式与肖像交换》Christine Mollier, *Buddhism and Taoism Face to Face: Scripture, Ritual, and Iconographic Exchange in Medieval China*. University of Hawai'i Press (2008)
37. 《孝道与救赎：两种观音宝卷》Translated and with an introduction by Wilt L. Idema（伊维德）, *Personal Salvation and Filial Piety: Two Precious Scroll Narratives of Guanyin and Her Acolytes* (Classics in East Asian Buddhism). Kuroda Institute (2008)
38. 《佛教征服中国：佛教在中国中世纪早期的传播与适应》E. Zurcher, *Buddhist Conquest of China: The Spread and Adaptation of Buddhism in Early Medieval China* (Sinica Leidensia). Brill (2007)
39. 《为佛而燃烧：中国佛教中的自焚》James A. Benn, *Burning for the Buddha: Self-Immolation in Chinese Buddhism* (Studies in East Asian Buddhis). University of Hawai'i Press (2007)
40. 《平常心即是道：洪州学派和禅宗佛教的发展》Mario Poceski, *Ordinary Mind as the Way: The Hongzhou School and the Growth of Chan Buddhism*. Oxford University Press (2007)
41. 《救世主菩萨的形成：中世纪中国的地藏菩萨》Zhiru, *The Making of a Savior Bodhisattva: Dizang in Medieval China* (Studies in East Asian Buddhism). University of Hawai'i Press (2007)
42. 《道元到过中国吗？他写了什么以及何时所写》Steven Heine, *Did Dogen Go to China? What He Wrote and When He Wrote It*. Oxford University Press, USA (2006)
43. 《八世纪至十世纪中国禅宗的洪州学派》Jinhua Jia（贾晋华）, *The Hongzhou School of*

Chan Buddhism in Eighth-through Tenth-century China. State University of New York Press (2006)

44. 《佛教：宗教研究中的关键概念。第六卷，密宗佛教（包括中国和日本）；佛教在尼泊尔和西藏》Paul Williams (ed.), *Buddhism: Critical Concepts in Religious Studies. Volume VI Tantric Buddhism (including China and Japan) ; Buddhism in Nepal and Tibet.* Routledge (2006)

45. 《中国佛教》Haicheng Ling, *Buddhism in China.* China Intercontinental Press (2005)

46. 《看破禅宗：中国禅宗的遭遇、改造与谱系》John R. McRae, *Seeing through Zen: Encounter, Transformation, and Genealogy in Chinese Chan Buddhism.* University of California Press (2004)

47. 《佛教对中国物质文化的影响》John Kieschnick, *The Impact of Buddhism on Chinese Material Culture.* Princeton University Press (2003)

48. 《空之帝国：佛教艺术与清政权》Patricia Berger（白瑞霞）, *Empire of Emptiness: Buddhist Art and Political Authority in Qing China.* Honululu: University of Hawaii Press (2003)

49. 《理解并接受中国佛教：〈宝藏论〉解读》Robert H. Sharf, *Coming to Terms with Chinese Buddhism: A Reading of the Treasure Store Treatise.* University of Hawai'i Press (2002)

50. 《〈妙法莲花经〉选本》Burton Watson, *The Essential Lotus: Selections from the Lotus Sutra.* Columbia University Press (2001)

51. 《走向现代中国佛教：太虚的改革》Don A. Pittman, *Toward a Modern Chinese Buddhism: Taixu's Reforms.* University of Hawaii Press (2001)

52. 《中国佛教后期的文化交汇》Marsha Smith Weidner, *Cultural Intersections in Later Chinese Buddhism.* University of Hawai'i Press (2001)

53. 《观音的汉化》Chün-fang Yü（于君方）, *Kuan-yin: The Chinese Transformation of Avalokitesvara.* Columbia University Press (2000)

54. 《早期佛教基本教义：基于Pali Samyutta-Nikaya和Chinese Samyuktagama经文部分的比较研究》Mun-keat Choong, *The Fundamental Teachings of Early Buddhism: A Comparative Study Based on the Sutranga Portion of the Pali Samyutta-Nikaya and the Chinese Samyuktagama* (Beitrage zur Indologie). Harra (2000)

55. 《〈维摩经〉中文英译》Kumarajiva, Burton Watson, *The Vimalakirti Sutra: From the Chinese Version by Kumarajiva.* Motilal Banarsidass (1999)

56. 《达摩文集：禅的最早记录》Jeffrey L. Broughton, *The Bodhidharma Anthology: The Earliest Records of Zen* (Philip E. Lilienthal Book). University of California Press (1999)

57. 《佛教汉梵大辞典》Akira Hirakawa, *A Buddhist Chinese-Sanskrit Dictionary.* The Reiyukai (1997)

58. 《中国僧侣在印度：大唐时期到西方世界寻求佛法的名僧传记》Latika Lahiri, *Chinese Monks in India: Biography of Eminent Monks Who Went to the Western World in Search of the Law During the Great Tang Dynasty.* Motilal Banarsidass (1995)

59. 《中国禅宗的故事》Nan Huai-Chin（南怀瑾）, Thomas Cleary (trans.), *The Story of*

Chinese Zen. Tuttle Publishing (1995)

60. 《佛教分类：包括印度、中国和日本佛教教义的分类》Bruno Petzold, *Classification of Buddhism: Comprising the Classification of Buddhist Doctrines in India, China and Japan*. Harrassowitz (1995)

61. 《寻找佛法：中国现代佛教朝圣者回忆录》Chen-hua (Zhenhua), Chün-fang Yü, *In search of the Dharma: memoirs of a modern Chinese Buddhist pilgrim*. SUNY (1992)

62. 《超越云彩的曲调：来自旧中国的禅宗教诲》J. C. Cleary (Translator and Editor), *A Tune Beyond the Clouds: Zen Teachings from Old China*. Asian Humanities Press (1991)

63. 《中国净土教义的黎明：净影慧远〈观经疏〉》Kenneth K. Tanaka, *The Dawn of Chinese Pure Land Buddhist Doctrine: Ching-Ying Hui-Yuan's Commentary on the Visualization Sutra*. State University of New York Press (1990)

64. 《中国佛教中的伪经》Robert E. Buswell, Jr. (ed.), *Chinese Buddhist Apocrypha*. University of Hawai'i Press (1990)

65. 《中国佛教禅修传统》Peter N. Gregory (ed.), *Traditions of Meditation in Chinese Buddhism*. University of Hawai'i Press (1986)

66. 《中国佛教之花》Daisaku Ikeda, Burton Watson, *The Flower of Chinese Buddhism* (Studies in East Asian Buddhism 4). Weatherhill (1986)

67. 《中国佛教著名的佛菩萨》Kuan Ming（观明）, *Popular Deities of Chinese Buddhism (Illustrated)*. Kuan Yin Contemplative Order (1985)

68. 《佛教哲学：一种"总体论"的综合》Alfonso Verdu, *The Philosophy of Buddhism: A "Totalistic" Synthesis*. Springer Netherlands (1981)

69. 《积极的自我：〈佛性论〉及其他中国佛教文本的哲学研究》（博士论文）Sallie B. King, *Active Self: A Philosophical Study of the Buddha Nature Treatise and Other Chinese Buddhist Texts*. Ph. D. Dissertation, Temple University (1981)

70. 《妙善传说：观音菩萨缘起考》Glen Dudbridge（杜德桥）, *The Legend of Miaoshan*. Oxford University Press (1978, 2004)

71. 《佛教思想中的辩证观：中日大乘佛教理想主义研究》Alfonso Verdu, *Dialectical Aspects in Buddhist Thought: Studies in Sino-Japanese Mahayana Idealism*. Center for East Asian Studies, The University of Kansas (1974)

72. 《中国禅定的秘密》Lu K'uan Yu (Charles Luk), *The Secrets of Chinese Meditation*. Samuel Weiser (1972)

73. 《禅宗的原始教诲》Chang Chung-Yuan, *Original Teachings of Ch'an Buddhism*. Vintage Books (1971)

74. 《禅者的初心》Shunryu Suzuki, *Zen Mind: Beginner's Mind*. Weatherhill (1970, 1973, 1995)

75. 《中国佛教实践（1900—1950）》(Harvard East Asian Studies 26) Holmes Welch, *The Practice of Chinese Buddhism, 1900—1950*. Harvard University Press (1967)

76. 《法显〈佛国记〉：中国僧人法显在印度和锡兰的旅行（399—414年）》Fa Xian, James Legge（理雅各）, *A Record of Buddhistic Kingdoms: Being An Account by the Chinese Monk Fâ-Hien of His Travels in India and Ceylon (A.D. 399—414)*. Paragon Book Reprint (1965)

77. 《佛教在中国的历史考察》Kenneth K. S. Ch'en, *Buddhism in China: A Historical Survey*. Princeton University Press (1964)

78. 《中国禅宗发展史》Chou Hsiang-Kuang（周祥光）, *Dhyana Buddhism in China: Its History and Teaching*. Indo-Chinese Literature Publications (1960)

79. 《中国历史中的佛教》Arthur F. Wright（芮沃寿）, *Buddhism in Chinese History*. Stanford University Press (1959)

80. 《中国早期佛教艺术的文学证据》Alexander Coburn Soper, *Literary Evidence for Early Buddhist Art in China*. Artibus Asiae Publishers (1959)

81. 《中国佛教史》Chou Hsiang-Kuang（周祥光）, *A History of Chinese Buddhism*. Indo-Chinese Literature Publications (1956)

82. 《玄奘的一生：大慈恩寺三藏法师传》Huili（慧立）, San Shih Buddhist Institute (Tr), *The life of Hsuan-Tsang, the Tripitaka-master of the Great Tzu En Monastery*. Chinese Buddhist Association (1959)

83. 《泉州（刺桐港）双塔：中国晚近佛教雕塑研究》Gustav Ecke（艾锷风）, Paul Demiéville（戴密微）, *The Twin Pagodas of Zayton: A Study of Later Buddhist Sculpture in China*. Cambridge, Mass., Harvard University Press (1935)

84. 《中国皇帝忽必烈汗的僧侣们》E. A. Wallis Budge, *The Monks of Kublai Khan, Emperor of China*. Harrison & Sons (1928)

85. 《中国佛教与佛教徒》Lewis Hodus, *Buddhism and Buddhists in China*. New York: Macmillan (1924)

86. 《禅宗及其与艺术的关系》Arthur Waley（阿瑟·韦利）, *Zen Buddhism and its Relation to Art*. London: Luzac and Co. (1922)

87. 《佛教中国/佛教徒的中国》Reginald Fleming Johnston（庄士敦）, *Buddhist China*. London: John Murray (1913)

88. 《伟大的东方宗教导师》Alfred W. Martin, *Great Religious Teachers of the East*. New York: The Macmillan Co. (1911)

89. 《中国佛教》Rev. S. Beal, *Buddhism in China*. London: Society for Promoting Christian Knowledge (1884)

90. 《法显佛国记》Samuel Beal, *Travels of Fah Hian and Sung Yun, Buddhist Pilgrims, from China to India (400 A.D. and 518 A.D.)*; Translated from the Chinese. Trubner & Co. (1869)

3.2.5 道教

1. 《性别、权力和才华：中国唐代女道士的生命历程》Jinhua Jia（贾晋华）, *Gender, Power, and Talent: The Journey of Daoist Priestesses in Tang China*. Columbia University Press (2018)

2. 《中国早期道教：从出土文本看黄老思想》Feng Cao, *Daoism in Early China: Huang-Lao Thought in Light of Excavated Texts*. Palgrave Macmillan US (2017)
3. 《中国炼金术：道教、黄金之力与追求不朽》Jean Cooper, *Chinese Alchemy: Taoism, the Power of Gold, and the Quest for Immortality*. Weiser Books (2016)
4. 《无君—道教与无政府主义：古代和现代中国对国家自治的批评》John A. Rapp, *Daoism and Anarchism: Critiques of State Autonomy in Ancient and Modern China*. Bloomsbury Academic: Continuum (2012)
5. 《20世纪的道教》(New Perspectives on Chinese Culture and Society) David A. Palmer, Liu Xun, *Daoism in the Twentieth Century*. University of California Press (2012)
6. 《创意与道教：中国哲学、艺术和诗歌研究》Chung-yuan Chang, Zhao Xian Batt, *Creativity and Taoism: A Study of Chinese Philosophy, Art and Poetry*. Jessica Kingsley Publishers Ltd; Singing Dragon (2011)
7. 《天庭：中国道教绘画（1200—1400）》Lennert Gesterkamp, *The Heavenly Court: Daoist Temple Painting in China, 1200—1400*. Brill (2011)
8. 《梅红：中国古代道教故事》Stuart Wilde, *Plum Red: Taoist Tales of Old China*. Tolemac (2011)
9. 《坐忘：道教冥想的心境》Livia Kohn, *Sitting in Oblivion: The Heart of Daoist Meditation*. Three Pines Press (2010)
10. 《寻找华北的民间道家》Stephen Jones, *In Search of the Folk Daoists of North China*. Ashgate (2010)
11. 《祖先与焦虑：道教与投胎重生》Stephen R. Bokenkamp, *Ancestors and Anxiety: Daoism and the Birth of Rebirth in China* (Philip E. Lilienthal Books). University of California Press (2009)
12. 《内丹术》Livia Kohn, Robin R. Wang, *Internal Alchemy*. Three Pines Press (2009)
13. 《道教导论》Livia Kohn, *Introducing Daoism* (World Religions: Routledge). Routledge (2008)
14. 《修真：早期全真教的神秘主义和自我转化》Louis Komjathy, *Cultivating Perfection: Mysticism and Self-transformation in Early Quanzhen Daoism*. Brill (2007)
15. 《道家的身体修养：传统模式与当代实践》Livia Kohn (ed.), *Daoist Body Cultivation: Traditional Models and Contemporary Practices*. Three Pines Press (2006)
16. 《大彻：中世纪早期中国的道教和炼丹术》Fabrizio Pregadio, *Great Clarity: Daoism and Alchemy in Early Medieval China*. Stanford University Press (2005)
17. 《原道：早期道家话语中的形而上学》Thomas Michael, *The Pristine Dao: Metaphysic in Early Daoist Discourse*. State University of New York Press (2005)
18. 《中国旅游：道教》Yin Zhihua, *Chinese Tourism: Taoism*. Foreign Languages Press (2005)
19. 《道家：不朽的传统》Russell Kirkland, *Taoism: The Enduring Tradition*. Routledge (2004)
20. 《道教手册》Livia Kohn, *The Daoist Monastic Manual: A Translation of the Fengdao kejie* (American Academy of Religion texts and translations series). Oxford University Press (2004)
21. 《道藏通考：从古代到中世纪》（第一卷）Kristofer Schipper, Franciscus Verellen, *The

Taoist Canon: A Historical Companion to the Daozang. Vol. 1, Antiquity through the middle Ages. The University of Chicago Press (2004)

22. 《道藏通考：现代时期》（第二卷）Kristofer Schipper, Franciscus Verellen, *The Taoist Canon: A Historical Companion to the Daozang. Vol. 2, The Modern Period*. The University of Chicago Press (2004)

23. 《道藏通考：传记、参考书目、索引》（第三卷）Kristofer Schipper, Franciscus Verellen, *The Taoist Canon: A Historical Companion to the Daozang. Vol. 3, Biographies, Bibliography, Indexes*. The University of Chicago Press (2004)

24. 《七真史传：中国民间小说》Eva Wong (translator), *Seven Taoist Masters: A Folk Novel of China*. Shambhala (2004)

25. 《道教初学者指南》James Miller, *Daoism: A Beginner's Guide*. Oneworld Publications (2003)

26. 《无为：中国早期的概念隐喻和精神理想》Edward Slingerland, *Effortless Action: Wu-wei as Conceptual Metaphor and Spiritual Ideal in Early China*. Oxford University Press (2003)

27. 《道家身份：历史、谱系、仪式》Livia Kohn, Harold D. Roth (eds.), *Daoist Identity: History, Lineage and Ritual*. University of Hawai'i Press (2002)

28. 《道与迂回：宋代和近代中国的道教、地方宗教与神性模式》Robert Hymes, *Way and byway: Taoism, Local Religion, and Models of Divinity in Sung and Modern China*. University of California Press (2002)

29. 《道教手册》(Handbook of Oriental Studies: Section 4 China 〈Book 14〉) Livia Kohn, *Daoism Handbook (Handbook of Oriental Studies: Handbuch der Orientalisk-Part 4: China, 14)*. Brill (2000)

30. 《原道：内业与道教秘传的基础》Harold D. Roth, *Original Tao: Inward Training (Nei-yeh) and the Foundations of Taoist Mysticism*. Columbia University Press (1999)

31. 《唐代道教：中国黄金历史时代的宗教与帝国》Timothy Hugh Barrett, *Taoism Under the Tang: Religion and Empire During a Golden Age of Chinese History*. Wellsweep (1996)

32. 《列子：实践生活的道教指引》Eva Wong, *Lieh-tzu: A Taoist Guide to Practical Living*. Hambhala Publications, Inc. (1995)

33. 《中国思想的道家理论：一个哲学的解释》Chad Hansen（陈汉生）, *A Daoist Theory of Chinese Thought: A Philosophical Interpretation*. Oxford University Press (1992)

34. 《中国早期神秘主义：道家传统中的哲学与救赎论》Livia Kohn, *Early Chinese Mysticism: Philosophy and Soteriology in the Taoist Tradition*. Princeton University Press (1992)

35. 《中国道家巫术：扯平的艺术》Min Tzu, *Chinese Taoist Sorcery: The Art of Getting Even*. Vision Press Films (1992, 2000)

36. 《10—17世纪道教文学概观》AJudith M. Boltz, *Survey of Taoist Literature: Tenth to Seventeenth Centuries*. Institute of East Asian Studies [and] Center for Chinese Studies, University of California, Berkeley (1987)

37. 《道与魔：宗教调查的片段》Robert C. Neville（南乐山）, *The Tao and the Daimon: Segments of a Religious Inquiry*. SUNY Press (1982)
38. 《道教与中国宗教》Henri Maspero（马伯乐）, translated by Frank A. Kierman Jr., *Taoism and Chinese Religion*. University of Massachusetts Press (1981)
39. 《道教面面观：中国宗教文集》Holmes Welch, Anna Seidel (eds.), *Facets of Taoism: Essays in Chinese Religions*. Yale University Press (1979)
40. 《创意与道教：中国哲学、艺术与诗歌研究》Chung-yuan Chang, *Creativity and Taoism: A Study of Chinese Philosophy, Art and Poetry*. Singing Dragon (1965; 2011)
41. 《金花的秘密：一本关于生命的中国书》Huayang Liu, Dongbin Lü, Richard Wilhelm（卫礼贤）, C. G. Jung, *The Secret of the Golden Flower: A Chinese Book of Life*. Harcourt, Brace, & World (1962)

4. 中国文学与艺术

4.1 文学

1. 《中国现代文学中的个体构成》Qin Wang, *Configurations of the Individual in Modern Chinese Literature*. Springer Singapore: Palgrave Macmillan (2020)

2. 《现代主义的边缘：徐讦、无名氏与20世纪40年代中国通俗文学》(Edinburgh East Asian Studies) Christopher Rosenmeier, *On the Margins of Modernism: Xu Xu, Wumingshi and Popular Chinese Literature in the 1940s*. Edinburgh University Press (2019)

3. 《碎星：当代中国科幻小说翻译》(Chinese Science Fiction in Translation 2) Translated and edited by Ken Liu, *Broken Stars: Contemporary Chinese Science Fiction in Translation*. Tor Books (2019)

4. 《近代中国儿童文学与跨国知识：教育、宗教与童年》Shih-Wen Sue Chen, *Children's Literature and Transnational Knowledge in Modern China: Education, Religion, and Childhood*. Springer Singapore: Palgrave Macmillan (2019)

5. 《重新定义中国文学艺术》(Key Concepts in Chinese Thought and Culture) Jixi Yuan, *Redefining Chinese Literature and Art*. Springer Singapore: Palgrave Pivot (2019)

6. 《中国文学中的鼠与猫：故事与评论》Translated and introduced by Wilt L. Idema（伊维德）, Foreword by Haiyan Lee, *Mouse vs. Cat in Chinese Literature: Tales and Commentary*. University of Washington Press (2019)

7. 《中国文学与文化》（第十三卷）Timothy Huson, Craig Gallup, Zhou Zhengjie, Yu Hua, *Chinese Literature and Culture*. Vol. 13. IntLingo Inc., Westbury, New York & Zilin Limited, Guangzhou (2018)

8. 《中西通俗小说叙事》Yonglin Huang, *Narrative of Chinese and Western Popular Fiction*. Springer Berlin Heidelberg (2018)

9. 《中国韵律学视野中的比较文学》Shudong Chen, *Comparative Literature in the Light of Chinese Prosody*. Lexington Books (2018)

10. 《20世纪中国文学的诞生：语言、历史与文化的革命》Yu Gao, *The Birth of Twentieth-Century Chinese Literature: Revolutions in Language, History, and Culture*. Palgrave Macmillan US (2018)

11. 《中国抗日战争时期的文学期刊（1931—1938）》Sunny Han Han (auth.), *Literature Journals in the War of Resistance against Japanese Aggression in China (1931—1938)*. Springer Singapore (2018)

12. 《劳特利奇中国现代文学手册》Ming Dong Gu（顾明栋）, *Routledge Handbook of Modern*

Chinese Literature. Routledge (2018)

13. 《射雕英雄传》（第一卷）Jin Yong（金庸），Anna Holmwood（郝玉青），*A Hero Born: Legends of the Condor Heroes*. Vol. 1. MacLehose Press (2018)

14. 《豆棚闲话：17世纪中国故事集》Aina jushi（艾衲居士），Robert E. Hegel (ed.), *Idle Talk under the Bean Arbor: A Seventeenth-Century Chinese Story Collection*. University of Washington Press (2017)

15. 《牛津中国古典文学手册（公元前1000—公元900年）》Wiebke Denecke, Wai-Yee Li, Xiaofei Tian（田晓菲），*The Oxford Handbook of Classical Chinese Literature (1000 Bce—900ce)*. Oxford University Press, USA (2017)

16. 《中国文学中的色情与其他文学习俗：〈石头记〉的互文性》(Cambria Sinophone World Series) I-Hsien Wu, *Eroticism and Other Literary Conventions in Chinese Literature: Intertextuality in the Story of the Stone*. Cambria Press (2017)

17. 《当代中国文学与文学理论》Zhang Jiong, *Literature and Literary Theory in Contemporary China* (China Perspectives). Routledge (2017)

18. 《林语堂与中国寻找现代重生》Qian Suoqiao, *Lin Yutang and China's Search for Modern Rebirth* (Canon and World Literature).Palgrave Macmillan (2017)

19. 《中国现代文学、林纾与改良主义运动：古典与白话之间》César Guarde-Paz, *Modern Chinese Literature, Lin Shu and the Reformist Movement: Between Classical and Vernacular Language*. Palgrave Macmillan (2017)

20. 《中国文学纲要》（第一、二卷）Yuan Xingpei（袁行霈），*An Outline of Chinese Literature I, II* (China Perspectives). Routledge (2017)

21. 《知识的边缘：现代中国文学的梦想、历史和现实主义》Roy Bing Chan, *The Edge of Knowing: Dreams, History, and Realism in Modern Chinese Literature* (Modern Language Initiative Books). University of Washington Press (2017)

22. 《社会主义的世界主义：中国文学的宇宙（1945—1965）》Nicolai Volland, *Socialist Cosmopolitanism: The Chinese Literary Universe, 1945—1965* (Studies of the Weatherhead East Asian Institute, Columbia University). Columbia University Press (2017)

23. 《当代中国文学与文学理论》Zhang Jiong, *Literature and Literary Theory in Contemporary China* (China Perspectives). Routledge (2017)

24. 《来自唐代中国的故事：〈太平广记〉选》Alexei Ditter, Jessey Choo, Sarah Allen (eds.), *Tales from Tang Dynasty China: Selections from the Taiping Guangji*. Hackett Publishing Company, Inc. (2017)

25. 《中国现代文学新史》David Der-wei Wang（王德威，ed.），*A New Literary History of Modern China*. Belknap Press (2017)

26. 《三遂平妖传》Guanzhong Luo（罗冠中），Patrick Hanan（韩南，tr.），Ellen Widmer（魏爱莲，Intro.），Dewei Wang（王德威，Intro.），*Quelling the Demons' Revolt: A Novel*

from Ming China. Columbia University Press (2017)

27. 《东方往事：成长的故事》Xiaolu Guo, *Once Upon A Time in the East: A Story of Growing up*. Chatto & Windus (2017)

28. 《许愿灯：新中国的年轻人》Alec Ash（阿修）, *Wish Lanterns: Young Lives in New China*. Picador (2016)

29. 《中国现代文学指南》Yingjin Zhang（张英进）, *A Companion to Modern Chinese Literature* (Blackwell Companions to Literature and Culture). Wiley Blackwell (2016)

30. 《牛津现代中国文学手册》Carlos Rojas, Andrea Bachner (eds.), *The Oxford Handbook of Modern Chinese Literatures*. Oxford University Press (2016)

31. 《自己的问题：关于在当今中国制造麻烦的杂文》Han Han（韩寒）, edited and translated by Alice Xin Liu（刘欣）and Joel Martinsen（周华）, *The Problem with Me: And Other Essays About Making Trouble in China Today*. Simon & Schuster (2016)

32. 《无国界的美国华裔文学：性别、体裁和形式》King-Kok Cheung, *Chinese American Literature without Borders: Gender, Genre, and Form*. Palgrave Macmillan US (2016)

33. 《文学与社会：现代汉语高级读本》Xuedong Wang, Ying Wang, Zhiping Zhou, *Literature and Society: An Advanced Reader of Modern Chinese*. Princeton University Press (2016)

34. 《20世纪中国文学的意识形态转型》Xie Mian, *The Ideological Transformation of 20th Century Chinese Literature*. Silkroad Press (2016)

35. 《在十字路口的中国和西方：比较文学与文化随笔》Daiyun Yue（乐黛云）, *China and the West at the Crossroads: Essays on Comparative Literature and Culture* (China Academic Library). Springer Singapore (2016)

36. 《被焚藏书之精选》Li Zhi (Author), Rivi Handler-Spitz (Editor), Pauline Lee (Editor), Haun Saussy (Editor), *A Book to Burn and a Book to Keep (Hidden): Selected Writings* (Translations from the Asian Classics). Columbia University Press (2016)

37. 《小说中的事实：20世纪20年代的中国与巴金的〈家〉》Kristin Stapleton, *Fact in Fiction: 1920s China and Ba Jin's Family*. Stanford University Press (2016)

38. 《黑暗的闸门：中国左翼运动文学研究》Tsi-an Hsia（夏济安）, *The Gate of Darkness: Studies on the Leftist Literary Movement*. The Chinese University Press (2016)

39. 《中国的文学世界主义者：钱锺书、杨绛和文学世界》Christopher Rea, *China's Literary Cosmopolitans: Qian Zhongshu, Yang Jiang, and the World of Letters*. Brill (2015)

40. 《中国网络文学》Michel Hockx, *Internet Literature in China*. Columbia University Press (2015)

41. 《桃花扇》K'ung Shang-Jen, Judith T. Zeitlin, Chen Shih-Hsiang, Harold Acton, Cyril Birch（白之）, *The Peach Blossom Fan* (New York Review Books). New York Review Books Classics (2015)

42. 《中世纪中国一个醉汉的谈话故事》Alister D. Inglis, Luo Ye, Wilt L. Idema（伊维德）, *The Drunken Man's Talk Tales from Medieval China*. University of Washington Press (2015)

43. 《当真爱来到中国》Lynn Pan, *When True Love Came to China*. Hong Kong University

Press (2015)

44. 《中国互联网文学》Michel Hockx, *Internet literature in China*. Columbia University Press (2015)

45. 《20世纪初中国文学与文化中的性别与主体性》Ping Zhu, *Gender and Subjectivities in Early Twentieth-Century Chinese Literature and Culture* (Chinese Literature and Culture in the World). Palgrave Macmillan US (2015)

46. 《王佐良：论契合—比较文学研究集》Zuoliang Wang, *Degrees of Affinity: Studies in Comparative Literature and Translation* (China Academic Library). Springer-Verlag Berlin Heidelberg (2015)

47. 《中国早期文学形式的争论》Joachim Gentz, Dirk Meyer, *Literary Forms of Argument in Early China*. Brill Academic Publishing (2015)

48. 《从比较到世界文学》Longxi Zhang（张隆溪）, *From Comparison to World Literature* (SUNY Series in Chinese Philosophy and Culture). State University of New York Press (2015)

49. 《中国富豪女友》Kevin Kwan, *China Rich Girlfriend* (Crazy Rich Asian 2). Doubleday (2015)

50. 《基于语料库的中国文学散文翻译名词化研究：〈红楼楼〉的三版本》Yu Hou, *A Corpus-Based Study of Nominalization in Translations of Chinese Literary Prose: Three Versions of: Dream of the Red Chamber*. Peter Lang AG (2014)

51. 《古代和中世纪早期中国文学参考指南：第三部分》David R. Knechtges, Taiping Chang (Editors), *Ancient and Early Medieval Chinese Literature: A Reference Guide*. Part Three. Brill (2014)

52. 《中国文学史》Herbert A. Giles（翟理斯）, *A History of Chinese Literature* (reprint). Createspace Independent Publishing (2014)

53. 《三国演义：一部历史小说》Guanzhong Luo（罗贯中）, Moss Roberts（罗慕士, tr.）, *Three Kingdoms: A Historical Novel*. Abridged Edition. NUniversity of California Press, Foreign Languages Press (2014)

54. 《未来故事的消逝：当代中国文学的希望与终结》Paola Iovene, *Tales of Futures Past: Anticipation and the Ends of Literature in Contemporary China*. Stanford University Press (2014)

55. 《三体：地球往事》(Remembrance of Earth's Past 1) Cixin Liu（刘慈欣）, Ken Liu (translator), *The Three-Body Problem*. Tor Books (2014)

56. 《〈三国演义〉第三卷：迎虎》(With Footnotes) Guanzhong Luo（罗贯中）, Sumei Yu (trans.), Ronald C. Iverson (ed.), *The Three Kingdoms, Volume 3: Welcome the Tiger: The Epic Chinese Tale of Loyalty and War in a Dynamic New Translation*. Tuttle Publishin (2014)

57. 《〈三国演义〉第二卷：睡龙》(With Footnotes) Guanzhong Luo（罗贯中）, Sumei Yu (trans.), Ronald C. Iverson (ed.), *The Three Kingdoms, Volume 2. The Sleeping Dragon: The Epic Chinese Tale of Loyalty and War in a Dynamic New Translation*. Tuttle Publish (2014)

58. 《〈三国演义〉第一卷：圣誓》(With Footnotes) Guanzhong Luo（罗贯中）, Sumei Yu (trans.), Ronald C. Iverson (ed.), *The Three Kingdoms, Volume 1: The Sacred Oath: An Epic Chinese Tale of Loyalty and War in a Dynamic New Translations*. Tuttle Publishing (2014)

59. 《胡适英文文存：文学与社会》（第一卷）Hu Shih (auth.), Chih-P'ing Chou（周质平）(eds.), *English Writings of Hu Shih: Literature and Society* (Volume 1) (China Academic Library). Springer-Verlag Berlin Heidelberg (2013)

60. 《古代和中世纪早期中国文学参考指南：第二部分》David R. Knechtges, Taiping Chang (Editors), *Ancient and Early Medieval Chinese Literature: A Reference Guide*. Part Two. Brill Academic Pub (2013)

61. 《古典世界文学：中—日与格列柯—罗马比较》Wiebke Denecke, *Classical World Literatures: Sino-Japanese and Greco-Roman Comparisons*. Oxford University Press (2013)

62. 《碎片化现代主义：中国战时文学、艺术和电影（1937—1949）》Carolyn FitzGerald, *Fragmenting Modernisms: Chinese Wartime Literature, Art, and Film, 1937—49*. Brill (2013)

63. 《雪峰山脚下的生与死：一个湖南农村少年的童年》Yin Dalong（尹大龙）with CK Stuart, *Living and Dying at the Feet of the Snowy Mountains: A Contemporary Childhood in Rural Hunan, China*. AHP22 (2013)

64. 《中国文学与儿童：20世纪晚期中国小说中的儿童与童年》Kate Foster, *Chinese Literature and the Child: Children and Childhood in Late-Twentieth-Century Chinese Fiction*. Palgrave Macmillan UK (2013)

65. 《超越月亮门：1920年代中国的真实故事》Elizabeth Quan, *Beyond the Moongate: True Stories of 1920s China*. Random House; Tundra; Tundra Books (2013)

66. 《英国儿童小说中的中国描绘（1851—1911）》Shih-Wen Chen, *Representations of China in British Children's Fiction, 1851—1911* (Studies in Childhood, 1700 to the Present). Ashgate (2013)

67. 《人民喜爱的文学：阅读毛泽东时代早期中文文本（1949—1966）》Krista Van Fleit Hang (auth.), *Literature the People Love: Reading Chinese Texts from the Early Maoist Period (1949—1966)* (Chinese Literature and Culture in the World). Palgrave Macmillan US (2013)

68. 《文学史学的另一面：宇文所安与中国学者的文学史比较研究》Min Wang, *The Alter Ego Perspectives of Literary Historiography: A Comparative Study of Literary Histories by Stephen Owen and Chinese Scholars*. Springer Berlin Heidelberg (2013)

69. 《〈金瓶梅〉第五卷：解体》(Princeton library of Asian translations) David Tod Roy（芮效卫，translator）, *The Plum in the Golden Vase, or, Chin P'ing Mei: Volume 5: The Dissolution*. Princeton University Press (2013)

70. 《中国文学简介》Sabina Knight, *Chinese Literature: A Very Short Introduction* (Very Short Introductions 302). Oxford University Press (2012)

71. 《中国文学》Dan Yao, Jinhui Deng, Feng Wang, Huiyun Tang, *Chinese Literature* (Introductions to Chinese Culture). Cambridge University Press (2012)

72. 《中国语文素养教学透视》Liqing Tao, Gaoyin Qian (auth.), Cynthia B. Leung, Jiening Ruan (eds.), *Perspectives on Teaching and Learning Chinese Literacy in China*. Springer Netherlands (2012)

73. 《老舍在伦敦》Anne Witchard, *Lao She in London* (RAS Shanghai). Hong Kong University Press (2012)
74. 《中国梦》（小说）Irene Mahoney, O.S.U., *China Dreams*. Authorhouse (2012)
75. 《弄潮儿：中国崛起中的行动者和推动者》Jianying Zha（查建英）, *Tide Players: The Movers and Shakers of a Rising China*. The New Press (2011)
76. 《简明中国文学史》Luo Yuming（骆玉明）, translated with Annotations and an Introduction by Ye Yang, *A Concise History of Chinese Literature*. Koninklijke Brill NV, Leiden, The Netherlands (2011)
77. 《哥伦比亚中国民间通俗文学选读》Victor H. Mair（梅维恒）, Mark Bender, *The Columbia Anthology of Chinese Folk and Popular Literature*. Columbia University Press (2011)
78. 《中国现代白话在跨国文学中的运用》Gang Zhou, *Placing the Modern Chinese Vernacular in Transnational Literature*. Palgrave Macmillan (2011)
79. 《炳在西汉：从农民的儿子到县令》Michael Loewe（鲁惟一）, *Bing: From Farmer's Son to Magistrate in Han China*. Hackett Publishing Company, Inc. (2011)
80. 《〈金瓶梅〉第四卷：高潮》(Princeton library of Asian translations) David Tod Roy（芮效卫, translator), *The Plum in the Golden Vase or, Chin P'ing Mei, Volume 4: The Climax*. Princeton University Press (2011)
81. 《长恨歌》Wang Anyi（王安忆）, translated by Michael Berry and Susan Chan Egan, *The Song of Everlasting Sorrow: A Novel of Shanghai*. Columbia University Press (2011)
82. 《不列颠的中华眼：19世纪英国文学、帝国与审美》Elizabeth Chang, *Britain's Chinese Eye: Literature, Empire, and Aesthetics in Nineteenth. Century Britain* (2010)
83. 《苏童和余华的当代中国小说：长于乱世》Hua Li, *Contemporary Chinese Fiction by Su Tong and Yu Hua: Coming of Age in Troubled Times*. Koninklijke Brill NV, Leiden, The Netherlands (2010)
84. 《中国俄罗斯文学阅读：道德榜样与实践手册》Mark Gamsa, *The Reading of Russian Literature in China: A Moral Example and Manual of Practice*. Palgrave Macmillan (2010)
85. 《中国"大跃进"英雄故事两则》Richard King, *Heroes of China's Great Leap Forward: Two Stories*. University of Hawai'I Press (2010)
86. 《早期希腊和中国的作者与文化认同：文学流通模式》Alexander Beecroft, *Authorship and Cultural Identity in Early Greece and China: Patterns of Literary Circulation*. Cambridge University Press (2010)
87. 《北京来人》Henning Mankell, *The Man from Beijing*. Harvill Secker (2010)
88. 《中国文学（至1375年）》（第一卷）Kang-I Sun Chang（孙康宜）, Stephen Owen（宇文所安）(eds.), *Chinese Literature. vol. 1, To 1375 (The Cambridge History of Chinese literature)*. Cambridge University Press (2010)
89. 《中国文学（自1375年）》（第二卷）Kang-I Sun Chang（孙康宜）, Stephen Owen

（宇文所安）(eds.), *Chinese Literature. vol. 2, From 1375* (The Cambridge History of Chinese literature). Cambridge University Press (2010)

90. 《中国珍珠》Anchee Min, *Pearl of China*. Bloomsbury USA (2010)

91. 《唐代传奇故事选译》William H Nienhauser Jr.（倪豪士）, *Tang Dynasty Tale: A Guided Reader*. World Scientific Publishing (2010)

92. 《东亚故事搜索：468个中国、日本、韩国故事、主题和来源指南》Sharon Barcan Elswit, *East Asian Story Finder: A Guide to 468 Tales from China, Japan and Korea, Listing Subjects and Sources*. McFarland & Company, Inc., Publishers (2009)

93. 《拉里的肾脏：我在中国如何发现自己》Daniel Asa Rose, *Larry's Kidney: Being the True Story of How I Found Myself in China with My Black Sheep Cousin and His Mail*. HarperCollins Publishers Ltd. (2009)

94. 《绿牡丹与中国武侠小说的兴起》Margaret B. Wan, *Green Peony and the Rise of the Chinese Martial Arts Novel*. State University of New York Press, Albany, NY (2009)

95. 《行尸走肉：中国自下而上的现实生活故事》Liao Yiwu, *The Corpse Walker: Real Life Stories: China From the Bottom Up*. Anchor (2009)

96. 《动态文本帝国：日本文学中的中国、韩国和"台湾"文化嫁接》Karen Laura Thornber, *Empire of Texts in Motion: Chinese, Korean, and Taiwanese Transculturations of Japanese Literature* (Harvard-Yenching Institute Monograph Series). Harvard University Asia Center (2009)

97. 《超越笔谈：两次世界大战之间的中日文学交流》Christopher Keaveney, *Beyond Brushtalk: Sino-Japanese Literary Exchange in the Interwar Period*. Hong Kong University Press (2008)

98. 《塑造"新人"：从启蒙运动理想到社会主义现实》Yinghong Cheng（程映虹）, *Creating the "New Man": From Enlightenment Ideals to Socialist Realities* (Perspectives on the Global Past). University of Hawai'i Press (2008)

99. 《大娱乐：何景明的世界》（莱顿汉学）Daniel Bryant, *The Great Recreation: Ho Ching-ming (1483—1521) and His World*. Brill (2008)

100. 《小品文与中国现代性》Charles A. Laughlin, *The Literature of Leisure and Chinese Modernity*. University of Hawai'i Press (2008)

101. 《重塑邓小平时代的中国历史小说（1979—1997）》Howard Yuen Fung Choy, *Remapping the Past Fictions of History in Deng's China, 1979—1997*. Brill Academic Publishers (2008)

102. 《中国小说/英国语言：移民社群、记忆和故事中的文学随笔》Robert A. Lee, *China Fictions/ English Language: Literary Essays in Diaspora, Memory, Story*. Textxet Studies in Comparative Literature.Editions Rodopi B.V. (2008)

103. 《疼痛史：中国现代文学与电影的创伤》Michael Berry, *A History of Pain: Trauma in Modern Chinese Literature and Film* (Global Chinese Culture).Columbia University Press (2008)

104. 《当代中国文学：从"文革"到未来》Yibing Huang, *Contemporary Chinese Literature: From the Cultural Revolution to the Future*. Palgrave Macmillan (2007)

105. 《晚清青楼小说研究》Chloe F. Starr, *Red-light Novels of the late Qing* (China Studies). Koninklijke Brill NV, Leiden, The Netherlands (2007)
106. 《文学、现代性与反抗的实践：日本和"台湾"小说（1960—1990）》Margaret Hillenbrand, *Literature, Modernity, and the Practice of Resistance: Japanese and Taiwanese Fiction, 1960—1990* (China Studies). Brill (2007)
107. 《阅读中国：小说、历史和话语的动力——杜德桥教授纪念文集》Daria Berg (ed.), *Reading China: Fiction, History And the Dynamics of Discourse: Essays In Honor of Professor Glen Dudbridge*. Koninklijke Brill NV, Leiden, The Netherlands (2007)
108. 《中国文学新型实用入门》Paul Rouzer, *A New Practical Primer of Literary Chinese* (Harvard East Asian Monographs).Harvard University Asia Center (2007)
109. 《中国现代文学选集》Joseph S.M. Lau, Howard Goldblatt, *The Columbia Anthology of Modern Chinese Literature*.Columbia University Press (2007)
110. 《狄公传奇之迷宫谋杀案》Robert van Gulik（高罗佩）, *The Chinese Maze Murders: A Judge Dee Mystery* (Gulik, Robert Hans, Judge Dee Mystery).The University of Chicago Press (2007)
111. 《创新与排斥：美国现代诗歌中的中国文学融入》（博士论文）James InnisMcDougall, *Innovations and Exclusions: The Incorporation of Chinese Literature in Modern American Poetry*. Ph. D. Dissertation, University of Florida (2007)
112. 《猴子与和尚：〈西游记〉删节本》Anthony C. Yu, *The Monkey and the Monk: An Abridgment of The Journey to the West*.University of Chicago Press (2006)
113. 《中国社会主义晚期的腐败与现实主义：政治小说的回归》Jeffrey Kinkley（金介甫）, *Corruption and Realism in Late Socialist China: The Return of the Political Novel*. Stanford University Press (2006)
114. 《恋爱与革命：一本关于宋庆龄与孙中山的小说》（《行道天涯》英译）Ping Lu（平路）, *Love and Revolution: A Novel About Song Qingling and Sun Yat-sen* (Modern Chinese Literature from Taiwan). Columbia University Press (2006)
115. 《中国叙事：贾平凹和他的小说世界》Yiyan Wang, *Narrating China: Jia Pingwa and his Fictional World* (Routledge Contemporary China Series). Routledge (2006)
116. 《汉族人看魔幻莲灯及其他故事》Haiwang Yuan, *The Magic Lotus Lantern and Other Tales from the Han Chinese*.Libraries Unlimited (2006)
117. 《〈我爱美元〉及其他中国故事》(Weatherhead Books on Asia) Wen Zhu（朱文）, Julia Lovell（蓝诗玲，translator）, *I Love Dollars and Other Stories of China*. Columbia University Press (2006)
118. 《聊斋志异》Pu Songling（蒲松龄）, John Minford (tr.), *Strange Tales from a Chinese Studio*. Penguin Classics (2006)
119. 《〈金瓶梅〉第三卷：春药》(Princeton library of Asian translations) Roy, David Tod

Roy（芮效卫，translator）, *The Plum in the Golden Vase or, Chin P'ing Mei: Vol. 3, The Aphrodisiac.* Princeton University Press (2006)

120. 《雪花与秘扇》Lisa See, *Snow Flower and the Secret Fan: A Novel.* Random House (2006)

121. 《青春万岁：民族复兴与教育小说》（博士论文）Mingwei Song, *Long Live Youth: National Rejuvenation and the Bildungsroman, 1900—1958.* Ph. D. Dissertation, Columbia University (2005)

122. 《妇女、战争和家庭生活：1940年代的上海文学与通俗文化》Nicole Huang, *Women, War, Domesticity: Shanghai Literature and Popular Culture of the 1940s* (China Studies). Brill Academic Publishers (2005)

123. 《中国文学中有争议的现代性》Charles A. Laughlin (ed.), *Contested Modernities in Chinese Literature.* Palgrave Macmillan (2005)

124. 《消费文学：畅销书与当代中国文学生产商业化》Shuyu Kong, *Consuming Literature: Best Sellers and the Commercialization of Literary Production in Contemporary China.* Stanford University Press (2005)

125. 《陶元明与手稿文化：一个满是灰尘的表格记录》Xiaofei Tian（田晓菲）, *Tao Yuanming and Manuscript Culture: The Record of a Dusty Table* (China Program Books). University of Washington Press (2005)

126. 《文化、身份与商品：英语中的侨居地华文文学》Tseen Khoo, Kam Louie, *Culture, Identity, Commodity: Diasporic Chinese Literatures in English.* Hong Kong University Press (2005)

127. 《读写的中国理论：诠释学与开放诗学的进路》Ming Dong Gu (author), editor of Roger T. Ames（安乐哲）, *Chinese Theories of Reading and Writing: A Route to Hermeneutics and Open Poetics.* State University of New York (2005)

128. 《三国演义》（全本）Luo Guanzhong（罗冠中）, Translated by CH Brewitt-Taylor, *The Romance of Three Kingdoms* (complete and unbridged), Volumes 1 & 2. Disruptive Publishing (2005)

129. 《19世纪和20世纪初的中国小说》（中译本名：中国近代小说的兴起）Patrick Hanan（韩南）, *Chinese Fiction of the Nineteenth and Early Twentieth Centuries.* Columbia University Press (2004)

130. 《文学与乌托邦政治》Robert Appelbaum, *Literature and Utopian Politics.* Cambridge University Press (2004)

131. 《最后的黄埔》Pang-yuan Chi（齐邦媛）, David Der-Wei Wang（王德威）, *The Last of the Whampoa Breed* (Modern Chinese Literature from Taiwan). Columbia University Press (2004)

132. 《夏志清论中国文学》Chih-tsing Hsia（夏志清）, *C. T. Hsia on Chinese Literature* (Masters of Chinese Studies, V. 1). Columbia University Press (2004)

133. 《狄公案之黄金谋杀案》Robert Van Gulik（高罗佩）, *The Chinese Gold Murders: A Judge Dee Detective Story.* Harper Paperbacks (2004)

134. 《狄公案之广州谋杀案》Robert van Gulik, *Murder in Canton: A Judge Dee Mystery*. University of Chicago Press (2004)
135. 《跨文化解读：华裔和犹太裔美国文学的身份创建》Judith Oster, *Crossing Cultures: Creating Identity in Chinese and Jewish American Literature*. University of Missouri (2003)
136. 《哥伦比亚东亚现代文学指南》Kirk A. Denton, Bruce Fulton, Sharalyn Orbaugh, *The Columbia Companion to Modern East Asian Literature*. Columbia University Press (2003)
137. 《中国文学思想：〈文心雕龙〉的文化、创造力和修辞》Zong-qi Cai, *A Chinese Literary Mind: Culture, Creativity, and Rhetoric in Wenxin Diaolong*. Stanford University Press (2002)
138. 《孟称舜的〈娇红记〉》Cyril Birch（白之）, *Mistress and Maid (Jiaohong ji) by Meng Chengshun*. Columbia University Press (2001)
139. 《哥伦比亚中国文学史》Victor H. Mair（梅维恒）, *The Columbia History of Chinese Literature*. Columbia University Press (2001)
140. 《走出边缘：中国白话小说的兴起》Liangyan Ge, *Out of the Margins: the Rise of Chinese Vernacular Fiction*. University of Hawai'i Press (2001)
141. 《理论时代的中国现代文学与文化研究：重塑一个领域》Rey Chow（周蕾）(ed.), *Modern Chinese Literary and Cultural Studies in the Age of Theory: Reimagining a Field* (Asia-Pacific Culture, Politics, and Society). Duke University Press (2000)
142. 《现代性声音的失落：以中国通俗小说杂志为语境》Denise Gimpel, *Lost Voices of Modernity: A Chinese Popular Fiction Magazine in Context*. Honolulu: University of Hawai'i Press (2001)
143. 《〈金瓶梅〉第二卷：情敌》(Princeton library of Asian translations) David Tod Roy（芮效卫, translator）, *The Plum in the Golden Vase or, Chin P'ing Mei: Vol. 2, The Rivals*. Princeton University Press (2001)
144. 《中国传统文学短篇集》Victor H. Mair（梅维恒）, *The Shorter Columbia Anthology of Traditional Chinese Literature*. Columbia University Press (2000)
145. 《中国现代：英雄与平凡》Xiaobing Tang, *Chinese Modern: The Heroic and the Quotidian* (Post-Contemporary Interventions). Duke University Press (2000)
146. 《20世纪下半叶的中国文学：一个批评的概述》Pang-yuan Chi（齐邦媛）, David Der-wei Wang（王德威）, *Chinese Literature in the Second Half of a Modern Century: A Critical Survey*. Indiana University Press (2000)
147. 《中国古典文学》André Lévy, trans. by William H. Nienhauser, Jr.（倪豪士）, *Chinese Literature, Ancient and Classical*. Indiana University Press (2000)
148. 《20世纪中国文学界》Michel Hockx, *The Literary Field of Twentieth-century China*. Honolulu: University of Hawai'i Press (1999)
149. 《现代中国文学史》Tang Tao, *History of Modern Chinese Literature*. Foreign Languages Press, China (1998)

150. 《中华帝制晚期的插图小说阅读》Robert E. Hegel, *Reading Illustrated Fiction in Late Imperial China*. Stanford University Press (1998)

151. 《王氏之死》Jonathan D. Spence（史景迁）, *Death of Woman Wang*. Penguin Books (1998)

152. 《中国传统文学指南》（第三卷）William H. Nienhauser Jr.（倪豪士）, *The Indiana Companion to Traditional Chinese Literature*. Volume 2. Indiana University Press (1998)

153. 《紫禁城：一部现代中国小说》William Bell, *Forbidden City: A Novel of Modern China*. Laurel Leaf (1996)

154. 《毛主席不会被逗乐：今日中国小说》Howard Goldblatt, *Chairman Mao Would Not Be Amused: Fiction from Today's China*. Grove Press (1996)

155. 《〈金瓶梅〉第一卷：相聚》(Princeton library of Asian translations) David Tod Roy（芮效卫, translator), *The Plum in the Golden Vase or, Chin P'ing Mei: Vol. 1, The Gathering*. Princeton University Press (1993)

156. 《中国文学选读》Stephen Owen（宇文所安）, *Readings in Chinese Literary*. Harvard University Press (1992)

157. 《〈石头记〉：互文性、古代中国的石头传说，以及〈红楼梦〉〈水浒传〉〈西游记〉中的石头象征》Jing Wang（王瑾）, *The Story of Stone: Intertextuality, Ancient Chinese Stone Lore, and the Stone Symbolism in Dream of the Red Chamber, Water Margin, and The Journey to the West*. Duke University Press (1991)

158. 《现实主义界限：革命年代的中国小说》Marston Anderson, *The Limits of Realism: Chinese Fiction in the Revolutionary Period*. University of California Press (1990)

159. 《如何阅读中国小说》(Princeton Legacy Library) David L. Rolston, *How to Read the Chinese Novel*. Princeton University Press (1990)

160. 《北京：中国革命小说（1921—1978）》Anthony Grey, *Peking: A Novel of China's Revolution 1921—1978*. Pan Books Ltd (1989)

161. 《袁宏道与公安派》（剑桥汉学）Chih-P'ing Chou（周质平）, *Yüan Hung-tao and the Kung-an School* (Cambridge Studies in Chinese History, Literature and Institutions). Cambridge University Press (1988)

162. 《中国现代小说中的俄罗斯英雄》Mau-sang Ng, *The Russian Hero in Modern Chinese Fiction*. SUNY Press (1988)

163. 《中国小说中的知识分子》Yue Daiyun, *Intellectuals in Chinese Fiction*. Institute of East Asian Studies, University of California, Berkeley, Center for Chinese studies (1988)

164. 《创造李渔》Patrick Hanan（韩南）, *The Invention of Li Yu*. Harvard University Press (1988)

165. 《明代小说四大杰作：四大奇书》Andrew H. Plaks, *The Four Masterworks of the Ming Novel: SsuTa Ch'i-Shu*. Princeton University Press (1987)

166. 《追忆：中国古典文学中的往事再现》Stephen Owen（宇文所安）, *Remembrance: Experience of Past in Classical Chinese Literature*. Harvard University Press (1986)

167. 《中国传统文学指南》（修订二版）William H. Nienhauser Jr.（倪豪士），*The Indiana Companion to Traditional Chinese Literature*. Second Revised Edition. Indiana University Press (1986)
168. 《鹊桥：一个从未有过的中国古代小说》Barry Hughart, *Bridge of Birds: A Novel of an Ancient China That Never Was*. St. Martin's Press (1985)
169. 《与中国作家相遇》Annie Dillard, *Encounters with Chinese Writers*. Wesleyan University Press (1984)
170. 《中国白话小说史》Patrick Hanan（韩南），*The Chinese Vernacular Story*. Harvard University Press (1981)
171. 《〈红楼梦〉英译》Cao Xueqin, O Kao, David Hawkes（大卫·霍克斯，translator），*The Story of the Stone*. In Five Volumes. Penguin Classics (1974)
172. 《中国作家的浪漫一代》Leo Ou-fan Lee（李欧梵），*The Romantic Generation of Chinese Writers* (Harvard East Asian series). Harvard University Press (1973)
173. 《中国历史与文学研究文集》Jaroslav Průšek, *Chinese History and Literature: Collection of Studies*. Springer Netherlands (1970)
174. 《中国古典小说史论》Hsia Chih-tsing（夏志清），*The Classic Chinese Novel: A Critical Introduction*. Companions to Asian Studies. Reprinted 1980; 1996. New York: Columbia University Press (1968)
175. 《文言文入门》（第三册）Harold Shadick（谢迪克），Ch'iao Chien（乔健），*A First Course in Literary Chinese*. Volume III. Cornell University Press (1968)
176. 《中国文学研究》John L. Bishop, *Studies in Chinese Literature*. Harvard University Press (1965)
177. 《武则天传》Lin Yutang（林语堂），*Lady Wu: A Novel*. G. P Putnam's Sons (1965)
178. 《中国现代小说史》Hsia Chih-tsing（夏志清），*A History of Modern Chinese Fiction*. Yale University Press (1961)
179. 《文心雕龙：中国文学思想与模式研究》Liu Hsieh; Translated with an Introduction and Notes by Vincent Yu-chung Shih, *The Literary Mind and the Carving of Dragons: A Study of Thought and Pattern in Chinese Literature*. Columbia University Press (1959)
180. 《中国绅士：一部小说》Robert Standish, *Gentleman of China: A Novel*. London: Peter Davies (1949)
181. 《战时中国故事》Chi-Chen Wang, *Stories of China at War*. Geoffrey Cumberlege, London (1947)
182. 《故事绘话中国》（一本用蜡笔记录中国印象的画集）Emily Hahn（项美丽），*The Picture Story of China*. New York: D. McKay Co. (1946)
183. 《中国生活：近代短篇小说选》Edgar Snow（斯诺）Compiled and Edited, *Living China: Modern Chinese Short Stories*. John Day (1936)

184. 《中国文学：包括孔子〈论语〉〈诗经〉〈孟子〉〈汉宫秋〉〈法显游记〉》Epiphanius Wilson, *Chinese Literature: Comprising the Analects of Confucius, the Shi-King, the Sayings of Mencius, the Sorrows of Han, and the Travels of Fa-Hien*.New York: The Colonial Press (1900)

185. 《中国文学札记》A. Wylie, *Notes on Chinese Literature*. With introductory remarks on the progressive advancement of the art; and a list of translations from the Chinese into various European languages. Presbyterian Mission Press (1867, 1922)

鲁迅研究

186. 《铁屋之外：鲁迅与中国现代文学圈》Saiyin Sun, *Beyond the Iron House: Lu Xun and the Modern Chinese Literary Field* (China Perspectives). Routledge (2016)

187. 《复活的骨架：从庄子到鲁迅》Wilt L. Idema（伊维德）, *The Resurrected Skeleton: From Zhuangzi to Lu Xun* (Translations from the Asian Classics). Columbia University Press (2014)

188. 《鲁迅的革命：暴力时代的写作》Gloria Davies, *Lu Xun's Revolution: Writing in a Time of Violence*. Harvard University Press (2013)

189. 《阿Q正传及其他中国故事：鲁迅小说全集》Lu Xun, Julia Lovell（蓝诗玲, translator), *The Real Story of Ah-Q and Other Tales of China: The Complete Fiction of Lu Xun* (Penguin Classics). Penguin Books Ltd (2009)

190. 《狂人和其他幸存者：读鲁迅小说》Jeremy Tambling, *Madmen and Other Survivors: Reading Lu Xun's Fiction*. Hong Kong University Press (2007)

191. 《近代中国的情书和隐私权：鲁迅与许广平的私密生活》Bonnie S. McDougall, *Love-Letters and Privacy in Modern China: The Intimate Lives of Lu Xun and Xu Guangping* (Studies on Contemporary China). Oxford University Press (2002)

192. 《鲁迅与进化》James Reeve Pusey, *Lu Xun and Evolution*.State University of New York Press (1998)

193. 《〈狂人日记〉及其他故事》Lu Xun, William A. Lyell, *Diary of a Madman and Other Stories*. University of Hawaii Press (1990)

194. 《作为译者的鲁迅：鲁迅对文学及文学理论的翻译与介绍（1903—1936）》Lennart Lundberg, *Lu Xun as a Translator: Lu Xun's Translation and Introduction of Literature and Literary Theory, 1903—1936*.Stockholm University, Orientaliska Studier (1989)

195. 《逝去的时代：鲁迅家族的衰落》Zhou Jianren, Zhou Ye, *An Age Gone by: Lu Xun's Clan in Decline*.New World Press (1988)

196. 《鲁迅：永远的中国作家》Ruth F. Weiss, *Lu Xun: A Chinese Writer for All Times*.New World Press (1985)

197. 《鲁迅和他的遗产》Leo Ou-Fan Lee（李欧梵）, *Lu Xun and His Legacy*. University of California Press (1985)

4.2 诗歌

1. 《放逐的仙人：李白的一生》Ha Jin, *The Banished Immortal: A Life of Li Bai*. Pantheon (2019)
2. 《英译唐诗西方鉴赏史》Lan Jiang, *A History of Western Appreciation of English-translated Tang Poetry* (China Academic Library). Springer Berlin Heidelberg (2013)
3. 《心灵之鹰：诗集》Yang Mu, *Hawk of the Mind: Collected Poems* (Modern Chinese Literature from Taiwan). Columbia University Press (2018)
4. 《楚辞：屈原等中国古诗选集》Gopal Sukhu (ed.and tr.), *The Songs of Chu: An Anthology of Ancient Chinese Poetry by Qu Yuan and Others*. Columbia University Press (2017)
5. 《二百年满族女诗人诗选》Wilt L. Idema（伊维德）, *Two Centuries of Manchu Women Poets: An Anthology*. University of Washington Press (2017)
6. 《重新审视改革后的中国城市公众：广州的诗学与政治》Qian, Junxi, *Re-visioning the Public in Post-reform Urban China: Poetics and Politics in Guangzhou*.Springer Verlag (2017)
7. 《杜甫（712—770）及其诗歌在中国的接受》Ji Hao, *The Reception of Du Fu (712—770) and His Poetry in Imperial China* (Sinica Leidensia). Brill (2017)
8. 《大雁归来：中国的可逆诗》Jody Gladding, Michèle Métail, Jeffrey Yang, *Wild Geese Returning: Chinese Reversible Poems* (Calligrams). The Chinese University of Hong Kong Press (2017)
9. 《〈诗经—国风〉新译》Ha Poong Kim, *Joy and Sorrow: Songs of Ancient China: A New Translation of Shi Jing Guo Feng* (A Chinese-English Bilingual Edition). Sussex Academic Press (2016)
10. 《无法翻译的东西太多：20世纪美国之中国古典诗歌英译》（硕士论文）Ahui Yu, *There Is So Much You Can't Translate: English Translation of Chinese Classic Poetry in Twentieth Century America*. Thesis for the Degree of Master of Arts, State University of New York at Albany (2016)
11. 《缔造选本：〈花间集〉的文化语境与诗学实践》Anna M. Shields（田安）, *Crafting a Collection: The Cultural Contexts and Poetic Practice of Huajian ji (Collection from among Flowers)*. Harvard University Asia Center (2016)
12. 《杜甫诗》Stephen Owen（宇文所安）, *The Poetry of Du Fu*：杜甫诗(Library of Chinese Humanities). De Gruyter (2015)
13. 《幻想与现实：帝国晚期中国女性旅游诗》Yanning Wang, *Reverie and Reality: Poetry on Travel by Late Imperial Chinese Women*. Lexington Books (2014)
14. 《中国私语：诗歌》John Ashbery, *Chinese Whispers: Poems*. Open Road Media (2014)
15. 《诗人郑珍（1806—1864）与中国现代性的兴起》Jerry D. Schmidt, *The Poet Zheng Zhen (1806—1864) and the Rise of Chinese Modernity*. Brill (2013)
16. 《李白诗选》David Hinton (Trans.), *The Selected Poems of Li Po*. New York: New Directions Publishing Corporation (2013)
17. 《大师们的诗歌：中国唐宋诗歌经典选本〈千家诗〉》Red Pine (transl.), *Poems of the Masters: China's Classic Anthology of T'ang and Sung Dynasty Verse Qian Jia Shi*. Copper

Canyon Press (2012)

18. 《巫师和异教：〈离骚〉的新解释》Gopal Sukhu, *The Shaman and the Heresiarch: A New Interpretation of the Li Sao* (SUNY Series in Chinese Philosophy and Culture). State University of New York Press (2012)
19. 《透过诗歌看中国诞生》Chan Hong-Mo, *The Birth of China: Seen Through Poetry*. World Scientific (2011)
20. 《显以文，书于纸：唐代诗歌的产生与流传》Christopher M. B. Nugent, *Manifest in Words, Written on Paper: Producing and Circulating Poetry in Tang Dynasty China* (Harvard-Yenching Institute Monograph Series). Harvard University Asia Center (2011)
21. 《晴山古道：马来亚—新加坡文学先驱作家陈晴山中国古典诗歌和散文选集》Peter Min-liang Chen, Michael Tan, Chiu Ming Chan, *A Scholar's Path: An Anthology of Classical Chinese Poems and Prose of Chen Qing Shan, a Pioneer Writer of Malayan-Singapore Literature*. World Scientific (2010)
22. 《空虚诗学：美国诗歌中亚洲思想的转变》Jonathan Stalling, *Poetics of Emptiness: Transformations of Asian Thought in American Poetry*. New York: Fordham University Press (2010)
23. 《革命之声：现代中国诗歌与听觉想象》John A. Crespi, *Voices in Revolution: Poetry and the Auditory Imagination in Modern China*. University of Hawai'i Press (2009)
24. 《中国当代诗歌新视角》Christopher Lupke, *New Perspectives on Contemporary Chinese Poetry*. Palgrave Macmillan (2008)
25. 《英译乐府诗精华》Wang Rongpei（汪榕培）, *Gems of Yuefu Ballads* (SFLEP Bilingual Chinese Culture Series). Foreign Languages Education Press (2008)
26. 《如何阅读中国诗歌：导读选集》Zong-qi Cai, *How to Read Chinese Poetry: A Guided Anthology*. Columbia University Press (2008)
27. 《中国古典诗选》David Hinton, *Classical Chinese Poetry: An Anthology*. Farrar, Straus and Giroux (2008)
28. 《中国早期古典诗词的形成》Stephen Owen（宇文所安）, *The Making of Early Chinese Classical Poetry*. Harvard University Press (2006)
29. 《香巴拉中国诗歌选集》Jerome P. Seaton, *The Shambhala Anthology of Chinese Poetry*. Shambhala Publications (2006)
30. 《文言文（补编2）：诗歌和散文读物》(Princeton Language Program: Modern Chinese.) Naiying Yuan, Hai-tao Tang, *Classical Chinese (Supplement 2): Readings in Poetry and Prose*. Princeton University Press (2005)
31. 《北宋中期诗歌的社会循环：情感能量与文人自我培养》Colin S. C. Hawes, *The Social Circulation of Poetry in the Mid-Northern Song: Emotional Energy and Literati Self-Cultivation* (SUNY Series in Chinese Philosophy and Culture). State University of New York Press (2005)
32. 《中国诗歌与预言：东亚甲骨文》Michel Strickmann, Bernard Faure, *Chinese Poetry and*

Prophecy: The Written Oracle in East Asia. Stanford University Press (2005)

33. 《杜甫诗选》Burton Watson, *The Selected Poems of Du Fu*. Columbia University Press (2002)
34. 《寒山诗》Translated by Red Pine, with an Introduction by John Blofeld, *The Collected Songs of Cold Mountain*. Revised and Expanded. Copper Canyon Press (2000)
35. 《颓废的诗学：南朝与晚唐中国诗歌》Fusheng Wu, *The Poetics of Decadence: Chinese Poetry of the Southern Dynasties and Late Tang Periods*. State University of New York Press (1998)
36. 《反思杜甫：文学的伟大与文化语境》Eva Shan Chou, *Reconsidering Tu Fu: Literary Greatness and Cultural Context*. Cambridge University Press (1995)
37. 《看待王维的十九种方式：中国诗歌的翻译》Eliot Weinberger, Octavio Paz, *19 Ways of Looking at Wang Wei: How a Chinese Poem is Translated*. Asphodel Press (1995)
38. 《孤舟自横：中国禅诗选集》Jerome P. Seaton & Dennis Maloney, *A Drifting Boat: An Anthology of Chinese Zen Poetry*. White Pine Press (1994)
39. 《论宋词》Pauline Yu (ed.), *Voices of the Song Lyric in China*. BerkeleyUniversity of California Press (1994)
40. 《三位中国诗人：王维、李白、杜甫诗歌翻译》Vikram Seth, *Three Chinese Poets: Translations of Poems by Wang Wei, Li Bai, and Du Fu*. HarperPerennial (1992)
41. 《文字和图像：中国诗歌、书法、绘画》Alfreda Murck, Wen C. Fong, *Words and Images: Chinese Poetry, Calligraphy, and Painting*. Princeton University Press (1991)
42. 《〈楚辞〉英译选集》(Penguin Classics) David Hawkes（大卫·霍克斯）, *The Songs of the South: An Anthology of Ancient Chinese Poems by QuYuan and Other Poets*. Penguin (1985)
43. 《卞之琳：中国现代诗歌研究》Lloyd Haft, *Pien Chih-lin: A Study in Modern Chinese Poetry* (Publications in modern Chinese language and literature 3). De Gruyter (1983)
44. 《盛唐诗》Stephen Owen（宇文所安）, *The Great Age of Chinese Poetry. The High T'ang*. New Haven and London, Yale University Press (1981)
45. 《庾信〈哀江南赋〉》William T. Graham, *'The Lament for the South': Yu Hsin's 'Ai Chiang-Nan Fu'* (Cambridge Studies in Chinese History, Literature and Institutions). Cambridge University Press (1980, 2008)
46. 《关于〈尔雅〉中植物和动物部分的语言学研究》（博士论文）Michael Edward Carr, *A Linguistic Study of the Flora and Fauna Sections of the Erh-Ya*. Ph. D. Dissertation, The University of Arizona (1979)
47. 《诗歌与政治：阮籍生平与作品（210—263）》Donald Holzman, *Poetry and Politics: The Life and Works of Juan Chi, A.D. 210–263* (Cambridge Studies in Chinese History, Literature and Institutions). Cambridge University Press (1976)
48. 《北宋重要词人（公元960—1126年）》James J.Y. Liu, *Major Lyricists of the Northern Sung: 960—1126 A.D.* (Princeton Legacy Library). Princeton University Press (1974)
49. 《苏东坡传》Lin Yutang（林语堂）, *The Gay Genius: The Life and Times of Su Tungpo*.

Praeger (1971)

50. 《中国诗歌艺术》James J. Y. Liu, *The Art of Chinese Poetry*. University of Chicago Press (1966)

51. 《晚唐诗歌》Translated with an Introduction by A. C. Graham（葛瑞汉）, *Poems of the Late T'ang*. Penguin Classics (1965, 1968)

52. 《中国诗歌》A. R. Davis (Author), Robert Kotewall (Translator), Norman L. Smith (Translator), *Chinese Verse* (Poets). Penguin Classics; Fifth Impression Edition (1962)

53. 《遇见中国》（英文诗画集）Leila Pirani, Illustrated by Ruth Shackel, *I Met Them in China*. Robertson and Mullens (1944)

54. 《群玉山头：唐诗三百首》Translated by Witter Bynner From the Texts of Kiang Kang-Hu (Author), *The Jade Mountain: A Chinese Anthology, Being Three Hundred Poems of the T'ang Dynasty, 618-906*. Alfred A. Knopf (1929)

55. 《松花笺》Florence Ayscough（艾思柯）, Amy Lowell, *Fir-flower Tablets: Poems from the Chinese*. Houghton Mifflin Company, Boston (1921)

56. 《英译中国诗》Arthur Waley（阿瑟·韦利）, *Poems from the Chinese*. London: Ernest Benn Ltd. (1920)

57. 《英译唐诗选》Translated into English verse by W. J. B. Fletcher, *Gems of Chinese Verse*. Shanghai Commercial Press (1919)

58. 《汉诗170首》Translated by Arthur Waley（阿瑟·韦利）, *A Hundred And Seventy Chinese Poems*. Alfred A. Knopf, Inc. (1919)

59. 《更多中国（诗歌）的翻译》Arthur Waley（阿瑟·韦利）, *More Translations from the Chinese*. Geogre Allen & Unwin Ltd (1919)

60. 《诗人李白（701—762）》Arthur Waley（阿瑟·韦利）, *The Poet Li Po, A.D. 701—762. A Paper Read before the China Society at the School of Oriental Studies on November 21, 1918*. London, East and West, Ltd. (1919)

61. 《中国诗选》Arthur Waley（阿瑟·韦利）, *Chinese Poems*. London, Printed by Lowe Bros (1916)

62. 《华夏集》（大部分翻译内容来自李白，注释来自已故的欧内斯特·费诺罗萨，译解来自森海南教授和有贺永雄教授）Ezra Pound, *Cathay. Translations by Ezra Pound for the Most Part from the Chinese of Rihaku, from the Notes of the Late Ernest Fenollosa, and the Decipherings of Professors Mori and Ariga*. London: Elkin Mathews (1915)

63. 《中国诗歌》Charles Budd, *Chinese Poems*. London, New York etc.: Henry Frowde, Oxford University Press (1912)

64. 《中国异教徒：东西方诗歌与模仿》Bret Harte, *The Heathen Chinee: With East and West Poems and Parodies*. London: Ward, Lock & Co. (1884)

4.3 戏剧

1. 《中国剧本：历史、人物与书法》Thomas O. Höllmann, *Chinese Script: History, Characters,*

Calligraphy. Columbia University Press (2017)

2. 《多面目莲：明清时期宝卷》Rostislav Berezkin（白若思）, *Many Faces of Mulian: The Precious Scrolls of Late Imperial China.* University of Washington Press (2017)

3. 《舞台中国：21世纪新剧院》Li Ruru (ed.), *Staging China: New Theatres in the Twenty-First Century.* Palgrave Macmillan US (2016)

4. 《在伦敦舞台上表演中国：中国戏剧与全球大国（1759—2008）》Ashley Thorpe, *Performing China on the London Stage: Chinese Opera and Global Power, 1759—2008.* Palgrave Macmillan UK (2016)

5. 《1616：莎士比亚与汤显祖的中国》Paul Edmondson, Shih-pe Wang, Tian Yuan Tan, *1616: Shakespeare and Tang Xianzu's China.* Bloomsbury Arden Shakespeare (2016)

6. 《赵氏孤儿与其他元杂剧》Stephen H. West, Wilt L. Idema（伊维德）, *Orphan of Zhao and Other Yuan Plays.* Columbia University Press (2015)

7. 《都市政治与文化资本：中国戏曲的个案》Ma Haili, *Urban Politics and Cultural Capital: The Case of Chinese Opera.* Ashgate Publishing Company (2015)

8. 《粤剧的兴起》Wing Chung Ng, *The Rise of Cantonese Opera.* University of Illinois Press (2015)

9. 《中国现代戏剧哥伦比亚文集（摘编）》Chen Xiaomei, *The Columbia Anthology of Modern Chinese Drama, Abridged.* Columbia University Press (2014)

10. 《现代中国的前卫与流行：田汉与表演和政治的交集》Liang Luo, *The Avant-Garde and the Popular in Modern China: Tian Han and the Intersection of Performance and Politics.* University of Michigan Press (2014)

11. 《京剧秦香莲》Chen Rong, *Qin Xianglian: A Beijing Opera* (The Project for Disseminating Chinese Operatic Dramas Overseas by Renmin University of China). Foreign Language Teaching and Research Press (2014)

12. 《哥伦比亚元杂剧选集》C. T. Hsia（夏志清）, Wai-yee Li（李惠仪）, George Kao, *Columbia Anthology of Yuan Drama.* Columbia University Press (2014)

13. 《殖民地摩登中国时期的表演杂糅》（加拿大）Liu Siyuan（刘思远）, *Performing Hybridity in Colonial-Modern China.* Palgrave Macmillan (2013)

14. 《歌剧与城市：北京的文化政治（1770—1900）》Andrea S. Goldman, *Opera and the City: The Politics of Culture in Beijing, 1770—1900.* Stanford University Press (2012)

15. 《梅兰芳与20世纪国际舞台：中国戏剧的入场与出场》Min Tian, *Mei Lanfang and the Twentieth-Century International Stage: Chinese Theatre Placed and Displaced.* Palgrave and Macmillan (2012)

16. 《中式英语》（老汇新喜剧）David Henry Hwang（黄哲伦）, *Chinglish: A Play.* Theatre Communications Group (2012)

17. 《全球化时代的另类中国戏曲：零表演》Daphne P. Lei, *Alternative Chinese Opera in the Age of Globalization: Performing Zero* (Studies in International Performance). Palgrave

Macmillan (2011)

18. 《现代中国早期的小说与戏剧想象》Mei Chun, *The Novel and Theatrical Imagination in Early Modern China* (Sinica Leidensia). Brill (2011)

19. 《逃离血池地狱：目连及黄氏女的传说》Beata Grant（管佩达）, Wilt L. Idema（伊维德）, *Escape from Blood Pond Hell: The Tales of Mulian and Woman Huang*. University of Washington Press (2011)

20. 《约翰·亚当斯的尼克松在中国：音乐分析、历史和政治角度》Timothy A. Johnson, *John Adams's Nixon in China: Musical Analysis, Historical and Political Perspectives*. Ashgate Pub Co. (2011)

21. 《京剧之魂：变化世界中的戏剧创作和连续性》Ruru Li, *Soul of Beijing Opera: Theatrical Creativity and Continuity in the Changing World*. Hong Kong University Press (2010)

22. 《北京戏曲服饰：人物与文化视觉传播》Alexandra B. Bonds, *Beijing Opera Costumes: The Visual Communication of Character and Culture*. University of Hawai'i Press (2008)

23. 《中国电视剧》Ying Zhu, *TV Drama in China* (TransAsia: Screen Cultures). Hong Kong University Press (2008)

24. 《差异与位移诗学：20世纪中西文化戏剧》Min Tian, *The Poetics of Difference and Displacement: Twentieth-century Chinese-Western Intercultural Theatre*. Hong Kong: Hong Kong University Press; London: Eurospan distributor (2008)

25. 《表演"国家"：1880—1940年中国和日本的文学、戏剧、视觉艺术中的性别政治》Doris Croissant, Catherine Vance Yeh, Joshua S. Mostow, *Performing "Nation": Gender Politics in Literature, Theater, and the Visual Arts of China and Japan, 1880—1940*. Brill Academic (2008)

26. 《过去之永恒存在：明万历年间的插图、戏剧与阅读（1573—1619）》Li-ling Hsiao, *The Eternal Present of the Past: Illustration, Theater, and Reading in the Wanli Period, 1573—1619*. Brill (2007)

27. 《戏剧之王：1870—1937年京剧再创造过程中的玩家与公众》Joshua Goldstein, *Drama Kings: Players and Publics in the Re-creation of Peking Opera, 1870—1937*. University of California Press (2007)

28. 《歌剧中国：横跨太平洋的舞台中国认同》Daphne Pi-Wei Lei, *Operatic China: Staging Chinese Identity Across the Pacific* (Palgrave Studies in Theatre and Performance History). Palgrave Macmillan US (2006)

29. 《明代中国的精英戏剧（1368—1644）》Grant Guangren Shen（沈广仁）, *Elite Theatre in Ming China, 1368—1644* (Routledgecurzon Studies on the Early History of Asia). Routledge (2005)

30. 《重要的他者：中国舞台上的美国人》Claire Conceison, *Significant Other: Staging the American in China*. University of Hawaii Press (2004)

31. 《莎士比亚在中国》Murray J. Levith, *Shakespeare in China*. Continuum (2004)

32. 《京剧》Xu Chengbei, *Peking Opera*. Cambridge University Press (2003)

33. 《毛泽东时代最后的舞者》Li Cunxin（李存信）, *Mao's Last Dancer*. Berkley Trade (2003)
34. 《欲望剧场：中国早期歌剧的作者、读者与再生产（1300—2000）》Patricia Sieber（夏颂）, *Theaters of Desire: Authors, Readers, and the Reproduction of Early Chinese Song-Drama, 1300—2000*. Palgrave Macmillan US (2003)
35. 《中国戏曲中的变装》Siu Leung Li, *Cross-Dressing in Chinese Opera*. Hong Kong University Press (2003)
36. 《戏剧与社会：当代中国戏剧选集》Haiping Yan, *Theater and Society: An Anthology of Contemporary Chinese Drama*. M.E. Sharpe (1998)
37. 《蝴蝶君》David Henry Hwang（黄哲伦）, *M. Butterfly*. Dramatists Play Service, Inc. (1998)
38. 《边缘景象：美国舞台上的华人》James S. Moy, *Marginal Sights: Staging the Chinese in America* (Studies Theatre Hist & Culture). University Of Iowa Press (1994)
39. 《"长子"（1897）：关于弗朗西斯·鲍尔斯与大卫·贝拉斯科未发表的美国华裔生活剧的文化、历史和文学研究》（博士论文）Sheryl Fern Nadler, *"The First Born" (1897): A Cultural, Historical, and Literary Study of Francis Powers and David Belasco's Unpublished Drama of Chinese Life in America*. Ph. D. Dissertation, The Florida State University (1994)
40. 《听剧：京剧的听觉维度》Elizabeth Wichmann, *Listening to Theatre: The Aural Dimension of Beijing Opera*. University of Hawai'i Press (1991)
41. 《中国当代历史剧研究四论》Rudolf G. Wagner, *The Contemporary Chinese Historical Drama: Four Studies*. Berkeley: University of California Press (1990)
42. 《中华人民共和国戏剧》Constantine Tung, Colin Mackerras（马克林）, *Drama in the People's Republic of China*. State University of New York Press (1987)
43. 《中国戏剧：从起源至今》Colin Mackerras（马克林）, *Chinese Theater: From Its Origins to the Present Day*. University of Hawai'i Press (1983)
44. 《杜鹃山：一部现代革命京剧》Wang Shu-yuan etc., *Azalea Mountain: A Modern Revolutionary Peking Opera*. Foreign Languages Press (1976)
45. 《样板戏五部》Martin Ebon, *Five Chinese Communist Plays*. John Day Co. (1975)
46. 《梅兰芳：一位京剧演员的生活与时代》A. C. Scott, *Mei Lan-Fang: The Life and Times of a Peking Actor*. Hong Kong University Press (1971)
47. 《共产党中国的现代戏剧》Walter J. Meserve, Ruth I. Meserve, *Modern Drama from Communist China*. New York University Press (1970)
48. 《中国戏剧》Adolf Eduard Zucker, *The Chinese Theater*. Little, Brown, and Company (1925)
49. 《中国戏剧研究》Kate Buss, *Studies in the Chinese Drama*. Boston: The Four Seas Company (1922)
50. 《中国戏谈》Chu Chia-Chien（朱家健）, translated from the French by James A. Graham, with Illustrations from Paintings, Sketches and Crayon Drawings by Alexandre Jacovleff, *The Chinese Theatre*. John Lane the Bodley Head Limited, London (1922)

51.《中国之谜：四幕原创剧本》Marian Bower, Leon M. Lion, *The Chinese Puzzle: An Original Play in Four Acts*. Hutchinson (1919)

4.4 神话/传说

1. 《隐秘又可见的领域：中古早期中国的超自然奇幻故事》(Translations from the Asian Classics) Liu Yiqing, Zhenjun Zhang, *Hidden and Visible Realms: Early Medieval Chinese Tales of the Supernatural and the Fantastic*. Columbia University Press (2018)

2. 《我们从中国神话中得到什么》Katie Marsico, *What We Get From Chinese Mythology* (21st Century Skills Library: Mythology and Culture). Cherry Lake Publishing (2014)

3. 《关于中国的49个神话》Marte Kjær Galtung, Stig Stenslie, *49 Myths about China*. Rowman & Littlefield Publishers (2012)

4. 《中国和美国的木兰传奇与遗产》Lan Dong, *Mulan's Legend and Legacy in China and the United States*. Temple University Press (2011)

5. 《发展性童话：进化思维与中国现代文化》Andrew F. Jones, *Developmental Fairy Tales: Evolutionary Thinking and Modern Chinese Culture*. Harvard University Press (2011)

6. 《中国神话大全》Jeremy Roberts, *Chinese Mythology A to Z*. Chelsea House (2010)

7. 《神话与象征的宇宙起源：从多贡和古埃及到印度、西藏和中国》Laird Scranton, *The Cosmological Origins of Myth and Symbol: From the Dogon and Ancient Egypt to India, Tibet, and China*. Inner Traditions (2010)

8. 《龙王：中国民间故事》Wang Ping, Teng Ge, *The Dragon Emperor: A Chinese Folktale*. Millbrook Press (2008)

9. 《古代中国的洪水神话》Mark Edward Lewis, *The Flood Myths Of Early China*. State University of New York Press (2006)

10. 《中国神话手册》Lihui Yang, Deming An, Jessica Anderson Turner, *Handbook of Chinese Mythology* (World Mythology). ABC-CLIO (2005)

11. 《中国民和土族民间故事》Coll., *Folktales of China's Minhe Mangghuer* (Languages of the World). Lincom Europa (2005)

12. 《与天地齐寿：葛洪〈神仙传〉翻译与研究》Robert Ford Campany（康儒博）, *To live as Long as Heaven and Earth: A Translation and Study of Ge Hong's Traditions of Divine Transcendents*. University of California Press (2002)

13. 《山海经研究》Edited and translated with commentary by Richard E. Strassberg, *A Chinese Bestiary: Strange Creatures from the Guideways through Mountains and Seas* [Shan hai jing]. University of California Press (2002)

14. 《中国神话》Irene Dea Collier, *Chinese Mythology*. Enslow (2001)

15. 《中国回族穆斯林的神话与民间传说》Shujiang Li, Karl W. Luckert, *Mythology and Folklore of the Hui, a Muslim Chinese People*. State University of New York Press (1994)

16. 《乌龟的形状：中国早期神话、艺术和宇宙》Sarah Allan, *The Shape of the Turtle: Myth, Art, and Cosmos in Early China*. State University of New York Press (1991)
17. 《中日神话传说》Donald A. Mackenzie, *Myths of China and Japan*. The Gresham Publishing Company Ltd (1937)
18. 《古伊朗和中国的崇拜与传说》Jehangir Cooverjee Coyajee, *Cults & Legends of Ancient Iran & China*. J. B. Karani's & Sons (1936)
19. 《各种族神话：中国与日本神话学》（第八卷）Edited by Canon John A. MacCulloch and George F. Moore, *The Mythology of All Races*. Volume VIII Chinese, by John C. Ferguson. Japanese, by Masaharu Anesaki. Marshall Jones Company, Boston, Mass., (1928)
20. 《中国与日本的神话》Donald A. Mackenzie, *Myths of China and Japan*. The Gresham Publ. (1923)
21. 《中国神话和传说》E. T. C. (Edward Theodore Chalmers) Werner, *Myths and Legends of China*. H.B.M. Consul Foochow (Retired), Barrister at law, Middle Temple. Late Member of The Chinese Government Historiographical Bureau Peking, Author of "Descriptive Sociology: Chinese" "China of the Chinese" Etc. George G. Harrap & Co. Ltd., London, Bombay, Sydney (1922)
22. 《中国童话：民间故事四十篇》Adele Marion Fielde, *Chinese Fairy Tales: Forty Stories Told by Almond-Eyed Folk*. G. P. Putnam's Sons (1912)
23. 《神话、传说、艺术和年鉴中的中国故事》William Elliot Griffis, *China's Story in Myth, Legend, Art, and Annals*. Boston and New York: Houghton Mifflin (1911)
24. 《中国寓言与民间故事》Mary Hayes Davis, Chow-Leung, *Chinese Fables and Folk Stories*. American Book Company (1908)

4.5 艺术、创意、收藏

1. 《石砚里的社会百态：清初的匠人与学者》Dorothy Ko（高彦颐）, *The Social Life of Inkstones: Artisans and Scholars in Early Qing China*. University of Washington Press (2017)
2. 《纠缠的风景：近代早期的中国和欧洲》Yue Zhuang, Andrea Riemenschnitter, *Entangled Landscapes: Early Modern China and Europe*. National University of Singapore Press (2017)
3. 《抵抗的艺术：毛泽东时代的烛光绘画》（原书题词：依惜烛光画丹青）Shelley Drake Hawks, *The Art of Resistance: Painting by Candlelight in Mao's China*. University of Washington Press (2017)
4. 《中国艺术指南》Martin J. Powers, Katherine R. Tsiang, *A Companion to Chinese Art*. Wiley-Blackwell (2016)
5. 《中国艺术文化中的变形想象》Jerome Silbergeld, Eugene Y. Wang, *The Zoomorphic Imagination in Chinese Art and Culture*. University of Hawaii Press (2016)
6. 《解构当代中国艺术：2007—2014年批判性著作与对话精选》Paul Gladston,

Deconstructing Contemporary Chinese Art: Selected Critical Writings and Conversations, 2007—2014 (Chinese Contemporary Art Series). Springer-Verlag Berlin Heidelberg (2016)

7. 《伟大的中国艺术转移：中国艺术如何来到美国》Michael St. Clair, *The Great Chinese Art Transfer: How So Much of China's Art Came to America*. Madison: Fairleigh Dickinson University Press (2016)

8. 《姬子及其艺术在当代中国》David Adam Brubaker（大卫·布鲁贝克）, Chunchen Wang（王春辰）, *Jizi and His Art in Contemporary China: Unification*-Springer Berlin Heidelberg (2015)

9. 《文化冒险：谷文达及其艺术》Yan Zhou, *Odyssey of Culture: Wenda Gu and His Art* (Chinese Contemporary Art Series).Springer-Verlag Berlin Heidelberg (2015)

10. 《把"文化"带到克利夫兰：东亚艺术、同情拨款与克利夫兰艺术博物馆（1914—1930）》（博士论文）Christa Adams, *Bringing "Culture" to Cleveland: East Asian Art, Sympathetic Appropriation, and the Cleveland Museum of Art, 1914—1930*. Ph. D. Dissertation, The University of Akron (2015)

11. 《趣味中国结：打造自己的时尚配饰》Lydia Chen, *Fun with Chinese Knotting: Making Your Own Fashion Accessories & Accents*. Tuttle Publishing (2014)

12. 《国王的屏风：明代中国的皇家艺术和权力》Craig Clunas（柯律格）, *Screen of Kings: Royal Art and Power in Ming China*. Reaktion Books (2013)

13. 《教育和文化的创意艺术：大中国视角》Patricia Shehan Campbell (auth.), Samuel Leong, Bo Wah Leung (eds.), *Creative Arts in Education and Culture: Perspectives from Greater China*. Springe (2013)

14. 《生与死：当代中国的艺术与身体》Silvia Fok, *Life and Death: Art and the Body in Contemporary China*. Intellect Books (2013)

15. 《1979—1989年中国"前卫"艺术团体》Paul Gladston, *'Avant-garde' Art Groups in China, 1979—1989*.Intellect Ltd (2013)

16. 《超越西方的艺术：伊斯兰世界，印度和东南亚，中国，日本和韩国，太平洋，非洲和美洲的艺术》Michael Kampen O'Riley, *Art Beyond the West: The Arts of the Islamic World, India and Southeast Asia, China, Japan and Korea, the Pacific, Africa, and the Americas*.Pearson Education (2013)

17. 《重要关头的身体：中国当代艺术与戏剧的实验》Jörg Huber（约格·胡伯）, Zhao Chuan（赵川）, *The Body at Stake: Experiments in Chinese Contemporary Art and Theatre*. Transcript Verlag (2013)

18. 《中国宗教艺术》Patricia Eichenbaum Karetzky, *Chinese Religious Art*. Lexington Books (2013)

19. 《土生华人之家：日常生活中的艺术与文化》Ronald G. Knapp, A. Chester Ong (photo), *The Peranakan Chinese Home: Art and Culture in Daily Life*. Tuttle Publishing (2013)

20. 《日本在中国现代艺术中的作用》(New Perspectives on Chinese Culture and Society) Joshua A. Fogel（傅佛果）, *The Role of Japan in Modern Chinese Art*. University of California Press (2013)
21. 《神和仪式：莫尔斯珍藏中国古代艺术》Virginia L. Bower, Robert L. Thorp, *Spirit and Ritual: The Morse Collection of Ancient Chinese Art*. Metropolitan Museum of Art (2012)
22. 《中国艺术》Stephen W. Bushell（卜士礼）, *Chinese Art* (Temporis collection). Parkstone International (2012)
23. 《中国家庭：灵感设计创意》Michael Freeman, *China Home: Inspirational Design Ideas*. Tuttle (2012)
24. 《现代中国艺术》Julia F. Andrews, Kuiyi Shen, *The Art of Modern China*. University of California Press (2012)
25. 《中国家具：古玩收藏指南》Karen Mazurkewich, A. Chester Ong (photo), *Chinese Furniture: A Guide to Collecting Antiques*. Tuttle Publishing (2012)
26. 《中国物品：古董、工艺品、收藏品》Ronald G. Knapp, Michael Freeman (photo), *Things Chinese: Antiques, Crafts, Collectibles*. Tuttle Publishing (2012)
27. 《1500种中国设计图案》(Dover Pictorial Archive) Pan Wuhua, *1500 Chinese Design Motifs*. Dover Publications (2012)
28. 《创意联结》Zheng Shuyang, et. al., *Creative Junctions*. National Museum of China (2011)
29. 《中国艺术及其与世界的相遇》David Clarke, *Chinese Art and Its Encounter with the World*. Hong Kong University Press (2011)
30. 《中国好设计》Clifford Pearon, *Good Design in China*. Design Media Publishing Ltd (2011)
31. 《智慧之展示：大都会艺术博物馆的中国佛教与道教雕塑》Denise Patry Leidy, Donna Strahan, *Wisdom Embodied: Chinese Buddhist and Daoist Sculpture in The Metropolitan Museum of Art*. Metropolitan Museum of Art (2011)
32. 《当代中国艺术的颠覆策略》Mary Bittner Wiseman, Liu Yuedi, *Subversive Strategies in Contemporary Chinese Art* (Philosophy of History and Culture). Brill Academic Pub (2011)
33. 《20世纪中国艺术中的全面现代性与先锋派》Gao Minglu, *Total Modernity and the Avant-garde in Twentieth-Century Chinese Art*. MIT Press (2011)
34. 《徐冰与当代中国艺术：文化与哲学反思》Bing Xu, Roger T. Ames,（安乐哲）, Hsingyuan Tsao, *Xu Bing and Contemporary Chinese Art: Cultural and Philosophical Reflections*. State University of New York Press (2011)
35. 《中国器物：古董、工艺品、收藏品》Michael Freeman, Ronald G. Knapp, *Things Chinese: Antiques, Crafts, Collectibles*. Tuttle Publishing (2011)
36. 《古代茶艺：中国古代茶师的智慧》Warren Peltier, John T. Kirby, *The Ancient Art of Tea: Wisdom from the Old Chinese Tea Masters*. Tuttle Publishing (2011)
37. 《当代中国新思虑：艺术与美学的批判声音》Jörg Huber（约格·胡伯）, Zhao Chuan

（赵川）, *A New Thoughtfulness in Contemporary China: Critical Voices in Art and Aesthetics.* Transcript Verlag (2011)

38. 《艺术的友谊：傅雷和黄宾虹》Claire Roberts, *Friendship in Art: Fou Lei and Huang Binhong.* Hong Kong University Press (2010)

39. 《中国与中亚早期的佛教艺术：第三卷，十六国时期的甘肃西秦与犍陀罗佛教艺术的相互关系》Marylin Martin Rhie, *Early Buddhist Art of China and Central Asia, Volume 3: the Western Chin in Kansu in the Sixteen Kingdoms Period and Inter-relationships with the Buddhist Art of Gandhāra.* Koninklijke Brill NV, Leiden (2010)

40. 《中国艺术与文化政策：艾未未、乌力·西克与张永和对谈》Ai Weiwei, Uli Sigg, Yung Ho Chang, *Art and Cultural Policy in China: A Conversation between Ai Weiwei, Uli Sigg and Yun Ho Chang,* moderated by Peter Pakesch. Springer Vienna (2009)

41. 《文字景观：中国早期和中世纪的石刻》Robert E. Harrist Jr., *The Landscape of Words: Stone Inscriptions in Early and Medieval China.* University of Washington Press (2008)

42. 《变体学之第三卷：论中国及其他地区艺术、科学和技术的深层时间关系》Siegfried Zielinski, Eckhard Fürlus (eds.), *Variantology 3: On Deep Time Relations of Arts, Sciences and Technologies in China and Elsewhere.* Walther König (2008)

43. 《中国：3000年艺术与文学》Jason Steuber, *China: 3000 Years of Art and Literature.* Welcome Books (2007)

44. 《中国象征主义与艺术主题：中国历代艺术象征主义综合手册》Charles Alfred Speed Williams, *Chinese Symbolism and Art Motifs: A Comprehensive Handbook on Symbolism in Chinese Art through the Ages.* Tuttle Publishing (2006)

45. 《名闻遐迩的迪尔菲尔德中国出口艺术》Amanda E. Lange, *Chinese Export Art at Historic Deerfield.* Deerfield, MA: Historic Deerfield (2005)

46. 《收藏其物品，排斥其人民：中国主题与美国艺术话语（1879—1900）》（博士论文）Lenore Metrick-Chen, *Collecting Objects, Excluding People: Chinese Subjects and the American Art Discourse, 1879—1900.* Ph. D. Dissertation, The University of Chicago (2005)

47. 《中国皇家艺术珍品的奇幻之旅》Jeannette Shambaugh Elliott, David Shambaugh（沈大伟）, *The Odyssey of China's Imperial Art Treasures.* University of Washington Press (2005)

48. 《中国：黄金时代的黎明（公元200—750年）》James C. Y. Watt, An Jiayao, Angela F. Howard, Boris I. Marshak, Su Bai, Zhao Feng, *China: Dawn of a Golden Age, 200-750 A.D.* The Metropolitan Museum of Art; Yale University Press (2004)

49. 《中世纪中国的艺术、宗教与政治：翟氏家族的敦煌洞》Qiang Ning, *Art, Religion and Politics in Medieval China: The Dunhuang Cave of the Zhai Family.* University of Hawaii Press (2004)

50. 《后现代主义与后社会主义条件：后社会主义时代的政治化艺术》Martin Jay, Ales Erjavec, *Postmodernism and the Postsocialist Condition: Politicized Art under Late Socialism* (Ahmanson-Murphy Fine Arts Book). University of California Press (2003)

51. 《中国风格》Sharon Leece, Michael Freeman (photo), *China Style*. Periplus Editions (2002)
52. 《中国艺术：现代表达》Maxwell K. Hearn, Ms. Judith E. Smith, *Chinese Art: Modern Expressions*. Metropolitan Museum of Art (2001)
53. 《两种文化之间：大都会博物馆安思远收藏19世纪末至20世纪的中国画》Wen Fong, *Between Two Cultures: Late-Nineteenth-And Twentieth-Century Chinese Paintings from the Robert H. Ellsworth Collection in the Metropolitan Museum of Art*. Museum of Art (2001)
54. 《中国与中亚早期的佛教艺术：第一卷，中国东汉、三国、西秦与中亚的大夏至鄯善》Marylin Martin Rhie, *Early Buddhist Art of China and Central Asia. Volume one, Later Han, Three Kingdoms and Western Chin in China and Bactria to Shan-shan in Central Asia* (Handbook of Oriental Studies). Brill Academic Publishers (1999)
55. 《宋元艺术》Maxwell K. Hearn and Judith G. Smith, *Arts of the Sung and Yuan*. The Metropolitan Museum of Art (1996)
56. 《中国艺术的光辉》Stephen Solovy, *Splendors of Chinese Art*. Stephen Solovy Fine Art (1996)
57. 《美国收藏中国家具的历史》（硕士论文）Juliet Yung-Yi Chou, *A History of Collecting Chinese Furniture in America*. Thesis for the Degree of Master of Arts, State University of New York (1995)
58. 《中国艺术》Hugo Munsterberg, The Arts of China. C.E. Tuttle Co. (1989)
59. 《艺术、神话与仪式：古代中国政治权威之路》K. C. Chang, *Art, Myth and Ritual: The Path to Political Authority in Ancient China*. Harvard University Press (1988)
60. 《中国艺术与建筑》Laurence Sickman and Alexander Soper, *The Art and Architecture of China*. Penguin Books (1988)
61. 《中国古代艺术：大都会艺术博物馆厄内斯特—埃里克森收藏品》Maxwell K. Hearn, *Ancient Chinese Art: The Ernest Erickson Collection in the Metropolitan Museum of Art*. Metropolitan Museum of Art (1987)
62. 《中国茶艺》John Blofeld, *The Chinese Art of Tea*. Shambala (1985)
63. 《古代中国艺术、神话与仪式：通往权力之路》Chang Kwang-chih（张光直）, *Art, Myth and Ritual: Path to Political Authorities*. Harvard University Press (1983)
64. 《上海博物馆珍品：6000年中国艺术》Rene Yvon Lefebvre d'Argence, *Treasures from the Shanghai Museum: 6,000 Years of Chinese Art*. Shanghai Museum (1983)
65. 《夜光山水：中国艺术与诗歌》Richard Lewis, *The Luminous Landscape: Chinese Art and Poetry*. Doubleday & Company, Inc. (1981)
66. 《如何认识中国艺术》Dr Sian Franco Malafarina, *How to Recognize Chinese Art*. Penguin Books (1980)
67. 《中国地毯》Adolf Hackmack, *Chinese Carpets and Rugs*. Charles E. Tuttle Company (1980)
68. 《中国艺术：佛教石窟寺庙的新研究》Akiyama Terukazu, Yonezawa Yoshiho, Alexander C. Soper (tr.), *Arts of China: Buddhist Cave Temples: New Researches*. Kodansha

International LTD.（讲谈社）(1978)

69.《中国艺术：绘画、雕塑、陶瓷、纺织品、青铜器和小艺术入门手册》Roger Eliot Fry, *Chinese Art: An Introductory Handbook to Painting, Sculpture, Ceramics, Textiles, Bronzes & Minor Arts*. B. T. Batsford Ltd (1976)

70.《中国艺术手册》Margaret Medley, *Handbook of Chinese Art*. Harper & Row Publishers (1975)

71.《中国陶器手册》Suzanne G. Valenstein, *A Handbook of Chinese Ceramics*. The Metropolitan Museum of Art (1975, 1989)

72.《中国艺术风格》William Watson, *Style in the Arts of China*. Penguin Books (1974)

73.《中国古代艺术》Maxwell Hearn, Wen Fong, *The Arts of Ancient China*. The Metropolitan Museum of Art (1973—1974)

74.《中国艺术》Michael Sullivan, *The Arts of China*. University of California Press (1973)

75.《中国艺术》Francesco Abbate, *Chinese Art*. Octopus Books (1972)

76.《中国艺术》Thomas Froncek, Hugh Honour, *The Horizon Book of the Arts of China*. American Heritage (1969)

77.《中国艺术简史》Michael Sullivan, *A Short History of Chinese Art*. University of California (1967)

78.《中国艺术理论》Yutang Lin（林语堂）, *The Chinese Theory of Art*. G. P. Putnam's Sons (1967)

79.《弗瑞尔美术馆藏中国青铜器》（第一卷：目录）Freer Gallery of Art; John Alexander Pope; Rutherford John Gettens, James Cahill, Noel Barnard, *The Freer Chinese Bronzes*. Volume I, Catalogue. Washington, Smithsonian Institution (1967)

80.《中国艺术》R. L. Hobson, Soame Jenyns, *Chinese Art*. Spring Books (1964)

81.《中国、韩国和日本艺术》Peter C. Swann, *Art of China, Korea, and Japan*. Frederick A. Praeger, Inc. (1963)

82.《中国不朽的艺术》Claude Arthaud, *Chinese Monumental Art*. Viking Press (1963)

83.《中国艺术研究与印度影响》J. Hackin, *Studies in Chinese Art and Some Indian Influences*. The India Society; London (1961)

84.《中国艺术：精神与社会》Werner Speiser, *The Art of China: Spirit and Society*. Greystone Press (1960)

85.《中国艺术概论》Michael Sullivan, *An Introduction to Chinese Art*. University of California Press (1960)

86.《中国艺术与文化》Rene Grousset, *Chinese Art and Culture*. The Orion Press (1959)

87.《中国艺术》（第一、二卷）William Willetts, *Chinese Art*. vol.1; vol.2. Penguin Books (1958)

88.《中国艺术》Judith Burling, Arthur Hart Burling, *Chinese Art*. Studio Publications; Thomas Y. Crowell (1953)

89.《沙逊中国象牙目录简介》Sydney Edward Lucas, *Catalogue of Sassoon Chinese Ivories: Prospectus*. Country Life (1950)

90.《弗瑞尔美术馆藏中国青铜器图录》Freer Gallery of Art, *A Descriptive and Illustrative*

Catalogue of Chinese Bronzes: Acquired during the Administration of John Ellerton Lodge. Washington (1946).

91. 《中国丝织艺术：中国皇袍的象征意义》Bernard Vuilleumier, Robert Fazy (Pref.), *The Art of Silk Weaving in China: Symbolism of Chinese Imperial Robes*. China Institute (1939)

92. 《烂漫的中国艺术》R. L. Hobson, Laurence Binyon, *The Romance of Chinese Art*. Garden City Publishing (1936)

93. 《恢弘的中国五千年艺术》Dagny Carter, *China Magnificent: Five Thousand Years of Chinese Art*. Reynal&Hitchcock (1936)

94. 《中国艺术概论》Arnold Silcock, *Introduction to Chinese Art*. Oxford University Press (1935)

95. 《华西协和大学博物馆图录》Pictures of Objects in the West China Union University Museum of Archaeology, 3 Volumes; 385 Photographs in 4 Albums. Some Photographs Possibly Taken by David Crockett Graham（葛维汉）. (1934)

96. 《George Eumorfopoulos藏品：中国和朝鲜的青铜器、雕塑、玉器、珠宝、杂货目录》W. Perceval Yetts, *George Eumorfopoulos Collection: Catalogue of the Chinese & Corean Bronzes, Sculpture, Jades, Jewellery and Miscellaneous Objects*. Vol 3. Ernest Benn (1932)

97. 《中国艺术收藏》American Art Association, Anderson Galleries, *Collection of Chinese Art*. New York: American Art Association, Anderson Galleries (1931)

98. 《东方艺术与文化年鉴（1924—1925）：文本》（第一卷）Arthur Waley（阿瑟·韦利）, *The Year Book of Oriental Art And Culture: 1924—1925*. Vol 1: Text. London: Ernest Benn, Limited (1925)

99. 《东方艺术与文化年鉴（1924—1925）：图片》（第二卷）Arthur Waley（阿瑟·韦利）, *The Year Book of Oriental Art And Culture: 1924—1925. Vol 2: Plates* London: Ernest Benn, Limited (1925)

100. 《蓝色中国书：当时陶器中描绘的美国早期场景和历史》Ada Walker Camehl, *The Blue-China Book: Early American Scenes and History Pictured in the Pottery of the Time*. Reprint, New York: Dover (1916, 1971)

101. 《翡翠：中国考古与宗教研究》Berthold Laufer, *Jade: A Study in Chinese Archaeology and Religion*. Chicago: Field Museum of Natural History (1912)

102. 《东方瓷器/中国杂谈》J. F. Blacker, *Chats on Oriental China*. T. Fisher Unwin (1908)

103. 《历代名瓷图谱》Yuanbian Xiang（项元汴）, Stephen W. Bushell（卜士礼, Translator）, *Chinese Porcelain: Sixteenth-Century Illustrations with Chinese Ms. Text*. Oxford: Clarendon Press (1908)

104. 《美国的中国收藏》Alice Morse Earle, *China Collecting in America*. New York: Charles Scribner's Sons (1892, 1906)

105. 《中国钱币目录：公元前7世纪到公元621年，包括大英博物馆系列》Terrien de Lacouperie, *Catalogue of Chinese Coins from the VIIth Century B.C. to A.D. 621.*

Including the Series in the British Museum. Gilbert and Rivington (1892)

106.《青花瓷》Alexander T. Hollingsworth, *Blue and White China*. The Chiswick Press (1891)

107.《弗兰克·莱斯利1876年世纪博览会插图历史记录》Frank Norton (Ed.), Frank Leslie, *Frank Leslie's Illustrated Historical Register of the Centennial Exposition 1876*. New York: Frank Leslie's Publishing House (1877)

108.《世纪博览会插图史》James McGabe, *The Illustrated History of the Centennial Exhibition*. Philadelphia: The National Publishing Company (1876)

109.《中国收藏家袖珍手册》Mrs. Bury Palliser, *The China Collector's Pocket Companion*. Sampson, Low, Marston (1874)

110.《中国纹样集锦》Owen Jones, *Examples of Chinese Ornament: Selected from Objects in the South Kensington Museum and other Collections*. S. & T. Gilbert, London (1867)

111.《邓恩先生关于中国制度和习俗的收藏品一瞥》E. C. Wines, *A Peep at China in Mr. Dunn's Chinese Collection with Miscellaneous Notices Relating to the Institutions and Customs of the Chinese, and Our Commercial Intercourse with them*. Philadelphia (1839)

4.6 绘画、书法、摄影、服饰

1.《中国消费者与时装市场》Yingjiao Xu, Ting Chi, Jin Su, *Chinese Consumers and the Fashion Market* (Springer Series in Fashion Business). Springer Singapore (2018)

2.《漫画中国：代表共同立场（1890—1945）》Wendy Gan, *Comic China: Representing Common Ground, 1890—1945*. Temple University Press (2018)

3.《中国漫画艺术》John A. Lent, Xu Ying, *Comics Art in China*. University Press of Mississippi (2017)

4.《初学毛笔：发现中国传统国画艺术》(How to Draw & Paint 343) Monika Cilmi, *Beginning Chinese Brush: Discover the Art of Traditional Chinese Brush Painting*. Walter Foster Publishing (2017)

5.《毛笔精神：中国毛笔画技法——朴素、精神、个人之旅》Sungsook Hong Setton, *The Spirit of the Brush: Chinese Brush Painting Techniques: Simplicity, Spirit, and Personal Journey*. Rockport Publishers (2017)

6.《广州工厂图像（1760—1822）：艺术阅读史》Paul A. Van Dyke, Maria Kar-wing Mok, *Images of the Canton Factories 1760—1822: Reading History in Art*. Hong Kong: Hong Kong University Press (2016)

7.《聚焦：中国摄影史》Wu Hung（巫鸿）, *Zooming In: Histories of Photography in China*. Reaktion Books (2016)

8.《中国水彩画之旅》Lian Quan Zhen, *Chinese Watercolor Journeys with Lian Quan Zhen*. F. W. Media: North Light Books (2015)

9.《褪色的记忆，消逝的生命：来自中国青海的蒙古照片》Limusishiden, Jugui, Kelly

Ward, and Ck Stuart, *Fading Memories, Faded Lives: Mongghul (Tu) Photographs from Qinghai China*. Asian Highlands Perspectives (2014)

10. 《中国反貌：时尚、表演与种族》Sean Metzger, *Chinese Looks: Fashion, Performance, Race*. Indiana University Press (2014)
11. 《中国山水画：水彩技法》Lian Quan Zhen, *Chinese Landscape Painting Techniques for Watercolor*. North Light Bks (2013)
12. 《摄影与中国》Claire Roberts, *Photography and China*. Reaktion Books (2013)
13. 《当代中国书法》Zhang Gongzhe（张公者）, *Contemporary Chinese Calligraphy*. China Intercontinental Press（五洲传播出版社）(2013)
14. 《中国文人论画：从苏轼到董其昌》Susan Bush, *The Chinese Literati on Painting: Su Shih (1037—1101) to Tung Ch'i-ch'ang (1555—1636)*. Hong Kong University Press (2012)
15. 《书中的艺术：晚明绘画手册与休闲生活》J. P. Park, *Art by the Book: Painting Manuals and the Leisure Life in Late Ming China* (China Program Books). University of Washington Press (2012)
16. 《中国水墨画：传统与现代技法完整教程》(Dover Art Instruction) Jane Evans, *Chinese Brush Painting: A Complete Course in Traditional and Modern Techniques*. Dover Publications (2012)
17. 《笔法之道：中日绘画技术》Fritz van Briessen, *The Way of the Brush: Painting Techniques of China and Japan*. Tuttle Publishing (2011)
18. 《中国书法、印刷和图书馆工作的历史与文化遗产》Jan Bos, *The History and Cultural Heritage of Chinese Calligraphy, Printing and Library Work*. IFLA Publications (2010)
19. 《数字化中国书画的计算方法》Songhua Xu, Francis C. M. Lau, Yunhe Pan, *A Computational Approach to Digital Chinese Painting and Calligraphy*. Springer-Verlag Berlin Heidelberg (2009)
20. 《中国毛笔画艺术：水墨、纸张、灵感》Caroline Self, Susan Self, *The Art of Chinese Brush Painting: Ink, Paper, Inspiration*. Tuttle Publishing (2009)
21. 《中国服装变迁：时尚、历史、民族》Antonia Finnane, *Changing Clothes in China: Fashion, History, Nation*. Columbia University Press (2008)
22. 《从清代至今的中国服装》Valery Garrett, *Chinese Dress From the Qing Dynasty to the Present*. Tuttle Publishing (2008)
23. 《道德之镜：中国叙事性绘画与儒家意识形态》Julia K. Murray, *Mirror of Morality: Chinese Narrative Illustration and Confucian Ideology*. University of Hawai'i Press (2007)
24. 《中国毛笔画：传统艺术入门》Caroline Self, Susan Self, *Chinese Brush Painting: A Hands-On Introduction to the Traditional Art*. Tuttle Publishing (2007)
25. 《纹饰与人物：古代中国的装饰、社会与自我》Martin J. Powers（包华石）, *Pattern and Person: Ornament, Society, and Self in Classical China* (Harvard East Asian Monographs). Harvard University Asia Center (2006)
26. 《模式与人：古典中国的装饰、社会与自我》Martin J. Powers, *Pattern and Person:*

Ornament, Society, and Self in Classical China. Harvard University Asia Center (2006)

27. 《当代中国社会的书法与权力》Yuehping Yen, *Calligraphy and Power in Contemporary Chinese Society* (Anthropology in Asia).RoutledgeCurzon (2005)

28. 《中国画之优雅：装饰画》Priscilla Hauser, *China Painting Elegance: Decorative Painting*. Plaid (2004)

29. 《中国服饰》Hua Mei（华梅）, *Chinese Clothing*. China Intercontinental Press (2004)

30. 《中国书法》Chen Tingyou（陈廷祐）, *Chinese Calligraphy*. China Intercontinental Press (2003)

31. 《两种文化之间：大都会博物馆安思远收藏19世纪末至20世纪的中国画》Wen Fong, *Between Two Cultures: Late-Nineteenth-And Twentieth-Century Chinese Paintings from the Robert H. Ellsworth Collection in the Metropolitan Museum of Art*. Museum of Art (2001)

32. 《中国画的本真性》Judith G. Smith and Wen C. Fong, *Issues of Authenticity in Chinese Painting*. The Metropolitan Museum of Art (1999)

33. 《明代的图像与视觉性》Craig Clunas（柯律格）, *Pictures and Visuality in Early Modern China* (Picturing History). Reaktion Books (1997)

34. 《中华人民共和国的画家和政治》Julia F. Andrews（安雅兰）, *Painters and Politics in the People's Republic of China, 1949—1979*. University of California Press (1995)

35. 《中国书写系统的起源与早期发展》William G. Boltz, *The Origin and Early Development of the Chinese Writing System*. American Oriental Society (1994)

36. 《中国贸易的装饰艺术：绘画、家具和异国情调》Carl L. Crossman, *The Decorative Arts of the China Trade: Paintings, Furnishings, and Exotic Curiosities*. Woodbridge, Suffolk: Antique Collectors' Club (1991)

37. 《权力刷：现代政治与中国书法艺术》Richard Curt Kraus, *Brushes with Power: Modern Politics and the Chinese Art of Calligraphy*. University of California Press (1991)

38. 《沉思古人：中国早期肖像画中的审美与社会问题》Audrey Spiro, *Contemplating the Ancients: Aesthetic and Social Issues in Early Chinese Portraiture*. University of California Press (1990)

39. 《中国水墨绘画技法》Jean Long, *Chinese Ink Painting: Techniques In Shades Of Black*. Blandford (1984)

40. 《桃花泉：中国画中的园林与花卉》Richard M. Barnhart, *Peach Blossom Spring: Gardens and Flowers in Chinese Paintings*. Metropolitan Museum of Art (1983)

41. 《中国隋唐山水画》Michael Sullivan, *Chinese Landscape Painting in the Sui and T'ang dynasties*. University of California Press, Berkeley (1980)

42. 《离岸临别：明朝中早期的国画（1368—1580）》James Francis Cahill, *Parting at the Shore: Chinese Painting of the Early and Middle Ming Dynasty, 1368—1580* (A History of Later Chinese Painting, 1279—1950, V. 2). Weatherhill (1978)

43. 《河外山丘：元代的国画（1279—1368）》James Francis Cahill, *Hills Beyond a River: Chinese Painting of the Yuan Dynasty, 1279—1368* (History of Later Chinese Painting,

1279—1950 vol. 1). Weatherhill (1976)

44. 《中国贸易：出口绘画、家具、银器及其他物品》Carl L. Crossman, *The China Trade: Export Paintings, Furniture, Silver & Other Objects*. Princeton N.J Pyne Press (1972)

45. 《中国山水画艺术》Anil de Silva-Vigier, *The Art of Chinese Landscape Painting*. Crown Publishers (1967)

46. 《中国人论绘画艺术》Osvald Siren, *The Chinese on the Art of Painting*. Schocken Books (1963)

47. 《中国绘画之道》Mai-mai Sze, *The Way of Chinese Painting*. Vintage Books (1959)

48. 《斯坦因爵士从敦煌回收的绘画目录》Arthur Waley（阿瑟·韦利）, *A Catalogue of Paintings Recovered From Tun Huang by Sir Aurel Stein*. Preserved in the Sub-Department of Oriental Prints and Drawings in the British Museum, and in the Museum of Central Asian Antiquites, Delhi. British Museum, Government of India (1931)

49. 《中国画研究概论》Arthur Waley（阿瑟·韦利）, *Introduction to the Study of Chinese Painting*. London: Ernest Benn Ltd. (1923)

50. 《千佛洞：中国西部边境敦煌石窟寺所获之古代佛教绘画》Marc Aurel Stein, *The Thousand Buddhas: Ancient Buddhist Paintings from the Cave-temples of Tun-Huang on the Western Frontier of China*. London: Bernard Quaritch, Ltd (1921)

51. 《中国画：硬瓷装饰中业余爱好者实用手册》M. Louise McLaughlin, *China Painting: A Practical Manual for the Use of Amateurs in the Decoration of Hard Porcelain*. Cincinnati: The Robert Clarke Company (1911)

52. 《中国绘画实用提示》A. B. (Albert B.) Cobden, *Practical Hints on China Painting*. Press of Comegys & Bro. (1890)

53. 《中国绘画》Florence Lewis, *China Painting*. London (etc.) : Cassell & Co., Ltd. (1883)

54. 《中国衣冠风俗图解》William Alexander, *Picturesque Representations of the Dress and Manners of the Chinese*. London: John Murray (1814)

55. 《中国服装、艺术、制造业》Translated from the French by Jean-Baptiste Joseph Breton, *China: Its Costume, Arts, Manufactures, &c*. Edited principally from the originals in the cabinet of the late M. Bertin; with observations explanatory, historical, and literary. London, J. J. Stockdale (1812)

56. 《中国服饰》William Alexander, *The Costume of China*. London: Published by William Miller, Albemarle Street (1805)

57. 《中国服饰》George Henry Mason, *The Costume of China*. London: Printed for W. Miller (1800)

4.7 音乐、舞蹈

1. 《革命的身体：中国舞蹈与社会主义遗产》Emily Wilcox, *Revolutionary Bodies: Chinese Dance and the Socialist Legacy*. University of California Press (2018)

2. 《我没有赚一百万：爵士乐如何来到中国》Whitey Smith, with a New Foreword by

Andrew Field, *I Didn't Make A Million: How Jazz Came to China*. Earnshaw Books (2018)

3. 《中国与西方：音乐、表现与接受》Michael Saffle, Hon-Lun Yang, *China and the West: Music, Representation, and Reception*. University of Michigan Press (2017)

4. 《广场舞：公共空间中舞蹈的民族志研究》（硕士论文）Qianni Wang, *Guangchang Wu: An Ethnographic Study of Dance in Public Spaces*. Thesis for the Degree of Master of Arts, The Chinese University of Hong Kong (2015)

5. 《不敬的时代：中国笑声新史》Christopher Rea, *The Age of Irreverence: A New History of Laughter in China*. University of California Press (2015)

6. 《20世纪的中国音乐创作：阿炳的音乐与意义》Jonathan P. J. Stock, *Musical Creativity in Twentieth Century China: Abing, His Music, and Its Changing Meanings*. University of Rochester Press (2014)

7. 《音乐、宇宙学和中国早期的和谐政治》Erica Fox Brindley, *Music, Cosmology, and the Politics of Harmony in Early China*. State Univ of New York Pr (2012)

8. 《名叫忠梅的女孩：一个中国舞者及其如何实现梦想的真实故事》Maarten Jacobus Laurens Nierop, Giselher Wirsing, *A girl Named Faithful Plum: the True Story of a Dancer from China and How She Achieved Her Dream*. Random House Children's Books: Lann (2011)

9. 《山歌：中国明代情歌》Oki Yasushi and Paolo Santangelo Shange, *the Mountain Songs: Love Songs in Ming China*. Brill (2011)

10. 《打口中国：全球化、城市青年与流行音乐》Jeroen de Kloet, *China with a Cut: Globalisation, Urban Youth and Popular Music*. Amsterdam University Press (2010)

11. 《华南器乐丝竹：民族精神、理论与实践》Alan R. Thrasher, *Sizhu: Instrumental Music of South China: Ethos, Theory and Practice*. Brill Academic Publishers (2008)

12. 《中国音乐：体验音乐，表达文化》(Global Music Series) Frederick Lau, *Music in China: Experiencing Music, Expressing Culture*. Oxford University Press (2008)

13. 《中国新音乐与香港大学刘靖之作品集》Helen Woo, *New Music in China and The C.C. Liu Collection at the University of Hong Kong*. Hong Kong University Press (2005)

14. 《红色狂想曲：西方古典音乐的中国化历程》Sheila Melvin & Jindong Cai, *Rhapsody in Red: How Classical Music Became Chinese*. Algora Publishing (2004)

15. 《黄脸种：1850年代至1920年代美国流行音乐和表演中创造的中国人》Krystyn R. Moon, *Yellowface: Creating the Chinese in American Popular Music and Performance, 1850s—1920s*. Rutgers University Press (2004)

16. 《中国新声音：流行音乐、民族、性别与政治（1978—1997）》Nimrod Baranovitch（尼曼）, *China's New Voices: Popular Music, Ethnicity, Gender, and Politics, 1978—1997*. University of California Press (2003)

17. 《黄色音乐：中国爵士时代的媒体文化及殖民时代的现代性》（中译本名《留声中国：摩登音乐文化的形成》) Andrew F. Jones, *Yellow Music: Media Culture and Colonial*

Modernity in the Chinese Jazz Age. Duke University Press Books (2001)

18. 《历史的回声：现代中国纳西族音乐》Helen Rees, *Echoes of History: Naxi Music in Modern China*. Oxford University Press (2000)

19. 《上海的丝竹音乐：江南丝竹合奏传统》J. Lawrence Witzleben, *Silk and Bamboo Music in Shanghai: The Jiangnan Sizhu Instrumental Ensemble Tradition*. Kent State University Press (1995)

20. 《悬浮的音乐：中国青铜时代文化中的编钟》Lothar von Falkenhausen, *Suspended Music: Chime-Bells in the Culture of Bronze Age China*. University of California Press (1993)

21. 《金山歌集：来自旧金山唐人街的粤语韵律》Marlon K. Hom, *Songs of Gold Mountain: Cantonese Rhymes from San Francisco Chinatown*. University of California Press (1992)

22. 《中国的钢琴与政治：中产阶级的野心与西方音乐的斗争》Richard Curt Kraus, *Pianos and Politics in China: Middle-Class Ambitions and the Struggle over Western Music*. Oxford University Press (1989)

23. 《中国经典中的音乐参考文献》Walter A. Kaufmann, *Musical References in the Chinese Classics* (Detroit Monographs in Musicology 5). Harmonie Park Press (1976)

24. 《中国琵琶的传说：秦代思想随笔（中国古琴研究）》R.H.Van Gulik（高罗佩）, *The Lore of the Chinese Lute: An Essay in the Ideology of the Ch'in*. Sophia University (1968)

25. 《音乐在中国文化中的特征与作用》Bliss Wiant, *The Character and Function of Music in Chinese Culture*. Nashville: McQuiddy Printing Co. (1946)

26. 《中国音乐》Jules A. Van Aalst（阿理嗣）, *Chinese Music*. Shanghai: The Statical Department of the Inspectorate General of Customs (1884)

5. 中国语言与文字

5.1 语言

1. 《劳特利奇汉语教学手册》(Routledge Handbooks) Chris Shei, Monica E. McLellan Zikpi, Der-Lin Chao, *The Routledge Handbook of Chinese Language Teaching*. Routledge (2020)
2. 《从西到东的语法：欧洲和中国传统中的语言意义考察》(The M. A. K. Halliday Library Functional Linguistics Series) Edward McDonald, *Grammar West To East: The Investigation of Linguistic Meaning in European and Chinese Traditions*. Springer (2020)
3. 《从社会认知角度理解中国多语学者的英语写作和出版经验》Congjun Mu, *Understanding Chinese Multilingual Scholars' Experiences of Writing and Publishing in English: A Social-Cognitive Perspective*. Palgrave Macmillan (2020)
4. 《跨学科视角下的亚洲中文写作体系》Yu Li, *The Chinese Writing System in Asia: An Interdisciplinary Perspective*. Routledge (2020)
5. 《作为多语种通用语的汉英互动：语境、实践与感知》Weihua Zhu, *Interaction in Mandarin Chinese and English as a Multilingua Franca: Context, Practice, and Perception*. Routledge (2019)
6. 《中国崛起中的语言意识形态与秩序》Minglang Zhou（周明朗）, *Language Ideology and Order in Rising China*. Springer Singapore, Palgrave Macmillan (2019)
7. 《藏语、缅甸语和汉语的历史音韵学》Nathan W. Hill, *The Historical Phonology of Tibetan, Burmese, and Chinese*. Cambridge University Press (2019)
8. 《通过经典掌握现代高级汉语》Shu-Ling Wu, Haiwang Yuan, *Mastering Advanced Modern Chinese through the Classics*. Routledge (2019)
9. 《阅读写作：高级汉语教科书》Zu-yan Chen, *Reading to Write: A Textbook of Advanced Chinese*. Routledge (2019)
10. 《劳特利奇汉语话语分析手册》(Routledge International Handbooks) Chris Shei (ed.), *The Routledge Handbook of Chinese Discourse Analysis*. Routledge (2019)
11. 《普通话和粤语的焦点表现：比较的视角》Peppina Po Lee, *Focus Manifestation in Mandarin Chinese and Cantonese: A Comparative Perspective*. Routledge (2019)
12. 《汉语韵律句法学：历史与变迁》(Chinese linguistics) Feng Shengli, *Prosodic Syntax in Chinese: History and Changes*. Routledge (2019)
13. 《汉语学习的计算指令与语料库方法》(Chinese Language Learning Sciences) Xiaofei Lu, Berlin Chen, *Computational and Corpus Approaches to Chinese Language Learning*. Springer (2019)

14. 《中国历史语言学中的体与情态新论》(Frontiers in Chinese Linguistics 5) Barbara Meisterernst, *New Perspectives on Aspect and Modality in Chinese Historical Linguistics*. Springer Singapore (2019)
15. 《认知语言学与汉语研究》(Human Cognitive Processing, 67) Dingfang Shu, Hui Zhang, Lifei Zhang, *Cognitive Linguistics and the Study of Chinese*. John Benjamins Publishing Company (2019)
16. 《汉语讲习者的英文读写能力指导》Barry Lee Reynolds, Mark Feng Teng（滕锋）(eds.), *English Literacy Instruction for Chinese Speakers*. Palgrave MacMillan (2019)
17. 《汉字学：汉字的借用与改编》(Language Writing and Literary Culture in the Sinographic Cosmopolis) Zev Joseph Handel, *Sinography: The Borrowing and Adaptation of the Chinese Script*. Brill (2019)
18. 《汉语课堂中的多语种与音译》(Palgrave Studies in Teaching and Learning Chinese) Danping Wang, *Multilingualism and Translanguaging in Chinese Language Classrooms*. Springer International Publishing, Palgrave Macmillan (2019)
19. 《科技强化的对外汉语教学》(Routledge Chinese Language Pedagogy) Amber Navarre, *Technology-Enhanced Teaching and Learning of Chinese as a Foreign Language*. Routledge (2019)
20. 《语法中的显著性与局部性：Wh疑问句与反身代词的句法和语义》(Routledge Studies in Chinese Linguistics) Jianhua Hu（胡建华）, *Prominence and Locality in Grammar: The Syntax and Semantics of Wh-Questions and Reflexives*. Routledge (2019)
21. 《普通话外来语》(Routledge Studies in Chinese Linguistics) Tae Eun Kim, *Mandarin Loanwords*. Routledge (2019)
22. 《韵律研究：挑战与展望》(Routledge studies in Chinese linguistics) Youyong Qian, Hongming Zhang, *Prosodic Studies: Challenges and Prospects*. Routledge (2019)
23. 《当前汉语语言与话语研究：全球语境与多元视角》(Studies in Chinese language and discourse (SCLD) volume 10) Yun Xiao, Linda T. H. Tsung, *Current Studies in Chinese Language and Discourse: Global Context and Diverse Perspectives*. John Benjamins Publishing Company (2019)
24. 《普通话的受事—主语结构：句法、语义、话语》(Studies in Chinese language and discourse (SCLD), 12) Xiaoling He, *Patient-Subject Constructions in Mandarin Chinese: Syntax, Semantics, Discourse*. John Benjamins Publishing Company (2019)
25. 《中国双语教育与少数民族语言维护：学校在拯救彝语中的作用》(Multilingual Education 31) Lubei Zhang, Linda Tsung, *Bilingual Education and Minority Language Maintenance in China: The Role of Schools in Saving the Yi Language*. Springer International Publishing (2019)
26. 《词汇本体语义学》(Routledge Studies in Chinese Linguistics) Yulin Yuan, Guoxiang Wu, *Lexical Ontological Semantics*. Routledge (2019)

27. 《汉语运动事件编码的认知功能研究》(Studies in Chinese Language and Discourse (SCLD) 11) Jingxia Lin, *Encoding Motion Events in Mandarin Chinese: A Cognitive Functional Study*. John Benjamins (2019)

28. 《汉语文化词典：500谚语、成语和格言》Liwei Jiao, *A Cultural Dictionary of the Chinese Language: 500 Proverbs, Idioms and Maxims*. Routledge: Taylor & Francis Group (2019)

29. 《当代汉语专题词典》Liwei Jiao, Yan Yang, Wei Liu, *A Thematic Dictionary of Contemporary Chinese*. Routledge (2019)

30. 《专业汉语：理论、教学应用与实践》(Chinese Language Learning Sciences) Hongyin Tao, Howard Hao-Jan Chen, *Chinese for Specific and Professional Purposes: Theory, Pedagogical Applications, and Practices*. Springer Singapore (2019)

31. 《计算机支持的汉语第二语言协作学习：超越头脑风暴》(Chinese Language Learning Sciences) Yun Wen, *Computer-Supported Collaborative Chinese Second Language Learning: Beyond Brainstorming*. Springer Singapore (2019)

32. 《中国的语文学转向：18世纪的学者、考据学和道家》Ori Sela（石敖睿），*China's Philological Turn: Scholars, Textualism, and the DAO in the Eighteenth Century*. Columbia University Press (2018)

33. 《学习使用汉语动态助词》Jian Kang Loar, *Learn to Use Chinese Aspect Particles*. Routledge (2018)

34. 《〈马氏文通〉：附汉英词汇原文》Muhammad Wolfgang G. A. Schmidt, *Mister Ma's Grammar Guide to Literary Chinese: The Original Chinese Text of the Mashi Wentong with Chinese-English Character and Word Glossaries*. Disserta Verlag (2018)

35. 《汉语普通话的强化和情态必要性》(Routledge Studies in Chinese Linguistics) Jiun-Shiung Wu, *Intensification and Modal Necessity in Mandarin Chinese*. Routledge (2018)

36. 《写作系统、阅读过程和跨语言影响：来自中文、日文和韩文的反思》(Bilingual Processing and Acquisition 7) Hye K. Pae (ed.), *Writing Systems, Reading Processes, and Cross-Linguistic Influences: Reflections from the Chinese, Japanese and Korean Languages*. John Benjamins (2018)

37. 《中文问题的语义接口方法》(Routledge Studies in Chinese Linguistics) Hongyuan Dong, *Semantics of Chinese Questions: An Interface Approach*. Routledge (2018)

38. 《现代汉语词类：系统研究》Guo Rui, *Modern Chinese Parts of Speech: Systems Research* (Chinese Linguistics). Routledge (2018)

39. 《现代汉语词汇学》Ge Benyi, *Modern Chinese Lexicology* (China Perspectives). Routledge (2018)

40. 《学校汉语教学》Robyn Moloney, Hui Ling Xu, *Teaching and Learning Chinese in Schools* (Palgrave Studies in Teaching and Learning Chinese). Springer International Publishing:

Palgrave Pivot (2018)

41. 《作为中国早期身体实践的语言：中国语法学》Jane Geaney, *Language as Bodily Practice in Early China: A Chinese Grammatology* (SUNY series in Chinese philosophy and culture). State University of New York Press (2018)

42. 《汉语本土化：通过服务学习培养教师》Michael Singh, Thị Hồng Nhung Nguyễn, *Localising Chinese: Educating Teachers through Service-Learning* (Palgrave Studies in Teaching and Learning Chinese). Palgrave Macmillan (2018)

43. 《语言哲学、汉语、中国哲学：建设性的接触》Bo Mou (ed.), *Philosophy of Language, Chinese Language, Chinese Philosophy: Constructive Engagement* (Philosophy of History and Culture 37). Brill (2018)

44. 《对外汉语教学手册》Bo Hu, *Manual for Teaching and Learning Chinese as a Foreign Language* (Routledge Chinese language pedagogy). Routledge (2018)

45. 《划分与数量：汉语中的量词、量度和分词结构》Jing Jin, *Partition and Quantity: Numerical Classifiers, Measurement, and Partitive Constructions in Mandarin Chinese* (Routledge studies in Chinese linguistics). Routledge (2018)

46. 《汉语书面叙事话语基础》Wendan Li, *Grounding in Chinese Written Narrative Discourse* (Utrecht Studies in Language and Communication). Brill Rodopi (2018)

47. 《汉语语境下的第二语言演说行为研究与教学》Cynthia Lee, *Researching and Teaching Second Language Speech Acts in the Chinese Context*. Springer Singapore (2018)

48. 《中国外语学习焦虑：英语教学中的理论与应用》Deyuan He, *Foreign Language Learning Anxiety in China: Theories and Applications in English Language Teaching*. Springer Singapore (2018)

49. 《后共产主义时代的语言规划：东欧、欧亚和中国新秩序下的语言控制斗争》Ernest Andrews, (eds.), *Language Planning in the Post-Communist Era: The Struggles for Language Control in the New Order in Eastern Europe, Eurasia and China*. Palgrave Macmillan (2018)

50. 《词汇增长与搭配学习：基于语料库的中国英语学习者横断面研究》Haiyan Men, *Vocabulary Increase and Collocation Learning: A Corpus-Based Cross-sectional Study of Chinese Learners of English*. Springer Singapore (2018)

51. 《让我们说汉语：1001个现实短语和成语》Wendy Abraham, *Let's Talk Mandarin Chinese: 1,001 Real-life Phrases and Idioms*. Fall River Press (2018)

52. 《中国大学学术英语》Xiaofei Rao, *University English for Academic Purposes in China*. Springer Singapore (2018)

53. 《傻瓜汉语》（第3版）Wendy Abraham, *Chinese for Dummies*. 3rd Edition. For Dummies (2018)

54. 《连读变调的历时性：来自闽南语的证据》Qing Lin, *The Diachrony of Tone Sandhi: Evidence from Southern Min Chinese* (Frontiers in Chinese linguistics 6). Springer (2018)

70. 《文言基础读本：文本、词汇与分析》Naiying Yuan（袁乃瑛）, Haitao Tang（唐海涛）, James Geiss（盖杰民）, *Classical Chinese: A Basic Reader. Texts, Glossaries, Analyses*. Princeton University Press (2017)

71. 《中国魅力的语言和图像：解密过去的信仰体系》Alex Chengyu Fang, François Thierry (eds.), *The Language and Iconography of Chinese Charms: Deciphering a Past Belief System*. Springer Singapore (2016)

72. 《孟子与亚里士多德修辞的深层生态学：身体指南》Douglas Robinson, *The Deep Ecology of Rhetoric in Mencius and Aristotle: A Somatic Guide* (SUNY series in Chinese philosophy and culture). State University of New York Press (2016)

73. 《欧洲早期文本中的汉语》Dinu Luca, *The Chinese Language in European Texts: The Early Period*. Palgrave Macmillan (2016)

74. 《美国华文教育》Jiening Ruan, Jie Zhang, Cynthia B. Leung (eds.), *Chinese Language Education in the United States*. Springer International Publishing (2016)

75. 《来自汉语的两千壮族谚语，附注释和英汉翻译》Zhou Yanxian, *Two Thousand Zhuang Proverbs from China with Annotations and Chinese and English Translation* (International Folkloristics). Peter Lang Inc. (2016)

76. 《远东生活华语》（第一册）Yeh Teh-Ming（叶德明）, *Far East Everyday Chinese. Book 1: Traditional Character*. The Far East Book Co., Ltd (2016)

77. 《整合中国语言研究与语言教学》Hongyin Tao (ed.), *Integrating Chinese Linguistic Research and Language Teaching and Learning* (Studies in Chinese Language and Discourse 7). John Benjamins Publishing Company (2016)

78. 《古汉语语法新探》Barbara Meisterernst, *New Aspects of Classical Chinese Grammar* (Asien-Und Afrika-studien Der Humboldt-universitat Zu Berlin). Harrassowitz Verlag (2016)

79. 《美国K-16汉语学习者汉语教材中的文化表征：汉语教育中的文化素养考察》（博士论文）Ying Li, *Representations of Culture in Chinese Language Textbooks for K-16 Chinese Language Learners in the United States: Examining Cultural Literacy in Chinese Language Education*. Ph. D. Dissertation, University of Texas at San Antonio (2016)

80. 《中国人英语学习的语料库搭配研究》(China Perspectives) Yuanwen Lu, *A Corpus Study of Collocation in Chinese Learner English*. Routledge (2016)

81. 《基于认知的汉语语法研究》(Routledge Studies in Chinese Linguistics) Yulin Yuan, *Cognition-Based Studies on Chinese Grammar*. Routledge (2016)

82. 《大中华区的语言作用与企业沟通：从学术到从业者的观点》Patrick P.K. Ng, Cindy S.B. Ngai (eds.), *Role of Language and Corporate Communication in Greater China: From Academic to Practitioner Perspectives*. Springer-Verlag Berlin Heidelberg (2015)

83. 《中国语言的空间与量化》Dan Xu, Jingqi Fu (eds.), *Space and Quantification in Languages of China*. Springer International Publishing (2015)

84. 《中国现代语法研究史》Peter Peverelli, *The History of Modern Chinese Grammar Studies*. Springer-Verlag Berlin Heidelberg (2015)

85. 《中国语言规划》Li Yuming（李玉明）, *Language Planning in China*. De Gruyter Mouton (2015)

86. 《中国多种语的语言态度与认同：语言民族志》Sihua Liang, *Language Attitudes and Identities in Multilingual China: A Linguistic Ethnography*. Springer International Publishing (2015)

87. 《汉语动词和语法要点》Julian K Wheatley, *Chinese Verbs & Essentials of Grammar*. McGraw-Hill Education (2015)

88. 《理解中文：综合语言导论》Chris Shei, *Understanding the Chinese Language: A Comprehensive Linguistic Introduction*. Taylor and Francis (2014)

89. 《古汉语重构》William H. Baxter, Laurent Sagart, *Old Chinese: A New Reconstruction*. Oxford University Press (2014)

90. 《中国语言学手册》Cheng-Teh James Huang, Yen-hui Audrey Li, Andrew Simpson, *The Handbook of Chinese Linguistics*. Wiley Blackwell (2014)

91. 《中国语言状况：第二卷》Li Yuming, Zhou Qingsheng, Guo Xi, Zhou Hongbo, Li Wei, *The Language Situation in China*, Volume 2. De Gruyter Mouton (2014)

92. 《汉代汉语的时与体》Barbara Meisterernst, *Tense and Aspect in Han Period Chinese* (Trends in Linguistics. Studies and Monographs). De Gruyter Mouton (2014)

93. 《英语和汉语关于悲伤的表述：语料库语言学对比语义分析》Ruihua Zhang, *Sadness Expressions in English and Chinese: Corpus Linguistic Contrastive Semantic Analysis*. Bloomsbury Academic (2014)

94. 《英语教育与评估：香港及中国内地最新发展》David Coniam (eds.), *English Language Education and Assessment: Recent Developments in Hong Kong and the Chinese Mainland*. Springer-Verlag Singapur (2014)

95. 《现代汉语实用语法练习》Claudia Ross, Jing-Heng Sheng Ma, Baozhang He, Pei-Chia Chen, *Modern Mandarin Chinese Grammar Workbook* (Modern Grammar Workbooks). Routledge (2014)

96. 《中国语言史》Hongyuan Dong, *A History of the Chinese Language*. Routledge (2014)

97. 《分裂的语言？日本、中国与斯拉夫世界的双语制、翻译和现代性的兴起》Jadranka Gvozdanović, Darja Miyajima (eds.), *Divided Languages? Diglossia, Translation and the Rise of Modernity in Japan, China, and the Slavic World*. Springer International Publishing (2014)

98. 《跨语言视角下的汉语句法》Wei-Tien Dylan Tsai, Audrey Li, Andrew Simpson (eds.), *Chinese Syntax in a Cross-Linguistic Perspective* (Oxford Studies in Comparative Syntax). Oxford University Press (2014)

99. 《思维的语言塑造：语言对中西思维影响研究》Alfred H. Bloom, *The Linguistic Shaping of Thought: A Study in the Impact of Language on Thinking in China and the West.*

Lawrence Erlbaum Associates (2014)

100. 《理解汉语：综合语言学导论》Chris Shei, *Understanding the Chinese Language: A Comprehensive Linguistic Introduction* (English and Chinese Edition). Routledge (2014)

101. 《反思东亚语言、白话和读写能力（1000—1919）》Benjamin A. Elman（艾尔曼）, *Rethinking East Asian Languages, Vernaculars, and Literacies, 1000—1919*. Brill (2014)

102. 《更多中文俚语：汉语术语和短语趣味视觉指南》Mike Ellis, *More Chinese Slanguage: A Fun Visual Guide to Mandarin Terms and Phrases*. Gibbs Smith (2014)

103. 《中国西南柔勒仡佬语语法》Xia Li, Jinfang Li（李锦芳）, Yongxian Luo, *A Grammar of Zoulei, Southwest China*. Peter Lang (2014)

104. 《文化纵横观：高级中文多媒体课程》Kunshan Carolyn Lee, Hsin-hsin Liang, Liwei Jiao, Julian K Wheatley, *The Routledge Advanced Chinese Multimedia Course: Crossing Cultural Boundaries*. Routledge (2014)

105. 《提升汉语能力：避免常见错误的策略》(Speed Up Your Language Skills) Shin Yong Robson, *Speed Up Your Chinese: Strategies to Avoid Common Errors*. Routledge (2013)

106. 《汉语剖析：节奏、隐喻与政治》Perry Link（林培瑞）, *An Anatomy of Chinese: Rhythm, Metaphor, Politics*. Harvard University Press (2013)

107. 《汉语与纳西族语言变化研究》Jung-yao Lu, *An Investigation of Various Linguistic Changes in Chinese and Naxi*. Cambridge Scholars Publishing (2013)

108. 《中国语言叙事：文化、认知和情感》Allyssa McCabe, Chien-ju Chang, *Chinese Language Narration: Culture, Cognition, and Emotion*. John Benjamins Publishing Company (2013)

109. 《中国少数民族学生的语言、文化与认同：以回族为例》Yuxiang Wang, *Language, Culture, and Identity among Minority Students in China: The Case of the Hui*. Routledge (2013)

110. 《汉语语气词A（啊）：语用和语义研究》Ying Xian Wang, *On Chinese Modal Particle A（啊）: A Pragmatic and Semantic Study*. Peter Lang AG, Internationaler Verlag der Wissenschaften (2013)

111. 《中国谚语与俗语：对文化与语言的观察》Qin Xue Herzberg, Larry Herzberg, *Chinese Proverbs and Popular Sayings: with Observations on Culture and Language*. Stone Bridge Press (2012)

112. 《汉语词汇9000字》Andrey Taranov, *Chinese Vocabulary for English Speakers: 9000 Words*. T&P Books (2012)

113. 《柯林斯中国语言与文化：现代中国普通话与生活指南》Duncan Poupard, *Collins Chinese Language and Culture: Your Essential Guide to Mandarin and Life in Modern China*. HarperCollins Publishers (2012)

114. 《外来汉语词：认知语义学方法》Suogui Li, *Foreign-inspired Chinese Terms: A Cognitive Semantic Approach*. Mellen (2012)

115. 《中国官话中的做梦：生活、爱情、语言的教训》Deborah Fallows, *Dreaming in Chinese Mandarin: Lessons in Life, Love, and Language*. Walker & Company (2011)

116. 《事事关心：现代汉语高级读本》Chih-p'ing Chou, Yan Xia, Meow Hui Goh, *All Things Considered: An Advanced Reader of Modern Chinese* (The Princeton Language Program: Modern Chinese). Princeton University Press (2011)

117. 《"礼貌"在历史与当代汉语中的比较分析》Daniel Z. Kadar, Yuling Pan, *Politeness in Historical and Contemporary Chinese: A Comparative Analysis*. Continuum (2011)

118. 《中国之旅：现代汉语的中级读本》Chih-p'ing Chou, Der-lin Chao, Chen Gao, *A Trip to China: An Intermediate Reader of Modern Chinese* (The Princeton Language Program: Modern Chinese). Princeton University Press (2011)

119. 《哦，中国！现代汉语高阶初学者初级读本》Chih-p'ing Chou, Perry Link（林培瑞）, Xuedong Wang, *Oh, China! An Elementary Reader of Modern Chinese for Advanced Beginners* (The Princeton Language Program: Modern Chinese). Princeton University Press (2011)

120. 《中国语言文化史》Sharron Gu, *A Cultural History of the Chinese Language*. McFarland & Company (2011)

121. 《用魔鬼语言写作：中国英文写作史》Xiaoye You, *Writing in the Devils Tongue: A History of English Composition in China*. Southern Illinois University Press (2010)

122. 《汉语习惯含义与语用标记理论》Guangwu Feng, *A Theory of Conventional Implicature & Pragmatic Markers in Chinese* (Current Research in the Semantics: Pragmatics Interface). Emerald Group Publishing Limited (2010)

123. 《口语广东话：初学者完整教程》Dana Scott Bourgerie, Keith S T Tong, Gregory James, *Colloquial Cantonese: The Complete Course for Beginners* (Colloquial Series). Routledge (2010)

124. 《脏话：日常俚语》Matt Coleman, Edmund Backhouse, *Dirty Chinese: Everyday Slang from What's Up: to F: %# Off!* (Dirty Everyday Slang). Ulysses Press (2010)

125. 《定义与告知：中国和丹麦英语学习者使用的词典信息分析》Saihong Li Rasmussen, *To Define and Inform: An Analysis of Information Provided in Dictionaries Used by Learners of English in China and Denmark*. Cambridge Scholars Publishing (2010)

126. 《中文天地》（简体版）Sue-mei Wu, *Chinese link: Simplified Character Version*. Level 1, Part 1. Pearson, Prentice Hall (2010)

127. 《汉语句法学》C.-T. James Huang, Y.-H. Audrey Li, Yafei Li, *The Syntax of Chinese*. Cambridge University Press (2009)

128. 《普通话频率词典：初学者核心词汇》Richard Xiao, Paul Rayson, Tony McEnery, *A Frequency Dictionary of Mandarin Chinese: Core Vocabulary for Learners* (Routledge Frequency Dictionaries). Routledge (2009)

129. 《中文听说读写》Daozhong Yao, Yuehua Liu, *Integrated Chinese* (Cheng & Tsui Chinese language series. Integrated Chinese series.). Cheng & Tsui (2009)

130. 《中国辞书：从公元前1046年到公元1911年》Heming Yong, Jing Peng, *Chinese Lexicography: A History from 1046 BC to AD 1911*.Oxford University Press (2008)
131. 《中国的语言空间：跨语言、共时和历时的角度》Dan Xu, *Space in Languages of China: Cross-linguistic, Synchronic and Diachronic Perspectives*. Springer (2008)
132. 《唱歌学中文！歌曲和图片让学习变得有趣》coll., Sing and Learn Chinese! Songs and Pictures to Make Learning Fun! ABC Melody (2008)
133. 《汉语教育中的语言政治学（1895—1919）》Elisabeth Kaske, *The Politics of Language in Chinese Education, 1895—1919* (Sinica Leidensia 82).Brill Academic Publishers (2007)
134. 《汉语系统功能语法：基于文本的分析》Eden Sum-hung Li, *A Systemic Functional Grammar of Chinese: A Text-based Analysis*. Continuum (2007)
135. 《当代中文媒体地域性语言的呈现》Edward M. Gunn, *Rendering the Regional: Local Language in Contemporary Chinese Media*. University of Hawaii Press (2005)
136. 《广东话俗语辞典》Christopher Hutton, Kingsley Bolton, *A Dictionary of Cantonese Slang: The Language of Hong Kong Movies, Street Gangs And City Life*. London: Hurst & Company (2005)
137. 《汉语区的写作教学》Mark Shiu Kee Shum, De Lu Zhang, *Teaching Writing in Chinese Speaking Areas* (Studies in Writing). Springer (2005)
138. 《汉语中的体：基于语料库的研究》Richard Xiao, Tony McEnery, *Aspect In Mandarin Chinese: A Corpus-based Study* (Studies in Language Companion Series). John Benjamins Publishing Co. (2004)
139. 《中华人民共和国的语言政策：1949年以来的理论与实践》Minglang Zhou, Hongkai Sun, *Language Policy in the Peoples Republic of China: Theory and Practice since 1949*. Springer (2004)
140. 《一字千金：通过中国谚语成长》Adeline Yen Mah（严君玲）, *A Thousand Pieces of Gold: Growing up Through China's Proverbs*.Harper Collins Publishers (2003)
141. 《Mangghuer语法：中国青藏语系中的一种蒙古语言》Keith Slater, *Grammar of Mangghuer: A Mongolic Language of China's Qinghai-Gansu Sprachbund* (Curzon Asian Linguistics). RoutledgeCurzon (2003)
142. 《中国多语现象》Minglang Zhou, *Multilingualism in China* (Contributions to the Society of Language).De Gruyter Mouton (2003)
143. 《语言工程：毛泽东时代的中国语言与政治》Ji Fengyuan, *Linguistic Engineering: Language and Politics in Mao's China*. University of Hawaii Press (2003)
144. 《大山的声音：来自中国西南和东北的口头证词》Panos Publications, *Voices from the Mountain: Oral Testimonies from Southwest and Northeast China*.The Panos Institute (2002)
145. 《现代汉语语法的建立：动补结构的形成及其影响》Yuzhi Shi, *Establishment of Modern Chinese Grammar: The Formation of the Resultative Construction and Its Effects* (Studies in Language Companion Series 59). John Benjamins (2002)

146.《汉语语法》(Schaum's outline series) Claudia Ross, *Chinese Grammar*. McGraw-Hill (2002)

147.《普通话语法》(Languages of the world: materials 344) Hua Lin, *A Grammar of Mandarin Chinese*. Lincom Europa (2001)

148.《中国语言文化的政治：阅读龙的艺术》Bob Hodge, Kam Louie, *The Politics of Chinese Language and Culture: The Art of Reading Dragons* (Culture and Communication in Asia). Routledge (1998)

149.《中国文言语法大纲》Edwin G. Pulleyblank, *Outline of Classical Chinese Grammar*. University of British Columbia Press (1995)

150.《初学者和高级初学者汉语：汉语口语和书面完整课程》Ellie Mao Mok, *Chinese for Beginners and Advanced Beginners: A Complete Course of Spoken and Written Chinese*. Gould Publications (1990)

151.《中国语言》S. Robert Ramsey, *The Languages of China*. Princeton University Press (1992)

152.《汉语》Jerry Norman, *Chinese*. Cambridge University Press (1988)

153.《普通话口语变体》（第二卷）Cornelis C Kubler, George Ho, *Varieties of Spoken Standard Chinese. Volume 2: A Speaker from Taipei 2* (Publications in modern Chinese language and literature 1). Foris Publications (1984)

154.《中古汉语：历史音韵学研究》Edwin G. Pulleyblank, *Middle Chinese: A Study in Historical Phonology*. University of British Columbia Press (1984)

155.《自学汉语》(Teach Yourself Books) Henry Raymond Williamson, *Teach Yourself Chinese*. English Universities Press (1974)

156.《你可以写中文》Kurt Wiese, *You Can Write Chinese*. The Viking Press (1973)

157.《中国语文浅说》Richard Newnham（牛恩汉）, Tan Lin-tung（谭林通）, *About Chinese*. Penguin Books (1971)

158.《语言和符号系统》Yuen Ren Chao（赵元任）, *Language and Symbolic Systems*. Cambridge University Press (1968)

159.《中国话的文法》Yuen Ren Chao（赵元任）, *Grammar of Spoken Chinese*. Berkeley: University of California Press (1968)

160.《普通话入门》Yuen Ren Chao（赵元任）, *Mandarin Primer*. Harvard University Press (1961)

161.《中国"元朝秘史"的语言》M. A. K. Halliday, *The Language of the Chinese "Secret history of the Mongols" (Yuan chao bi shi)* (Publications of the Philological Society, 17). Blackwell (1959)

162.《初学者的会话汉语》Morris Swadesh, *Conversational Chinese for Beginners* (Dover Language Guides). Dover Publications (1948)

163.《语言学与古代中国》Bernhard Karlgren（高本汉）, *Philology and Ancient China*.

OSLO: H. Aschehoug & Co. (1926)

164.《新疆出土佉卢文文书之语言》T. Burrow, *The Language of the Kharoṣṭhi Documents from Chinese Turkestan*. Cambridge University Press (1937)

165.《汉语谚语熟语集》Arthur H. Smith（明恩溥）, *Proverbs and Common Sayings from the Chinese: Together with much Related and unrelated Matter, Interspersed with Observations on Chinese Things in General*. Shanghai: Printed at the American Presbyterian Mission Press (1914)

166.《汉语句子结构与习语论述》Absalom Sydenstricker, *An Exposition of the Construction and Idioms of Chinese Sentences*. American Presbyterian Mission Press (1889)

167.《中国谚语合集》William Scarborough, *A Collection of Chinese Proverbs*. American Presbyterian Mission Press (1875)

168.《论中国书写系统的性质和特征：致约翰···沃恩的信》Peter Stephen Du Ponceau, *A Dissertation on the Nature and Character of the Chinese System of Writing: In a Letter to John Vaughan, Esq*. Philadelphia: Published for the American Philosophical Society (1838)

169.《汉语语法要素：兼论汉字和口语交际》Joshua Marshman. *Elements of Chinese Grammar, with a Preliminary Dissertation on the Characters, and the Colloquial Medium of the Chinese*. Serampore: Mission Press (1814)

5.2 文字、词典

1.《从最小对比到意义建构：基于语料库的近义词驱动的汉语词汇语义学方法》(Frontiers in Chinese Linguistics 9) Qi Su, Weidong Zhan, *From Minimal Contrast to Meaning Construct: Corpus-based, Near Synonym Driven Approaches to Chinese Lexical Semantics*. Springer Singapore (2020)

2.《汉语多词表达的理论与实践》Shan Wang, *Chinese Multiword Expressions: Theoretical and Practical Perspectives*. Springer Singapore (2020)

3.《体现概念化或神经实现：汉语通感形容词的语料库驱动研究》(Frontiers in Chinese Linguistics 10) Qingqing Zhao, *Embodied Conceptualization or Neural Realization: A Corpus-Driven Study of Mandarin Synaesthetic Adjectives*. Springer Singapore (2020)

4.《汉字书写达人迷》(For Dummies) Wendy Abraham, Jing Li, *Chinese Character Writing For Dummies*. John Wiley & Sons, Inc. (2019)

5.《汉字的起源：历史与文字指南》Kihoon Lee, *The Origin of Chinese Characters: An Illustrated History and Word Guide*. Algora Publishing (2018)

6.《另一种希腊语：中日文字及其历史与影响导论》Arthur R. V. Cooper, Imre Galambos, *The Other Greek: An Introduction to Chinese and Japanese Characters, Their History and Influence*. Brill (2018)

7.《常规字形：汉字的书写》Harvey Dam, *Regular Script Graphemics: How Chinese Characters Are Written*. Harvey Dam (2018)

8. 《袖珍汉语词典：汉英—英汉》Philip Yungkin Lee, Jiegang Fan, *Periplus Pocket Mandarin Chinese Dictionary: Chinese-English, English-Chinese* (Fully Romanized)（Periplus Pocket Dictionaries）. Periplus Editions (2017)

9. 《基础汉语常用语手册词典》Catherine Dai, *Essential Mandarin Chinese Phrasebook & Dictionary* (Essential Phrasebook & Disctionary Series). Tuttle Publishing (2017)

10. 《汉语词汇和词类：基于语料库的研究》Chu-Ren Huang, Shu-Kai Hsieh, Keh-Jiann Chen, *Mandarin Chinese Words and Parts of Speech: A Corpus-based Study*. Routledge (2017)

11. 《汉字词典：安排、解释、查找汉字的新途径》Adrian Van Amstel, *Chinese Character Dictionary: A New Approach to Arranging, Explaining and Looking Up Chinese Characters*. Createspace Independent Publishing Platform (2016)

12. 《汉英初阶词典：涵盖六级汉语水平考试全部词汇》Muhammad Wolfgang G. A. Schmidt, *A Learner's Chinese-English Dictionary: Covering the Entire Vocabulary for All the Six Levels of the Chinese Language Proficiency Exam*. Disserta Verlag (2016)

13. 《中国语言学牛津手册》William S-Y Wang, Chaofen Sun, *The Oxford Handbook of Chinese Linguistics*. Oxford University Press (2015)

14. 《中国语言学手册》Cheng-Teh James Huang, Yen-hui Audrey Li, Andrew Simpson, *The Handbook of Chinese Linguistics*. Wiley Blackwell (2014)

15. 《中文、韩语和日语的书写与识字》Insup Taylor, M. Martin Taylor, *Writing and Literacy in Chinese, Korean and Japanese*, Revised edition. John Benjamins Publishing Company (2014)

16. 《汉语识字新法》ShaoLan Hsueh, Noma Bar, *Chineasy: The New Way to Read Chinese*. Harper Design (2014)

17. 《说文写字：汉字书写与文化印迹》Andrea Bachner, *Beyond Sinology: Chinese Writing and the Scripts of Culture*. Columbia University Press (2014)

18. 《满英综合词典》Jerry Norman, *A Comprehensive Manchu-English Dictionary* (Harvard-Yenching Institute Monograph Series). Harvard University Asia Center (2013)

19. 《书写中国生活（1600—2010）：难以捉摸的自我历史》Marjorie Dryburgh, Sarah Dauncey (eds.), *Writing Lives in China, 1600—2010: Histories of the Elusive Self*. Palgrave Macmilla (2013)

20. 《中国表意文字》Henri Michaux, *Ideograms in China*. New Directions (2013)

21. 《用魔鬼语言写作：中国英文写作史》Xiaoye You, *Writing in the Devils Tongue: A History of English Composition in China*. Southern Illinois University Press (2010)

22. 《定义与告知：中国和丹麦英语学习者使用的词典信息分析》Saihong Li Rasmussen, *To Define and Inform: An Analysis of Information Provided in Dictionaries Used by Learners of English in China and Denmark*. Cambridge Scholars Publishing (2010)

23. 《蒙文总汇：1891年蒙—汉—满三语词典》Kuribayashi Hitoshi (comp.), *Mengwen Zonghui: Mongolian-Chinese-Manchu Triglot Dictionary of 1891*. Center for Northeast

Asian Studies, Tohoku University (2010)

24. 《中日阅读入门词典》Victor H. Mair（梅维恒）, *ABC Dictionary of Sino-Japanese Readings*. University of Hawai'i Press (2010)

25. 《牛津汉语词典》Julie Kleeman, Harry Yu, *The Oxford Chinese Dictionary*. Oxford University Press (2010)

26. 《普通话频率词典：初学者核心词汇》Richard Xiao, Paul Rayson, Tony McEnery, *A Frequency Dictionary of Mandarin Chinese: Core Vocabulary for Learners* (Routledge Frequency Dictionaries). Routledge (2009)

27. 《250个運用汉字》（第一册）Philip Yungkin Lee, Darell Tibbles, *250 Essential Chinese Characters* (HSK Level 1) Vol. 1. Tuttle Publishing (2009)

28. 《Sinographies：书写中国》Eric Hayot, Haun Saussy（苏源熙）, Steven G. Yao, *Sinographies: Writing China*. University of Minnesota Press (2008)

29. 《汉字规划：反应、进化还是革命》Shouhui Zhao, Richard B. Baldauf Jr., *Planning Chinese Characters: Reaction, Evolution or Revolution*. Springer US (2008)

30. 《中国辞书：从公元前1046年到公元1911年》Heming Yong, Jing Peng, *Chinese Lexicography: A History from 1046 BC to AD 1911*. Oxford University Press (2008)

31. 《汉语学习词典：汉英—英汉》Bin Liu (compiler), Chris A. Warnasch (editor), *Mandarin Chinese Learner's Dictionary: Chinese-English: English-Chinese* (Living Language). Random House (2008)

32. 《首要100汉字：学习100个最基本汉字的快捷方法》Laurence Matthews, Alison Matthews, *The First 100 Chinese Characters: The Quick and Easy Method to Learn the 100 Most Basic Chinese Characters* (Tuttle language library). Tuttle Publishing (2007)

33. 《广东话俗语辞典》Christopher Hutton, Kingsley Bolton, *A Dictionary of Cantonese Slang: The Language of Hong Kong Movies, Street Gangs And City Life*. London: Hurst & Company (2005)

34. 《汉语区的写作教学》Mark Shiu Kee Shum, De Lu Zhang, *Teaching Writing in Chinese Speaking Areas* (Studies in Writing). Springer (2005)

35. 《把弄文字：解读中国早期文献》Pauline Yu（余宝琳）(ed.), *Ways with Words: Writing about Reading Texts from Early China*. University of California Press (2000)

36. 《文字的力量：华南扫盲与革命（1949—1995）》Glen Peterson, *The Power of Words Literacy and Revolution in South China, 1949—95*. University of British Columbia Press (1997)

37. 《古汉语音韵学手册》William H. Baxter, *A Handbook of Old Chinese Phonology* (Trends in Linguistics. Studies and Monographs, Vol. 64). Mouton De Gruyter (1992)

38. 《汉字的乐趣》（第一至三卷）Tan Huay Peng, *Fun With Chinese Characters* (vol 1-3). Federal Publications (1983)

39. 《简明满—英词典》Norman Jerry, *A Concise Manchu-English Lexicon*. University of

Washington Press (1978)

40. 《6000汉字，附日语发音、日英文翻译》J. Ira Jones, *6000 Chinese Characters with Japanese Pronunciation and Japanese and English Renderings*. Kyo Bun Kwan (1915)

41. 《学生四千字通用袖珍字典》William Edward Soothill（苏慧廉）, *The Student's Four Thousand Tzu and General Pocket Dictionary*. American Presbyterian Mission Press (1908)

42. 《汉英词典：广东话客家话》D. MacIver, M.C. MacKenzie, *A Chinese-English Dictionary: Hakka-Dialect, as Spoken in Kwang-Tung Province*. Presbyterian Mission Press (1905)

43. 《汉英潮州方言字典》Josiah Goddard, *A Chinese and English Vocabulary, in the Tie-chiu Dialect*. American Presbyterian Mission press (1883)

44. 《英汉词典读本》Ira M. Condit, *English and Chinese Reader with a Dictionary*. American Tract Society (1882)

45. 《字学举隅》Herbert Allen Giles（翟理斯）, *Synoptical Studies in the Chinese Character*. Shanghai, Kelly & Co. (1874)

46. 《分析型读本：学习中文读写的简便方法》William Alexander Parsons Martin（丁韪良）, *The Analytical Reader: A Short Method for Learning to Read and Write Chinese*. Shanghai, China: Presbyterian Mission Press (1863)

47. 《论中国文字系统的性质和特征：致约翰·沃恩的信》Peter Stephen Du Ponceau, *A Dissertation on the Nature and Character of the Chinese System of Writing: In a Letter to John Vaughan, Esq*. Philadelphia: Published for the American Philosophical Society (1838)

5.3 翻译学

1. 《中文语境下基于语料库的翻译研究：现状与未来》(Palgrave Studies in Translating and Interpreting) Kaibao Hu, Kyung Hye Kim, *Corpus-based Translation and Interpreting Studies in Chinese Contexts: Present and Future*. Springer International Publishing (2020)

2. 《英汉翻译中的新闻构架：中英文媒体话语比较研究》(Routledge Studies in Chinese Discourse Analysis) Nancy Xiuzhi Liu, *News Framing Through English-Chinese Translation: A Comparative Study of Chinese and English Media Discourse*. Routledge (2019)

3. 《中国新闻翻译的话语分析》(Routledge Studies in Chinese Translation) Liang Xia, *A Discourse Analysis of News Translation in China*. Routledge (2019)

4. 《重构翻译教育：中国对世界其他地区的启示》Feng Yue, Youlan Tao, Huashu Wang, Qiliang Cui, Bin Xu, *Restructuring Translation Education: Implications from China for the Rest of the World*. Springer Singapore (2019)

5. 《从后殖民视角看晚清英汉翻译中的征服与反抗（1811—1911）》Xiaojia Huang, *English-Chinese Translation as Conquest and Resistance in the Late Qing, 1811—1911: A Postcolonial Perspective*. Springer Singapore (2019)

6. 《电影字幕中译的多模式研究》Yuping Chen, *Translating Film Subtitles into Chinese: A*

Multimodal Study. Springer Singapore (2019)

7. 《中国翻译研究最新进展》Ziman Li, Dengfeng Li (eds.), *Translation Studies in China: The State of the Art*. Springer (2019)

8. 《翻译异域他者：近代中国的跨文化焦虑》Yifeng Sun, *Translating Foreign Otherness: Cross-Cultural Anxiety in Modern China* (Routledge Advances in Translation and Interpreting Studies). Routledge (2018)

9. 《歌王：当代中国人、地方和过去的联系》Levi S Gibbs, *Song King: Connecting People, Places, and Past in Contemporary China*. University of Hawaii Press (2018)

10. 《劳特利奇中文翻译手册》Chris Shei, Zhao-Ming Gao (eds.), *The Routledge Handbook of Chinese Translation*. Routledge (2017)

11. 《中国翻译与健康风险知识建构》Meng Ji, *Translation and Health Risk Knowledge Building in China*. Springer Singapore (2017)

12. 《普鲁斯特、中国与互文性参与：翻译与跨文化对话》Marcel Proust, Shuangyi Li, *Proust, China and Intertextual Engagement: Translation and Transcultural Dialogue*. Palgrave Macmillan (2017)

13. 《中英文学间的翻译诗学》David Jasper, Geng Youzhuang, Wang Hai, *A Poetics of Translation: Between Chinese and English Literature*. Baylor University Press (2016)

14. 《翻译中国：反思、批判与实践文选》Rainer Schulte, Ming Dong Gu, *Translating China for Western Readers: Reflective, Critical, and Practical Essays*. State University of New York Press (2015)

15. 《近代中国和西方：翻译与文化调解》(East Asian Comparative Literature and Culture) Peng Hsiao-yen, Isabelle Rabut, *Modern China and the West: Translation and Cultural Mediation*. Brill (2014)

16. 《中国学生的英语写作：语料库的启示》(Routledge Research in Education) Maria Leedham, *Chinese Students' Writing in English: Implications from a Corpus*. Driven Study-Routledge (2014)

17. 《中国文化翻译：汉英翻译的过程》Valerie Pellatt, Eric T. Liu, Yalta Ya-Yun Chen, *Translating Chinese Culture: The Process of Chinese-English Translation*. Routledge (2013)

18. 《西方文学在中国：一个民族的翻译》Shouhua Qi, *Western Literature in China and the Translation of a Nation*. Palgrave Macmillan (2012)

19. 《汉英字幕中的礼貌与观众反应》(New trends in translation studies 10) Xiaohui Yuan, *Politeness and Audience Response in Chinese-English Subtitling*. Peter Lang (2012)

20. 《中国翻译小说的读者、阅读与接受：小说的遭遇》Leo Tak-Lung Chan, *Readers, Reading and Reception of Translated Fiction in Chinese: Novel Encounters*. Routledge (2010)

21. 《翻译中国：翻译的主题》Xuanmin Luo, Yuanjian He, *Translating China: Topics in Translation*. Multilingual Matters (2009)

22. 《中文和希腊文圣经翻译：理论与实践的口头表达》Toshikazu S. Foley, *Biblical Translation in Chinese and Greek: Verbal Aspect in Theory and Practice* (Linguistic Biblical Studies).Brill (2009)
23. 《翻译、全球化与本土化》Wang Ning（王宁）and Sun Yifeng, *Translation, Globalizationa and Localization-a Chinese perspective.* Multilingual Matters Ltd (2008)
24. 《中国的维多利亚翻译：理雅各的东方朝圣》Norman J. Girardot, *The Victorian Translation of China: James Legge's Oriental Pilgrimage.* University of California Press (2002)
25. 《传统的呼唤：龙的传人之歌》Easton Lee, *Heritage Call: Ballad for the Children of the Dragon.* Ian Randle Publishers (2001)
26. 《抛砖引玉：相互理解的关键事件》Mary M. Wang, *Turning Bricks into Jade: Critical Incidents for Mutual Understanding.* Yarmouth, Me.: Intercultural Press (2000)
27. 《翻译与创作：1840—1918年代现代中国早期的西方文学读物》David E. Pollard, *Translation and Creation: Readings of Western Literature in Early Modern China, 1840—1918.* John Benjamins Publishing Company (1998)
28. 《通过敞开的大门：美国对中国诗歌的翻译与帝国译介》（博士论文）Steven Edgar Bradbury, *Through the Open Door: American Translation of Chinese Poetry and the Translations of Empire.* Ph. D. Dissertation, University of Hawai'i at Manoa (1997)
29. 《跨语际实践：文学、民族文化与翻译的现代性：1900—1937年的中国》Lydia H. Liu, *Translingual Practice: Literature, National Culture, and Translated Modernity-China, 1900—1937.* Stanford University Press (1995)
30. 《西方通过翻译对中国的影响：书目研究》（硕士论文）Tsien Tsuen-Hsuin（钱存训）, *Western Impact On China through Translation: A Bibliographical Study.* Thesis for the Degree of Master of Arts, University of Chicago (1952)

6. 中国文化与文明

6.1 文化总论

1. 《文化理论化的中国视角》(Palgrave Studies in Teaching and Learning Chinese) Jinghe Han, *Theorising Culture: A Chinese Perspective*. Springer International Publishing: Palgrave Pivot (2020)
2. 《中国现代文明文化观》(Key Concepts in Chinese Thought and Culture) Weigui Fang, *Modern Notions of Civilization and Culture in China*. Springer Singapore: Palgrave Pivot (2019)
3. 《中国文化简明读本》(China Insights) Chunsong Gan, *A Concise Reader of Chinese Culture*. Springer Singapore (2019)
4. 《中国文化产业的发展》(Research Series on the Chinese Dream and China's Development Path) Chang Jiang, Jialian Li, Tao Xu, Haijun Yang, *Development of China's Cultural Industry*. Springer Singapore (2019)
5. 《中国智慧文化》Keping Wang, *Chinese Culture of Intelligence*. Springer Singapore: Palgrave Macmillan (2019)
6. 《对中国文化认同的再思考：以"华礼人"为创新理念》Min Ding, *Rethinking Chinese Cultural Identity: "The Hualish" as an Innovative Concept*. Springer Singapore (2019)
7. 《中国文化导论：文化历史、艺术、节日和仪式》Guobin Xu, Yanhui Chen, Lianhua Xu, *Introduction to Chinese Culture: Cultural History, Arts, Festivals and Rituals*. Palgrave Macmillan, Singapore (2018)
8. 《了解中国文化：哲学、宗教和科技》Guobin Xu, Yanhui Chen, Lianhua Xu, *Understanding Chinese Culture: Philosophy, Religion, Science and Technology*. Palgrave Macmillan, Singapore (2018)
9. 《正在形成中的中国遗产：经验、谈判与争辩》Marina Svensson, Christina Maags, *Chinese Heritage in the Making: Experiences, Negotiations and Contestations*. Amsterdam University Press (2018)
10. 《中国大陆的文化、音乐教育和中国梦》Wai-Chung Ho, *Culture, Music Education, and the Chinese Dream in Mainland China* (Cultural Studies and Transdisciplinarity in Education 7). Springer Singapore (2018)
11. 《文化对中国中小企业管理的影响》Rubens Pauluzzo, Bin Shen, *Impact of Culture on Management of Foreign SMEs in China* (International Series in Advanced Management Studies). Springer International Publishing (2018)

12. 《跨文化体验与认同：在英国的中国博士生叙事》Lily Lei Ye, *Intercultural Experience and Identity: Narratives of Chinese Doctoral Students in the UK* (Palgrave Studies on Chinese Education in a Global Perspective). Springer International Publishing: Palgrave Macmillan (2018)

13. 《中国文化遗产的形成：经验、谈判与争鸣》Christina Maags, Marina Svensson (eds.), *Chinese Cultural Heritage in the Making: Experiences, Negotiations and Contestations*. Amsterdam University Press (2018)

14. 《中国文化概论》Guobin Xu, Yanhui Chen, Lianhua Xu, *Introduction to Chinese Culture*. Springer Singapore: Palgrave Macmillan (2018)

15. 《了解中国文化》Guobin Xu, Yanhui Chen, Lianhua Xu, *Understanding Chinese Culture*. Springer Singapore: Palgrave Macmillan (2018)

16. 《当代中国的朋克文化》Jian Xiao, *Punk Culture in Contemporary China*. Palgrave Macmillan (2018)

17. 《中国智慧与现代管理》Aimin Yan, Binghan Zheng, *Chinese Wisdom and Modern Management*. Cambridge Scholars Publishing (2018)

18. 《中国古代记忆与代理：塑造物品生命史》Francis Allard, Yan Sun, Kathryn M. Linduff, *Memory and Agency in Ancient China: Shaping the Life History of Objects*. Cambridge University Press (2018)

19. 《中国：承诺还是威胁？文化的比较》Horst J. Helle, *China: Promise or Threat? A Comparison of Culture*. Brill (2017)

20. 《中国新年：为所有人祈福》Jen Sookfong Lee, *Chinese New Year: A Celebration for Everyone* (Orca Origins). Orca Book Publishers (2017)

21. 《中国文化消费需求年度评估报告》Ya'nan Wang, Puning Hao, Ting Liu, Juan Zhao, Yu Fang, *Annual Evaluation Report of China's Cultural Consumption Demand*. Spring (2017)

22. 《中国文化软实力研究纲要》Guozuo Zhang, *Research Outline for China's Cultural Soft Power*. Springer Singapore (2017)

23. 《现代中国的文化研究》Dongfeng Tao, Lei He, Yugao He, *Cultural Studies in Modern China* (Research Series on the Chinese Dream and China's Development Path). Springer Singapore (2017)

24. 《与中国跨文化交流：超越（逆向）本质主义与文化主义》Fred Dervin, Regis Machart (eds.), *Intercultural Communication with China: Beyond (Reverse) Essentialism and Culturalism* (Encounters between East and West). Springer Singapore (2017)

25. 《中国传统休闲文化与经济发展：力量的冲突》Huidi Ma, Er Liu, *Traditional Chinese Leisure Culture and Economic Development: A Conflict of Forces*. Palgrave Macmillan US (2017)

26. 《中华民族精神：精神家园的核心》Kang Ouyang, *The Chinese National Spirit: The Core of a Spiritual Home*. Springer Singapore (2017)

27. 《中国文明的核心价值》Lai Chen（陈来）, *The Core Values of Chinese Civilization*. Springer Singapore (2017)
28. 《论中国文化》Deshun Li（李德顺）, *On Chinese Culture*. Springer (2016)
29. 《中国文物遣返案例》Zuozhen Liu, *The Case for Repatriating China's Cultural Objects*. Springer Singapore (2016)
30. 《当代中国语境中的人文精神》Evelyn T. Y. Chan, Michael O'sullivan (eds.), *The Humanities in Contemporary Chinese Contexts*. Springer Singapore (2016)
31. 《萧伯纳：中国文化桥梁》Kay Li, *Bernard Shaw's Bridges to Chinese Culture* (Bernard Shaw and His Contemporaries). Palgrave Macmillan (2016)
32. 《中国茶文化的兴起：独特的发明》Bret Hinsch, *The Rise of Tea Culture in China: The Invention of the Individual* (Asia Pacific Perspectives). Rowman & Littlefield Publishers (2016)
33. 《魅影礼仪：全球化中国的发展与位移》Carlos Rojas, Ralph A. Litzinger (eds.), *Ghost Protocol: Development and Displacement in Global China*. Duke University Press (2016)
34. 《多元文化中国：统计年鉴（2014）》Rongxing Guo, Uradyn E. Bulag, Michael A. Crang, Thomas Heberer, *Multicultural China: A Statistical Yearbook (2014)*. Springer-Verlag Berlin Heidelberg (2015)
35. 《中国历史文化概论》Qizhi Zhang（张岂之）, *An Introduction to Chinese History and Culture* (China Academic Library). Springer-Verlag Berlin Heidelberg (2015)
36. 《全球化与文化自觉》Xiaotong Fei（费孝通）, *Globalization and Cultural Self-Awareness*. Springer-Verlag Berlin Heidelberg (2015)
37. 《近来中国文化转型研究导论》Yunzhi Geng（耿云志）, *An Introductory Study on China's Cultural Transformation in Recent Times* (China Academic Library). Springer Berlin Heidelberg (2015)
38. 《中国茶叶：一部宗教文化史》James A. Benn, *Tea in China: A Religious and Cultural History*. University of Hawaii Press (2015)
39. 《清代与中国传统文化》Richard J. Smith, *The Qing Dynasty and Traditional Chinese Culture*. Rowman & Littlefield Publishers (2015)
40. 《多元文化中国》Rongxing Guo, Uradyn E. Bulag, Michael A. Crang, Thomas Heberer, Eui-Gak Hwang, James A Millward, Morris Rossabi（罗茂锐）, Gerard A. Postiglione, Chih-yu Shih（石之瑜）, *Multicultural China*. Springer (2015)
41. 《物化：中国传统中的知识》Barry Allen, *Vanishing into Things: Knowledge in Chinese Tradition*. Harvard University Press (2015)
42. 《当代中国视觉文化：范式与转变》Xiaobing Tang, *Visual Culture in Contemporary China: Paradigms and Shifts*. Cambridge University Press (2015)
43. 《中国文化创意产业报告（2013）》Hardy Yong Xiang (auth.), Hardy Yong Xiang, Patricia Ann Walker (eds.), *China Cultural and Creative Industries Reports 2013*

(Understanding China). Springer Berlin Heidelberg (2014)

44. 《中国风俗文化手册》May-Lee Chai, Winberg Chai, *China A to Z: Everything You Need to Know to Understand Chinese Customs and Culture*. Plume (2014)

45. 《改革时代的道德中国》Jiwei Ci, *Moral China in the Age of Reform*. Cambridge University Press (2014)

46. 《纠缠的历史：交叉的东北文化》Dan Ben-Canaan, Frank Grüner, Ines Prodöhl, *Entangled Histories: The Transcultural Past of Northeast China*. Springer (2014)

47. 《中美文化与音乐的交流影响》（硕士论文）Jianyu Fan, *Exchanging Influence between American and Chinese Culture and Music*. Thesis for the Degree of Master of Arts, Dartmouth College (2014)

48. 《六大秘笈：中国经典战略手册》Thomas Cleary (Translator), *Six Secrets: A Classic Chinese Manual of Strategy*. Amazon Digital Services LLC (2014)

49. 《中国创意产业：艺术、设计和媒体》Michael Keane, *Creative Industries in China: Art, Design and Media* (China today). Polity (2013)

50. 《中国文化遗产的政治学》Helaine Silverman, Tami Blumenfield (auth.), Tami Blumenfield, Helaine Silverman (eds.), *Cultural Heritage Politics in China*. Springer New York (2013)

51. 《中国文化研究的新视角》Longxi Zhang（张隆溪）, Pei-kai Cheng, Ka Wai Fan, *New Perspectives on the Research of Chinese Culture*. Springer Singapore (2013)

52. 《我们这个时代的价值观：中国当代价值研究》Deshun Li, *Values of Our Times: Contemporary Axiological Research in China*. Springer-Verlag Berlin Heidelberg (2013)

53. 《围棋国家：中国男性气质与中国围棋博弈》Marc L. Moskowitz, *Go Nation: Chinese Masculinities and the Game of Weiqi in China*. University of California Press (2013)

54. 《永恒的帝国：古代中国的政治文化和帝国遗产》Yuri Pines, *The Everlasting Empire: The Political Culture of Ancient China and Its Imperial Legacy*. Princeton University Press (2012)

55. 《寻踪达摩：中国文化核心和旅行》Andy Ferguson, *Tracking Bodhidharma: A Journey to the Heart of Chinese Culture*. Counterpoint (2012)

56. 《中世纪早期的多元文化中国》Sanping Chen, *Multicultural China in the Early Middle Ages*. University of Pennsylvania Press (2012)

57. 《拼图中国与管理世界：帝制晚期的文化、制图和宇宙学》Richard J. Smith, *Mapping China and Managing the World: Culture, Cartography and Cosmology in Late Imperial Times*. Routledge (2012)

58. 《中文耳语：文化散文》Nicholas Jose, *Chinese Whispers: Cultural Essays*. Wakefield Press (2012)

59. 《文化构成》Yunhe Pan, *Cultural Composition*. Springer-Verlag Berlin Heidelberg (2012)

60. 《跨文化史与他者的归化》Michal Jan Rozbicki and George O. Ndege, *Cross-Cultural History and the Domestication of Otherness*. Palgrave Macmillan (2012)

61. 《宫廷文化中的修辞学与权力话语：中国、欧洲和日本》David R. Knechtges, Eugene Vance, *Rhetoric and the Discourses of Power in Court Culture: China, Europe, and Japan*. University of Washington Press (2012)
62. 《中国文化论文集》Tsuen-Hsuin Tsien（钱存训）, *Collected Writings on Chinese Culture*. The Chinese University Press (2011)
63. 《中国文化》Kathleen Kuiper, *The Culture of China*. Britannica Educational Publishing (2011)
64. 《解读中国人，解读中国》Robin Setton (ed.), *Interpreting Chinese, Interpreting China* (Benjamins Current Topics). John Benjamins Publishing Company (2011)
65. 《文化冲击！中国风俗礼仪生存指南》Angie Eagan, Rebecca Weiner, *Culture Shock! China: A Survival Guide to Customs and Etiquette*. Marshall Cavendish International (2011)
66. 《婚礼风水：中国策划婚礼星座指南》Laura Lau, Theodora Lau, *Wedding Feng Shui: The Chinese Horoscopes Guide to Planning Your Wedding*. HarperCollins (2011)
67. 《中国历史上的知识技术文化》Dagmar Schäfer, *Cultures of Knowledge Technology in Chinese History*. Brill (2011)
68. 《中国文化》Shi Zhongwen, Chen Qiaosheng, *China's Culture*. Cengage Learning Asia (2010)
69. 《中国改革年代的文化社会转型》Cao Tian Yu, Zhong Xueping, Liao Kebin, *Culture and Social Transformations in Reform Era China*. Brill Academic Publishers (2010)
70. 《遇见中国：现代国家，古代文化》Wenzhong Hu（胡文仲）, Cornelius N. Grove, Cornelius Lee Grove, Zhuang Enping, *Encountering the Chinese: A Modern Country, an Ancient Culture*. Nicholas Brealey Publishing (2010)
71. 《中国文化》Kenneth Pletcher, *The Culture of China*. Encyclopaedia Britannica; Britannica Educational Publishing (2010)
72. 《中国传统渊源》（第二卷）William Theodore De Bary（狄百瑞）, Richard Lufrano, *Sources of Chinese Tradition: Volume 2: From 1600 Through the Twentieth Century*. Columbia University Press (2010)
73. 《中国文化优势：六城记》Fu Yuhua, Florentin Smarandache, V. Christianto (eds.), *Cultural Advantages in China: Tale of Six Cities*. InfoLearnQuest Publisher (2009)
74. 《中国人的心灵：理解中国传统信仰及其对当代文化的影响》Boye Lafayette De Mente, *The Chinese Mind: Understanding Traditional Chinese Beliefs and their Influence on Contemporary Culture*. Tuttle Publishing (2008)
75. 《中国发展：新兴社会的文化身份》George Fusun Ling, *China Developing: Cultural Identity of Emerging Societies*. World Scientific Publishing Company (2008)
76. 《中国的文化排斥：国家教育、社会流动与文化差异》Lin Yi, *Cultural Exclusion in China: State Education, Social Mobility and Cultural Difference* (Comparative Development and Policy in Asia). Routledge (2008)
77. 《中国礼仪指南：了解不同的规则》Boye Lafayette De Mente, *Etiquette Guide to China:*

Know the Rules that Make the Difference! Tuttle Publishing (2008)

78. 《剑桥现代中国文化指南》Kam Louie, *The Cambridge Companion to Modern Chinese Culture.* Cambridge University Press (2008)

79. 《中国：穿越时光的世界文化》M. A. Gisela Lee, *China: World Cultures through Time* (Primary Source Readers). Rachelle Cracchiolo, M. S. Ed (2008)

80. 《寻求中国文雅：超越性别和阶级的谈判》Daria Berg, Chloë Starr, *The Quest for Gentility in China: Negotiations Beyond Gender and Class*. Routledge (2008)

81. 《〈洛书〉的遗产：四千年寻找三阶魔方的意义》Frank J. Swetz, *Legacy of the Luoshu: The 4,000 Year Search for the Meaning of the Magic Square of Order Three*. A K Peters (2008)

82. 《三国与中国文化》Kimberly Besio, Constantine Tung (eds.), *Three Kingdoms and Chinese Culture*. State University of New York (2007)

83. 《中国文化遗产管理》Hilary du Cros, Yok-shiu F. Lee, *Cultural Heritage Management in China* (Routledge Contemporary China Series). Routledge (2007)

84. 《皇帝的新衣：中国在寻求全球地位过程中的文化特殊主义和普世价值》Jeremy T. Paltiel, *The Empire's New Clothes: Cultural Particularism and Universal Value in China's Quest for Global Status*. Palgrave Macmillan (2007)

85. 《个案思考：中国文化史中的专家知识》Charlotte Furth（费侠莉）, *Thinking with Cases: Specialist Knowledge in Chinese Cultural History*. University of Hawai'i Press (2007)

86. 《意外的契合：跨文化阅读》Zhang Longxi（张隆溪）, *Unexpected Affinities: Reading across Cultures* (Alexander Lectures). University of Toronto Press (2007)

87. 《古代世界与现代反思：希腊与中国科学文化的哲学透视》G. E. R. Lloyd, *Ancient Worlds, Modern Reflections: Philosophical Perspectives on Greek and Chinese Science and Culture*. Oxford University Press, USA (2006)

88. 《体现现代性：身体、表征、中国文化》Fran Martin, Larissa Heinrich (eds.), *Embodied Modernities: Corporeality, Representation, and Chinese Cultures*. University of Hawai'i Press (2006)

89. 《英释中国传统文化》He Qi Liang（何其亮）, Zhang Ye（张晔）, *A Talk on Traditional Chinese Culture: the Language Perspective*. Zhejiang University Publishing House (2006)

90. 《位移的欲望：中国旅游与大众文化》Beth E. Notar, *Displacing Desire: Travel and Popular Culture in China*. University of Hawai'i Press (2006)

91. 《文化资本政治：中国寻求诺贝尔文学奖》Julia Lovell（蓝诗玲）, *The Politics of Cultural Capital: China's Quest for a Nobel Prize in Literature*. University of Hawaii Press (2006)

92. 《中文写作：重塑中国文化身份》Lingchei Letty Chen, *Writing Chinese: Reshaping Chinese Cultural Identity*. Palgrave Macmillan US (2006)

93. 《中国星相学：探索东方星座》Shelly Wu, *Chinese Astrology: Exploring the Eastern Zodiac*. New Page Books (2005)

94. 《当代中国文化百科全书》Edward L. Davis (ed.), *Encyclopedia of Contemporary Chinese*

Culture. Routledge (2005)

95. 《中国历史与文化》W. Scott Morton, Charlton M. Lewis, *China: Their History and Culture*. McGraw-Hill (2004; 2005)

96. 《定位中国：空间、场所和流行文化》Jing Wang（王瑾）, *Locating China: Space, Place, and Popular Culture*. Routledge (2005)

97. 《中国关系：制度、文化和"关系"的流变本质》Thomas Gold, Doug Guthrie, David Wank (eds), *Social Connections in China: Institutions, Culture, and the Changing Nature of Guanxi*. Cambridge University Press (2004)

98. 《中国文物》Li Li（李力）, *China's Cultural Relics* (Cultural China). China Intercontinental Press (2004)

99. 《命的大小：中国文化中的命令、分配与命运》Christopher Lupke, *The Magnitude of Ming: Command, Allotment, and Fate in Chinese Culture*. University of Hawaii Press (2004)

100. 《中国风水：国家正统与民间宗教间的风水占卜》Ole Bruun, *Fengshui In China: Geomantic Divination Between State Orthodoxy And Popular Religion*. NIAS Press (2004)

101. 《自我的他性：当代中国的自我系谱》Liu Xin（流心）, *The Otherness of Self: A Genealogy of Self in Contemporary China*. University of Michigan Press (2002)

102. 《文化好奇：中国寻根13个故事》Josephine M.T. Khu, *Cultural Curiosity: Thirteen Stories about the Search for Chinese Roots*. University of California Press (2001)

103. 《关系：中国背景下的关系营销》Y. H. Wong, Thomas K. P. Leung, *Guanxi: Relationship Marketing in a Chinese Context*. Routledge (2001)

104. 《中国新文化景观：变革手册》Claire Huot, *China's New Cultural Scene: A Handbook of Changes*. Duke University Press Books (2000)

105. 《中国青铜时代的轮式车辆（公元前2000年至公元前741年）》Anthony J. Barbieri-Low, *Wheeled Vehicles in the Chinese Bronze Age (c. 2000—741 B.C.)*. Princeton University (2000)

106. 《中华帝国晚期科举考试文化史》Benjamin A. Elman（艾尔曼）, *A Cultural History of Civil Examinations in Late Imperial China*. University of California Press (2000)

107. 《风水艺术与科学：塑造命运的中国古代传统》Henry B. Lin, *The Art & Science of Feng Shui: The Ancient Chinese Tradition of Shaping Fate*. Llewellyn Publications (2000)

108. 《探索楚文化：古代中国的图像与现实》John S. Major, Constance A. Cook, *Defining Chu: Image and Reality in Ancient China*. University of Hawaii Press (1999)

109. 《红色：论当代中国文化》Geremie R. Barme（白杰明）, *In the Red: On Contemporary Chinese Culture*. Columbia University Press (1999)

110. 《道家风水：中国布局艺术的古老根源》Susan Levitt, *Taoist Feng Shui: The Ancient Roots of the Chinese Art of Placement*. Destiny Books (1999)

111. 《神秘主义和王权：中国智慧的核心》Julia Ching（秦家懿）, *Mysticism and Kingship in China: The Heart of Chinese Wisdom*. Cambridge University Press (1997)

112. 《统一与差异：中国的本土文化与身份》Tao Tao Liu, David Faure (ed.), *Unity and Diversity: Local Cultures and Identities in China*. Hong Kong University Press (1996)

113. 《从古代传统至今：中国文化遗产资源指南》Ching Fang Chen, Amy Lee, *From an Ancient Tradition to the Present: Chinese Cultural Heritage Resource Guide*. New York City Board of Education, Brooklyn, NY. Office of Bilingual Education (1996)

114. 《文化热：邓小平时代中国的政治、美学和意识形态》Jing Wang, *High Culture Fever: Politics, Aesthetics, and Ideology in Deng's China*. University of California Press (1996)

115. 《中国波普：肥皂剧、小报和畅销书如何改变一种文化》Jianying Zha（查建英）, *China Pop: How Soap Operas, Tabloids and Bestsellers Are Transforming a Culture*. The New Press (1996)

116. 《科学主义与人文主义：毛泽东时代后中国两种文化（1978—1989）》Shiping Hua, *Scientism and Humanism: Two Cultures in Post-Mao China (1978—1989)*. State University of New York Press (1995)

117. 《中国历史和文化》（第三版）Scott W. Morton, *China: Its History and Culture* (Third Edition). McGraw-Hill (1995)

118. 《教室中的文化交流：两位美国教师在中国》Lois Baker Muehl, Siegmar Muehl, *Trading Cultures in the Classroom: Two American Teachers in China*. University of Hawaii Press (1993)

119. 《中国茶：中国民族饮料史》John C. Evans, *Tea in China: The History of China's National Drink*. Greenwood Press (1992)

120. 《长物志：早期现代中国的物质文化与社会状况》Craig Clunas（柯律格）, *Superfluous Things: Material Culture and Social Status in Early Modern China*. Polity Press (1991)

121. 《中国暴力：文化与反文化散文》Jonathan Neaman Lipman, Stevan Harrell, *Violence in China: Essays in Culture and Counterculture*. State University of New York Press (1990)

122. 《西方遇到东方：中国物质文化在19世纪美国的展出》（硕士论文）Charlotte Elizabeth Smith, *West Meets East: Exhibitions of Chinese Material Culture in Nineteenth-Century America*. Thesis for the Degree of Master of Arts, University of Delaware (Winterthur Program) (1987)

123. 《从中国到美国：中国文化与遗产（1923—1980）》Young Oy Bo Lee, *From China to America: Chinese Culture and Heritage, 1928—1980*. (Oral History Transcript and Related Material). University of California (1987)

124. 《帝制中国晚期的大众文化》David Johnson（姜士彬）, Andrew Nathan（黎安友）, Evelyn Rawski（罗友枝）, *Popular Culture in Late Imperial China*. University of California Press (1985)

125. 《中国文化中的正常和异常行为》Thomas A. Metzger（墨子刻）, Arthur Kleinman, Tsung-Yi Lin (eds.), *Normal and Abnormal Behavior in Chinese Culture*. Springer Netherlands (1981)

126. 《中国文化在美国：附注释书目》Alberto R. Sanchez, *Chinese Culture in the United States*

of Amreica: An Annotated Bibliography. Cross Cultural Resource Center, California State University (1977)

127. 《中国文化资料读本（供初级双语教师）》Irene Kwok, *Chinese Cultural Resource Book* (For Elementary Bilingual Teachers). ERIC (1974)

128. 《中国心灵：中国哲学与文化精要》Charles Alexander Mocre, *The Chinese Mind: Essentials of Chinese Philosophy and Culture*. Honolulu: East-West Center Press (1967)

129. 《12生肖：通过中国古代智慧在日常生活中创造和谐》Zhongxian Wu, *The 12 Chinese Animals: Create Harmony in Your Daily Life Through Ancient Chinese Wisdom*. Singing Dragon (1965, 2011)

130. 《中国文物》Collective, *Chinese Art Treasures*. Skira (1961)

131. 《中国传统渊源》（第一卷）William Theodore De Bary（狄百瑞）, Wing-Tsit Chan（陈荣捷）, Burton Watson（伯顿·沃森）, *Sources of Chinese Tradition* (Unesco Collection of Representative Works. Chinese Series). Volume I. Columbia University Press (1960)

132. 《中国文化》Francis C. M. Wei, *The Spirit of Chinese Culture*. New York: Charles Scribner's Sons, USA (1947)

133. 《中国智慧》Yutang Lin（林语堂）, *Wisdom of China*. Michael Joseph Ltd (1944)

134. 《中国人的历史与文化》Kenneth Scott Latourette（赖德烈）, *The Chinese: Their History and Culture*. The Macmillan Company (1943, 1964)

135. 《中国早期文化研究》Herrlee Glessner Creel（顾立雅）, *Studies in Early Chinese Culture*. The American Council of Learned Societies (1938)

136. 《中国文化简史》C. P. Fitzgerald (author), C. G. Seligman (editor), *China: A Short Cultural History*. New York: D. Appleton-Century Co. (1938)

137. 《吾国与吾民》Lin Yutang（林语堂）, *My Country and My People*. London: William Heinemann Ltd. (1936)

138. 《中国文化简史》C. P. Fitzgerald, *China: A Short Cultural History*. Praeger publishers, New York (1935, 1942, 1950, 1954, 1958, 1961, 1965, 1970)

139. 《中国人的世界观演变研究》Herrlee Glessner Creel（顾立雅）, *Sinism: A Study of the Evolution of the Chinese World-View*. Chicago, Illinois: The Open Court Publishing Co. (1929)

140. 《中国的风俗》Lewis Hodous（何乐益）, *Folkways in China*. London: Arthur Probsthain (1929)

141. 《中国（茶叶）》S. W. Harris, *China*. Irwin-Harrisons & Crosfield, Inc. (1919)

142. 《远东的七个女仆》Bing Ding, Mary Forman Ledyard, Abertine D. Mandall, *Seven Maids of Far Cathay: Being English Notes from a Chinese Class Book*. San Francisco: Paul Elder and Company (1916)

143. 《中国问题》Bertrand Russell（罗素）, *The Problem of China*. George Allen & Unwin (1922; 1993)

144. 《中国人的素质》Arthur H. Smith（明恩溥）, *Chinese Characteristics*. EastBridge (1894)
145. 《中国茶叶栽培与加工报告》Samuel Ball, *An Account of the Cultivation and Manufacture of Tea in China*. London: Printed for Longman, Brown, Green, and Longmans (1848)
146. 《世界主要国家的风俗习惯》Samuel Griswold Goodrich, *Manners and Customs of the Principal Nations of the Globe*. Boston: Bradbury, Soden (1845)

6.2 儒学与经典

6.2.1 儒学

1. 《当代中国的国家社会关系与儒家复兴》Qin Pang, *State-Society Relations and Confucian Revivalism in Contemporary China*. Springer Singapore: Palgrave Macmillan (2019)
2. 《韩国儒家哲学读本》(Dao Companions to Chinese Philosophy 11) Young-chan Ro, *Dao Companion to Korean Confucian Philosophy*. Springer Netherlands (2019)
3. 《儒家的政治想象》Eske J. Møllgaard, *The Confucian Political Imagination*. Springer International Publishing: Palgrave Macmillan (2018)
4. 《儒家资本主义》John H. Sagers, *Confucian Capitalism* (Palgrave Studies in Economic History). Springer International Publishing: Palgrave Macmillan (2018)
5. 《儒家的疑虑：梁漱溟的法律叙事》Zhangrun Xu, *The Confucian Misgivings: Liang Shuming's Narrative About Law*. Springer Singapore (2017)
6. 《西方话语中的儒家伦理》Wai-ying Wong, *Confucian Ethics in Western Discourse*. Bloomsbury Academic (2017)
7. 《儒学与美国哲学》Mathew A. Foust, *Confucianism and American Philosophy* (SUNY series in Chinese Philosophy and Culture). Albany, New York: SUNY Press (2017)
8. 《儒学与中国的自我：重新审视马克斯·韦伯的中国》Jack Barbalet, *Confucianism and the Chinese Self: Re-examining Max Weber's China*. Palgrave Macmillan (2017)
9. 《公共理性儒学：民主完美主义与东亚宪政》Sungmoon Kim, *Public Reason Confucianism: Democratic Perfectionism and Constitutionalism in East Asia*. Cambridge University Press (2017)
10. 《早期儒家思想中的诚信脆弱性》Michael David Kaulana Ing, *The Vulnerability of Integrity in Early Confucian Thought*. Oxford University Press (2017)
11. 《唐君毅：儒家哲学与现代性的挑战》Thomas Fröhlich, *Tang Junyi: Confucian Philosophy and the Challenge of Modernity*. Leiden; Boston: Brill (2017)
12. 《儒教宪政秩序：中国古代的历史如何塑造其政治未来》(Princeton-China series) Jiang Qing（蒋庆）, Edmund Ryden（雷敦龢）, Ruiping Fan, Daniel A. Bell（淡贝宁）, *A Confucian Constitutional Order: How China's Ancient Past can Shape Its Political Future*. Princeton University Pres (2017)
13. 《儒学，心灵的习惯：贝拉、民间宗教与东亚》Philip J. Ivanhoe, Sungmoon Kim (eds.), *Confucianism, a Habit of the Heart: Bellah, Civil Religion, and East Asia*. State University

of New York Press (2016)

14. 《现代性视域：新儒家哲学的主体性与社会结构》(Modern Chinese Philosophy) Ady Van den Stock, *The Horizon of Modernity: Subjectivity and Social Structure in New Confucian Philosophy*. Brill (2016)

15. 《三条溪流：中、韩、日儒家对学问与道德心智的思考》Philip J. Ivanhoe, *Three Streams: Confucian Reflections on Learning and the Moral Heart-Mind in China, Korea, and Japan*. Oxford University Press (2016)

16. 《古典儒家政治思想新论》Loubna El Amine, *Classical Confucian Political Thought: A New Interpretation*. Princeton University Press (2015)

17. 《儒家的社会生物学影响》Guangdan Pan（潘光旦）, *Socio-biological Implications of Confucianism*. Springer Berlin Heidelberg (2015)

18. 《儒家的礼与礼教》Geir Sigurosson, *Confucian Propriety and Ritual Learning: A Philosophical Interpretation*. State University of New York Press (2015)

19. 《圣人归来：当代中国的儒家复兴》Kenneth J. Hammond, Jeffrey L Richey, *The Sage Returns: Confucian Revival in Contemporary China*. State University of New York Press (2015)

20. 《儒教、佛教、道教、基督教与中国文化》Yijie Tang（汤一介）, *Confucianism, Buddhism, Daoism, Christianity and Chinese Culture*. Springer Berlin Heidelberg (2015)

21. 《儒—法国家：中国历史新论》Dingxin Zhao（赵鼎新）, *The Confucian-Legalist State: A New Theory of Chinese History*. Oxford University Press (2015)

22. 《美德家庭：儒家思想与西方对童年发展的看法》Erin M. Cline, *Families of Virtue: Confucian and Western Views on Childhood Development*. Columbia University Press (2015)

23. 《儒家礼仪学习：哲学阐释》Geir Sigurosson & Geir Sigursson, *Confucian Propriety and Ritual Learning: A Philosophical Interpretation*. State University of New York Press (2015)

24. 《圣人与民众：中国儒学的复兴》Sébastien Billioud, *The Sage and the People: The Confucian Revival in China*. New York: Oxford University Press (2015)

25. 《思想与行动中的当代儒学》Guy Alitto（艾恺）(eds.), *Contemporary Confucianism in Thought and Action*. Springer-Verlag Berlin Heidelberg (2015)

26. 《经典儒家哲学之道》Vincent Shen, *Dao Companion to Classical Confucian Philosophy*. Springer Netherlands (2014)

27. 《日本儒家哲学指南》Chun-chieh Huang, John Allen Tucker (eds.), *Dao Companion to Japanese Confucian Philosophy*. Springer Netherlands (2014)

28. 《道德修养与儒家特质》Chenyang Li and Peimin Ni, *Moral Cultivation and Confucian Character: Engaging Joel J. Kupperman*. State University of New York Press (2014)

29. 《儒家文化与民主》John Fuh-sheng Hsieh, *Confucian Culture and Democracy*. World Scientific Publishing Company (2014)

30. 《儒学简介》Daniel K. Gardner, *Confucianism: A Very Short Introduction*. Oxford

University Press (2014)

31. 《重建儒家之道：朱熹对周敦颐的盗用》Joseph Alan Adler, Dunyi Zhou, Xi Zhu, *Reconstructing the Confucian Dao: Zhu Xi's Appropriation of Zhou Dunyi*. State University of New York Press (2014)

32. 《实施跨文化教学：儒家传统文化的合作学习》Pham Thi Hong Thanh, *Implementing Cross-Culture Pedagogies: Cooperative Learning at Confucian Heritage Cultures*. Springer-Verlag Singapur (2014)

33. 《东亚的性别和福利国家：儒家还是两性平等》Sirin Sung, Gillian Pascall (eds.), *Gender and Welfare States in East Asia: Confucianism or Gender Equality*. Palgrave Macmillan UK (2014)

34. 《爱默生与理学：跨越太平洋的道路》Yoshio Takanashi, *Emerson and Neo-Confucianism: Crossing Paths over the Pacific*. Palgrave Macmillan US (2014)

35. 《东亚地区的儒家遗产及其现代适应》Gilbert Rozman（饶济凡）, *The East Asian Region: Confucian Heritage and Its Modern Adaptation*. Princeton University Press (2014)

36. 《儒家礼仪与中国乡民：1368—1949年闽西四堡的礼仪变革与社会转型》Yonghua Liu（刘永华）, *Confucian Rituals and Chinese Villagers: Ritual Change and Social Transformation in a Southeastern Chinese Community, 1368—1949*. Brill (2013)

37. 《作为世界宗教的儒学：有争议的历史与当代现实》Anna Xiao Dong Sun, *Confucianism as a World Religion: Contested Histories and Contemporary Realities*. Princeton University Press (2013)

38. 《儒家完美主义：现代政治哲学》Joseph Chan, *Confucian Perfectionism: A Political Philosophy for Modern Times*. Princeton University Press (2013)

39. 《韩国经济发展道路：儒家传统、情感网络》Seok-Choon Lew (eds.), *The Korean Economic Developmental Path: Confucian Tradition, Affective Network*. Palgrave Macmillan US (2013)

40. 《经典儒家哲学指南》Qingsong Shen, *Dao companion to Classical Confucian Philosophy*. Springer (2013)

41. 《美德伦理与儒家思想》Stephen Angle, Michael Slote, *Virtue Ethics and Confucianism*. Routledge (2013)

42. 《儒学百科全书》（二卷本）Xinzhong Yao, *The Encyclopedia of Confucianism*, 2-volume set. Routledge (2013)

43. 《伟大的平等社会：儒学、中国和21世纪》Young-Oak Kim, Jung-Kyu Kim, *The Great Equal Society: Confucianism, China and the 21st Century*. World Scientific Publishing Company (2013)

44. 《人类有未来吗？与最后的儒家对话》Shu Ming Liang（梁漱溟）, Guy S. Alitto（艾恺）, *Has Man a Future? Dialogues with the Last Confucian*. Springer Berlin Heidelberg (2013)

45. 《早期儒学中的仪式失灵》(Oxford Ritual Studies) Michael David Kaulana Ing, *The Dysfunction of Ritual in Early Confucianism*. Oxford University Press (2012)

46. 《当代儒家政治哲学》Stephen Angle, *Contemporary Confucian Political Philosophy*. Polity Press (2012)
47. 《李贽、儒家和欲望之德》Lee Pauline C., *Li Zhi, Confucianism, and the Virtue of Desire*. State University of New York Press (2012)
48. 《儒学、民主化与台湾人权》Joel Fetzer, J. Christopher Soper, *Confucianism, Democratization, and Human Rights in Taiwan*. Lexington Books (2012)
49. 《儒家民族主义的社会性别政治：妇女与日本民族国家》Nicole L. Freiner, *The Social and Gender Politics of Confucian Nationalism: Women and the Japanese Nation-State*. Palgrave Macmillan US (2012)
50. 《中国的儒家改造：国家赞助的儒家思想和谐话语与作为国家形象管理的中国"和平崛起"》Rachael Gary, *China's Confucian Makeover: The Discourse of Harmony in State-Sponsored Confucianism and China's "Peaceful Rise" as National Image Management*. University of Puget Sound (2011—2012)
51. 《孔子、罗尔斯与正义意识》Erin M. Cline, *Confucius, Rawls, and the Sense of Justice*. Fordham University Press (2012)
52. 《当代中国儒学复兴》Ruiping Fan, *The Renaissance of Confucianism in Contemporary China*. Springer (2011)
53. 《董仲舒的儒家传承和〈春秋繁露〉》Michael Loewe（鲁惟一）, *Dong Zhongshu, A 'Confucian' Heritage and the Chunqiu Fanlu*. Brill (2011)
54. 《儒家思想与东亚民主化》Doh Chull Shin, *Confucianism and Democratization in East Asia*. Cambridge University Press (2011)
55. 《朝鲜的妇女与儒学：新观点》Youngmin Kim, Michael J. Petid, *Women and Confucianism in Chosŏn Korea: New Perspectives*. State University of New York Press, Albany (2011)
56. 《儒学概论》Ronnie Littlejohn, *Confucianism: An Introduction*. I.B.Tauris & Co Ltd (2011)
57. 《顽强：中国儒家资本主义、美国坚韧品格与下一次经济复兴》Christopher D. Brooke, *Tenacious: The Confucian Capitalism of China, the Tenacity of the American Character, and the Next Economic Renaissance*. Zionsville, Ind.: Wealth Shift Pub. (2011)
58. 《儒家统治的时代：宋的转型》(History of Imperial China) Dieter Kuhn (Sinologe), *The Age of Confucian Rule: The Song Transformation of China*. Belknap Press of Harvard University Press (2011)
59. 《儒学语境：传统哲学与当代问题、东亚及超越》Wonsuk Chang, Leah Kalmanson (Editors), *Confucianism in Context: Classic Philosophy and Contemporary Issues, East Asia and Beyond*. State University of New York (2010)
60. 《圣贤：新儒家哲学的当代意义》Stephen C. Angle, *Sagehood: The Contemporary Significance of NeoConfucian Philosophy*. Oxford University Press (2010)
61. 《和谐与战争：儒家文化与中国强权政治》Yuan-kang Wang, *Harmony and War:*

Confucian Culture and Chinese Power Politics. Columbia University Press (2010)

62. 《想象和谐：德川中期儒学与本土主义的诗歌、移情和社区》Peter Flueckiger, *Imagining Harmony: Poetry, Empathy, and Community in Mid-Tokugawa Confucianism and Nativism.* Stanford University Press (2010)

63. 《重建儒家思想：西方之后重新思考道德》Ruiping Fan, *Reconstructionist Confucianism: Rethinking Morality after the West.* Springer Netherlands (2010)

64. 《新儒家哲学指南》Tze-ki Hon (auth.), John Makeham (eds.), *Dao Companion to Neo-Confucian Philosophy.* Springer Netherlands (2010)

65. 《儒学》（第3版）Dorothy Hoobler, Thomas Hoobler, *Confucianism, 3rd Edition* (World Religions). Chelsea House Publications (2009)

66. 《和平和政治：以弗所书、Dio Chrysostom和儒家四书》Te-Li Lau, *The Politics of Peace: Ephesians, Dio Chrysostom, and the Confucian Four Books.* Brill (2009)

67. 《历史上的新儒家》Peter K. Bol（包弼德）, *Neo-Confucianism in history.* Harvard University Press (2008)

68. 《儒家教学》Jeffrey L. Richey, *Teaching Confucianism* (AAR Teaching Religious Studies Series). Oxford University Press (2008)

69. 《儒家政治伦理》Daniel A. Bell（淡贝宁）(ed.), *Confucian Political Ethics* (Ethikon Series in Comparative Ethics). Princeton University Press (2008)

70. 《中国新儒学：变动社会中的政治和日常生活》Daniel A. Bell（淡贝宁）, *China's New Confucianism: Politics and Everyday Life in a Changing Society* (New in Paper). Princeton University Press (2008)

71. 《儒家伦理观的回顾与展望》Qingsong Shen（沈清松）, Kwong-loi Shun, *Confucian Ethics in Retrospect and Prospect.* Council for Research in Values & Philosophy (2007)

72. 《真正的儒家，勇敢的基督徒：韩国传教士的经验，第三个千年典范》Antton Egiguren Iraola, *True Confucians, bold Christians: Korean missionary experience. A model for the third millennium.* (Studies in World Christianity and Interreligious Realtions). Editions Rodopi B.V. (2007)

73. 《儒家权威文化》Peter D. Hershock, Roger T. Ames（安乐哲）, *Confucian Cultures of Authority* (Suny Series in Asian Studies Development). State University of New York Press (2006)

74. 《儒家与女性：一种哲学解读》Li-hsiang Lisa Rosenlee, *Confucianism And Women: A Philosophical Interpretation.* State University of New York (2006)

75. 《日本财富与权力的起源：调和儒家与资本主义（1830—1885）》John H. Sagers, *Origins of Japanese Wealth and Power: Reconciling Confucianism and Capitalism, 1830—1885.* Palgrave Macmillan US (2006)

76. 《早期儒家智慧和以色列传统：比较研究》Xinzhong Yao, *Wisdom in Early Confucian And Israelite Traditions: A Comparative Study* (Ashgate World Philosophies Series). Ashgate

Publishing (2006)

77. 《转型时期的东亚福利制度：从儒学到全球化》Alan Walker, Chack-Kie Wong, *East Asian Welfare Regimes in Transition: From Confucianism to Globalisation*. The Policy Press (2005)
78. 《图解儒学百科全书》Rodney Leon Taylor, Howard Y. F. Choy, *The Illustrated Encyclopedia of Confucianism*. The Rosen Publishing Group (2005)
79. 《儒家》Rodney Leon Taylor, *Confucianism*. Chelsea House Publishers (2004)
80. 《儒家伦理：自我、自治和社区的比较研究》Kwong-Loi Shun, David B. Wong, *Confucian Ethics: A Comparative Study of Self, Autonomy, and Community*. Cambridge University Press (2004)
81. 《儒家民主：杜威式重建》Sor-Hoon Tan, *Confucian Democracy: A Deweyan Reconstruction*. State University of New York (2004)
82. 《埃兹拉·庞德与儒学：面向现代性的人文主义重建》Feng Lan, *Ezra Pound and Confucianism: Remaking Humanism in the Face of Modernity*. University of Toronto Press (2004)
83. 《古代儒家思想中描绘的美国文明》Wei-Bin Zhang, *American Civilization Portrayed in Ancient Confucianism*. Algora Publishing (2003)
84. 《当代新儒家哲学的本质》Shu-hsien Liu（刘述先）, *Essentials of Contemporary Neo-Confucian Philosophy*. Praeger Publishers (2003)
85. 《中国新儒学：批判性的审视》John Makeham（梅约翰）, *China's New Confucianism: A Critical Examination*. Palgrave Macmillan (2003)
86. 《现代世界之儒家思想》Daniel A. Bell（淡贝宁）, Hahm Chaibong (eds.), *Confucianism for the Modern World*. Cambridge University Press (2003)
87. 《儒家生命伦理》Ruiping Fan, *Confucian Bioethics*. Springer Netherlands (2002)
88. 《儒家思想基础：春秋时期的知识分子生活》Yuri Pines, *Foundations of Confucian Thought: Intellectual Life in the Chunqiu Period, 722–453 B. C. E.* University of Hawai'i Press (2002)
89. 《越南儒学》Hồ Chí Minh City, *Confucianism in VietNam*. Vietnam National University and Hồ Chí Minh City Publishing House (2002)
90. 《波士顿儒学：晚期现代世界的可移植传统》Robert Cummings Neville（南乐山）, *Boston Confucianism: Portable Tradition in the Late Modern World*. State University of New York Press (2000)
91. 《儒学简介》Berthron, *Confucianism: A Short Introduction*. Oneworld Publications (2000)
92. 《儒学入门》Xinzhong Yao（姚新中）, *An Introduction to Confucianism*. Cambridge University Press (2000)
93. 《儒学与现代化：儒家文化圈的工业化与民主化》Wei-Bin Zhang, *Confucianism and Modernization: Industrialization and Democratization of the Confucian Regions*. Palgrave Macmillan UK (2000)
94. 《儒学与朝鲜思想》Keum Jang-tae, *Confucianism and Korean Thoughts*. Jmoondang Pub.

Co. (2000)

95. 《理学精要：宋明八大哲学家》Siu-Chi Huang, *Essentials of Neo-Confucianism: Eight Major Philosophers of the Song and Ming Periods*. Greenwood (1999)

96. 《儒学与家庭》George A. De Vos, Walter H. Slote, *Confucianism and the Family*. State University of New York Press (1998)

97. 《编造儒学：中国传统与普世文明》Lionel M. Jensen, *Manufacturing Confucianism: Chinese Traditions and Universal Civilization*. Durham, NC, USA Duke University Press (1998)

98. 《正统与异端的建构：新儒家、伊斯兰、犹太与早期基督教模式》John B. Henderson, *The Construction of Orthodoxy and Heresy: Neo-Confucian, Islamic, Jewish, and Early Christian Patterns*. State University of New York Press (1998)

99. 《埃兹拉·庞德的儒学翻译》Mary Paterson Cheadle, *Ezra Pound's Confucian Translations*. Ann Arbor: University of Michigan Press (1997)

100. 《儒家治国之道与朝鲜制度：Yu Hyongwon与朝鲜王朝后期》James B. Palais, *Confucian Statecraft and Korean Institutions: Yu Hyongwon and the Late Choson Dynasty*. University of Washington Press (1996)

101. 《儒家的困境》Wm. Theodore de Bary（狄百瑞）, *The Trouble with Confucianism* (The Tanner Lectures on Human Values). Harvard University Press (1996)

102. 《专制之限制：从宋朝新儒家思想到政治权力学说》Alan T. Wood, *Limits to Autocracy: From Sung Neo-Confucianism to a Doctrine of Political Rights*. University of Hawai'i Press (1995)

103. 《中华帝制晚期儒家礼教的兴起：伦理、经典和血统话语》Kai-Wing Chow（周启荣）, *The Rise of Confucian Ritualism in Late Imperial China-Ethics, Classics, and Lineage Discourse*. Stanford University Press (1994)

104. 《轴心时代的儒家伦理：突破后传统思维方式的重建》Heiner Roetz, *Confucian Ethics of the Axial Age: A Reconstruction under the Aspect of the Breakthrough toward Postconventional Thinking* (Suny Series in Chinese Philosophy & Culture). State Univ of New York (1993)

105. 《儒家话语与朱熹的影响》Hoyt Cleveland Tillman, *Confucian Discourse and Chu His's Ascendancy*. Honolulu: University of Hawaii Press (1992)

106. 《儒教、佛教、道教、基督教与中国文化》Tang Yi-Jie（汤一介）, *Confucianism, Buddhism, Daoism, Christianity and Chinese Culture*. The Council for Research in Values and Philosophy (1991)

107. 《中华帝国的儒家与家庭仪式：礼仪写作的社会史》Patricia Buckley Ebrey（伊沛霞）, *Confucianism and Family Rituals in Imperial China: A Social History of Writing about Rites*. Princeton University Press (1991)

108. 《儒家和新儒家哲学观的新维度》Chung-Ying Cheng（成中英）, *New Dimensions of Confucian and Neo-Confucian Philosophy*. State University of New York Press (1991)

109. 《儒家的天国创造》Robert Eno, *The Confucian Creation of Heaven: Philosophy and the*

Defense of Ritual Mastery. State University of New York Press (1990)

110. 《李栗谷的韩国新儒学》Young-Chan Ro, *The Korean Neo-Confucianism of Yi Yulgok*. State University of New York Press (1989)

111. 《核心和共性：论儒家宗教性》Wei-ming Tu（杜维明）, *Centrality and Commonality: An Essay on Confucian Religiousness* (SUNY Series in Chinese Philosophy and Culture). State University of New York Press (1989)

112. 《朱熹与新儒家》Wing-Tsit Chan（陈荣捷）, *Chu Hsi and Neo-Confucianism*. University of Hawaii Press (1986)

113. 《儒家思想：创意转化的个性》Wei-ming Tu（杜维明）, *Confucian Thought: Selfhood As Creative Transformation* (SUNY Series in Philosophy). State University of New York Press (1985)

114. 《儒学与专制：明代建国的职业精英》John W. Dardess, *Confucianism and Autocracy: Professional Elites in the Founding of the Ming Dynasty*. University of California Press (1984)

115. 《从理学到朴学：中华帝国晚期思想与社会变化面面观》Benjamin A. Elman（艾尔曼）, *From Philosophy to Philology: Intellectual and Social Aspects of Change in Late Imperial China*. Harvard University Press (1984)

116. 《儒家与基督教：首次相遇》John D. Young, *Confucianism and Christianity: The First Encounter*. Hong Kong University Press (1983)

117. 《最后的儒家：梁漱溟与中国现代化的两难》Guy Alitto（艾恺）, *The Last Confucian: Liang Shu-ming and the Chinese Dilemma of Modernity*. University of California Press (1979)

118. 《莱布尼茨与儒学：寻求共识》David E. Mungello（孟德卫）, *Leibniz and Confucianism: The Search for Accord*. Honolulu: University Press of Hawaii (1977)

119. 《摆脱困境：新儒学与中国政治文化的演进》Thomas A. Metzger（墨子刻）, *Escape from Predicament: Neo-Confucianism and China's Evolving Political Culture*. New York: Columbia University Press (1977)

120. 《征服者与儒家：中国元代晚期政治变迁的几个方面》John W. Dardess, *Conquerors and Confucians: Aspects of Political Change in Late Yüan China*. Columbia University Press (1973)

121. 《孔子与儒学》Richard Wilhelm（卫礼贤）, George H. Danton, Annina Periam Danton, *Confucius and Confucianism*. Routledge & Kegan Paul PLC (1972)

122. 《儒教中国及其现代命运：思想继承性问题》（第一卷）Joseph R. Levenson（列文森）, *Confucian China and its Modern Fate: A Trilogy. Volume 1: The Problem of Intellectual Continuity*. University of California Press (1968)

123. 《儒教中国及其现代命运：君主制衰亡问题》（第二卷）Joseph R. Levenson（列文森）, *Confucian China and Its Modern Fate: A Trilogy. Volume 2: The Problem of Monarchial Decay*. University of California Press (1968)

124. 《儒教中国及其现代命运：历史意义问题》（第三卷）Joseph R. Levenson（列文森）, *Confucian China and Its Modern Fate: A Trilogy. Volume 3: The Problem of Historical*

Significance. University of California Press (1968)

125. 《中国福音》（《四书》摘译本，由法文译本 Confucius et Mencius 重译为英文）M. G. Pauthier (author), Duncan Greenlees (editor and translator), *The Gospel of China: "Love Virtue, and then the People will be virtuous."* The Theosophical Publishing House (1949)

126. 《儒家政治哲学：孔子及其先辈、早期弟子的社会政治思想解读》Leonard Shih-lien Hsü, *The Political Philosophy of Confucianism: An Interpretation of the Social and Political Ideas of Confucius, His Forerunners, and His Early Disciples.* New York, E.P. Dutton (1932)

127. 《儒学及其竞争对手》Herbert A. Giles（翟理斯）, *Confucianism and its Rivals.* London: Williams and Norgate (1915)

128. 《圣书：儒家、希伯来人、基督教、佛教、印度教、穆罕默德》Charles William Eliot, *Sacred Writings: Confucian, Hebrew, Christian, Buddhist, Hindu, Mohammedan.* New York Collier & Sons (1910)

129. 《儒学汇纂：〈论语〉〈中庸〉〈大学〉》（第二版）Ernst Faber（花之安）, Paul Georg von Möllendorff, *A Systematical Digest of the Doctrines of Confucius: According to the Analects, Great Learning, and Doctrine of the Mean.* Second Edition. Shanghai: The General Evangelical Protestant Missionary Society of Germany (1902)

130. 《中国圣书：儒学文本。第一部：〈书经〉》（第二版）Translated by James Legge（理雅各）, *The Sacred Books of China: The Texts of Confucianism. Part 1: The Shu King.* Second Edition. Oxford Clarendon Press (1899)

131. 《中国圣书：儒学文本。第三部：〈礼记〉》Translated by James Legge（理雅各）, *The Sacred Books of China: The Texts of Confucianism. Part 3: The Li Ki.* Oxford, the Clarendon Press (1885)

132. 《儒学汇纂：〈论语〉〈中庸〉〈大学〉》Ernst Faber（花之安）, P. G. von Moellendorff, *A Systematical Digest of the Doctrines of Confucius: According to the Analects, Great Learning and Doctrine of the Mean, with an introduction on the authorities upon Confucius and Confucianism.* Hong Kong: The China Mail Office (1875)

6.2.2 孔子

1. 《中国思想：从孔子到庖丁》Roel Sterckx（胡司德）, *Chinese Thought: From Confucius to Cook Ding* (Pelican Books). Pelican (2019)

2. 《简明孔子手册》Confucius, Paul Rakita Goldin, *A Concise Companion to Confucius* (Blackwell companions to philosophy). John Wiley & Sons Ltd (2017)

3. 《历史解读：孔子到汤因比》(Routledge Library Editions Historiography) Alban G. Widgery, *Interpretations of History: Confucius to Toynbee.* Routledge (2016)

4. 《孔子及其开创的世界》Michael Schuman, *Confucius and the World He Created.* Basic Books (2015)

5. 《谁的传统？哪个道？孔子和维特根斯坦论道德学习与思考》James F. Peterman, *Whose*

Tradition? Which Dao? Confucius and Wittgenstein on Moral Learning and Reflection. State University of New York Press (2015)

6. 《基督徒的孔子：中国古代世界观能教会我们怎样在基督里生活》Gregg A. Ten Elshof, *Confucius for Christians: What an Ancient Chinese Worldview Can Teach Us about Life in Christ.* Wm. B. Eerdmans Publishing Co. (2015)

7. 《孔子》Charlene Tan, *Confucius*.Bloomsbury Academic (2013)

8. 《孔子：迷惘者的向导》Yong Huang, Qiu Kong, *Confucius: A Guide for the Perplexed.* Bloomsbury Academic (2013)

9. 《孔子：无冕之王》Meher McArthur, *Confucius: A Throneless King.* Open Road Integrated Media (2012)

10. 《孔子》Meher McArthur, *Confucius.* Quercus (2010)

11. 《孔子与儒学精要》Lee Dian Rainey, *Confucius and Confucianism: The Essentials.* Wiley-Blackwell (2010)

12. 《孔子的一生：历代文明最伟大的圣人》Michael Nylan, Thomas Wilson, *Lives of Confucius: Civilization's Greatest Sage Through the Ages.*Crown Archetype (2010)

13. 《孔子：中国哲学家》Wendy Conklin, M.A., Gisela Lee, *Confucius: Chinese Philosopher.* World Cultures through Time (2008)

14. 《用亚里士多德和孔子重建道德》May Sim, *Remastering Morals with Aristotle and Confucius.*Cambridge University Press (2007)

15. 《孔子《中庸》》Kung Fu Tsu, James Legge（理雅各，Translator), *Confucius, The Doctrine of The Mean.* Kessinger Publishing, LLC (2004)

16. 《孔子精要》Thomas Cleary, *Essential Confucius.*Castle Books, US (2000)

17. 《聚焦孔子：中国经典与文化价值》Linda Arkin, *Spotlight on Confucius: Chinese Classics and Cultural Values.* Updated. American Forum for Global Education New York (2000)

18. 《住在隔壁的孔子：东方生活教会我们如何在西方生活》T. R. Reid, *Confucius Lives Next Door: What Living in the East Teaches Us about Living in the West.*Vintage Books (1999)

19. 《如何在韩国取得商业成功：穿着三件套西装的孔子》Chong Ju Choi, Nigel Wright, *How to Achieve Business Success in Korea: Where Confucius Wears a Three-Piece Suit.* Palgrave Macmillan UK (1994)

20. 《孔子哲学思微》David L. Hall（郝大维）, Roger T. Ames（安乐哲）, *Thinking Through Confucius.* State University of New York Press (1987)

21. 《孔子教育制度的若干问题》Robert V. Schnucker, *Some Aspects of the Educational System of Confucius.* U. S. Department of Health, Education and Welfare, National Institute of Education (1974)

22. 《孔子》Shigeki Kaizuka, Translated by Geoffrey Bownas, *Confucius.* London: George Allen and Unwin Ltd; New York: The Macmillan Company (1956)

23. 《孔子的生平与时代》Liu Wu-Chi, *Confucius: His Life and Time*. Philosophical Library, New York (1955).

24. 《孔子其人与神话》Herrlee G. Creel（顾立雅）, *Confucius: The Man & the Myth*. Routledge & Kegan Paul Ltd (1949).

25. 《孔子塑造的中国：西部之光照耀下的中国道路》Tien-hsi Cheng（郑天锡）, *China Moulded by Confucius: The Chinese Way in Western Light*. London: Stevens and Sons Limited (1947).

26. 《鲜活的孔子思想》Alfred Doeblin, *The Living Thoughts of Confucius*. Cassell and Company, Limited (1945).

27. 《孔子的智慧》Yutang Lin（林语堂）, *The Wisdom of Confucius*. Karlton House, New York (1938).

28. 《日本印象：孔子笔记》Paul Louis Couchoud, Frances Rumsey, *Japanese Impressions: With a Note on Confucius*. London: John Lane; New York: John Lane Company (1921).

29. 《孔子伦理》Confucius; American Institute for Scientific Research; Miles Menander Dawson, *The Ethics of Confucius*. New York, London, G. P. Putnam's sons (1915).

30. 《生命规范：孔子伦理》Confucius; Miles Menander Dawson, *The Conduct of Life: The Ethics of Confucius*. New York: Carlton House (1915).

31. 《孔夫子：一首戏剧诗》Paul Carus, *K'ung Fu Tze: A Dramatic Poem*. The Open Court Publishing Co. (1915).

32. 《孔子之前的中国道德情怀：伦理评价起源研究》Herbert Finley Rudd, *Chinese Moral Sentiments before Confucius: A Study in the Origin of Ethical Valuations*. Shanghai, Christian Literature Society Depot (1914).

33. 《孔子经济思想及其学派/孔门理财学》（博士论文）Chen Huan-Chang（陈焕章）, *The Economic Principles of Confucius and his School*. Ph. D. Dissertation, New York, Columbia University (1911).

34. 《孔子与儒学四讲》W. Gilbert Walshe, *Confucius and Confucianism: Four Lectures*. Shanghai: Kelly & Walsh (1911).

35. 《孔孟中国经典引论》James Legge（理雅各）, *The Prologomena to the Chinese Classics of Confucius and Mencius*. Oxford University Press (1907).

36. 《孔子的智慧》Epiphanius Wilson, *The Wisdom of Confucius* (Classic Reprint). Forgotten Books (1900, 2017).

37. 《孔子的智慧》Epiphanius Wilson, *The Wisdom of Confucius*. The Colonial Press (1900).

38. 《孔子生平、成就和学说》Edward Harper Parker（庄延龄）, *The Life, Labours and Doctrines of Confucius*. Oriental university institute, Woking (1897).

39. 《伟大的教师孔子研究》George Gardiner Alexander, *Confucius, the Great Teacher: A Study*. London, K. Paul, Trench, Trübner (1890).

40. 《孔子的生平与教义，附解释性说明》（第六版）James Legge（理雅各）, *The Life and Teaching of Confucius, with Explanatory Notes*. Sixth Edition. London, Trübner and Co. (1887)

41. 《孔子与中国经典：中国文学读物》A. W. (Augustus Ward) Loomis, Confucius; Mencius; James Legge（理雅各）(tr.), *Confucius and the Chinese Classics: Or, Readings in Chinese Literature*. San Francisco, A. Roman; Boston, Lee and Shepard (1882)

42. 《孔庙碑文指南》Thomas Watters, *A Guide to the Tablets in a Temple of Confucius*. Shanghai, China-America Presbyterian Mission Press (1879)

43. 《孔子的生平与教义，附解释性说明》（第四版）James Legge（理雅各）, *The Life and Teaching of Confucius, with Explanatory Notes*. Fourth Edition. London, Trübner and Co. (1875)

44. 《孔子的音乐课及其他诗歌》Charles Godfrey Leland, *The Music-lesson of Confucius, and other Poems*. Boston: James R. Osgood and Company, late Ticknor and Fields, and Fields, Osgood, and Co. (1872)

45. 《中国哲学家孔子的道德箴言》Confucius, L. E. Barnard, *Moral Sayings of Confucius: A Chinese Philosopher*. Cleveland, Ohio, A. B. & Co. (1855)

46. 《中国哲学家孔子的道德箴言》Translated from the Chinese by R. F. Incorcetta and Couplet, *The phenix: A Collection of Old and Rare Fragments; Viz. The Morals of Confucius: The Chinese Philosopher, Who Flourished about Five Hundred Years before Christ*. New York: William Govan (1835)

47. 《孔子著作，含原文和翻译》（第一卷）Joshua Marshman, *The Works of Confucius, Containing the Original Text, with a Translation*, Vol.1. Serampore: the Mission Press (1809)

48. 《中国哲学家孔子的道德箴言》Confucius, *The Morals of Confucius: A Chinese Philosopher, Who Flourished Above Five Hundred Years Before the Coming of Our Lord and Saviour Jesus Christ. Being one of the most Choicest Pieces of Learning Remaining of That Nation*. London: printed for F. Fayram (1724)

49. 《西文四书直解（中国哲学家孔子）》Confucius; Prospero Intorcetta（殷铎泽）, Chrétien R. Herdtrich（恩理格）, Franciscode Rougemont（鲁日满）, Philippe Couplet（柏应理）, *Confucius sinarum philosophus, sive, Scientia sinensis latine exposita, Scientia sinensis latine exposita*. Parisiis, Apud Danielem Horthemels (1687)

6.2.3 《论语》

1. 《插图本孔子〈论语〉》(The Illustrated Library of Chinese Classics) C. C. Tsai, Brian Bruya, Michael Puett, *Confucius: The Analects: An Illustrated Edition*. Princeton University Press (2018)

2. 《耶稣会士的孔子阅读：1687年西方出版的首部〈论语〉全译本》Confucius, Thierry Meynard, *The Jesuit Reading of Confucius: The First Complete Translation of the Lunyu (1687) Published in the West*. Brill Academic Pub (2015)

3. 《〈论语〉：在线教学翻译》Robert Eno, *Analects of Confucius: An Online Teaching Translation*. (2015) http://www.indiana.edu/~p374/Analects: of: Confucius: (Eno-2015).pdf

4. 《〈论语〉指南》Amy Olberding, *Dao Companion to the Analects*. Springer Netherlands (2014)

5. 《〈论语〉英译》Translated by James Legge（理雅各）, *The Analects of Confucius*. Createspace (2014)

6. 《孔子〈论语〉》Translated with An Introduction and Commentary by Annping Chin（金安平）, *Confucius: The Analects* (Penguin Classics). Penguin Classics (2014)

7. 《孔子〈论语〉读本》Henry Rosemont, Jr.（罗思文）, *A Reader's Companion to the Confucian Analects*. Palgrave Macmillan US (2013)

8. 《孔子〈论语〉与西方教育》Frank M. Flanagan, *Confucius, the Analects, and Western Education*. Continuum International Publishing Group (2011)

9. 《孔子〈论语〉》Confucius, Translated by Burton Watson（华兹生）, *Confucius: The Analects of Confucius* (Translations from the Asian classics: Columbia Asian studies series). Columbia University Press (2007)

10. 《谢良佐与〈论语〉：作为一种宗教追求的人文学习》Thomas W. Selover, *Hsieh Liang-tso and the Analects of Confucius: Humane Learning as a Religious Quest* (American Academy of Religion: Academy Series). Oxford University Press (2005)

11. 《论朱熹对〈论语〉的解读：准则、评论与古典传统》Daniel K. Gardner, *Zhu Xi's Reading of the Analects: Canon, Commentary, and the Classical Tradition*. Columbia University Press (2003)

12. 《〈论语〉：附传统评论精选》Confucius; Translated by Edward Slingerland, *Analects with Selections from Traditional Commentaries* (Hackett Classics Series). Hackett Publishing Company, Inc. (2003)

13. 《传播者与创作者：〈论语〉的中国评论者和评论》John Makeham, *Transmitters and Creators: Chinese Commentators and Commentaries on the Analect*. Cambridge: Harvard University Asia Center: Distributed by Harvard University Press (2003)

14. 《孔子与〈论语〉》Bryan W. Van Norden, *Confucius and the Analects: New Essays*. Oxford University Press (2002)

15. 《论语辩》E. Bruce Brooks（白牧之）, A. Taeko Brooks（白妙子）, *The Original Analects: Sayings of Confucius and His Successors*. Columbia University Press (2001)

16. 《孔子〈论语〉》Translated and annotated by Arthur Waley（阿瑟·韦利）, *The Analects of Confucius*. London: George Allen and Unwin Ltd. (1938)

17. 《论语》Leonard A. lyall, *The Sayings of Confucius*. Longmans, Green and Co. (1925)

18. 《孔子〈论语〉新译》Confucius; Lionel Giles（翟林奈）, *The Sayings of Confucius: A New Translation of the Greater Part of the Confucian Analects*. New York, E. P. Dutton and Company (1910, 1915)

19. 《〈论语〉英译》William Edward Soothill（苏慧廉）, *The Analects of Confucius*. Yokohama: Printed by the Fukuin Printing Co. (1910)

20. 《〈论语〉新译》Lionel Giles（翟林奈）, *The Sayings of Confucius: A New Translation of the*

Greater Part of the Confucian Analects, with Introduction and Notes. London: John Murray. (1907)

21. 《鸿铭先生集译：〈论语〉译英文》Ku Hung-ming, *The Discourses and Sayings of Confucius: A New Special Translation, Illustrated with Quotations from Goethe and other Writers*. Shanghai: Kelly and Walsh, Limited (1898)

6.2.4 老子、庄子与《道德经》

1. 《老子〈道德经〉：中国古代道书精译》Translated with an Introduction and Commentary by John Minford, *Lao Tzu: Tao Te Ching: The Essential Translation of the Ancient Chinese Book of the Tao*. Viking (4 Dec 2018)
2. 《中国早期道教：从出土文献看黄老思想》Feng Cao, *Daoism in Early China: Huang-Lao Thought in Light of Excavated Texts*. Palgrave MacMillan (2017)
3. 《道：关于美好生活中国哲学家可以教给我们什么》Michael Puett, Christine Gross-Loh, *The Path: What Chinese Philosophers Can Teach Us About the Good Life*. Simon & Schuster (2016)
4. 《庄子新译（附郭象哲学解释）》Chuang Tzu, Yu-lan Fung（冯友兰）, *Chuang-Tzu: A New Selected Translation with an Exposition of the Philosophy of Kuo Hsiang*. Springer-Verlag Berlin Heidelberg (2016)
5. 《道家哲学指南》Xiaogan Liu (ed.), *Dao Companion to Daoist Philosophy*. Springer Netherlands (2015)
6. 《老子〈道德经〉》David Hinton, *Lao Tzu: Tao Te Ching*. Counterpoint (2015)
7. 《庄子全集》(Translations from the Asian Classics) Burton Watson（华兹生）, *The Complete Works of Zhuangzi*. Columbia University Press (2013)
8. 《道：一种新的思维方式——〈道德经〉的译介与评论》Yuan Chang Chung, *Tao: A New Way of Thinking: A Translation of the Tao Te Ching with an Introduction and Commentaries*. Singing Dragon (2013)
9. 《老子〈道德经〉》Translated with notes by Edmund Ryden（雷敦龢）, *Daodejing-Laozi*. Oxford University Press (2008)
10. 《道德经》Lao Tse（老子）, James Legge（理雅各）, *The Tao Te Ching* (Laminated Hardcover). Arc Manor (2008)
11. 《作为断言的解脱：老子和尼采的宗教性》Geling Shang, *Liberation as Affirmation: The Religiosity of Zhuangzi and Nietzsche*. State University of New York (2006)
12. 《〈道德经〉的哲学》Hans-Georg Moellerr, *The Philosophy of the Daodejing*. Columbia University Press (2006)
13. 《〈道德经〉的中国解读：王弼关于老子的评论，附批评性文本和翻译》Rudolf G. Wagner, *A Chinese Reading of the Daodejing: Wang Bi's Commentary On the Laozi With Critical Text and Translation*. State University of New York Press (2003)
14. 《庄子基本著作》Zhuangzi, Burton Watson, *Zhuangzi: Basic Writings* (Translations from the Asian classics). Columbia University Press (2003)

15. 《〈道德经〉今生更有意义：一种哲学翻译》Roger T. Ames（安乐哲）, David L. Hall （郝大维）, *Daodejing "Making This Life Significant": A Philosophical Translation*. Ballantine Books (2003)

16. 《老子〈道德经〉》Lau Tzu & Moss Roberts（罗慕士）, *Dao De Jing: The Book of the Way*. University of California Press (2001)

17. 《中国评论家的技艺：王弼论老子》Rudolf G. Wagner, *The Craft of a Chinese Commentator: Wang Bi on the Laozi* (SUNY Series in Chinese Philosophy and Culture). State University of New York Press (2000)

18. 《老子的宗教和哲学》Mark Csikszentmihalyi, Philip J. Ivanhoe, *Religious and Philosophical Aspects of the Laozi*. State University of New York Press (1999)

19. 《〈道德经〉精华选译》Sam Hamill and J. P. Seaton, *The Essential Chuang Tzu*. Shambhala Publications, Inc. (1999)

20. 《老子道德经》Ursula K. Le Guin（娥苏拉·勒瑰恩）, *Lao Tzu Tao Te Ching: A Book about the Way and the Power of the Way* (New edition). Shambhala (1998)

21. 《艾兰：水之道与德之端》Sarah Allan, *The Way of Water and Sprouts of Virtue*. State University of New York Press (1997)

22. 《庄子基本著作》Burton Watson, *Chuang Tzu: Basic Writings*. Columbia University Press (1996)

23. 《逍遥于道：庄子早期道教寓言故事》Translated with an introduction and commentary by Victor H. Mair（梅维恒）, *Wandering on the way: Early Taoist tales and parables of Chuang Tzu*. Bantam Books (1994)

24. 《道及其力量：老子〈道德经〉及其在中国思想中的地位》Lao Tzu, Arthur Waley（阿瑟·韦利）, *The Way and Its Power: Lao Tzus Tao Te Ching and Its Place in Chinese Thought*. Grove Press (1994)

25. 《根本之道》Translated and presented by Thomas Cleary, *The essential Tao*. San Francisco (1993)

26. 《道德经》Lao-Tzu, Stephen Addiss, Stanley Lombardo, Burton Watson, *Tao Te Ching* (Hackett Classics). Hackett Publishers (1993)

27. 《道之二解：王弼与河上公〈老子〉注研究》Alan Kam-Leung Chan, *Two Visions of the Way: A Study of the Wang Pi and the Ho-Shang Kung Commentaries on the Lao-Tzu* (Suny Series in Chinese Philosophy & Culture). State University of New York Press (1991)

28. 《老子道德经：基于马王堆新发现文本的翻译》(Classics of Ancient China) Lao Tzu, Robert G. Henricks, *Lao Tzu: Te-Tao Ching: A New Translation Based on the Recently Discovered Ma-wang-tui Texts* (Classics of Ancient China). Ballantine Books (1989)

29. 《庄子·内篇》(Mandala Books) A. C. Graham（葛瑞汉）(trans.), *Chuang-Tzu: The Inner Chapters*. Harpercollins (1987)

30. 《宋代收藏道书考》Piet van der Loon（龙彼德），*Taoist Books in the Libraries of the Sung Period*. Ithaca Press, University of Oxford (1984)

31. 《庄子初探》Victor H. Mair（梅维恒）(Editor), *Experimental Essays on Chuang-Tzu*. Univ. of Hawaii Pr. (1983)

32. 《庄子全集》Chuang Tzu, Burton Watson, *The Complete Works of Chuang Tzu* (UNESCO Collection of Representative Works: Chinese Series). Columbia University Press (1968)

33. 《庄子之道》Thomas Merton, *The Way of Chuang Tzu*. New Directions (1965)

34. 《东方圣书：道教文献》（第一部分：老子《道德经》；庄子著作）Translated by James Legge（理雅各），*The Sacred Books of the East: The Texts of Taoism. In Two Parts, Part I. The Tao Te Ching of Lao Tzu, The Writings of Chuang Tzu* (Books I-XVII). New York: Dover Publications, Inc. (1962)

35. 《〈道德经〉新译》Lao Tzu, R. B. Blakney, *The Way of Life, Lao Tzu, a New Translation of the Tao Te Ching*. USA Mentor Books (1955)

36. 《庄子：神秘、道德主义的社会改革者》Herbert A. Giles（翟里斯），*Chuang Tzu: Mystic, Moralist and Social Reformer*. London: Bernard Quaritch (1889)

37. 《东方圣书：道教文献》Edited by F. Max Muller, Translated by James Legge, *The Sacred Books of the East: The Texts of Taoism*. Clarendon Press (1891)

6.2.5 《易经》

1. 《〈易经〉：古代文本的批判性翻译》Geoffrey Redmond, *The I Ching (Book of Changes: A Critical Translation of the Ancient Text*. Bloomsbury Academic (2017)

2. 《秸秆占卜：一种新发现的〈易经〉替代品》Constance A. Cook, Zhao Lu, *Stalk Divination: A Newly Discovered Alternative to the I Ching*. Oxford University Press (2017)

3. 《〈易经〉核心精华》Lars Bo Christensen, *Book of Changes: The Original Core of the I Ching*. Lars Bo Christensen (2015)

4. 《〈易经〉教学》Tze-Ki Hon, Geoffrey P. Redmond, *Teaching the I Ching (Book of changes)* (AAR Teaching Religious Studies). Oxford University Press (2014)

5. 《〈易经〉：中国古代神谕和智慧之书的精译》John Minford, *I Ching: The Essential Translation of the Ancient Chinese Oracle and Book of Wisdom*. Viking (2014)

6. 《〈易经〉：汉英词典的整合与翻译》Daniel Bernardo, *YiJing (I Ching) : Chinese-English Dictionary with Concordance and Translation*. Bersoft Software & Technology (2012)

7. 《〈易经〉：中国的萨满神谕》Translated with commentary by Richard Bertschinger, *YiJing, Shamanic Oracle of China: A New Book of Change*. Singing Dragon (2012)

8. 《〈易经〉的真实翻译》Margaret J. Pearson, *The Original I Ching: An Authentic Translation of the Book of Changes*. Tuttle Publishing (2011)

9. 《〈易经〉与中国政治：北宋时期的古典评论与文人激进主义（960—1127）》Tze-Ki Hon, *The Yijing And Chinese Politics: Classical Commentary And Literati Activism in the*

Northern Song Period, 960—1127. State University of New York Press (2005)

10. 《〈易经〉：青铜器时代的文献，附导论与注释的翻译》Richard Rutt, *The Book of Changes (Zhouyi): A Bronze Age Document Translated with Introduction and Notes.* Routledge (2002)

11. 《易经》Edward L. Shaughnessy（夏含夷）, *I Ching: The Classic of Changes.* New York: Ballantyne Books (1997)

12. 《〈易经〉中的天、地、人：7场爱诺思讲座》Hellmut Wilhelm（卫德明）, *Heaven, Earth, and Man in The Book of Changes: Seven Eranos Lectures.* University of Washington Press (1997)

13. 《插图本〈易经〉》Li Yan, *The Illustrated Book of Changes: I Ching.* Foreign Language Press (1997)

14. 《了解〈易经〉：关于〈易经〉的讲座》Hellmut Wilhelm（卫德明）, Richard Wilhelm（卫礼贤）, *Understanding the I Ching: The Wilhelm Lectures on the Book of Changes.* Princeton University Press (1995)

15. 《宋代对〈易经〉的使用》(Princeton Legacy Library) Kidder Smith, Peter K. Bol（包弼德）, Joseph A. Adler, Don J. Wyatt, *Sung Dynasty Uses of the I Ching.* Princeton University Press (1990)

16. 《〈易经〉与不变的真理》Hua Ching Ni, *Book of Changes and the Unchanging Truth = Tian di bu yi zhi jing.* Sevenstar Communications (1990)

17. 《易经》Kerson Huang, Rosemary Huang, *I Ching.* Workman Publishing Company (1987)

18. 《"周易"的构成》（博士论文）Edward L. Shaughnessy（夏含夷）, *The Composition of the "Zhouyi".* Ph. D. Dissertation, Stanford University (1983)

19. 《易经》Richard Wilhelm（卫礼贤）, Cary F. Baynes, Hellmut Wilhelm（卫德明）, C. G. Jung, *The I Ching or Book of Changes.* Princeton University Press (1967)

20. 《易经》James Legge（理雅各）(translator), *The I Ching: The Book of Changes.* Republication of 2nd edition (1899)（Sacred Books of the East Vol XVI) [2 ed.]. Dover Publications (1963)

6.2.6 传统经典与诸子百家

1. 《左传：关于〈春秋〉的评论》Andrew Plaks, *Zuo Tradition: Zuozhuan: Commentary on the 'Spring and Autumn Annals'.* University of Washington Press (2016)

2. 《经由儒学的自我实现：荀子伦理的当代重构》(SUNY series in Chinese philosophy and culture.) Siu-Fu Tang（邓小虎）, *Self-Realization through Confucian Learning: A Contemporary Reconstruction of Xunzi's Ethics.* State University of New York Press (2016)

3. 《列子：冲虚至德真经》(Lionshare Chinese Classics) Lionel Giles（翟林奈）, *Taoist Teachings from the Book of Lieh Tzŭ* (Bilingual Edition, English and Chinese). Lionshare Media (2015)

4. 《商君书》Shang Yang（商鞅）, J. J. L. Duyvendak（戴闻达, translator), *The Book of*

Lord Shang：商君書 (Study Guide). Lionshare Media (2014)

5. 《荀子的仪式与宗教》(SUNY series in Chinese philosophy and culture) T. C. Kline, Justin Tiwald, *Ritual and Religion in the Xunzi*. State University of New York Press (2014)

6. 《文本体现：中国早期手稿中文本身份的确立》Matthias L. Richter, *The Embodied Text: Establishing Textual Identity in Early Chinese Manuscripts*. Brill (2013)

7. 《文本演变中的墨子：中国早期思想中的不同声音》Carine Defoort, Nicolas Standaert（钟鸣旦）, *The Mozi as an Evolving Text: Different Voices in Early Chinese Thought*. Brill (2013)

8. 《尸子：中国第一位杂家》Paul Fischer（方破）, *Shizi: China's First Syncretist*. Columbia University Press (2012)

9. 《〈黄帝内经素问〉译注全本》Paul U. Unschuld and Hermann Tessenow in collaboration with Zheng Jinsheng, *An Annotated Translation of Huang Di's Inner Classic*. University of California Press (2011)

10. 《从东亚经典中的寻找智慧》William Theodore De Bary（狄百瑞）, *Finding Wisdom in East Asian Classics*. Columbia University Press (2011)

11. 《Xun Xu与中国三世纪的精密政治》Howard L Goodman, *Xun Xu and the politics of precision in third-century AD China*. BRILL (2010)

12. 《墨子全译》Translated and Annotated by Ian Johnston, *The Mozi-A Complete Translation*. The Chinese University Press (2010)

13. 《孙子兵法》Sun Zi, Victor H. Mair（梅维恒）, *The Art of War: Sun Zi's Military Methods*. Columbia University Press (2009)

14. 《孙子兵法》Sun-tzu, Lionel Giles（翟林奈）, John Minford, *Sun Tzu's The Art of War*. Bilingual Edition, Complete Chinese and English Text. Tuttle Publishing (2008)

15. 《孟子和男子气概：权力、道德与母性思维》Joanne D. Birdwhistell, *Mencius and Masculinities: Dynamics of Power, Morality, and Maternal Thinking*. State University of New York Press (2007)

16. 《重写中国古代文献》Edward L. Shaughnessy（夏含夷）, *Rewriting Early Chinese Texts* (Suny Series in Chinese Philosophy & Culture). State University of New York Press (2006)

17. 《荀子基本著作》Xunzi, Burton Watson, *Xunzi: Basic Writings* (Translations from the Asian Classics). Columbia University Press (2003)

18. 《韩非子基本著作》Han Feizi (Author), Burton Watson (Translator), *Han Feizi: Basic Writings* (Translations from the Asian Classics). Columbia University Press (2002)

19. 《〈世说新语〉英译》(Michigan monographs in Chinese studies volume 95) Liu I-ch'ing（刘义庆）, Liu Chun, Richard B. Mather（马瑞志）, *Shih-shuo Hsin-Yu: A New Account of Tales of the World*. Center for Chinese Studies, The University of Michigan (2002)

20. 《五经》Michael Nylan, *The Five "Confucian" Classics*. Yale University Press (2001)

21. 《中世纪的中国精神与自我：〈世说新语〉及其遗产》Nanxiu Qian, *Spirit and Self in*

22. 《〈孙子兵法〉和〈商君书〉》Sun-tzu, Shang Yang, *The Art of War* and *The Book of Lord Shang* (Wordsworth Classics of World Literature). Wordsworth Editions Ltd (1999)

Medieval China: The Shih-Shuo Hsin-Yu and Its Legacy. University of Hawaii Press (2001)

23. 《勇士之道、王者密码：中国经典中的领导经验》Thomas Cleary (translator), *Ways of Warriors, Codes of Kings: Lessons in Leadership from the Chinese Classics*. Shambhala (1999)

24. 《荀子的自然与天：〈天论〉研究》(Suny series in Chinese philosophy and culture) Edward J. Machle, *Nature and Heaven in the Xunzi: A Study of the Tian Lun*. State University of New York Press (1993)

25. 《中国早期文本：参考书目指南》Micheal Loewe (ed.), *Early Chinese Texts: A Bibliographical Guide*. Institute of East Asian Studies (1993)

26. 《最高神秘经典〈太玄经〉》Hsiung Yang（杨雄）, Michael Nylan（戴梅可）(trans.), *The Canon of Supreme Mystery "Tài HsüAn Ching"* (SUNY series in Chinese philosophy and culture). State University of New York Press (1993)

27. 《〈临济路〉英译》Translated by Burton Watson（华兹生）, *The Zen Teachings of Master Lin-Chi* (Shambhala dragon editions). Shambhala (1993)

28. 《〈孙子兵法〉：结合新发现的银雀山汉墓竹简的第一个英译本》Sunzi, Roger T. Ames（安乐哲）, *Sun-tzu "The Art of Warfare": The First English Translation Incorporating the Recently Discovered Yin-chüeh-shan Texts*. Ballantine Books (1993)

29. 《中国经典第二卷：孟子》Translated by James Legge（理雅各）, *The Chinese Classics: The Works of Mencius*. SMC Publishing Inc. (1991)

30. 《列子书：道家经典》(Translations from the Oriental classics) Translated by A. C. Graham,（葛瑞汉）*The Book of Lieh-tzu: A Classic of the Tao*. Columbia University Press (1990)

31. 《荀子》（第一至三卷）Xunzi, trans. by John Knoblock, *Xunzi: A Translation and Study of the Complete Works*. vol.1-3. Stanford University Press (1988, 1990, 1994)

32. 《管子：中国古代政治、经济、哲学的文章》Rickett Allyn (translator), *Guanzi: Political, Economic, and Philosophical Essays from Early China*. Princeton University Press (1985, 1998)

33. 《盐铁论：中国古代关于国家控制商业和工业的辩论（第一至二十八章）》Esson Gale, *Discourses on Salt and Iron: A Debate on State Control of Commerce and Industry in Ancient China, Chapter I-XXVIII*. Ch'eng-Wen Tai-pei Publishing Co. (1967)

34. 《墨子、荀子、韩非子基本著述》Translated by Burton Watson, *Basic Writings of Mo Tzu, Hsün Tzu, and Han Fei Tzu*. Columbia University Press (1963, 1964)

35. 《韩非子基本著作》Watson Burton, Han Fei Tzu, *Han Fei Tzu: Basic Writings* (UNESCO collection of representative works, Chinese series). Columbia University Press (1964)

36. 《诗经》Translated from the Chinese by Arthur Waley（阿瑟·韦利）, *The Book of Songs: The Ancient Chinese Classic of Poetry*. Grove Press (1960)

37. 《〈荀子〉译本》Homer H. Dubs（德效骞, translator）, *The Works of Hsuntze*. London:

Arthur Probsthain (1928)

38. 《〈荀子〉：古代儒学的塑造者》Homer H. Dubs（德效骞）, *Hsüntze: The Moulder of Ancient Confucianism*. London: Arthur Probsthain (1927)

39. 《〈中庸〉英译》Hongming Gu（辜鸿铭）, *The Conduct of Life, or, The universal Order of Confucius: A Translation of One of the Four Confucian Books, Hitherto Known as The Doctrine of the Mean*. London, J. Murray (1920)

40. 《〈诗经〉英译》James Legge（理雅各）, *The She King: The Book of Anciant Poetry*. London: Trubner and Co. (1876)

41. 《中国经典：孟子》（第二卷）James Legge（理雅各）, *The Chinese Classics: The Life and Works of Mencius*. Vol. 2. London: Trubner and Co. (1875)

6.3 思想与文明

6.3.1 思想传统

1. 《天之路：中国思想概论》Roel Sterckx, *Ways of Heaven: An Introduction to Chinese Thought*. Basic Books (2019)

2. 《权力的转移：近代中国思想与社会》Zhitian Luo, *Shifts of Power: Modern Chinese Thought and Society* (Brill's Humanities in China Library). Brill (2017)

3. 《世界古代政治思想史：意义与后果》Antony Black, *A World History of Ancient Political Thought: Its Significance and Consequences*. Oxford University Press (2016)

4. 《通过中国思考》Jerusha Hull McCormack, John G. Blair, *Thinking Through China*. Rowman & Littlefield Publishers (2016)

5. 《构建和谐世界：中国传统思维理想》Baoxu Zhao（赵宝煦）, *To Build a Harmonious World: Ideal of Traditional Chinese Thinking*. Springer Berlin Heidelberg (2014)

6. 《生命、自由与道的追求：现代美国生活中的古代中国思想》Sam Crane, *Life, Liberty, and the Pursuit of Dao: Ancient Chinese Thought in Modern American Life*. Wiley-Blackwell (2013)

7. 《野蛮的智慧：中国古代思想36大策略述评》Master "Dutch" Hinkle, *Brutal Wisdom: Comments on the 36 Strategies of Ancient Chinese Thought*. Whispers of Bushido, LLC (2013)

8. 《中国传统思想中的道德》Amy Olberding and Philip J. Ivanhoe, *Mortality in Traditional Chinese Thought*. State University of New York (2011)

9. 《古代中国思想，现代中国实力》Yan Xuetong（阎学通）, Daniel A. Bell（淡贝宁）, Sun Zhe, Edmund Ryden（雷敦龢）, *Ancient Chinese Thought, Modern Chinese Power*. Princeton University Press (2011)

10. 《十个词汇里的中国》Yu Hua（余华）, Allan H. Barr, *China in Ten Words*. Random House Inc (2011)

11. 《远东的灵魂》Percival Lowell, *The Soul of the Far East*. Kessinger Publishing (2010)

12. 《中国早期的个人主义：思想政治中的人性代理与自我》Erica Fox Brindley, *Individualism*

in Early China: Human Agency and the Self in Thought and Politics. University of Hawai'i Press (2010)

13. 《海德格尔、罗蒂和东方思想家：跨文化理解的诠释学》Wei Zhang, *Heidegger, Rorty, and the Eastern Thinkers: A Hermeneutics of Cross-cultural Understanding*. State University of New York Press (2006)

14. 《中国汉代思想选读》Edited and translated by Mark Csikszentmihalyi, *Readings in Han Chinese Thought*. Hackett Publishing Company (2006)

15. 《尼采、海德格尔与道家思想：中间交叉的路径》Martin Heidegger, Katrin Froese, Friedrich Wilhelm Nietzsche, *Nietzsche, Heidegger, and Daoist Thought: Crossing Paths In-between* (SUNY series in Chinese philosophy and culture). State University of New York Press (2006)

16. 《莱布尼茨与中国：思想的交流》Franklin Perkins, *Leibniz and China: A Commerce of Light*. Cambridge University Press (2004)

17. 《现代心灵：20世纪思想史》Peter Watson, *The Modern Mind: An Intellectual History of the 20th Century*. Harper Perennial (2002)

18. 《中国早期思想中的意识认识论》Jane Geaney, *On the Epistemology of the Senses in Early Chinese Thought*. Honolulu: University of Hawaii Press (2002)

19. 《50位东方思想家》Diané Collinson, Kathryn Plant and Robert Wilkinson, *Fifty Eastern Thinkers*. Routledge (2000)

20. 《洛阳隐士：邵雍与北宋思想的道德发展》Don J. Wyatt, *The Recluse of Loyang: Shao Yung and the Moral Evolution of Early Sung Thought*. University of Hawai'i Press (1996)

21. 《中国与其他》Benjamin I. Schwartz（史华慈）, *China and other Matters*. Harvard University Press (1996)

22. 《天、地与其间的生活和谐》Benjamin I. Schwartz（史华慈）(auth.), Anna-Teresa Tymieniecka (eds.), *Heaven, Earth, and In-Between in the Harmony of Life*. Springer Netherlands (1995)

23. 《柳宗元与唐代思想的转变（773—819）》Jo-shui Chen, *Liu Tsung-yuan and Intellectual Change in Tang Dynasty, 773—819*. Cambridge University Press (1992)

24. 《中国思想之渊源》Frederick W. Mote（牟复礼）, *Intellectual Foundations of China*. McGraw-Hill Higher Education (1989)

25. 《古代中国的思想世界》Benjamin I. Schwartz（史华慈）, *The World of Thought in Ancient China*. Belknap Press of Harvard University Press (1985)

26. 《梁启超与中国思想的过渡：1890—1907》Hao Chang（张灏）, *Liang Ch'i-ch'ao and Intellectual Transition in China, 1890—1907*. Harvard University Press (1971)

27. 《明代思想中的自我与社会》Wm. Theodore de Bary（狄百瑞）, and the Conference on Ming Thought, *Self and Society in Ming Thought*. Columbia University Press (1970)

28. 《中国意识的危机：“五四”时期激烈的反传统主义》（博士论文）Yu-sheng Lin（林毓生），*The Crisis of Chinese Consciousness: Radical Antitraditionalism in the May Fourth Era*. Ph D. Dissertation, University of Chicago (1970)

29. 《中国现代思想中的唯科学主义》D. W. Y. Kwok（郭颖颐），*Scientism in Chinese Thought: Nineteen Hundred to Nineteen Fifty*. New Haven, C. T.: Yale University Press (1965)

30. 《梁启超与中国近代思想》Joseph R. Levenson（列文森：），*Liang Ch'i-ch'ao and the Mind of Modern China*. Harvard University Press (1953)

31. 《中国思想研究》Arthur F. Wright（芮沃寿，ed.），*Studies in Chinese Thought*. The University of Chicago (1953)

32. 《中国古代思想的三种路径》Arthur Waley（阿瑟·韦利），*Three Ways of Thought in Ancient China*. Geogre Allen & Unwin Ltd (1939, 1946, 1953)

6.3.2 中外思维

1. 《普通百科新大辞典（新全球知识中国百科全书（1870—1930） 思维方式的转变）》Rudolf G. Wagner (auth.), Milena Doleželová-Velingerová, Rudolf G Wagner (eds.), *Chinese Encyclopaedias of New Global Knowledge (1870—1930): Changing Ways of Thought*. Springer (2014)

2. 《思维地理：亚洲人和西方人如何不同的思考，以及为什么》Richard E Nisbett, *The Geography of Thought: How Asians and Westerners Think Differently, And Why*. Nicholas Brealey Publishing (2011)

3. 《东西方两分法》Thorsten Pattberg, *The East-West Dichotomy*. LoD Press (2009)

4. 《功效论：中西思维》François Jullien, *A Treatise on Efficacy: Between Western and Chinese Thinking*. University of Hawaii Press (2004)

5. 《关于东方的思考》Thomas Merton, *Thoughts on the East*. Burns & Oates (1996)

6. 《约翰·杜威中国演讲集（1919—1920）》Robert W. Clopton, Tsuin-chen Ou, *John Dewey, lectures in China, 1919—1920*. The University Press of Hawaii (1973)

7. 《东方民族的思维方式：印度、中国、西藏、日本》Hajime Nakamura, *Ways of Thinking of Eastern Peoples: India, China, Tibet, Japan* (Revised).University of Hawai'i Press (1964)

6.3.3 现代主义

1. 《全球现代性危机：亚洲传统与可持续发展的未来》Prasenjit Duara（杜赞奇），*The Crisis of Global Modernity: Asian Traditions and a Sustainable Future* (Asian Connections). Cambridge University Press (2015)

2. 《中国转向现代性：戴震的新古典视野》Minghui Hu, *China's Transition to Modernity: The New Classical Vision of Dai Zhen*. University of Washington Press (2015)

3. 《中国现代性与个人精神》Andrew B. Kipnis (eds.), *Chinese Modernity and the Individual Psyche*. Palgrave Macmillan US (2012)

4. 《东亚文明、民族与现代性》(Routledge Advances in Asia-Pacific Studies) Chih-Yu Shih

（石之瑜）, *Civilization, Nation and Modernity in East Asia*. Routledge (2012)

5. 《表意的现代主义：中国、写作、媒体》Christopher Bush, *Ideographic Modernism: China, Writing, Media*. Oxford University Press, USA (2010)

6. 《传统与现代：人文主义观》Chen Lai（陈来）, *Tradition and Modernity: A Humanist View* (Brills Humanities in China Library). Brill (2010)

7. 《革命的终结：中国与现代性的界限》Wang Hui（汪晖）, *The End of the Revolution: China and the Limits of Modernity*. Verso (2010)

8. 《中国现代性的思想基础：民国时期的文化与政治思想》Edmund S. K. Fung, *The Intellectual Foundations of Chinese Modernity: Cultural and Political Thought in the Republican Era*. Cambridge University Press (2010)

9. 《哈哈镜：中国视觉现代性》Laikwan Pang（彭丽君）, *The Distorting Mirror: Visual Modernity in China*. University of Hawai'i Press (2007)

10. 《中国现代性与全球生命政治学：文学与视觉文化研究》Sheldon H. Lu, *Chinese Modernity and Global Biopolitics: Studies in Literature and Visual Culture*. University of Hawai'i Press (2007)

11. 《失落的现代性：中国、越南、韩国以及世界历史的危害》Alexander Woodside, *Lost Modernities: China, Vietnam, Korea, and the Hazards of World History* (The Edwin O. Reischauer Lectures). Harvard University Press (2006)

12. 《现代的诱惑：书写半殖民地中国的现代主义（1917—1937）》Shu-mei Shih, *The Lure of the Modern: Writing Modernism in Semicolonial China, 1917—1937*. University of California Press (2001)

13. 《偶像破坏：现代主义、施蛰存与上海边界》（博士论文）Stephen William Schaefer, *Relics of Iconoclasm-Modernism, Shi Zhecun, and Shanghai's Margins*. Ph. D. Dissertation, The University of Chicago (2000)

14. 《做中国人：现代性及其后的途径》Wen-hsin Yeh（叶文心）(ed.), *Becoming Chinese: Passages to Modernity and Beyond* (Studies on China). University of California Press (2000)

6.3.4 左派与后现代

1. 《新古典现实主义与中国核学说的不发达》Paolo Rosa, *Neoclassical Realism and the Underdevelopment of China's Nuclear Doctrine*. Springer International Publishing: Palgrave Pivot (2018)

2. 《革命本土论：中国法西斯主义和文化（1925—1937）》Maggie Clinton, *Revolutionary Nativism: Fascism and Culture in China, 1925—1937*. Duke University Press (2017)

3. 《无声的革命：左派政治权力和文化优势如何上升》Barry Rubin, *Silent Revolution: How the Left Rose to Political Power and Cultural Dominance*. Broadside Books (2014)

4. 《中国与新左派想象：政治文化的干预》Ban Wang（王斑）, Jie Lu, *China and New Left Visions: Political and Cultural Interventions*. Lexington Books (2012)

5. 《德里达：声音与现象：胡塞尔现象学中的符号问题导论》Jacques Derrida; Translated from the French by Leonard Lawlor, *Voice and Phenomenon: Introduction to the Problem of the Sign in Husserl's Phenomenology*. Northwestern University Press (2011)
6. 《英美历史、历史学家和保守主义：对撒切尔和里根的大战》Reba Soffer, *History, Historians And Conservatism In Britain And America: The Great War to Thatcher and Reagan*. Oxford University Press (2009)
7. 《超越资本主义和社会主义：旧理想之新声明：为21世纪社会和经济理智辩解》Tobias J. Lanz, *Beyond Capitalism and Socialism-A New Statement of an Old Ideal: A Twenty-First Century Apologia for Social and Economic Sanity*. IHS Press (2008)
8. 《新教伦理与资本主义精神》Max Weber（马克思.韦伯），*The Protestant Ethic and the Spirit of Capitalism*. Routledge (2005)
9. 《资本主义简介》James Fulcher, *Capitalism: A Very Short Introduction*. Oxford University Press (2004)
10. 《缔造民主：欧洲左派史（1850—2000）》Geoff Eley, *Forging Democracy: The History of the Left in Europe, 1850—2000*. Oxford University Press (2002)
11. 《空中的革命：60年代激进派转向列宁、毛泽东和切·格瓦拉》（美国新左派）Max Elbaum, *Revolution in the Air: Sixties Radicals Turn to Lenin, Mao and Che*. Verso (2002)
12. 《汉娜·阿伦特读本》Peter Baehr, *The Portable Hannah Arendt*. Pergiun Books (2000)
13. 《后现代主义与中国》Arif Dirlik（阿里夫·德里克），Wang Ning, Anthony D. King, Ping-Hui Liao, Xiaoying Wang, Sheldon Hsiao-Peng Lu, Sebastian Hsiao-peng Lu, *Postmodernism and China*. Duke University Press (2000)
14. 《法西斯意识形态的诞生：从文化反抗到政治变革》Zeev Sternhell, Mario Sznajder, Maia Asheri, *The Birth of Fascist Ideology: From Cultural Rebellion to Political Revolution*. Princeton University Press (1994)
15. 《海地，国家对民族：杜瓦利埃主义的起源和遗产》Michel-Rolph Trouillot, *Haiti, State against Nation: The Origins and Legacy of Duvalierism*. Monthly Review Press (1990)
16. 《极权主义的起源》Hannah Arendt（汉娜·阿伦特），*The Origins of Totalitarianism*. Harcourt, Brace, Jovanovich (1973)
17. 《科学革命的结构》Thomas S. Kuhn, *The Structure of Scientific Revolutions* (International encyclopedia of unified science. Foundations of the unity of science, v.II, no.2). The University of Chicago Press (1970)

6.3.5 乌托邦

1. 《乌托邦的前景》Edward Rothstein, Herbert Muschamp, Martin E. Marty, *Visions of Utopia*. Oxford University Press (2003)
2. 《马克思主义与自由王国的飞跃：共产主义乌托邦的兴衰》Andrzej Walicki, *Marxism and the Leap to the Kingdom of Freedom: The Rise and Fall of the Communist Utopia*. Stanford

University Press (1995)

3.《社会主义：活跃的乌托邦》Zygmunt Bauman（鲍曼）, *Socialism: The Active Utopia*. Holmes & Meier Publishers Inc (1976)

6.3.6 东方主义

1.《中国和东方主义：西方知识生产与中华人民共和国》Daniel Vukovich, *China and Orientalism: Western Knowledge Production and the PRC*. Routledge (2013)

2.《法律东方主义：中国、美国与现代法》Teemu Ruskola, *Legal Orientalism: China, the United States, and Modern Law*. Harvard University Press (2013)

3.《品味中国：英语主体性与东方主义史前史》Eugenia Zuroski Jenkins, *A Taste for China: English Subjectivity and the Prehistory of Orientalism*. Oxford University Press (2013)

4.《中国与东方主义：西方知识生产与中华人民共和国》Daniel F. Vukovich, *China and Orientalism: Western knowledge production and the P.R.C*. Routledge (2012)

5.《法国路易十四时代的东方主义》Nicholas Dew, *Orientalism in Louis XIV's France* (Oxford Historical Monographs). Oxford University Press (2009)

6.《近代早期法国的东方主义：欧亚贸易、异国情调与古希腊》Ina Baghdiantz McCabe, *Orientalism in Early Modern France: Eurasian Trade, Exoticism, and the Ancien Re'gime*. London: Bloomsbury Publishing PLC (2008)

7.《描绘唐人街：旧金山的艺术和东方主义》Anthony W. Lee, *Picturing Chinatown: Art and Orientalism in San Francisco*. University of California Press (2001)

8.《玛丽安·穆尔与中国：东方主义与美国书写》Cynthia Stamy, *Marianne Moore and China: Orientalism and a Writing of America* (Oxford English monographs). Oxford, UK; New York: Oxford University Press (1999)

9.《唐人街之前的纽约：东方主义与美国文化的塑造（1776—1882）》John Kuo Wei Tchen, *New York before Chinatown: Orientalism and the Shaping of American Culture, 1776—1882*. Baltimore, Md.: Johns Hopkins University Press (1999)

10.《东方主义与现代主义：庞德与威廉姆斯的中国遗产》Zhaoming Qian, *Orientalism and Modernism: The Legacy of China in Pound and Williams*. Durham: Duke University Press (1995)

6.3.7 人类文明

1.《东亚史：从文明起源到21世纪》Charles Holcombe, *A History of East Asia: From the Origins of Civilization to the Twenty-First Century*. Cambridge University Press (2016)

2.《历史：定义世界历史的古代文明》Roman Collins, *History: The Ancient Civilizations That Defined World History* (Egypt, Roman, SPQR, Aztec, Ancient China, Ancient Greece, Julius Caesar, Jesus, Human History Book 1). Amazon Digital Services LLC (2016)

3.《30秒解读古代中国：一个永恒文明的50项最重要成就，每一项用半分钟解释》Yijie Sung, *30-Second Ancient China: The 50 Most Important Achievements of a Timeless Civilization, Each Explained in Half a Minute*. The Ivy Press (2015)

4. 《智人：人类简史》Yuval Harari, *Sapiens: A Brief History of Humankind*. Signal (2014)

5. 《龙与鹰：中国与罗马帝国的兴衰》Sunny Y. Auyang, *The Dragon and the Eagle: The Rise and Fall of the Chinese and Roman Empires*. Routledge (2014)

6. 《想象中的文明：中国、西方及其首次相遇》Roger Hart, *Imagined Civilizations: China, the West, and Their First Encounter*. Johns Hopkins University Press (2013)

7. 《文明中国：2013中国故事年鉴》Geremie R. Barmé, Jeremy Goldkorn, *Civilising China: China Story Yearbook 2013*. Australian Centre on China in the World, The Australian National University (2013)

8. 《中国人的生活：创造文明的人民》Victor H. Mair（梅维恒）, Sanping Chen, Frances Wood, *Chinese Lives: The People Who Made a Civilization*. Thames Hudson (2013)

9. 《希腊和奥古斯都的文化革命》A. J. S. Spawforth, *Greece and the Augustan Cultural Revolution*. Cambridge University Press (2012)

10. 《中日文明简史》Conrad Schirokauer, Miranda Brown, David Lurie, Suzanne Gay, *A Brief History of Chinese and Japanese Civilizations*. Wadsworth Publishing (2012)

11. 《文明：西方与其他》Niall Ferguson, *Civilization: The West and the Rest*. Penguin Books (2012)

12. 《亚洲文明思想与艺术：印度、中国和日本》Kenneth R. Stunkel *Ideas and Art in Asian Civilizations: India, China and Japan*. Routledge (2011)

13. 《西方文明：历史与文化》Judith Coffin, Robert Stacey, Joshua Cole, Carol Symes, *Western Civilizations: Their History & Their Culture* (Seventeenth Edition, Vol. 1). W. W. Norton & Company (2011)

14. 《中国文明史》Jacques Gernet, *A History of Chinese Civilization*. Cambridge University Press (2008)

15. 《古代文明：中国、印度、非洲、美索不达米亚》Wendy Conklin *Ancient Civilizations: China, India, Africa, Mesopotamia*. Scholastic, Inc. (2006)

16. 《黑色雅典娜：古典文明的亚非之根—语言学证据》（第三卷）Martin Bernal, *Black Athena: The Afroasiatic Roots of Classical Civilization: The Linguistic Evidence*. Vol. 3. Rutgers University Press (2006)

17. 《爱、恨和其他激情：中国文明中的情感问题与主题》Donatella Guida, Paolo Santangelo, *Love, Hatred, and other Passions: Questions and Themes on Emotions in Chinese Civilization*. Brill (2006)

18. 《文明之敌：古代美索不达米亚、埃及和中国对外国人的态度》Mu-Chou Poo, *Enemies Of Civilization: Attitudes Toward Foreigners In Ancient Mesopotamia, Egypt, And China*. State University of New York Press (2005)

19. 《亚洲文明史上的政治竞争、创新与增长》Peter Bernholz, Roland Vaubel (eds.), *Political Competition, Innovation and Growth in the History of Asian Civilizations*. Edward

Elgar Publishing Limited (2004)

20. 《旧世界的早期文明：埃及、地中海东部、美索不达米亚、印度和中国的形成史》Charles Keith Maisels, *Early Civilizations of the Old World: The Formative Histories of Egypt, The Levant, Mesopotamia, India and China.* Routledge (2001)

21. 《中国早期文明研究：宗教、社会、语言和古文书学》Michiharu Ito, Ken-klli Takashima, *Studies in Early Chinese Civilization: Religion, Society, Language, and Palaeography.* IRI, M. Ito & K. Takashima (1996)

22. 《中国文明在形成中（公元前1766—221）》Jun Li, *Chinese Civilization in the Making, 1766—221 BC.* Palgrave Macmillan UK (1996)

23. 《中国、韩国和日本：东亚文明的崛起》Gina L. Barnes, *China Korea and Japan: The Rise of Civilization in East Asia.* Thames & Hudson (1993)

24. 《中国文明：资料手册》（第2版）Patricia Buckley Ebrey（伊沛霞）, *Chinese Civilization: A Sourcebook.* 2nd Ed. The Free Press (1993)

25. 《黑色雅典娜：古典文明的亚非之根—考古和文献证据》（第二卷）Martin Bernal, *Black Athena: The Afroasiatic Roots of Classical Civilization: The Archaeological and Documentary Evidence.* Vol. II. Rutgers University Press (1991)

26. 《东亚文明：五个阶段的对话》Wm. Theodore de Bary（狄百瑞）, *East Asian Civilizations: A Dialogue in Five Stages* (The Edwin O. Reischauer Lectures). Harvard University Press (1988)

27. 《黑色雅典娜：古典文明的亚非之根—构造的古希腊（1785—1985）》（第一卷）Martin Bernal, *Black Athena: The Afroasiatic Roots of Classical Civilization: The Fabrication of Ancient Greece, 1785—1985.* vol. 1. Rutgers University Press (1987)

28. 《中华文明的起源》David N. Keightley, *Origins of Chinese Civilization* (Studies on China). University of California Press (1983)

29. 《中国的文明和官僚体制》Etienne Balazs（白乐日）, trans. from the French by H.M. Wright, *Chinese Civilization and Bureaucracy.* Yale University Press (1964)

30. 《中国文明》Marcel Granet（葛兰言）, *Chinese Civilization.* Meridian Books (1958)

31. 《中国的诞生：中华文明形成时期的考察》Herrlee Glessner Creel（顾立雅）, *Birth of China: Survey of the Formative Period of Chinese Civilization.* London: Jonathan Cape (1936); New York: Frederick Ungar Publishing (1937)

32. 《劳作的中国：中国劳苦大众生活的原始工业图志——中国文明记录》Rudolf P. Hommel, *China at Work: An Illustrated Record of the Primitive Industries of China's Masses, Whose Life is Toil, and thus an Account of Chinese Civilization.* John Day (1937)

33. 《中国文明》Herbert A. Giles（翟里斯）, *The Civilization of China.* Henry Holt and Company (1911)

34. 《中国文明及西方与中国关系概观》From the French of Pierre Laffitte; Translated by John

Carey Hall, *A General View of Chinese Civilization and of the Relations of the West with China*. Trübner, Kelly & Walsh, Maruya (1887)

6.3.7.1 长城

1. 《伟大的长城：沿着历史边界从中国到墨西哥》Ian Volner, *The Great Great Wall: Along the Borders of History from China to Mexico*. Abrams Press (11 Jun 2019)
2. 《制造中国长城工程》(Building by Design) Yvette Lapierre, *Engineering the Great Wall of China*. Core Library (2017)
3. 《中国长城》Cindy Jenson-Elliott, *The Great Wall of China*. ReferencePoint Press (2014)
4. 《长城：文化史》Carlos Rojas, *The Great Wall: A Cultural History*. Harvard University Press (2010)
5. 《长城：中国世界奇迹的非凡故事》John Man, *The Great Wall: The Extraordinary Story of China's Wonder of the World*. Da Capo Press (2008)
6. 《中国长城（公元前221—公元1644年）》Stephen Turnbull, *The Great Wall of China: 221 BC-1644 AD* (Fortress 057). Osprey Publishing (2007)
7. 《长城：中国与世界为敌（公元前2000—公元2000年）》Julia Lovell（蓝诗玲）, *The Great Wall: China Against the World, 1000 BC-AD 2000*. Grove Press (2006)
8. 《中国长城 从历史到神话》Arthur Waldron, *The Great Wall of China: From History to Myth*. Cambridge University Press (1990)
9. 《中国长城》William Edgar Geil, *The Great Wall of China*. London John Murray, Albemarle Street, W. (1909)

6.3.7.2 瓷器

1. 《墨西哥殖民地时期的中国瓷器：早期现代贸易的物质世界》Meha Priyadarshini, *Chinese Porcelain in Colonial Mexico: The Material Worlds of an Early Modern Trade* (Palgrave Studies in Pacific History). Palgrave Macmillan (2018)
2. 《瓷盗：寻找埋葬瓷器的中国》Huan Hsu, *The Porcelain Thief: Searching the Middle Kingdom for Buried China*. Crown (2015)
3. 《朝圣者的艺术：世界历史中的陶瓷文化》Robert Finlay, *The Pilgrim Art: Cultures of Porcelain in World History*. University of California Press (2010)
4. 《陶瓷与荷中贸易》C. J. A. Jörg, *Porcelain and the Dutch China Trade*. Springer Netherlands (1982)
5. 《中国贸易瓷器》Clare Le Corbeiller, *China Trade Porcelain*. Metropolitan Museum of Art (1975)
6. 《陶器与陶瓷》（第一、二卷）Warren Cox, *The Book of Pottery and Porcelain*. Vols. 1-2. New York: L. Lee and Shepard; distributed by Crown Publishers (1944)
7. 《中国陶瓷图录》R. L. Hobson, *A Catalogue of Chinese Pottery and Porcelain: In the Collection of Sir Percival David*. London: The Stourton Press (1934)
8. 《瓷器通史》William Burton, *A General History of Porcelain*. Cassell and company, Ltd. (1921)

9. 《瓷器与陶器打标》（作者不详），*China and Pottery Marks*. Gilman Collamore & Company, Inc. New York (1920)

10. 《瓷器小传》Onondaga Pottery Company, *Little Romances of China*. Privately Printed for the Onondaga Pottery Company (1919)

11. 《中国瓷器的起源》Berthold Laufer, Henry W. (Henry Windsor) Nichols, *The Beginnings of Porcelain in China*. Chicago (1917)

12. 《古代中国和波斯的瓷器、陶器收藏》The Anderson Galleries, *Collection of Ancient Chinese & Persian Porcelain & Pottery*. (1915)

13. 《德累斯顿瓷器：迈森瓷》Egan Mew, *Dresden China: Meissen Porcelain*. London: T. C. & E. C. Jack; Newyork: Dodd Mead &Co. (1909)

14. 《中国瓷器摩根收藏目录》Stephen Wootton Bushell, William Mackay Laffan, John Pierpont Morgan, *Catalogue of the Morgan Collection of Chinese Porcelains*. The Metropolitan Museum of Art (1907)

15. 《老瓷器》*Old China*, Volume Three, Numbers One Through Twelve. Syracuse: Keramic Studio Publishing Company (1903, 1904)

16. 《东方陶瓷艺术》Stephen W. Bushell（卜士礼）, *Oriental Ceramic Art: Illustrated by Examples from the Collection of W. T. Walters*. NO.14. New York: D. Appleton and Company (1897)

17. 《瓷器搜寻者俱乐部》Annie Trumbull Slosson, *The China Hunters Club*. New York: Harper & Brothers (1878)

6.4 教育

1. 《中国世界一流大学的全球综合竞争力：背景、概念、模式与评价》(Perspectives on Rethinking and Reforming Education) Jian Li, *Comprehensive Global Competence for World-Class Universities in China: Context, Concept, Model and Evaluation*. Springer Singapore (2020)

2. 《中国课堂文化：集体的个人主义学习模式》(Perspectives on Rethinking and Reforming Education) Xudong Zhu, Jian Li, *Classroom Culture in China: Collective Individualism Learning Model*. Springer Singapore (2020)

3. 《理解中国学校领导：术语解读》Daming Feng, *Understanding China's School Leadership: Interpreting the Terminology*. Springer Singapore (2020)

4. 《中国高等教育与职业前景》Felicia F. Tian, Lin Chen, *Higher Education and Career Prospects in China*. Springer Singapore: Palgrave Macmillan (2020)

5. 《全球化世界中对幼儿教育的投资：中国、印度和美国的政策、实践和父母理念》Guangyu Tan, Amita Gupta, Gay Wilgus, *Investment in Early Childhood Education in a Globalized World: Policies, Practices, and Parental Philosophies in China, India, and the United States*. Palgrave Macmillan US (2019)

6. 《杜威的民主教育及其对中国教育学的影响（1917—1937）》Lei Wang, *John Dewey's Democratic Education and its Influence on Pedagogy in China 1917—1937*. Springer Fachmedien Wiesbaden: Springer VS (2019)

7. 《中国和芬兰对自闭症谱系障碍学生的教育》(New Frontiers of Educational Research) Xiaoyi Hu, Eija Kärnä, *Educating Students with Autism Spectrum Disorder in China and Finland*. Springer Singapore (2019)

8. 《北欧—中国教育的交叉点》(Palgrave Studies on Chinese Education in a Global Perspective) Haiqin Liu, Fred Dervin, Xiangyun Du, *Nordic-Chinese Intersections within Education*. Springer International Publishing: Palgrave Macmilla (2019)

9. 《中国教育政策格局：附加概念的政策链分析》(Perspectives on Rethinking and Reforming Education) Eryong Xue, Jian Li, *The Chinese Education Policy Landscape: A Concept-Added Policy Chain Analysis*. Springer Singapore (2019)

10. 《全球高等教育共享社区：中国重点大学的努力和关注》(Perspectives on Rethinking and Reforming Education) Jian Li, *Global Higher Education Shared Communities: Efforts and Concerns from Key Universities in China*. Springer Singapore (2019)

11. 《中国高等教育师资队伍建设：理念、实践与策略》(Perspectives on Rethinking and Reforming Education) Xudong Zhu, Jian Li, *Faculty Development in Chinese Higher Education. Concepts, Practices, and Strategies*. Springer Singapore (2019)

12. 《中国小学生学业成绩评价报告：以小学六年级四个科目为例》Huisheng Tian, Zhichang Sun, *Assessment Report on Chinese Primary School Students' Academic Achievement: 4 Subjects of Grade 6 in Primary School Taken as Examples*. Springer Berlin Heidelberg (2019)

13. 《中国教育政策与改革》Guangli Zhou, Xiang Zhou, *Education Policy and Reform in China*. Springer Singapore: Palgrave Macmillan (2019)

14. 《中国教育治理的范式转换：两次义务教育立法插曲——1986与2006年》Yan Wang, *Paradigm Shift of Education Governance in China: Two Compulsory Education Legislation Episodes: 1986 vs 2006*. Springer Berlin Heidelberg (2019)

15. 《理解在职教师培训（INSET）对中国教师变革的影响》Ming Li, *Understanding the Impact of INSET on Teacher Change in China*. Springer Singapore, Palgrave Pivot (2019)

16. 《中国教育治理》Ming Yang, Hao Ni, *Educational Governance in China*. Springer Singapore (2018)

17. 《中国高等教育》Jianmin Gu, Xueping Li, Lihua Wang, *Higher Education in China*. Springer Singapore (2018)

18. 《导航中国教育变革：当代历史与现实经验》Fang Wang, Leslie N.K. Lo, *Navigating Educational Change in China: Contemporary History and Lived Experiences* (Curriculum Studies Worldwide). Palgrave Macmillan (2018)

19. 《教育旅程、斗争与族群认同：国家教育对中国农村穆斯林回族的影响》Xinyi Wu,

Educational Journeys, Struggles and Ethnic Identity: The Impact of State Schooling on Muslim Hui in Rural China (Palgrave Studies on Chinese Education in a Global Perspective). Palgrave Macmillan (2018)

20. 《慕课在中国的发展》Qinhua Zheng, Li Chen, Daniel Burgos, *The Development of MOOCs in China* (Lecture Notes in Educational Technology). Springer Singapore (2018)

21. 《中国女大学校长的形成》Kai Yu, Yinhan Wang, *The Making of Female University Presidents in China*. Springer Singapore (2018)

22. 《中国城市公立学校入学不平等现象》Jing Liu, *Inequality in Public School Admission in Urban China* (Education in the Asia-Pacific Region: Issues, Concerns and Prospects 43). Springer Singapore (2018)

23. 《专业学习团体中的教师教育》Xuefeng Huang, *Teacher Education in Professional Learning Communities* (Intercultural Reciprocal Learning in Chinese and Western Education). Springer International Publishing: Palgrave Macmillan (2018)

24. 《中国留学生》Fred Dervin, Xiangyun Du, Anu Härkönen, *International Students in China* (Palgrave Studies on Chinese Education in a Global Perspective). Springer International Publishing: Palgrave Macmillan (2018)

25. 《中国城市公立学校流动儿童教育》Bo Hu, *Educating Migrant Children in Urban Public Schools in China* (SpringerBriefs in Education). Springer Singapore (2018)

26. 《中国母语和非母语英语教师的认知与实践》Zheng Huang, *Native and Non-Native English Speaking Teachers in China: Perceptions and Practices*. Springer Singapore (2018)

27. 《中国西南地区职前教师教育与入职培训》 (Intercultural Reciprocal Learning in Chinese and Western Education) Ju Huang, *Pre-Service Teacher Education and Induction in Southwest China*. Springer International Publishing: Palgrave Macmillan (2018)

28. 《中国民办教育》 (Perspectives on Rethinking and Reforming Education) Haitao Zhou, Qiang Liu, Jing Tian, Qian Li, *Private Education in China*. Springer Singapore (2018)

29. 《中国教育政策与立法》Xiaozhou Xu, Weihui Mei, *Educational Policies and Legislation in China*. Springer Singapore (2018)

30. 《美国在华大学：日本的启示》Dennis T. Yang, *American Universities in China: Lessons from Japan*. Lexington Books (2018)

31. 《中国的职业技术教育》Xueping Wu, Yiqun Ye, *Technical and Vocational Education in China*. Springer Singapore (2018)

32. 《中国农村、牧区、民族、私立学校基础教育体制改革六例》Ling Li, Jiafu Zheng (eds.), *Chinese Elementary Education System Reform in Rural, Pastoral, Ethnic, and Private Schools: Six Case Studies*. Springer Singapore (2017)

33. 《21世纪的中国科学教育：政策、实践与研究》Ling L. Liang, Xiufeng Liu, Gavin W. Fulmer (eds.), *Chinese Science Education in the 21st Century: Policy, Practice, and Research*

(Contemporary Trends and Issues in Science Education 45). Springer Netherlands (2017)

34. 《国际化教学与本土化学习：中国英语教学改革与英语使用的考察》Paul McPherron, *Internationalizing Teaching, Localizing Learning: An Examination of English Language Teaching Reforms and English Use in China.* Palgrave Macmillan UK (2017)

35. 《中国西部高校英语教师职业发展研究》Yuhong Jiang, *A Study on Professional Development of Teachers of English as a Foreign Language in Institutions of Higher Education in Western China.* Springer-Verlag Berlin Heidelberg (2017)

36. 《了解美国机构中的中国工程博士生：个人认识论视角》Jiabin Zhu, *Understanding Chinese Engineering Doctoral Students in U.S. Institutions: A Personal Epistemology Perspective.* Springer Singapore (2017)

37. 《美国华裔留学生压力源及应对策略》Kun Yan, *Chinese International Students' Stressors and Coping Strategies in the United States.* Springer Singapore (2017)

38. 《中国学校画像》Mingyuan Gu, Jiansheng Ma, Jun Teng, *Portraits of Chinese Schools.* Springer Singapore (2017)

39. 《全球化与跨国学术流动：中国学术归国人士的经验》Qiongqiong Chen, *Globalization and Transnational Academic Mobility: The Experiences Of Chinese Academic Returnees.* Springer Singapore (2017)

40. 《中国大学研究效率评估》Yongmei Hu, Wenyan Liang, Yipeng Tang, *Evaluating Research Efficiency of Chinese Universities.* Springer Singapore (2017)

41. 《中国英语学习者听力评价：大学英语考试听力理解测试成套工具的开发》Zhixin Pan, *Assessing Listening for Chinese English learners: Developing a Communicative Listening Comprehension Test Suite for CET.* Routledge (2017)

42. 《中国移民家庭的跨文化教育经历：转型时期的家园寻求》Shijing Xu, *Cross-Cultural Schooling Experiences of Chinese Immigrant Families: In Search of Home in Times of Transition* (Intercultural Reciprocal Learning in Chinese and Western Education). Springer International Publishing (2017)

43. 《聚焦中国：中国市场经济下的教育变革》Shibao Guo, Yan Guo (eds.), *Spotlight on China: Changes in Education under China's Market Economy* (Spotlight on China). SensePublishers (2016)

44. 《全球化时代的中国教育模式》Chuing Prudence Chou, Jonathan Spangler (eds.), *Chinese Education Models in a Global Age* (Education in the Asia-Pacific Region: Issues, Concerns and Prospects 31). Springer Singapore (2016)

45. 《寻求世界一流教师教育？中国政策执行模式的多目标研究》Jun Li (auth.), *Quest for World-Class Teacher Education? A Multiperspectival Study on the Chinese Model of Policy Implementation* (Education in the Asia-Pacific Region: Issues, Concerns and Prospects 34). Springer (2016)

46.《中国西部教育发展：迈向素质与公平》John Chi-Kin Lee, Zeyuan Yu, Xianhan Huang, Edmond Hau-Fai Law (eds.), *Educational Development in Western China: Towards Quality and Equity*. Sense Publishers (2016)

47.《中国义务教育财政研究》Yuhong Du, Zhijun Sun, *Research on Compulsory Education Financing in China*. Springer-Verlag Berlin Heidelberg (2016)

48.《聚焦中国：全球化世界中的中国教育》Shibao Guo, Yan Guo (eds.), *Spotlight on China: Chinese Education in the Globalized World*. Sense Publishers (2016)

49.《教育的多学科研究观点：澳大利亚和中国的共同经验》Indika Liyanage, Badeng Nima (eds.), *Multidisciplinary Research Perspectives in Education: Shared Experiences from Australia and China*. SensePublishers (2016)

50.《中国的高等教育、精英政治和不平等》Ye Liu, *Higher Education, Meritocracy and Inequality in China*. Springer Singapore (2016)

51.《中国的学校领导、公民教育与政治：上海初级中学的经验》Shuqin Xu, *School Leadership, Citizenship Education and Politics in China: Experiences from Junior Secondary Schools in Shanghai*. Springer Singapore (2016)

52.《当代中国农民式子弟学校的政治、实践和可能性》Min Yu, *The Politics, Practices, and Possibilities of Migrant Children Schools in Contemporary China*. Palgrave Macmillan US (2016)

53.《中国留学生与跨文化学习环境：学术调整、适应与体验》Jiani Zhu, *Chinese Overseas Students and Intercultural Learning Environments: Academic Adjustment, Adaptation and Experience*. Palgrave Macmillan UK (2016)

54.《中国农村基础教育二十年：发展变迁与挑战》Lu Wang, Keith Lewin (auth.), *Two Decades of Basic Education in Rural China: Transitions and Challenges for Development* (New Frontiers of Educational Research). Springer Singapore (2016)

55.《国际流动与教育愿望：新加坡的中国天才留学生》Peidong Yang, *International Mobility and Educational Desire: Chinese Foreign Talent Students in Singapore*. Palgrave Macmillan US (2016)

56.《职场英语培训：中国企业项目案例研究》Qing Xie, *English Language Training in the Workplace: Case Studies of Corporate Programs in China*. Springer International Publishing (2016)

57.《乡村中的"国家"：审视中国农村学校》Shulei Li, *The "States" in Villages: A Look at Schools in Rural China*. Springer Singapore (2016)

58.《中国高等教育、精英政治与不平等》Ye Liu, *Higher Education, Meritocracy and Inequality in China* (Higher Education in Asia: Quality, Excellence and Governance). Springer Singapore (2016)

59.《中国西部教育发展走向质量与公平》John Chi-Kin Lee, Zeyuan Yu, Xianhan Huang, Edmond Hau-Fai Law (eds.), *Educational Development in Western ChinaTowards Quality and Equity*. SensePublishers (2016)

6. 中国文化与文明 | 185

60. 《美国、欧洲、亚洲文科教育经验：跨洲对话》William C. Kirby 柯伟林，Marijk C. van der Wende (eds.), *Experiences in Liberal Arts and Science Education from America, Europe, and Asia: A Dialogue across Continents*. Palgrave Macmillan US (2016)

61. 《中国的三语教育：模式与挑战》Anwei Feng, Bob Adamson (eds.), *Trilingualism in Education in China: Models and Challenges* (Multilingual Education 12).Springer Netherlands (2015)

62. 《教习评估：中国学生的教学经验》Heng Jiang, *Learning to Teach with Assessment: A Student Teaching Experience in China*.Springer-Verlag Singapur (2015)

63. 《作为一个复杂系统的教师信仰：中国英语教师》Hongying Zheng, *Teacher Beliefs as a Complex System: English Language Teachers in China*.Springer International Publishing (2015)

64. 《中国教育改革中的教师调解机构》Hongzhi Yang, *Teacher Mediated Agency in Educational Reform in China*.Springer International Publishing Switzerland (2015)

65. 《班级工作：职业学校与中国城市青年》Terry Woronov, *Class Work: Vocational Schools and China's Urban Youth*.Stanford University Press (2015)

66. 《中、日、美三种文化中的幼儿教育：》Liyan Huo, Susan B. Neuman, Atsushi Nanakida, *Early Childhood Education in Three Cultures: China, Japan and the United States*. Springer (2015)

67. 《燕京大学新视角（1916—1952）：新中国的自由教育》Arthur Lewis Rosenbaum, *New Perspectives on Yenching University, 1916—1952: A Liberal Education for a New China*. Brill (2015)

68. 《谁怕大恶龙：为什么中国拥有世界上最好（和最坏）的教育体系》Yong Zhao, *Who's Afraid of the Big Bad Dragon: Why China Has the Best (and Worst) Education System in the World*. Jossey-Bass (2014)

69. 《公务员考试：中国的考试地狱》Miyazaki Ichisada, *The Civil Service Examination: China's Examination Hell*. Chinese Education (2014)

70. 《我承认有错：在中国如何教西方礼仪成为自己难忘的教训》Eden Collinsworth, *I Stand Corrected: How Teaching Western Manners in China Became Its Own Unforgettable Lesson*. Nan A. Talese (2014)

71. 《中国高等教育私有化之路：新"文化大革命"》Li Wang, *The Road to Privatization of Higher Education in China: A New Cultural Revolution*.Springer-Verlag Berlin Heidelberg (2014)

72. 《适者生存：中国和美国高等教育的转移轮廓》Mimi Wolverton (auth.), Qi Li, Cynthia Gerstl-Pepin (eds.), *Survival of the Fittest: The Shifting Contours of Higher Education in China and the United States*.Springer-Verlag Berlin Heidelberg (2014)

73. 《中国课程研究：思想史与目前境遇》William F. Pinar (eds.), *Curriculum Studies in China: Intellectual Histories, Present Circumstances*.Palgrave Macmillan US (2014)

74. 《北京大学元培计划：课程创新案例研究》Wanying Wang, *The Yuanpei Program in Peking University: A Case Study of Curriculum Innovation*.Springer-Verlag Berlin Heidelberg (2014)

75. 《跟妈妈学习：中国家庭教育研究》Xiaoming Sheng, *Learning with Mothers: A Study of*

Home Schooling in China. SensePublishers (2014)

76. 《变化社会中的课程创新：来自香港、台湾和大陆的中国视角》Kerry J. Kennedy, Edmond Hau-Fai Law, Chenzhi Li (eds.), *Curriculum Innovations in Changing Societies: Chinese Perspectives from Hong Kong, Taiwan and Mainland China.* Sense Publishers (2013)

77. 《儿童、哲学与开放社会：儒家文化传承中的教育意蕴》Chi-Ming Lam, *Childhood, Philosophy and Open Society: Implications for Education in Confucian Heritage Cultures.* Springe (2013)

78. 《将跨课程写作引入中国：可行性与适应性》Dan Wu, *Introducing Writing Across the Curriculum into China: Feasibility and Adaptation.* Springer-Verlag Berlin Heidelberg (2013)

79. 《德国和中国职前教育：课程比较及其启示》Jun Li, *Pre-vocational Education in Germany and China: A Comparison of Curricula and Its Implications.* VS Verlag für Sozialwissenschaften (2013)

80. 《测试一个国家：中国大学英语考试的社会教育影响》Mark Garner, Dayong Huang, *Testing a Nation: The Social and Educational Impact of the College English Test in China.* Peter Lang AG, Internationaler Verlag der Wissenschaften (2013)

81. 《中国融资教育的政治学》Tingjin Lin, *The Politics of Financing Education in China.* Palgrave Macmillan UK (2013)

82. 《中国公民教育：为"中国世纪"准备公民》Kerry J. Kennedy, Gregory Fairbrother, Zhenzhou Zhao, *Citizenship Education in China: Preparing Citizens for the "Chinese Century".* Routledge (2013)

83. 《教育年轻的巨人：孩子们在中国和美国学什么（以及不学什么）》Nancy Pine, *Educating Young Giants: What Kids Learn (And Don't Learn) in China and America.* Palgrave Macmillan US (2012)

84. 《中国高等教育概览》Kai Yu, Andrea Lynn Stith, Li Liu, Huizhong Chen, *Tertiary Education at a Glance: China.* SensePublishers (2012)

85. 《西方人在中国教英语的批判性民族志：在上海"上贼船"》Phiona Stanley, *A Critical Ethnography of 'Westerners' Teaching English in China: Shanghaied in Shanghai* (Routledge Critical Studies in Asian Education). Routledge (2012)

86. 《中国学者论西方教育思想、领导、改革与发展》Nie Tingwu (author), Sylvester Chen, Michael Kompf (eds.), *Chinese Scholars on Western Ideas about Thinking, Leadership, Reform and Development in Education.* Sense Publishers (2012)

87. 《中国大陆、中国香港、中国台湾的学校音乐教育与社会变革》Wai-chung Ho, *School Music Education and Social Change in Mainland China, Hong Kong and Taiwan.* Brill (2011)

88. 《中国的教育发展与政策（1978—2008）》Xiulan Zhang (Editor), *China's Education Development and Policy, 1978—2008.* Brill (2011)

89. 《大中华区的英语教育》Anwei Feng, *English Language Education Across Greater China.*

Multilingual Matters (2011)

90. 《21世纪中国大学肖像：迈向高等教育大众化》Ruth Hayhoe（许美德）, Jun Li, Jing Lin, Qiang Zha, *Portraits of 21st Century Chinese Universities: In the Move to Mass Higher Education*. Springer Netherlands (2011)

91. 《中国教育政策的影响与转型》Tiedan Huang, Alexander W. Wiseman (eds.), *The Impact and Transformation of Education Policy in China*.Emerald Group Publishing Limited (2011)

92. 《重新定义天堂：跨国华人学生与发达国家灵活公民权追求》Vanessa Fong, *Paradise Redefined: Transnational Chinese Students and the Quest for Flexible Citizenship in the Developed World*.Stanford University Press (2011)

93. 《美国和中国教师发展的连续性：研讨会纪要》Ana Ferreras and Steve Olsen, Rapporteurs A. Ester Sztein, (ed.), *The Teacher Development Continuum in the United States and China: Summary of a Workshop*.National Academies Press (2010)

94. 《中国职业技术教育与培训体系国际比较》Zhenyi Guo, Stephen Lamb, *International Comparisons of China's Technical and Vocational Education and Training System*.Springer Netherlands (2010)

95. 《作为一项研究领域的中国高等教育：定义知识和课程结构》Xin Wang, *Higher Education as a Field of Study in China: Defining Knowledge and Curriculum Structure*. Lexington Books (2010)

96. 《中国和美国的平权行动：不平等与少数民族教育对话》Minglang Zhou, Ann Maxwell Hill (eds.), *Affirmative Action in China and the U.S.: A Dialogue on Inequality and Minority Education*. Palgrave Macmillan US (2009)

97. 《中国大学自治、国家和社会变迁》Su-Yan Pan, *University Autonomy, the State, and Social Change in China*.Hong Kong University Press (2009)

98. 《美中教育交流：国家、社会和文化间关系（1905—1950）》Hongshan Li, *U.S.-China Educational Exchange: State, Society, and Intercultural Relations, 1905—1950*. Rutgers University Press (2008)

99. 《中国的性别与教育：20世纪初期的性别话语与女性就学》Paul John Bailey, *Gender and Education in China: Gender Discourses and Women's Schooling in the Early Twentieth Century*. Routledge (2007)

100. 《中国双语教育：实践、政策与理念》Anwei Feng, *Bilingual Education in China: Practices, Policies and Concepts*.Multilingual Matters (2007)

101. 《通过终身学习提升中国的竞争力》Carl Dahlman, Douglas Zhihua Zeng, Shuilin Wang, *Enhancing China's Competitiveness Through Lifelong Learning* (WBI Development Studies). The World Bank (2007)

102. 《思想肖像：中国知名教育家的故事》Ruth Hayhoe（许美德）, *Portraits of Influential Chinese Educators* (CERC Studies in Comparative Education). Springer (2007)

103. 《通过内容竞争：中华帝国的文官考试标准（1127—1279）》Hilde De Weerdt, *Competition over Content Negotiating: Standards for the Civil Service Examinations in Imperial China（1127—1279）*. Harvard University Asia Center (2007)

104. 《中国投资大学的利润》Investment U, Alexander Green, Horacio MA-rquez, Louis Bass, Mark Whistler, *Investment University's Profit from China*.John Wiley & Sons (2007)

105. 《中国远程教育：2007战略参考》Philip M. Parker, *Distance Education in China: A Strategic Reference, 2007*. Icon Group International, Inc. (2007)

106. 《中国教育与社会变迁：市场经济中的不平等》Gerard A. Postiglione, *Education and Social Change in China: Inequality in a Market Economy*. M.E.Sharpe (2006)

107. 《中国商业与管理教育：转型、教育学、培训与联盟》Ilan Alon; John R. McIntyre, *Business and Management Education in China: Transition, Pedagogy, Training and Alliances*. World ScientificPublishing Co. Re. Ltd. (2005)

108. 《集权与分权：中国社会的教育改革与变革治理》Ka Ho Mok (eds.), *Centralization and Decentralization: Educational Reforms and Changing Governance in Chinese Societies*. Springer Netherlands (2004)

109. 《中国、日本和新加坡的英语教育》Rita Silver, Guangwei Hu, & Masakazu Iino, *English Language Education in China, Japan, and Singapore*. Nanyang Technological University (2002)

110. 《文化之县：从山东邹平乡村学校看20世纪中国》Stig Thøgersen, *A County of Culture: Twentieth-Century China Seen from the Village Schools of Zouping, Shandong*. University of Michigan Press (2002)

111. 《中国教育改革（1880—1910）：李提摩太及其高等教育观》（博士论文）Eunice V. Johnson, *Educational Reform in China, 1880—1910: Timothy Richard and His Vision for Higher Education*. Ph. D. Dissertation, University of Florida (2001)

112. 《中国传统教育史》Thomas H C Lee, *Education in Traditional China: A History* (Handbook of Oriental Studies: Handbuch Der Orientalistik). Brill (2000)

113. 《中国少数民族教育：文化、学校训练与发展》Gerard A. Postiglione, *China's National Minority Education: Culture, Schooling, and Development*.Falmer Press (1999)

114. 《中国体育运动和体育教育》James Riordan, Robin E. Jones, *Sport and Physical Education in China*.Taylor & Francis (1999)

115. 《中国社会转型与私立教育》Jing Lin, *Social Transformation and Private Education in China*.Praeger (1999)

116. 《联大：战争与革命中的中国大学》John Israel, *Lianda: A Chinese University in War and Revolution*. Stanford University Press (1999)

117. 《北京的教训：中国西南少数民族教育与民族认同》Mette Hansen, *Lessons in Being: Chinese Minority Education and Ethnic Identity in Southwest China*. Hong Kong University Press (1999)

6. 中国文化与文明 | 189

118. 《后毛泽东时代的中国高等教育》Michael Agelasto, Bob Adamson, *Higher Education in Post-Mao China*. Hong Kong University Press (1998)

119. 《中国图书馆事业教育》Guangwei Wu, Lili Zheng, *Education for Librarianship in China* (Education of Library and Information Professionals). Mansell Publishing Limited (1997)

120. 《中国高等教育改革》World Bank, *China: Higher Education Reform*. World Bank Publications (1997)

121. 《中国大学（1895—1995）：文化冲突的世纪》Ruth Hayhoe, *China's Universities, 1895—1995: A Century of Cultural Conflict* (Garland Reference Library of Social Science). (1996)

122. 《基础汉语课本》Sinolingua, *Elementary Chinese Readers* China Books Periodical (1994)

123. 《失落的改革者：1906—1931年在美中国留学生》（博士论文）Jan Stacey Bieler, *The lost Reformers: Chinese Students in the United States from 1906—1931*. Ph. D. Dissertation, Michigan State University (1994)

124. 《中国大陆学生在美国：社区与边缘》（硕士论文）Koji Hoshino, *Mainland Chinese Students in America: Community and Marginality*. Thesis for the Degree of Master of Arts, University of Montana (1994)

125. 《中国高等教育：改革发展的十年（1978—1988）》Ruiqing Du, *Chinese Higher Education: A Decade of Reform and Development (1978—1988)*. Palgrave Macmillan UK (1992)

126. 《20世纪80年代中国教育改革：政策、问题和历史视角》Suzanne Pepper, *China's Education Reform in the 1980s: Policies, Issues, and Historical Perspectives*. Institute of East Asian Studies, University of California at Berkeley, Center for Chinese Studies (1990)

127. 《教育交流：中美经验论文集》Joyce K. Kallgren, Denis Fred Simon (eds.), *Educational Exchanges: Essays on the Sino-American Experience*. Institute of East Asian Studies, University of California (1987)

128. 《中国教育与工业化世界：文化转移研究》Ruth Hayhoe（许美德），Marianne Bastid (eds.), *China's Education and the Industrialized World: Studies in Cultural Transfer*. Armonk, NY: M. E. Sharpe (1987)

129. 《恢复关系：美中教育交流趋势（1978—1984）》David M. Lampton（蓝普顿），Joyce A. Madancy, Kristen M. Williams, *A Relationship Restored: Trends in U.S.–China Educational Exchanges, 1978—1984*. National Academy Press (1986)

130. 《竞争的同志：中国的职业动机与学生策略》Susan Shirk（谢淑丽），*Competitive Comrades: Career Incentives and Student Strategies in China*. University of California Press (1982)

131. 《一个中国社区的双语教育》Sau-Lim Tsang, *Bilingual Education in a Chinese Community*. Final Research Report. National Institute of Education, Washington, DC. (1982)

132. 《1949以来的中国教育：学术与革命模式》Theodore Hsi-en Chen, *Chinese Education Since 1949. Academic and Revolutionary Models*. Elsevier Inc, Pergamon Press (1981)

133. 《不断变化的中国学校：美中关系全国委员会国家教育领导代表团报告》Ronald N.

Montaperto, Jay Henderson, *China's Schools in Flux: Report by the State Education Leaders Delegation, National Committee on United States-China Relations*. Palgrave Macmillan UK (1979)

134. 《燕京大学与中美关系（1916—1952）》Philip West, *Yenching University and Sino-American Relations, 1916—1952*. Harvard University Press (1976)

135. 《张之洞与中国教育改革》William Ayers, *Chang Chih-tung and Educational Reform in China* (Harvard East Asian series). Harvard University Press (1971)

136. 《中国共产党的少数民族教育》Changdu Hu, *Education of National Minorities in Communist China*. U.S. Office of Education, Institute of International Studies (1970)

137. 《中国社会、学校与进步》Chiu-Sam Tsang and Edmund King, *Society, Schools and Progress in China*. Elsevier Ltd, Pergamon Press (1968)

138. 《供1—12年级使用的亚洲国家教学指南和材料准备》John U. Michaetis, *Preparation of Teaching Guides and Materials on Asian Countries for Use in Grades I-XII. Final Report*. Office of Education (DHEW), Washington, D.C. Bureau of Research (1968)

139. 《福建协和大学：历史回顾》Roderick Scott, *Fukien Christian University: A Historical Sketch*. New York: United Board for Christian Colleges in China (1954)

140. 《年轻的中国》Arthur Evans Moule（慕雅德）, *Young China*. Hodder and Stoughton (1908)

141. 《鲍留云：一位新东方的创造者，中国、美国和日本教育先驱，其生活和工作的故事》William Elliot Griffis, *A Maker of the New Orient: Samuel Robbins Brown, Pioneer Educator in China, America, and Japan, the Story of His Life and Work*. New York: Fleming H. Revell (1902)

142. 《翰林院论文集：他们的教育、哲学和文字》William Alexander Parsons Martin（丁韪良）, *Hanlin Papers: Their Education, Philosophy, and Letters*. Trubner & Co. (1880)

6.4.1 孔子学院

1. 《中国在世界：孔子学院的人类学、软实力与全球化》Jennifer Hubbert, *China in the World: An Anthropology of Confucius Institutes, Soft Power, and Globalization*. University of Hawaii Press (2019)

2. 《外包给中国：美国高等教育中的孔子学院与软实力》Rachelle Peterson, *Outsourced to China. Confucius Institutes and Soft Power in American Higher Education*. National Association of Scholars (2017)

3. 《软实力与中国语言学习观念的全球推广和实践：孔子学院项目》Jeffrey Gil, *Soft Power and the Worldwide Promotion of Chinese Language Learning Beliefs and Practices: The Confucius Institute Project*. Multilingual Matters (2017)

4. 《中国软实力议程在美国高等教育中的表现：以美国孔子学院项目为例》（博士论文）Jiaying Song, *The Manifestation of China's Soft Power Agenda in American Higher Education: The Case of the Confucius Institute Project in America*. Ph.D. Dissertation, Education 0249, UCLA (2017)

5. 《孔子学院的后果：理解反对派》（硕士论文）Andrew Switzer, *The Consequences of*

Confucius Institutes: Understanding the Opposition. Thesis for the Degree of Master of Arts, Georgetown University (2017)

6. 《中国公共外交：孔子学院的兴起》Falk Hartig, *Chinese Public Diplomacy: The Rise of the Confucius Institute*. Routledge (2016)

6.4.2 心理学

1. 《近代早期中国人的情感空间：从梦境到戏剧》Ling Hon Lam, *The Spatiality of Emotion in Early Modern China: From Dreamscapes to Theatricality*. Columbia University Press (2018)
2. 《幽默与中国文化：心理学视角》Xiaodong Yue, *Humor and Chinese Culture: A Psychological Perspective* (Routledge Studies in Asian Behavioural Sciences). Routledge (2017)
3. 《心理健康与不平等：作为心理健康公共医疗卫生服务使用者的中国少数民族》Lynn Tang, Recovery, *Mental Health and Inequality: Chinese Ethnic Minorities as Mental Health Service Users* (Routledge studies in the sociology of health and illness). Routledge (2017)
4. 《了解中国文化情感：心理学思考》Louise Sundararajan, *Understanding Emotion in Chinese Culture: Thinking Through Psychology*. Springer International Publishing (2015)
5. 《道德萌芽与自然目的论：21世纪道德心理学与中国古典哲学的相遇》Owen J. Flanagan, *Moral Sprouts and Natural Teleologies: 21st Century Moral Psychology Meets Classical Chinese Philosophy*. Marquette University Press (2014)
6. 《面术读本：通过道家相面术发现任何人的真实个性》（第二版）Patrician McCarthy, *The Face Reader: Discover Anyone's True Personality Through Taoist Chinese Face Reading, Second Edition*. Tao House Press (2014)
7. 《中国心理学基础：儒家社会关系》Kwang-Kuo Hwang（黄光国，台湾）, *Foundations of Chinese Psychology: Confucian Social Relations* (International and Cultural Psychology 1). Springer-Verlag New York (2012)
8. 《中国开发的心理健康相关评估工具》Lawrence T. Lam (ed.), *Psychological and Health-Related Assessment Tools Developed in China*. Bentham Science (2010)
9. 《弗洛伊德与远东：中、日、韩人民和文化的精神分析视角》Salman Akhtar, June Cai, *Freud and the Far East: Psychoanalytic Perspectives on the People and Culture of China, Japan, and Korea*. Jason Aronson (2009)
10. 《从阿Q到雷锋：20世纪中国的弗洛伊德和革命精神》Wendy Larson（文棣）, *From Ah Q to Lei Feng: Freud and Revolutionary Spirit in 20th Century China*. Stanford University Press (2008)
11. 《中国超级心理学》Paul Dong, Thomas E. Raffill, Ph. D. Karen S. Kramer, *China's Super Psychics*. Marlowe & Company (1997)
12. 《思想改造和极权主义心理学：中国洗脑研究》Robert Jay Lifton（利夫顿）, *Thought Reform and the Psychology of Totalism: A Study of Brainwashing in China*. University of North Carolina Press (1989)
13. 《中国文化与心理健康》Wen-Shing Tseng, David Y. H. Wu (eds.), *Chinese Culture and*

Mental Health. Academic Press, Inc. (1985)

14. 《当代中国心理学》L. B. Brown, *Psychology in Contemporary China.* Franklin Book Co. (1981)

15. 《红色中国的洗脑》Edward Hunter（洪德）, *Brain Washing in Red China.* New York: Vanguard Press (1951)

6.5 知识分子

1. 《创造知识分子：中国共产主义与等级类别的兴起》Eddy U, *Creating the Intellectual: Chinese Communism and the Rise of a Classification.* University of California Press (2019)

2. 《民间：中国草根知识分子的崛起》Sebastian Veg, *Minjian: The Rise of China's Grassroots Intellectuals.* Columbia University Press (2019)

3. 《20世纪初中国女性知识分子的教育记忆》Lijing Jiang, *Educational Memory of Chinese Female Intellectuals in Early Twentieth Century.* Springer Singapore (2018)

4. 《阅读哲学与创作诗歌：早期中古中国的意义构建互文性模式》Wendy Swartz（田菱）, *Reading Philosophy, Writing Poetry: Intertextual Modes of Making Meaning in Early Medieval China.* Harvard University Asia Center (2018)

5. 《跨太平洋共同体：美国、中国与一个文化网络的兴衰》Richard Jean So, *Transpacific Community: America, China, and the Rise and Fall of a Cultural Network.* Columbia University Press (2016)

6. 《中世纪晚期中国文人的故事讲述》Manling Luo, *Literati Storytelling in Late Medieval China.* University of Washington Press (2015)

7. 《史诗时代的抒情：1949年危机中的现代中国知识分子与艺术家》David Der-Wei Wang（王德威）, *The Lyrical in Epic Time: Modern Chinese Intellectuals and Artists through the 1949 Crisis.* Columbia University Press (2015)

8. 《晚清学者与作为政治话语的国家小说》Liangyan Ge, *The Scholar and the State Fiction as Political Discourse in Late Imperial China.* University of Washington Press (2014)

9. 《清初国家与士绅（1644—1699）》Harry Miller, *State versus Gentry in Early Qing Dynasty China, 1644—1699.* Palgrave Macmillan US (2013)

10. 《明末国家与士绅（1572—1644）》Harry Miller, *State versus Gentry in Late Ming Dynasty China, 1572—1644.* Palgrave Macmillan US (2009)

11. 《燕卜荪传：在精英们中间》John Haffenden, *William Empson: Among the Mandarins.* Oxford University Press, USA (2009)

12. 《最后的中国文人：蔡德允的音乐、诗歌和人生》Bell Yung, *The Last of China's Literati: The Music, Poetry and Life of Tsar Teh-yun.* Hong Kong University Press (2008)

13. 《当代中国大陆知识分子的生活快照》Arif Dirlik（阿里夫·德里克）, *Snapshots of Intellectual Life in Contemporary PR China.* Duke University Press (2008)

14. 《埃兹拉·庞德的中国朋友们：书信中的故事》Zhaoming Qian, *Ezra Pound's Chinese*

Friends. Stories in Letters. Oxford University Press, USA (2008)

15. 《杜威在中国：教与学》Jessica Ching-Sze Wang, *John Dewey in China: To Teach and to Learn* (SUNY Series in Chinese Philosophy and Culture).State University of New York Press (2007)

16. 《中国宋元明时代的吉安文人与地方》A. T. Gerritsen, *Ji'an Literati and the Local in Song-Yuan-Ming China* (China Studies). Brill (2007)

17. 《书籍的社会史：中华帝国晚期的书籍与士人文化》Joseph McDermott, *A Social History of the Chinese Book: Books and Literati Culture in Late Imperial China* (Understanding China: New Viewpoints on History and Culture). Hong Kong University Press (2006)

18. 《阮元（1764—1849）：一位19世纪鸦片战争前中国重要士大夫的生平与作品》Betty Wai, *Ruan Yuan, 1764—1849: The Life and Work of a Major Scholar-Official in Nineteenth-Century China before the Opium War*. Hong Kong University Press (2005)

19. 《革命中国的知识分子》Hung-yok Ip, *Intellectuals in Revolutionary China: Leaders, Heroes and Sophisticates*. RoutledgeCurzon (2005)

20. 《1761年的课堂：中国18世纪的考试、国家和精英》Iona Man-Cheong, *The Class of 1761: Examinations, State, and Elites in Eighteenth-Century China*. Stanford University Press (2004)

21. 《国家与市场之间的中国知识分子》Edward Gu, Merle Goldman（梅谷）, *Chinese Intellectuals between State and Market* (Routledgecurzon Studies on China in Transition, 17). Routledgecurzon (2004)

22. 《权力源自地位：北京大学、知识分子与中国政治文化（1898—1929）》Timothy B. Weston（魏定熙）, *The Power of Position: Beijing University, Intellectuals, and Chinese Political Culture, 1898—1929*. University of California Press (2004)

23. 《中国科研精英》Cong Cao, *China's Scientific Elite* (Routledgecurzon Studies on China in Transition). Routledgecurzon (2004)

24. 《十字路口的知识分子：中国知识工作者不断变化的政治》Zhidong Hao, *Intellectuals at a Crossroads: The Changing Politics of China's Knowledge Workers*. State University of New York Press (2003)

25. 《中华帝制晚期的阅读（1000—1800）》（博士论文）Li Yu, *A History of Reading in Late Imperial China, 1000—1800*. Ph. D. Dissertation, the Ohio State University (2003)

26. 《傅斯年传》Fan-sen Wang（王汎森）, *Fu Ssu-nien: A Life in Chinese History and Politics* (Cambridge Studies in Chinese History, Literature and Institutions). Cambridge University Press (2000)

27. 《拒仕的模式：中世纪早期中国隐逸的实践与写照》Alan Berkowitz, *Patterns of Disengagement: The Practice and Portrayal of Reclusion in Early Medieval China*. Stanford University Press (2000)

28. 《后毛泽东时代的中国知识分子与国家》Ka-ho Mok, *Intellectuals and the State in Post-*

Mao China. Palgrave Macmillan (1998)

29. 《陈独秀最后的文章和信件（1937—1942）》Gregor Benton（班国瑞）(ed.), Chen Duxiu, *Chen Duxiu's Last Articles and Letters, 1937—1942*. University of Hawai'i Press (1998)

30. 《梁思成与林徽因：探索中国建筑史的伴侣》Wilma Fairbank（费慰梅）, *Liang and Lin: Partners in Exploring China's Architectural Past*. University of Pennsylvania Press (1994)

31. 《最高级的权力：专业人士与新官员秩序的兴起》Charles Derber, William A. Schwartz, Yale Magrass, *Power in the Highest Degree: Professionals and the Rise of a New Mandarin Order*. Oxford University Press, USA (1990)

32. 《中国地方精英与支配模式》Joseph W. Esherick（周锡瑞）, Mary Backus Rankin, *Chinese Local Elites and Patterns of Dominance*. Berkeley: University of California Press (1990)

33. 《危机中的中国知识分子：寻求秩序与意义》Chang Hao（张灏）, *Chinese Intellectuals in Crisis: Search for Order and Meaning (1890—1911)*. University of California Press (1987)

34. 《官宦与乡绅：宋代江西抚州精英》Robert Hymes, *Statesmen and Gentlemen: The Elite of Fu-Chou Chiang-Hsi, in Northern and Southern Sung*. Cambridge University Press (1987)

35. 《中国精英行动主义与政治转变：1865—1911年之浙江》Mary Backus Rankin, *Elite Activism and Political Transformation in China: Zhejiang Province, 1865—1911*. Stanford University Press (1986)

36. 《楚国狂人：忠诚与异议的中国神话》（屈原的故事）Laurence A. Schneider, *Madman of Ch'u: The Chinese Myth of Loyalty and Dissent*. University of California Press (1980)

37. 《中华人民共和国的精英》Robert A. Scalapino（斯卡拉皮诺）, *Elites in the People's Republic of China* (Studies in Chinese government and politics). Seattle: University of Washington Press (1972)

38. 《梁启超与近代中国自由主义》Philip C. C. Huang（黄宗智）, *Liang Ch'i-ch'ao and Modern Chinese Liberalism*. University of Washington Press (1972)

39. 《胡适与中国文艺复兴：中国革命中的自由主义（1917—1937）》Jerome B. Grieder, *Hu Shih and the Chinese Renaissance: Liberalism in the Chinese Revolution, 1917—1937*. Harvard University Press (1970)

40. 《共产主义中国的文学异议者》Merle Goldman（梅谷）, *Literary Dissent in Communist China* (Harvard East Asian Series). Harvard University Press (1967)

41. 《百花运动与中国知识分子》Roderick MacFarquhar（马若德）, *The Hundred Flowers Campaign and the Chinese Intellectuals*. New York: Praeger (1960)

42. 《中国的青年运动》Tsi Chang Wang（王苢章）, *The Youth Movement In China*. New Republic (1927)

6.6 传媒与网络

6.6.1 新闻媒体

1. 《现实与媒体建设：德国对华媒体形象的框架分析》Fengmin Yan, *Image, Reality and Media Construction: A Frame Analysis of German Media Representations of China*. Springer Singapore (2020)
2. 《中国社会舆论与危机管理研究报告》(Research Series on the Chinese Dream and China's Development Path) Yungeng Xie, *Report on Chinese Social Opinion and Crisis Management*. Springer Singapore (2019)
3. 《中国传媒政治：共识与论争》Bingchun Meng, *The Politics of Chinese Media: Consensus and Contestation* (China in Transformation). Palgrave Macmillan US (2018)
4. 《中澳重要新闻中的新闻立场》Changpeng Huan, *Journalistic Stance in Chinese and Australian Hard News*. Springer Singapore (2018)
5. 《中国社交媒体》(Sociology, Media and Journalism in China) Wenbo Kuang, *Social Media in China*. Springer Singapore: Palgrave Macmillan (2018)
6. 《汉英政府新闻发布会口译的情态重构》(Corpora and Intercultural Studies 1) Xin Li, *The Reconstruction of Modality in Chinese-English Government Press Conference Interpreting*. Springer Singapore (2018)
7. 《中国新媒体发展报告》Xujun Tang, Xinxun Wu, Chuxin Huang Ruisheng Liu (eds.), *Development Report on China's New Media*. Springer Singapore (2017)
8. 《网络公众：当代中国的社会媒体与社会变迁》Wei He, *Networked Public: Social Media and Social Change in Contemporary China*. Springer-Verlag Berlin Heidelberg (2017)
9. 《新媒体与中国社会》Ke Xue, Mingyang Yu (eds.), *New Media and Chinese Society* (Communication, Culture and Change in Asia 5). Springer Singapore (2017)
10. 《新媒体与中国社会发展》Yungeng Xie (eds.), *New Media and China's Social Development* (Research Series on the Chinese Dream and China's Development Path). Springer Singapore (2017)
11. 《中国社交媒体与电子外交：审视微博的力量》Ying Jiang, *Social Media and e-Diplomacy in China: Scrutinizing the Power of Weibo*. Palgrave Pivot, New York (2017)
12. 《政府新闻发布会汉英口译中的情态重构：基于语料库的研究》Xin Li, *The Reconstruction of Modality in Chinese-English Government Press Conference Interpreting: A Corpus-Based Study* (Corpora and Intercultural Studies 1). Springer (2017)
13. 《中国传媒素养教育》Chi-Kim Cheung, *Media Literacy Education in China*. Springer Singapore (2016)
14. 《微博记忆：微博与当代中国的集体记忆》Eileen Le Han, *Micro-blogging Memories: Weibo and Collective Remembering in Contemporary China*. Palgrave Macmillan UK (2016)

15. 《中国战地记者：报道21世纪的战争与冲突》Shixin Ivy Zhang, *Chinese War Correspondents: Covering Wars and Conflicts in the Twenty-First Century*. Palgrave Macmillan (2016)
16. 《工业中国的社交媒体》Xinyuan Wang, *Social Media in Industrial China*. UCL Press (2016)
17. 《中国的新闻调查、环境问题与现代化》Jingrong Tong, *Investigative Journalism, Environmental Problems and Modernisation in China*. Palgrave Macmillan UK (2015)
18. 《网络化中国：数字媒体与公民参与的全球动力》Wenhong Chen, Stephen D. Reese (eds.), *Networked China: Global Dynamics of Digital Media and Civic Engagement*. Routledge (2015)
19. 《中国城市的社会化媒体代际：青少年社会化媒体使用和成瘾研究》Hanyun Huang, *Social Media Generation in Urban China: A Study of Social Media Use and Addiction among Adolescents*. Springer Berlin Heidelberg (2014)
20. 《当代中国大众传媒、社会情感与公共话语》Shuyu Kong, *Popular Media, Social Emotion and Public Discourse in Contemporary China* (Routledge Contemporary China Series). Routledge (2014)
21. 《中国新闻的政治经济学：制造和谐》Jesse Owen Hearns-Branaman, *The Political Economy of News in China: Manufacturing Harmony*. Lexington Books (2014)
22. 《中国独立纪录片：从工作室到街头》Luke Robinson, *Independent Chinese Documentary: From the Studio to the Street*. Palgrave Macmillan UK (2013)
23. 《中国媒体商业化与专制统治》Daniela Stockmann, *Media Commercialization and Authoritarian Rule in China*. Cambridge University Press (2012)
24. 《电视节目的文化差异：中国的外国电视节目》Zhuo Feng, *Cultural Difference in Television Programs: Foreign Television Programs in China*. Peter Lang GmbH (2012)
25. 《中国流行电视剧中的视觉政治传播》Florian Schneider, *Visual Political Communication in Popular Chinese Television Series*. Brill (2012)
26. 《美国广播电台在中国：技术通信的国际遭遇（1919—1941）》Michael A. Krysko, *American Radio in China: International Encounters with Technology and Communications, 1919—41*. Palgrav (2011)
27. 《中国新闻调查：新闻权力与社会》Jingrong Tong, *Investigative Journalism in China: Journalism Power and Society*. Continuum (2011)
28. 《新闻媒体与中国—欧盟关系》Li Zhang, *News Media and EU-China Relations* (Palgrave Macmillan Series in International Political Communication). Palgrave Macmillan (2011)
29. 《新中国的新闻媒体》James F. Scotton, William A. Hachten, *New Media for a New China*. Wiley-Blackwell (2010)
30. 《变动中的媒体与变动中的中国》Susan L. Shirk（谢淑丽）, *Changing Media, Changing China*. Oxford University Press, USA (2010)
31. 《电视中国》Ying Zhu, Christopher Berry, *TV China*. Indiana University Press (2009)

32. 《中国媒体与文化转型》Haiqing Yu, *Media and Cultural Transformation in China*. Routledge (2009)
33. 《雾锁中国：中国媒体控制》He Qinglian（何清涟）, *The Fog of Censorship: Media Control in China*. Human Rights in China (2008)
34. 《加入全球大众：早期中国报纸中的世界、图像与城市》Rudolf G. Wagner, *Joining the Global Public: World, Image and City in Early Chinese Newspapers, 1870—1910*. State University of New York Press (2007)
35. 《中国纪录片：从教条到多种声音》Yingchi Chu, *Chinese Documentaries: From Dogma to Polyphony*. Routledge (2007)
36. 《近代中国新闻的起源：晚清新教传教士新闻的影响》Xiantao Zhang, *The Origins of the Modern Chinese Press: The Influence of the Protestant Missionary Press in Late Qing China*. Routledge (2007)
37. 《美国新闻杂志中的蒋介石形象》（博士论文）Amy Giovanetti, *Image-making in United States-China relations: Images of Chiang Kai-Shek in American newsmagazines*. Ph. D. Dissertation, St. John's University (2007)
38. 《全球化、文化认同与媒体再现》Natascha Gentz（费南山）, Stefan Kramer, *Globalization, Cultural Identities, and Media Representation*. State University of New York Press (2006)
39. 《一位在中国早期革命中的美国编辑：约翰·威廉·鲍威尔与〈密勒氏评论报〉》Neil O'Brien, *An American Editor in Early Revolutionary China: John William Powell and the China Weekly Monthly Review*. Routledge (2003)
40. 《国家与市场之间：当代中国媒体改革与公共话语变迁》（博士论文）Qing Liu（刘擎）, *Between the State and Market: Media Reform and the Change of Public Discourse in Contemporary China*. Ph. D. Dissertation, The University of Minnesota (2003)
41. 《中国媒体与全球语境》Lee Chin-Chuan, *Chinese Media, Global Contexts* (Asia's Transformations). RoutledgeCurzon (2003)
42. 《中国报道：美国精英新闻媒体内容分析（1990—1995）》（博士论文）Chun-Lei Wang, *Reporting on China: What the Elite American News Media Say-A Content Analysis (1990—1995)*. Ph. D. Dissertation, Ohio University (2001)
43. 《多种声音交响乐：论扩大中国的言论与新闻自由》Sun Xupei（孙旭培）, Elizabeth C. Michel, Eric B. Easton, *An Orchestra of Voices: Making the Argument for Greater Speech and Press Freedom in the People's Republic of China*. Praeger (2001)
44. 《中国情景：高级汉语多媒体课程》Hong Gang Jin, De Bao Xu, James Hargett, *China Scene: An Advanced Chinese Multimedia Course*. Cheng & Tsui Company (2000)
45. 《中国新闻工作者在改革年代的斗争》Allison Liu Jernow, *The Struggle of Chinese Journalists in the Reform Era*. University of Maryland (1994)
46. 《中国报道：20世纪30—40年代美国新闻口述史》Stephen R. MacKinnon, Oris Friesen,

China Reporting: An Oral History of American Journalism in the 1930s and 1940s. University of California Press (1990)

47. 《纽约时报：来自红色中国的报告》Tillman Durdin, James Reston, Seymour Topping; with photographs and additional articles by Audrey Topping; edited with an introduction by Frank Ching, *The New York Times: Report from Red China*. Quadrangle Books (1971)

48. 《中国青年的革命化：〈中国青年〉研究》James R. Townsend, *The Revolutionization of Chinese Youth: A study of Chungkuo Ch'ing-nien*. Center for Chinese Studies, University of California (1967)

6.6.2 电影

1. 《中国革命电影：宣传、美学和国际主义（1949—1966）》(International Library of the Moving Image) Jessica Ka Yee Chan, *Chinese Revolutionary Cinema: Propaganda, Aesthetics and Internationalism 1949—1966*. I. B. Tauris (2019)

2. 《基于区块链和智能合约的中国在线电影制作：新兴创意人才合作平台的开发》(International Series on Computer Entertainment and Media Technology) Patrice Poujol, *Online Film Production in China Using Blockchain and Smart Contracts: The Development of Collaborative Platforms for Emerging Creative Talents*. Springer International Publishing (2019)

3. 《中国新潮电影中的意识形态与乌托邦》Xiaoping Wang, *Ideology and Utopia in China's New Wave Cinema* (Chinese Literature and Culture in the World). Springer International Publishing, Palgrave Macmillan (2018)

4. 《中国艺术电影的形成（1990—2003）》Li Yang, *The Formation of Chinese Art Cinema: 1990—2003*. Springer International Publishing, Palgrave Macmillan (2018)

5. 《全球化与当代中国电影：张艺谋的流派电影》Xuelin Zhou, *Globalization and Contemporary Chinese Cinema: Zhang Yimou's Genre Films*. Palgrave Macmillan (2017)

6. 《舞台表演中国革命：剧院、电影和宣传的来生》Xiaomei Chen, *Staging Chinese Revolution: Theater, Film, and the Afterlives of Propaganda*. Columbia University Press (2017)

7. 《当代中国电影和著名导演》Shenshen Cai, *Contemporary Chinese Films and Celebrity Directors*. Palgrave Macmillan (2017)

8. 《中国电影节：翻译网站》Chris Berry, Luke Robinson (eds.), *Chinese Film Festivals: Sites of Translation*. Palgrave Macmillan US (2017)

9. 《中国制造的好莱坞》Aynne Kokas, *Hollywood Made in China*. University of California Press (2017)

10. 《大众电影中的中国和中国人：从傅满洲到陈查理》Jeffrey Richards, *China and the Chinese in Popular Film: From Fu Manchu to Charlie Chan*. I. B. Tauris & Company (2017)

11. 《中国电影诗学》Gary Bettinson, James Udden (eds.), *The Poetics of Chinese Cinema*. Palgrave Macmillan US (2016)

12. 《拍摄日常：中国21世纪的独立纪录片》Paul G. Pickowicz（毕克伟）, Yingjin Zhang

（张英进）(eds.), *Filming the Everyday: Independent Documentaries in Twenty-First-Century China*. Rowman & Littlefield (2016)

13. 《中国电影的国际视角》Felicia Chan, Andy Willis (eds.), *Chinese Cinemas: International Perspectives*. Routledge (2016)

14. 《中国动画：历史、美学与媒体》Sean Macdonald, *Animation in China: History, Aesthetics, Media*. Routledge (2016)

15. 《世界影院中国目录2》Gary Bettinson, *Directory of World Cinema China 2*. Intellect Books (2015)

16. 《火热的影院：1915—1945年中国情感媒体的出现》Weihong Bao, *Fiery Cinema: The Emergence of an Affective Medium in China, 1915—1945*. University of Minnesota Press (2015)

17. 《筛选1989年后的中国：华语影视的批判性分析》Wing Shan Ho, *Screening Post-1989 China: Critical Analysis of Chinese Film and Television*. Palgrave Macmillan US (2015)

18. 《数码摄像中国：电影独立后的数字主题和社会变革》Zhen Zhang, Angela Zito, *DV-Made China: Digital Subjects and Social Transformations after Independent Film*. University of Hawaii Press (2015)

19. 《中国的iGeneration: 21世纪电影和移动影像文化》Matthew D. Johnson, Luke Vulpiani, Keith B. Wagner, Kiki Tianqi Yu, *China's iGeneration: Cinema and Moving Image Culture for the Twenty-First Century*. Bloomsbury Academic (2014)

20. 《中国电影的革命周期（1951—1979）》Zhuoyi Wang, *Revolutionary Cycles in Chinese Cinema, 1951—1979*. Palgrave Macmillan US (2014)

21. 《破碎的现代主义：战时中国文学、艺术、电影（1937—1949）》Carolyn FitzGerald, *Fragmenting Modernisms: Chinese Wartime Literature, Art, and Film, 1937—49*. Brill (2013)

22. 《想象大众独裁：文学和电影中的个人和群众》Michael Schoenhals（沈迈克），Karin Sarsenov (eds.), *Imagining Mass Dictatorships: The Individual and the Masses in Literature and Cinema* (Mass Dictatorship in the 20th Century). Palgrave Macmillan UK (2013)

23. 《电影里的中国：一个世纪的探索、对抗与争论》Paul G. Pickowicz（毕克伟），*China on Film: A Century of Exploration, Confrontation, and Controversy*. Rowman & Littlefield Publishers (2012)

24. 《世界华语电影指南》Yingjin Zhang（张英进）(ed.), *A Companion to Chinese Cinema*. Wiley-Blackwell (2012)

25. 《李连杰：中国男性气质与跨国电影明星》Sabrina Qiong Yu, *Jet Li: Chinese Masculinity and Transnational Film Stardom*. Edinburgh University Press (2012)

26. 《中国海外移民武侠电影：李安、吴宇森和成龙在好莱坞》Kin-Yan Szeto, *The Martial Arts Cinema of the Chinese Diaspora: Ang Lee, John Woo, and Jackie Chan in Hollywood*. Southern Illinois University Press (2011)

27. 《东亚电影与文化遗产：从中国大陆、中国香港、中国台湾到日本和韩国》Yau Shuk-

ting Kinnia (eds.), *East Asian Cinema and Cultural Heritage: From China, Hong Kong, Taiwan to Japan and South Korea*. Palgrave Macmillan (2011)

28. 《中国女性电影：跨国语境》Lingzhen Wang, *Chinese Women's Cinema: Transnational Contexts*. Columbia University Press (2011)

29. 《屏幕左侧：好莱坞的共产党和左翼思想（1929—2009）》Bob Herzberg, *The Left Side of the Screen: Communist and Left-Wing Ideology in Hollywood, 1929—2009*. McFarland (2011)

30. 《中国女性电影：跨国语境》Lingzhen Wang, *Chinese Women's Cinema: Transnational Contexts* (Film and Culture Series). Columbia University Press (2011)

31. 《适应屏幕：中国小说和电影中的文化政治学》Hsiu-Chuang Deppman, *Adapted for the Screen: The Cultural Politics of Modern Chinese Fiction and Film*. University of Hawai'i Press (2010)

32. 《城市边缘的电影院：东亚的电影与城市网络》Yomi Braester, *Cinema at the City's Edge: Film and Urban Networks in East Asia*. Hong Kong University Press (2010)

33. 《全球华语电影："英雄"的文化与政治》Gary D. Rawnsley, Ming-Yeh T. Rawnsley, *Global Chinese Cinema: The Culture and Politics of "Hero"*. Routledge (2010)

34. 《地铁电影：后毛泽东时代的中国电影都市化》Harry H. Kuoshu, *Metro Movies: Cinematic Urbanism in Post-Mao China*. Southern Illinois University Press (2010)

35. 《为了荧幕而改变：中国小说和电影中的文化政治学》Hsiu-Chuang Deppman, *Adapted for the Screen: The Cultural Politics of Modern Chinese Fiction and Film*. University of Hawai'i Press (2010)

36. 《马克思与可口可乐之子：中国前卫艺术和独立电影》Xiaoping Lin, *Children of Marx and Coca-Cola: Chinese Avant-Garde Art and Independent Cinema*. University of Hawai'i Press (2009)

37. 《罗马帝国的堕落：电影与历史》Martin M. Winkler, *The Fall of the Roman Empire: Film and History*. Blackwell Publishing Ltd (2009)

38. 《中国全球化过程中的电影、空间和多维地点》Yinghin Zheng, *Cinema, Space and Polylocality in Globalizing China*. University of Hawai'i Press (2009)

39. 《中国电影的未来：中国银幕文化的技术和时间性》Olivia Khoo, Sean Metzger, *Futures of Chinese Cinema: Technologies and Temporalities in Chinese Screen Cultures*. Intellect Ltd (2009)

40. 《冯小刚电影：1989年后中国电影的商业化与审查》Rui Zhang, *The Cinema of Feng Xiaogang: Commercialization and Censorship in Chinese Cinema after 1989*. Hong Kong University Press (2008)

41. 《中国台湾与中国大陆影院的现代性冲突》Tonglin Lu, *Confronting Modernity in the Cinemas of Taiwan and Mainland China*. Cambridge University Press (2007)

42. 《当代中国电影的感伤魅力：全球可见度的依恋》Rey Chow（周蕾）, *Sentimental Fabulations, Contemporary Chinese Films: Attachment in the Age of Global Visibility* (Film

and Culture Series). Columbia University Press (2007)

43. 《当代中国电影中的年轻反叛者》Xuelin Zhou, *Young Rebels in Contemporary Chinese Cinema*. Hong Kong University Press (2007)

44. 《导演杜琪峰与香港动作片》Stephen Teo, *Director in Action: Johnnie To and the Hong Kong Action Film*. Hong Kong University Press (2007)

45. 《迎合世界最大观众：中国影视全球化》Michael Curtin, *Playing to the World's Biggest Audience: The Globalization of Chinese Film and TV*. University of California Press (2007)

46. 《银幕上的中国：电影与民族》Christopher J. Berry, Mary Ann Farquhar, *China on Screen: Cinema and Nation*. Columbia University Press (2006)

47. 《银幕上的同志：当代中国电影中的男性同性恋代表》Song Hwee Lim, *Celluloid Comrades: Representations of Male Homosexuality in Contemporary Chinese Cinemas*. University of Hawai'i Press (2006)

48. 《台湾电影导演（李安、侯孝贤等）》Emilie Yueh-yu Yeh and Darrell William Davis, *Taiwan Film Directors: A Treasure Island*. Columbia University Press (2005)

49. 《中国左翼电影的起源（1932—1937）》Vivian Shen, *The Origins of Leftwing Cinema in China, 1932—37*. Routledge (2005)

50. 《后毛泽东时代的中国社会主义电影："文革"后的"文革"》Chris Berry, *Postsocialist Cinema in Post-Mao China: The Cultural Revolution after the Cultural Revolution*. Routledge (2004)

51. 《中国电影研究注释书目》Jim Cheng, *An Annotated Bibliography of Chinese Film Studies*. Hong Kong University Press (2004)

52. 《镜头中的女性：中国电影百年中的性别和民族》Cui, Shuqin, *Women Through the Lens: Gender and Nation in a Century of Chinese Cinema*. University of Hawai'i Press (2003)

53. 《香港电影：殖民者、祖国、自我》Yingchi Chu, *Hong Kong Cinema: Coloniser, Motherland, and Self*. RoutledgeCurzon (2003)

54. 《建构盗版行为：大中华区的全球化与电影发行》Shujen Wang, *Framing Piracy: Globalization and Film Distribution in Greater China*. Rowman & Littlefield Publishers (2003)

55. 《展现一个国家：1949之前的中国民族电影》Jubin Hu, *Projecting A Nation: Chinese National Cinema Before 1949*. Hong Kong University Press (2003)

56. 《在上海和香港之间：中国电影政治》（中译本《双城故事：早期中国电影的文化政治》）Poshek FU（傅葆石）, *Between Shanghai and Hong Kong: The Politics of Chinese Cinemas*. Stanford University Press (2003)

57. 《中国对1949年之前美国电影中描写中国和中国人的反应》（博士论文）M. S. Michael C. Wall, *Chinese Reaction to the Portrayal of China and Chinese in American Motion Pictures Prior to 1949*. Ph. D. Dissertation, Georgetown University (2000)

58. 《中国现代文学与电影中的城市：空间、时间与性别构形》Yingjin Zhang（张英进）, *The City in Modern Chinese Literature and Film: Configurations of Space, Time, and Gender*.

Stanford University Press (1996)

59. 《从"五四"到"六四":20世纪中国小说与电影》Ellen Widmer, David Der-wei Wang（王德威）, *From May Fourth to June Fourth: Fiction and Film in Twentieth-Century China*. Harvard University Press (1993)

60. 《当代中国电影：批评性辩论（1979—1989年）》George S. Semsel, Xia Hong, Chen Xihe, *Film in Contemporary China: Critical Debates, 1979—1989*. Praeger (1993)

61. 《中国现代文学与电影中的城市构形》（博士论文）Yingjin Zhang（张英进）, *Configurations of the City in Modern Chinese Literature and Film*. Ph. D. Dissertation, Stanford University (1992)

62. 《中国电影理论：新时代指南》Edited by George S. Semsel, Xia Hong, and Hou Jianping; foreword by Luo Yijun, *Chinese Film Theory: A Guide to the New Era*. Praeger Publishers (1990)

63. 《中国电影：1949年后的文化与政治》Paul Ckark, *Chinese Cinema: Culture and Politics since 1949*. Cambridge University Press (1987)

64. 《中国政治文化主题：中国共产党电影研究》John H. Weakland, *Chinese Political and Cultural Themes: A Study of Chinese Communist Films*. U. S. Naval Ordnance Test Station (1966)

6.6.3 互联网

1. 《中国网络社会研究报告（2016）》(Sociology, Media and Journalism in China) Shaojie Liu, Jianmin Wang, *The Internet Society in China: A 2016 Report*. Palgrave Macmillan (2020)

2. 《中国网络少年的网瘾：风险因素和干预策略》Qiaolei Jiang, *Internet Addiction Among Cyberkids in China: Risk Factors and Intervention Strategies*. Springer Singapore (2019)

3. 《2017年中国互联网发展报告》Chinese Academy of Cyberspace Studies, *China Internet Development Report 2017*. Springer Berlin Heidelberg (2019)

4. 《中国的网络安全》Greg Austin, *Cybersecurity in China* (SpringerBriefs in Cybersecurity). Springer International Publishing (2018)

5. 《"互联网+"中国房地产业转型的路径》Shusong Ba, Xianling Yang, *"Internet Plus" Pathways to the Transformation of China's Property Sector*. Springer Singapore (2016)

6. 《中国网络安全和网络防御》Daniel Ventre, *Chinese Cybersecurity and Cyberdefense*. Wiley-ISTE (2015)

7. 《中国在线：网络空间的社会定位》Peter Marolt, David Kurt Herold, *China Online: Locating Society in Online Spaces*. Routledge (2015)

8. 《联盟资本主义、创新与中国国家：全球无线领域》Victoria Higgins, *Alliance Capitalism, Innovation and the Chinese State: The Global Wireless Sector*. Palgrave Macmillan, London (2015)

9. 《网络战争：21世纪的权力斗争》Fergus Hanson, *Internet Wars: The Struggle for Power in the 21st Century*. Longueville Media (2015)

10. 《中国网络政策》Greg Austin, *Cyber Policy in China*. Polity (2014)

11. 《中国新连通性：虚拟、现实和地方互动》Boxu Yang (auth.), Pui-lam Law (eds.), *New Connectivities in China: Virtual, Actual and Local Interactions*. Springer Netherlands (2012)
12. 《中国在线社会：创造、庆祝和在线狂欢的工具化》David Kurt Herold, Peter Marolt (eds.), *Online Society in China: Creating, Celebrating, and Instrumentalising the Online Carnival*. Routledge (2011)
13. 《红色有线：中国互联网革命》Sherman So, J. Christopher Westland, *Red Wired: China's Internet Revolution*. Marshall Cavendish Business (2010)
14. 《互联网管辖权和法律选择：欧盟、美国和中国的法律实践》Faye Fangfei Wang, *Internet Jurisdiction and Choice of Law: Legal Practices in the EU, US and China*. Cambridge University Press (2010)
15. 《中国城市青年：现代性、互联网和自我》Fengshu Liu, *Urban Youth in China: Modernity, the Internet and the Self*. Routledge (2010)
16. 《中国网络战能力》Elisabette M. Marvel, *China's Cyberwarfare Capability*. Nova Science Publishers (2010)
17. 《中国的通信和网络》Patrick Bond, *Communications and Networking in China*. 1st International Business Conference, Chinacombiz 2008, Hangzhou China, August 2008, Revised Selected Papers. Springe (2009)
18. 《中国互联网的力量：公民行动主义在线》Guobin Yang（杨国斌）, *The Power of the Internet in China: Citizen Activism Online*. Columbia University Press (2009)
19. 《中国宽带设备和服务：战略参考（2007）》Philip M. Parker, *Broadband Equipment and Services in China: A Strategic Reference, 2007*. Icon Group International, Inc. (2007)
20. 《中国互联网：网络空间与公民社会》Zixue Tai, *The Internet in China: Cyberspace And Civil Society*.Routledge (2006)
21. 《在线政治的历史化：电报、互联网与中国的政治参与》Yongming Zhou, *Historicizing Online Politics: Telegraphy, the Internet, and Political Participation in China*. Stanford University Press (2005)
22. 《网络中国：信息时代的国民身份重塑》Francoise Mengin, *Cyber China: Reshaping National Identities in the Age of Information*. Palgrave Macmillan (2004)
23. 《中国与互联网：数字化跃进的政治学》Christopher R. Hughes, Gudrun Wacker (eds.), *China and the Internet: Politics of the Digital Leap Forward* (Politics in Asia). Routledge (2003)

6.6.4 出版印刷

1. 《盗版与出版商：中国近代版权社会史》(Histories of Economic Life) Fei-Hsien Wang, *Pirates And Publishers: A Social History of Copyright in Modern China*. Princeton University Press (2019)
2. 《印刷在近代中国的力量：从帝制末期到毛泽东国家社会主义的知识分子和工业出版》Robert Culp, *The Power of Print in Modern China: Intellectuals and Industrial Publishing*

from the End of Empire to Maoist State Socialism. Columbia University Press (2019)

3. 《为印刷而写作：中华帝制晚期的出版与文本权威的形成》Suyoung Son, *Writing for Print: Publishing and the Making of Textual Authority in Late Imperial China* (Harvard-Yenching Institute Monograph Series 112). Harvard University Asia Center (2018)

4. 《中国打字机的历史》Thomas S. Mullaney, *The Chinese Typewriter: A History*. The MIT Press (2017)

5. 《互联网之前的中国公民出版物》Shao Jiang, *Citizen Publications in China Before the Internet*. Palgrave Macmillan US (2015)

6. 《帝制下中国地方志的书写、出版和阅读（1100—1700）》(Harvard East Asian Monographs) Joseph R. Dennis（戴思哲）, *Writing, Publishing, and Reading Local Gazetteers in Imperial China, 1100—1700*. Harvard University Asia Center (2015)

7. 《家与世界：16—17世纪刻本中对"大明"的编写》Yuming He（何予明）, *Home and the World: Editing the 'Glorious Ming' in Woodblock-Printed Books of the Sixteenth and Seventeenth Centuries*. Harvard University, Asia Center (2013)

8. 《中国印刷时代的知识与文本制作（900—1400）》Edited by Lucille Chia（贾晋珠）and Hilde De Weerdt, *Knowledge and Text Production in an Age of Print China, 900—1400* (Sinica Leidensia). Brill (2011)

9. 《明日广场的明信片：来自中国的报道》James Fallows, *Postcards from Tomorrow Square: Reports from China*. Vintage (2009)

10. 《中国帝制晚期的印刷与书籍文化》Cynthia J. Brokaw, *Printing and Book Culture in Late Imperial China* (Studies on China 27). University of California Press (2006)

11. 《古滕堡在上海：中国印刷资本主义（1876—1937）》Christopher A. Reed（芮哲非）, *Gutenberg in Shanghai: Chinese Print Capitalism, 1876—1937*. The University of British Columbia Press (2004)

12. 《印刷牟利：11—17世纪福建建阳的出版商》Lucille Chia（贾晋珠）, *Printing for Profit: The Commercial Publishers of Jianyang, Fujian (11th—17th Centuries)*. Harvard University Asia Center (2003)

13. 《印刷与政治：〈时报〉与中国晚清的改革文化》Joan Judge, *Print and Politics: 'shibao' and the Culture of Reform in Late Qing China*. Stanford University Press (1996)

14. 《古代中国之彩色书》Bellerophon Books, *A Coloring Book of Ancient China*. Bellerophon Books (1985)

15. 《中国印刷术的发明及其西传》Thomas Francis Carter（卡特）, *The Invention of Printing in China and Its Spread Westward*. New York: Columbia University Press (1931)

6.6.5 传播学

1. 《中国广播电视网络国际传播策略初步观察》Duan Peng, *International Communication Strategies of Chinese Radio and TV Networks: Initial Observations*. Springer Singapore (2017)

2. 《符号传播里的中国》Sui Yan, *China in Symbolic Communication* (China Perspectives). Routledge (2017)
3. 《中国广告的批评性话语分析：1981—1996年家电广告案例研究》Chong Wang, *Critical Discourse Analysis of Chinese Advertisement: Case Studies of Household Appliance Advertisements from 1981 to 1996*. Springer Singapore (2017)
4. 《中国市场经济时代的传播活动与国家整合：振兴民族之魂》Yanru Chen, *Communication Campaigns and National Integration in China's Market Economy Era: Reviving the National Soul*. Springer (2016)
5. 《中国侨民的媒体与传播：反思跨国主义》Wanning Sun, John Sinclair (eds.), *Media and Communication in the Chinese Diaspora: Rethinking Transnationalism* (Media, Culture and Social Change in Asia Series). Routledge (2016)
6. 《中国城市传播、舆论与全球化》Francis L.F. Lee, Chin-Chuan Lee, Mike Z. Yao, Tsan-Kuo Chang, Fen Jennifer Lin, Chris Fei Shen, *Communication, Public Opinion, and Globalization in Urban China*. Routledge (2014)
7. 《中国信息通信技术高速公路》Jiang Yu, Richard Li-Hua, *China's Highway of Information and Communication Technology*. Palgrave Macmillan (2010)
8. 《主流文化再聚焦：改革时期中国电视剧、社会以及意义的生产》Zhong Xueping, *Mainstream Culture Refocused: Television Drama, Society, and the Production of Meaning in Reform-Era China*. University of Hawaii Press (2010)
9. 《中国传播：政治经济学、权力和冲突》Yuezhi Zhao, *Communication in China: Political Economy, Power, and Conflict*. Rowman & Littlefield Publishers, Inc. (2008)
10. 《中国电信革命》Eric Harwit, *China's Telecommunications Revolution*. Oxford University Press (2008)
11. 《全新中国：广告、媒体和商业文化》Jing Wang（王瑾）, *Brand New China: Advertising, Media, and Commercial Culture*. Harvard University Press (2008)
12. 《大中华圈的政治传播：身份的建构与反思》Gary D. Rawnsley & Ming-Yeh T. Rawnsley, *Political Communications in Greater China: The Construction and Reflection of Identity*. RoutledgeCurzon (2003)

6.7 医学

6.7.1 医学与医疗

1. 《中国公共卫生概论》(Public Health in China 4) Liming Li, Qingwu Jiang, *Introduction to Public Health in China*. Springer Singapore (2019)
2. 《理解跨文化历史中的健康、疾病和环境：阿拉伯—伊斯兰世界、中国、欧洲和北美》(Boston Studies in the Philosophy and History of Science 333) Florence Bretelle-Establet, Marie Gaille, Mehrnaz Katouzian-Safadi, *Making Sense of Health, Disease, and the Environment*

in Cross-Cultural History: The Arabic-Islamic World, China, Europe, and North America. Springer International Publishing (2019)

3.《中国环境温度与健康》Hualiang Lin, Wenjun Ma, Qiyong Liu, *Ambient Temperature and Health in China*. Springer Singapore (2019)

4.《当代中国的医疗保健转型》Jiong Tu, *Health Care Transformation in Contemporary China*. Springer Singapore (2019)

5.《中国医疗改革：从暴力到数字化医疗》Carine Milcent, *Healthcare Reform in China: From Violence to Digital Healthcare*. Palgrave Pivot (2018)

6.《转型中的中国卫生系统》(Research Series on the Chinese Dream and China's Development Path) Lijie Fang, *The Chinese Health System in Transition*. Springer Singapore (2018)

7.《史迪威的外科医生：John H. Grindlay与第二次世界大战中—缅—印战区的战斗医学》Alan K Lathrop, *A Surgeon with Stilwell: Dr. John H. Grindlay and Combat Medicine in the China-Burma-India Theater of World War II*. McFarland & Company (2018)

8.《亲密的团体：战时医疗与现代中国的诞生（1937—1945）》Nicole Elizabeth Barnes, *Intimate Communities: Wartime Healthcare and the Birth of Modern China, 1937—1945*. University of California Press (2018)

9.《今日中国和印度医学：亚洲品牌》Md. Nazrul Islam, *Chinese and Indian Medicine Today: Branding Asia*. Springer Singapore (2017)

10.《社会医疗保险改革对中国人医疗保健现金支出的影响：制度安排的中介作用》Kai Liu, *The Effects of Social Health Insurance Reform on People's Out-of-Pocket Health Expenditure in China: The Mediating Role of the Institutional Arrangement*. Springer Singapore (2016)

11.《中国大型公立医院改革调查报告》Lulu Zhang, Meina Li, Feng Ye, Tao Ding, Peng Kang, *An Investigation Report on Large Public Hospital Reforms in China*. Springer Singapore (2016)

12.《当代中国公共卫生面临的挑战：跨学科视角》MD. Nazrul Islam (eds.), *Public Health Challenges in Contemporary China: An Interdisciplinary Perspective*. Springer-Verlag Berlin Heidelberg (2016)

13.《中国研究解决方案：使用全食、植物饮食减肥和逆转疾病的简单方法》Thomas Campbell, *The China Study Solution: The Simple Way to Lose Weight and Reverse Illness, Using a Whole-Food, Plant-Based Diet*. Rodale Inc. (2016)

14.《新医学：中国近代早期的疗愈、文学与大众知识》Andrew Schonebaum, *Novel Medicine: Healing, Literature, and Popular Knowledge in Early Modern China*. University of Washington Press (2016)

15.《中国饮食药材：化学、药理学和临床证据》Yanze Liu, Junzeng Zhang, Zhimin Wang, *Dietary Chinese Herbs: Chemistry, Pharmacology and Clinical Evidence*. Springer (2015)

16.《20世纪中国医学变迁》Mary Brown Bullock, Bridie Andrews（吴章）, *Medical Transitions in Twentieth-Century China*. Indiana University Press (2014)

17. 《现代中国医学的形成（1850—1960）》Bridie Andrews（吴章）, *The Making of Modern Chinese Medicine, 1850—1960*. University of Washington Press (2014)
18. 《非驴非马：中国争取现代性过程中的医学》Sean Hsiang-Lin Lei, *Neither Donkey nor Horse: Medicine in the Struggle over China's Modernity*. The University of Chicago Press (2014)
19. 《第二春：毛博士为任何年龄女性恢复生机和再生的数百个自然秘密》Maoshing Ni, *Second Spring: Dr. Mao's Hundreds of Natural Secrets for Women to Revitalize and Regenerate at Any Age*. Atria Books (2014)
20. 《毛泽东时代的中国无私精神：社会主义医学与新人》Christos Lynteris, *The Spirit of Selflessness in Maoist China: Socialist Medicine and the New Man*. Palgrave Macmillan UK (2013)
21. 《中国药品证据与理性研究》H. Wagner (auth.), Hildebert Wagner, Gudrun Ulrich-Merzenich (eds.), *Evidence and Rational Based Research on Chinese Drugs*. Springer-Verlag Wien (2013)
22. 《为呼吸而战：一个癌症村生与死的故事》Anna Lora-Wainwright, *Fighting for Breath: Living Morally and Dying of Cancer in a Chinese Village*. University of Hawai'i Press (2013)
23. 《中国体育与保健》Wang Kaiwen, Qu Jianmei, Sun Lixia, *Chinese Physical Exercises and Health Care* (Chinese Lifestyle). China Intercontinental Press (2011)
24. 《中国参与全球卫生治理：负责任的利益相关者还是系统变革者？》Lai-Ha Chan, *China Engages Global Health Governance: Responsible Stakeholder or System-Transformer?* Palgrave Macmillan US (2011)
25. 《新反射学：一种独特的中医与西医反射学结合的混合实践，更好地实现保健与康复》Inge Dougans, *The New Reflexology: A Unique Blend of Traditional Chinese Medicine and Western Reflexology Practice for Better Health and Healing*. Da Capo Press (2009)
26. 《中国临床实验室：战略参考（2006）》Philip M. Parker, *Clinical Laboratories in China: A Strategic Reference, 2006*. Icon Group International, Inc. (2007)
27. 《中国的科学与文明。第六卷，生物学和生物技术。第六部分，医学》Gwei-Djen Lu（鲁桂珍）, Nathan Sivin, Joseph Needham（李约瑟）, *Science and Civilisation in China. Volume 6, Biology and Biological Technology. Part VI, Medicine*. Cambridge University Press (2004)
28. 《洗冤：中国13世纪的法医学》Brian E. McKnight, *The Washing away of Wrongs: Forensic Medicine in Thirteenth-century China*. Center for Chinese Studies, The University of Michigan (1981)
29. 《赤脚医生手册》Hu-Nan Chung I Yao Yen Chiu So, U.S. Dept. of Health, Education, and Welfare, *A Barefoot Doctor's Manual: The American Translation of the Official Chinese Paramedical Manual*. Running Press Book Publis (1977)
30. 《中国医学》China Medical Commission of the Rockefeller Foundation, *Medicine in China*. Chicago: The University of Chicago Press (1914)

6.7.2 中医与中药

1. 《中国12世纪的医学实践：许叔微〈伤寒九十论〉的翻译》（Archimedes 54）Asaf Goldschmidt（郭志松）, *Medical Practice in Twelfth-century China: A Translation of Xu Shuwei's Ninety Discussions (Cases) on Cold Damage Disorders*. Springer International Publishing (2019)

2. 《中医核心概念》Li Zhaoguo, Wu Qing, Xing Yurui, *Key Concepts in Traditional Chinese Medicine*. Springer Singapore: Palgrave Pivot (2019)

3. 《养生：中国自愈的艺术——现代问题的古老解决方案》Katie Brindle, *Yang Sheng: The Art of Chinese Self-Healing: Ancient Solutions to Modern Problems*. Hardie Grant Publishing (18 Apr 2019)

4. 《中医的传承与改造》Paul U. Unschuld, Bridie Andrews（吴章）, *Traditional Chinese Medicine: Heritage and Adaptation*. Columbia University Press (2018)

5. 《中医与阿育吠陀手册：古代治疗传统的综合实践》Bridgette Shea, *Handbook of Chinese Medicine and Ayurveda: An Integrated Practice of Ancient Healing Traditions*. Healing Arts Press (2018)

6. 《克服阿片类药物依赖性的自然疗法：用中药、针灸、草药、营养补充剂、冥想和生活方式实践来控制疼痛和戒毒》Catherine Browne, *Natural Therapies for Overcoming Opioid Dependency: Control Pain and Recover from Addiction with Chinese Medicine, Acupuncture, Herbs, Nutritional Supplements & Meditation and Lifestyle Practices*. Storey Publishing (2018)

7. 《以中国拍打拉筋法自愈》Hongchi Xiao, Lan Ziegler, Jean Vangua, Candida Kutz, *Heal Yourself Naturally Now: With the Established Chinese Technique of PaidaLajin*. Pailala Institute (2018)

8. 《推拿手册：中式按摩唤醒身心》Maria Mercati, *The Tui Na Manual: Chinese Massage to Awaken Body and Mind*. Healing Arts Press (2018)

9. 《中药的分子结构、天然来源及应用》George W. A. Milne, Guirong Xie, Xinjian Yan, Jiaju Zhou, *Traditional Chinese Medicines: Molecular Structures, Natural Sources and Applications*. Routledge (2018)

10. 《非凡的中医：非凡的脉管、器官和做人艺术》Thomas Richardson, William R. Morris, *Extraordinary Chinese Medicine: The Extraordinary Vessels, Extraordinary Organs, and the Art of Being Human*. Singing Dragon (2018)

11. 《中药与植物药：传统用法与现代科学方法》Raymond Cooper, Chun-Tao Che, Daniel Kam-Wah Mok, Charmaine Wing-Yee Tsang, *Chinese and Botanical Medicines: Traditional Uses and Modern Scientific Approaches*. CRC Press, Taylor & Francis Group (2017)

12. 《活力中医：能量医疗与中医的综合》D.Pfeiffer, *Energetic Chinese Medicine: A Synthesis of Pranic Healing and Chinese Medicine*. Books on Demand (2017)

13. 《中医治眼：针灸、穴位按摩和中草药》Andy Rosenfarb, *Healing Your Eyes with Chinese*

Medicine: Acupuncture, Acupressure, & Chinese Herbs. North Atlantic Books (2017)

14. 《中医历史与哲学》 (International Medical Library of Chinese Medicine) Tu Ya, Shelley Ochs, Fang Ting-yu, *History and Philosophy of Chinese Medicine*. People's Medical Publishing House (2016)

15. 《中医药理论与原理》Dongpei Hu, *Traditional Chinese Medicine: Theory and Principles*. De Gruyter (2016)

16. 《中医诊断学图书与DVD》 (International Standard Library of Chinese Medicine) Chen Jia-xu, Jane Frances Wilson, *Diagnostics in Chinese Medicine Book and Dvd*. People's Medical Publishing House (2016)

17. 《黄帝内经》（英文版中医卡通书）Damo Mitchell, Spencer Hill, *The Yellow Monkey Emperor's Classic of Chinese Medicine*. Singing Dragon (2016)

18. 《追求生命灵药：中医养生》Hong Hai, Karen Wee, *Pursuing the Elixir of Life: Chinese Medicine for Health*. World Scientific Publishing Company (2016)

19. 《石疗：中医宝石和矿物治疗指南》Leslie J. Franks, *Stone Medicine: A Chinese Medical Guide to Healing with Gems and Minerals*. Healing Arts Press (2016)

20. 《中成药临床手册：伦理与纯中成药指南》Will Maclean, Kathryn Taylor, *The Clinical Manual of Chinese Herbal Patent Medicines: A Guide to Ethical and Pure Patent Medicines*. Pangolin Press (2016)

21. 《中医治疗癌症：草药、针灸、气功、营养和预防》Niko Trian, *Chinese Medicine in Cancer Care: Herbs, Acupuncture, Qi Gong, Nutrition, Prevention*. Create Space Independent Publishing Platform (2016)

22. 《巴哈花精与中药》Pablo Noriega, Loey Colebeck, *Bach Flower Essences and Chinese Medicine*. Healing Arts Press (2016)

23. 《新中医手册：东方智慧与西方现代治疗实践相结合的创新指南》Misha Ruth Cohen, *The New Chinese Medicine Handbook: An Innovative Guide to Integrating Eastern Wisdom with Western Practice for Modern Healing*. Fair Winds Press (2015)

24. 《中草药及其基本成分、临床应用和健康效益》Brian L. Duke, *Chinese Herbs and Herbal Medicine Essential Components, Clinical Applications and Health Benefits*. Nova Science Pub Inc (2015)

25. 《中国耳针》Skya Abbate, *Chinese Auricular Acupuncture, Second Edition*. CRC Press, Taylor & Francis Group (2015)

26. 《中国古代医学艺术：现代档案的古代和中世纪起源》Miranda Brown, *The Art of Medicine in Early China: The Ancient and Medieval Origins of a Modern Archive*. Cambridge University Press (2015)

27. 《道与法：中医和阿育吠陀》Robert Svoboda, Arnie Lade, *Tao and Dharma: Chinese Medicine and Ayurveda*. Lotus Press (2015)

28. 《气候危机的阴和阳：用中医治疗个人、文化和生态失衡》Brendan Kelly, *The Yin and Yang of Climate Crisis: Healing Personal, Cultural, and Ecological Imbalance with Chinese Medicine*. North Atlantic Books (2015)

29. 《艾灸：阴阳疗法的中医康复艺术》Candra M. Linfoot, *Moxibustion: Traditional Chinese Medicine Healing Art of Yin Yang Therapy*. Amazon.com (2015)

30. 《孕期进食：以中药、真正食物和整体健康生活方式培养健康怀孕的指南》Emily Bartlett, Laura Erlich, *Feed Your Fertility: Your Guide to Cultivating a Healthy Pregnancy with Chinese Medicine, Real Food, and Holistic Living*. Fair Winds Press (2015)

31. 《古代中医理论基础：〈伤寒论〉与当代医学文献》Guohui Liu, Charles Buck, *Foundations of Theory for Ancient Chinese Medicine: Shang Han Lun and Contemporary Medical Texts*. Singing Dragon (2015)

32. 《蕴含在中国古代智慧中的美容实践》Joanna M. Burton, *Beauty Practices: Embedded in Ancient Chinese Wisdom* (Beautiful & Healthy YOU! Anti-Aging and Longevity Secrets of the Ancients Revealed. Book 3). Joanna M. Burton (2015)

33. 《中医综合指南》Ping-Chung Leung, *A Comprehensive Guide to Chinese Medicine* (Second Edition). World Scientific Publishing Company (2015)

34. 《美容针灸：中医治疗美容和皮肤病的方法》（第二版）Radha Thambirajah, *Cosmetic Acupuncture: A Traditional Chinese Medicine Approach to Cosmetic and Dermatological Problems*. Second Edition. Singing Dragon (2015)

35. 《中医经典：〈黄帝内经〉》Richard Bertschinger, *Essential Texts in Chinese Medicine: The Single Idea in the Mind of the Yellow Emperor*. Singing Dragon (2015)

36. 《中医案例研究：内科》(International Standard Library of Chinese Medicine) Bayan Liu, Suzanne Robidoux, Xiao Ye, *TCM Case Studies: Internal Medicine*. People's Medical Publishing House (2014)

37. 《中医基础》(International Standard Library of Chinese Medicine) Sun Guang-ren (Author), Doug Eisenstark (Author), Zhang Qing-rong (Editor), *Fundamentals of Chinese Medicine*. People's Medical Publishing House (2014)

38. 《中古中国佛教医学的翻译》C. Pierce Salguero, *Translating Buddhist Medicine in Medieval China*. University of Pennsylvania Press (2014)

39. 《中医治疗人体寄生虫》Heinz Mehlhorn (auth.), Heinz Mehlhorn, Zhongdao Wu, Bin Ye (eds.), *Treatment of Human Parasitosis in Traditional Chinese Medicine*. Springer-Verlag Berlin Heidelberg (2014)

40. 《刺穿血管：中医放血疗法》Henry McCann, *Pricking the Vessels: Bloodletting Therapy in Chinese Medicine*. Jessica Kingsley (2014)

41. 《中国传统医学拔罐疗法》Ilkay Zihni Chirali, *Traditional Chinese Medicine Cupping Therapy*. Churchill Livingstone (2014)

42. 《中医研究数据分析》Josiah Poon, Simon K. Poon (eds.), *Data Analytics for Traditional Chinese Medicine Research*. Springer International Publishing (2014)

43. 《中国传统医学及其应用的科学基础》James D Adams, Eric J Lien, *Traditional Chinese Medicine: Scientific Basis for Its Use*. Cambridge: The Royal Society of Chemistry (2013)

44. 《中医临床手册》Bob Xu, Chun-Su Yuan, *Clinical Handbook of Chinese Medicine*. World Scientific Publishing Company (2013)

45. 《中医治疗不孕不育》Jane Lyttleton, *Treatment of Infertility with Chinese Medicine*. Churchill Livingstone (2013)

46. 《中医学原理：是什么、如何发挥作用以及能为你做什么》Angela Hicks, *Principles of Chinese Medicine: What It Is, How It Works, and What It Can Do for You*. Second Edition. Singing Dragon (2013)

47. 《中医学原理：是什么、如何发挥作用以及能为你做什么》（注：同上书题目、出版社相同，但作者和内容不同）John Hicks, *Principles of Chinese Herbal Medicine: What it Is, How It Works, and What It Can Do for You*. Revised Edition. Singing Dragon (2013)

48. 《中药概论》Jin Yang, Matthew Huang, Li-Jiang Zhu, Yunhui Chen, *Introduction to Chinese Materia Medica*. World Century (2013)

49. 《中医内科概论》Xiang Xia, Xiao-Heng Shen, Min Chen, *Introduction to Chinese Internal Medicine*. World Scientific Publishing Company (2013)

50. 《古中医治疗不孕症：以混元功实现孕育健康》Yaron Seidman, *Curing Infertility with Ancient Chinese Medicine: How to Become Pregnant and Healthy with the Hunyuan Method*. Skyhorse (4 Jun 2013)

51. 《针灸治疗失眠：中医之睡眠与梦》Hamid Montakab, *Acupuncture for Insomnia: Sleep and Dreams in Chinese Medicine*. Thieme (2012)

52. 《中医系统生物学》Guoan Luo, Yiming Wang, Qionglin Liang, Qingfei Liu, *Systems Biology for Traditional Chinese Medicine*. Wiley (2012)

53. 《沈鹤峰医师中药方剂》Leon I. Hammer（汉默）, Hamilton Rotte, *Chinese Herbal Medicine: The Formulas of Dr. John H. F. Shen*. Thieme (2012)

54. 《内在之美：通过中国传统健康疗法，寻找、感受和成为最好的你》Pauline Couture, Xiaolan Zhao, *Inner Beauty: Looking, Feeling and Being Your Best Through Traditional Chinese Healing*. Random House of Canada (2011)

55. 《中世纪日本的医学融合：佛教治疗、中国知识、伊斯兰教配方和战争创伤》Andrew Edmund Goble, *Confluences of Medicine in Medieval Japan: Buddhist Healing, Chinese Knowledge, Islamic Formulas, and Wounds of War*. University of Hawai'i Press (2011)

56. 《中医药在生育障碍中的应用》Andreas A. Bew, Sabine Wilms, Simon Becker, *Chinese Medicine in Fertility Disorders* (Complementary Medicine (Thieme Hardcover)). Thieme: TPS (2010)

57. 《中药材的比较与特点》Yifan Yang, *Chinese Herbal Medicines: Comparisons and Characteristics*. Elsevier (2010)

58. 《中医诊断学》Zhu Bing, Wang Hongcai, *Diagnostics of Traditional Chinese Medicine*. Singing Dragon (2010)

59. 《无人编织的网：理解中医》Ted Kaptchuk, *The Web That Has No Weaver: Understanding Chinese Medicine*. RosettaBooks (2010)

60. 《中医基础理论》Zhu Bing, *Basic Theories of Traditional Chinese Medicine*. Singing Dragon (2010)

61. 《中医诊断学》Zhu Bing, Wang Hongcai, *Diagnostics of Traditional Chinese Medicine*. Singing Dragon (2010)

62. 《永生的秘诀：〈参同契〉之初译》Richard Bertschinger, *The Secret of Everlasting Life: The First Translation of the Ancient Chinese Text on Immortality*. Singing Dragon (2011)

63. 《宋代中医发展（960—1200）》Asaf Goldschmidt, *The Evolution of Chinese Medicine: Song Dynasty, 960—1200*. Routledge (2009)

64. 《中国与北美相关草本：植物药理与治疗价值》Thomas S. C. Li, *Chinese & Related North American Herbs: Phytopharmacology & Therapeutic Values*, Second Edition. CRC Press, Taylor & Francis Group (2009)

65. 《中医治疗癌症：直面老虎的和谐》Henry McGrath, *Traditional Chinese Medicine Approaches to Cancer: Harmony in the Face of the Tiger*. Singing Dragon (2009)

66. 《美容针灸：关于化妆和皮肤问题的中医方法》Radha Thambirajah, *Cosmetic Acupuncture: A Traditional Chinese Medicine Approach to Cosmetic and Dermatological Problems*. Churchill Livingstone (2009)

67. 《比照中医的西方草药：从业者指南》Thomas Avery Garran, *Western Herbs according to Traditional Chinese Medicine: A Practitioner's Guide*. Healing Arts (2008)

68. 《中国康复练习：导引的传统》Livia Kohn, *Chinese Healing Exercises: The Tradition of Daoyin* (A Latitude 20 Book). University of Hawaii Press (2008)

69. 《以中药转化情感：当代中国民族志的记述》Yanhua Zhang, *Transforming Emotions With Chinese Medicine: An Ethnographic Account from Contemporary China*. State University of New York Press (2007)

70. 《中医治疗现代西方疾病：教材与临床手册》Philippe Sionneau, Bob Flaws, *The Treatment of Modern Western Medical Diseases with Chinese Medicine: A Textbook & Clinical Manual*. Blue Poppy Press (2007)

71. 《瘀血大成》Gunter R. Neeb（内龙道）, *Blood Stasis: China's Classical Concept in Modern Medicine*. Churchill Livingstone (2006)

72. 《中医药研究现状：中草药质量控制》Ping-Chung Leung, Harry Hong Sang Fong, Charlie Changli Xue, *Current Review of Chinese Medicine: Quality Control of Herbs and*

Herbal Material (Annals of Traditional Chinese Medicine). World Scientific (2006)

73. 《中医男人：中国和东南亚的消费文化》Sherman Cochran, *Chinese Medicine Men: Consumer Culture in China and Southeast Asia*. Harvard University Press (2006)

74. 《中国康复之道：通向健康的多种途径》Misha Ruth Cohen, Kalia Doner, *The Chinese Way to Healing: Many Paths to Wholeness*. iUniverse (2006)

75. 《早期共产主义中国的中医（1945—1963）：医学革命》Kim Taylor, *Chinese Medicine in Early Communist China, 1945—1963: A Medicine of Revolution* (Needham Research Institute). Routledge (2005)

76. 《中医基础学：针灸与中医学综合教材》Giovanni Maciocia, *The Foundations of Chinese Medicine: A Comprehensive Text for Acupuncturists and Herbalists* 2nd Ed. Churchill Livingstone (2005)

77. 《中医：现代实践》Ping-Chung Leung, Charlie Chang-li Xue, *Chinese Medicine: Modern Practice* (Annals of Traditional Chinese Medicine). World Scientific Publishing Company (2005)

78. 《中医诊断综合指南》Giovanni Maciocia, Julian Scott, *Diagnosis in Chinese Medicine: A Comprehensive Guide*. Churchill Livingstone (2004)

79. 《中医百科参考》Xinrong Yang, Anmin Chen, Yingfu Ma (eds.), *Encyclopedic Reference of Traditional Chinese Medicine*. Springer-Verlag Berlin Heidelberg (2003)

80. 《实用中医药》Penelope Ody, *Practical Chinese Medicine*. New Age Books (2003)

81. 《中医之道》Donald Kendall, *Dao of Chinese Medicine*. Oxford University Press (2002)

82. 《道与言：古代中国、希腊的科学和医药》Geoffrey Lloyd, Nathan Sivin, *The Way and the Word: Science and Medicine in Early China and Greece*. Yale University Press (2002)

83. 《养生五要素计划：完美的中国保健体系》Barbara Temelie, *The Five-Elements Wellness Plan: A Chinese System for Perfect Health*. Sterling (2002)

84. 《神奇的中国医学》Michel Strickmann, edited by Bernard Faure, *Chinese Magical Medicine*. Stanford University Press (2002)

85. 《针灸手册》Peter Deadman and Mazin Al-Khafaji, *A Manual of Acupuncture*. Journal of Chinese Medicine Publications (2001)

86. 《单穴针灸治疗100病》Cheng Decheng, *100 Diseases Treated by Single Point of Acupuncture Moxibustion*. Foreign Languages Press, China (2001)

87. 《中国生草药揭秘》（西班牙语）Stefan Chmelik, *Hierbas Medicinales Chinas*. The Ivy Press Limited (1999)

88. 《身体的表现力和希腊与中医的分歧》Shigehisa Kuriyama, *The Expressiveness of the Body and the Divergence of Greek and Chinese Medicine*. Zone Books (1999)

89. 《中药药理学》Kee Chang Huang, *The Pharmacology of Chinese Herbs*. CRC Press (1999)

90. 《周易与中医学》Yang Li（杨力）, *Book of Changes and Traditional Chinese Medicine*. Beijing Science & Technology Press, China (1998)

91. 《针灸手册》Peter Deadman, Mazin Al-Khafaji, Kevin Baker, *A Manual of Acupuncture*. Journal of Chinese Medicine (1998)

92. 《翡翠疗法：中国草药为西方提供借鉴》（第一、二卷）Peter Holmes, *Jade Remedies: A Chinese Herbal Reference for the West*, Vol. 1. and 2. Snow Lotus Press (1997)

93. 《中国古代名医》(Science stories of ancient China) Zhu Kang, *Distinguished Doctors of Ancient China*. Dolphin Books (1996)

94. 《黄帝医学经典：附评注的〈内经素问〉新译》Maoshing Ni, *The Yellow Emperor's Classic of Medicine: A New Translation of the Neijing Suwen with Commentary*. Shambhala Publications (1995)

95. 《中国自然疗法体系》Henry C. Lu, *Chinese System of Natural Cures*. Sterling (1994)

96. 《针灸标准命名法》World Health Organization, *Standard Acupuncture Nomenclature: A Brief Explanation of 361 Classical Acupuncture Point Names and Their Multilingual Comparative List* (Second Edition).World Health Organization (1993)

97. 《生命之草：中西医结合的健康养生》Lesley Tierra, *The Herbs of Life: Health and Healing Using Western and Chinese Techniques*. Crossing Press (1992)

98. 《天地之间：中医指南》Harriet Beinfield, *Between Heaven and Earth: A Guide to Chinese Medicine*. Ballantine Books (1991)

99. 《传奇中草药》Henry C. Lu, *Legendary Chinese Healing Herbs*. Sterling Publishing Company (1991)

100. 《中国保健球：实操练习》Hans Hoting, *Chinese Health Balls: Practical Exercises*. Weiser Books (1990)

101. 《中医文献方法：翻译方法与术语国际学术研讨会论文集》Wolfgang Bauer (auth.), Prof. Dr. Paul U. Unschuld (eds.), *Approaches to Traditional Chinese Medical Literature: Proceedings of an International Symposium on Translation Methodologies and Terminologies*. Kluwer Academic Publishers (1989)

102. 《中国农村的医药：个人记述》C. C. Chen, *Medicine in Rural China: A Personal Account*. University of California Press (1989)

103. 《秉风：中国针灸穴位名称意义探析》Andrew Ellis, N. Wiseman, K. Boss, *Grasping the Wind: An Exploration into the Meaning of Chinese Acupuncture Point Names* (English and Chinese Edition). Paradigm Publications (MA) (1989)

104. 《中国精选常见药用植物150种》(WHO Regional Publications) Institute of Chinese Materia Medica, *Medicinal Plants in China: A Selection of 150 Commonly Used Species*. World Health Organization (1989)

105. 《中医基础学：针灸师和中医师综合教材》Giovanni Maciocia, Forword by Su Xin Ming, *The Foundations of Chinese Medicine: A Comprehensive Text for Acupuncturists and Herbalists*. Churchill Livingstone (1989, 2005)

106. 《中草药》Daniel Reid, *Chinese Herbal Medicine*. Shambhala (1987)

107. 《脏腑：中医器官系统》Jeremy Ross, *Zang Fu: The Organ Systems of Traditional Chinese Medecine*. Churchill Livingstone (1985)

108. 《中国补药》Ron Teeguarden, *Chinese Tonic Herbs*. Kodansha (1985)

109. 《中华人民共和国草药药理学：美国草药药理学代表团出访报告》The Committee on Scholarly Communication with the People's Republic of China, *Herbal Pharmacology in the People's Republic of China: A Trip Report of the American Herbal Pharmacology Delegation*. National Academy of Sciences (1982)

110. 《近代中国的传统医学：科学、民族主义与文化变迁的张力》Ralph C. Croizier, *Traditional Medicine in Modern China: Science, Nationalism, and the Tensions of Cultural Change* (East Asian). Harvard University Press (1968)

111. 《中药之兽药》Bernard E. Read, *Chinese Materia Medica: Animal Drugs*. Peking Natural History Bulletin (1931)

112. 《针灸学回忆录》J. Morand, *Memoir on Acupunturation, Embracing a Series of Cases, Drawn up under the Inspection of M. Julius Cloquet*. Philadelphia: Published by Robert Desilver, Clark & Raser, Printers (1825)

6.7.3 疾病与防控

1. 《中国血吸虫病防治：江西省成功的范例》(Parasitology Research Monographs 11) Zhongdao Wu, Yiwen Liu, Heinz Mehlhorn, *Schistosomiasis Control in China: The Successful Example of Jiangxi Province*. Springer International Publishing (2019)

2. 《中国突发事件应急能力综合评估》(Research Series on the Chinese Dream and China's Development Path) Lan Xue, Guang Zeng, *A Comprehensive Evaluation on Emergency Response in China*. Springer Singapore (2019)

3. 《中国地方病》(Public Health in China 2) Dianjun Sun, *Endemic Disease in China*. Springer Singapore (2019)

4. 《中国免疫规划》(Public Health in China 3) Xiaofeng Liang, *Immunization Program in China*. Springer Singapore (2019)

5. 《"疯癫"的发明：现代中国的国家、社会和疯狂》(Studies of the Weatherhead East Asian Institute, Columbia University) Emily Baum, *The Invention of Madness: State, Society, and the Insane in Modern China*. University of Chicago Press (2018)

6. 《中国艾滋病：数字之外》Zunyou Wu (eds.), *HIV: AIDS in China: Beyond the Numbers* (Public Health in China 1). Springer Singapore (2017)

7. 《被遗忘的疾病：中医疾病的转化》Hilary A. Smith, *Forgotten Disease: Illnesses Transformed in Chinese Medicine* (Studies of the Weatherhead East Asian Institute, Columbia University). Stanford University Press (2017)

8. 《疾病话语：现代中国的疾病写作与身心》Howard Y. F. Choy, *Discourses of Disease:*

Writing Illness, the Mind and the Body in Modern China. Brill (2016)

9. 《中国和印度的艾滋病：健康安全管理》Catherine Yuk-ping Lo, *HIV-AIDS in China and India: Governing Health Security*. Palgrave Macmillan US (2015)

10. 《在道路建设背景下实施艾滋病防治：以广西壮族自治区为例》Asian Development Bank, *Implementing HIV Prevention in the Context of Road Construction: A Case Study from Guangxi Zhuang Autonomous Region in the people's Republic of China*. Asian Development Bank (2014)

11. 《中华人民共和国疟疾防治计划》Randall Kramer, Wei-Zhong Yang, Xiao-nong Zhou, *Malaria Control and Elimination Programme in the People's Republic of China* (Advances in Parasitology Volume 86). Academic Press, Elsevier (2014)

12. 《战时中国的生命拯救：医疗改革者如何在战争和流行病中建立现代医疗系统（1928—1945）》John R. Watt, *Saving Lives in Wartime China: How Medical Reformers Built Modern Healthcare Systems Amid War and Epidemics, 1928—1945*. Brill (2013)

13. 《农村医疗保健的提供：从疾病政治角度看现代中国》Yi Hu, *Rural Health Care Delivery: Modern China from the Perspective of Disease Politics*. Springer-Verlag Berlin Heidelberg (2013)

14. 《全球卫生治理的形成：中国与全球基金抗击艾滋病、结核病和疟疾》Nicole A. Szlezák, *The Making of Global Health Governance: China and the Global Fund to Fight AIDS, Tuberculosis, and Malaria*. Palgrave Macmillan US (2012)

15. 《肥胖的中国：腰围扩大如何改变一个国家》Paul French, Matthew Crabbe, *Fat China: How Expanding Waistlines are Changing a Nation*. Anthem Press (2010)

16. 《中国毒品实践与政策：全球背景下的控制物管理》Hong Lu, Terance D. Miethe, Bin Liang, *China's Drug Practices and Policies: Regulating Controlled Substances in a Global Context*. Ashgate Publishing Company (2009)

17. 《中国麻风病史》Angela Ki Che Leung, *Leprosy in China: A History* (Studies of the Weatherhead East Asian Institute, Columbia University). Columbia University Press (2008)

18. 《SARS：三个中国城市的接受与解读》Deborah Davis, Helen F. Siu, *Sars: Reception and Interpretation in Three Chinese Cities*. Routledge (2007)

19. 《吃春米：中国西南艾滋病的文化政治》Sandra Teresa Hyde, *Eating Spring Rice: The Cultural Politics of AIDS in Southwest China*. University of California Press (2007)

20. 《近代早期欧洲想象中的传染病》Claire L. Carlin (ed.), *Imagining Contagion in Early Modern Europe*. Palgrave Macmillan (2005)

21. 《身体差异：现代中国关于残疾与制度宣传的经验》Matthew Kohrman, *Bodies of Difference: Experiences of Disability and Institutional Advocacy in the Making of Modern China*. University of California Press (2005)

22. 《卫生的现代性：中国通商口岸的卫生与疾病》Ruth Rogaski（罗芙芸）, *Hygienic*

Modernity: Meanings of Health and Disease in Treaty-Port China. University of California Press (2004)

23. 《虎口拔牙：如何以中国武士秘诀疗伤》Tom Bisio, Xue Zhu, *A Tooth from the Tiger's Mouth: How to Treat Your Injuries with Powerful Healing Secrets of the Great Chinese Warrior.* Atria Books (2004)

24. 《汪机与〈石山医案〉》Joanna Grant, *A Chinese Physician: Wang Ji and the "Stone Mountain Medical Case Histories".* New York: RoutledgeCurzon (2003)

25. 《日本和中国冠心病的危险因素》Gerd Stehle, Ralph Bernhardt, *Coronary Risk Factors in Japan and China.* Springer-Verlag Berlin Heidelberg (1987)

26. 《中国医疗保健》(Modern China Series No. 8) Robin Stott, Joshua Horn, *Health Care in China.* Anglo-Chinese Educational Institute (1976)

6.7.4 气功

1. 《气功——中国体操：入门指南》Paul Powell, *Qigong-Chinese Gymnastics: A Beginner Guide.* Amazon.com (2017)

2. 《15天内终结早泄的中国气功：阴茎增大、活力和长寿的古老秘诀》Channing Chang, *Chinese Qigong For Ending Premature Ejaculation in 15 Days: Ancient Secret For Penis Enlargement, Vitality, and Longevity.* Amazon.com (2017)

3. 《中国萨满教宇宙轨道气功：治疗和内修中的神秘护身符、咒语和手印》Zhongxian Wu, *Chinese Shamanic Cosmic Orbit Qigong: Esoteric Talismans, Mantras, and Mudras in Healing and Inner Cultivation.* Singing Dragon (2011)

4. 《中医气功》Tianjun Liu, Kevin W. Chen, *Chinese Medical Qigong.* Singing Dragon (2010)

5. 《呼吸空间：中国气功、精神病学和治疗》Nancy N. Chen, *Breathing Spaces: Qigong, Psychiatry, and Healing in China.* Columbia University Press (2003)

6. 《气功：中国的治疗、能量与自然魔法》L.V. Carnie, *Chi Gung: Chinese Healing, Energy and Natural Magick.* Llewellyn Publications (2002)

7. 《气功完整指南：中国古代养生、活力和长寿之道的原则与实践》Daniel Reid, *A Complete Guide to Chi-Gung: The Principles and Practice of the Ancient Chinese Path to Health, Vigor, and Longevity.* Shambhala (2000)

8. 《气功：中医或伪科学？》Zixin Lin, *Qigong: Chinese Medicine or Pseudoscinece.* Prometheus Books (March 2000)

9. 《气功之道：中国能量疗法的艺术与科学》Kenneth S. Cohen, *The Way of Qigong: The Art and Science of Chinese Energy Healing.* Ballantine Books Inc (29 April 2000)

10. 《中国气功外气疗法》Yongsheng Bi, *Chinese Qigong Outgoing: Qi Therapy.* Shandong Science and Technology Press (1997)

11. 《气功：中国的健身运动与冥想》Danny Connor, Michael Tse, *Qigong: Chinese Movement & Meditation for Health.* Weiser Books (1992)

12. 《原呼吸：中国古代通过控制呼吸的延年益寿之道，第二卷〈道藏〉关于胚胎呼吸的另外九项条约译文》Jane Huang, *The Primordial Breath: An Ancient Chinese Way of Prolonging Life Through Breath Control, Vol. 2: Additional Translations of Nine Treaties on Embryonic Breathing from the Taoist Canon, the Tao Tsang*. Original Books (1990)

13. 《中国气功疗法》Zhang Mingwu, Sun Xingyuan, *Chinese Qigong Therapy*. 2nd Edition. Shandong Science Technology Pub. (1988)

14. 《原呼吸：中国古代通过控制呼吸的延年益寿之道，第一卷〈道藏〉之七项条约》Jane Huang, *Primordial Breath: An Ancient Chinese Way of Prolonging Life Through Breath Control, Vol. 1: Seven Treaties from the Taoist Canon, the Tao Tsang*. Original Books (1987)

6.8 园林建筑

1. 《福建土楼：中国传统民居的瑰宝》Hanmin Huang, *Fujian's Tulou: A Treasure of Chinese Traditional Civilian Residence*. Springer Singapore (2020)

2. 《中国外围建筑：制图与极简主义》(Routledge Studies in Chinese Linguistics) Victor Junnan Pan, *Architecture of the Periphery in Chinese: Cartography and Minimalism*. Routledge (2019)

3. 《澳大利亚和新西兰的中国市场园艺：繁荣的花园》Joanna Boileau, *Chinese Market Gardening in Australia and New Zealand: Gardens of Prosperity* (Palgrave Studies in the History of Science and Technology). Palgrave Macmillan (2017)

4. 《失落的圆明园》Young-tsu Wong（汪荣祖）, *A Paradise Lost: The Imperial Garden Yuanming Yuan*. Springer Singapore (2016)

5. 《奇迹花园：中世纪初期中国传奇故事》Robert Ford Campany（康儒博）, *A Garden of Marvels: Tales of Wonder from Early Medieval China*. University of Hawaii Press (2015)

6. 《美国和中国的绿色建筑：发展与政策比较》Brenden Forester, *Green Buildings in the U.S. and China: Development and Policy Comparisons*. Nova Science Pub Inc (2015)

7. 《陆谦受：被遗忘的中国现代建筑师》Edward Denison, Guang Yu Ren（广裕仁）, *Luke Him Sau: Architect: China's Missing Modern*. John Wiley & Sons Ltd (2014)

8. 《中国皇帝的花园：乾隆年间的帝制创作（1739—1796）》Victoria M. Siu, *Gardens of a Chinese Emperor: Imperial Creations of the Qianlong Era, 1736—1796*. Lehigh University Press (2013)

9. 《自由主义者的野蛮行为：欧洲人对中国皇宫的毁灭》Erik Ringmar, *Liberal Barbarism: The European Destruction of the Palace of the Emperor of China*. Palgrave Macmillan US (2013)

10. 《中国庭园：大都会艺术博物馆的阿斯特庭》Alfreda Murck, Wen C. Fong, *A Chinese Garden Court: The Astor Court at the Metropolitan Museum of Art*. Metropolitan Museum of Art (2012)

11. 《木材与接头：欧洲、日本和中国的建筑传统》Klaus Zwerger, *Wood and Wood Joints:*

Building Traditions of Europe, Japan and China.Birkhäuser (2012)

12. 《中国桥梁：中国过去的活建筑》Ronald G. Knapp, A. Chester Ong (photo), *Chinese Bridges: Living Architecture from China's Past*. Tuttle Publishing (2012)

13. 《花园世界》John Dixon Hunt, *A World of Gardens*. Reaktion Books (2012)

14. 《中国园林》Yu Sui, Wei Xun, *Chinese Gardens*. Design Media Publishing Ltd (2011)

15. 《中国建筑与美术》(Spatial Habitus: Making and Meaning in Asia's Architecture) Nancy Shatzman Steinhardt, Jeffrey W. Cody, Tony Atkin, *Chinese Architecture and the Beaux-Arts*. University of Hawai'i Press (2011)

16. 《中国民居》Shan Deqi（单德启）, *Chinese Vernacular Dwellings: People's Daily Life with Their Houses*. China Intercontinental Press (2010)

17. 《清代建筑画册》Compiled by Peking University Library, *A Pictorial Record of the Qing Dynasty: Qing Dynasty Architecture*.Cengage Learning Asia Pte Ltd (2010)

18. 《创新与未来：中国当代新建筑》Kai Cui, Sophia Song, Li Yang, *Creation and Future: Chinese Contemporary New Architectue*. Profession Design Press Co., Ltd (2009)

19. 《中国建筑设计服务：2006战略参考》Philip M. Parker, *Architectural Design Services in China: A Strategic Reference, 2006*. ICON Group International, Inc. (2007)

20. 《中国建筑》(Contemporary Architecture by Country) Philip Jodidio, *Architecture in China*. Taschen (2007)

21. 《建筑革命：1980年以来的中国建筑》Charlie Q. L. Xue, *Building a Revolution: Chinese Architecture since 1980*. University of Washington Press (2006)

22. 《中国建筑项目：建筑师和工程师手册》Bert Bielefeld, Lars-Phillip Rusch, *Building Projects in China: A Manual for Architects and Engineers*.Birkhäuser Basel (2006)

23. 《中国早期的景观与权力》Li Feng, *Landscape and Power in Early China*. Cambridge University Press (2006)

24. 《秘密花园》Frances Hodgson Burnett, *The Secret Garden* (Webster's Chinese-Traditional Thesaurus Edition).ICON Group International, Inc. (2005)

25. 《中国园林》Lou Qingxi（楼庆西）, *Chinese Gardens*. China Intercontinental Press (2003)

26. 《围墙内的自然景观：大都会艺术博物馆的中国花园庭院，教育工作者的资源》Elizabeth Hammer, *Nature within Walls: The Chinese Garden Court at The Metropolitan Museum of Art: A Resource for Educators* (Metropolitan Museum of Art Series). Metropolitan Museum of Art (2003)

27. 《私人领域的变形：唐宋诗歌中的园林与玩好》(Harvard University East Asian Series) Xiaoshan Yang（杨晓山）, *Metamorphosis of the Private Sphere: Gardens and Objects in Tang-Song Poetry*. Harvard University Asia Center (2003)

28. 《遭遇体用冲突的现代中国建筑》Peter G. Rowe, Seng Kuan, *Architectural Encounters with Essence and Form in Modern China*. Massachusetts Institute of Technology Press (2002)

29. 《作为建筑的花园：日本、中国和韩国花园的形式与精神》Toshiro Inaji, Pamela Virgilio, *The Garden as Architecture: Form and Spirit in the Gardens of Japan, China and Korea*. Kodansha International (JPN) (1998)

30. 《明代中国园林文化》Craig Clunas（柯律格）, *Fruitful Sites: Garden Culture in Ming Dynasty China*. Duke University Press (1996)

31. 《中华人民共和国的土地、财产和建筑》Anthony Walker, *Land, Property and Construction in the Peoples Republic of China*. Hong Kong University Press (1991)

32. 《图像中国建筑史：关于中国建筑结构体系的发展及其形制的研究》Ssu-ch'eng Liang（梁思成）, Edited by Wilma Fairbank, *A Pictorial History of Chinese Architecture: A Study of the Development of Its Structural System and the Evolution of Its Types*. MIT Press (1984)

33. 《中国园林：历史、艺术和意义》Edwin T. Morris, *The Gardens of China: History, Art, and Meanings*. Charles Scribner&Sons (1983)

34. 《中国传播与帝国控制：宫殿纪念制度的演变（1693—1735）》Silas H. L. Wu, *Communication and Imperial Control in China: Evolution of the Palace Memorial System, 1693—1735* (Harvard East Asian Series, 51). Harvard University Press (1970)

35. 《中国园林》Osvald Siren, *Gardens of China*. The Ronald Press Company, New York (1949)

36. 《清朝皇家园林史》Carroll Brown Malone, *History of The Peking Summer Palaces under The Ching Dynasty*. Urbana: The University of Illinois (1934); rpt. New York: Paragon Book Reprint Corp. (1966)

37. 《东方园艺论》William Chambers, *A Dissertation on Oriental Gardening*. London: Printed by W. Griffin, Printer to the Royal Academy (1772)

38. 《中国建筑、家具、服装、机器和器物的设计》William Chambers, *Designs of Chinese Buildings, Furniture, Dresses, Machines and Utensils*. London (1757)

39. 《中国风的乡村建筑》William Halfpenny, *Rural Architecture in the Chinese Taste: Being Designs Entirely New for the Decoration of Gardens, Parks, Forrests, Insides of Houses, &c. on Sixty Copper Plates, with Full Instructions for Workmen, Also a Near Estimate of the Charge and Hints Where Proper to Be Erected the Whole Invented & Drawn by Willm. & Inn. Halfpenny, Architects. The 3rd. Edition. With the Addition of 4 Plates in Quarto of Roofs for Chinese & Indian Temples, the Manner of Fixing Their Ornaments, Covering and Carrying off the Water, their Cornices with the Several Members Adjusted to Regular Proportion*. London: Printed for Robert Sayer (1755)

40. 《英汉园艺词汇》The Hongkong Horticultural Society, *A Gardening Vocabulary in English and Chinese*. 香港园艺学会编印，出版时间不详。

6.9 食品与饮食

1. 《中国连锁餐饮业：标准化与真实性的两难选择》Guojun Zeng, Henk J. de Vries, Frank

M. Go, *Restaurant Chains in China: The Dilemma of Standardisation versus Authenticity*. Springer Singapore: Palgrave Macmillan (2019)

2. 《巴西对华食品出口的法律经济分析》(Springer Briefs in Law) Dan Wei, Ângelo Patrício Rafael, Almeida Zacarias Machava, Ana Cândida Muniz Cipriano, Daniel Freire e Almeida, *Food Exports from Brazil to China: A Legal and Economic Analysis*. Springer International Publishing (2019)

3. 《炒杂烩之国：加拿大中餐馆的军团咖啡馆和其他故事》Ann Hui（许平安），*Chop Suey Nation: The Legion Cafe and Other Stories from Canada's Chinese Restaurants*. Douglas & McIntyre (2 Feb 2019)

4. 《中国外卖食谱：从杂烩到糖醋，重新打造您最爱的70多个菜谱》Kwoklyn Wan, *Chinese Takeaway Cookbook: From Chop Suey to Sweet 'n' Sour, over 70 Recipes to Re-create Your Favourites*. Quadrille Publishing Ltd (2019)

5. 《喂养大众：中国监管失灵的剖析》John K. Yasuda, *On Feeding the Masses: An Anatomy of Regulatory Failure in China*. Cambridge University Press (2018)

6. 《中国美食：自制饺子、炒菜、汤类等指南》Hsiao-Ching Chou, *Chinese Soul Food: A Friendly Guide for Homemade Dumplings, Stir-Fries, Soups, and More*. Sasquatch Books (2018)

7. 《另一种牛奶：民国时期的大豆再造》Jia-Chen Fu, *The Other Milk: Reinventing Soy in Republican China*. University of Washington Press (2018)

8. 《中国有机食品和农业：自上而下和自下而上的生态举措》Aijuan Chen, Theresa Schumilas, Steffanie Scott, Zhenzhong Si, *Organic Food and Farming in China: Top-Down and Bottom-Up Ecological Initiatives*. Routledge (2018)

9. 《中国研究食谱：修订和扩展版，包含超过175种基于植物的全面膳食配方》LeAnne Campbell, *The China Study Cookbook: Revised and Expanded Edition with Over 175 Whole Food, Plant-Based Recipes*. BenBella Books (2018)

10. 《中国食品安全：科学、技术、管理和监管》Joseph J. Jen, Junshi Chen, *Food Safety in China: Science, Technology, Management and Regulation*. John Wiley & Sons, Incorporated (2017)

11. 《最全面的中国营养研究》T. Colin Campbell, Thomas M. Campbell, *The China Study: The Most Comprehensive Study of Nutrition* (Revised and Expanded Edition). BenBella Books (2016)

12. 《杂烩：食物与华裔美国人之旅》Anne Mendelson, *Chow Chop Suey: Food and the Chinese American Journey* (Arts and Traditions of the Table: Perspectives on Culinary History). Columbia University Press (2016)

13. 《华裔美国的美食：1965年以来中国烹饪文化在美国的转型》Xiachui Liu, *Foodscapes of Chinese America: The Transformation of Chinese Culinary Culture in the U.S. since 1965*. Peter Lang (2016)

14. 《鱼米之乡：来自江南的美味食谱》Fuchsia Dunlop, *Land of Fish and Rice: Recipes from*

the Culinary Heart of China. W. W. Norton & Co. (2016)

15. 《从广州餐馆到熊猫快餐：美国中餐史》Haiming Liu, *From Canton Restaurant to Panda Express: A History of Chinese Food in the United State*s (Asian American Studies Today). Rutgers University Press (2015)

16. 《中国食谱》Del Sroufe, LeAnne Campbell, M. D. Thomas M. Campbell, *The China Study: Quick & Easy Cookbook: Cook Once, Eat All Week with Whole Food, Plant-Based Recipes.* BenBella Books (2015)

17. 《潮州传统烹饪：中式安胃食物食谱宝库》Chef Eric Low, *Teochew Heritage Cooking: A Treasury of Recipes for Chinese Comfort Food.* Marshall Cavendish International (Asia) Pte Ltd (2015)

18. 《中国早期与中世纪的食物与环境》E. N. Anderson, *Food and Environment in Early and Medieval China.*University of Pennsylvania Press (2014)

19. 《亚洲泡菜：来自韩国、日本、中国、印度及其他国家的甜、酸、咸、固化和发酵保鲜》Karen Solomon, *Asian Pickles: Sweet, Sour, Salty, Cured, and Fermented Preserves from Korea, Japan, China, India, and Beyond.*Ten Speed Press (2014)

20. 《中国食品安全综述》Linhai Wu, Dian Zhu, *Food Safety in China: A Comprehensive Review.* CRC Press (2014)

21. 《中国研究全明星系列：整个食品来自你最喜爱的素食主厨植物食谱》LeAnne Campbell, T. Colin Campbell, *The China Study All-Star Collection: Whole Food, Plant-Based Recipes from Your Favorite Vegan Chefs.*BenBella Books (2014)

22. 《每一粒米：简单中国家庭烹饪》Fuchsia Dunlop, *Every Grain of Rice: Simple Chinese Home Cooking.* W. W. Norton & Company (2013)

23. 《中国研究食谱：超过120种全食品和植物配方》LeAnne Campbell, Steven Campbell Disla, T. Colin Campbell, *The China Study Cookbook: Over 120 Whole Food, Plant-Based Recipes.* BenBella Books (2013)

24. 《中国食品安全管理：以食品质量管理体系为视角》Jiehong Zhou, Shaosheng Jin, *Food Safety Management in China: A Perspective from Food Quality Control System.* World Scientific Publishing Company (2013)

25. 《毛博士的长寿秘诀食谱：吃出茁壮、长寿、健康》Maoshing Ni, *Dr. Mao's Secrets of Longevity Cookbook: Eat to Thrive, Live Long, and Be Healthy.* Andrews McMeel Publishing (2013)

26. 《美食文士：中华帝国文学中的饮食描写》Isaac Yue, Siu-fu Tang, *Scribes of Gastronomy: Representations of Food and Drink in Imperial Chinese Literature.* Hong Kong University Press (2013)

27. 《大湄公河次区域：从中国到越南的美食之旅》Luke Nguyen, *Greater Mekong: A Culinary Journey from China to Vietnam.* Hardie Grant Books (2012)

28. 《喂龙：中国食谱烹饪游记》Nate Tate, Mary Kate Tate, *Feeding the Dragon: A Culinary Travelogue Through China with Recipes*. Andrews McMeel Publishing (2011)
29. 《古代中国的食品、祭祀和圣人》Roel Sterckx（胡司德）, *Food, Sacrifice, and Sagehood in Early China*. Cambridge University Press (2011)
30. 《中国烹饪》Matthew Locricchio, *The Cooking of China* (Superchef). Marshall Cavendish Children's Books (2011)
31. 《从中国进口：食品接触研究》Michael Stanbrough, *Importing from China: A Food Contact Study*. Pira International Ltd (2010)
32. 《东看西望：亚洲和欧洲有机食品与优质食品营销》Rainer Haas, Maurizio Canavari, Bill Slee, Chen Tong, Bundit Anurugsa, *Looking East, Looking West: Organic and Quality Food Marketing in Asia and Europe*. Wageningen Pers (2010)
33. 《世界食物：中国和印度》Zangwill Kaufman, Twila Byers, *Food of the World: China & India*. Gloabl Media (2009)
34. 《营养之道》Maoshing Ni, *Tao of Nutrition*. Sevenstar Communications (2009)
35. 《如何烹龙：中国生活、爱和吃》Linda Furiya, *How to Cook a Dragon: Living, Loving, and Eating in China*. Seal Press (2008)
36. 《中国美食的魅力》F. T. Cheng, *Musings of a Chinese Gourmet*. China Economic Review Publishing Ltd (2008)
37. 《中国食谱：从馄饨汤到糖醋鸡，远东300种多汁食谱》(Everything) Rhonda Lauret Parkinson, *The Everything Chinese Cookbook: From Wonton Soup to Sweet and Sour Chicken, 300 Succulent Recipes from the Far East*. Adams Media (2008)
38. 《鱼翅与花椒：吃在中国的酸甜回忆录》Fuchsia Dunlop, *Shark's Fin and Sichuan Pepper: A Sweet-Sour Memoir of Eating in China*. W. W. Norton & Co. (2008)
39. 《变化的饭碗：中国经济发展与饮食》Elizabeth Leppman, *Changing Rice Bowl: Economic Development and Diet in China*. Hong Kong University Press (2005)
40. 《三脚架与口感：传统中国的食品、政治与宗教》Roel Sterckx（胡司德）(eds.), *Of Tripod and Palate: Food, Politics, and Religion in Traditional China*. Palgrave Macmillan US (2005)
41. 《中国研究：有史以来最全面的营养研究，对饮食，减肥和长期健康的惊人影响》T. Colin Campbell, Thomas M Campbell, *The China Study: The most Comprehensive Study of Nutrition ever Conducted and the Startling Implications for Diet, Weight Loss and Long-term Health*. Benbella Books (2005)
42. 《中国味道：地方烹饪权威指南》Ken Hom, *A Taste of China: The Definitive Guide to Regional Cooking* (Pavilion Classic Cookery). Pavilion (2005)
43. 《中国正宗食谱》Kenneth Law, Lee Cheng Meng, Luca Invernizzi Tettoni, Max Zhang, *Authentic Recipes from China*. Penptus Edltlons (HK) Ltd. (2004)
44. 《国际美食：中国篇》Christine Yau, Norman Fu, Deh-Ta Hsiung, *International Cuisine:*

China. Hodder & Stoughton (2004)

45. 《炒锅的气息：通过烹饪知识掌握中国炒菜的精髓》Alan Richardson, Grace Young, *The Breath of a Wok: Unlocking The Spirit of Chinese Wok Cooking through Recipes And Lore.* Simon & Schuster (2004)

46. 《丰腴之地：地道四川菜》Fuchsia Dunlop, *Land of Plenty: A Treasury of Authentic Sichuan Cooking.* W. W. Norton & Company (2003)

47. 《从中国到唐人街：中国食品在西方》J. A. G. Roberts, *China to Chinatown: Chinese Food in the West.* Reaktion Books Ltd (2002)

48. 《中国食品的全球化》David Y. H. Wu, Sidney C. H. Cheung, *The Globalization of Chinese Food.* University of Hawai'i Press (2002)

49. 《亚洲食品：来自缅甸、中国、印度、印度尼西亚、日本、韩国、马来西亚、菲律宾、新加坡、斯里兰卡、泰国、越南厨艺大师的正宗配方》Kong Foong Ling, *The food of Asia: Featuring Authentic Recipes from Master Chefs in Burma, China, India, Indonesia, Japan, Korea, Malaysia, the Philippines, Singapore, Sri Lanka, Thailand, and Vietnam.* Periplus Editions (2002)

50. 《食品安全与经济改革：中国粮食流通体制面临的挑战》Christopher Findlay, Andrew Watson (eds.), *Food Security and Economic Reform: The Challenges Facing China's Grain Marketing System.* Palgrave Macmillan UK (1999)

51. 《中国食物和食谱》Theresa M. Beatty, *Food and Recipes of China* (Kids in the Kitchen). The Rosen Publishing Group (1999)

52. 《中国康复烹饪法：300种充满活力的健康长寿食谱》Zhuo Zhao, George Ellis, *The Healing Cuisine of China: 300 Recipes for Vibrant Health and Longevity.* Healing Arts Press (1998)

53. 《中国餐桌：食品安全选项》Albert Nyberg, World Bank, *At China's Table: Food Security Options*, Volume 113. World Bank Publications (1997)

54. 《谁来养活中国：唤醒地球的呼唤》Lester Russell Brown, *Who Will Feed China: Wake-Up Call for a Small Planet.* W. W. Norton & Company (1995)

55. 《中国食物》E. N. Anderson（安德森）, *The Food of China.* Yale University Press (1990)

56. 《长寿的艺术：中国长寿美食》Henry C. Lu, *The Art of Long Life: Chinese Food For Longevity.* Pelanduk Publications (1990)

57. 《中国文化中的饮食：人类学与历史的视角》K. C. Chang, *Food in Chinese Culture: Anthropological and Historical Perspectives.* Yale University Press (1977)

58. 《卡萨诺瓦的中国餐馆》Anthony Powell, *Casanova's Chinese Restaurant* (Dance to the Music of Time). Arrow (1960)

59. 《中日烹饪书》Sara Bosse, Onoto Watanna, *Chinese-Japanese Cook Book.* Rand McNally (1914)

6.10 武术

1. 《咏春拳创作：华南武术社会史》Benjamin N. Judkins, Jon Nielson, *The Creation of Wing Chun: A Social History of the Southern Chinese Martial Arts*. State University of New York Press (2015)
2. 《咏春之道：中国最具爆发力的武术的历史与原则》John Little, Danny Xuan, *The Tao of Wing Chun: The History and Principles of China's Most Explosive Martial Art*. Skyhorse Publishing (2015)
3. 《武当剑法大要：中国剑术手册选编》Scott M. Rodell, *Fundamentals of the Wudang Sword Method: Selected Translations with Commentary from a Manual of Chinese Swordsmanship*. Seven Stars Books & Video (2015)
4. 《纸上升音：19世纪武侠小说与中国人听觉想象》Paize Keulemans, *Sound Rising from the Paper: Nineteenth-Century Martial Arts Fiction and the Chinese Acoustic Imagination*. Harvard University Press (2014)
5. 《墨派德内功》Shifu Lin, *The Meritocratic Standards of Mozi: Why Nei Kung Cannot Be Limited Only to Chinese Students & Discussion On the Role of Karma in the First Four Levels of Mo Pai Nei Kung*. Lung Hu Shan Publications (2012)
6. 《中国武术：从古代到21世纪》Peter Lorge, *Chinese Martial Arts: From Antiquity to the Twenty-First Century*. Cambridge University Press (2011)
7. 《少林寺：历史、宗教与中国武术》Meir Shahar, *The Shaolin Monastery: History, Religion and the Chinese Martial Arts*. University of Hawai'i Press (2008)
8. 《少林擒拿法：擒拿格斗艺术（浙江省警察学院教师手册）》(Shanghai, 1936) Liu Jin Sheng, Andrew Timofeevich, *Shaolin Chin Na Fa: Art of Seizing and Grappling. Instructor's Manual for Police Academy of Zhejiang Province*. CreateSpace (2008)
9. 《中国摔跤法》Tong Zhongyi, *The Method of Chinese Wrestling*. North Atlantic, Publishers Group UK (2007)
10. 《太极拳与寻找小个老年中华男子：通过武术理解身份》Adam D. Frank, *Taijiquan and the Search for the Little Old Chinese Man: Understanding Identity through Martial Arts*. Palgrave Macmillan US (2006)
11. 《站桩与求物：揭示内愈和拳击的终极秘密》Yu Yongnian, *Zhan Zhuang & the Search of Wu: Ultimate Secret of Internal Healing & Boxing Revealed*. China Martial Arts Ltd (2006)
12. 《形意拳》Robert W. Smith, *Hsing-I: Chinese Mind-body Boxing*. North Atlantic Books (2003)
13. 《杨氏太极拳秘要：中国古典、翻译与评论》Yang Jwing-Ming（杨俊敏）, *Tai Chi Secrets of the Yang Style: Chinese Classics, Translations, Commentary*. YMAA Publication Center (2001)
14. 《李小龙功夫之道：关于中国武术的研究》John Little (ed.), *Bruce Lee: The Tao of Gung Fu: A Study in the Way of Chinese Martial Art* (Bruce Lee Library). Tuttle Publishing (1997)

15.《中国式快速摔跤：散手快步投掷、起跳和地面对抗的艺术》Liang Shou-Yu, Tai D. Ngo, *Chinese Fast Wrestling for Fighting: The Art of San Shou Kuai Jiao Throws, Takedowns, & Ground-Fighting*. Ymaa Publication Center (1997)

16.《基本中国拳法》Bruce Lee, *Chinese Gung Fu: The Philosophical Art of Self Defense*. Ohara Publications (1987)

17.《山东黑虎：华北少林武术》Leo Budiman Prakarsa, Khek Kiong Tjoa, Donn F. Draeger, Quintin T. G. Chambers, *Shantung Black Tiger: A Shaolin Fighting Art of North China (*Martial Arts Self Defense). John Weatherhill, Inc. (1976)

7. 中国社会与族群

7.1 儿童

1. 《中国0～3岁儿童的开发与教育研究》(*New Frontiers of Educational Research*) Xin Liu, Xiumin Hong, Wanzhen Feng, Xiaowei Li, Xinghua Wang, Yuejuan Pan, *Research on the Development and Education of 0~3-Year-Old Children in China*. Springer (2019)

2. 《培育中国革命者：20世纪20年代至50年代世界民族主义者和被解放的同志的童年现代化》Margaret Mih Tillman, *Raising China's Revolutionaries: Modernizing Childhood for Cosmopolitan Nationalists and Liberated Comrades, 1920s—1950s*. Columbia University Press (2018)

3. 《全部关于中国：儿童故事、歌曲、工艺品等》(All About...countries) Allison Branscombe, *All About China: Stories, Songs, Crafts and More for Kids*. Tuttle Publishing (17 Apr 2018)

4. 《好孩子：中国学前班的道德开发》Jing Xu（许晶）, *The Good Child: Moral Development in a Chinese Preschool*. Stanford University Press (2017)

5. 《中国社会早期儿童教育》Nirmala Rao, Jing Zhou, Jin Sun (eds.), *Early Childhood Education in Chinese Societies*. Springer Netherlands (2017)

6. 《中国独生子女如何成长：生态系统视角》Weiping Liu, *How Are Chinese Only Children Growing: A Bioecological Systems Perspective*. VS Verlag für Sozialwissenschaften (2017)

7. 《中国转型期的青少年犯罪：紧张的一代》Wan-Ning Bao, *Delinquent Youth in a Transforming China: A Generation of Strain* (Palgrave Advances in Criminology and Criminal Justice in Asia). Palgrave Macmillan (2017)

8. 《中国残疾人政策：儿童与家庭经验》Xiaoyuan Shang, Karen R. Fisher, *Disability Policy in China: Child and Family Experiences*. Routledge (2016)

9. 《中国城市儿童保健与家长媒介参与：一种文化焦虑》Qian Gong, *Children's Healthcare and Parental Media Engagement in Urban China: A Culture of Anxiety*. Palgrave Macmillan UK (2016)

10. 《中国黑孩：遗弃、收养与一孩政策的人力成本》Kay Ann Johnson, *China's Hidden Children: Abandonment, Adoption, and the Human Costs of the One-child Policy*. University of Chicago Press (2016)

11. 《迁移背景下生活的弱点与机遇：中国流动儿童和留守儿童》Guanglun Michael Mu, Yang Hu, *Living with Vulnerabilities and Opportunities in a Migration Context: Floating Children and Left-Behind Children in China*. SensePublishers (2016)

12. 《爱的不确定性：当代中国育儿的政治伦理》Teresa Kuan, *Love's Uncertainty: The*

Politics and Ethics of Child Rearing in Contemporary China. University of California Press (2015)

13. 《中国千禧一代》Eric Fish, *China's Millennials: The Want Generation*. Rowman & Littlefield Publishers (2015)

14. 《独生：中国最激进的实验故事》Mei Fong（方凤美）, *One Child: The Story of China's Most Radical Experiment*. Houghton Mifflin Harcourt (2015)

15. 《我要天上的星星：中国一胎化世代的真实样貌》Xinran（薛欣然）, *Buy Me the Sky: The Remarkable Truth of China's One-Child Generations*. Rider (2015)

16. 《生死之间：中国19世纪的溺杀女婴》Michelle King, *Between Birth and Death: Female Infanticide in Nineteenth-Century China*. Stanford University Press (2014)

17. 《中国儿童、权利与现代性：培育自治公民》Orna Naftali, *Children, Rights and Modernity in China: Raising Self-Governing Citizens*. Palgrave Macmillan UK (2014)

18. 《小皇帝的新玩具：中国儿童与电视的批判性考察》Bin Zhao, *The Little Emperors' New Toys: A Critical Inquiry into Children and Television in China*. Springer-Verlag Berlin Heidelberg (2013)

19. 《中国早期儿童发展：打破贫困周期与提高未来竞争力》Kin Bing Wu, Mary Eming Young, Jianhua Cai, *Early Child Development in China: Breaking the Cycle of Poverty and Improving Future Competitiveness*. The World Bank (2012)

20. 《民国时期的分娩：婴儿接生的现代性》Tina Phillips Johnson, *Childbirth in Republican China: Delivering Modernity*. Lexington Books (2011)

21. 《无声的眼泪：一个中国孤儿院的希望之旅》Kay Bratt, *Silent Tears: A Journey of Hope in a Chinese Orphanage*. Mariner Books (2011)

22. 《中国独生子女政策与多重照料：厦门的"小太阳"抚养》Esther Goh, *China's One-Child Policy and Multiple Caregiving: Raising Little Suns in Xiamen* (Routledge Contemporary China Series).Routledge (2011)

23. 《非自然选择：重男轻女，世上有那么多男人的后果》Mara Hvistendahl, *Unnatural Selection: Choosing Boys Over Girls, and the Consequences of a World Full of Men*. Public Affairs (2011)

24. 《小皇帝：与中国的未来生活一年》Joann Dionne, *Little emperors: A Year with the Future of China*. Dundurn Press (2008)

25. 《幸运儿：我们从中国领养儿童的故事》Ann Rauhala, *The Lucky Ones: Our Stories of Adopting Children from China*. ECW Press (2008)

26. 《溺杀女婴：清代的女婴杀害》D. E. Mungello（孟德卫）, *Drowning Girls in China: Female Infanticide in China since 1650*. Rowman & Littlefield Publishers, Inc. (2008)

27. 《美国和中国的儿童养育价值观：信仰体系与社会结构比较》Hong Xiao, *Childrearing Values in the United States and China: A Comparison of Belief Systems and Social Structure*. Praeger Publishers (2001)

28. 《中国聋儿》Alison Callaway, *Deaf Children in China*.Gallaudet University Press (2000)

29. 《中国人的儿童观》Anne Behnke Kinney, *Chinese Views of Childhood*. University of Hawaii Press (1995)
30. 《中国独生子女政策》Elisabeth Croll, Delia Davin, Penny Kane (eds.), *China's One-Child Family Policy*. Palgrave Macmillan UK (1985)
31. 《中国的男孩和女孩》Isaac Taylor Headland（何德兰）, *The Chinese Boy and Girl*. New York; Chicago; Toronto: Fleming H. Revell Co. (1901)
32. 《孺子歌图》Translated and illustrated by Isaac Taylor Headland（何德兰）, *Chinese Mother Goose Rhymes*. New York, Chicago [etc.], Fleming H. Revell Co. (1900)

7.2　婚姻家庭

1. 《诺言：现代中国的爱情与失落》Xinran（薛欣然）, *The Promise: Love and Loss in Modern China*. I. B. Tauris (2019)
2. 《呜呜：我如何在冰球、毒品袭击、恶魔和疯狂的中国家庭中幸存》Lindsay Wong, *The Woo-Woo: How I Survived Ice Hockey, Drug Raids, Demons, and My Crazy Chinese Family*. Arsenal Pulp Press (2018)
3. 《当代中国电视相亲：身份、爱情和亲密关系》Chao Yang (auth.) *Television and Dating in Contemporary China: Identities, Love and Intimacy*. Springer Singapore (2017)
4. 《改变父权制：21世纪中国家庭》Gonçalo Santos, Stevan Harrell, *Transforming Patriarchy: Chinese Families in the Twenty-First Century*. University of Washington Press (2017)
5. 《今日中国家庭》Anqi XU, John DeFrain, Wenrong LIU, *The Chinese Family Today*. Routledge (2016)
6. 《规范中国人类胚胎干细胞：美国和欧盟的人类胚胎干细胞专利性与道德比较研究》Li Jiang, *Regulating Human Embryonic Stem Cell in China: A Comparative Study on Human Embryonic Stem Cell's Patentability and Morality in US and EU*. Springer Singapore (2016)
7. 《中英婚姻：摆脱性别与种族歧视》Yang Hu, *Chinese-British Intermarriage: Disentangling Gender and Ethnicity*. Palgrave Macmillan (2016)
8. 《中国城市的工作与家庭：毛泽东时代以来不断变化的女性体验》Jiping Zuo, *Work and Family in Urban China: Women's Changing Experience since Mao*. Palgrave Macmillan US (2016)
9. 《双杯之爱：追踪中国的家庭、食品以及破碎的心》Eddie Huang, *Double Cup Love: On the Trail of Family, Food, and Broken Hearts in China*. Spiegel & Grau (2015)
10. 《中国太太指南：如何找到模特型的中国女友或妻子》Julian Bernard Stiles, *Chinese Wife Guide: How to Find a Model-Type Chinese Girlfriend or Wife*. Amazon.com Services LLC (2016)
11. 《你还是中国人吗？（跨国）领养的中国青年及其家庭的身份和文化谈判》Andrea Louie, *How Chinese Are You? Adopted Chinese Youth and Their Families Negotiate Identity and Culture*. New York University Press (2015)

12. 《法庭上的小妾：20世纪中国的婚姻与一夫一妻制》Lisa Tran, *Concubines in Court: Marriage and Monogamy in Twentieth-Century China*. Rowman & Littlefield (2015)

13. 《清代中国的一妻多夫与卖妻：生存策略与司法介入》Matthew H. Sommer, *Polyandry and Wife-Selling in Qing Dynasty China: Survival Strategies and Judicial Interventions*. University of California Press (2015)

14. 《家庭革命：当代中国文学与视觉文化中的婚姻冲突》Hui Faye Xiao, *Family Revolution: Marital Strife in Contemporary Chinese Literature and Visual Culture*. University of Washington Press (2014)

15. 《中国社会中的家庭与社会变迁》Chien-Liang Chen (auth.), Dudley L. Poston, Jr., Wen Shan Yang, Demetrea Nicole Farris (eds.), *The Family and Social Change in Chinese Societies*. Springer (2014)

16. 《丑妻是家中宝：共产主义中国真实的爱情与婚姻故事》Melissa Margaret Schneider, *The Ugly Wife Is a Treasure at Home: True Stories of Love and Marriage in Communist China*. Potomac Books Inc. (2014)

17. 《家庭和生活安排预测：美国和中国的扩展队列组件方法与应用》Yi Zeng, Kenneth C. Land, Danan Gu, Zhenglian Wang, *Household and Living Arrangement Projections: The Extended Cohort-Component Method and Applications to the U.S. and China*. Springer Netherlands (2014)

18. 《中国城市的住房支付能力和住房政策》Zan Yang, Jie Chen, *Housing Affordability and Housing Policy in Urban China*. Springer-Verlag Berlin Heidelberg (2014)

19. 《中国全球化进程中的爱情和婚姻》Wang Pan, *Love and Marriage in Globalizing China*. Routledge (2014)

20. 《中国家庭国际手册》Chan Kwok-bun, Chan Nin (auth.), Chan Kwok-bun (eds.), *International Handbook of Chinese Families*. Springer-Verlag New York (2013)

21. 《中国经济特区的性别、工作和家庭：劳作在天堂》Nancy E Riley (auth.), *Gender, Work, and Family in a Chinese Economic Zone: Laboring in Paradise*. Springer Netherlands (2013)

22. 《作为战略游戏的在线约会：香港男性为何以及如何使用QQ追逐中国大陆女性》Maurice Kwok-to Choi, Kwok-bun Chan, *Online Dating as A Strategic Game: Why and How Men in Hong Kong Use QQ to Chase Women in Mainland China*. Springer-Verlag Berlin Heidelberg (2013)

23. 《从西部好莱坞到中国西部地区的剩男剩女爱情、婚姻和家庭价值观》Judith Stacey, *Unhitched Love, Marriage, and Family Values from West Hollywood to Western China* (NYU Series in Social and Cultural Analysis). NYU Press (2011)

24. 《叶：百年动荡中的一个中国家庭》Joseph W. Esherick（周锡瑞）, *Ancestral Leaves: A Family Journey through Chinese History*. University of California Press (2011)

25. 《了解中国家庭：中国台湾与中国东南地区比较研究》C. Y. Cyrus Chu, Ruoh-Rong Yu, *Understanding Chinese Families: A Comparative Study of Taiwan and Southeast China*.

Oxford University Press (2010)

26. 《移动的中国：迁徙、国家与家庭》C. Cindy Fan, *China on the Move: Migration, the State, and the Household*. Routledge (2008)

27. 《表演悲伤：中国农村新娘的悲痛》Anne E. McLaren, *Performing Grief: Bridal Laments in Rural China*. University of Hawai'i Press (2008)

28. 《中国中世纪的婚礼著述：8—14世纪的文本和礼仪实践》Christian De Pee, *The Writing of Weddings in Middle Period China: Text and Ritual Practice in the Eighth Through Fourteenth Centuries*. State University of New York Press (2007)

29. 《中国中世纪的婚礼书写：8—14世纪的文本与仪式实践》Christian De Pee, *The Writing of Weddings in Middle Period China: Text and Ritual Practice in the Eighth through Fourteenth Centuries* (SUNY Series in Chinese Philosophy and Culture). State University of New York Press (2007)

30. 《心灵的革命：1900—1950年中国恋爱谱系》Haiyan Lee（李海燕）, *Revolution of the Heart: A Genealogy of Love in China, 1900—1950*. Stanford University Press (2006)

31. 《无私的后代：中国中世纪的孝子与社会秩序》Keith Nathaniel Knapp, *Selfless Offspring: Filial Children and Social Order in Medieval China*. Honolulu: University of Hawai'i Press (2005)

32. 《私人生活的变革：一个中国村庄里的爱情、家庭与亲密关系（1949—1999）》Yunxiang Yan（阎云翔）, *Private Life under Socialism: Love, Intimacy and Family Change in a Chinese Village, 1949—1999*. Stanford University Press (2003)

33. 《中国人对家庭和国家的看法（1915—1953）》Susan L. Glosser, *Chinese Visions of Family and State, 1915—1953*. University of California Press (2003)

34. 《郑振满：明清福建家族组织与社会变迁》Zheng Zhenman, *Family Lineage Organization and Social Change in Ming and Qing Fujian*. University of Hawai'i Press (2001)

35. 《家庭革命：中国城乡的政治、爱情和离婚（1949—1968）》Neil J. Diamant, *Revolutionizing the Family: Politics, Love, and Divorce in Urban and Rural China, 1949—1968*. University of California Press (2000)

36. 《重新界定中国的工作、家庭和性别》Barbara Entwisle, Gail E. Henderson, *Re-Drawing Boundaries: Work, Households, and Gender in China*. University of California Press (2000)

37. 《中国住房政策与实践》Ya Ping Wang, Alan Murie, *Housing Policy and Practice in China*. Palgrave Macmillan UK (1999)

38. 《分家：清代及民国时期的分家与继承》David Wakefield, *Fenjia: Household Division and Inheritance in Qing and Republican China*. University of Hawaii Press (1998)

39. 《后毛泽东时代的中国家庭》Deborah Davis, Stevan Harrell (eds.), *Chinese Families in the Post-Mao Era*. Berkeley: University of California Press (1993)

40. 《内闱：宋代的婚姻和妇女生活》Patricia Buckley Ebrey（伊沛霞）, *The Inner Quarters:*

Marriage and the Lives of Chinese Women in the Sung Period. University of California Press (1993)

41.《中国社会中的婚姻与不平等》Rubie S. Watson, Patricia Buckley Ebrey（伊佩霞）(eds.), *Marriage and Inequality in Chinese Society*. University of California Press (1991)

42.《中国家庭与亲属关系》Hugh D. R. Baker, *Chinese Family and Kinship*.Macmillan Education UK (1979)

43.《早期中华帝国的贵族家庭：博陵崔氏个案研究》Patricia Buckley Ebrey（伊沛霞）, *The Aristocratic Families of Early Imperial China: A Case Study of the Po-Ling Ts'ui Family*. Cambridge University Press (1978)

44.《中国计划生育的方式》Leo A. Orleans (eds.), *Chinese Approaches to Family Planning*. Palgrave Macmillan UK (1979)

45.《中国沿海家庭》John C. Caldwell, *China Coast Family*. Henry Regnery Company (1953)

46.《中国之家庭与社会》Olga Lang, *Chinese Family and Society*. New Haven: Yale University Press (1946)

47.《中国传统家庭》H. P. Wilkinson（成金生）, *The Family in Classical China*. London: Macmillan (1923)

48.《中国的家庭生活》Isaac Taylor Headland（何德兰）, *Home Life In China. With Four Plates in Colour and Twelve Other Illustrations*. Methuen & Co. Ltd (1914)

7.3 女性

1.《妇女与中国革命》(Critical Issues in World and International History) Gail Hershatter（贺萧）, *Women and China's Revolutions*. Rowman & Littlefield Publishers (2019)

2.《作为时尚的缠足：传统中国的种族、劳力与地位》John Robert Shepherd, *Footbinding as Fashion: Ethnicity, Labor, and Status in Traditional China*. University of Washington Press (2019)

3.《当代中国社会女性名人》Shenshen Cai, *Female Celebrities in Contemporary Chinese Society*. Springer Singapore: Palgrave Macmillan (2019)

4.《中国的易卜生主义：妇女、阶级与民族的重塑》Kwok-kan Tam, *Chinese Ibsenism: Reinventions of Women, Class and Nation*. Springer Singapore (2019)

5.《背叛大哥：中国女权主义的觉醒》Leta Hong Fincher, *Betraying Big Brother: The Feminist Awakening in China*. Verso (2018)

6.《性别、权力与天资：中国唐代道教女祭司的旅程》Jinhua Jia, *Gender, Power, and Talent: The Journey of Daoist Priestesses in Tang China*. Columbia University Press (2018)

7.《中国城市女儿》Patricia O'Neill, *Urban Chinese Daughters* (St Antony's Series). Springer Singapore: Palgrave Macmillan (2018)

8.《20世纪初中国的女权主义、女性代理与传播》Qiliang He, *Feminism, Women's Agency, and Communication in Early Twentieth-Century China* (Chinese Literature and Culture in the World). Springer International Publishing: Palgrave Macmillan (2018)

9. 《中国的剩女：塑造世界下一个超级大国的女性》Roseann Lake, *Leftover in China: The Women Shaping the World's Next Superpower*. W. W. Norton & Company (2018)

10. 《世界之家：清末民初的妇女与慈善事业》Xia Shi, *At Home in the World: Women and Charity in Late Qing and Early Republican China*. Columbia University Press (2018)

11. 《世界之家：清末民初的妇女与慈善》Xia Shi, *At Home in the World: Women and Charity in Late Qing and Early Republican China*. Columbia University Press (2018)

12. 《毛泽东时代的性别遗产：当代中国女性的生活故事》Xin Huang, *The Gender Legacy of the Mao Era: Women's Life Stories in Contemporary China*. State University of New York Press (2018)

13. 《中国帝制晚期的女性诗歌与诗学：对话参与》Haihong Yang, *Women's Poetry and Poetics in Late Imperial China: A Dialogic Engagement*. Lexington Books (2017)

14. 《女儿国：中国大山中深藏的生命、爱情与死亡》Choo Wai Hong, *The Kingdom of Women: Life, Love and Death in China's Hidden Mountains*. I.B. Tauris & Co (2017)

15. 《小脚与年轻的手：追踪中国乡村缠足的消亡》Laurel Bossen and Hill Gates, *Bound Feet, Young Hands: Tracking the Demise of Footbinding in Village China*. Stanford University Press (2017)

16. 《中华帝国晚期文学中的放荡女人：模式、类型、颠覆与传统》(Women and Gender in China Studies) Edited by Mark Stevenson, Wu Cuncun (eds.), *Wanton Women in Late-Imperial Chinese Literature: Models, Genres, Subversions and Traditions*. Brill (2017)

17. 《选择女儿：中国农村的家庭变迁》Lihong Shi, *Choosing Daughters: Family Change in Rural China*. Stanford University Press (2017)

18. 《中国城市的工作与家庭：毛泽东去世以来女性的变化经历》Jiping Zuo, *Work and Family in Urban China: Women's Changing Experience since Mao* (Politics and Development of Contemporary China). Palgrave Macmillan US (2016)

19. 《中国新女权主义：中国上海的年轻中产阶级女性》Jiaran Zheng, *New Feminism in China: Young Middle-Class Chinese Women in Shanghai*. Springer Singapore (2016)

20. 《穿越大门：宋代福建女性的日常生活（960—1279）》Man Xu, *Crossing the Gate: Everyday Lives of Women in Song Fujian (960—1279)* (Suny Series in Chinese Philosophy and Culture). State University of New York Press (2016)

21. 《清代女英雄：模范女人讲述自己的故事》Binbin Yang, *Heroines of the Qing: Exemplary Women Tell Their Stories* (Modern Language Initiative Books). University of Washington Press (2016)

22. 《在国家中寻找女性：中华人民共和国的社会主义女权革命（1949—1964）》Zheng Wang, *Finding Women in the State: A Socialist Feminist Revolution in the People's Republic of China, 1949—1964*. University of California Press (2016)

23. 《革命的母爱：前线之爱》Alexis Pauline Gumbs, China Martens, Mai'a Williams, *Revolutionary Mothering: Love on the Front Lines*. PM Press (2016)

24. 《性别与中国历史：变革的遭遇》Beverly Jo Bossler, *Gender and Chinese History: Transformative Encounters*. University of Washington Press (2015)

25. 《当代中国之冒犯妇女：性别与犯罪道路》Anqi Shen, *Offending Women in Contemporary China: Gender and Pathways into Crime*. Palgrave Macmillan UK (2015)

26. 《中国数字化后的女性色情余晖》Katrien Jacobs, *The Afterglow of Women's Pornography in Post-Digital China*. Palgrave Macmillan US (2015)

27. 《翻译中国女性主义：性别、性欲望与审查制度》(Routledge Advances in Translation and Interpreting Studies) Zhongli Yu, *Translating Feminism in China: Gender, Sexuality and Censorship*. Routledge (2015)

28. 《剩女：中国社会性别不平等的复苏》Leta Hong Fincher, *Leftover Women: The Resurgence of Gender Inequality in China*. Zed Books (2014)

29. 《现代中国年轻女性的迁移：从农村到城市工厂》（博士论文）Juan Zhong, *Young Women's Migration in Modern China: From Rural Villages to Factories in Urban Cities*. Ph. D. Dissertation, Clark University (2014)

30. 《中华帝国晚期的纳妾和奴役》Hsieh Bao Hua, *Concubinage and Servitude in Late Imperial China*. Lexington Books (2014)

31. 《中国女性主义的诞生：跨国理论中的基本文本》Lydia H. Liu（刘禾）, Rebecca E. Karl（柯瑞佳）, Dorothy Ko（高彦颐）, *The Birth of Chinese Feminism: Essential Texts in Transnational Theory*. Columbia University Press (2013)

32. 《购买美貌：中国的整容手术》Wen Hua, *Buying Beauty: Cosmetic Surgery in China*. Hong Kong University Press (2013)

33. 《家妾：一个中国家族传奇》Amy S. Kwei, *A Concubine for the Family: A Family Saga in China*. TATS Publishing (2013)

34. 《妓女、妾与女性忠诚崇拜：中国的性别与社会变迁（1000—1400）》Beverly Bossler, *Courtesans, Concubines, and the Cult of Female Fidelity: Gender and Social Change in China, 1000—1400* (Harvard-Yenching Institute Monograph Series). Harvard University Asia Center (2013)

35. 《女性不可统治：从汉到辽的中国妃嫔》Keith McMahon, *Women Shall Not Rule: Imperial Wives and Concubines in China from Han to Liao*. Rowman & Littlefield Publishers (2013)

36. 《北京太太：中国首都的生活、欢笑与母性》Tania McCartney, *Beijing Tai Tai: Life, Laughter and Motherhood in China's Capital*. Exisle Publishing, Australia (2012)

37. 《不朽的女人：中国文明中"阴"的一面》Brian Griffith, *A Galaxy of Immortal Women: The Yin Side of Chinese Civilization*. Exterminating Angel Press (2012)

38. 《中国内地（大陆）、香港、台湾的失踪女孩和妇女：杀婴、强迫卖淫、政治监禁，"鬼新娘"、逃亡与抛弃"的社会学研究（1900—2000s）》Hua-Lun Huang, *The Missing Girls and Women of China, Hong Kong and Taiwan: A Sociological Study of*

Infanticide, Forced Prostitution, Political Imprisonment, "Ghost Brides," Runaways and Thrownaways, 1900—2000s. McFarland (2012)

39. 《市场与身体：女性、服务工作与中国不平等的形成》Eileen M. Otis, Markets and Bodies: Women, Service Work, and the Making of Inequality in China. Stanford University Press (2012)

40. 《寻找美女：中国和日本的美女文化史》Cho Kyo, Kyoko Iriye Selden, The Search for the Beautiful Woman: A Cultural History of Japanese and Chinese Beauty. Rowman & Littlefield Publishers (2012)

41. 《超越范例故事：中国历史上的女性传记》Joan Judge and Hu Ying, (eds.), Beyond Exemplar Tales: Women's Biography in Chinese History. University of California Press (2011)

42. 《征服朝代的女性：中国辽金的性别与身份》Linda Cooke Johnson, Women of the Conquest Dynasties: Gender and Identity in Liao and Jin China. University of Hawaii Press (2011)

43. 《贪得无厌的女人与过失的权威：唐代初期的性别与权力建设》（博士论文）Rebecca Esther Doran, Insatiable Women and Transgressive Authority: Constructions of Gender and Power in Early Tang China. Ph. D. Dissertation, Harvard University (2011)

44. 《中国女权主义的多维度》Ya-chen Chen, The Many Dimensions of Chinese Feminism (Breaking Feminist Waves). Palgrave Macmillan (2011)

45. 《记忆的性别：农村妇女和中国集体化历史》Gail Hershatter（贺萧）, The Gender of Memory: Rural Women and China's Collective Past. University of California Press (2011)

46. 《曾经的铁姑娘：后毛泽东时代中国文学女性随笔》Hui Wu, Once Iron Girls: Essays on Gender by Post-Mao Chinese Literary Women. Lexington Books (2010)

47. 《帝制早期的中国妇女》Bret Hinsch, Women in Early Imperial China. Rowman & Littlefield Publishers, Inc. (2010)

48. 《商人的女儿们：女性、商业与华南的地域文化》Helen F. Siu（萧凤霞）, Merchants' Daughters: Women, Commerce and Regional Culture in South China. Hong Kong University Press (2010)

49. 《自我赋权的故事：中华帝制晚期和20世纪早期之侦察女性弹词》（博士论文）Li Guo, Tales of Self Empowerment: Reconnoitering Women's Tanci in Late Imperial and Early Twentieth-Century China. Ph. D. Dissertation, University of Iowa (2010)

50. 《内闱与超越：明清女性作家》Grace Fong, Ellen Widmer, The Inner Quarters and Beyond: Women Writers from Ming Through Qing (Women and Gender in China Studies). Brill Academic Publishing (2010)

51. 《水中月的反思：用中国传统智慧治愈女性身心》Kanae Kinoshita, Xiaolan Zhao, Reflections of the Moon on Water: Healing Women's Bodies and Minds through Traditional Chinese Wisdom. Random House of Canada Vintage Canada (2010)

52. 《女性再生：中华帝国晚期的医学、隐喻与生育》Yi-Li Wu, Reproducing Women: Medicine, Metaphor, and Childbirth in Late Imperial China. University of California Press (2010)

53.《从远古时代至今的中国女性：西文书目研究》Robin D.S. Yates, *Women in China from Earliest Times to the Present: a Bibliography of Studies in Western Languages*. Brill (2009)

54.《打工女孩：从乡村到城市的变动中国》Leslie T. Chang（张彤禾）, *Factory Girls: From Village to City in a Changing China*. Spiegel & Grau (2008)

55.《历史宝筏：过去、西方与中国妇女问题》Joan Judge, *The Precious Raft of History: The Past, the West, and the Woman Question in China*. Stanford University Press (2008)

56.《妻子、母亲与红色威胁：保守派妇女与反共产主义十字军》Mary C. Brennan, *Wives, Mothers, and the Red Menace: Conservative Women and the Crusade against Communism*. University Press of Colorado (2008)

57.《中国侍女：媒体、道德和边界的文化政治》Wanning Sun, *Maid in China: Media, Morality, and the Cultural Politics of Boundaries*. Routledge (2008)

58.《自己即作者：中华帝国晚期的性别、代理和写作》Grace S. Fong, *Herself an Author: Gender, Agency, and Writing in Late Imperial China*. University of Hawai'i Press (2008)

59.《中国妇女与网络空间》Khun Eng Kuah-Pearce, *Chinese Women and the Cyberspace*. Amsterdam University Press (2008)

60.《性别、政治与民主：中国妇女参政权》Louise Edwards, *Gender, Politics, and Democracy: Women's Suffrage in China*. Stanford University Press (2008)

61.《中国妇女在漫长的20世纪》Gail Hershatter（贺萧）, *Women in China's Long Twentieth Century* (Global, Area, and International Archive). University of California Press (2007)

62.《女鬼：17世纪中国文学中的鬼魂与性别》Judith T. Zeitlin, *The Phantom Heroine: Ghosts and Gender in Seventheenth-century Chinese Literature*. University of Hawai'i Press (2007)

63.《中国城市的性别与工作：不幸的一代女工》Jieyu Liu, *Gender and Work in Urban China: Women Workers of the Unlucky Generation* (Routledge Contemporary China Series). Routledge (2007)

64.《文艺复兴时期女性百科：意大利、法国和英国》Edited by Diana Robin, Anne R. Larsen, Carole Levin, *Encyclopedia of Women in the Renaissance: Italy, France, and England*. ABC-CLIO (2007)

65.《中国妇女传记辞典：古代到隋（公元前1600—公元618年）》Lily Xiao Hong Lee, A. D. Stefanowska, Sue Wiles, *Biographical Dictionary of Chinese Women: Antiquity through SUI, 1600 B.C.E.-618 C.E.* M.E. Sharpe (2007)

66.《张家才女》Susan Mann, *The Talented Women of the Zhang Family*. University of California Press (2007)

67.《儒家与女性：一种哲学解读》Li-hsiang Lisa Rosenlee, *Confucianism And Women: A Philosophical Interpretation*. State University of New York (2006)

68.《英国殖民主义下的性别与社区：中国乡村的情感、斗争与政治》Siu Keung Cheung,

Gender and Community Under British Colonialism: Emotion, Struggle and Politics in a Chinese Village. Routledge (2006)

69. 《中国帝制时代的女性医学》Angela Ki Che Leung, *Medicine for Women in Imperial China*. Brill (2006)

70. 《儒家思想与妇女的哲学解读》Li-hsiang Lisa Rosenlee, *Confucianism and Women: A Philosophical Interpretation*. State University of New York (2006)

71. 《中国女性作家与女权主义的想象（1905—1948）》Yan Haiping, *Chinese Women Writers and the Feminist Imagination, 1905—1948*. Routledge (2006)

72. 《中国制造：全球工场之女工》Pun Ngai, *Made in China: Women Factory Workers in a Global Workplace*. Duke University Press and Hong Kong University Press (2005)

73. 《20世纪中国女性的文学女权主义》Amy D. Dooling, *Women's Literary Feminism in Twentieth Century China*. Palgrave Macmillan US (2005)

74. 《现代中国妇女、体育与社会：远超撑起半边天》Dong Jinxia, *Women, Sport and Society in Modern China: Holding up More than Half the Sky* (Sport in the Global Society). Frank Cass Publishers (2005)

75. 《金发美女张玛珠医生：战时名人生活》Judy Tzu-Chun Wu, *Doctor Mom Chung of the Fair-Haired Bastards: The Life of a Wartime Celebrity*. University of California Press (2005)

76. 《中国城市中的农村妇女：性别、迁移与社会变迁》Tamara Jacka, *Rural Women in Urban China: Gender, Migration, And Social Change* (East Gate Books). M E Sharpe Inc (2005)

77. 《灰姑娘姐妹：一部缠足的修正史》（中文译名：缠足："金莲崇拜"盛极而衰的演变）Dorothy Ko（高彦颐）, *Cinderella's Sisters: A Revisionist History of Footbinding*. University of California Press (2005)

78. 《现代中国的女性书写：革命年代（1936—1976）》Amy D. Dooling (ed.), *Writing Women in Modern China: The Revolutionary Years, 1936—1976*. Columbia University Press (2005)

79. 《中国女权主义中的妇女问题》Tani E Barlow, *The Question of Women in Chinese Feminism*. Duke University Press (2004)

80. 《亚洲妇女选举权：性别、民族主义与民主》Louise Edwards, *Women's Suffrage in Asia: Gender, Nationalism and Democracy*. Routledge (2004)

81. 《流动中：当代中国女性与农村向城市的迁移》Arianne M. Gaetano, Tamara Jacka, *On the Move: Women and Rural-to-Urban Migration in Contemporary China*. Columbia University Press (2004)

82. 《红色毛笔：中华帝国的女性书写》Wilt L. Idema, Beata Grant, *The Red Brush: Writing Women of Imperial China*. Harvard University Press (2004)

83. 《边缘拍摄：被遗忘的香港女导演唐书璇》Ching Yau（游静）, *Filming Margins: Tang Shu Shuen, A Forgotten Hong Kong Woman Director*. Hong Kong University Press (2004)

84. 《现代中国女性》Helen F. Snow, *Women in Modern China*. Foreign Languages Press, China (2004)

85. 《20世纪初中国小说中的新女性》Jin Feng, *The New Woman in Early Twentieth-Century Chinese Fiction* (Comparative Cultural Studies). Purdue University Press (2004)

86. 《女性与中、日、韩三国的儒家文化》Dorothy Ko（高彦颐）, JaHyun Kim Haboush, Joan R. Piggott (eds.), *Women and Confucian Cultures in Premodern China, Korea, and Japan*. University of California Press (2003)

87. 《斩首红龙：中国女性内丹史》（博士论文）Elena Valussi (Italy), *Beheading the Red Dragon: A History of Female Inner Alchemy in China*. Ph. D. Dissertation, University of London, SOAS (2003)

88. 《革命加爱情：20世纪中国小说中的文学史、女性身体与主题重复》Jianmei Liu, *Revolution Plus Love: Literary History, Women's Bodies, and Thematic Repetition in Twentieth-Century Chinese Fiction*. University of Hawai'i Press (2003)

89. 《中国好女人：隐藏的声音》Xinran（薛欣然）, *The Good Women of China: Hidden Voices*. Vintage (2003)

90. 《降低孕产妇死亡率：来自玻利维亚、中国、埃及、洪都拉斯、印度尼西亚、牙买加和津巴布韦的经验》A. Koblinsky Marjorie, *Reducing Maternal Mortality: Learning from Bolivia, China, Egypt, Honduras, Indonesia, Jamaica, and Zimbabwe* (Health, Nutrition and Population Series). The World Bank (2003)

91. 《中国女性与中国男性读本》Susan Brownell（包素姗）and Jeffrey N. Wasserstrom（华志坚）(eds.), *Chinese Femininities, Chinese Masculinities: A Reader*. University of California Press (2002)

92. 《中国女性主义面临全球化》Sharon Wesoky, *Chinese Feminism Faces Globalization*. Routledge (2002)

93. 《宋、元中国的女性财产和儒家反应（960—1368）》Bettine Birge, *Women, Property, and Confucian Reaction in Sung and Yuan China: 960—1368*. Cambridge University Press (2002)

94. 《中国女权主义面临全球化》Sharon Wesoky, *Chinese Feminism Faces Globalization* (East Asia: History, Politics, Sociology and Culture). Routledge (2002)

95. 《中国历史上的女性与家庭》Patricia Buckley Ebrey（伊沛霞）, *Women and the Family in Chinese History*. Routledge (2002)

96. 《我们中的一些人：成长于毛泽东时代的中国妇女》Xueping, Zhong, Zheng, Wang, Bai, Di, *Some of Us: Chinese Women Growing Up in the Mao Era*. Rutgers University Press (2001)

97. 《为美而痛：中国缠足》Ping Wang, *Aching for Beauty: Footbinding in China*. University of Minnesota Press (2000)

98. 《中国经济改革中的女性农民工》Feng Xu, *Women Migrant Workers in China's Economic Reform*. Palgrave Macmillan (2000)

99. 《中国妇女：经济与社会转型》Jackie West, Zhao Minghua, Chang Xiangqun, Cheng Yuan

(eds.), *Women of China: Economic and Social Transformation*. Palgrave Macmillan UK (1999)

100. 《中国启蒙运动中的女性：口头述和文本史》Zheng Wang, *Women in the Chinese Enlightenment: Oral and Textual Histories*. University of California Press (1999)

101. 《繁盛之阴：中国医学史中的性（960—1665）》Charlotte Furth（费侠莉）, *A Flourishing Yin: Gender in China's Medical History, 960—1665*. University of California Press (1999)

102. 《中国传统女性作家：诗歌与批评选集》Kang-i Sun Chang（孙康宜）, Haun Saussy, Charles Yim-tze Kwong, *Women Writers of Traditional China: An Anthology of Poetry and Criticism*. Stanford University Press (1999)

103. 《性别和华南奇迹：女工的两个世界》Ching Kwan Lee, *Gender and the South China Miracle: Two Worlds of Factory Women*. University of California Press (1998)

104. 《中国妇女研究指南》Gail Hershatter（贺萧）, *Guide to Women's Studies in China*. Institute of East Asian Studies, University of California, Berkeley, Center for Chinese Studies (1998)

105. 《中国农村妇女工作：改革时代的变化和连续性》Tamara Jacka, *Women's Work In Rural China: Change And Continuity In An Era Of Reform*. Cambridge University Press (1997)

106. 《中国的女性与性相：1949年以来的性别话语》Harriet Evans（艾华）, *Women and Sexuality in China: Dominant Discourses of Female Sexuality and Gender since 1949*. London: Blackwell (1997)

107. 《放脚：中国妇女在旧金山的社会史》Judy Yung, *Unbound Feet: A Social History Of Chinese Women In San Francisco*. University of California Press (1995)

108. 《鸿：三代中国女人的故事》Jung Chang（张戎）, *Wild Swans: Three Daughters of China*. Chivers Audio Books (1995)

109. 《造就中国革命：20世纪20年代的激进妇女、共产主义政治与群众运动》Christina Kelley Gilmartin, *Engendering the Chinese Revolution: Radical Women, Communist Politics, and Mass Movements in the 1920s*. University of California Press (1995)

110. 《闺塾师：17世纪中国妇女与文化》Dorothy Ko（高彦颐）, *Teachers of the Inner Chambers: Women and Culture in Seventeenth-Century China*. Stanford University Press (1994)

111. 《儒家女性的见证：聂曾纪芬夫人自传（1852—1942）》Thomas L. Kennedy, Micki Kennedy, *Testimony of a Confucian Woman: The Autobiography of Mrs. Nie Zeng Jifen, 1852—1942*. University of Georgia Press (1993)

112. 《姐妹们与陌生人：上海棉纱厂女工（1919—1949）》Emily Honig（韩起澜）, *Sisters and Strangers: Women in the Shanghai Cotton Mills, 1919—1949*. Stanford University Press (1992)

113. 《妇女与中国现代性：西方和东方之间的阅读政治》Rey Chow（周蕾）, *Woman and Chinese Modernity: The Politics of Reading between West and East*. University of Minnesota Press (1991)

114.《背阴盛放：中日绘画史上的女性》Marsha Weidner（魏玛莎）, *Flowering in the Shadows: Women in the History of Chinese and Japanese Painting*. University of Hawaii Press (1990)

115.《妾与奴仆的社会史》Maria Jaschok, *Concubines and Bondservants: A Social History*. Zed Books (1988)

116.《个人的声音：20世纪80年代的中国妇女》Emily Honig（韩起澜）, Gail Hershatter（贺萧）, *Personal Voices: Chinese Women in the 1980's*. Stanford University Press (1988)

117.《走向风暴：中国女性革命的奥德赛》Recounted by Yue Daiyun（乐黛云）; Written by Carolyn Wakeman, *To the Storm: The Odyssey of a Revolutionary Chinese Woman*. University of California Press (1985, 1987)

118.《延迟的革命：当代中国妇女》Margery Wolf, *Revolution Postponed: Women in Contemporary China*. Stanford University Press (1985)

119.《中国妇女、家庭和农民革命》Kay Ann Johnson, *Women, the Family, and Peasant Revolution in China*. The University of Chicago Press (1985)

120.《中国劳动妇女的生活》Mary Sheridan and Janet W. Salaff, *Lives: Chinese Working Women*. Indiana University Press (1984)

121.《中国的女权主义与社会主义》Elisabeth Croll, *Feminism and Socialism in China*. Routledge and Kegan Paul (1980)

122.《中国妇女解放》Claudie Broyelle, *Women's liberation in China*. Humanities Press (1977)

123.《妇女工作：革命中国的妇女与党》Delia Davin, *Woman-Work: Women and the Party in Revolutionary China*. Clarendon Press (1976)

124.《中国妇女的革命肖像》Agnes Smedley（史沫特莱）, *Portraits of Chinese Women in Revolution*. The Feminist Press (1976)

125.《中国社会中的女性》Margery Wolf and Roxane Witke, *Women in Chinese Society*. Stanford University Press (1975)

126.《汉家女儿：一位中国劳动妇女的自传》Ida Pruitt, from the story told her by Ning Lao T'ai-t'ai. *A Daughter of Han: The Autobiography of a Chinese Working Woman*. Yale University Press (1945)

127.《中国妇女的战时工作》*Women's Wartime Work in China*. The China Information Publishing Company (1940)

128.《近代中国著名女性》Margaret E. Burton, *Notable Women of Modern China*. Fleming H. Revell Company (1912)

129.《中华女儿：晚清帝国家庭生活素描》Eliza Jane Gillett Bridgman, *Daughters of China: Or the Sketches of Domestic Life in the Celestial Empire*. Robert Carter and Brothers (1853)

7.4　男性

1.《大都会梦想：全球化时代的跨国华人男子气概》(Transnational Asian masculinities.

Hong Kong scholarship online.) Derek Hird, Geng Song (eds.), *The Cosmopolitan Dream: Transnational Chinese Masculinities in a Global Age*. Hong Kong University Press (2018)

2. 《优质：中国精子库的常规化》Ayo Wahlberg, *Good Quality: The Routinization of Sperm Banking in China*. University of California Press (2018)

3. 《中国父亲、性别与家庭：父亲使命》Mario Liong, *Chinese Fatherhood, Gender and Family: Father Mission*. Palgrave Macmillan UK (2017)

4. 《中国家庭的父权、青春期与性别》Qiong Xu, *Fatherhood, Adolescence and Gender in Chinese Families* (Palgrave Macmillan Studies in Family and Intimate Life). Palgrave Macmillan UK (2016)

5. 《世界全球化中的中国男子气概》(Routledge Culture, Society, Business in East Asia) Kam Louie, *Chinese Masculinities in a Globalizing World*. Routledge (2015)

6. 《当代中国的男性和男人气概》Geng Song, Derek Hird, *Men and Masculinities in Contemporary China*. Brill (2014)

7. 《中国变性人》Howard Chiang (eds.), *Transgender China*. Palgrave Macmillan US (2012)

8. 《中国帝制晚期的男性气概》Martin W. Huang, *Negotiating Masculinities in Late Imperial China*. University of Hawai'i Press (2006)

9. 《男性焦虑与女性贞洁：明清时代中国伦理价值观的比较研究》T'ien Ju-K'ang, *Male Anxiety and Female Chastity: A Comparative Study of Chinese Ethical Values in Ming-Ch'ing Times*. Brill (1988)

7.5　性别

1. 《泪水与欢颜背后：中国服务业的性别与移民》(New Perspectives on Chinese Politics and Society) Yang Shen（沈洋）, *Beyond Tears and Laughter: Gender, Migration, and the Service Sector in China*. Springer Singapore: Palgrave Macmillan (2019)

2. 《跨越性别中国：跨阴阳、跨文化、超越京剧》Huai Bao, *Cross-Gender China: Across Yin-Yang, Across Cultures, and Beyond Jingju* (Routledge Advances in Theatre & Performance Studies). Routledge (2017)

3. 《回顾性别不平等：来自中华人民共和国的视角》Qi Wang, Min Dongchao, Bo Ærenlund Sørensen (eds.), *Revisiting Gender Inequality: Perspectives from the People's Republic of China*. Palgrave Macmillan US (2016)

4. 《重新审视性别不平等：来自中华人民共和国的视角》Qi Wang, Min Dongchao, Bo Ærenlund Sørensen (eds.), *Revisiting Gender Inequality: Perspectives from the People's Republic of China* (Comparative Feminist Studies Series). Palgrave Macmillan US (2016)

5. 《20世纪初中国文学与文化中的性别与主体性》Ping Zhu, *Gender and Subjectivities in Early Twentieth-Century Chinese Literature and Culture*. Palgrave Macmillan US (2015)

6. 《性别话语：中国农村变化中的情感与表达》Fei-wen Liu, *Gendered Words: Sentiments*

and Expression in Changing Rural China. Oxford University Press (2015)

7. 《中国性别政策和艾滋病：促进政策变革》Dudley L. Poston, Joseph Tucker, Qiang Ren, Baochang Gu, Xiaoying Zheng, Stephanie Wang, Chris Russell (eds.), Gender Policy and HIV in China: Catalyzing Policy Change. Springer Netherlands (2009)

8. 《变动中的性别：帝制晚期与近代中国的劳动分工与文化变迁》Bryna Goodman, Wendy Larson, Gender in Motion: Divisions of Labor and Cultural Change in Late Imperial and Modern China. Rowman & Littlefield Publishers (2005)

9. 《筷子成双才能用：中国西南拉祜族的性别统一与性别平等》Shanshan Du, Chopsticks Only Work in Pairs: Gender Unity & Gender Equality Among the Lahu of Southwest China. Columbia University Press (2003)

10. 《中华帝制晚期的性别、法律和社会》Matthew Sommer, Sex, Law, and Society in Late Imperial China (Law, Society, and Culture in China). Stanford University Press (2002)

11. 《其他现代性：后社会主义中国的性别渴望》Lisa Rofel, Other Modernities: Gendered Yearnings in China after Socialism. University of California Press (1999)

7.6　性文化

1. 《中国的商业性景观：对亲密、阳刚之气和刑事司法的反思》Eileen Yuk Tsang, China's Commercial Sexscapes: Rethinking Intimacy, Masculinity, and Criminal Justice. University of Toronto Press (2019)

2. 《中国的性：权力和愉悦的历史》Howard Chiang, Sexuality in China: Histories of Power and Pleasure. University of Washington Press (2018)

3. 《太监之后：科学、医学与近代中国的性别转变》Howard Chiang, After Eunuchs: Science, Medicine, and the Transformation of Sex in Modern China. Columbia University Press (2018)

4. 《中国企业中的性别、性与权力：美女在工作》Liu Jieyu, Gender, Sexuality and Power in Chinese Companies: Beauties at Work. Palgrave Macmillan (2017)

5. 《北美和中国的性工作者与定罪：排斥制度中的伦理和法律问题》Susan Dewey, Tiantian Zheng, Treena Orchard, Sex Workers and Criminalization in North America and China: Ethical and Legal Issues in Exclusionary Regimes. Springer International Publishing (2016)

6. 《情色按摩：道教士的性感秘密》Wang-puh Wei, Chris Evans, Erotic Chinese Massage: The Sexy Secrets of Taoist Teachers. Skyhorse Publishing (2015)

7. 《阳痿流行：当代中国的男性药物和性欲》Everett Yuehong Zhang, The Impotence Epidemic: Men's Medicine and Sexual Desire in Contemporary China. Duke University Press Books (2015)

8. 《规范中国卖淫：性别与地方政权建设（1900—1937）》Elizabeth Remick, Regulating Prostitution in China: Gender and Local Statebuilding, 1900—1937. Stanford University Press (2014)

9. 《妓女、妾与女性忠贞崇拜》Beverly Bossler, *Courtesans, Concubines, and the Cult of Female Fidelity*. Harvard University Asia Center (2013)

10. 《关于中国性工作合法化：HIV与病人权利》Jinmei Meng, *On the Decriminalization of Sex Work in China: HIV and Patients' Rights*.Palgrave Macmillan US (2013)

11. 《红门背后：中国的性》Richard Burger, *Behind the Red Door: Sex in China*. Earnshaw Books (2012)

12. 《黄帝基本问题中的性别：中国早期的性、长寿和医学》Jessieca Leo, *Sex in the Yellow Emperor's Basic Questions: Sex, Longevity, and Medicine in Early China*.Three Pines Press (2011)

13. 《现代中国的性别与性》Susan L. Mann, *Gender and Sexuality in Modern Chinese History*. Cambridge University Press (2011)

14. 《毛主义模范剧院：中国"文化大革命"中的性别与性符号学》Rosemary A. Roberts, *Maoist Model Theatre: The Semiotics of Gender and Sexuality in the Chinese Cultural Revolution*. Brill (2010)

15. 《一夫多妻与升华的激情：中国现代性边缘的性》Keith McMahon, *Polygamy and Sublime Passion: Sexuality in China on the Verge of Modernity*. University of Hawai'i Press (2010)

16. 《红灯区：后社会主义中国性工作者的生活》Tiantian Zheng, *Red Lights: The Lives of Sex Workers in Postsocialist China*. University of Minnesota Press (2009)

17. 《歌妓与唐宋词》（硕士学位论文）Tse Wai Lok, *Female Singers and the Ci Poems of the Tang and Song Periods*. The University of Hong Kong (2007)

18. 《渴望的中国：新自由主义、性和公共文化的实验》Lisa Rofel, *Desiring China: Experiments in Neoliberalism, Sexuality, and Public Culture*. Duke University Press Books (2007)

19. 《亚洲春药：从曼谷到北京，寻找终极刺激》Jerry Hopkins, *Asian Aphrodisiacs: From Bangkok to Beijing: The Search for the Ultimate Turn-on*.Periplus Editions (2007)

20. 《中国的性与性别》Elaine Jeffreys, *Sex and Sexuality in China*.Routledge (2006)

21. 《中国之性占星学：性幻觉的东方秘密》Shelly Wu, *Chinese Sexual Astrology: Eastern Secrets to Mind-Blowing Sex*. New Page Books (2006)

22. 《不光彩之事：18世纪中国的贞洁观与政治》Janet M. Theiss, *Disgraceful Matters: The Politics of Chastity in Eighteenth-Century China*.University of California Press (2005)

23. 《帝制晚期中国的同性恋情结》Wu Cuncun, *Homoerotic Sensibilities in Late Imperial China*.RoutledgeCurzon (2004)

24. 《中国、性与卖淫的故事》Elaine Jeffreys, *China, Sex and Prostitution: Telling Tales*. Routledgecurzon (2004)

25. 《秘戏图考》Robert Hans Van Gulik（高罗佩）, *Erotic Colour Prints of the Ming Period: With an Essay on Chinese Sex Life from the Han to the Ching Dynasty, B.C. 206-A.D. 1644* Brill Academic Pub (2004)

26. 《中国古代房内考：中国的性与社会的初步考察（公元前1500年至公元1644年）》

Robert Hans van Gulik（高罗佩）, *Sexual Life in Ancient China: A Preliminary Survey of Chinese Sex and Society from ca. 1500 B.C. till 1644 A.D.* (Sinica Leidensia 57). Brill (2003)

27. 《中国古代性文化》Paul Rakita Goldin, *The Culture of Sex in Ancient China*. University of Hawai'i Press (2001)

28. 《坚强不屈的女人：19世纪旧金山的中国妓女》Benson Tong, *Unsubmissive Women: Chinese Prostitutes in Nineteenth-century San Francisco*. University of Oklahoma Press (2000)

29. 《危险的愉悦：20世纪上海的娼妓问题与现代性》Gail Hershatter（贺萧）, *Dangerous Pleasures: Prostitution and Modernity in Twentieth-Century Shanghai*. University of California Press (1999)

30. 《道教瑜伽：中国古代大师的性教育》Lu Kuan (Charles Luk) Yu, *Taoist Yoga: The Sexual Teachings of the Ancient Chinese Masters*. Ebury Publishing: Rider (1996)

31. 《性、文化与现代化：民国时期的医学与性控制》Frank Dikotter, *Sex, Culture and Modernity in Modern China: Medical Science and the Construction of Racial Identities in the Early Republican Period*. Hurst: Hong Kong University Press (1995)

32. 《20世纪中国文学与社会中的性别与性》Tonglin Lu, *Gender and Sexuality in Twentieth-Century Chinese Literature and Society*. State University of New York Press (1993)

33. 《卧房的艺术：中国性感瑜伽经典，包括女性个人冥想文本》Douglas Wile, *Art of the Bedchamber: The Chinese Sexual Yoga Classics Including Women's Solo Meditation Texts*. State University of New York Press (1992)

34. 《性事：中国文化中的性学研究》Fang Fu Ruan, *Sex in China: Studies in Sexology in Chinese Culture*. Springer US (1991)

35. 《阴阳之道：中国古代的迷幻之道》Jolan Chang, *The Tao of Love and Sex: The Ancient Chinese Way to Ecstasy*. Dutton (1977)

7.7 人口

1. 《中国和印度的女性稀缺与人口过剩：宏观人口统计与地方动态》Sharada Srinivasan, Shuzhuo Li (eds.), *Scarce Women and Surplus Men in China and India: Macro Demographics versus Local Dynamics* (Demographic Transformation and Socio-Economic Development 8). Springer International Publishing (2018)

2. 《中国人口老龄化与"中等收入陷阱"风险》Xueyuan Tian (eds.), *China's Population Aging and the Risk of 'Middle-income Trap'* (Research Series on the Chinese Dream and China's Development Path). Springer Singapore (2017)

3. 《贩卖人口：华北地区的贩卖者和家庭生活》Johanna S. Ransmeier, *Sold People: Traffickers and Family Life in North China*. Harvard University Press (2017)

4. 《中国、印度和印度尼西亚的当代人口变化》Christophe Z. Guilmoto, Gavin W. Jones (eds.), *Contemporary Demographic Transformations in China, India and Indonesia*. Springer

International Publishing (2016)

5. 《中国人口流动、城市规划与管理》Tai-Chee Wong, Sun Sheng Han, Hongmei Zhang (eds.), *Population Mobility, Urban Planning and Management in China*. Springer International Publishing (2015)

6. 《中国人口分析：新人口时代的社会变迁》Isabelle Attané, Baochang Gu (eds.), *Analysing China's Population: Social Change in a New Demographic Era*. Springer Netherlands (2014)

7. 《人口大国的希望：中国人口转型的理论与实践》Xueyuan Tian, *The Hope of the Country with a Large Population: Theories and Practices of China's Population Transformation*. Springer-Verlag Berlin Heidelberg (2014)

8. 《中国人口男性化：希望有个儿子》Isabelle Attané, *The Demographic Masculinization of China: Hoping for a Son*. Springer International Publishing Switzerland (2013)

9. 《培育世界公民：中国崛起中的人口》Susan Greenhalgh（葛苏珊）, *Cultivating Global Citizens: Population in the Rise of China*. Harvard University Press (2010)

10. 《近代中国的黑人》Don J. Wyatt, *The Blacks of Premodern China*. University of Pennsylvania Press (2010)

11. 《培育全球公民：中国崛起中的人口》Susan Greenhalgh, *Cultivating Global Citizens: Population in the Rise of China* (Edwin O. Reischauer Lectures, 2008). Harvard University Press (2010)

12. 《只生一个好：邓小平时代的科学与政策》Susan Greenhalgh（葛苏珊）, *Just One Child: Science and Policy in Deng's China*. University of California Press (2008)

13. 《转型与挑战：21世纪初的中国人口》Zhongwei Zhao, Fei Guo, *Transition and Challenge: China's Population at the Beginning of the 21st Century*. Oxford University Press, USA (2007)

14. 《中国的生育能力、计划生育和人口控制》Dudley Poston, *Fertility, Family Planning and Population Control in China*. Routledge Studies in Asias Transformations. Routledge (2006)

15. 《真实中国：中华人民共和国的人们》Sang Ye（桑晔）, Miriam Lang, Geremie Randall Barmé, *China Candid: The People on the People's Republic*. University of California Press (2006)

16. 《中国人口治理：从列宁主义到新自由主义的生物政治学》Susan Greenhalgh（葛苏珊）, Edwin Winckler, *Governing China's Population: From Leninist to Neoliberal Biopolitics*. Stanford University Press (2005)

17. 《人口增长与风景变化：来自印度、中国和美国的研究》Indian National Science Academy, Chinese Academy of Sciences, *Growing Populations, Changing Landscapes: Studies from India, China, and the United States*. National Academies Press (2001)

18. 《中国农村的命运与财富：辽宁的社会组织与人口行为（1774—1873）》James Z. Lee, Cameron D. Campbell, *Fate and Fortune in Rural China: Social Organization and Population Behavior in Liaoning 1774—1873*. Cambridge University Press (1997)

19. 《现代中国人口》Li Muzhen (auth.), Dudley L. Poston Jr., David Yaukey (eds.), *The

Population of Modern China. Springer US (1992)

20.《中国饥荒（1959—1961）：人口与社会影响》Penny Kane, *Famine in China, 1959—61: Demographic and Social Implications.* Palgrave Macmillan UK (1988)

21.《中国历史人口学（公元2—1982年）》Hans Bielenstein, *Chinese Historical Demography (AD 2—1982)* (Bulletin of the Museum of Far Eastern Antiquities 59). Elanders (1987)

22.《中国人口的急剧变化（1952—1982）》Ansley J. Coale, *Rapid Population Change in China, 1952—1982.* National Academies Press (1984)

23.《中国人口研究（1368—1953）》Ping-ti Ho（何炳棣）, *Studies on the Population of China, 1368—1953.* Harvard University Press (1959)

7.8 老龄、保健

1.《老龄福利与社会政策：中国与北欧国家的比较研究》(International Perspectives on Aging 20) Tian-kui Jing, Stein Kuhnle, Yi Pan, Sheying Chen, *Aging Welfare and Social Policy: China and the Nordic Countries in Comparative Perspective.* Springer Interna (2019)

2.《中国农村养老、代际关系与社会变迁》Fang Cao, *Elderly Care, Intergenerational Relationships and Social Change in Rural China.* Springer Singapore, Palgrave Macmillan (2019)

3.《中国老年人保障与全程护理制度的发展》Yanzhong Wang (eds.), *The Development of Security and Whole Care System for the Aged in China.* Springer Singapore (2018)

4.《中国养老融资年度报告（2017）》Keyong Dong, Yudong Yao (eds.), *Annual Report on Financing Old Age Care in China (2017).* Social Sciences Academic Press and Springer Nature Singapore Pte Ltd. (2018)

5.《当代中国的老年人看护演变：两代人与一项决定》Lin Chen, *Evolving Eldercare in Contemporary China: Two Generations, One Decision.* Palgrave Macmillan US (2016)

6.《中国老年人的精神健康：概念化、测量和干预》Vivian W. Q. Lou, *Spiritual Well-Being of Chinese Older Adults: Conceptualization, Measurement and Intervention.* Springer-Verlag Berlin (2015)

7.《中国11世纪的卫生保健》Nathan Sivin, *Health Care in Eleventh-Century China.* Springer (2015)

8.《中国健康慈善事业》Jennifer Ryan, Lincoln C. Chen, Anthony J. Saich, *Philanthropy for Health in China.* Indiana University Press (2014)

9.《中国老龄化：对转型期经济国家的社会政策影响》Sheying Chen, Jason L. Powell (eds.), *Aging in China: Implications to Social Policy of a Changing Economic State.* Springer (2012)

10.《当代中国保健治理》Yanzhong Huang, *Governing Health in Contemporary China.* Routledge (2012)

11.《中国长寿资料手册》Livia Kohn, *A Sourcebook in Chinese Longevity.* Three Pine Press (2012)

12.《77种改善健康的方法：如何运用中国古代智慧来提高你的身心健康》Angela Hicks,

77 Ways to Improve Your Wellbeing: How to Use Ancient Chinese Wisdom to Enhance Your Physical, Mental and Spiritual Health. Spring Hill How to Books (2009)

13. 《中国的健康长寿：人口、社会经济和心理层面》Zeng Yi, Dudley L. Poston Jr, Denese Ashbaugh Vlosky, Danan Gu (eds.), *Healthy Longevity in China: Demographic, Socioeconomic, and Psychological Dimensions.* Springer Netherlands (2008)

14. 《中国传统健康秘诀：和谐生活基本指南》Xu Xiangcai, *Traditional Chinese Health Secrets: The Essential Guide to Harmonious Living.* YMAA Publication Center (2001)

15. 《中国医疗保健问题与选择》World Bank, Financing *Health Care Issues and Options for China.* World Bank Publications (1997)

7.9　就业、阶层与移民

1. 《中国城乡移民与政策干预》Li Sun, *Rural Urban Migration and Policy Intervention in China.* Springer Singapore: Palgrave Macmillan (2019)

2. 《中国国内和国际移民发展》(International Talent Development in China) Huiyao Wang（王辉耀）, Lu Miao, *China's Domestic and International Migration Development.* Springer Singapore (2019)

3. 《运动中的公民：跨越中国国界的出境、移民和再迁移》Elaine Lynn Ho, *Citizens in Motion: Emigration, Immigration, and Re-Migration Across China's Borders.* Stanford University Press (2018)

4. 《中国中产阶级的形成：小舒适与大期望》Jean-Louis Rocca, *The Making of the Chinese Middle Class: Small Comfort and Great Expectations.* Palgrave Macmillan US (2017)

5. 《中国民工》Pun Ngai, *Migrant Labor in China* (China Today). Polity (2015)

6. 《劳动收入份额：理解中国收入不平等的另一个关键》Minghai Zhou, *Labor's Share of Income: Another Key to Understand China's Income Inequality.* Springer Singapore (2016)

7. 《技术移民、期望与现实：中国专业人才与全球劳动力市场》Ying Lu, Ramanie Samaratunge, Charmine E.J. Härtel, *Skilled Migration, Expectation and Reality: Chinese Professionals and the Global Labour Market.* Gower (2015)

8. 《中国和亚洲移民：经验与政策》Jijiao Zhang, Howard Duncan (eds.), *Migration in China and Asia: Experience and Policy* (International Perspectives on Migration 10). Springer Netherlands (2014)

9. 《中国农村劳动力流动、歧视和新型双重劳动力市场》Guifu Chen, Shigeyuki Hamori, *Rural Labor Migration, Discrimination, and the New Dual Labor Market in China.* Springer-Verlag Berlin Heidelberg (2014)

10. 《庶民中国：农村移民、媒体与文化实践》Wanning Sun, *Subaltern China: Rural Migrants, Media, and Cultural Practices* (Asia Pacific Perspectives). Rowman & Littlefield Publishers (2014)

11.《当代中国的阶层》David S. G. Goodman, *Class in Contemporary* China (China Today). Polity (2014)

12.《中国中产阶级：身份与行为》Minglu Chen, David S. G. Goodman (eds.), *Middle Class China: Identity and Behaviour* (CSC China Perspectives series). Edward Elgar Pub (2013)

13.《中国的性别、现代性和男性农民工：成为"现代"人》Xiaodong Lin, *Gender, Modernity and Male Migrant Workers in China: Becoming a "Modern" Man*. Routledge (2013)

14.《吃苦：中国城市移民前沿的故事》Michelle Dammon Loyalka, *Eating Bitterness: Stories from the Frontline of China's Urban Migration*. University of California Press (2012)

15.《中国十亿城市人：人类历史上最大迁移背后的故事》Tom Miller, *China's Urban Billion: The Story Behind the Biggest Migration in Human History*. Zed Books Ltd. (2012)

16.《散沙：中国农民工的故事》Hsiao-Hung Pai, *Scattered Sand: The Story of China's Rural Migrants*. Verso (2012)

17.《中国的移居和社会保护》Ingrid Nielsen, *Migration and Social Protection in China*. World Scientific Publishing Company (2008)

18.《新主人和新仆人：中国的迁移、发展与女工》Hairong Yan, *New Masters, New Servants: Migration, Development, and Women Workers in China*. Duke University Press Books (2008)

19.《中国新富人：未来统治者和目前生活》David Goodman, *The New Rich in China: Future Rulers, Present Lives*. Routledge (2008)

20.《中国城市失业、不平等与贫困》Shi Li, Hiroshi Sato, *Unemployment, Inequality and Poverty in Urban China* (Routledge Studies on the Chinese Economy). Routledge (2006)

21.《超越边界的社区：北京"浙江村"的生活史》Biao Xiang, *Transcending Boundaries: Zhejiangcun: The Story of a Migrant Village in Beijing* (China Studies). Koninklijke Brill NV, Leiden, The Netherlands (2005)

22.《中国改革中的国家与下岗职工：被裁员者的沉默和集体行动》Yongshun Cai, *State and Laid-Off Workers in Reform China: The Silence and Collective Action of the Retrenched*. Routledge (2005)

23.《中国的分离生活：人类学考察》Charle Stafford, *Living with Separation in China: Anthropological Accounts*. RoutledgeCurzon (2003)

24.《农民工如何改变中国农村》Rachel Murphy, *How Migrant Labor is Changing Rural China*. Cambridge University Press (2002)

25.《劳工改革的悖论：从社会主义到市场的中国劳工理论与实践》Luigi Tomba, *Paradoxes of Labour Reform: Chinese Labour Theory and Practice from Socialism to Market*. Honolulu, Hawai'i: University of Hawai'i Press (2002)

26.《当代中国的内部移民》Delia Davin, *Internal Migration in Contemporary China*. Palgrave Macmillan UK (1999)

7.10 贫困

1. 《中国扶贫开发政策的演变（2001—2015）》(Research Series on the Chinese Dream and China's Development Path) Changsheng Zuo, *The Evolution of China's Poverty Alleviation and Development Policy (2001—2015)*. Springer Singapore (2019)

2. 《福利、工作与贫困：中国的社会救助》Qin Gao, *Welfare, Work And Poverty: Social Assistance in China*. Oxford University Press (2017)

3. 《中国扶贫：理论与实证研究》Kun Yan, *Poverty Alleviation in China: A Theoretical and Empirical Study*. Springer-Verlag Berlin Heidelberg (2016)

4. 《中国如何摆脱贫困陷阱》Yuen Yuen Ang, *How China Escaped the Poverty Trap* (Cornell Studies in Political Economy). Cornell University Press (2016)

5. 《中国经济发展代价：权力、资本和权利贫困》Zhaohui Hong, *The Price of China's Economic Development: Power, Capital, and the Poverty of Rights* (Asian In The New Millennium). University Press of Kentucky (2015)

6. 《中国扶贫投资与民营经济：光彩事业的探索》Lin Wang, *Poverty Alleviation Investment and Private Economy in China: An Exploration of The Guangcai Programme*. Springer-Verlag Berlin Heidelberg (2014)

7. 《中国增长质量与减贫》Xiaolin Wang, Limin Wang, Yan Wang, *The Quality of Growth and Poverty Reduction in China* (International Research on Poverty Reduction). Springer-Verlag Berlin Heidelberg (2014)

8. 《人的幽灵：中国东北的城市贫困》Mun Young Cho, *The Specter of the People: Urban Poverty in Northeast China*. Cornell University Press (2013)

9. 《穷困之罪：中国的城市贫民（1900—1953）》Janet Y. Chen, *Guilty of Indigence: the Urban Poor in China, 1900—1953*. Princeton University Press (2012)

10. 《中国农村扶贫与可持续发展》Edited by Zheng Yisheng, *Poverty Reduction and Sustainable Development in Rural China* (Social Scientific Studies in Reform Era China). Brill (2011)

11. 《中国城市贫困》Fulong Wu, Chris Webster, Shenjing He and Yuting Liu, *Urban Poverty in China*. Edward Elgar Publishing Limited (2010)

12. 《中国城市边缘化的比较视角》Fulong Wu, Chris Webster (eds.), *Marginalization in Urban China: Comparative Perspectives* (International Political Economy Series). Palgrave Macmillan UK (2010)

13. 《中华人民共和国贫困地区农村金融：平衡政府和市场》Asian Development Bank, *Rural Finance in Poverty-stricken Areas in the People's Republic of China: Balancing Government and Market* (International Atomic Energy Agency Tecdoc). Intl Atomic Energy Agency (2010)

14. 《面对中国歧视与不平等：中国和加拿大视角》Errol P. Mendes, Sakunthala Srighanthan, *Confronting Discrimination and Inequality in China: Chinese and Canadian Perspectives*.

University of Ottawa Press (2009)

15. 《后社会主义中国的财富创造与贫困形成》Deborah Davis, Wang Feng, *Creating Wealth and Poverty in Postsocialist China*. Stanford University Press (2009)

16. 《了解中国不平等与贫困：方法和应用》Guanghua Wan (eds.), *Understanding Inequality and Poverty in China: Methods and Applications* (Studies in Development Economics and Policy). Palgrave Macmillan UK (2008)

17. 《现代中国的不平等与发展》Guanghua Wan, *Inequality and Growth in Modern China*. Oxford University Press (2008)

18. 《中国的不平等与公共政策》Björn A. Gustafsson, Li Shi, Terry Sicular, *Inequality and Public Policy in China*. Cambridge University Press (2008)

19. 《兄弟间的不平等：华南的阶层与亲属关系》Rubie S. Watson, *Inequality Among Brothers: Class and Kinship in South China* (Cambridge Studies in Social and Cultural Anthropology). Cambridge University Press (2007)

20. 《中国进步的代价：公共财政、人类福利与不平等的变化模式》Vivienne Shue（许慧文）, Christine Wong (Eds.), *Paying for Progress in China: Public Finance, Human Welfare and Changing Patterns of Inequality*. Routledge (2007)

21. 《中国的收入差距：经合组织的视角》Organisation for Economic Co-Operation and Development, *Income Disparities In China: An OECD Perspective* (China in the Global Economy). OECD publications (2004)

22. 《中国的城市贫困、住房与社会变迁》Ya Ping Wang, *Urban Poverty, Housing and Social Change in China* (Housing and Society). Routledge (2004)

23. 《中国贫困地区：城乡迁移、贫困、经济改革与城市化》Mei Zhang, *China's Poor Regions: Rural-Urban Migration, Poverty, Economic Reform and Urbanisation* (Routledgecurzon Studies on the Chinese Economy). Routledgecurzon (2003)

24. 《全球化时代中国的不平等与贫困》Azizur Rahman Khan, Carl Riskin, *Inequality and Poverty in China in the Age of Globalization*. Oxford University Press (2001)

7.11 社会生活/社会学

1. 《转型期的中国社会福利》(Sociology, Media and Journalism in China) Keqing Han, *Social Welfare in Transitional China*. Springer Singapore: Palgrave Macmillan (2020)

2. 《嵌入过程中的实体与结构：政企关系变迁的社会学分析》(Social Development Experiences in China) Qingong Wei, Hanlin Li, *Entities and Structures in the Embedding Process: A Sociological Analysis of Changes in the Government-enterprise Relations*. Springer Singapore (2019)

3. 《红色天空下：中国三代人的生活、失落与希望》Karoline Kan, *Under Red Skies: Three Generations of Life, Loss, and Hope in China*. Hachette Books (2019)

4. 《当代中国社会心态》(Research Series on the Chinese Dream and China's Development

Path) Yiyin Yang, Social Mentality in Contemporary China. Springer Singapore (2019)

5. 《中国普通民众的日常生活（1850—1950）：了解抄本文化》Ronald Suleski（薛龙），*Daily Life for the Common People of China, 1850 to 1950: Understanding Chaoben Culture*. Brill (2018)

6. 《中国社会学：国家建构与全球流通知识的制度化》Hon Fai Chen, *Chinese Sociology: State-Building and the Institutionalization of Globally Circulated Knowledge* (Sociology Transformed). Palgrave Macmillan UK (2018)

7. 《走向全民保障社会：近代中国社会保障转型简史》Jia Hui, Hong Zhou, *Towards a Society with Social Protection for All: A Concise History of Social Security Transformation in Modern China* (China Insights). Springer Nature (2017)

8. 《中国社会保障：论中国公平分配的可能性》Yanzhong Wang, *Social Security in China: On the Possibility of Equitable Distribution in the Middle Kingdom* (Research Series on the Chinese Dream and China's Development Path). Springer Singapore (2017)

9. 《中国关系、社会资本与学校选择：仪式资本的兴起》Ji Ruan (auth.), *Guanxi, Social Capital and School Choice in China: The Rise of Ritual Capital*. Palgrave Macmillan (2017)

10. 《中国古代和中世纪的不良行为》N. Harry Rothschild, Leslie V. Wallace, *Behaving Badly in Early and Medieval China*. University of Hawai'i Press (2017)

11. 《当代中国大变迁与社会治理》Peilin Li (eds.), *Great Changes and Social Governance in Contemporary China*. Springer-Verlag Berlin Heidelberg (2016)

12. 《理解中国社会（第二版）》Xiaowei Zang（臧小伟），*Understanding Chinese Society* (Second edition). Routledge (2016)

13. 《中国城市犯罪与社会混乱：三个广州社区案例研究》Haiyan Xiong, *Urban Crime and Social Disorganization in China: A Case Study of Three Communities in Guangzhou*. Springer Singapore (2016)

14. 《现代中国社会学》Gregory Elliott, Jean-Louis Rocca, *A Sociology of Modern China* (Comparative politics and international studies series). Oxford University Press (2015)

15. 《中国社会福利：第三个转折点》Joe C. B. Leung, Yuebin Xu, *China's Social Welfare: The Third Turning Point*. Polity Press (2015)

16. 《中国社会问题：性别、种族、劳动和环境》Sheying Chen, Zhidong Hao, *Social Issues in China: Gender, Ethnicity, Labor, and the Environment*. Springer-Verlag New York (2014)

17. 《当代中国社会变迁》Tamara Jacka, *Contemporary China: Society and Social Change*. Cambridge University Press (2013)

18. 《中国养老金制度的愿景》Mark C. Dorfman, Robert Holzmann, Philip O'Keefe, Dewen Wang, Yvonne Sin, Richard Hinz, *China's Pension System: A Vision*. World Bank Publications (2013)

19. 《当代中国民生：变迁、挑战与展望》Peilin Li, *People's Livelihood in Contemporary China: Changes, Challenges and Prospects* (Series on Chinese Economics Research 6). World Scientific

(2013)

20. 《社区服务的动态配置》Li Qi, Hai Jin, *Dynamic Provisioning for Community Services*. Springer-Verlag Berlin Heidelberg (2013)

21. 《闲话：传统中国的八卦与轶事》(New Perspectives on Chinese Culture and Society) Jack W. Chen, David Schaberg, *Idle Talk: Gossip and Anecdote in Traditional China*. University of California Press (2013)

22. 《通过中国和蒙古以社区为基础的牧场管理恢复社区与土地建设弹性联系》María Edith Fernández-Giménez; et al, *Restoring Community Connections to the Land Building Resilience through Community-based Rangeland Management in China and Mongolia*. CABI (2012)

23. 《国家根源：北京和台北的社区组织与社交网络》Benjamin Read, *Roots of the State: Neighborhood Organizations and Social Networks in Beijing and Taipei*. Palo Alto: Stanford University Press (2012)

24. 《变动的中国混合福利：本地视角》Beatriz Carrillo Garcia, Jane Duckett, *China's Changing Welfare Mix: Local Perspectives*. Routledge (2011)

25. 《中国生活与文学中的幽默：古典与传统方法》Jocelyn Chey, Jessica Milner Davis (eds.), *Humour in Chinese Life and Letters: Classical and Traditional Approaches*. Hong Kong University Press (2011)

26. 《中国城市的休闲与权力：一个中国城市的日常生活》Unn Målfrid Rolandsen, *Leisure and Power in Urban China: Everyday Life in a Chinese City*. Routledge (2011)

27. 《烧钱：中国生活世界的物质精神》C. Fred Blake（柏桦）, *Burning Money: The Material Spirit of the Chinese Lifeworld*. University of Hawai'i Press (2011)

28. 《中国社会的复兴：新社会行动主义》You-tien Hsing（邢幼田）, Ching Kwan Lee, *Reclaiming Chinese Society: The New Social Activism*. Routledge (2010)

29. 《iChina：现代中国社会个体的兴起》Mette Halskov Hansen, Rune Svarverud, *iChina: The Rise of the Individual in Modern Chinese Society*. Nordic Institut of Asian Studies (2010)

30. 《2006年中国社会年鉴：中国社会发展；分析与预测》RU Xin, LU Xueyi, LI Peilin, HUANG Ping, CHEN Guangjin, *The China Society Yearbook 2006: China's Social Development; Analysis and Forecast*. Koninklijke Brill NV, Leiden (2007)

31. 《鸦片在中国的社会生活》Zheng Yangwen, *The Social Life of Opium in China*. Cambridge University Press (2005)

32. 《1949—1994年中国城市状态与生活机遇：再分配和分层》Xueguang Zhou, *The State and Life Chances in Urban China: Redistribution and Stratification, 1949—1994*. Cambridge University Press (2004)

33. 《中国的社会关系：制度、文化与关系性质的变化》Thomas Gold, Doug Guthrie, David Wank, *Social Connections in China: Institutions, Culture, and the Changing Nature of Guanxi* (Structural Analysis in the Social Sciences). Cambridge University Press (2002)

34. 《宋代中国的社会与超自然》Edward L. Davis, Society and the Supernatural in Song China. University of Hawai'i Press (2001)
35. 《中国城市生活改革：变化中的社会契约》Wenfang Tang, William L. Parish, *Chinese Urban Life under Reform: The Changing Social Contract* (Cambridge Modern China Series).Cambridge University Press (2000)
36. 《中国生活》Mike Chinoy, *China Live*.Rowman & Littlefield Publishers (1999)
37. 《改革开放与中国社会：西方社会学文献述评》Zhao-qing Tu（涂肇庆），Yi-min Lin（林益民），Andrew G. Walder（魏昂德），Richard Madson（赵文词），etc., *Social Change in China's Reform Era*. Cambridge University Press (1999)
38. 《中国的边缘化群体与社会福利》Linda Wong, *Marginalization and Social Welfare in China*.Routledge (1998)
39. 《礼物、恩惠与宴会：中国社会关系的艺术》（中译本《礼物、关系学与国家：中国人际关系与主体性建构》）Mayfair Mei-Hui Yang（杨美惠），*Gifts, Favors, and Banquets: The Art of Social Relationships in China*. Cornell University Press (1994)
40. 《邻里互助的神话：基于中国城市社区的福利制度》Cecilia Chan, *The Myth of Neighbourhood Mutual Help: The Community-Based Urban Welfare System of China*.Hong Kong University Press (1993)
41. 《乡土中国》Xiaotong Fei（费孝通），Gary G. Hamilton, Wang Zheng, *From the Soil: The Foundations of Chinese Society*.University of California Press (1992)
42. 《社区、贸易和网络：3至13世纪的闽南》(Cambridge Studies in Chinese History, Literature and Institutions) Hugh R. Clark, *Community, Trade, and Networks: Southern Fujian Province from the Third to the Thirteenth Century*. Cambridge University Press (1991)
43. 《中世纪的中国社会与当地"社区"》Michio Tanigawa, *Medieval Chinese Society and the Local "Community"*. University of California Press (1985)
44. 《中国人生活品质的变化》Dennis Duncanson, *Changing Qualities of Chinese Life*. Palgrave Macmillan UK (1982)
45. 《被土地束缚的中国：云南乡村经济研究》（又名《云南三村》）Hsiao-tung Fei（费孝通）; Tse-i Chang（张之毅）; Paul L. Cooper, Margaret Park Redfield, *Earthbound China: A Study of Rural Economy in Yunnan*. London: Routledge & Kegan Paul (1948)
46. 《来自爪哇和华南的早期巨人》Franz Weidenreich, *Giant Early Man from Java and South China* (Anthrpological papers of the American museum of natural history). The American Museum of Natural History (1945)
47. 《江村经济》Hsiao-tung Fei（费孝通），*Peasant Life In China: A Field Study of Country Life in the Yangtze Valley*. Kegan Paul, Trench, Trubner &Amp; Co., Ltd (1939)
48. 《中国人的生活》Adam Grainger（钟秀芝），*Studies in Chinese Life*. Chengtu, West China: Canadian Methodist Mission Press (1921)

49. 《中国乡村生活：社会学研究》Arthur H. Smith（明恩溥），*Village Life in China: A Study in Sociology*. Fleming H. Revell Company (1899)

50. 《中国一隅：对中国人之间生活的考察》Adele M. Fielde, *A Corner of Cathay: Studies from Life among the Chinese*. New York, London: Macmillan and Co. (1894)

51. 《中国社会》Robert K. Douglas, *Society in China*. London: A. D. Innes & Co. (1894)

52. 《中国人的社会生活：关于宗教、政府、教育、商业习俗和观点的记述》Rev. Justus Doolitle, *Social life of the Chinese: With some Account of The Religious, Governmental, Educational, and Business Customs and Opinions*. London: Sampson Low, Son, & Marston (1866)

7.12 仪式、丧葬、巫术与民俗

7.12.1 仪式与丧葬

1. 《古希腊与中国先秦的哀悼仪式》Xiaoqun Wu, *Mourning Rituals in Archaic & Classical Greece and Pre-Qin China*. Springer Singapore: Palgrave Pivot (2018)

2. 《丧曲：中国西南地区的死尸、文本与世界》Erik Mueggler, *Songs for Dead Parents: Corpse, Text, and World in Southwest China*. University Of Chicago Press (2017)

3. 《中国西南梁山地区的史前丧葬记录：作为混合对象的坟墓》Anke Hein, *The Burial Record of Prehistoric Liangshan in Southwest China: Graves as Composite Objects*. Springer International Publishing (2017)

4. 《逝者剧场：中国丧葬艺术的社会转折（1000—1400）》Jeehee Hong（洪知希），*Theater of the Dead: A Social Turn in Chinese Funerary Art, 1000—1400*. University of Hawai'i Press (2016)

5. 《中国中世纪早期的墓葬碑文与纪念文化：早期墓志铭史》Timothy M. Davis, *Entombed Epigraphy and Commemorative Culture in Early Medieval China: A History of Early Muzhiming*. Brill Academic Pub (2015)

6. 《欧亚大陆对岸的死亡："台湾"与荷兰的死亡率趋势（1850—1945）》Theo Engelen, John R. Shephard, Wen-shan Yang (Ed.), *Death at the Opposite Ends of Eurasian Continent: Mortality Trends in Taiwan and the Netherlands 1850—1945*. Amsterdam University Press (2011)

7. 《天裂地动：唐山地震和毛泽东时代的中国死亡》James Palmer, *Heaven Cracks, Earth Shakes: The Tangshan Earthquake and the Death of Mao's China*. Basic Books (2012)

8. 《中国古代丧葬：一个人的旅行故事（包山楚墓）》Constance A. Cook（柯鹤立），*Death in Ancient China: The Tale of One Man's Journey*. Brill (2006)

9. 《中国唐代帝王陵墓》Tonia Eckfeld, *Imperial Tombs in Tang China* (Routledgecurzon Studies in the Early History of Asia, 1). RoutledgeCurzon (2005)

10. 《中国小乘佛教徒的葬礼如何进行》Venerable Suvanno, *How a Theravadin Buddhist Chinese Funeral May Be Conducted*. Sukhi Hotu (1996)

7.12.2 巫术、鬼神

1. 《中国古代的神与女神》Trenton Campbell, *Gods & Goddesses of Ancient China* (Gods and goddesses of mythology). Britannica Educational Publishing (2015)
2. 《巫术与首个儒家帝国的兴起》Cai, Liang, *Witchcraft and the Rise of the First Confucian Empire*. State University of New York Press (2014)
3. 《中国宋代的社会与超自然力量》Edward L. Davis, *Society and the Supernatural in Song China*. University of Hawai'i Press (2001)
4. 《野鬼时代：中国西南地区的记忆、暴力和场所》Erik Mueggler, *The Age of Wild Ghosts: Memory, Violence, and Place in Southwest China*. University of California Press (2001)
5. 《莆田平原的仪式联盟（上册）：神的回归历史介绍》Kenneth Dean（丁荷生），Zheng Zhenman（郑振满）, *Ritual Alliances of the Putian Plain (Volume One): Historical Introduction to the Return of the Gods* (Handbook of Oriental Studies). Brill (2009)
6. 《莆田平原的仪式联盟（下册）：村庙和祭祀活动调查》Kenneth Dean（丁荷生），Zheng Zhenman（郑振满）, *Ritual Alliances of the Putian Plain (Volume Two): A Survey of Village Temples and Ritual Activities* (Handbook of Oriental Studies). Brill (2009)
7. 《鬼魂附身的医生：一个中国女医生的家族传奇》Li Qunying, Louis Han, *The Doctor Who Was Followed by Ghosts: The Family Saga of a Chinese Woman Doctor*. ECW Press (2007)
8. 《为了神灵、鬼魂与祖先：中国传统纸祭》Janet Lee Scott, *For Gods, Ghosts and Ancestors: The Chinese Tradition of Paper Offerings*. Hong Kong University Press (2007)
9. 《针灸、草药、神仙和鬼怪：1848年前的中国、医疗和西方》Linda L. Barnes, *Needles, Herbs, Gods, and Ghosts: China, Healing, and the West to 1848*. Harvard University Press (2005)
10. 《唐代纳贤之礼》Oliver J. Moore, *Rituals Of Recruitment In Tang China: Reading An Annual Programme In The Collected Statements By Wang Dingbao 870-940* (Sinica Leidensia). Brill Academic Publishers (2004)
11. 《记忆的圣殿：中国乡村的历史、权力和道德》Jun Jing, *The Temple of Memories: History, Power, and Morality in a Chinese Village*. Stanford University Press (1998)
12. 《叫魂：1768年中国妖术大恐慌》Philip A. Kuhn（孔飞力）, *Soulstealers: The Chinese Sorcery Scare of 1768*. Harvard University Press (1990)
13. 《中国中世纪的鬼节》Stephen F. Teiser, *The Ghost Festival in Medieval China*. Princeton University Press (1988)
14. 《中国古代医生、占卜师和魔术师：方士传记》Kenneth J. DeWoskin, *Doctors, Diviners, and Magicians of Ancient China: Biographies of Fang-shih*. Columbia University Press (1983)
15. 《川苗族故事与歌谣》David Crockett（葛拉汉）, *The Tribal Songs and Tales of the Ch'uan Miao* (Asian Folklore and Social Life Monographs, 102). Chinese Association for Folklore (1978)

7.12.3 秘密会社、民俗

1. 《袍哥：1940年代川西乡村的暴力与秩序》Di Wang（王笛），*Violence and Order on the Chengdu Plain: The Story of a Secret Brotherhood in Rural China, 1939—1949*. Stanford University Press (2018)

2. 《白莲教叛乱与华南海盗：清帝国的危机与改革》Wensheng Wang, *White Lotus Rebels and South China Pirates: Crisis and Reform in the Qing Empire*. Harvard University Press (2014)

3. 《天地会的起源：传说和历史中的中国三合会》Dian Murray, Qin Baoqi, *The Origins of the Tiandihui: The Chinese Triads in Legend and History*. Stanford University Press (1994)

4. 《中国赌博社会学》Cheng Tijie, *The Sociology of Gambling in China*. Paths International Ltd (2010)

5. 《古代中国和希腊的节日、盛会与性别关系》Yiqun Zhou, *Festivals, Feasts, and Gender Relations in Ancient China and Greece*. Cambridge University Press (2010)

7.13 人类学

1. 《踏迹寻中：40年华南田野之旅》Helen F. Siu（萧凤霞），*Tracing China: A Forty-Year Ethnographic Journey*. Hong Kong University Press (2017)

2. 《中国人类学：作为民族志与理论批判的中国》Charlotte Bruckermann, Stephan Feuchtwang, *The Anthropology of China: China as Ethnographic and Theoretical Critique*. Imperial College Press (2016)

3. 《中国多民族语言学习者的付出和收获：人种学个案研究》Ge Wang, *Pains and Gains of Ethnic Multilingual Learners in China: An Ethnographic Case Study*. Springer Singapore (2016)

4. 《亚洲古人类：从非洲到中国及其外》Christopher J. Norton, David R. Braun (auth.), Christopher J. Norton, David R. Braun (eds.), *Asian Paleoanthropology: From Africa to China and Beyond*. Springer (2010)

5. 《中国亲属关系：当代人类学视角》Susanne Brandtstadter, Goncalo D. Santos, *Chinese Kinship: Contemporary Anthropological Perspectives* (Routledge Contemporary China Series). Routledge (2009)

6. 《人民的北京人：20世纪中国的大众科学和人类身份》Sigrid Schmalzer, *The People's Peking Man: Popular Science and Human Identity in Twentieth-Century China*. University Of Chicago Press (2008)

7. 《人类学、政治和国家：南亚民主与暴力》Jonathan Spencer（乔纳森·斯宾塞），*Anthropology, Politics, and the State: Democracy and Violence in South Asia*. Cambridge University Press (2007)

8. 《社会文化人类学百科全书》Alan Barnard, Jonathan Spencer（乔纳森·斯宾塞），*Encyclopedia of Social and Cultural Anthropology* (Routledge World Reference). Routledge (2002)

9. 《近代中国的分离与团圆》Charles Stafford, *Separation and Reunion in Modern China*. Cambridge University Press (2000)

10. 《中国人类进化：化石度量描述与遗址评论》Xinzhi Wu, Frank E. Poirier, *Human Evolution in China: A Metric Description of Fossils and a Review of the Sites*. Oxford University Press, USA (1995)

11. 《中国风水的人类学分析》Stephan D. Feuchtwang, *An Anthropological Analysis of Chinese Geomancy*. Vithagma (1974)

7.14 族群与宗族

7.14.1 族群

1. 《种族变迁：当代中国的民族政治》Zhitian Guo, *Changing Ethnicity: Contemporary Ethno-Politics in China*. Springer Singapore: Palgrave Macmillan (2020)

2. 《中国民族问题的解决》(China Insights) Shiyuan Hao, *China's Solution to Its Ethno-national Issues*. Springer Singapore (2020)

3. 《中国南方少数民族叙事：政治、纪律与公共史》Guo Wu, *Narrating Southern Chinese Minority Nationalities: Politics, Disciplines, and Public History*. Palgrave Macmillan (2019)

4. 《虔诚的中国少数民族文化、认知与情感：彝族苦难之声》Rachel Sing-Kiat Ting, Louise Sundararajan, *Culture, Cognition, and Emotion in China's Religious Ethnic Minorities: Voices of Suffering among the Yi*. Palgrave Macmillan (2018)

5. 《身份、政策与繁荣：朝鲜族侨民的边疆民族性与中国东北区域发展》Jeongwon Bourdais Park, *Identity, Policy, and Prosperity: Border Nationality of the Korean Diaspora and Regional Development in Northeast China*. Palgrave Macmillan (2018)

6. 《蒙古如何重要：战争、法律和社会》Morris Rossabi（罗茂锐）, *How Mongolia Matters: War, Law, and Society* (Brill's Inner Asian Library). Brill Academic Pub. (2017)

7. 《蛮族与中国人身份的诞生：五代十国至元朝（907—1368）》Jing Liu, *Barbarians and the Birth of Chinese Identity: The Five Dynasties and Ten Kingdoms to the Yuan Dynasty (907—1368)*, (Understanding China Through Comics). Stone Bridge Press (2017)

8. 《上游之旅：1570—1850年华南的侨民与帝国》Steven B. Miles, *Upriver Journeys: Diaspora and Empire in Southern China, 1570—1850*. Harvard University Asia Center (2017)

9. 《一个有我名字的村庄：中国对外开放的家族史》Scott Tong（童致刚）, *A Village with My Name: A Family History of China's Opening to the World*. University of Chicago Press (2017)

10. 《茶叶生产、土地利用的政治与少数民族：中国西南边疆的困境挣扎》Po-Yi Hung, *Tea Production, Land Use Politics, and Ethnic Minorities: Struggling over Dilemmas in China's Southwest Frontier*. Palgrave Macmillan US (2015)

11. 《汉族：中国多元化的大多数》Agnieszka Joniak-Luthi, *The Han: China's Diverse Majority*. University of Washington Press (2015)

12. 《中国民族问题的去政治化》Lizhong Xie, Lizhong Xie, *De-Politicization of Ethnic Questions in China*. World Scientific Publishing Company (2014)

13. 《中国和印度少数民族的贫困与放逐》A. S. Bhalla, Dan Luo, *Poverty and Exclusion of Minorities in China and India*. Palgrave Macmillan UK (2013)

14. 《汉民族研究：多数中国人的历史、代表和身份》(New Perspectives on Chinese Culture and Society) Thomas S. Mullaney, James Patrick Leibold, Stéphane Gros, Eric Armand Vanden Bussche (eds.), *Critical Han Studies: The History, Representation, and Identity of China's Majority*. University of California Press (2012)

15. 《蒙古人简介》Morris Rossabi（罗茂锐）, *The Mongols: A Very Short Introduction* (Very Short Introductions 314). Oxford University Press (2012)

16. 《与国家接轨：近代中国的民族分类》Mullaney Thomas Shawn, *Coming to Terms with the Nation: Ethnic Classification in Modern China* (Asia-Local studies: global themes 18). University of California Press (2011, 2012)

17. 《匈奴考古：内亚第一草原帝国的多学科视角》Ursula Brosseder, Bryan K. Miller, *Xiongnu Archaeology: Multidisciplinary Perspectives of the First Steppe Empire in Inner Asia*. Vor-und Fruhgeschichtliche Archaologie (2011)

18. 《近代中国的民族边疆：西部旅行》Hsiao-ting Lin（林孝庭）, *Modern China's Ethnic Frontiers: A Journey to the West*. Routledge (2010)

19. 《中国民族认同与民族冲突》Arabinda Acharya, Rohan Gunaratna, Wang Pengxin, *Ethnic Identity and National Conflict in China*. Palgrave Macmillan (2010)

20. 《中国民族与宗教》Zheng Qian, *China's Ethnic Groups and Religions*. Cengage Learning Asia (2010)

21. 《民族适应：近代中国的族群分类》Thomas Mullaney, *Coming to Terms with the Nation: Ethnic Classification in Modern China*. University of California Press (2010)

22. 《移山：中国高原、越南、老挝的种族和生计》Jean Michaud, Tim Forsyth, *Moving Mountains: Ethnicity and Livelihoods in Highland China, Vietnam, and Laos*. University of British Columbia Press (2010)

23. 《中国与加拿大少数民族发展比较研究》Reza Hasmath, *A Comparative Study of Minority Development in China and Canada*. Palgrave Macmillan (2010)

24. 《国际民族网络与种族间冲突：韩国人在中国》Hyejin Kim, *International Ethnic Networks and Intra-Ethnic Conflict: Koreans in China*. Palgrave Macmillan (2010)

25. 《立国之道：现代中国的民族识别》Thomas Mullaney（墨磊宁）, *Coming to Terms with the Nation: Ethnic Classification in Modern China*. University of California Press (2010)

26. 《民族认同：近代中国的民族分类》Thomas S. Mullaney, *Coming to Terms with the Nation: Ethnic Classification in Modern China*. University of California Press (2010)

27. 《隐形中国：民族边疆之旅》Colin Legerton, Jacob Rawson, *Invisible China: A Journey*

through Ethnic Borderlands. Chicago Review Press (2009)

28. 《中国纳木依藏族：生活、语言与民间文学（第一卷）》Libu Lakhi, Tsering Bum, Charles Kevin Stuart, *China's Namzi Tibetan Life, Language and Folklore*. Asian Highlands Perspectives Vol. 1 (2009)

29. 《中国少数民族语言、教育和社区》Linda Tsung, *Minority Languages, Education and Communities in China* (Palgrave Studies in Minority Languages and Communities). Palgrave Macmillan (2009)

30. 《中国边缘化：重塑少数民族政治》Siu-Keung Cheung, Joseph Tse-Hei Lee, Lida V. Nedilsky, *Marginalization in China: Recasting Minority Politics*. Palgrave Macmillan (2009)

31. 《在启蒙运动中阅读并看到民族差异：从中国到非洲》Birgit Tautz, *Reading and Seeing Ethnic Differences in the Enlightenment: From China to Africa*. Palgrave Macmillan (2007)

32. 《中国西南地区自治、种族和贫困》Chih-yu Shih（石之瑜）, *Autonomy, Ethnicity, and Poverty in Southwestern China: The State Turned Upside Down*. Palgrave Macmillan (2007)

33. 《帝国之于边缘：近代中国文化、族群性与边界》Pamela Kyle Crossley（柯娇燕）, Helen F. Siu, Donald S. Sutton, *Empire at the Margins: Culture, Ethnicity, and Frontier in Early Modern China*. University of California Press (2006)

34. 《中国国家的创立：民族性与明代疆域的拓展》Leo K. Shin（单国钺）, *The Making of the Chinese State: Ethnicity and Expansion on the Ming Dynasty*. Cambridge University Press (2006)

35. 《维吾尔族人和维吾尔人的身份》Dolkun Kamberi, *Uyghurs and Uyghur identity*. Deptment of East Asian Languages and Civilizations, University of Pennsylvania (2005)

36. 《歌唱与沉默：中国西南边界的民族复兴》Sara L. M. Davis, *Song and Silence: Ethnic Revival on China's Southwest Borders*. Columbia University Press (2005)

37. 《中国的少数民族和全球化》Colin Mackerras（马克林）, *China's Ethnic Minorities and Globalisation*. Routledge (2003)

38. 《中国历史之政治前沿、民族界限与人文地理》Nicola Di Cosmo（狄宇宙）, Don J. Wyatt, *Political Frontiers, Ethnic Boundaries and Human Geographies in Chinese History*. RoutledgeCurzon (2003)

39. 《中国古代及其敌人：游牧力量东亚崛起史》Nicola Di Cosmo（狄宇宙）, *Ancient China and its Enemies: The Rise of Nomadic Power in East Asian History*. Cambridge University Press (2002)

40. 《议定中国种族：作为国家回应的公民身份》Chih-yu Shih（石之瑜）, *Negotiating Ethnicity in China: Citizenship as a Response to the State*. Routledge (2002)

41. 《中国苗族：语境、中介与想像》Nicholas Tapp, *The Hmong of China: Context, Agency, and the Imaginary*. Brill Academic Pub (2002)

42. 《成为中国西南少数民族的途径》Stevan Harrell, *Ways of Being Ethnic in Southwest China*. University of Washington Press (2002)

43. 《中国西南彝族》Stevan Harrell, *Perspectives on the Yi of Southwest China*. University of

California Press (2001)

44.《无父无夫社会：中国纳人》Cai Hua（蔡华），translated by Asti Hustvedt, *A Society without Fathers or Husbands: The Na of China*.Zone Books (2001)

45.《满与汉：清末民初的民族关系与政治权力（1861—1928）》Edward J. M. Rhoads（路康乐）, *Manchus & Han: Ethnic Relations and Political Power in Late Qing and Early Republican China, 1861—1928*. University of Washington Press (2000)

46.《他者中国：瑶族与国家归属的政治》Ralph Litzinger, *Other Chinas: The Yao and the Politics of National Belonging*. Duke University Press (2000)

47.《中国壮族政治的创建》Katherine Palmer Kaup, *Creating the Zhuang-Ethnic Politics in China*. Lynne Rienner Publishers (2000)

48.《中国民族史学词典》James S. Olson, *An Ethnohistorical Dictionary of China*.Greenwood (1998)

49.《中国历史上的移民与族群性：客家人，棚民及其邻居》Sow-Theng Leong（梁肇庭）, *Migration and Ethnicity in Chinese History: Hakkas, Pengmin and Their Neighbors*. Stanford University Press (1997)

50.《中国民族边疆的文化遭遇》Stevan Harrell (ed.), *Cultural Encounters on China's Ethnic Frontiers*. University of Washington Press (1995)

51.《中国蒙古族：民族志与民间故事》Kevin Stuart, and Limusishiden, *China's Monguor Minority: Ethnography and Folktales*.Sino-Platonic Papers (1994)

52.《后共产主义世界的种族与冲突：苏联、东欧和中国》Kumar Rupesinghe, Peter King, Olga Vorkunova (eds.), *Ethnicity and Conflict in a Post-Communist World: The Soviet Union, Eastern Europe and China*. Palgrave Macmillan UK (1992)

53.《孤军：满洲三代家族与清世界之灭亡》Pamela Kyle Crossley（柯娇燕）, *Orphan Warriors: Three Manchu Generations and the End of the Qing World*. Princeton University Press (1990)

54.《进化理论与文化多样性：中国少数民族学研究》（博士论文）Wei Yang Chao, *Evolutionary Theory and Cultural Diversity: A Study of the Ethnology of China's National Minorities*. Ph. D. Dissertation, University of California, Berkeley (1986)

55.《中华人民共和国的民族政策》*Policy Toward Nationalities of the People's Republic of China*. Foreign Languages Press (1953)

56.《中国和满族》Herbert Allen Giles（翟理斯）, *China and the Manchus*. Project Gutenberg (1912, 2009)

7.14.2 宗族

1.《金鹅：中国西部一个农民家庭的故事》Xu Liu, David Burnett, *Golden Goose: The Story of a Peasant Family in Western China*. Palgrave Macmillan (2019)

2.《孝的困扰：中国父系继嗣及其不满》P. Steven Sangren, *Filial Obsessions: Chinese Patriliny and Its Discontents*.Palgrave Macmillan (2017)

3.《华南地区新农村秩序的形成（第一卷）：惠州的村庄、土地和宗族（900—1600）》

Joseph P. McDermott, *The Making of a New Rural Order in South China (Volume 1): Village, Land, and Lineage in Huizhou, 900—1600.* Cambridge University Press (2014)

4. 《制造伪装亲属关系：中韩间婚姻和劳动力迁移》Caren Freeman, *Making and Faking Kinship: Marriage and Labor Migration between China and South Korea.* Cornell University Press (2011)

5. 《皇帝与祖先：华南的国家与宗族》David Faure, *Emperor and Ancestor: State and Lineage in South China.* Stanford University Press (2007)

6. 《种族差异与本地含义：中国文化认同谈判》Mary Rack, *Ethnic Distinctions, Local Meanings: Negotiating Cultural Identities in China.* Pluto Press (2005)

7. 《中国人的身份认同、族群与世界主义》Kwok-bun Chan, *Chinese Identities, Ethnicity and Cosmopolitanism* (Chinese Worlds).Routledge (2005)

8. 《祖先崇拜：中国的肖像纪念》Jan Stuart, Evelyn Sakakida Rawski（罗友枝）, *Worshiping the Ancestors: Chinese Commemorative Portraits.* Stanford University Press (2001)

9. 《明清时期的悼念仪式：孝与国家》Norman Kutcher, *Mourning in Late Imperial China: Filial Piety and the State.*Cambridge University Press (1999)

10. 《强大的关系：宋代的亲属关系、地位与国家（960—1279）》Beverly Bossler, *Powerful Relations: Kinship, Status, and the State in Sung China (960—1279)* (Harvard-Yenching Institute Monograph Series). Harvard University Asia Center (1998)

11. 《中华帝国晚期的亲属组织（1000—1940）》Patricia Buckley Ebrey（伊沛霞）, James L. Watson, *Kinship Organization in Late Imperial China, 1000—1940* (Studies on China). University of California Press (1986)

12. 《传统的中国族规》Hui-chen Wang Liu, *The Traditional Chinese Clan Rules.* Locust Valley, N.Y., Published for the Association for Asian Studies by J. J. Augustin (1959)

7.14.3 犹太人

1. 《中国犹太难民研究（1933—1945）：历史、理论与中国模式》Guang Pan, *A Study of Jewish Refugees in China (1933—1945): History, Theories and the Chinese Pattern.* Springer Singapore (2019)

2. 《中国人对犹太人和犹太教的认识：一部犹太史》Zhou Xun, *Chinese Perceptions of the Jews' and Judaism: A History of the Youtai.* Routledge (2013)

3. 《主要的外来者：东南亚和中欧现代转型中的中国人和犹太人》Daniel Chirot, *Essential Outsiders: Chinese and Jews in the Modern Transformation of Southeast Asia and Central Europe.* University of Washington Press (2011)

4. 《中国开封犹太人的哈加达》Fook-Kong Wong, Dalia Yasharpour, *The Haggadah of the Kaifeng Jews of China.* Brill (2011)

5. 《当代中国的犹太人和犹太教》M. Avrum Ehrlich, *Jews and Judaism in Modern China* (Routledge Jewish studies series). Routledge (2010)

6. 《二战时期中国的犹太难民》Edited, translated and with an introduction by Irene Eber, *Voices*

from Shanghai: Jewish Exiles in Wartime China. The University of Chicago Press (2008)

7. 《犹太人与中国人的联结：文明的会合》M. Avrum Ehrlich, *The Jewish-Chinese Nexus: A Meeting of Civilizations* (Routledge Jewish Studies Series). Routledge (2008)

8. 《近代犹太人历史》Lloyd P. Gartner, *History of the Jews in Modern Times*. Oxford University Press (2001)

9. 《中国犹太人：历史和比较视角》Jonathan Goldstein, *The Jews of China: Historical and Comparative Perspectives*.Vol. 1. M E Sharpe Inc. (1999)

10. 《尊严与绝望之间：纳粹德国的犹太人生活》Marion A. Kaplan, *Between Dignity and Despair: Jewish Life in Nazi Germany*. Oxford University Press (1998)

11. 《中国梦：在天津长大的犹太人》Isabelle Maynard, *China Dreams: Growing Up Jewish in Tientsin* (Singular Lives). University of Iowa Press (1996)

12. 《中国犹太人历史》S. M. Perlmann, *The History of the Jews in China*. R. Mazin & Co. Ltd., (1913)

13. 《开封府的犹太人纪念碑》William Alexander Parsons Martin（丁韪良）, *The Jewish Monument at Kaifungfu*. Shanghai (1906)

8. 中国政治与外交

8.1 政治

8.1.1 研究总论

1. 《中国故事年鉴：权势威力》Jane Golley, Linda Jaivin, Paul J. Farrelly, Sharon Strange (eds.), *China Story Year Book: Power*. The Australian National University (ANU) Press (2019)
2. 《中国的世界：中国想要什么？》Kerry Brown（凯瑞·布朗）, *China's World: What Does China Want?* I. B. Tauris (2017)
3. 《中国嘉年华：胡锦涛和习近平时代的中国》Kerry Brown（凯瑞·布朗）, *Carnival China: China in the Era of Hu Jintao and Xi Jinping*. Imperial College Press (2014)
4. 《中国政治寻论》（第2、3版）William A. Joseph（邹伟兼）, *Politics in China: An Introduction*. Second Edition; Third Edition. Oxford University Press (2014, 2019)
5. 《政治学与中国政治研究：学科发展现状评析》Sujian Guo（郭苏建）(eds.), *Political Science and Chinese Political Studies: The State of the Field*, Springer Berlin Heidelberg (2013)
6. 《中华人民共和国政治60年》(3rd Edition) Roderick MacFarquhar（马若德）(ed.), *The Politics of China: Sixty Years of the People's Republic of China*. Cambridge University Press (2011)
7. 《当代中国政治学：新来源、新方法与田野策略》Allen Carlson, Mary E. Gallagher, Kenneth Lieberthal（李侃如）, and Melanie Manion（墨宁）, *Contemporary Chinese Politics: New Sources, Methods, and Field Strategies*. New York: Cambridge University Press (2010)
8. 《当代中国基层政治改革》Elizabeth J. Perry（裴宜理）, Merle Goldman（梅谷）, *Grassroots Political Reform in Contemporary China* (Harvard Contemporary China Series). Harvard University Press (2007)
9. 《中国进入胡温时代：政策倡议和挑战》John Wong（黄朝翰）, Lai Hongyi, *China into the Hu-wen Era: Policy Initiatives and Challenges*, World Scientific (2006)
10. 《中国与社会主义：市场改革与阶级斗争》Martin Hart-Landsberg, Paul Burkett, *China and Socialism: Market Reforms and Class Struggle*, Monthly Review Press (2005)
11. 《中国政治：移动的前沿》Françoise Mengin, Jean-Louis Rocca (eds.), *Politics in China: Moving Frontiers* (The CERI Series in International Relations and Political Economy). Palgrave Macmillan US (2002)
12. 《当代中国的政治、经济和社会》Bill Brugger, Stephen Reglar, *Politics, Economy and Society in Contemporary China*. Macmillan Education UK (1994)
13. 《当代中国政治的历史透视》Brantly Womack（沃马克）(ed.), *Contemporary Chinese*

Politics in Historical Perspective. Cambridge University Press (1991)

14. 《中世纪早期中国的国家与社会》Albert Dien, *State and Society in Early Medieval China*. Stanford University Press (1991)

15. 《"文革"后的中国：两次党代会之间的政治》Jürgen Domes, Marie-Luise Nath, *China after the Cultural Revolution: Politics between Two Party Congresses*. University of California Press (1977)

8.1.2 中国共产党

1. 《讲述中国治理：习近平讲话中的故事》（《习近平讲故事》英译本）Department of Commentary People's Daily（人民日报评论部）, Translated by Jing Luo, *Narrating China's Governance: Stories in Xi Jinping's Speeches*. Springer Singapore (2020)

2. 《中国共产主义的来世：从毛泽东到习近平的政治观念》Christian Sorace, Ivan Franceschini, Nicholas Loubere, *Afterlives of Chinese Communism: Political Concepts from Mao to XI*. ANU Press, Verso Books (2019)

3. 《使中国现代化：从大清到习近平》Klaus Mühlhahn（余凯思）, *Making China Modern: From the Great Qing to Xi Jinping*. The Belknap Press (2019)

4. 《习近平所说的世界：关于新中国你需要知道的一切》Kerry Brown, *The World According to Xi: Everything You Need to Know About the New China*. I. B. Tauris & Co. Ltd (2018)

5. 《第三次革命：习近平与新中国》Elizabeth Economy, *The Third Revolution: XI Jinping and the New Chinese State*. Oxford University Press (2018)

6. 《习近平的内心世界》François Bougon, *Inside the Mind of Xi Jinping*. Context (2018)

7. 《习近平的新发展哲学》Angang Hu（胡鞍钢）, Yilong Yan, Xiao Tang, *Xi Jinping's New Development Philosophy*. Springer Singapore (2018)

8. 《党统治的地方：中国共产主义国家的等级制度》Daniel Koss, *Where The Party Rules: The Rank And File Of China's Communist State*. Cambridge University Press (2018)

9. 《中国共产党手册》Willy Wo Lam（林和立）, *Routledge Handbook of the Chinese Communist Party*.Routledge (2018)

10. 《红心：中国共产党人是如何爱上俄国革命的》Elizabeth McGuire, *Red at Heart: How Chinese Communists Fell in Love with the Russian Revolution*. Oxford University Press (2017)

11. 《中国反腐败运动论文》（博士论文）Xi Lu, *Essays in China's Anti-corruption Campaign*. Ph. D. Dissertation, Agricultural & Resource Economics, UC Berkeley (2017)

12. 《中国的伦理革命与合法性恢复：通过公务员改革共产党》Shaoying Zhang, Derek McGhee, *China's Ethical Revolution and Regaining Legitimacy: Reforming the Communist Party through Its Public Servants* (Politics and Development of Contemporary China). Palgrave Macmillan (2017)

13. 《习近平时代的中国：国内和外交政策挑战》Robert S. Ross（陆伯彬）, Jo Inge Bekkevold, *China in the Era of Xi Jinping: Domestic and Foreign Policy Challenges*. Georgetown

University Press (2016)

14. 《中国CEO：习近平的崛起》Kerry Brown（凯瑞·布朗）, *CEO, China: The Rise of Xi Jinping*. I. B. Tauris (2016)

15. 《中国共产党如何解决民族问题》Shiyuan Hao, *How the Communist Party of China Manages the Issue of Nationality: An Evolving Topic*. Springer-Verlag Berlin Heidelberg (2016)

16. 《意识形态的回归：寻求后共产主义俄罗斯和中国的政权认同》Cheng Chen, *The Return of Ideology: The Search for Regime Identities in Postcommunist Russia and China*. University of Michigan Press (2016)

17. 《当代中日关系的起源：周恩来与日本》Mayumi Itoh, *The Origins of Contemporary Sino-Japanese Relations: Zhou Enlai and Japan*. Palgrave Macmillan US (2016)

18. 《党的培训：改革时代党的适应和精英培训》Charlotte P. Lee, *Training the Party: Party Adaptation and Elite Training in Reform-era China*. Cambridge University Press (2015)

19. 《潘佐夫：邓小平的革命生涯》Alexander V. Pantsov, Steven I. Levine, *Deng Xiaoping: A Revolutionary Life*. Oxford University Press (2015)

20. 《习近平统治下的中国：经济挑战与外交政策倡议》Shao Binhong, *China Under Xi Jinping: Its Economic Challenges and Foreign Policy Initiatives* (China in the World). Brill (2015)

21. 《习近平：如何阅读孔子等中国古典思想家》Fenzhi Zhang, *Xi Jinping: How to Read Confucius and Other Chinese Classical Thinkers*. CN Times Books (2015)

22. 《中国执政党新范式：政治重建和民族复兴的追求》Timothy R. Heath, *China's New Governing Party Paradigm: Political Renewal and the Pursuit of National Rejuvenation*. Ashgate Publishing Company (2014)

23. 《中国领导人选拔》Chien-wen Kou, Xiaowei Zang, *Choosing China's Leaders*. Routledge (2014)

24. 《红色上帝：韦拔群及其华南农民革命（1894—1932）》Xiaorong Han, *Red God: Wei Baqun and His Peasant Revolution in Southern China, 1894—1932* (SUNY Series in Chinese Philosophy and Culture). State University of New York Press (2014)

25. 《第四次革命：国家重塑的全球竞赛》John Micklethwait, Adrian Wooldridge, *The Fourth Revolution: The Global Race to Reinvent the State*. The Penguin Press (2014)

26. 《中国集体领导体制》Angang Hu（胡鞍钢）, *China's Collective Presidency*. Springer Berlin Heidelberg (2014)

27. 《跟随领导：统治中国，从邓小平到习近平》David M. Lampton（蓝普顿）, *Following the Leader: Ruling China, from Deng Xiaoping to Xi Jinping*. University of California Press (2014)

28. 《共产国际时期的中国共产党（1919—1943）》Tony Saich（托尼·赛奇）, *The Chinese Communist Party During the Era of the Comintern (1919—1943)*. International Institute of Social History, Amsterdam (2014)

29. 《邓小平：现代中国的缔造者》Michael Dillon, *Deng Xiaoping: The Man who Made*

Modern China. I. B. Tauris (2014)

30. 《选择中国领导人》Chien-wen Kou, Xiaowei Zang, *Choosing China's Leaders* (Routledge Studies on China in Transition). Routledge (2013)

31. 《"文革"前的邓小平：毛泽东的副帅（1956—1966）》zhong yan lin, *Deng Xiaoping before the Cultural Revolution: Mao's "Vice Marshal" (1956—1966)*. Info Rainbow LTD (2013)

32. 《共产党中国的资本家》Keming Yang, *Capitalists in Communist China* (International Political Economy Series). Palgrave Macmillan (2013)

33. 《中国共产党成立史》Ishikawa Yoshihiro（石川祯浩）, Joshua A. Fogel（傅佛果）, *The Formation of the Chinese Communist Party*. Columbia University Press (2012)

34. 《中国共产党的思想改造运动》Hu Ping, Philip F. Williams, Yenna Wu, *The Thought Remolding Campaign of the Chinese Communist Party-State*. Amsterdam University Press (2012)

35. 《中国共产党历史辞典》Lawrence R. Sullivan, *Historical Dictionary of the Chinese Communist Party*. Scarecrow Press (2012)

36. 《最暗的红角：1926—1945年中共情报及其在党内的地位》（博士论文）Matthew James Brazil, *The Darkest Red Corner: Chinese Communist Intelligence and Its Place in the Party, 1926—1945*. Ph. D. Dissertation, University of Sydney thesis (2012)

37. 《中国领导力》Barbara Xiaoyu Wang, Harold Chee, *Chinese Leadership*. Palgrave Macmillan (2011)

38. 《邓小平时代》Ezra F. Vogel（傅高义）, *Deng Xiaoping and the Transformation of China*. Belknap Press of Harvard University Press (2011)

39. 《毛式经济学：为何中国共产党人比我们资本家做得更好》Loretta Napoleoni, Stephen Twilley, *Maonomics: Why Chinese Communists Make Better Capitalists Than We Do*. Seven Stories Press (2011)

40. 《被遗忘的毛泽东接班人：华国锋政治生涯》Robert Weatherley, *Mao's Forgotten Successor: The Political Career of Hua Guofeng*. Palgrave Macmillan (2010)

41. 《中国的精英政治：治理与民主化》Bo Zhiyue（薄智跃）, *China's Elite Politics: Governance and Democratization*. World Scientific (2010)

42. 《地下阵线：中国共产党在香港》Christine Loh, *Underground Front: The Chinese Communist Party in Hong Kong*. Hong Kong University Press (2010)

43. 《莫斯科与中共政权的出现（1925—1930）：南昌起义和红军诞生》Bruce Elleman, *Moscow and the Emergence of Communist Power in China, 1925—30: The Nanchang Uprising and the Birth of the Red Army*. Routledge (2009)

44. 《共产党的多元文化：中国西南地区的民族复兴》Susan K. McCarthy, *Communist Multiculturalism: Ethnic Revival in Southwest China*. University of Washington Press (2009)

45. 《优秀共产党员：当下中国精英培训和国家建设》Frank N. Pieke（彭柯）, *The Good*

Communist: Elite Training and State Building in Today's China. Cambridge University Press (2009)

46. 《胡锦涛》Daniel K. Davis, *Hu Jintao*. Chelsea House Publishers (2008)
47. 《中国领导与管理：哲学、理论和实践》Chao-Chuan Chen, Yueh-Ting Lee, *Leadership and Management in China: Philosophies, Theories, and Practices*. Cambridge University Press (2008)
48. 《21世纪中国的党—国：适应和合法性的重塑》Andre Laliberte, Marc Lanteigne (eds), *The Chinese Party-State in the 21st Century: Adaptation and the reinvention of legitimacy*. Routledge (2008)
49. 《中国共产党：收缩与调适》Shambaugh David（沈大伟）, *China's Communist Party: Atrophy and Adaptation*. University of California Press (2008)
50. 《晚年周恩来》Gao Wenqian（高文谦）(author), Translated by Peter Rand and Lawrence R. Sullivan, *Zhou Enlai: The Last Perfect Revolutionary*. PublicAffairs (2008)
51. 《中国的精英政治：政治转型与权力平衡》Bo Zhiyue（薄智跃）, *China's Elite Politics Political Transition and Power Balancing*. World Scientific (2007)
52. 《胡锦涛时代的中国政治：新领导 新挑战》(East Gate Books) Willy Wo-Lap Lam, *Chinese Politics in the Hu Jintao Era. New Leaders, New Challenges* M. E. Sharpe (2006)
53. 《胡锦涛统治下的中国：机遇、危险和困境》Tun-jen Cheng, *China under Hu JinTao: Opportunities, Dangers, and Dilemmas*. World Scientific Publishing Company (2006)
54. 《改革中的中国共产党》Kjeld Brodsgaard（柏思德）, Zheng Yongnian（郑永年）, *The Chinese Communist Party in Reform*. Routledge (2006)
55. 《中共政治中的宗派主义》Jing Huang（黄靖）, *Factionalism in Chinese Communist Politics*. Cambridge University Press (2006)
56. 《高地上的革命：中国井冈山根据地》Stephen C. Averill（韦思谛）, *Revolution in the Highlands: China's Jinggangshan Base Area*. Rowman & Littlefield Publishers (2005)
57. 《他改变了中国：江泽民传》Robert Lawrence Kuhn（罗伯特·劳伦斯·库恩）, *The Man Who Changed China: The Life and Legacy of Jiang Zemin*. Crown (2005)
58. 《中国的党和艺术：新文化政治》Richard Curt Kraus, *The Party and the Arty in China: The New Politics of Culture* (State and Society in East Asia). Rowman & Littlefield Publishers (2004)
59. 《中国的二元精英和领导选择》Xiaowei Zang, *Elite Dualism and Leadership Selection in China*. Routledge (2003)
60. 《中国新一代领导人》Cheng Li（李成）, *China's Leaders: The New Generation*. Rowman & Littlefield Publishers (2001)
61. 《"南巡"讲话遗产与后邓小平时代中国的发展》John Wong（黄朝翰）, Zheng Yongnian（郑永年）, *The Nanxun Legacy and China's Development in the Post-Deng Era*. Singapore University Press; World Scientific Publishing (2001)

62. 《螺旋之路：一个共产党领导人眼中的中国村庄变迁—福建林庄》Huang Shu-min, *The Spiral Road: Change in a Chinese Village through the Eyes of a Communist Party Leader*. Westview Press (1998)

63. 《共产主义统治下的中国》Alan Lawrance（艾伦）, *China Under Communism* (Making of the Contemporary World). Routledge (1998)

64. 《李达与中国马克思主义哲学》Nick Knight（尼克·奈特）, *Li Da and Marxist Philosophy in China*. Westview Press (1998)

65. 《延安使团：1944—1947年美国与中国共产党人的联络》Carolle J. Carter, *Mission to Yenan: American Liaison with the Chinese Communists, 1944—1947*. The University Press of Kentucky (1997)

66. 《邓小平政治传记》Benjamin Yang（杨炳章）, *Deng: A Political Biography*. M. E. Sharpe Inc. (1997)

67. 《邓小平一代：20世纪80年代中国青年知识分子》Ruth Cherrington, *Deng's Generation: Young Intellectuals in 1980s China*. Palgrave Macmillan UK (1997)

68. 《邓小平时代：探索中国社会主义的命运》Maurice Meisner（莫里斯·迈斯纳）, *The Deng Xiaoping Era: An Inquiry into the Fate of Chinese Socialism, 1978—1994*. Hill and Wang (1996)

69. 《地方道路：文化、空间与中国共产主义的起源》Wen-hsin Yeh（叶文心）, *Provincial Passages: Culture, Space, and the Origins of Chinese Communism*. University of California Press (1996)

70. 《邓小平与中国革命：政治传记》David Goodman, *Deng Xiaoping and the Chinese Revolution: A Political Biography* (Routledge in Asia Series). Routledge (1994)

71. 《山火：红军在华南的三年战争（1934—1938）》Gregor Benton（班国瑞）, *Mountain Fires: The Red Army's Three-Year War in South China, 1934—1938*. University of California Press (1992)

72. 《从朋友到同志：中国共产党的成立（1920—1927）》Hans J. van de Ven（方德万）, *From Friend to Comrade: The Founding of the Chinese Communist Party, 1920—1927*. University of California Press (1991)

73. 《从革命到政治：长征途中的中国共产党人》（牛津大学中译本名《从革命到政治：长征与毛泽东的崛起》）Benjamin Yang（杨炳章）, *From Revolution to Politics: Chinese Communists on the Long March*. Westview Press (1990)

74. 《邓小平统治下的中国：政治和经济改革》David Wen-Wei Chang, *China under Deng Xiaoping: Political and Economic Reform*. Palgrave Macmillan UK (1988)

75. 《共产党社会的新传统主义：中国工业中的工作环境和权力结构》Andrew G. Walder（魏昂德）, *Communist Neo-Traditionalism: Work and Authority in Chinese Industry*. University of California Press (1986)

76. 《革命的形成：华东和华中的共产主义运动（1937—1945）》Chen Yung-fa（陈永发）,

Making Revolution: The Communist Movement in Eastern and Central China, 1937—1945. University of California Press (1986)

77. 《中国新一届党的领导：中国共产党第十二届中央委员会的传记与分析》Wolfgang Bartke, Peter Schier, *China's New Party Leadership: Biographies and Analysis of the Twelfth Central Committee of the Chinese Communist Party*. M. E. Sharpe, Inc. (1985)

78. 《陈云与中国政治制度》David M. Bachman, *Chen Yun and the Chinese Political System*. Institute of East Asian Studies [and] Center for Chinese Studies, University of California, Berkeley (1985)

79. 《彭德怀：其人与形象》Jürgen Domes, *Peng Te-huai: The Man and the Image*. Stanford University Press (1985)

80. 《中国共产党创始人陈独秀》Lee Feigon, *Chen Duxiu: Founder of the Chinese Communist Party*. Princeton University Press (1983)

81. 《延安妇女与共产党》Patricia Stranahan, *Yan'an Women and the Communist Party*. University of California, Center for Chinese Studies (1983)

82. 《中国共产党与农村社会（1927—1934）》Philip C. C Huang（黄宗智）, Lynda Schaefer Bell, Kathy Lemons Walker, *Chinese Communists and Rural Society, 1927—1934*. Berkeley: Center for Chinese Studies, University of California (1978)

83. 《干部、指挥员和政委：1920—1945年中国共产党领导力训练》(Columbia University, East Asian Institute Studies) Jane L. Price, *Cadres, Commanders and Commissars: The Training of the Chinese Communist Leadership, 1920—45*. Dawson (1976)

84. 《中国共产党基础知识》Danielle Bergeron, *A Basic Understanding of the Communist Party of China*. Translated from the French edition and published by Norman Bethune Institute, Toronto (1976)

85. 《运动：中国共产党领导的群众运动》Gordon Bennett, *Yundong: Mass Campaigns in Chinese Communist Leadership*. Berkeley: Center for Chinese Studies, University of California (1976)

86. 《中国共产主义政治：苏维埃时期的江西》Ilpyong J. Kim, *The Politics of Chinese Communism: Kiangsi under the Soviets*. University of California Press (1974)

87. 《共产主义中国的意识形态和组织》Franz Schurmann（舒尔曼）, *Ideology and Organization in Communist China*. University of California Press (1973)

88. 《1937年6月的延安：与共产党领导人会谈》T. A. Bisson, *Yenan in June 1937: Talks with the Communist Leaders*. Berkeley: Center for Chinese Studies, University of California (1973)

89. 《中国共产党历史》Jacques Guillermaz, translated by Anne Destenay, *A History of the Chinese Communist Party*. London: Methuen (1972)

90. 《共产党中国的传播与民族融合》Alan P.L. Liu, *Communications and National Integration in Communist China* (Michigan studies on China). University of California Press (1971)

91. 《中国的国共斗争（1922—1949）》Chung-Gi Kwei, *The Kuomintang-Communist Struggle in China 1922—1949*. Springer Netherlands (1970)

92. 《列宁主义与中国革命》Wang Ming-Lenin, *Leninism and the Chinese Revolution*. Moscow: Novosti Press Agency Publishing House (1970)

93. 《中国共产党的政治运作》A. Doak Barnett（鲍大可）(ed.), *Chinese Communist Politics in Action* (Studies in Chinese government and politics). Seattle: University of Washington Press (1969)

94. 《共产主义和中国：变动中的思想意识》Benjamin Isadore Schwartz（史华慈）, *Communism and China: Ideology in Flux*. Cambridge, Massachusetts: Harvard University Press (1968)

95. 《李大钊与中国马克思主义的起源》Maurice Meisner（莫里斯·迈斯纳）, *Li Ta-chao and the Origins of Chinese Marxism*. Harvard University Press (1967)

96. 《共产党中国的大众说服》Frederic T. C. Yu, *Mass Persuasion in Communist China*. Praeger (1964)

97. 《共产党接管前夕之中国》A. Doak Barnett（鲍大可）, *China on the Eve of Communist Takeover*. Frederick A. Praeger (1963)

98. 《中国共产党文献阅读：中文学生手册》Wen-shun Chi, *Readings in Chinese Communist Documents: Manual for Students of the Chinese Language*. University of California Press (1963)

99. 《今日中共》S. Chandresekhar, *Communist China Today*. Asia Publishing House (1961)

100. 《伟大的道路：朱德的生平和时代》Agnes Smedley, *The Great Road: The Life and Times of Chu Teh*. Monthly Review Press (1956)

101. 《共产主义统治下的中国前五年》Richard L. Walker, *China under Communism: The First Five Years*. Yale University Press (1955)

102. 《中国共产主义文献史》Conrad Brandt, Benjamin Schwartz（史华慈）, John K. Fairbank（费正清）, *A Documentary History of Chinese Communism*. Harvard University Press (1952)

103. 《中国共产主义者》Stuart Gelder, *The Chinese Communists*. Victor Gollancz Ltd (1946)

104. 《红色中国的挑战》Gunther Stein（冈瑟·斯坦因）, *The Challenge of Red China*. Whittlesey House (1945)

105. 《新中国的创造者》S. S. Batliwala, *Makers of New China*. People's Publishing House, Bombay (1943)

106. 《殖民地国家的革命运动：在共产国际七大上的讲话（1935）》Wang Ming（王明）, *The Revolutionary Movement in the Colonial Countrie: Speech at Seventh Comintern Congress, 1935*. Workers Library Publishers (1935)

107. 《中国共产党人与教会财产》*Chinese Communists and Mission Properties*. Publicity Bureau for South China (1926)

8.1.3 毛泽东

1. 《毛主义全球史》Julia Lovell（蓝诗玲）, *Maoism: A Global History*. Bodley Head (2019)

2. 《1934—1935年长征：毛泽东的崛起与近代中国的开端》Benjamin Lai, Adam Hook, *The Long March 1934—1935: The Rise of Mao and the Beginning of Modern China*. Osprey Publishing (2019)
3. 《斯大林与毛泽东：俄罗斯与中国革命之比较》Lucien Bianco, *Stalin and Mao: A Comparison of the Russian and Chinese Revolutions*. Chinese University Press (2018)
4. 《毛泽东的形象：艺术家与中国1949年转型》Yan Geng, *Mao's Images: Artists and China's 1949 Transition*. J. B. Metzler (2018)
5. 《被误解的友谊：毛泽东、金日成与1949—1976年的中朝关系》Zhihua Shen, Yafeng Xia, *A Misunderstood Friendship: Mao Zedong, Kim Il-Sung, and Sino-North Korean Relations, 1949—1976*. Columbia University Press (2018)
6. 《毛泽东：造就中国的人》Philip Short, *Mao: The Man Who Made China*. I. B. Tauris (2017)
7. 《如此迅速的力量：毛泽东、杜鲁门与现代中国的诞生（1949）》Kevin Peraino, *A Force So Swift: Mao, Truman, and the Birth of Modern China, 1949*. Crown (2017)
8. 《中国男孩：寻找毛泽东失踪之子》Richard Loseby, *A Boy of China: In Search of Mao's Lost Son*. HarperCollins (2017)
9. 《毛泽东的修辞学：改造中国及其人民》Xing Lu, *The Rhetoric of Mao Zedong: Transforming China and Its People*. University of South Carolina Press (2017)
10. 《从斯大林到毛泽东：阿尔巴尼亚和社会主义世界》Elidor Mechilli, *From Stalin to Mao: Albania and the Socialist World*. Cornell University Press (2017)
11. 《中国与新毛派》Kerry Brown（凯瑞·布朗）, Simone van Nieuwenhuizen, *China and the New Maoists*. Zed Books (2016)
12. 《天门风暴：印度毛主义运动的批判性研究（1972—2014）》Amit Bhattacharyya, *Storming the Gates of Heaven: The Maoist Movement in India: A Critical Study, 1972—2014*. Setu Prakashani (2016)
13. 《毛泽东时代的外国人：生活在中国的西方人（1949—1976）》Beverley Hooper, *Foreigners Under Mao: Western Lives in China, 1949—1976*. Hong Kong University Press (2016)
14. 《送瘟神：毛主席的中国灭虫运动》Miriam Gross, *Farewell to the God of Plague: Chairman Mao's Campaign to Deworm China*. (2016)
15. 《毛泽东的权力之路：革命著作（1942—1945）》（第八卷）Stuart R. Schram（施拉姆）, Timothy Cheek（齐慕实）, Roderick MacFarquhar（马若德）, *Mao's Road to Power: Revolutionary Writings (1942—1945)*. Volume VIII. Routledge (2016)
16. 《毛泽东思想与中国革命：批判性导论》Elliott Liu, *Maoism and the Chinese Revolution: A Critical Introduction* (Revolutionary Pocketbooks). PM Press (2016)
17. 《印度和尼泊尔的毛主义》Ranjit Bhushan, *Maoism in India and Nepal*. M-Routledge (2016)
18. 《毛主义在基层：中国社会主义高潮时代的日常生活》Jeremy Brown, Matthew D. Johnson (eds.), *Maoism at the Grassroots: Everyday Life in China's Era of High Socialism*.

Harvard University Press (2015)

19. 《施米特、毛泽东和转型政治》Qi Zheng, *Carl Schmitt, Mao Zedong and the Politics of Transition*. Palgrave Macmillan UK (2015)

20. 《毛泽东的文化军队：中国农村革命剧团》Brian James DeMare, *Mao's Cultural Army: Drama Troupes in China's Rural Revolution*. Cambridge University Press (2015)

21. 《天命：马克思和毛泽东在现代中国》Harris, Nigel, *The mandate of heaven: Marx and Mao in modern China*. Haymarket Books (2015)

22. 《毛泽东和麦卡锡之间：冷战时期的中美政治》Charlotte Brooks, *Between Mao and McCarthy: Chinese American Politics in the Cold War Years*. University of Chicago Press (2015)

23. 《毛泽东时代的博物馆画像：从"文革"到共产主义媚俗》Amy Jane Barnes, *Museum Representations of Maoist China: From Cultural Revolution to Commie Kitsch*. Ashgate Pub Co (2014)

24. 《中国规则：毛泽东的狗、邓小平的猫和来自中国一线的5个永不过时的教训》Tim Clissold, *Chinese Rules: Mao's Dog, Deng's Cat, and Five Timeless Lessons from the Front Lines in China*. Harper (2014)

25. 《子弹与票箱：尼泊尔毛主义者的革命故事》Aditya Adhikari, *The Bullet and the Ballot Box: The Story of Nepal's Maoist Revolution*. Verso (2014)

26. 《中国1945：毛泽东的革命与美国的致命选择》Richard Bernstein, *China 1945: Mao's Revolution and America's Fateful Choice*. Knopf (2014)

27. 《毛泽东简介》Delia Davin, *Mao: A Very Short Introduction*. Oxford University Press, USA (2013)

28. 《反巴迪欧：毛主义引入哲学》Francois Laruelle, Robin Mackay, *Anti-Badiou: The Introduction of Maoism into Philosophy*. Bloomsbury Academic (2013)

29. 《毛泽东统治下的生活》Zhang Da-Peng, George A. Fowler, *Life under Mao Zedong's Rule*. CreateSpace Independent Publishing Platform (2013)

30. 《毛泽东的真实故事》Alexander V. Pantsov（潘佐夫）, Steven I. Levine（罗思文）, *Mao: The Real Story*. Simon & Schuster (2012)

31. 《赛先生和毛主席的"文革"：近现代中国的科学技术》Chunjuan Nancy Wei (ed.), Darryl E. Brock (ed.), *Mr. Science and Chairman Mao's Cultural Revolution: Science and Technology in Modern China*. Lexington Books (2012)

32. 《毛泽东和尼赫鲁的国际雄心：国家效能信念与外交政策的制定》Andrew Kennedy, *The International Ambitions of Mao and Nehru: National Efficacy Beliefs and the Making of Foreign Policy*. Cambridge University Press (2011)

33. 《毛泽东：鲜为人知的故事》Jung Chang（张戎）, Jon Halliday, *Mao: The Unknown Story*. Anchor (2011)

34. 《毛式经济学：为何中国共产党人比我们资本家做得更好》Loretta Napoleoni, Stephen

Twilley, *Maonomics: Why Chinese Communists Make Better Capitalists Than We Do*. Seven Stories Press (2011)

35. 《20世纪世界中的毛泽东与中国》Rebecca E. Karl（柯瑞佳）, *Mao Zedong and China in the Twentieth-Century World: A Concise History*. Duke University Press Books (2010)

36. 《毛主席诗词35首》Mao Zedong, Willis Barnstone, *The Poems of Mao Zedong*. University of California Press (2010)

37. 《毛主义模范剧院：中国"文化大革命"中的性别与性符号学》Rosemary A. Roberts, *Maoist Model Theatre: The Semiotics of Gender and Sexuality in the Chinese Cultural Revolution*. Brill (2010)

38. 《印度的毛主义者：写作与访谈》Azad, *Maoists in India: Writings & Interviews*. Friends of Azad (2010)

39. 《印度毛主义：21世纪极左派极端主义的再生》Bidyut Chakrabarty, Rajat Kumar Kujur, *Maoism in India: Reincarnation of Ultra-Left Wing Extremism in the Twenty-First Century* (Routledge Contemporary South Asia Series).Routledge (2010)

40. 《毛主席徽章："文革"符号和口号》Helen Wang, *Chairman Mao Badges: Symbols and Slogans of the Cultural Revolution*. British Museum Press (2008)

41. 《尼克松和毛泽东：改变世界的一周》Margaret MacMillan, *Nixon and Mao: The Week That Changed the World*. Random House (2008)

42. 《毛泽东和中国革命》（第一卷）Gregor Benton（班国瑞）, *Mao Zedong and the Chinese Revolution,* Vol. 1. Routledge (2007)

43. 《毛泽东：政治与思想肖像》Maurice Meisner, *Mao Zedong: A Political and Intellectual Portrait*. Polity (2007)

44. 《毛主义者的"春雷"：纳萨里运动（1967—1972）》Arun Prosad Mukherjee, *Maoist 'Spring Thunder': The Naxalite Movement 1967—1972*. K. P. Bagchi & Company (2007)

45. 《实践论和矛盾论》Mao Tse-Tung, Slavoj Zizek, *On Practice and Contradiction*.Verso (2007)

46. 《毛泽东最后的革命》Roderick MacFarquhar（麦克法夸尔）, Michael Schoenhals（沈迈克）, *Mao's Last Revolution*. The Belknap Press of Harvard University Press (2006)

47. 《中国的变迁：从毛泽东到市场》John Gittings（约翰·吉廷斯）, *The Changing Face of China: From Mao to Market*. Oxford University Press, USA (2006)

48. 《从马克思、毛泽东到市场：农业转型的经济学与政治学》Johan Swinnen, Scott Rozelle, *From Marx and Mao to the Market: The Economics and Politics of Agricultural Transition*. Oxford University Press, USA (2006)

49. 《毛泽东与中国经济的斯大林化（1948—1953）》Hua-Yu Li（李华钰）, *Mao and the Economic Stalinization of China, 1948—1953* (The Harvard Cold War Studies Book Series). Rowman & Littlefield Publishers (2006)

50. 《从艾克到毛泽东及其他：我从美国主流到共产主义革命者的旅程》Bob Avakian,

From Ike to Mao and Beyond: My Journey from Mainstream America to Revolutionary Communist. Insight Press, Inc. (2005)

51. 《中国马克思主义哲学：从瞿秋白到毛泽东，1923—1945》Nick Knight（尼克·奈特），*Marxist Philosophy in China: From Qu Qiubai to Mao Zedong, 1923—1945.* Springer Netherlands (2005)

52. 《毛泽东的权力之路：新民主主义（1939—1941）》（第七卷）Stuart R. Schram（施拉姆），Nancy Jane Hodes, *Mao's Road to Power: New Democracy (1939—1941).* M.E. Sharpe (2005)

53. 《毛泽东的权力之路：新阶段（1937年8月至1938年）》（第六卷）Stuart R. Schram（施拉姆），Nancy Jane Hodes, *Mao's Road to Power: The New Stage (August 1937—1938).* M.E. Sharpe (2004)

54. 《毛泽东》Michael Lynch, *Mao.* Routledge (2004)

55. 《从尧到毛泽东：中国5000年史》（第一至三卷）Kenneth J. Hammond, *From Yao to Mao: 5000 Years of Chinese History (Part I-Part III).* The Teaching Company (2004)

56. 《从毛泽东到市场：中国寻租、地方保护主义和市场化》Andrew H. Wedeman, *From Mao to Market-Rent Seeking, Local Protectionism, and Marketization in China.* Cambridge University Press (2003)

57. 《重新解释毛泽东》Lee Feigon, *Mao: A Reinterpretation.* Chicago: Ivan R. Dee. (2002)

58. 《毛泽东与中国革命：文献简史》Timothy Cheek（齐慕实），*Mao Zedong and China's Revolutions: A Brief History with Documents* (The Bedford Series in History and Culture). Palgrave Macmillan US (2002)

59. 《政治哲学：从柏拉图到毛泽东》Martin Cohen, *Political Philosophy From Plato to Mao.* Pluto Press (2001)

60. 《发达世界的毛主义》Robert J. Alexander, *Maoism in the Developed World.* Praeger Publishers (2001)

61. 《毛泽东、马克思和市场：俄罗斯和中国资本主义的冒险》Dean LeBaron, *Mao, Marx, and the Market: Capitalist Adventures in Russia and China.* Wiley (2001)

62. 《毛泽东的中国与冷战》Jian Chen（陈兼），*Mao's China and the Cold war.* The University of North Carolina Press (2001)

63. 《毛泽东与自然的斗争：革命时代中国的政治与环境》Judith Shapiro（夏竹丽），*Mao's War against Nature: Politics and the Environment in Revolutionary China.* Cambridge University Press (2001)

64. 《成为毛泽东夫人》Anchee Min（闵安琪），*Becoming Madame Mao.* Mariner Books (2001)

65. 《毛泽东、周恩来与中国共产党领导体制的演变》Thomas Kampen, *Mao Zedong, Zhou Enlai and the Evolution of the Chinese Communist Leadership.* Nordic Institute of Asian

Studies (2000)

66. 《毛泽东传》Philip Short, *Mao: A Life*. Henry Holt and Company (1999)

67. 《毛泽东的中国及其后：人民共和国史》Maurice Meisner（莫旦斯·迈斯纳）, *Mao's China and After: A History of the People's Republic,* Third Edition. Free Press (1999)

68. 《毛泽东传》Jonathan D. Spence（史景迁）, *Mao*. Weidenfeld & Nicolson (1999)

69. 《毛泽东的权力之路：迈向第二次统一战线（1935年1月至1937年7月）》（第五卷）Nancy Jane Hodes, Stuart R. Schram（施拉姆）, *Mao's Road to Power: Toward the Second United Front (January 1935-July 1937)*. M. E. Sharpe (1999)

70. 《中国政治：毛泽东和邓小平时代》Roderick MacFarquhar（麦克法夸尔）(ed.), T*he Politics of China: The Eras of Mao and Deng*. Cambridge University Press (1997)

71. 《毛泽东的权力之路：中华苏维埃共和国的兴衰（1931—1934）》（第四卷）Stuart R. Schram（施拉姆）, Nancy Jane Hodes, Stephen C. Averill, *Mao's Road to Power: The Rise and Fall of the Chinese Soviet Republic (1931—1934)*. M. E. Sharpe (1997)

72. 《毛泽东私人医生回忆录》Li Zhi-Sui（李志绥）, *The Private Life of Chairman Mao*. Random House (1996)

73. 《毛主席不会被逗乐：今日中国小说》Howard Goldblatt, *Chairman Mao Would Not Be Amused: Fiction from Today's China*. Grove Press (1996)

74. 《毛泽东的权力之路：从井冈山到江西苏维埃的建立（1927—1930）》（第三卷）Stuart R. Schram（施拉姆）, Nancy Jane Hodes, *Mao's Road to Power: From the Jinggangshan to the Establishment of the Jiangxi Soviets (1927—1930)*. M.E. Sharpe (1995)

75. 《不确定的伙伴：斯大林、毛泽东和朝鲜战争》Sergei Goncharov, John Lewis, Litai Xue, *Uncertain Partners: Stalin, Mao, and the Korean War* (Studies in International Security and Arms Control). Stanford University Press (1995)

76. 《毛泽东的权力之路：国民革命与社会革命（1920—1927）》（第二卷）Stuart R. Schram（施拉姆）, *Mao's Road to Power: National Revolution and Social Revolution (1920—1927)*. M. E. Sharpe (1994)

77. 《赞扬毛主义经济计划：1931以来四川的生活水平和经济发展》（中译本名《毛时代经济再评价：四川，1930—1980s》）Chris Bramall（克里斯·布拉莫尔）, *In Praise of the Maoist Economic Planning: Living Standards and Economic Development in Sichuan since 1931*. Oxford: Clarendon Press (1993)

78. 《毛泽东：初学者读本》Rius and Friends, *Mao for Beginners*. Writers & Readers (1993)

79. 《寻乌调查》Mao Zedong, Roger Thompson, *Report from Xunwu*. Stanford University Press (1993)

80. 《毛泽东言论集》（第二卷）Zedong Mao, John K. Leung, Michael Y. M. Kau, *The Writings of Mao Zedong, 1949—1976. Volume II. January 1956-December 1957* M. E. Sharpe (1992)

81. 《毛泽东的权力之路：前马克思主义时期（1912—1920）》（第一卷）Stuart R.

Schram（施拉姆）, *Mao's Road to Power: The Pre-Marxist Period (1912—1920)*. M. E. Sharpe (1992)

82. 《毛泽东参考书目》Alan Lawrance（艾伦）, *Mao Zedong: A Bibliography (Bibliographies of World Leaders)*. Greenwood (1991)

83. 《没有毛泽东的中国：寻求新秩序》Immanuel C. Y. Hsu（徐中约）, *China without Mao: The Search for a New Order*. York: Oxford University Press (1990)

84. 《毛泽东论辩证唯物主义：1937年的哲学著作》Nick Knight（尼克·奈特）, *Mao Zedong on Dialectical Materialism: Writings on Philosophy, 1937* (Chinese Studies on China). M. E. Sharpe, Inc. (1990)

85. 《美国海军陆战队：毛泽东论游击战》Samuel B. Griffith, *Mao Tse-tung on Guerrilla Warfare*. U.S. Marine Corps (1989)

86. 《毛泽东的思想》Stuart Schram（施拉姆）, *The Thought of Mao Tse-Tung*. Cambridge University Press (1989)

87. 《托洛茨基主义与毛主义：法国与美国的理论和实践》A. Belden Fields, *Trotskyism and Maoism: Theory and Practice in France and the United States*. Autonomedia (1988)

88. 《毛泽东言论集（第一卷）》Tse-tung Mao, Michael Y. M. Kau, John K. Leung, *The Writings of Mao Zedong, 1949—1976.Vol.1 .September 1949-December 1955*. M. E. Sharpe (1986)

89. 《走向资本主义复辟：毛泽东去世后的中国社会主义》Michel Chossudovsky, *Towards Capitalist Restoration: Chinese Socialism after Mao*. Macmillan Education UK (1986)

90. 《中国的领导、合法性与冲突：从超凡魅力的毛泽东到继承政治》Frederick C. Teiwes（泰伟斯）, *Leadership, Legitimacy and Conflict in China: From a Charismatic Mao to the Politics of Succession*. Palgrave Macmillan UK (1984)

91. 《毛泽东的收获：来自中国新一代的声音》Helen F. Siu, Zelda Stern, *Mao's Harvest: Voices from China's New Generation*. Oxford University Press (1983)

92. 《毛主义的未来》Samir Amin, Norman H. Finkelstein, *The Future of Maoism*. Monthly Review Press (1983)

93. 《马克思主义、毛泽东思想与乌托邦主义》Maurice J. Meisner（莫里斯·迈斯纳）, *Marxism, Maoism, and Utopianism: Eight Essays*. Madison University of Wisconsin Press (1982)

94. 《中国政治与毛泽东的继承权》John Gardner, *Chinese Politics and the Succession to Mao* (China in Focus Series). Macmillan Education UK (1982)

95. 《毛泽东政治思想的基础：1917—1935》Womack Brantly, *The Foundations of Mao Zedong's Political Thought, 1917—1935*. Honolulu: University Press of Hawai'i (1982)

96. 《毛泽东的人民：革命中国的十六幅肖像》B. Michael Frolic, *Mao's People: Sixteen Portraits of Life in Revolutionary China*. Harvard University Press (1981)

97. 《毛泽东的辩证法理论》Francis Y. K. Soo, *Mao Tse-Tung's Theory of Dialectic* (Sovietica 44). Springer Netherlands (1981)

98.《毛泽东传》Ross Terrill（罗斯·特里尔）, *Mao: A biography*. Harper & Row (1980)

99.《毛主席论无产阶级教育》Don-Chean Chu, *Chairman Mao: Education of the Proletariat*. Philosophical Library, New York (1980)

100.《毛泽东和边区的政治经济学》Andrew Watson（安德鲁·沃森）, *Mao Zedong and the Political Economy of the Border Region: A Translation of Mao's Economic and Financial Problems*. Cambridge University Press (1980)

101.《揽月：毛泽东传》Ed Hammond, *To Embrace The Moon: An Illustrated Biography of Mao Zedong*. Lancaster-Miller, Inc. Asian Humanities Press (1980)

102.《毛泽东去世以来的中国》Kwan Ha Yim (eds.), *China since Mao*. Palgrave Macmillan UK (1980)

103.《继续革命：毛泽东的政治思想》John Bryan Starr, *Continuing the Revolution: The Political Thought of Mao*. Princeton University Press (1979)

104.《毛泽东的不朽贡献》Bob Avakian, *Mao Tsetung's Immortal Contributions*. RCP Publications (1979)

105.《纪念毛泽东：历史唯物主义论文》Philip Corrigan, Harvie Ramsay, Derek Sayer, *For Mao: Essays in Historical Materialism*. Palgrave Macmillan UK (1979)

106.《毛泽东的最后一场大战》Raymond Lotta, *And Mao Makes 5: Mao Tsetung's Last Great Battle*. Banner Press (1978)

107.《毛泽东逝世后的中国》Charles Bettelheim（夏尔·贝特兰）, Neill G. Burton, *China since Mao*. Monthly Review Press (1978)

108.《毛泽东思想中的爱与斗争》Raymond Whitehead, *Love and Struggle in Mao's Thought*. Orbiss Books (1977)

109.《革命暴力：印度毛主义运动研究》Manoranjan Mohanty（莫汉谛）, *Revolutionary Violence: A Study of the Maoist Movement in India*. Sterling Publishers (1977)

110.《毛泽东同志的早期革命活动》Rui Li（李锐）, Translated by Anthony W. Sariti, Edited by James C. Hsiung, Introduction by Stuart R. Schram（施拉姆）, *The Early Revolutionary Activities of Comrade Mao Tse-tung*. N.Y.: M. E. Sharpe (1977)

111.《中国经济与毛主义战略》John Gurley, *China's Economy and the Maoist Strategy*. Monthly Review Press (1976)

112.《毛泽东诗词10首》Zedong Mao, Wang Hui-Ming, *Ten Poems and Lyrics* (Poetry Paperbacks) (Mandarin Chinese and English Edition). Jonathan Cape Ltd (1976)

113.《作为领袖的毛泽东》（中译本名《毛泽东的心理分析》）Lucian W. Pye（白鲁恂）, *Mao Tse-Tung: The Man in the Leader*. New York: Basic Books (1976)

114.《毛泽东：来自长江流域的年轻人》Bernadette P. N. Shih, *Mao: A Young Man from the Yangtze Valley*. Ashley Books (1974)

115.《毛主席与人民的谈话：谈话与信件（1956—1971）》Stuart Schram（施拉姆），

Chairman Mao Talks to the People: Talk and Letters: 1956—1971. Pantheon Books (1974)

116. 《毛泽东》Jack Gray, *Mao Tse-tung* (Makers of modern though). Lutterworth Press (1973)

117. 《江西苏维埃共和国：毛泽东与1931、1934年全国代表大会》Derek J. Waller, *The Kiangsi Soviet Republic: Mao and the National Congresses of 1931 and 1934*. Berkeley, Center for Chinese Studies, University of California (1973)

118. 《毛泽东与甘地：社会转型的视角》Jayantanuja Bandyopadhyaya, *Mao Tse-tung and Gandhi: Perspectives on Social Transformation*. Allied Publishers (1973)

119. 《历史与意志：毛泽东思想的哲学透视》Frederic Wakeman, Jr.（魏斐德）, *History and Will: Philosophical Perspectives of Mao Tse-Tung's Thought* (Center for Chinese Studies, Uc Berkeley: No 9). University of California Press (1973)

120. 《毛泽东与林彪：革命后时代的著作》Edited by K. Fan, *Mao Tse-tung and Lin Piao: Post-Revolutionary Writings*. Anchor Books (1972)

121. 《毛泽东的"文革"》Tai Sung An, *Mao Tse-tung's Cultural Revolution*. Pegasus (1972)

122. 《毛泽东诗词》Paul Engle, Hua-ling Engle, *Poems of Mao Tse Tung*. Simon & Schuster (1972)

123. 《毛泽东理论概念的批判》F. V. Konstantinov, et al. (eds.), translated from the Russian by Yuri Sdobnikov, *A Critique of Mao Tse-tung's Theoretical Conceptions*. Progress Publishers, Moscow (1972)

124. 《毛主席的奇迹：文献概要，1966—1970》George Urban (ed.), *The miracles of Chairman Mao: A Compendium of Devotional Literature, 1966—1970*. Tom Stacey Ltd. (1971)

125. 《长期博弈：毛泽东革命战略的"围棋"解读》Scott Boorman, *The Protracted Game: A Wei-Ch'i Interpretation of Maoist Revolutionary Strategy* (Galaxy Books). Oxford University Press, USA (1971)

126. 《毛主席的奇迹：1966—1970年信仰文学纲要》Edited and introduced by George Urban, *The Miracles of Chairman Mao: A Compendium of Devotional Literature, 1966—1970*. Tom Stacey LTD (1971)

127. 《毛泽东文献：文选和文献目录》Jerome Ch'en（陈志让）, *Mao Papers: Anthology and Bibliography*. Oxford University Press (1970)

128. 《毛泽东》Jerome Ch'en（陈志让）, *Mao (Great Lives Observed)*. Prentice Hall (1969)

129. 《毛泽东论革命与战争》M. Regai, *Mao Tse-tung on revolution and war*. Anchor Books (1970)

130. 《五卷本毛泽东英语文选专有名词索引》Harry M. Lindquist, Roger D. Meyer, *Concordance of Proper Nouns in the Five-Volume English-Language Selected Works of Mao Tse-tung*. University of Kansas (1968)

131. 《印度尼西亚人民走毛泽东道路选集》Afro-Asian Writers, *Indonesian People Take Mao Tse-Tung's Road: Anthology*. Afro-Asian Writers Bureau (1968)

132. 《毛泽东的四篇哲学论文》Mao Tse-Tung, *Four Essays on Philosophy*. Foreign Languages Press (1968)

133. 《毛泽东以后的中国》A. Doak Barnett（鲍大可），*China after Mao*. Princeton University Press (1967)

134. 《在野的毛泽东：1927—1935》John E. Rue, *Mao Tse-tung in opposition, 1927—1935*. Stanford University Press (1966)

135. 《中国政治思想：毛泽东和刘少奇》Yung Ping Chen, *Chinese Political Thought: Mao Tse-Tung and Liu Shao-chi*. Springer Netherlands (1966)

136. 《毛主席语录》Mao Tse-tung, *Quotation from Chairman Mao*.Foreign Language Press (1966)

137. 《毛泽东与中国革命》Jerome Ch'en（陈志让），*Mao and the Chinese Revolution*. Oxford University Press (1965)

138. 《关于毛泽东与一群日本社会主义者的谈话》*In Connection with Mao Tse-tung's Talk with a Group of Japanese Socialists*. Moscow: Novosti Press Agency Publishing House (1964)（作者不详）

139. 《毛泽东和我曾是乞丐》Siao-Yu（萧瑜），*Mao Tse-Tung and I Were Beggars*. With a Foreword by Lin Yutang（林语堂），Preface by Raymond F. Piper, and Historical Commentary and Notes by Robert C. North. Syracuse University Press (1959)

140. 《毛泽东的中国：经济和政治调查》Ygael Gluckstein, *Mao's China: Economic and Political Survey*. Geogre Allen & Unwin Ltd (1957)

141. 《中国思想：从孔子到毛泽东》Herrlee Glessner Creel（顾立雅），*Chinese Thought, from Confucius to Mao Tse-Tung*. University Of Chicago Press (1953)

142. 《毛泽东治下的中国报道》Frank Moraes, *Report On Mao's China*.The Macmillan Company (1953)

143. 《中国的共产主义与毛泽东的崛起》Benjamin Schwartz（史华慈），*Chinese Communism and the Rise of Mao*. Harvard University Press (1951, 1979)

144. 《毛泽东：红色中国的统治者》Robert Payne, *Mao Tse Tung: Ruler of Red China*. New York: Henry Schuman (1950)

145. 《毛泽东思想》Anna Louise Strong（安娜·路易斯·斯特朗），*The Thought of Mao Tse-Tung*. Amerasia (1947)

8.1.4 中国道路/中国梦

1. 《论中国道路：寻找新的现代性》Honghua Men（门洪华），*On China's Road: In Search of a New Modernity*. Springer Singapore Palgrave Macmillan (2020)

2. 《一路多梦：中国重塑全球经济的大胆计划》Daniel Drache, A. T. Kingsmith, Duan Qi, *One Road, Many Dreams: China's Bold Plan to Remake the Global Economy*.Bloomsbury China (2019)

3. 《中国（1949—2019）：从贫困到世界强国》Paolo Urio（保罗·优利欧），*China 1949—2019: From Poverty to World Power*.Springer Singapore (2019)

4. 《中国的和平发展道路》(China Insights) Yuyan Zhang, Weijiang Feng, *Peaceful Development Path in China*.Springer Singapore (2019)

5. 《中国梦与浙江的实践：总论卷》(Research Series on the Chinese Dream and China's Development Path) Yingqiu Liu, Qunhui Huang, Jinling Wang, *The Chinese Dream and Zhejiang's Practice: General Report Volume*.Springer Singapore (2019)

6. 《中国梦与浙江的实践：经济》(Research Series on the Chinese Dream and China's Development Path) Changhong Pei, Jianfeng Xu, *Chinese Dream and Practice in Zhejiang: Economy*.Springer Singapore (2019)

7. 《中国梦与浙江的实践：文化》(Research Series on the Chinese Dream and China's Development Path) Dikun Xie, Ye Chen, *Chinese Dream and Practice in Zhejiang: Culture*. Springer Singapore (2019)

8. 《中国梦与浙江的实践：社会》(Research Series on the Chinese Dream and China's Development Path) Guangjin Chen, Jianhua Yang, *Chinese Dream and Practice in Zhejiang: Society*.Springer Singapore (2019)

9. 《中国梦与浙江的实践：政治》(Research Series on the Chinese Dream and China's Development Path) Ning Fang, Huaxing Chen, Jie Yun, *Chinese Dream and Practice in Zhejiang: Politics*.Springer Singapore (2019)

10. 《中国梦与浙江的实践：生态》(Research Series on the Chinese Dream and China's Development Path) Jiahua Pan, Manhong Shen, *Chinese Dream and Practice in Zhejiang: Ecology*.Springer Singapore (2019)

11. 《经济特区与中国发展道路》(Research Series on the Chinese Dream and China's Development Path) Yitao Tao, Zhiguo Lu, *Special Economic Zones and China's Development Path*.Springer Singapore (2018)

12. 《中国道路与中国梦：从党的全国代表大会分析中国政治决策过程》Angang Hu（胡鞍钢）, *China's Road and China's Dream: An Analysis of the Chinese Political Decision-Making Process Through the National Party Congress*. Springer Singapore (2018)

13. 《解密中国大趋势：撼动中国和世界的动力》Chi Lo, *Demystifying China's Mega Trends: The Driving Forces That Will Shake Up China and the World*. Emerald Publishing (2017)

14. 《中国的市场共产主义：挑战、困境与对策》Steven Rosefielde, Jonathan Leightner, *China's Market Communism: Challenges, Dilemmas, Solutions*. Routledge (2017)

15. 《中国新的战略布局》Ming Xin（辛鸣）, *China's New Strategic Layout* (China Insights). Springer (2017)

16. 《中国的共识、地方政府与发展：中国模式反思》Huihua Nie, *Collusion, Local Governments and Development in China: A Reflection on the China Model*. Palgrave Macmillan (2017)

17. 《中国的许多梦想：中国寻求民族复兴的比较视角》David Kerr (eds.), *China's Many Dreams: Comparative Perspectives on China's Search for National Rejuvenation*.Palgrave Macmillan (2015)

18. 《不可思议的中国三位一体："中国梦"的结构性挑战》Chi Lo, *China's Impossible*

Trinity: The Structural Challenges to the "Chinese Dream". Palgrave Macmillan (2015)

19. 《中国梦：后美国时代的大国思维与战略立场》Liu Mingfu, *The China Dream: Great Power Thinking and Stratigic Posture in the Post-American Era*. CN Times Books Inc. (2015)

20. 《中国模式：贤能政治与民主的局限》Daniel A. Bell（淡贝宁）, *The China Model: Political Meritocracy and the Limits of Democracy*. Princeton University Press (2015)

21. 《中国未来之路：难题、疑问和展望》Roland Benedikter, Verena Nowotny, *China's Road Ahead: Problems, Questions, Perspectives*. Springer New York (2014)

22. 《中国能领先吗？达到权力和增长的极限》Regina M.Abrami, William C. Kirby（柯伟林）, F. Warren McFarlan, *Can China Lead? Reaching the Limits of Power and Growth*. Harvard Business Review Press (2014)

23. 《中国创新绿色发展》Angang Hu（胡鞍钢）, *China: Innovative Green Development*. Springer Berlin Heidelberg (2014, 2017)

24. 《中国2030》Angang Hu（胡鞍钢）, Yilong Yan, Xing Wei, *China 2030*. Springer Berlin Heidelberg (2014)

25. 《中国梦与中国道路》Tianyong Zhou（周天勇）, *The China Dream and the China Path*. World Scientific Publishing Company (2013)

26. 《虎头蛇尾：今日中国如何形成，今后走向何方》Jonathan Fenby, *Tiger Head, Snake Tails: China Today, How It Got There, and Where It Is Heading*. Overlook TP (2013)

27. 《富强：中国迈向21世纪的长征》Orville Schell（夏伟）, John Delury（鲁乐汉）, *Wealth and Power: China's Long March to the Twenty-first Century*. Random House (2013)

28. 《中国试验：从地方创新到全国改革》Ann M. Florini, Hairong Lai（赖海榕）, Yeling Tan（陈业灵）, *China Experiments: From Local Innovations to National Reform*. Brookings Institution Press (2012)

29. 《全球经济衰退与中国政治经济学》Dali L. Yang (eds.), *The Global Recession and China's Political Economy*. Palgrave Macmillan US (2012)

30. 《中国震撼：一个文明型国家的崛起》Weiwei Zhang（张维维）, *The China Wave: Rise of a Civilizational State*. World Century Publishing Corporation (2012)

31. 《中国2020：新型超级大国》Angang Hu（胡鞍钢）, *China in 2020: A New Type of Superpower* (Thornton Center Chinese Thinkers). Brookings Institution Press (2011)

32. 《21世纪属于中国吗？基辛格等论辩中国》Henry Kissinger（基辛格）, Niall Ferguson（弗格森）, David Daokui Li（李稻葵）, Fareed Zakaria, *Does the 21st Century Belong to China Kissinger and Zakaria vs. Ferguson and Li. The Munk Debate on China*. House of Anansi Press (2011)

33. 《中国价值：西方是如何迷失的》Alex Mackinnon, Barnaby Powell, *China Counting: How the West Was Lost*. Palgrave Macmillan (2010)

34. 《中国：悲乐观主义者国度》William A. Callahan, *China: The Pessoptimist Nation*.Oxford

University Press (2010)

35. 《中国区域发展研究：路线图2050》Dadao Lu, Jie Fan (eds.), *Regional Development Research in China: A Roadmap to 2050*. Springer Berlin Heidelberg (2010)

36. 《中国复兴：未来的问题》Nazrul Islam, *Resurgent China: Issues for the Future*. Palgrave Macmillan (2009)

37. 《中国规则：全球化和政治转型》Ilan Alon, Julian Chang, Marc Fetscherin, Christoph Lattemann, John R. McIntyre (Editors), *China Rules: Globalization and Political Transformation*. Palgrave Macmillan (2009)

38. 《中国私有化：远方的社会主义》Aihwa Ong, Li Zhang, *Privatizing China: Socialism from afar*. Cornell University Press (2008)

39. 《中国道路：一个崛起大国的未来之路》Rob Gifford, *China Road: A Journey into the Future of a Rising Power*. Random House (2007)

40. 《21世纪的中国：挑战与机遇》Shiping Hua, Sujian Guo（郭苏建）, *China in the Twenty-First Century: Challenges and Opportunities*. Palgrave Macmillan (2007)

41. 《不满的奇迹：中国的增长、冲突和制度适应性》Dali L. Yang（杨大力）, *Discontented Miracle: Growth, Conflict, and Institutional Adaptations in China* (Series on Contemporary China). World Scientific Publishing Company (2007)

42. 《解读中国发展》Wang Gungwu（王赓武）, John Wong（黄朝翰）(eds.), *Interpreting China's Development*. World Scientific (2007)

43. 《中国：经济政治发展指南》Ian Jeffries, *China: A Guide to Economic and Political Develolpments*. Routledge (2006)

44. 《当代中国的关键问题》Cze Tubilewicz, *Critical Issues in Contemporary China*. Routledge (2006)

45. 《中国现代发展模式》Tian Yu Cao, *The Chinese Model of Modern Development* (Routledge Studies on the Chinese Economy). Routledge (2005)

46. 《中国复兴的动力》Jianrong Huang, *The Dynamics of China's Rejuvenation* (Studies on the Chinese Economy). Palgrave Macmillan UK (2004)

47. 《团结中国：邓小平时代后的多样性与民族融合》Barry J. Naughton, Dali L. Yang（杨大力）, *Holding China Together: Diversity and National Integration in the Post-Deng Era*. Cambridge University Press (2004)

48. 《一个中国，多条道路》Chaohua Wang (ed.), *One China, Many Paths*. Verso (2003)

49. 《红猫与白猫：中国与市场社会主义的矛盾》Robert Weil, *Red Cat, White Cat: China and the Contradictions of Market Socialism*. Monthly Review Press (1996)

50. 《中国重新评估社会主义（1976—1992）》Yan Sun, *The Chinese Reassessment of Socialism, 1976—1992*. Princeton University Press (1995)

51. 《从天到地：中国发展的形象与经验》Elizabeth Croll, *From Heaven to Earth: Images and*

Experiences of Development in China. Routledge (1993)
52. 《经济改革时代的中国国家：危机之路》Gordon White (eds.), *The Chinese State in the Era of Economic Reform: The Road to Crisis*. Palgrave Macmillan UK (1991)
53. 《中国变化的发展之路》Neville Maxwell, Bruce McFarlane (eds.), *China's Changed Road to Development*. Pergamon Press (1984)
54. 《中国发展道路》Neville Maxwell, *China's Road to Development*. 2nd ed., Pergamon Press (1979)

8.1.5 中国崛起

1. 《规范中国崛起：澳大利亚进军中等强国的经济学》(Studies in the Political Economy of Public Policy) Michael Peters, *Regulating the Rise of China: Australia's Foray into Middle Power Economics*. Springer International Publishing: Palgrave Macmillan (2019)
2. 《中国与西方之蒙克辩论：麦克马斯特与白邦瑞vs.马凯硕与王辉耀》H. R. McMaster, Michael Pillsbury（白邦瑞）, Kishore Mahbubani（马凯硕）, Huiyao Wang（王辉耀）, Rudyard Griffiths, *China and the West: McMaster and Pillsbury vs. Mahbubani and Wang: The Munk Debates*. House of Anansi Press (2019)
3. 《种族与中国崛起的话语》Yinghong Cheng（程映红）, *Discourses of Race and Rising China*. Palgrave Macmillan (2019)
4. 《国际法视野下决定中国兴衰的议题》Yuwa Wei, *Issues Decisive for China's Rise or Fall: An International Law Perspective*. Springer Singapore (2019)
5. 《中国在全球化时代的崛起：神话还是现实》Jianyong Yue, *China's Rise in the Age of Globalization: Myth or Reality* (Palgrave Studies in Economic History). Palgrave Macmillan (2018)
6. 《反思中国崛起：一种自由主义批判》(The Cambridge China library.) Jilin Xu（许纪霖）, David Ownby (edit and translate), *Rethinking China's Rise: A Liberal Critique*. Cambridge University Press (2018)
7. 《中国崛起与海外华人》Bernard P. Wong, Tan Chee-Beng (eds.), *China's Rise and the Chinese Overseas* (Routledge Contemporary China Series). Routledge (2018)
8. 《为什么中国没有文艺复兴，以及为什么重要：跨学科对话》Thomas Maissen, Barbara Mittler, *Why China did not Have a Renaissance, and Why that Matters: An Interdisciplinary Dialogue* (Critical Readings in Global Intellectual History 1). De Gruyter Oldenbourg (2018)
9. 《自由主义2.0与中国崛起：全球危机、创新与城市流动》David Tyfield, *Liberalism 2.0 and the Rise of China: Global Crisis, Innovation and Urban Mobility* (Routledge Advances in Sociology). Routledge (2018)
10. 《中国问题：对一个崛起大国的批判性见解》Jennifer Rudolph, Michael Szonyi（宋怡明）, *The China Questions: Critical Insights into a Rising Power*. Harvard University Press (2018)
11. 《红天鹅：非常规决策如何促进中国崛起》Sebastian Heilmann（韩博天）, *Red Swan: How*

Unorthodox Policy Making Facilitated China's Rise. The Chinese University Press (2018)

12. 《中国会和平崛起吗？一个大国崛起的理论、历史、政治和未来》Asle Toje, *Will China's Rise Be Peaceful: The Rise of a Great Power in Theory, History, Politics, and the Future*. Oxford University Press, USA (2018)

13. 《红星照耀太平洋：中国崛起对美国海洋战略的挑战》（修订版）Toshi Yoshihara, James R. Holmes, *Red Star over the Pacific, Revised Edition: China's Rise and the Challenge to U.S. Maritime Strategy*. Naval Institute Press (2018)

14. 《寻求亚洲平衡：中国在印太地区的崛起与平衡》Jeff M. Smith, *Asia's Quest for Balance: China's Rise and Balancing in the Indo-Pacific*. Rowman & Littlefield Publishers (2017)

15. 《中国：极地大国》Anne-Marie Brady, *China as a Polar Great Power*. Cambridge University Press (2017)

16. 《海上强国的形成：中国的挑战与政策回应》Zhiguo Kong, *The Making of a Maritime Power: China's Challenges and Policy Responses*. Springer Singapore (2017)

17. 《中国将和平崛起吗？一个大国崛起的理论、历史、政治和未来》Asle Toje, *Will China's Rise Be Peaceful? The Rise of a Great Power in Theory, History, Politics, and the Future*. New York, NY: Oxford University Press (2017)

18. 《面对中国作为新的全球超级大国：多学科视角的国内和国际动力学》Huhua Cao（曹沪华）, Jeremy Paltiel (eds.), *Facing China as a New Global Superpower: Domestic and International Dynamics from a Multidisciplinary Angle*. Springer-Verlag Singapur (2016)

19. 《中国读本：崛起的力量》（第六版）David Shambaugh（沈大伟）, *The China Reader: Rising Power*. Sixth Edition. Oxford University Press (2016)

20. 《中国鸟笼：中国崛起如何几乎颠覆西方》Heleen Mees, *The Chinese Birdcage: How China's Rise Almost Toppled the West*. Palgrave Macmillan US (2016)

21. 《鸡为何横扫世界：关于成功、财富和幸福来自中国的18个惊人秘密》Rachel Loui (a.k.a. Funky Chicken), *Why the Chicken Crossed the World: 18 Surprising Secrets from China on Success, Wealth, and Happiness*. Funky Chicken (2016)

22. 《中国对美国霸权的挑战：经济超级大国与崛起之星》John G. Glenn, *China's Challenge to US Supremacy: Economic Superpower versus Rising Star*. Palgrave Macmillan UK (2016)

23. 《百年马拉松：中国取代美国成为全球超级大国的秘密战略》Michael Pillsbury（白邦瑞）, *The Hundred-Year Marathon: China's Secret Strategy to Replace America as the Global Superpower*. Henry Holt and Company (2015)

24. 《应对中国崛起：美国和欧盟的战略》Vinod K. Aggarwal, Sara A. Newland (eds.), *Responding to China's Rise: US and EU Strategies*. Springer International Publishing (2015)

25. 《国家资本主义、制度适应与中国奇迹》Barry Naughton, Kellee S. Tsai（蔡欣怡）, *State Capitalism, Institutional Adaptation, and the Chinese Miracle* (Comparative Perspectives in

Business History). Cambridge University Press (2015)

26. 《中国经济崛起及其全球影响》Ken Moak, Miles W. N. Lee, *China's Economic Rise and Its Global Impact*. Palgrave Macmillan US (2015)

27. 《中国崛起：发展型金融与可持续发展》Lixing Zou, *China's Rise: Development-Oriented Finance and Sustainable Development*. World Scientific Publishing Company (2014)

28. 《中国崛起与东亚区域一体化：霸权还是共同体？》Yong Wook Lee, Key-Young Son, *China's Rise and Regional Integration in East Asia: Hegemony or Community?* Routledge (2014)

29. 《中国重要吗？再评估——纪念杰拉尔德·西格尔》Barry Buzan, Rosemary Foot, *Does China Matter: A Reassessment: Essays in Memory of Gerald Segal*. Routledge (2004)

30. 《全球政治中的知识、欲望与权力：中国崛起的西方陈述》Chengxin Pan, *Knowledge, Desire and Power in Global Politics: Western Representations of China's Rise*. Edward Elgar Publishing (2013)

31. 《揭秘中国奇迹：关系资本主义的兴起与未来》Wang Yongqin, *Demystifying the Chinese Miracle: The Rise and Future of Relational Capitalism* (Routledge Studies in the Modern World Economy). Routledge (2013)

32. 《无人关爱的美元本位：从布雷顿森林体系到中国崛起》Ronald I. McKinnon, *The Unloved Dollar Standard: From Bretton Woods to the Rise of China*. Oxford University Press (2013)

33. 《经济合作与发展组织：与中国互动》*Active with china*. OECD (2012)

34. 《红色崛起与红色黯淡：2012年中国故事年鉴》Geremie R. Barmé, Jeremy Goldkorn, Carolyn Cartier, Gloria Davies, *Red Rising, Red Eclipse: China Story Yearbook 2012*. Australian Centre on China in the World (2012)

35. 《中国化与中国崛起：超越东西方的文明进程》Peter J. Katzenstein, *Sinicization and the Rise of China: Civilizational Processes beyond East and West*. Milton Park; New York, NY: Routledge (2012)

36. 《中国2020：中华人民共和国未来十年》Kerry Brown（凯瑞·布朗）(ed.), *China 2020: The Next Decade for the People's Republic of China*. Chandos Publishing (2011)

37. 《美国的挑战：21世纪应对崛起的中国》Michael D. Swaine（迈克尔·史文）, *America's Challenge: Engaging a Rising China in the Twenty-First Century*. Carnegie Endowment for International Peace (2011)

38. 《亚太经合组织与中国的崛起》Lok Sang Ho, *APEC and the Rise of China*. World Scientific Publishing Company (2011)

39. 《中国崛起：全球挑战与机遇》Jane Golley, Ligang Song, *Rising China: Global Challenges and Opportunities*. Australian National University (2011)

40. 《跃过云层之马：间谍、丝绸之路和现代中国崛起的故事》Eric Enno Tamm, *The Horse That Leaps Through Clouds: A Tale of Espionage, the Silk Road, and the Rise of Modern*

China. Counterpoint (2011)

41. 《航点：中国崛起与零售业供应链管理的未来》Peter J. Levesque, *The Shipping Point: The Rise of China and the Future of Retail Supply Chain Management*. Wiley (2011)

42. 《入乡随俗：为什么中国崛起不会威胁西方》Edward S. Steinfeld（谢德华）, *Playing Our Game: Why China's Rise Doesn't Threaten the West*. Oxford University Press (2010)

43. 《红星照耀太平洋：中国崛起及其对美国海洋战略的挑战》Toshi Yoshihara（吉原恒淑）, James R. Holmes, *Red Star over the Pacific: China's Rise and the Challenge to U.S. Maritime Strategy*. Naval Institute Press (2010)

44. 《全球背景下的中国和平崛起：中国民主化路线图的国内看点》Jinghao Zhou, *China's Peaceful Rise in a Global Context: A Domestic Aspect of China's Road Map to Democratization*. Lexington Books (2010)

45. 《协调中国国家、市场与社会：走向繁荣的长征》Paolo Urio, *Reconciling State, Market and Society in China: The Long March toward Prosperity*. Routledge (2010)

46. 《中国大趋势：新社会的八大支柱》John Naisbitt, Doris Naisbitt, *China's Megatrends: The 8 Pillars of a New Society*. Harper Business (2010)

47. 《中国崛起与韩国、亚洲结构变化》Takatoshi Ito, Chin Hee Hahn, *The Rise of China and Structural Changes in Korea and Asia*. Edward Elgar Publishing Limited (2010)

48. 《与龙共处：美国公众如何看待中国崛起》Benjamin Page, Tao Xie, Andrew Nathan, *Living with the Dragon: How the American Public Views the Rise of China*. New York: Columbia University Press (2010)

49. 《中国：新的超级大国——权力、能源和安全的维度》Atilla Sandikli, *China: A New Superpower: Dimensions of Power, Energy and Security*. Bilgesam Publications (2010)

50. 《中国崛起及其后现代命运：新全球环境下的帝国记忆》Charles Horner（查尔斯·霍纳）, *Rising China and Its Postmodern Fate: Memories of Empire in a New Global Context* (Studies in Security and International Affairs). University of Georgia Press (2009)

51. 《管理混乱：中国奇迹的脆弱性》Prem Shankar Jha, *Managed Chaos: The Fragility of the Chinese Miracle*. Sage Publications Pvt. Ltd (2009)

52. 《崛起的中国：权力与保证》Ron Huisken, *Rising China: Power and Reassurance*. The Australian National University Press (2009)

53. 《当中国统治世界：西方世界的终结和全球新秩序的诞生》（中译本《大国雄心》，2016) Martin Jacques（马丁·雅克）, *When China Rules the World: The End of the Western World and the Birth of a New Global Order*. Allen Lane (2009)

54. 《中国崛起：西方能否应对？中国和亚洲总体崛起的真正长期挑战》Jan Willem Blankert, *China Rising: Will the West Be Able to Cope? The Real Long-term Challenge to the Rise of China and Asia in general*. World Scientific (2009)

55. 《中国崛起：挑战与机遇》C. Fred Bergsten, Charles Freeman, Nicholas R. Lardy（尼古

拉斯·拉迪）, Derek J. Mitchell, *China's Rise: Challenges and Opportunities*. Peterson Institute for International Economcis (2008)

56. 《"中国世纪"：挑战全球秩序》David Scott, *The 'Chinese Century': The Challenge to Global Order*. Palgrave Macmillan (2008)

57. 《现代中国：一个大国的兴衰（1850年至今）》Jonathan Fenby, *Modern China: The Fall and Rise of a Great Power, 1850 to the Present*. Ecco (2008)

58. 《中国崛起与资本主义世界经济的消亡》Minqi Li, *The Rise of China and the Demise of the Capitalist World-Economy*. Pluto Press (2008)

59. 《管理中国挑战的全球视角》Quansheng Zhao（赵全胜）, Guoli Liu, *Managing the China Challenge: Global Perspectives* (Asian Security Studies). Routledge (2008)

60. 《太平洋潮流：美国盟国和东亚安全伙伴对中国崛起的回应》Evan S. Medeiros（麦艾文）, *Pacific Currents: The Responses of U.S. Allies and Security Partners in East Asia to China's Rise*. RAND Corporation (2008)

61. 《龙的崛起：1978—2007年改革时期中国的内外投资》Kerry Brown（凯瑞·布朗）, *The Rise of the Dragon: Inward and Outward Investment in China in the Reform Period 1978—2007*. Chandos Publishing (2008)

62. 《中国密码：留给我们什么》Frank Sieren（弗郎克·泽林）, *The China Code: What's Left for Us*. Palgrave Macmillan (2007)

63. 《中国崛起：东亚的和平、权力与秩序》David C. Kang, *China Rising: Peace, Power, and Order in East Asia*. Columbia University Press (2007)

64. 《龙之崛起：看今日中国内部》Jasper Becker, *Dragon Rising: An Inside Look at China Today*. National Geographic (2006)

65. 《中国的繁荣与不满》Ross Garnaut, Ligang Song, *The China Boom and its Discontents*. Asia Pacific Press at the Australian National University (2005)

66. 《中国和平崛起：郑必坚演讲集（1997—2005）》Zheng Bijian, *China's Peaceful Rise: Speeches of Zheng Bijian 1997—2005*. Brookings Institution Press (2005)

67. 《中国公司：下一个超级大国的崛起是如何对美国和世界构成挑战的》Ted C. Fishman, *China, Inc.: How the Rise of the Next Superpower Challenges America and the World*. Scribner (2005)

68. 《中国的世纪：中国经济的崛起及其对全球经济、力量平衡和你的就业的影响》Oded Shenkar, *Chinese Century: The Rising Chinese Economy and Its Impact on the Global Economy, the Balance of Power, and Your Job*. Wharton School Publishing (2005)

69. 《中国作为崛起的世界大国及其对全球化的回应》Ronald Keith, *China as a Rising World Power and its Response to Globalization*. Routledge (2005)

70. 《中国超级大国：高增长的必要条件》Francis A. Lees, *China Superpower: Requisites for High Growth*. Palgrave Macmillan (1996)

71. 《中国崛起，俄罗斯衰落：斯大林主义转型中的政治、经济与规划》Peter Nolan, *China's*

Rise, Russia's Fall: Politics, Economics and Planning in the Transition from Stalinism*. Palgrave Macmillan (1995)

8.1.6 改革与转型

1. 《绿色转型与发展》(The Great Transformation Of China) Shuzhong Gu, Meie Xie, Xinhua Zhang, *Green Transformation And Development*. Palgrave Macmillan (2019)

2. 《中国改革以超越中等收入陷阱》Yining Li, Zhiqiang Cheng, *China's Reform to Overleap the Middle-Income Trap*. Springer Singapore (2019)

3. 《当代中国政治发展的再认识》Leizhen Zang, *Re-understanding of Contemporary Chinese Political Development*. Springer Singapore (2019)

4. 《中国转型：成功的故事与成功的陷阱》Manoranjan Mohanty, *China's Transfor-mation: The Success Story and the Success Trap*. Sage Publications India Pvt Ltd. (2018)

5. 《年轻的中国：不安的一代将如何改变其国家和世界》Zak Dychtwald, *Young China: How the Restless Generation Will Change Their Country and the World*. St. Martin's Press (2018)

6. 《中国如何改革：从计划向市场转变》Yingyi Qian, *How Reform Worked in China: The Transition from Plan to Market*. The MIT Press (2017)

7. 《工具性自治、政治社会化与公民身份：以后共产主义转型期中国朝鲜族少数民族身份、双语教育与现代媒体生活为例》Mengyan (Yolanda) Yu, *Instrumental Autonomy, Political Socialization, and Citizenship Identity: A Case Study of Korean Minority Citizenship Identity, Bilingual Education and Modern Media Life in the Post-Communism Transitioning China*. Springer Singapore (2017)

8. 《中国发展的成本》Guangyu Hu, *The Cost of Development in China*. Springer Singapore (2017)

9. 《中国人的内心体验：全球化、社会转型与社会心态的嬗变》Xiaohong Zhou (eds.), *Inner Experience of the Chinese People: Globalization, Social Transformation, and the Evolution of Social Mentality* (Research Series on the Chinese Dream and China's Development Path). Springer Singapore (2017)

10. 《中国的公平发展》Qingyun Jiang, Lixian Qian, Min Ding (eds.), *Fair Development in China*. Springer International Publishing (2017)

11. 《使中国向知识经济转型》OECD, *Enabling China's Transition towards a Knowledge-based Economy* (Better policies). OECD (2016)

12. 《中国向何处去：重启改革议程》Jinglian Wu, Guochuan Ma, *Whither China: Restarting the Reform Agenda*. Oxford University Press (2016)

13. 《中国共产主义的转型：新视角》Guoguang Wu（吴国光）, Helen Lansdowne (eds.), *China's Transition from Communism: New Perspectives* (China Policy Series). Routledge (2016)

14. 《中国公共预算改革：理论与实践》Xiaonan Liu (eds.), *Public Budgeting Reform in China: Theory and Practice*. Springer-Verlag Berlin Heidelberg (2015)

15. 《野心时代：在新中国追逐财富、真相和信仰》Evan Osnos（欧逸文）, *Age of Ambition:*

Chasing Fortune, Truth, and Faith in the New China. Farrar, Straus and Giroux (2014)

16. 《中国的挑战》Jacques deLisle（戴杰）, Avery Goldstein（金骏远）, *China's Challenges*. University of Pennsylvania Press (2014)

17. 《中美视角下的中国政治发展》Kenneth Liebertha l（李侃如）, Cheng Li（李成）, Keping Yu（俞可平）, *China's Political Development: Chinese and American Perspectives*. Brookings Institution Press (2014)

18. 《创新中国：东西方创新竞赛》Taco C.R. van Someren, Shuhua van Someren-Wang, *Innovative China: Innovation Race between East and West*. Springer-Verlag Berlin Heidelberg (2013)

19. 《文化与社会转型：理论框架与中国语境》Tianyu Cao, Xueping Zhong, Liao Kebin, Ban Wang（王斑）, *Culture and Social Transformations: Theoretical Framework and Chinese Context*. Brill Academic Pub (2013)

20. 《中国跨越鸿沟：政治与社会中的国内与全球》Rosemary Foot, *China Across the Divide: The Domestic and Global in Politics and Society*. Oxford University Press (2013)

21. 《真相与半真相：1978—2010年中国社会经济改革》Ferdinand Gul, Haitian Lu, *Truths and Half Truths: China's Socio-Economic Reforms from 1978—2010* (Chandos Asian Studies Series). Chandos Publishing (2011)

22. 《中国发展的挑战：经济脆弱性与公共部门改革》Richard Schiere, *China's Development Challenges: Economic Vulnerability and Public Sector Reform* (Routledge Studies on the Chinese Economy). Routledge (2010)

23. 《转型、区域发展与全球化：中国与中欧》Ken Morita, Yun Chen, *Transition, Regional Development And Globalization: China and Central Europe*. World Scientifc (2010)

24. 《中国国家转型：地方进程与竞争》Linda Chelan Li, *The Chinese State in Transition: Processes and contests in local China* (Routledge on China in Transition). Routledge (2009)

25. 《中国30年转型后的工作和组织》Lisa Keister, *Work and Organizations in China After Thirty Years of Transition*. Emerald Group Publishing Limited (2009)

26. 《中国转型时代：理解当代国家与社会行动者》Reza Hasmath, Jennifer Hsu, *China in an Era of Transition: Understanding Contemporary State and Society Actors*. Palgrave Macmillan (2009)

27. 《中国转型与发展》Yun Chen, *Transition and Development in China*. Ashgate Publishing Limited (2009)

28. 《中国改革30载：挑战与前景》Dali L. Yang（杨大力）, Litao Zhao（赵立涛）, *China's Reforms at 30: Challenges and Prospects* (Series on Contemporary China). World Scientific Publishing Company (2009)

29. 《激荡三十年（1978—2008）》Wu Xiao-bo（吴晓波）, *China Emerging (1978—2008)*. Cengage Learning (2008)

30. 《中国改革与国际政治经济》David Zweig, Chen Zhimin, *China's Reforms and International Political Economy* (Routledge Studies on China in Transition). Routledge (2007)

31. 《以改革为生：1989年以来的中国》Timothy Cheek（齐慕实）, *Living With Reform: China Since 1989*. Zed Books (2007)

32. 《中国社会主义转型》Lin Chun（林春）, *The Transformation of Chinese Socialism*. Duke University Press Books (2006)

33. 《中国经济和社会转型：机遇与挑战》Angang Hu（胡鞍钢）, *Economic and Social Transformation in China: Challenges and Opportunities* (Routledgecurzon Studies on the Chinese Economy). Routledge (2006)

34. 《探讨中国政治改革：法治与民主化》Suisheng Zhao（赵穗生）, *Debating Political Reform in China: Rule of Law VS. Democratization*. M. E. Sharpe (2006)

35. 《转型中的制度：中国土地所有权、产权和社会冲突》Peter Ho, *Institutions in Transition: Land Ownership, Property Rights and Social Conflict in China* (Studies on Contemporary China). Oxford University Press (2005)

36. 《中国的改革与改革者》Alfred K. Ho, *China's Reforms and Reformers*. Praeger Publishers (2004)

37. 《中国：进步与改革挑战》Organization for Economic Cooperation & Development, *China: Progress & Reform Challenges* (OECD Investment and Policy Reviews). OECD Publishing (2003)

38. 《中国国家合作与发展战略》Alexius Pereira, *State Collaboration and Development Strategies in China* (Routledgecurzon Studies in the Growth Economies of Asia). Routledgecurzon (2003)

39. 《中国城乡：认同与感知》David Faure, Tao Tao Liu (eds.), *Town and Country in China: Identity and Perception* (St Antony's Series). Palgrave Macmillan UK (2002)

40. 《改革、合法性和困境：中国政治与社会》Wang Gungwu（王赓武）, Yongnian Zheng（郑永年）(eds.), *Reform, Legitimacy, and Dilemmas: China's Politics and Society*. Singapore University Press and World Scientific Publishing (2001)

41. 《改革后中国社会政治发展》Ka-ho Mok, *Social and Political Development in Post-Reform China*. Palgrave Macmillan UK (2000)

42. 《中国简报（2000）：持续转型》Tyrene White, *China Briefing 2000: The Continuing Transformation*. M.E. Sharpe (2000)

43. 《转型中国：经济改革及其政治影响》Wei-Wei Zhang（张维维）, *Transforming China: Economic Reform and Its Political Implications* (Studies on the Chinese Economy). Palgrave Macmillan (2000)

44. 《20世纪90年代的中国》Robert Benewick, Paul Wingrove (eds.), *China in the 1990s*. Macmillan Education UK (1999)

45. 《中国制度与制度变迁：前现代性与现代化》Fei-Ling Wang, *Institutions and Institutional Change in China: Premodernity and Modernization*. Palgrave Macmillan UK (1998)

46. 《强化中国改革：国有工业的命运》Edward S. Steinfeld（谢德华）, *Forging Reform in*

China: The Fate of State-Owned Industry (Cambridge Modern China Series). Cambridge University Press (1998)

47. 《重新发现中国：改革的动力和困境》Cheng Li（李成）, A. Doak Barnett（鲍大可）, Rediscovering China: Dynamics and Dilemmas of Reform. Rowman & Littlefield Publishers (1997)

48. 《中国各省改革：阶级、社区和政治文化》David Goodman (ed.), China's Provinces in Reform: Class, Community and Political Culture (Routledge in Asia). Routledge (1997)

49. 《中国拥抱市场：成就、制约因素和机遇》East Asia Analytical Unit, Department of Foreign Affairs and Trade, Commonwealth of Australia, China Embraces the Market: Achievements, Constraints and Opportunities.EAAU (1997)

50. 《中国：从革命到改革》Sheng Hua, Xuejun Zhang, Xiaopeng Luo, China: From Revolution to Reform (Studies on the Chinese Economy). Palgrave Macmillan UK (1993)

51. 《骑虎：后毛泽东时代中国经济改革的政治学》Gordon White, Riding the Tiger: The Politics of Economic Reform in Post-Mao China. Macmillan Education UK (1993)

52. 《中国经济改革的政治逻辑》Susan L. Shirk（谢淑丽）, The Political Logic of Economic Reform in China (California Series on Social Choice and Political Economy). University of California Press (1993)

53. 《中国：从革命到改革》Sheng Hua, Xuejun Zhang, Xiaopeng Luo, China: From Revolution to Reform (Studies on the Chinese Economy). Palgrave Macmillan UK (1993)

54. 《中国价格改革（1979—1986）》Jiann-Jong Guo, Price Reform in China, 1979–86. Palgrave Macmillan UK (1992)

55. 《中国之现在：报告和评估》William Hinton（韩丁）, Hugh Deane, China Now: Reports & Appraisal. A Local USCPFA Chapter Pamphlet (1989)

8.1.7 中国革命

1. 《中国现代革命简史》Rebecca E. Karl（柯瑞佳）, China's Revolutions in the Modern World: A Brief Interpretive History. Verso (2020)

2. 《土地战争：中国土地革命的故事》Brian J. DeMare, Land Wars: The Story of China's Agrarian Revolution. Stanford University Press (2019)

3. 《中国革命诗人》Gregor Benton (Compiled), Translated by Feng Chongyi, Poets of the Chinese Revolution: Mao Zedong, Chen Duxiu, Zheng Chaolin, Chen Yi. Verso Books (2019)

4. 《策划革命：毛泽东时代的中国关于展示的政治》Denise Y. Ho, Curating Revolution: Politics on Display in Mao's China.Cambridge University Press (2018)

5. 《权利的政治与中国1911年革命》Xiaowei Zheng, The Politics of Rights and the 1911 Revolution in China. Stanford University Press (2018)

6. 《中国的保守主义革命：寻求新秩序（1927—1949）》(Studies of the Weatherhead East Asian Institute) Brian Tsui, China's Conservative Revolution: The Quest for a New Order,

1927—1949. Cambridge University Press (2018)

7. 《现代中国的空间、政治和文化代表：革命的绘画》Enhua Zhang, *Space, Politics, and Cultural Representation in Modern China: Cartographies of Revolution*. Routledge (2017)

8. 《革命及其叙事：中国社会主义文学和文化想象（1949—1966）》Xiang Cai, Rebecca E. Karl（柯瑞佳）, Xueping Zhong, *Revolution and Its Narratives: China's Socialist Literary and Cultural Imaginaries, 1949—1966*. Duke University Press Books (2016)

9. 《第二次中国革命》Eugenio Bregolat, *The Second Chinese Revolution*. Palgrave Macmillan UK (2015)

10. 《李劼人地缘诗学的消失视界：革命中国里书写成都的危机》Kenny Kwok-kwan Ng（吴国坤）, *The Lost Geopoetic Horizon of Li Jieren: The Crisis of Writing Chengdu in Revolutionary China* (Sinica Leidensia). Brill Academic Pub (2015)

11. 《复辟的革命：〈国粹学报〉与中国的现代性之路（1905—1911）》Tze-ki Hon, *Revolution as Restoration: Guocui xuebao and China's Path to Modernity, 1905—1911*. Brill (2013)

12. 《安源：发掘中国革命之传统》Elizabeth J. Perry（裴宜理）, *Anyuan: Mining China's Revolutionary Tradition*. University of California Press (2013)

13. 《上海怒火：革命中国的澳大利亚英雄》Peter Thompson, *Shanghai Fury: Australian Heroes of Revolutionary China*. William Heinemann (2012)

14. 《旧中国的新势力：一种必然的觉醒》Arthur Judson Brown, *New Forces in Old China: An Inevitable Awakening*. University of Virginia (2011)

15. 《孙中山与中国革命的起源》Harold Z. Schiffrin, *Sun Yat-Sen and the Origins of the Chinese Revolution*. University of California Press (2010)

16. 《中国从帝国到人民共和国（1900—1949）》Michael Lynch, *China from Empire to Peoples Republic 1900—1949*. Hodder (2010)

17. 《话语与故事：中国革命语言文集》Edited by Wang Ban（王斑）(ed.), *Words and Their Stories: Essays on the Language of the Chinese Revolution*. Brill (2010)

18. 《中国和俄国的革命与人民：比较史》S. A. Smith, *Revolution and the People in Russia and China: A Comparative History*. Cambridge University Press (2008)

19. 《不可避免的中国革命——美国失去中国的再反思》Thomas Lutze（罗其韬）, *China's Inevitable Revolution: Rethinking America's Loss to the Communists*. Palgrave Macmillan (2007)

20. 《中国农村的农民与革命：华北平原和长江三角洲的农村政治变革》Chang Liu（刘昶）, *Peasants and Revolution in Rural China: Rural Political Change in the North China Plain and the Yangzi Delta, 1850—1949*. Routledge (2007)

21. 《报道中国革命：瑞娜的来信》Baruch Hirson, Arthur J. Knodel, Gregor Benton（班国瑞）, *Reporting the Chinese Revolution: The Letters of Rayna Prohme*. Pluto Press (2007)

22. 《救国：民国时期的经济现代性》Margherita Zanasi, *Saving the Nation: Economic*

Modernity in Republican China. The University of Chicago Press (2006)

23. 《中国在战争与革命之中（1895—1949）》Peter Zarrow（沙培德）, *China in War and Revolution, 1895—1949*. Routledge (2005)

24. 《中国农村革命、反抗和改革》Edward Friedman（傅礼门）, Paul G. Pickowicz（毕克伟）, Mark Selden（赛尔登）, *Revolution, Resistance, and Reform in Village China* (Yale Agrarian Studies). Yale University Press (2005)

25. 《20世纪中国生物学与革命》Laurence Schneider, *Biology and Revolution in Twentieth-Century China* (Asia Pacific Perspectives). Roman & Littlefield Publishers, Inc. (2005)

26. 《痛苦的革命：中国走向现代世界的斗争》Rana Mitter（米德）, *A Bitter Revolution: China's Struggle with the Modern World*. Oxford University Press (2004)

27. 《中国革命的历史透视》（第二版）John E. Schrecker（石约翰）, *The Chinese Revolution in Historical Perspective*. Second Edition. Praeger Publishers (2004)

28. 《十里店：一个中国村庄的革命》David Crook（柯鲁克）, Isabel Crook, *Revolution in a Chinese Village: Ten Mile Inn*. Routledge (2003)

29. 《中国辛亥革命：莫理循和英日关系（1897—1920）》Eiko Woodhouse, *The Chinese Hsinhai Revolution: G. E. Morrison and Anglo-Japanese Relations, 1897—1920*. Routledge (2003)

30. 《阳光下的去处：中国漫长革命中的马克思主义和法西斯主义》A. James Gregor, *A Place in the Sun: Marxism and Fascism in China's Long Revolution*. Westview Press (2000)

31. 《布尔什维克与中国革命（1919—1927）》Alexander Pantsov, *The Bolsheviks and the Chinese Revolution, 1919—1927* (Chinese Worlds). University of Hawaii Press (2000)

32. 《重造中国无产阶级》Sally Sargeson, *Reworking China's Proletariat*. Palgrave Macmillan UK (1999)

33. 《现代化与中国革命》June M. Grasso, Jay P. Corrin, Michael Kort, *Modernization and Revolution in China*. M.E. Sharpe (1997)

34. 《地球之盐：中国农民抗议和共产主义革命的政治根源》Ralph A. Thaxton, *Salt of the Earth: The Political Origins of Peasant Protest and Communist Revolution in China*. University of California Press (1997)

35. 《革命与千禧年：中国、墨西哥和伊朗》James F. Rinehart, *Revolution and the Millennium: China, Mexico, and Iran*. Rraeger (1997)

36. 《唤醒中国：国民革命中的政治、文化与阶级》John Fitzgerald（费约翰）, *Awakening China: Politics, Culture, and Class in the Nationalist Revolution*. Stanford University Press (1996)

37. 《造就中国革命：20世纪20年代激进的共产主义妇女政治和群众运动》Christina K. Gilmartin（柯临清）, *Engendering the Chinese Revolution: Radical Women Communist Politics, and Mass Movements in the 1920s*. University of California Press (1995)

38. 《血路：革命中国中的沈定一传奇》R. Keith Schoppa（萧邦奇）, *The Blood Road: The Mystery of Shen Dingyi in Revolutionary China*. University of California Press (1995)

39. 《红星照耀中国》Edgar Snow（斯诺），John K. Fairbank（费正清），*Red Star over China: The Classic Account of the Birth of Chinese Communism*. Grove Press (1994)

40. 《中国革命者的退休：公共政策、社会规范与个人利益》Melanie Manion（墨宁），*Retirement of Revolutionaries in China: Public Policies, Social Norms, Private Interests*. Princeton, New Jersey: Princeton University Press (1993)

41. 《中国革命中的无政府主义》Arif Dirlik（阿里夫·德里克），*Anarchism in the Chinese Revolution*. University of California Press (1993)

42. 《革命传教士：苏联顾问与中国国民党（1920—1927）》C. Martin Wilbur（韦慕庭），Julie Lien-ying How（夏连荫），*Missionaries of Revolution: Soviet Advisers and Nationalist China, 1920—1927*. Harvard University Press (1989)

43. 《改革革命：转型期的中国》Robert Benewick, Paul Wingrove (eds.), *Reforming the Revolution: China in Transition*. Palgrave Macmillan UK (1988)

44. 《中国的不断革命：新中国成立的时代（1949—1981）》Lowell Dittmer（罗德明），*China's Continuous Revolution: The Post-Liberation Epoch, 1949—1981*. Berkeley: University of California Press (1987)

45. 《1923—1928年的中国民族革命》C. Martin Wilbur（韦慕庭），*The Nationalist Revolution in China, 1923—1928*. Cambridge University Press (1985)

46. 《深翻：中国一个村庄的继续革命纪实》William Hinton（韩丁），*Shenfan: The Continuing Revolution in a Chinese Village*. Random House (1983)

47. 《帝国主义与中国政治》Hu Sheng（胡绳），*Imperilism and Chinese Politics*. Foreign Language Press (1981)

48. 《鲍罗廷：斯大林的中国代理人》Dan Jacobs, *Borodin: Stalin's Man in China*. Harvard University Press (1981)

49. 《华北的叛乱者与革命者（1845—1945）》Elizabeth J. Perry（裴宜理），*Rebels and Revolutionaries in North China, 1845—1945*. Stanford University Press (1980)

50. 《中华人民共和国：革命的文献史》Mark Selden（赛尔登），*The People's Republic of China: A Documentary History of Revolutionary Change*. Monthly Review Press (1980)

51. 《国家与社会革命：法国、俄国和中国比较分析》Theda Skocpol, *States and Social Revolutions: A Comparative Analysis of France, Russia and China*. Cambridge University Press (1979)

52. 《革命与历史：中国马克思主义历史学的起源（1919—1937）》Arif Dirlik（阿里夫·德里克），*Revolution and History: Origins of Marxist Historiography in China, 1919—1937*. Berkeley: University of California Press (1978)

53. 《革命中国的工人与工作场所》Stephen Andors, *Workers and Workplaces in Revolutionary China*. M. E. Sharpe (1977)

54. 《破碎的波涛：中国共产主义农民运动（1922—1928）》Roy Hofheinz Jr., *The Broken

Wave: The Chinese Communist Peasant Movement, 1922—1928 (Harvard East Asian Series, No. 90). Harvard University Press (1977)

55. 《中国的共和革命：以1895到1913年间的广东省为例》 (Harvard East Asian Series, 81) Edward J. M. Rhoads, *China's Republican Revolution: The Case of Kwangtung, 1895—1913*. Harvard University Press (1975)

56. 《中国的抗战与革命：共产党与第二次统一战线》Tetsuya Kataoka, *Resistance and Revolution in China: The Communists and the Second United Front*. University of California Press (1974)

57. 《解放的囚徒：中国共产党监狱四年》（中文译本：两个美国间谍的自述，群众出版社，1958) Allyn Rickett（李克）, Adele Rickett（李又安）, *Prisoners of Liberation: Four Years in a Chinese Communist Prison*. Anchor Press (1973)

58. 《中国最高统帅部：共产主义军事政治史（1927—1971）》William W. Whitson, Chen-Hsia Huang, *The Chinese High Command: A History of Communist Military Politics, 1927—71*. Palgrave Macmillan UK (1973)

59. 《中国早期革命家：上海和浙江激进知识分子（1902—1911）》Mary Backus Rankin, *Early Chinese Revolutionaries: Radical Intellectuals in Shanghai and Chekiang, 1902—1911* (East Asian). Harvard University Press (1971)

60. 《革命中国的延安之路》Mark Selden, *The Yenan Way in Revolutionary China*. Harvard University Press (1971)

61. 《中国震撼世界》Jack Belden（杰克·贝尔登）, *China Shakes the World: A Classic Account of the Chinese Revolution*. Monthly Review Press (1970)

62. 《列宁、列宁主义与中国革命》Wang Ming（王明）, *Lenin, Leninism and the Chinese Revolution*. Moscow: Novosti Press Agency Publishing House (1970)

63. 《中国共产主义与中国犹太人》Itsvan Bakony, *Chinese Communism and Chinese Jews* (Library of Political Secrets 04). Sons of Liberty (1969)

64. 《红旗飘飘收藏指南》Robert Rinden, Roxane Witke, *The Red Flag Waves: A Guide to the Hung-ch'i P'Iao-p'iao Collection*. Berkeley, Center for Chinese Studies, University of California (1968)

65. 《中国革命问题》Leon Trotsky, *Problems of the Chinese Revolution*. University of Michigan Press (1967)

66. 《翻身：一个中国村庄的革命纪实》William Hinton（韩丁）, *Fanshen: A Documentary of Revolution in a Chinese Village*. Monthly Review Press (1966)

67. 《红色中国之崛起》Robert C. Goldston, *The Rise of Red China* Illustrated with Photos and Drawings by Donald Carrick. The Bobbs-merrill Company, INC. (1962)

68. 《中国散记》John Kenneth Galbraith, *A China Passage*. New Delhi: Vikas (1960)

69. 《有办法》Rewi Alley, Shirley Barton, *Yo Banfa!* China Monthly Review (1952)

70. 《中国故事》Freda Utley, *The China Story*. Chicago: Henry Regnery Company (1951)
71. 《中国从半殖民地到人民民主》G. Astafyev, *China from a Semi-colony to a People's Democracy*. Bombay, People's Pub. House (1950)
72. 《中国人民胜利》Anna Louise Strong（斯特朗）, *The Chinese Conquer China*. Doubleday & Company, Inc. (1949)
73. 《明日中国》Anna Louise Strong（斯特朗）, *Tomorrow's China*. Committee for a Democratic Far Eastern Policy (1948)
74. 《革命尚未成功》Israel Epstein（伊斯雷尔·爱泼斯坦）, *The Unfinished Revolution in China*. Boston: Little, Brown and Company (1947)
75. 《红色中国之旅》（涉及延安、黄河、毛泽东等）Robert Payne, *Journey to Red China*. London William Heinemann (1947)
76. 《中国惊雷》Theodore H. White（白修德）, Annalce Jacoby（贾安娜）, *Thunder Out of China*. London: Victor Gollancz (1947)
77. 《北行漫记》Harrison Forman, *Report From Red China*. London, Robert Hale Limited (1946)
78. 《阳光下的中国》Randall Gould, *China in the Sun*. New York: Doubleday & Company Inc. (1946)
79. 《中国觉醒》Robert Payne, *China Awake*. William Heinemann Ltd., London (1944)
80. 《中国抵抗》Edgar Snow（斯诺）, *China Resists*. Modern Publishers (1944)
81. 《红星照耀中国》Edgar Snow（斯诺）, *Red Star over China*. Random House (1944)
82. 《中国战歌》Agnes Smedley（史沫特莱）, *Battle Hymn of China*. New York: Alfred A Knopf (1944)
83. 《中国新危机》Anna Louise Strong, *China's New Crisis: With Other Authentic Documents*. Fore Publications Ltd. (1941)
84. 《为华北而斗争》George E. Taylor（戴德华）, *The Struggle For North China*. Institute of Pacific Relations (1940)
85. 《中国在战争中》Freda Utley（厄特利）, *China at War*. Faber and Faber (1939)
86. 《中国地主与农民：华南土地危机研究》Chen Han-Seng（陈翰笙）, *Landlord and Peasant in China: A Study of the Agrarian Crisis in South China*. International Publishers (1936)
87. 《黑暗之路：关于中国的真相》Ralph Townsend, *Ways That Are Dark: The Truth about China*. Barnes Review (1933)
88. 《中国发生了什么及为什么》Paul Hutchinson, *What And Why In China*. Willett, Clark&Colby, Chicago (1927)
89. 《中国觉醒》James H. Dolsen, *The Awakening of China*. The Daily Worker (1926)
90. 《中国为何走上红色之路》Putnam Weale, *Why China Sees Red*. Dodd, Mead and Company (1925)
91. 《经由中国革命：我在南北方的经历，社会生活的演变，对党员领导的访谈，以及违宪贷款》Fernand Farjenel, Margaret Cordelia Vivian, *Through the Chinese Revolution:*

My Experience in the South and North, the Evolution of Social Life, Interviews with Party Leaders, an Unconstitutional Loan. Frederick A. Stokes (1916)

92.《中国革命的启示：回顾与展望》John James Mullowney, *A Revelation of the Chinese Revolution: A Retrospect and Forecast*. New York: Fleming H. Revell (1914)

93.《北洋之始》John Stuart Thomson, *China Revolutionized*. Bobbs-Merrill Company (1913)

94.《中国革命（1911—1912）：内战历史和政治记录》Edwin J. Dingle（丁乐梅）, *China's Revolution 1911—1912: A Historical and Political Record of the Civil War*. New York: McBride, Nast and Company (1912)

95.《陷入中国革命：风险与救援记录》Ernest Frank Borst-Smith, *Caught in the Chinese Revolution: A Record of Risks and Rescue*. London (etc.) : T. F. Unwin (1912)

96.《旧中国的新力量：不受欢迎但不可避免的觉醒》Arthur Judson Brown, *New Forces in Old China: An Unwelcome But Inevitable Awakening*. New York: Fleming H. Revell Company (1904)

97.《中国在动乱中》Arthur H. Smith（明恩溥）, *China in Convulsion*. New York: Fleming H. Revell Company (1901)

98.《衰退中的中国》Alexis Krausse, *China in Decay*. 3rd Ed. Chapman and Hall, London (1900)

8.1.8 中国治理

1.《中国应急管理：理论、实践与政策》(Research Series on the Chinese Dream and China's Development Path) Xing Tong, Haibo Zhang, *China's Emergency Management: Theory, Practice and Policy*.Springer Singapore (2020)

2.《中国发展、治理与不动产税》(Politics and Development of Contemporary China) Yilin Hou, *Development, Governance, and Real Property Tax in China*. Springer International Publishing: Palgrave Macmillan (2019)

3.《当代中国地方治理手册》Jianxing Yu, Sujian Guo（郭苏建）, *The Palgrave Handbook of Local Governance in Contemporary China*. Springer Singapore: Palgrave Macmillan (2019)

4.《中国电子政务发展》(Research Series on the Chinese Dream and China's Development Path) Ping Du, Shiyang Yu, Daoling Yang, *The Development of E-governance in China*. Springer Singapore (2019)

5.《国家、政府间关系与市场发展：当代中国与19世纪美国资本主义增长比较》(Governing China in the 21st Century) Jinhua Cheng, *States, Intergovernmental Relations, and Market Development: Comparing Capitalist Growth in Contemporary China and 19th Century United States*. Palgrave Macmillan US (2019)

6.《绿化中国城市治理》(ARI-Springer Asia Series 7) Jørgen Delman, Yuan Ren, Outi Luova, Mattias Burell, Oscar Almén, *Greening China's Urban Governance*.Springer Singapore (2019)

7.《再访邹平：县域的适应性治理》Jean C. Oi（戴慕珍）, Steven Goldstein, *Zouping Revisited: Adaptive Governance in a Chinese County*.Stanford University Press (2018)

8.《中国治理、社会控制与法律改革：社区制裁与对策》Qi Chen, *Governance, Social*

Control and Legal Reform in China: Community Sanctions and Measures (Palgrave Advances in Criminology and Criminal Justice in Asia). Palgrave Macmillan (2018)

9. 《中国乡镇制度：治理与改革》Licai Wu, *China's Township System: Governance and Reform*. World Scientific Publishing Co. Pte. Ltd (2018)

10. 《中国治理：跨越垂直和水平联系》Peijie Wang, *China's Governance: Across Vertical and Horizontal Connexions*. Springer International Publishing (2017)

11. 《中国治理、国内变化与社会政策：辛亥革命后100年》Jean-Marc Blanchard, Kun-Chin Lin (eds.), *Governance, Domestic Change, and Social Policy in China: 100 Years after the Xinhai Revolution*. Palgrave Macmillan US (2017)

12. 《跨国行动主义、全球劳工治理与中国》Sabrina Zajak, *Transnational Activism, Global Labor Governance, and China*. Palgrave Macmillan US (2017)

13. 《治理理念与中国新自由主义精神》Quan Li, *The Idea of Governance and the Spirit of Chinese Neoliberalism*. Palgrave (2017)

14. 《中国治理困境：一党制国家如何实现透明和参与》Jonathan R. Stromseth, Edmund J. Malesky, Dimitar D. Gueorguiev (eds.), *China's Governance Puzzle: Enabling Transparency and Participation in a Single-Party State*. Cambridge University Press (2017)

15. 《治理中国：权力演变的实践》Vivienne Shue（许慧文）, Patricia M. Thornton, *To Govern China: Evolving Practices of Power*. Cambridge University Press (2017)

16. 《中国国家治理现代化》Angang Hu（胡鞍钢）, *The Modernization of China's State Governance*. Springer Singapore (2017)

17. 《中国经济特区研究》Yiming Yuan (eds.), *Studies on China's Special Economic Zones* (Research Series on the Chinese Dream and China's Development Path). Springer Singapore (2017)

18. 《中国西部大开发》Huiqin Yao, Zhangyong Xu (eds.), *Redevelopment of Western China* (Research Series on the Chinese Dream and China's Development Path). Springer Singapore (2017)

19. 《大中华区的管制政治》Sonny Shiu-Hing Lo, *The Politics of Policing in Greater China*. Palgrave Macmillan US (2016)

20. 《测量警察亚文化认知：关于中国一线警务人员的研究》Zheng Chen, *Measuring Police Subcultural Perceptions: A Study of Frontline Police Officers in China*. Springer Singapore (2016)

21. 《中国协同治理之路》Yijia Jing (eds.), *The Road to Collaborative Governance in China*. Palgrave Macmillan US (2015)

22. 《中国治理之变化：农村迁移制度的变迁》Jie Lu, *Varieties of Governance in China: Migration and Institutional Change in Chinese Villages*. Oxford University Press (2014)

23. 《邻家政府：中国城市中的社区政治》Luigi Tomba, *The Government Next Door Neighborhood Politics in Urban China*. Cornell University Press (2014)

24. 《权力与赞助：中国农村的地方政府网络与党—国适应力》Ben Hillman, *Power and*

Patronage: Local State Networks and Party-State Resilience in Rural China. Stanford University Press (2014)

25. 《中国乡镇治理与制度化》Shukai Zhao（赵树凯）, *Township Governance and Institutionalization in China*. World Scientific Publishing Company (2013)

26. 《中国户籍制度：市场、移民和制度变迁》Jason Young, *China's Hukou System: Markets, Migrants and Institutional Change*. Palgrave Macmillan (2013)

27. 《中国警察改革：警务理论与实践的进展》Kam C. Wong, *Police Reform in China: Advances in Police Theory and Practice*. CRC Press (2011)

28. 《治理中国（150—1850）》John W. Dardess（达第斯）, *Governing China: 150—1850*. Hackett Publishing Co. (2010)

29. 《中国海南省的政府、社会与商业》Kjel Brodsgaard, *Hainan: State, Society and Business in a Chinese Province* (China Policy). Routledge (2009)

30. 《人民代表大会与中国治理：走向网络化的治理模式》Ming Xia, *The People's Congresses and Governance in China: Toward a Network Mode of Governance*. Routledge (2008)

31. 《中国的开放社会：非国有部门与治理》Zheng Yongnian（郑永年）, Joseph Fewsmith（傅士卓）, *China's Opening Society: The Non-State Sector and Governance* (China Policy Series). Routledge (2008)

32. 《转型中国提供的公共产品》Tony Saich（托尼·赛奇）, *Providing Public Goods in Transitional China*. Palgrave Macmillan (2008)

33. 《追逐权力：欧洲帝国主义和中国治国方略的制定，1850—1927》（博士论文）Stephen Halsey, *Quest for Power: European Imperialism and the Making of Chinese Statecraft*. Ph. D. Dissertation, University of Chicago (2007)

34. 《中国空间政策：国内国际政治研究》Roger Handberg, Zhen Li, *Chinese Space Policy: A Study in Domestic and International Politics*. Routledge (2006)

35. 《跨地域中国：联系、身份和空间重新定位》Tim Oakes, Louisa Schein, *Translocal China: Linkages, Identities and the Reimagining of Space*. Routledge (2006)

36. 《重塑中国巨龙：市场转型与治理政治》Dali Yang（杨大力）, *Remaking the Chinese Leviathan: Market Transition and the Politics of Governance in China*. Stanford University Press (2006)

37. 《经济合作与发展组织：中国治理》*Governance in China*, OECD (2005)

38. 《中国城市的社会空间和治理：单位制从起源到改革》David Bray, *Social Space and Governance in Urban China: The Danwei System from Origins to Reform*, Stanford University Press (2005)

39. 《通过分工与排斥进行组织：中国户口制度》Fei-Ling Wang, *Organizing Through Division and Exclusion: China's Hukou System*. Stanford University Press (2005)

40. 《华北村治》Huaiyin Li（李怀印）, *Village Governance in North China: 1875—1936*.

Stanford University Press (2005)

41. 《中国治理》Organisation for Economic Co-operation and Develop, *Governance in China*. OECD (2005)

42. 《中国治理与政治》（第二版）Tony Saich（托尼·赛奇）, *Governance and Politics of China* (Comparative Government and Politics). Second Edition. Palgrave Macmillan (2004)

43. 《SARS疫情：对中国危机管理的挑战》John Wong（黄朝翰）, Zheng Yongnian（郑永年）, *The SARS Epidemic: Challenges To China's Crisis Management*. World Scientific Publishing (2004)

44. 《治理中国：从革命到改革》Kenneth Lieberthal（李侃如）, *Governing China: From Revolution Through Reform*. W. W. Norton & Company (2003)

45. 《中国治理与政治》Tony Saich（托尼·赛奇）, *Governance and Politics of China*. Palgrave, London (2001)

46. 《中国各省的竞争与比较优势的政治经济》H. Hendrischke, *Political Economy of China's Provinces Competitive and Comparative Advantage*. Routledge (1999)

47. 《中国政府间关系与经济管理》Jun Ma, *Intergovernmental Relations and Economic Management in China*. Palgrave Macmillan UK (1997)

48. 《20世纪80年代的中国：改革中的社会主义国家中央与省的关系》Shaun Gerard Breslin, *China in the 1980's: Centre-Province Relations in a Reforming Socialist State*. Palgrave Macmillan (1996)

49. 《中国的权力和政策》Yu-ming Shaw, *Power and policy in the PRC* (Westview special studies on East Asia). Boulder: Westview Press (1985)

50. 《中国盐政管理的现代化》S. A. M. Adshead, *The Modernization of the Chinese Salt Administration* (Harvard East Asian). Harvard University Press (1970)

8.1.9 政治体制

1. 《建设法治政府》(Research Series on the Chinese Dream and China's Development Path) Huaide Ma（马怀德）, Jingbo Wang, *Building a Government Based on the Rule of Law*. Springer Singapore (2018)

2. 《中国政治体制》Sebastian Heilmann（韩博天）, *China's Political System*. Rowman & Littlefield Publishers (2017)

3. 《当代中国中央政府与地方政府的关系》Feizhou Zhou, Mingzhi Tan, *Relationship between the Central Government and Local Governments of Contemporary China*. Springer Singapore (2017)

4. 《国家权力的关键：中国农村内聚性地方政权的兴亡》Wang, Juan, *The Sinews of State Power: The Rise and Demise of the Cohesive Local State in Rural China*. Oxford University Press (2017)

5. 《中国地方政府结构改革》Guo Qingwang（郭庆旺）, Jia Junxue（贾俊雪）, *Structural Reform in China's Regional Governments* (2-Volume Set). Enrich Professional Publishing (2015)

6. 《中国政府和政治的演变》Earle Rice, *The Evolution of Government and Politics in China*.

Mitchell Lane Publishers (2015)

7. 《中国政治与政府：权力、意识形态和组织》Sujian Guo（郭苏建），*Chinese Politics and Government: Power, Ideology and Organization*. Routledge (2012)

8. 《东亚政治体制：中国、韩国和日本》Louis D.Hayes, *Political Systems of East Asia: China, Korea, and Japan*. Routledge (2012)

9. 《转型的挑战：俄罗斯、中国和越南的工会》Simon Clarke, Tim Pringle, *The Challenge of Transition: Trade Unions in Russia, China and Vietnam* (Non-Governmental Public Action), Palgrave Macmillan (2011)

10. 《红色皇后的运行：中国政府、创新、全球化与经济发展》Dan Breznitz, Michael Murphree, *Run of the Red Queen: Government, Innovation, Globalization, and Economic Growth in China*. Yale University Press (2011)

11. 《当代中国的制度变迁与合法性》Thomas Herberer, *Institutional Change and Legitimacy in Contemporary China*, Routledge (2009)

12. 《理解中国政治体制》Kerry Dumbaugh, *Understanding China's Political System*, CRS Report for Congress (2009)

13. 《中国各省的反思》John Fitzgerald（费约翰）(ed.), *Rethinking China's Provinces*. Routledge (2002)

14. 《中国现代国家》Shambaugh David（沈大伟），*The Modern Chinese State* (Cambridge Modern China Series). Cambridge University Press (2000)

15. 《技术与性别：晚期帝制中国的权力经纬》Francesca Bray（白馥兰），*Technology and Gender: Fabrics of Power in Late Imperial China*. University of California Press (1997)

16. 《中国政治制度：现代化与传统》June Teufel Dreyer, *China's Political System: Modernization and Tradition*. Palgrave Macmillan UK (1993)

17. 《中国的政策制定》Kenneth Lieberthal（李侃如），Michel Oksenberg（奥克森伯格），*Policy Making in China*. Princeton University Press (1988)

18. 《中国政治与政府》Tony Saich（托尼·赛奇），*China: Politics and Government*. Macmillan Education UK (1981)

19. 《现代中国对政治形式的追求》Jack Gray (editor), *Modern China's Search for a Political Form*. Oxford University Press (1969)

20. 《现代中国政治制度》William L. Tung（童威廉），*The Political Institutions of Modern China*. Springer Netherlands (1964)

21. 《清代地方政府》Tung-tsu Chu（瞿同祖），*Local Government in China under the Ch'ing*. Harvard University Press (1962)

22. 《清代政府研究三题》John King Fairbank（费正清），Ssu-yü Teng（邓嗣禹），*Ch'ing Administration: Three Studies*. Cambridge: Harvard University Press (1960)

23. 《中国政府与政治》A. N. Agarwala, *The Government and Politics of China*. Kitab Mahal,

Allahabad（出版年不详）

8.1.10 民主建设/劳工关系

1. 《中国政治与劳工运动》(Politics and Development of Contemporary China) Jake Lin, *Chinese Politics and Labor Movements*. Springer International Publishing: Palgrave Macmillan (2020)

2. 《中国农民工与雇主支配：与香港、越南的比较》(Series in Asian Labor and Welfare Policies) Kaxton Siu, *Chinese Migrant Workers and Employer Domination: Comparisons with Hong Kong and Vietnam*. Springer Singapore: Palgrave Macmillan (2020)

3. 《中国大陆、中国台湾和中国香港的民主斗争：锐实力及其不满》(China Policy) Andreas Fulda, *The Struggle for Democracy in Mainland China, Taiwan and Hong Kong: Sharp Power and Its Discontents*. Routledge (2019)

4. 《罢工求生：中国工人对工厂搬迁的抵制》Fan Shigang, *Striking to Survive: Workers' Resistance to Factory Relocations in China*. Haymarket Books (2018)

5. 《中国民众抗议》Teresa Wright, *Popular Protest in China*. Polity Press (2018)

6. 《中国失地农民与地方政府间关系：融合、冲突及其相互作用》Hongping Lian, *The Relationship between Land-lost Farmers and Local Government in China: Integration, Conflict, and Their Interplay*. Springer Singapore (2017)

7. 《中国罢工：工人抵抗的叙述》Hao Ren, Zhongjin Li and Eli Friedman (eds.), *China on Strike: Narratives of Workers' Resistance*. Haymarket Books (2016)

8. 《建设中国：非正式工作与新的不稳定型无产者》Sarah Swider, *Building China: Informal Work and the New Precariat*. Cornell University Press (2016)

9. 《中国民主之路》Ning Fang（房宁）, *China's Democracy Path*. China Social Sciences Press and Springer-Verlag Berlin Heidelberg (2015)

10. 《劳工维权人士与中国新工人阶级：罢工领导人的斗争》Parry P. Leung, *Labor Activists and the New Working Class in China: Strike Leaders' Struggles*. Palgrave Macmillan US (2015)

11. 《解开心结：中国的失业问题与疗法治理》Jie Yang, *Unknotting the Heart: Unemployment and Therapeutic Governance in China*. ILR Press (2015)

12. 《中国和加拿大的基层公民参与》Andrew Sancton, Chen Zhenming, *Citizen Participation at the Local Level in China and Canada*, Taylor and Francis, CRC Press (2014)

13. 《中国的新中产阶级：消费、政治与市场经济》Eileen Yuk-Ha Tsang, *The New Middle Class in China: Consumption, Politics and the Market Economy*. Palgrave Macmillan UK (2014)

14. 《中国新兴中产阶级：超越经济转型》Cheng Li（李成）, *China's Emerging Middle Class: Beyond Economic Transformation*. Brookings Institution Press (2010)

15. 《信息时代的世界工厂：新工人阶级的网络社会》) Jack Linchuan Qiu（邱林川）, *Working-class Network Society: Communication Technology and the Information Have-less in Urban China*. The MIT Press (2009)

16. 《社会主义后的中国工人》William Hurst, *The Chinese Worker after Socialism*. Cambridge University Press (2009)
17. 《变化的中国政治图景：展望民主》Cheng Li（李成）, *China's Changing Political Landscape: Prospects for Democracy*. Brookings Institution Press (2008)
18. 《民主是个好东西：当代中国政治、社会和文化论集》Yu Keping（俞可平）, *Democracy is a Good Thing: Essays on Politics, Society, and Culture in Contemporary China* (The Thornton Center Chinese Thinkers), Brookings Institution Press (2008)
19. 《中国市场化与民主化》Jianjun Zhang, *Marketization and Democracy in China* (Routledge Studies on China in Transition).Routledge Studies (2008)
20. 《东亚人如何看待民主》Yun-han Chu（朱云汉）, Larry Diamond, Andrew J. Nathan（黎安友）, Doh Chull Shin, *How East Asians View Democracy*. Columbia University Press (2008)
21. 《中国农村民主：乡村选举的作用》Baogang He（何包钢）, *Rural Democracy in China: The Role of Village Elections*. Palgrave Macmillan (2007)
22. 《中国劳动争议及其解决》Jie Shen, *Labour Disputes and their Resolution in China*. Chandos Publishing (2007)
23. 《中国协商民主的探索》Ethan J. Leib, Baogang He（何包钢）, *The Search for Deliberative Democracy in China*. Palgrave Macmillan (2006)
24. 《中国农村的依法抗争》Kevin J. O'Brien（欧博文）, Lianjiang Li（李连江）, *Rightful Resistance in Rural China* (Cambridge Studies in Contentious Politics). Cambridge University Press (2006)
25. 《中国民主的未来：如何发生，走向哪里》Bruce Gilley（布鲁斯·吉利）, *China's Democratic Future: How It Will Happen and Where It Will Lead*, Columbia University Press (2004)
26. 《儒家民主：杜威式重建》Sor-Hoon Tan, *Confucian Democracy: A Deweyan Reconstruction*, State University of New York Press, Albany (2004)
27. 《中国社区参与：能力建设问题与进程》Jannelle Plummer, John G. Taylor, *Community Participation in China: Issues and Processes for Capacity Building*-Earthscan Publications Ltd. (2004)
28. 《中国民主转型中的国家与社会：儒学、列宁主义与经济发展》Xiaoqin Guo, *State and Society in China's Democratic Transition: Confucianism, Leninism, and Economic Development*. Routledge (2003)
29. 《寻求中国民主：国民党时期的民间反抗（1929—1949）》Edmund S. K. Fung, *In Search of Chinese Democracy: Civil Opposition in Nationalist China, 1929—1949*. Cambridge University Press (2000)
30. 《协商政治：民主与异议论文集》Stephen Macedo, *Deliberative Politics: Essays on Democracy and Disagreement*. Oxford University Press (1999)
31. 《中国工人新史》Jackie Sheehan, *Chinese Workers: A New History*. Routledge (1998)

32. 《中国工会与管理》Ng Sek Hong, Malcolm Warner, *China's Trade Unions and Management*. Macmillan Press Ltd (1998)

33. 《北京的政治参与》Tianjian Shi（史天健）, *Political Participation in Beijing*. Harvard University Press (1997)

34. 《北京以外：中国的自由化与区域》Dali L. Yang（杨大力）, *Beyond Beijing: Liberalization and the Regions in China* (Routledge Studies on China in Transition). Routledge (1997)

35. 《中国的民主化》Baogang He（何包钢）, *The Democratisation of China* (Routledge Studies on China in Transition). Routledge (1996)

36. 《中国工人》Charles Hoffmann, *The Chinese Worker*. State University of New York Press (1974)

8.1.11　公民社会/非政府组织

1. 《中国非政府组织与问责制》Jude Howell, Xiaoyuan Shang, Karen R. Fisher, *NGOs and Accountability in China*. Springer International Publishing: Palgrave Macmillan (2019)

2. 《公民意识在当代中国社会中的意义：基于西方视角的实证研究》Sicong Chen, *The Meaning of Citizenship in Contemporary Chinese Society: An Empirical Study through Western Lens* (Governance and Citizenship in Asia). Springer Singapore (2018)

3. 《公民社会对中国政策创新的贡献：环境、社会发展和国际合作》Andreas Fulda (eds.), *Civil Society Contributions to Policy Innovation in the PR China: Environment, Social Development and International Cooperation*. Palgrave Macmillan (2015)

4. 《中国公民社会：从古代到改革新时代的法律框架》Karla W. Simon, *Civil Society in China: The Legal Framework from Ancient Times to the New Reform Era*. Oxford University Press (2013)

5. 《中国公民社会与治理》Jianxing Yu, Sujian Guo（郭苏建）(eds.), *Civil Society and Governance in China*. Palgrave Macmillan (2012)

6. 《中国新兴公民社会（1978—2008）》Wang Ming, *Emerging Civil Society in China, 1978—2008*. Brill Academic Pub (2011)

7. 《国家与市民社会：中国视角》Zhenglai Deng（邓正来）, *State and Civil Society: The Chinese Perspective*. World Scientific (2010)

8. 《中国非政府组织》Yiyi Lu, *Non-Governmental Organisations in China* (China Policy Series), Routledge (2008)

9. 《当代中国非政府组织：为市民社会铺路？》Qiusha Ma, *Non-Governmental Organisations in Contemporary China: Paving the Way to Civil Society?* Routledge (2005)

10. 《中国公民社会的民主意蕴》Baogang He（何包钢）, *The Democratic Implications of Civil Society in China*. Palgrave Macmillan UK (1997)

8.1.12　公民权利

1. 《中国的人权保护制度》Pinghua Sun（孙平华）, *Human Rights Protection System in China*. Springer Berlin Heidelberg (2014)

2. 《中国的民众抗议》Kevin J. O'Brien（欧博文）(ed.), *Popular Protest in China*. Harvard University Press (2008)

3. 《传染性资本主义：全球化与中国劳工政治》（2010年出版中译本）Mary Elizabeth Gallagher（高敏）, *Contagious Capitalism: Globalization and the Politics of Labor in China*, Princeton University Press (2005)

4. 《体育、革命与北京奥运》Grant Jarvie, Dong-Jhy Hwang, Mel Brennan, *Sport, Revolution and the Beijing Olympics*. Berg Publishers (2008)

5. 《创造国民：中国的仪式和符号（1911—1929）》Henrietta Harrison（沈艾娣）, *The Making of the Republican Citizen: Political Ceremonies and Symbols in China 1911—1929*. Oxford University Press (2000)

6. 《劳改：中国古拉格》Hongda Harry Wu, Ted Slingerland, *Laogai, the Chinese Gulag*. Westview Press (1992)

8.1.13 政治思想

1. 《重新定义世界治理哲学》(Key Concepts in Chinese Thought and Culture) Tingyang Zhao（赵汀阳）, Liqing Tao (translator), *Redefining A Philosophy for World Governance*. Springer Singapore: Palgrave Pivot (2019)

2. 《启蒙初期的中国政治思想》(Routledge Studies in Social and Political Thought, 116) Simon Kow, *China in Early Enlightenment Political Thought*. Routledge (2018)

3. 《中国政治思想史》Youngmin Kim, *A History of Chinese Political Thought*. Polity Press (2017)

4. 《中国权力的政治与哲学：永恒与适时》R. James Ferguson, Rosita Dellios, *Politics and Philosophy of Chinese Power: The Timeless and the Timely*. Lexington Books (2016)

5. 《政治思想与中国转型：后毛泽东时代形塑中国改革的观念》He Li, *Political Thought and China's Transformation: Ideas Shaping Reform in Post-Mao China* (Politics and Development of Contemporary China). Palgrave Macmillan (2015)

6. 《章太炎的政治哲学：意识的抵抗》Viren Murthy（慕唯仁）, *The Political Philosophy of Zhang Taiyan: The Resistance of Consciousness*. Brill, Leiden (2011)

7. 《中国民主与精英思维》Rey-ching Lu（卢锐清）, *Chinese Democracy and Elite Thinking*. Palgrave Macmillan (2011)

8. 《创造政治性：章士钊政治理论的创立和行动》Leigh K. Jenco（李蕾）, *Making the Political: Founding and Action in the Political Theory of Zhang Shizhao*. Cambridge University Press (2010)

9. 《展望永恒帝国：中国战国时代的政治思想》Yuri Pines, *Envisioning Eternal Empire: Chinese Political Thought of the Warring States Era*. University of Hawai'i Press (2009)

10. 《解码中国政治：思想争议以及它们为何重要》（智库报告）Melissa Murphy, *Decoding Chinese Politics: Intellectual Debates and Why They Matter*. Center for Strategic and International Studies (2008)

11.《7世纪末中国的政治宣传与意识形态》Antonino Forte, *Political Propaganda and Ideology in China at the End of the Seventh Century*.The Italian School of East Asian Studies (2005)

12.《帝国主义研究》John Atkinson Hobson, *Imperialism: A Study*.Cosimo Classics (2005)

13.《人权与中国思想：跨文化探究》Stephen C. Angle, *Human Rights and Chinese Thought: A Cross-Cultural Inquiry*.Cambridge University Press (2002)

14.《孙中山的政治思想：发展与冲突》Audrey Wells, *The Political Thought of Sun Yat-Sen: Development and Impact*. Palgrave Macmillan (2001)

15.《中国政治思想：基于周代主要思想家的理论研究》Elbert Duncan Thmas, Eward Thomas William, *Chinese Political Thought: A Study Based upon the Theories of the Principal Thinkers of the Chou Period*. Williams and Norgate, Ltd. (1928)

8.1.14 政治文化

1.《中国城市的政治文化与参与》Yang Zhong, *Political Culture and Participation in Urban China* (New Perspectives on Chinese Politics and Society). Palgrave (2018)

2.《不仅是笑谈：中国政治幽默的跨学科方法》King-fai Tam, Sharon R. Wesoky (eds.), *Not Just a Laughing Matter: Interdisciplinary Approaches to Political Humor in China* (The Humanities in Asia 5). Springer Singapore (2018)

3.《当代中国的娱乐与政治》Jingsi Christina Wu, *Entertainment and Politics in Contemporary China* (East Asian Popular Culture). Palgrave Macmillan (2017)

4.《被统治的艺术：中国帝国晚期的日常政治》Michael Szonyi（宋怡明）, *The Art of Being Governed: Everyday Politics in Late Imperial China*. Princeton University Press (2017)

5.《中国早期宫廷的形成：仪式、空间、角色》Luke Habberstad, *Forming the Early Chinese Court: Rituals, Spaces, Roles*. University of Washington Press (2017)

6.《论争与调适：中国民族认同的政治学》Enze Han, *Contestation and Adaptation: The Politics of National Identity in China*. Oxford University Press (2013)

7.《和谐与战争：儒家文化与中国权力政治》Yuan-kang Wang, *Harmony and War: Confucian Culture and Chinese Power Politics*. Columbia University Press, New York Chichester, West Sussex (2011)

8.《中国怎么想》Mark Leonard（马克·莱昂纳德）, *What Does China Think*. Fourth Estate (2008)

9.《中国礼仪与政治》Emily Martin Ahern, *Chinese Ritual and Politics*. Cambridge University Press (2007)

10.《早期中国的宇宙观与政治文化》Aihe Wang, *Cosmology and Political Culture in Early China*. Cambridge University Press (2006)

11.《中国政治文明与现代化：中国转型的政治背景》Shiping Hua, Yang Zhong, *Political Civilization And Modernization in China: The Poltical Context of China's Transformation*. World Scientific (2005)

12. 《主术：中国古代政治艺术之研究》Roger T. Ames（安乐哲）, *The Art of Rulership: A Study of Ancient Chinese Political Thought.* State University of New York Press (1994)
13. 《中国政治的动力》（中译本名《中国政治的变与常》）Lucian W. Pye（白鲁恂）, *The Dynamics of Chinese Politics.* Cambridge, Massachusetts: Oelgeschlager, Gunn & Hain (1981)
14. 《中国的政治学习小组与政治仪式》Martin King Whyte（马丁·怀特）, *Small Groups and Political Rituals in China.* University of California Press (1974)

8.1.15 政治精英

1. 《中国的未来：中国精英辩论经济、政治与外交政策》Daniel C. Lynch, *China's Futures: PRC Elites Debate Economics, Politics, and Foreign Policy.* Stanford University Press (2015)
2. 《现代中国政治知识分子的崛起：五四社会与群众——政党政治的根源》Shakhar Rahav, *The Rise of Political Intellectuals in Modern China: May Fourth Societies and the Roots of Mass-party Politics.* Oxford University Press (2015)
3. 《中国军民变化：党的十六大后的精英、制度和观念》Andrew Scobell（施道安）, Larry Wortzel (eds.), *Civil-Military Change in China: Elites, Institutes, and Ideas after the 16th Party Congress.* Strategic Studies Institute (2004)
4. 《中国精英二元论与领导选择》Xiaowei Zang, *Elite Dualism and Leadership Selection in China* (Routledge Studies in China in Transition). Routledge (2003)
5. 《近代中国政治领袖传记词典》Edwin Leung, Edwin Pak-wah Leung, *Political Leaders of Modern China: A Biographical Dictionary.* Greenwood (2002)
6. 《基层魅力：四位中国地方领导人》Stephan Feuchtwang, Wang Mingming, *Grassroots Charisma: Four Local Leaders in China.* Routledge (2001)

8.1.16 话语建设

1. 《中国公共话语批判性实用研究》(China perspectives series.) Xinren Chen, *Critical Pragmatic Studies on Chinese Public Discourse.* Routledge (2020)
2. 《跨界非自然叙事：跨国和比较视角》(China perspectives) Biwu Shang, *Unnatural Narrative Across Borders: Transnational and Comparative Perspectives.* Routledge (2019)
3. 《民族与种族：中国历史、史学和民族主义话语（20世纪初—20世纪20年代）》Julia C. Schneider, *Nation and Ethnicity: Chinese Discourses on History, Historiography, and Nationalism (1900s—1920s)* (Leiden Series in Comparative Historiography). Brill (2017)
4. 《官话与异端：中国国家话语中"异端"的建构》Junqing Wu, *Mandarins and Heretics: The Construction of "Heresy" in Chinese State Discourse* (Religion in Chinese Societies). Brill (2016)
5. 《当代中国话语与社会实践》Linda Tsung, Wei Wang, *Contemporary Chinese Discourse and Social Practice in China* (Studies in Chinese Language and Discourse). John Benjamins Publishing Company (2015)
6. 《当代中国的公共话语：大众文学、电影、电视的国家叙事》Yipeng Shen, *Public Discourses of Contemporary China: The Narration of the Nation in Popular Literatures, Film,*

and Television. Palgrave Macmillan (2015)

7. 《当代中国的话语、政治与传媒》Qing Cao, Hailong Tian, Paul Chilton (eds.), *Discourse, Politics and Media in Contemporary China*. John Benjamins (2014)

8. 《中国古代的语言、话语及实践》Zhenbin Sun, *Language, Discourse, and Praxis in Ancient China*. Springer (2014)

9. 《中国话语研究》Shi-xu, *Chinese Discourse Studies*. Palgrave Macmillan UK (2014)

10. 《全球化时代文化中国的话语》Dorren D. Wu, *Discourses of Cultural China in the Globalizing Age*. Hong Kong University Press (2008)

11. 《中国崛起与东亚安全：身份构建与安全话语》Rex Li, *A Rising China and Security in East Asia: Identity Construction and Security Discourse*. Routledge (2008)

12. 《中华人民共和国的干部与话语》Michael Schoenhals（沈迈克）, Xiaolin Guo, *Cadres and Discourse in the People's Republic of China*. Central Asia-Caucasus Institute & Silk Road Studies Program, Johns Hopkins University (2007)

13. 《中国农民话语》Xiaorong Han, *Chinese Discourses on the Peasant, 1900—1949*. State University of New York Press (2005)

14. 《他者的话语世界：关于互文性的跨文化视角》Richard Bauman, *A World of Others' Words: Cross-Cultural Perspectives on Intertextuality*. Blackwell Publishing (2004)

15. 《中国寻求现代性：20世纪末的文化话语》He Ping, *China's Search for Modernity: Cultural Discourse in the Late 20th Century*. Palgrave Macmillan (2002)

16. 《话杀：呼吁消灭中国的阶级敌人（1949—1953）》Cheng-Chih Wang, *Words Kill: Calling for the Destruction of Class Enemies in China, 1949—1953*（East Asia New York, N.Y.）. Routledge (2002)

17. 《革命的教学法：文化政治学、教育与话语理论》Peter Pericles Trifonas, *Revolutionary Pedagogies: Cultural Politics, Education, and Discourse of Theory*. Routledge (2000)

18. 《中国的人权话语：历史和意识形态视角》Robert Weatherley, *The Discourse of Human Rights in China: Historical and Ideological Perspectives*. Palgrave Macmillan UK (1999)

19. 《代理叙述：中国、印度、日本的自我建构》Wimal Dissanayake, *Narratives of Agency: Self-Making in China, India, and Japan*. University of Minnesota Press (1996)

20. 《中国政治中的以言代行五论》Michael Schoenhals（沈迈克）, *Doing Things with Words in Chinese Politics: Five Studies*. Institute of East Asian Studies, University of California, Berkeley (1992)

8.1.17 软实力

1. 《中国制造的软实力：线上线下媒体与跨国受众的困境》Claire Seungeun Lee, *Soft Power Made in China: The Dilemmas of Online and Offline Media and Transnational Audiences*. Springer International Publishing: Palgrave Macmillan (2018)

2. 《谁惧怕中国：中国软实力的挑战》Michael Barr, *Who's Afraid of China: The Challenge*

of Chinese Soft Power. Zed Books Ltd (2011)
3. 《中日关系的软实力：国家、次国家和非国家关系》Utpal Vyas, Soft Power in Japan-China Relations: State, Sub-state and Non-state Relations. Routledge (2011)
4. 《中国软实力：通过传播开展公共外交》Jian Wang, Soft Power in China: Public Diplomacy through Communication. Palgrave Macmillan (2010)
5. 《软实力：国际政治中的中国新兴战略》Mingjiang Li, Soft Power: China's Emerging Strategy in International Politics. Lexington Books (2009)
6. 《魅力攻势：中国软实力如何改变世界》Joshua Kurlantzick, Charm Offensive: How China's Soft Power Is Transforming the World. Yale University Press (2007)

8.1.18 民族主义/民族国家

1. 《中国的数字民族主义》Florian Schneider, China's Digital Nationalism. Oxford University Press (2018)
2. 《中华民族的起源：宋代中国与东亚世界秩序的形成》Nicolas Tackett, The Origins of the Chinese Nation: Song China and the Forging of an East Asian World Order. Cambridge University Press (2017)
3. 《当代中国历史与民族主义合法性：一把双刃剑》Robert Weatherley, Qiang Zhang, History and Nationalist Legitimacy in Contemporary China: A Double-Edged Sword. Palgrave Macmillan (2017)
4. 《近代中国之种族观念》Frank Dikotter（冯客）, The Discourse of Race in Modern China. Oxford University Press (2015)
5. 《永远不要忘记民族耻辱：中国政治和对外关系的历史记忆》Zheng Wang, Never Forget National Humiliation: Historical Memory in Chinese Politics and Foreign Relations (Contemporary Asia in the World). Columbia University Press (2014)
6. 《强大的爱国者：中国对外关系中的民族主义抗议》Jessica Chen Weiss, Powerful Patriots: Nationalist Protest in China's Foreign Relations. New York: Oxford University Press (2014)
7. 《中国从帝国到民族国家》Hui Wang（汪晖）, Michael Gibbs Hill, China from Empire to Nation-State. Harvard University Press (2014)
8. 《帝国之后：中国国家概念的转变（1885—1924）》Peter Zarrow（沙培德）, After Empire: The Conceptual Transformation of the Chinese State, 1885—1924. Stanford University Press (2012)
9. 《现实的激情：社会调查与中国民族国家建设（1900—1949）》Tong Lam, A Passion for Facts: Social Surveys and the Construction of the Chinese Nation-State, 1900—1949. University of California Press (2011)
10. 《阅读〈申报〉：中国的民族主义、消费主义与个性（1919—1937）》Weipin Tsai, Reading Shenbao: Nationalism, Consumerism and Individuality in China 1919—1937. Palgrave Macmillan (2010)

11. 《合作的民族主义：中国蒙古边疆的友谊政治》Uradyn Bulag, *Collaborative Nationalism: The Politics of Friendship on China's Mongolian Frontier*. Rowman & Littlefield Publishers (2010)

12. 《中国城市中的爱国敬业精神：人才培养的城市生活、景观与政策》Lisa M. Hoffman, *Patriotic Professionalism in Urban China: Fostering Talent Urban Life, Landscape and Policy*. Temple University Press (2010)

13. 《英帝国的种族、法律和中国难题》Sascha Auerbach, *Race, Law and The Chinese Puzzle in Imperial Britain*. Palgrave Macmillan (2009)

14. 《奥林匹克之梦：中国与体育（1895—2008）》Guoqi Xu（徐国琦）, *Olympic Dreams: China and Sports, 1895—2008*. Harvard University Press (2008)

15. 《重审中国现代民族主义：中美关系与21世纪中国公共舆论的兴起》Simon Shen, *Redefining Nationalism in Modern China: Sino-American Relations and the Emergence of Chinese Public Opinion in the 21st Century*. Palgrave Macmillan (2007)

16. 《重构中国民族主义：清代边疆及其原居民如何成为中国人》James Leibold, *Reconfiguring Chinese Nationalism: How the Qing Frontier and its Indigenes Became Chinese*. Palgrave Macmillan (2007)

17. 《中国网络民族主义：演变、特点与启示》Xu Wu, *Chinese Cyber Nationalism: Evolution, Characteristics, and Implications*. Lexington Books (2007)

18. 《全球化时代的中国民族主义》Christopher Hughes, *Chinese Nationalism in a Global Era*. Routledge (2006)

19. 《阅读中国的跨国民族主义：社会、文学、电影》Maria N. Ng, Philip Holden, *Reading Chinese Transnationalisms: Society, Literature, Film*. Hong Kong University Press (2006)

20. 《中国里里外外：当代中国民族主义和跨国主义》Pal Nyiri, Joana Breidenbach, *China Inside Out: Contemporary Chinese Nationalism and Transnationalism*. Central European University Press (2005)

21. 《制造公民身份：欧洲、南亚和中国的教育与民族主义》Veronique Benei, *Manufacturing Citizenship: Education and Nationalism in Europe, South Asian and China* (Routledge Research in Education). Routledge (2005)

22. 《失败、民族主义与文学：现代中国认同的生成（1895—1937）》Jing Tsu, *Failure, Nationalism, and Literature: The Making of Modern Chinese Identity, 1895—1937*. Stanford University Press (2005)

23. 《中国新民族主义：骄傲、政治和外交》Peter Hays Gries（彼得·格里斯）, *China's New Nationalism: Pride, Politics, and Diplomacy*. University of California Press (2004)

24. 《民族国家的建构：现代中国民族主义的动力》Suisheng Zhao（赵穗生）, *A Nation-State by Construction: Dynamics of Modern Chinese Nationalism*. Stanford University Press (2004)

25. 《当代中国文化民族主义：寻求改革下的国家认同》Yingjie Guo, *Cultural Nationalism in Contemporary China: The Search for National Identity under Reform*. Routledgecurzon (2003)

26. 《中国民族主义、民主和民族融合》Leong H. Liew, *Nationalism, Democracy and National Integration in China*. RoutledgeCurzon (2003)
27. 《中国的民族主义和战争（1925—1945）》Hans van de Ven（方德万）, *War and Nationalism in China: 1925—1945*. RoutledgeCurzon (2003)
28. 《登上世界舞台：20世纪之交的中国民族主义》Rebecca E. Karl（柯瑞佳）, *Staging the World: Chinese Nationalism at the Turn of the Twentieth Century* (Asia-Pacific: Culture, Politics, and Society). Duke University Press Books (2002)
29. 《创建中国哈尔滨：一个国际城市的民族主义（1916—1932）》James H. Carter, *Creating a Chinese Harbin: Nationalism in an International City 1916—1932*. Cornell University Press (2002)
30. 《龙的回归：受伤的中国民族主义》Maria H Chang, Amy Joseph, Maria Hsia Chang, *Return of the Dragon: China's Wounded Nationalism*. Westview Press (2001)
31. 《中国：制造国族》Henrietta Harrison（沈艾娣）, *China: Inventing the Nation*. Arnold; Cambridge University Press (2001)
32. 《满洲神话：近代中国的民族主义、抵抗与合作》Rana Mitter（米德）, *The Manchurian Myth: Nationalism, Resistance, and Collaboration in Modern China*. University of California Press (2000)
33. 《无根帝国：现代中国跨国主义的文化政治》Aihwa Ong and Donald M. Nonini, *Ungrounded Empires: The Cultural Politics of Modern Chinese Transnationalism*. Routledge (1997)
34. 《从民族国家拯救历史》Prasenjit Duara（杜赞奇）, *Rescuing History from the Nation*. The University of Chicago Press (1995)
35. 《建设民族国家：40年后的中国》Joyce K. Kallgren (ed.), *Building a Nation-state: China after Forty Years*. Institute of East Asian Studies, University of California at Berkeley, Center for Chinese Studies (1990)
36. 《帝国主义与中国民族主义：德国人在山东》John E. Schrecker（石约翰）, *Imperialism and Chinese Nationalism: Germany in Shantung* (Harvard East Asian series). Harvard University Press (1971)

8.1.19　国家建设

1. 《中国的选择性身份：国家、意识形态与文化》(Global Political Transitions) Dominik Mierzejewski, Bartosz Kowalski, *China's Selective Identities: State, Ideology and Culture*. Springer Singapore: Palgrave Macmillan (2019)
2. 《中国的国家与社会："大国"与"新公民"的世纪长合奏》Yong Gao, Ying Wu, *The State and Society of China: A Century Long Ensemble of "Great Power" and "New Citizens"* (Social Development Experiences in China). Springer Singapore (2018)
3. 《领航半殖民主义：中国航运、主权与国家建设（1860—1937）》Anne Reinhardt, *Navigating Semi-Colonialism: Shipping, Sovereignty, and Nation-Building in China, 1860—*

1937. Harvard University Press (2018)

4. 《1949年后中华人民共和国的国家与社会关系》Tony Saich（托尼·赛奇）, *State-society Relations in the People's Republic of China Post-1949* (Brill Research Perspectives).Brill Academic Pub (2016)

5. 《近代中国国家的形成：纽带、法律人格与产业》Humphrey Ko, *The Making of the Modern Chinese State: Cement, Legal Personality and Industry*.Palgrave Macmillan (2016)

6. 《国家的魅力：晚清和"中华民国"的文化历史辩论》Tze-Ki Hon, *The Allure of the Nation: The Cultural and Historical Debates in Late Qing and Republican China*.Brill Academic Pub (2015)

7. 《写作与古代国家：比较视野中的早期中国》Haicheng Wang, *Writing and the Ancient State: Early China in Comparative Perspective*.Cambridge University Press (2014)

8. 《蒙古帝国：成吉思汗及其继承人与现代中国的建立》John Man, *The Mongol Empire: Genghis Khan, His Heirs and the Founding of Modern China*.Bantam Press (2014)

9. 《中国统治、资源与宗教：管理21世纪多民族国家》Elizabeth Van Wie Davis, *Ruling, Resources and Religion in China: Managing the Multiethnic State in the 21st Century*. Palgrave Macmillan UK (2013)

10. 《中国的国家安全：哲学、进化和政治》Xuezhi Guo, *China's Security State: Philosophy, Evolution, and Politics*.Cambridge University Press (2012)

11. 《中国在21世纪的安全利益》Russell Ong, *China's Security Interests in the 21st Century* (Routledgecurzon Security in Asia Series).Routledge (2007)

12. 《中国的"行为联邦制"：中央地方关系的变革与动力》Zheng Yongnian（郑永年）, *De Facto Federalism in China: Reforms and Dynamics of Central-Local Relations* (Series on Contemporary China). World Scientific Publishing (2007)

13. 《重塑中国国家：战略、社会与安全》Chien-Min Cao, *Remaking the Chinese State: Strategies, Society and Security (Asia's Transformations)*. Routledge (2001)

14. 《绥远建设：西北领土政治与20世纪早期中国发展》Justin Tighe, *Constructing Suiyuan: The Politics Of Northwestern Territory And Development in Early Twentieth China*. Brill's Inner Asian Library (2005)

15. 《中国现代国家的起源》Philip A. Kuhn（孔飞力）, *Origins of the Modern Chinese State*. Stanford University Press (2002)

16. 《制造多数：在日本、韩国、中国、马来西亚、斐济、土耳其和美国建立国家》Dru Gladney, *Making Majorities: Constituting the Nation in Japan, Korea, China, Malaysia, Fiji, Turkey, and the United States*.Stanford University Press (1998)

17. 《警察、公共秩序与国家：英国、北爱尔兰、爱尔兰共和国、美国、以色列、南非和中国的警务》John D. Brewer, Adrian Guelke, *The Police, Public Order and the State: Policing in Great Britain, Northern Ireland, the Irish Republic, the USA, Israel, South Africa*

and China. Macmillan Press Ltd (1996)

18. 《中世纪早期中国的国家与社会》Albert Dien, *State and Society in Early Medieval China*. Stanford University Press (1990)

19. 《地方商人与中国官僚机构（1750—1950）》Susan Mann, *Local Merchants and the Chinese Bureaucracy: 1750—1950*. Stanford University Press (1986)

8.1.20　长征

1. 《长征：中国共产党开国神话的真实历史》Sun Shuyun, *The Long March: The True History of Communist China's Founding Myth*. Anchor (2008)

2. 《选择革命：长征中的中国女战士》Helen Praeger Young, *Choosing Revolution: Chinese Women Soldiers on the Long March*. University of Illinois Press (2001)

3. 《长征中的女人》Lily Xiao Hong Lee, Sue Wiles, *Women of the Long March*. Allen & Unwin (1999)

4. 《刘伯承等：回顾长征》Liu Po-cheng etc., *Recalling the Long March*. Foreign Languages Press (1978)

8.1.21　国际共运

1. 《共产主义的兴起与衰落》Archie Brown, *The Rise and Fall of Communism*. HarperCollins (2009)

2. 《红色旗帜：共产主义历史》David Priestland, *The Red Flag: A History of Communism*. Penguin (2009)

8.1.22　马克思主义

1. 《剑桥〈共产党宣言〉指南》Terrell Carver, James Farr, *The Cambridge Companion to The Communist Manifesto*. Cambridge University Press (2015)

2. 《马克思主义与中国的形成：学说史》A. James Gregor, *Marxism and the Making of China: A Doctrinal History*. Palgrave Macmillan US (2014)

3. 《共产主义衰落后的黑格尔与马克思》David MacGregor, *Hegel and Marx after the Fall of Communism*. University of Wales Press (2014)

4. 《马克思之后的哲学：100年误读与政治哲学的规范转向》Christoph Henning, Frederic Jameson, Max Henninger, *Philosophy after Marx: 100 years of Misreadings and the Normative Turn in Political Philosophy*. BRILL (2014)

5. 《马尔库塞：马克思主义、革命和乌托邦》Herbert Marcuse, *Marxism, Revolution And Utopia*. Routledge (2014)

6. 《马克思、恩格斯〈德意志意识形态手稿〉的版本政治史》Terrell Carver, Daniel Blank, *A Political History of the Editions of Marx and Engels's "German ideology Manuscripts"*. Palgrave Macmillan US (2014)

7. 《马克思与恩格斯的〈德意志意识形态〉手稿："费尔巴哈篇"的介绍与分析》Terrell Carver, Daniel Blank, *Marx and Engels's "German ideology" Manuscripts: Presentation*

and Analysis of the "Feuerbach chapter". Palgrave Macmillan US (2014)

8. 《马克思主义和社会运动》Colin Barker, Laurence Cox, John Krinsky, Alf Gunvald, *Marxism and Social Movements*. Brill (2013)

9. 《卡尔·马克思》（全面修订，第五版）Isaiah Berlin, Henry Hardy, Terrell Carver, Alan Ryan, *Karl Marx* (Thoroughly Revised, Fifth edition). Princeton University Press (2013)

10. 《如何改变世界：关于马克思和马克思主义的反思》Eric Hobsbawm, *How to Change the World: Reflections on Marx and Marxism*. Yale University Press (2011)

11. 《弗里德里希·恩格斯与马克思主义政治经济学》Samuel Hollander, *Friedrich Engels and Marxian Political Economy*. Cambridge University Press (2011)

12. 《共产主义史学》Michael E. Brown, *The Historiography of Communism*. Temple University Press (2009)

13. 《红色行星：马克思主义与科幻小说》Mark Bould, China Miéville, *Red Planets: Marxism and Science Fiction*. Wesleyan University Press (2009)

14. 《卡尔·马克思的经济学：分析与应用》Samuel Hollander, *The Economics of Karl Marx: Analysis and Application*. Cambridge University Press (2008)

15. 《三大经济学派：亚当·斯密、马克思、约翰·梅纳德·凯恩斯》Mark Skousen, *The Big Three in Economics: Adam Smith, Karl Marx, And John Maynard Keynes*. M.E. Sharpe (2007)

16. 《探索马克思的资本：哲学、经济和政治维度》Jacques Bidet, *Exploring Marx's Capital: Philosophical, Economic and Political Dimensions*. Brill Academic Publishers (2007)

17. 《现代性之后的马克思主义：政治、技术与社会转型》Ross Abbinnett, *Marxism after Modernity: Politics, Technology and Social Transformation*. Palgrave Macmillan (2007)

18. 《21世纪的马克思》Hiroshi Uchida, *Marx for the 21st Century*. Routledge (2006)

19. 《马克思、批判理论和宗教：理性选择的批评》Warren S. Goldstein, *Marx, Critical Theory, and Religion: A Critique of Rational Choice*. Brill Academic Publishers (2006)

20. 《马克思主义理论的新启程》Stephen A. Resnick and Richard D. Wolff, *New Departures in Marxian Theory*. Routledge (2006)

21. 《马克思主义与生态经济：迈向红色和绿色的政治经济学》Paul Burkett, *Marxism and Ecological Economics: Toward a Red and Green Political Economy*. Brill Academic Publishers (2006)

22. 《平等权利之间：马克思主义国际法理论》China Mieville, *Between Equal Rights: A Marxist Theory of International Law*. Brill Academic Publishers (2005)

23. 《持不同政见的马克思主义：为当代需要的过去声音》David Renton, *Dissident Marxism: Past Voices for Present Times*. Zed Books (2004)

24. 《马克思—列宁主义在俄罗斯的消亡》Archie Brown (eds.), *The Demise of Marxism-Leninism in Russia* (St Antony's Series). Palgrave Macmillan UK (2004)

25. 《马克思与现代性：重点阅读与评论》Robert J. Antonio, *Marx and Modernity: Key*

Readings and Commentary. Blackwell Publishers Ltd (2003)

26. 《马克思主义的未来：阿尔都塞的分析转向与社会主义理论复兴》Andrew Levine, *A Future For Marxism: Althusser, the Analytical Turn and the Revival of Socialist Theory*. Pluto Press (2003)
27. 《中国马克思主义》Adrian Chan, *Chinese Marxism*. Bloomsbury Academic (2003)
28. 《马克思和马克思主义》Peter Worsley, *Marx and Marxism*. Routledge (2002)
29. 《马克思主义之后的马克思：卡尔·马克思的哲学》Tom Rockmore, *Marx After Marxism: The Philosophy of Karl Marx*. Wiley-Blackwell (2002)
30. 《新亚洲马克思主义》Tani E. Barlow, William Pietz, Douglas R. Howland, Marshall Johnson, Kang Liu, Sugiyama Mitsunobu, You-me Park, Li Dazhao, Gi-wook Shin, *New Asian Marxisms* (A Positions Book). Duke University Press (2002)
31. 《马克思主义思想词典》Tom Bottomore (ed.), *A Dictionary of Marxist Thought*. Blackwell (2001)
32. 《马克思论全球化》David Renton, *Marx on Globalisation*. Lawrence and Wishart Ltd (2001)
33. 《马克思的生态学：唯物主义与自然》John Bellamy Foster, *Marx's Ecology: Materialism and Nature*. Monthly Review Press (2000)
34. 《马克思主义在2000年：晚期马克思主义观点》Ronaldo Munck, *Marxism@2000: Late Marxist Perspectives*. Palgrave Macmillan (2000)
35. 《马克思与自然：红绿视角》Paul Burkett, *Marx and Nature: A Red and Green Perspective*. Haymarket Books (1999)
36. 《颠覆性制度：社会主义和国家的设计与破坏》Valerie Bunce, *Subversive Institutions: The Design and the Destruction of Socialism and the State*. Cambridge University Press (1999)
37. 《马克思主义与人的本质》Sean Sayers, *Marxism and Human Nature* (Routledge Studies in Social and Political Thought). Routledge (1998)
38. 《如何阅读卡尔·马克思》Ernst Fischer, Franz Marek, *How To Read Karl Marx*. Monthly Review Press (1996)
39. 《马克思主义与人类社会学：中国经济改革的视角》Boshu Zhang, *Marxism and Human Sociobiology: the Perspective of Economic Reforms in China*. SUNY Press (1994)
40. 《公意：卢梭、马克思与共产主义》Andrew Levine, *The General Will: Rousseau, Marx, Communism*. Cambridge University Press (1993)
41. 《重建马克思主义：关于历史解释与理论的文章》Erik Olin Wright, Andrew Levine, Elliott Sober, *Reconstructing Marxism: Essays on the Explanation and the Theory of History*. Verso (1992)
42. 《社会主义制度：社会主义政治经济学》Janos Kornai, *The Socialist System: The Political Economy of Socialism* (Clarendon Paperbacks). Clarendon Press (1992)

43. 《剑桥马克思指南》Terrell Carver, *The Cambridge Companion to Marx*. Cambridge University Press (1991)

44. 《弗里德里希·恩格斯：生平与思想》Terrell Carver, *Friedrich Engels: His Life and Thought*. Palgrave Macmillan UK (1990)

45. 《共产主义和后共产主义政治制度导论》Stephen White, John Gardner, George Schöpflin, Tony Saich（托尼·赛奇）, *Communist and Postcommunist Political Systems: An Introduction*. Macmillan Education UK (1990)

46. 《马克思主义与中国经验：当代中国社会主义问题》Arif Dirlik（阿里夫·德里克）, *Marxism and the Chinese Experience: Issues in Contemporary Chinese Socialism*. Routledge (1989)

47. 《黑格尔和马克思的共产主义理想》David MacGregor, *The Communist Ideal in Hegel and Marx*. University of Toronto Press (1984)

48. 《为社会主义辩论：理论思考》（修订版）Andrew Levine, *Arguing for Socialism: Theoretical Considerations*. Revised Edition. Routledge & Kegan Paul (1984)

49. 《已故马克思和俄国道路：马克思与资本主义的边缘》Teodor Shanin, *Late Marx and the Russian Road: Marx and the Peripheries of Capitalism*. Monthly Review Press (1983)

50. 《古义霖：无政府主义和马克思主义》Daniel Guerin, *Anarchism and Marxism*. Cienfuegos Press Ltd. (1981)

51. 《疏离：马克思的人性观与劳动分工》Isidor Wallimann, *Estrangement: Marx's Conception of Human Nature and the Division of Labor* (Contributions in Philosophy). Greenwood Press (1981)

52. 《马克思主义与亚洲：阅读导论》Helene Carrere D'Encausse, Stuart R. Schram（施拉姆）, *Marxism and Asia: An Introduction with Readings*. Allen Lane (1969)

8.1.23 中国与资本主义

1. 《揭秘中国奇迹：关系型资本主义的兴起与未来》Wang Yongqin, *Demystifying the Chinese Miracle: The Rise and Future of Relational Capitalism*. Routledge (2013)

2. 《红色资本主义：中国非凡崛起的脆弱金融基础（修订版）》Carl E. Walter, Fraser J. T. Howie, *Red Capitalism: The Fragile Financial Foundation of China's Extraordinary Rise*. Revised and Updated. John Wiley & Sons Singapore Pte. Ltd. (2012)

3. 《东亚资本主义：多样性、连续性和变化》Andrew Walter, Xiaoke Zhang (eds.), *East Asian Capitalism: Diversity, Continuity, and Change*. Oxford University Press (2012)

4. 《构建中国资本主义：上海与城乡工业联结》Daniel Buck, *Constructing China's Capitalism: Shanghai and the Nexus of Urban-Rural Industries*. Palgrave Macmillan US (2012)

5. 《超越"中国"：中国资本主义转型的比较视角》Scott Kennedy (ed.), *Beyond the Middle Kingdom: Comparative Perspectives on China's Capitalist Transformation* (Contemporary Issues in Asia and Pacific). Stanford University Press (2011)

6. 《中国资本主义：历史崛起与政治意义》Yin-wah Chu, *Chinese Capitalisms: Historical*

Emergence and Political Implications. Palgrave Macmillan (2010)
7. 《中国与全球资本主义转型》Ho-fung Hung, *China and the Transformation of Global Capitalism*. The Johns Hopkins University Press (2009)
8. 《中国资本主义的未来：选择与机遇》Gordon Redding, Michael A. Witt, *The Future of Chinese Capitalism. Choices and Chances*.Oxford University Press (2008)
9. 《中国特色的资本主义：创业与国家》Yasheng Huang（黄亚生）, *Capitalism with Chinese Characteristics: Entrepreneurship and the State*. Cambridge University Press (2008)
10. 《资本主义起源与西方崛起》Eric H. Mielants, *The Origins of Capitalism and the Rise of the West*. Temple University Press (2007)
11. 《没有民主的资本主义：当代中国的私营部门》Kellee S. Tsai（蔡欣怡）, *Capitalism without Democracy: The Private Sector in Contemporary China*. Cornell University Press (2007)
12. 《中国与资本主义：现代中国工商企业史》David Faure, *China And Capitalism: A History of Business Enterprise in Modern China*. Hong Kong University Press (2006)
13. 《中国资本主义与现代主义视野》Satya Gabriel, *Chinese Capitalism and the Modernist Vision*.Routledge (2006)
14. 《全球化时代的中国资本主义：走向混合资本主义》Wai-Chung Yeung, *Chinese Capitalism in a Global Era: Towards a Hybrid Capitalism* (Routledge Advances Ininternational Political Economy, 12). Routledge (2003)

8.1.24 智库

1. 《对当代中国智库的反思》Silvia Menegazzi, *Rethinking Think Tanks in Contemporary China*. Palgrave Macmillan (2018)
2. 《中国对外国研发的管理：世界新智库》Zheng Han, *Managing Foreign Research and Development in the People's Republic of China: The New Think-Tank of the World*. Chandos Publishing (2008)

8.2 外交

1. 《国际发展援助与金砖国家》(Governing China in the 21st Century) Jose A. Puppim de Oliveira, Yijia Jing, *International Development Assistance and the BRICS*. Springer Singapore: Palgrave Macmillan (2020)
2. 《中国与联合国安全理事会的干预：和解状况》Courtney J. Fung, *China and Intervention at the UN Security Council: Reconciling Status*. Oxford University Press (2019)
3. 《中国外交政策中的新区域举措：即将到来的全球治理多元化》Matteo Dian, Silvia Menegazzi, *New Regional Initiatives in China's Foreign Policy: The Incoming Pluralism of Global Governance*. Palgrave Macmillan (2018)
4. 《中国外交政策的多边取向》Joseph Yu-shek Cheng, *Multilateral Approach in China's Foreign Policy*. World Scientific Publishing Co. Pte. Ltd. (2018)

5. 《清代外交使臣在西方：晚清外交与信息秩序》Jenny Huangfu Day, *Qing Travelers to the Far West: Diplomacy and the Information Order in Late Imperial China*. Cambridge University Press (2018)
6. 《中国的全球认同：考虑大国责任》Tiang Boon Hoo, *China's Global Identity: Considering the Responsibilities of Great Power*. Georgetown University Press (2018)
7. 《中国大使馆：鸦片战争之前的外交与文化遭遇》Michael Keevak, *Embassies to China: Diplomacy and Cultural Encounters Before the Opium Wars*. Palgrave Macmillan (2017)
8. 《中国对外援助60年回顾》Hong Zhou, Hou Xiong (eds.), *China's Foreign Aid: 60 Years in Retrospect*. Springer Singapore (2017)
9. 《天下万物：历史如何帮助中国力争成为全球强国》Howard W. French（傅好文）, *Everything under the Heavens: How the Past Helps Shape China's Push for Global Power*. Knopf (2017)
10. 《中国在南亚的软实力外交：神话还是现实？》B. M. Jain, *China's Soft Power Diplomacy in South Asia: Myth or Reality?* Lexington Books (2017)
11. 《中国新外交政策：军队现代化、多边主义和中国"威胁"》Tilman Pradt, *China's New Foreign Policy: Military Modernisation, Multilateralism and the "China Threat"*. Palgrave Macmillan (2016)
12. 《中国追求：中华人民共和国对外关系史》John W. Garver（高龙江）, *China's Quest: The History of the Foreign Relations of the People's Republic of China*. Oxford University Press (2016)
13. 《中国追求大国地位：船舶、石油与外交政策》Bernard D. Cole, *China's Quest for Great Power: Ships, Oil, and Foreign Policy*. Naval Institute Press (2016)
14. 《中国对外援助和投资外交（第一卷）：性质、范围和起源》John F. Copper, *China's Foreign Aid and Investment Diplomacy, Volume I: Nature, Scope, and Origins*. Palgrave Macmillan US (2016)
15. 《中国对外援助和投资外交（第二卷）：1950年至今在亚洲的历史与实践》John F. Copper, *China's Foreign Aid and Investment Diplomacy, Volume II: History and Practice in Asia, 1950-Present*. Palgrave Macmillan US (2016)
16. 《中国对外援助和投资外交（第三卷）：超越亚洲战略及对美国和国际秩序的挑战》John F. Copper, *China's Foreign Aid and Investment Diplomacy, Volume III: Strategy Beyond Asia and Challenges to the United States and the International Order*. Palgrave Macmillan US (2016)
17. 《评估中国力量》Jae Ho Chung (ed.), *Assessing China's Power*. Palgrave Macmillan (2015)
18. 《中国公共外交》Ingrid d'Hooghe, *China's Public Diplomacy*. Brill-Nijhoff (2015)
19. 《中国对外援助》Hong Zhou, *Foreign Aid in China*. Springer Berlin Heidelberg (2015)
20. 《和谐干预：中国对关系安全的追求》Chiung-chiu Huang, Chih-Yu Shih（石之瑜）, *Harmonious Intervention: China's Quest for Relational Security*. Ashgate Pub Co (2014)

21. 《与过去决裂：海关服务与中国现代性的全球起源》Hans van de Ven（方德万），*Breaking with the Past: The Maritime Customs Service and the Global Origins of Modernity in China*. Columbia University Press (2014)
22. 《胡适英文文存：国家危机与公共外交》（第三卷）Hu Shih (auth.), Chih-P'ing Chou（周质平）(eds.), *English Writings of Hu Shih: National Crisis and Public Diplomacy* (Volume 3) (China Academic Library). Springer-Verlag Berlin Heidelberg (2013)
23. 《中国走向全球：部分权力》David Shambaugh（沈大伟），*China Goes Global: The Partial Power*. Oxford University Press, USA (2013)
24. 《中国安全状态：理念、演变与政治》Xuezhi Guo, *China's Security State: Philosophy, Evolution, and Politics*. Cambridge University Press (2012)
25. 《中国对外关系：冷战后的权力与政策》Robert G. Sutter, *Chinese Foreign Relations: Power and Policy since the Cold War* (Asia in world politics), 3rd Edition. Rowman & Littlefield Publishers (2012)
26. 《美国国务院研究报告：维护美国与中国战略稳定》William J. Perry, *Maintaining U.S.-China Strategic Stability*. International Security Advisory Board (2012)
27. 《中国亲善大使：熊猫泰山》Patricia Eireann Holz, *China's Goodwill Ambassador-Tai Shan the Panda*. Washington International (2012)
28. 《中国外交与联合国安理会：超越否决权》Joel Wuthnow, *Chinese Diplomacy and the UN Security Council: Beyond the Veto*. Routledge (2012)
29. 《中国在非洲的资源外交：发展力量？》Marcus Power, Giles Mohan, May Tan-Mullins, *China's Resource Diplomacy in Africa: Powering Development?* Palgrave Macmillan UK (2012)
30. 《中国追求全球秩序：从和平崛起到和谐世界》Rosita Dellios, R. James Ferguson, *China's Quest for Global Order: From Peaceful Rise to Harmonious World*.Lexington Books (2012)
31. 《中国的外交政策：谁制定及如何制定？》Gilbert Rozman（饶济凡）(eds.), *China's Foreign Policy: Who Makes It, and How Is It Made?* Palgrave Macmillan US (2012)
32. 《帝国心灵：中国历史和现代外交》Christopher A. Ford, *The Mind of Empire: China's History and Modern Foreign Relations*. The University Press of Kentucky (2010)
33. 《亚太地区中国的多边合作：北京"睦邻政策"制度化》Chien-peng Chung, *China's Multilateral Co-operation in Asia and the Pacific: Institutionalizing Beijing's "Good Neighbour Policy"* (Politics in Asia). Routledge (2010)
34. 《中国外交政策辩论》Zhu Liqun, *China's Foreign Policy Debates*.Chaillot Paper (2010)
35. 《中国外交》Zhang Qingmin, *China's Diplomacy*.Cengage Learning Asia (2010)
36. 《中国全球战略：世界多极化》Jenny Clegg, *China's Global Strategy: Toward a Multipolar World*. Pluto Press (2009)

37. 《从唐代初期朝廷辩论到中国和平崛起》Friederike Assandri, Dora Martins, *From Early Tang Court Debates to China's Peaceful Rise*. Amsterdam University Press (2009)

38. 《中国外交政策导论》Marc Lanteigne, *Chinese Foreign Policy: An Introduction*. Routledge (2009)

39. 《蓝色外交官：1922—1933年在中国的美国海军军官》William R. Braisted, *Diplomats in Blue: U.S. Naval Officers in China, 1922—1933*. University Press of Florida (2009)

40. 《中国的国际行为：行动主义、机会主义和多样化》Evan S. Medeiros（麦艾文）, *China's International Behavior: Activism, Opportunism, and Diversification*. RAND Publishing (2009)

41. 《美国国务院：美国外交关系（1969—1976），第十八卷：中国（1973—1976）》David P. Nickles, Edward C. Keefer, *Foreign Relations of the United States, 1969—1976, Volume XVIII, China, 1973—1976*. U.S. Government Printing Office (2008)

42. 《中国"新"外交：战术或根本变革？》Pauline Kerr, Stuart Harris, Yaqing Qin (eds.), *China's "New" Diplomacy: Tactical or Fundamental Change?* (Palgrave Series in Asian Governance). Palgrave Macmillan US (2008)

43. 《社会国家：国际组织中的中国（1980—2000）》Alastair Iain Johnston（江忆恩）, *Social States: China in International Institutions, 1980—2000*. Princeton University Press (2008)

44. 《中国与国际新秩序》Wang Gungwu（王赓武）, Zheng Yongnian（郑永年）(eds.), *China and the New International Order* (China Policy Series). Routledge (2008)

45. 《21世纪中国的安全利益》Russell Ong, *China's Security Interests in the 21st Century*. Routledgecurzon (2007)

46. 《中国战略文化与外交决策：儒家、领导与战争》Huiyun Feng, *Chinese Strategic Culture and Foreign Policy Decision-Making: Confucianism, Leadership and War*. Routledge (2007)

47. 《新星—中国的新安全外交》Bates Gill（季北慈）, *Rising Star: China's New Security Diplomacy*. Brookings Institution Press (2007)

48. 《中国遵守全球事务：贸易、武器控制、环境保护、人权》Gerald Chan, *China's Compliance in Global Affairs: Trade, Arms Control, Environmental Protection, Human Rights*. World Scientific Publishing (2006)

49. 《中国外交政策研究新方向》Alastair Iain Johnston（江忆恩）, Robert S. Ross（陆伯彬）, *New Directions in the Study of China's Foreign Policy*. Stanford University Press (2006)

50. 《中国世界的外交与贸易（589—1276）》Hans Bielenstein（毕汉斯）, *Diplomacy and Trade in the Chinese World, 589—1276*. Brill Academic Pub. (2005)

51. 《渐增的挑战：中国大战略与国际安全》Avery Goldstein（金骏远）, *Rising to the Challenge: China's Grand Strategy and International Security*. Stanford University Press (2005)

52. 《让外国人为中国服务：中华人民共和国的外国人管理》Anne-Marie Brady, *Making the Foreign Serve China: Managing Foreigners in the People's Republic* (Asia Pacific Perspectives). Rowman & Littlefield (2003)
53. 《中国对外关系人权：定义和维护国家利益》Ming Wan, *Human Rights in Chinese Foreign Relations: Defining and Defending National Interests*.University of Pennsylvania Press (2001)
54. 《改革时期中国外交与安全政策的制定（1978—2000）》David M. Lampton（蓝普顿）, *The Making of Chinese Foreign and Security Policy in the Era of Reform, 1978—2000*. Stanford University Press (2001)
55. 《解读中国大战略：过去、现在和未来》Michael D. Swaine（迈克尔·史文）, Ashley J. Tellis, *Interpreting China's Grand Strategy: Past, Present, and Future*. RAND (2000)
56. 《参与中国：新兴大国的管理》Alastair Iain Johnston（江忆恩）, Robert S. Ross（陆伯彬）, *Engaging China: The Management of an Emerging Power* (Politics in Asia Series). Routledge (1999)
57. 《中国对外关系》Denny Roy, *China's Foreign Relations*. Macmillan Education UK (1998)
58. 《革命国家、领导人和外交：中国、古巴和伊朗比较研究》Houman A. Sadri, *Revolutionary States, Leaders, and Foreign Relations: A Comparative Study of China, Cuba, and Iran*. Praeger Publishers (1997)
59. 《相互依存世界中的新兴中国：给三边委员会的报告》Yōichi Funabashi, Michel Oksenberg（奥克森伯格）, Heinrich Weiss, *An Emerging China in a World of Interdependence: A Report to the Trilateral Commission*. Trilateral Commission (1994)
60. 《薛福成欧洲日记：中华帝国特派公使》Helen Hsieh Chien, *The European Diary of Hsieh Fucheng: Envoy Extraordinary of Imperial China*. Palgrave Macmillan US (1993)
61. 《赫德日记（1863—1866）：赫德与中国早期现代化》Richard J. Smith, John K. Fairbank（费正清）, Katherine F. Bruner, *Robert Hart and China's Early Modernization: His Journals, 1863—1866*. Council on East Assian Studies, Harvard University (1991)
62. 《中国外交政策精神：心理文化观》Chih-yu Shih（石之瑜）, *The Spirit of Chinese Foreign Policy: A Psychocultural View*. Palgrave Macmillan UK (1990)
63. 《中国海关总税务司赫德札记（1854—1863）》Katherine F. Bruner, John K. Fairbank（费正清）, Richard J. Smith, *Entering China's Service: Robert Hart's Journals, 1854—1863*. Council on East Asian Studies, Harvard University (1986)
64. 《中国与东南亚关系变化的政治经济学》John Wong（黄朝翰）, *The Political Economy of China's Changing Relations with Southeast Asia*. Macmillan Education UK (1984)
65. 《孤立主义的终结：毛泽东后的中国外交政策》Michael Yahuda（亚胡达）, *Towards the End of Isolationism: China's Foreign Policy after Mao*. Macmillan Education UK (1983)
66. 《中国外交政策中的中东（1949—1977）》Yitzhak Shichor, *The Middle East in China's*

Foreign Policy, 1949—1977 (LSE Monographs in International Studies). Cambridge University Press (1979)

67.《革命外交：中国外交政策与统一战线理论》James David Armstrong, *Revolutionary Diplomacy: Chinese Foreign Policy and the United Front Doctrine.* University of California Press (1977)

68.《中国海关总税务司赫德书信集（1868—1907）》（共两卷）John King Fairbank（费正清）, Katherine Frost Bruner, Elizabeth MacLeod Matheson, *The I. G. in Peking: Letters of Robert Hart, Chinese Maritime Customs, 1868—1907.* Two Vols. Belknap Press of Harvard University Press (1975)

69.《伊犁危机：中俄外交研究（1871—1881）》Immanuel Chung-Yueh Hsü（徐中约）, *The Ili Crisis: A Study of Sino-Russian Diplomacy 1871—1881.* Oxford University Press (1965)

70.《中国加入国际大家庭：外交阶段（1858—1880）》Immanuel C. Y. Hsü（徐中约）, *China's Entrance into the Family of Nations: The Diplomatic Phase 1858—1880* (Harvard Eeast Asian Series 5). Harvard University Press (1960)

71.《中国沿海的贸易与外交：1842—1854年通商口岸的开埠》（第二卷）John King Fairbank（费正清）, *Trade and Diplomacy on the China Coast: The Opening of Treaty Ports, 1842—1854.* Volume II. Harvard University Press (1956)

72.《中国沿海的贸易与外交：1842—1854年通商口岸的开埠》（第一卷）John King Fairbank（费正清）, *Trade and Diplomacy on the China Coast: The Opening of Treaty Ports, 1842—1854.* Volume I. Harvard University Press (1953)

73.《现代中国外交政策》Werner Levi, *Modern China's Foreign Policy.* University of Minnesota Press (1953)

74.《中国的对外关系（1917—1931）》Robert T. Pollard, *China's Foreign Relations, 1917—1931.* New York: Macmillan (1933)

75.《我们的首任驻华大使：乔治·马戛尔尼伯爵生平述略》Helen H. Robbins, *Our First Ambassador to China: An Account of the Life of George, Earl of Macartney, with Extracts from His Letters, and the Narrative of His Experiences in China, as Told by Himself, 1737—1806.* London (1908)

76.《中国与门户开放》Charles Coates, China and the Open Door. T. D. Taylor, Sons, and Hawkins, Printers (1899)

77.《中华帝国海关：截至1896年3月31日的半年医疗报告》Robert Hart, *China: Imperial Maritime Customs. Medical Reports For The Half-Year Ended March 31st, 1896.* Shanghai (1886)

8.3 国际关系

8.3.1 中国与美国

1.《中国战略研究报告（2018年）：国内发展、中美关系与中国大战略》Honghua Men

（门洪华, ed.), *Report of Strategic Studies in China (2018): Domestic Development, Sino-American Relations and China's Grand Strategy*. Springer Singapore (2020)

2. 《鹰与龙：力量与重塑的故事》Chris Duffin, *The Eagle and the Dragon: A Story of Strength and Reinvention*. Lioncrest Publishing (2019)

3. 《金山鬼魂：华工建造美国洲际铁路史诗般的故事》Gordon H. Chang, *Ghosts of Gold Mountain: The Epic Story of the Chinese Who Built the Transcontinental Railroad*. Houghton Mifflin Harcourt (2019)

4. 《分裂：中国、美国与全球贸易体系的破裂》Paul Blustein, *Schism: China, America, and the Fracturing of the Global Trading System*. CIGI Press (10 Sept 2019)

5. 《隐形战争：美国精英熟睡时中国如何占领》Robert Spalding, *Stealth War: How China Took Over While America's Elite Slept*. Portfolio (2019)

6. 《中国写生：美国陆军诗歌集》A. L. Crouch, *China Sketchbook: A Book of U.S. Army Verse*. Earnshaw Books (2019)

7. 《中国人与铁道：建设洲际铁路》Gordon H. Chang, Shelley Fisher Fishkin, Hilton Obenzinger, Roland Hsu, *The Chinese and the Iron Road: Building the Transcontinental Railroad*. Stanford University Press (2019)

8. 《资本主义冲突：在美中国公司》Ji Li, *The Clash of Capitalisms: Chinese Companies in the United States*. Cambridge University Press (2018)

9. 《中国使命：乔治·马歇尔未完成的战争（1945—1947）》Daniel Kurtz-Phelan, *The China Mission: George Marshall's Unfinished War, 1945—1947*. W. W. Norton & Company (2018)

10. 《艾森·豪威尔与美国对华舆论》Mara Oliva, *Eisenhower and American Public Opinion on China*. Palgrave Macmillan (2018)

11. 《中国处方：揭露美国依赖中国医药的风险》Rosemary Gibson, Janardan Prasad Singh, *China Rx: Exposing the Risks of America's Dependence on China for Medicine*. Prometheus Books (2018)

12. 《奥巴马执政期间美国与中国的军事国防关系》James Johnson, *The US-China Military and Defense Relationship during the Obama Presidency* (New Security Challenges). Springer International Publishing: Palgrave Macmillan (2018)

13. 《世界政治中两极性的回归：中国、美国与地缘结构现实主义》Øystein Tunsjø, *The Return of Bipolarity in World Politics: China, the United States, and Geostructural Realism*. Columbia University Press (2018)

14. 《美国天下：中国金钱、美国权力与历史的终结》Salvatore J. Babones, *American Tianxia: Chinese Money, American Power, and the End of History*. Policy Press (2017)

15. 《超越天意：1783以来亚太地区的大国战略与美国力量》Michael J. Green, *By More than Providence: Grand Strategy and American Power in the Asia Pacific since 1783* (A

Nancy Bernkopf Tucker and Warren I. Cohen Book on American-East Asian Relations). Columbia University Press (2017)

16. 《注定一战：美国和中国能避免修昔底德陷阱吗？》Graham Allison, *Destined for War: Can America and China Escape Thucydides's Trap?* Houghton Mifflin Harcourt (2017)

17. 《从长城到华尔街：跨文化视角看中美两国的领导和管理》Wei Yen, *From the Great Wall to Wall Street: A Cross-Cultural Look at Leadership and Management in China and the US*. Palgrave Macmillan (2017)

18. 《美国对中国、古巴和伊朗外交政策：承认的政治》Greg Ryan, *US Foreign Policy towards China, Cuba and Iran: The Politics of Recognition*. Routledge (2017)

19. 《新的中央王国：中国与美国早期自由贸易的浪漫史》Kendall Johnson, *The New Middle Kingdom: China and the Early American Romance of Free Trade*. Baltimore, Maryland: Johns Hopkins University Press (2017)

20. 《中国梦—美国梦：中国女性科学家和工程师在美国的生活》Diane Yu Gu, *Chinese Dreams-American Dreams: The Lives of Chinese Women Scientists and Engineers in the United States*. SensePublishers (2016)

21. 《与敌贸易：美国对华出口管制政策的形成》Hugo Meijer, *Trading with the Enemy: The Making of US Export Control Policy toward the People's Republic of China*. Oxford University Press (2016)

22. 《美丽的国家与中央王国：美国与中国，1776年至今》John Pomfret, *The Beautiful Country and the Middle Kingdom: America and China, 1776 to the Present*. Henry Holt and Co. (2016)

23. 《美国、中国与世界秩序的斗争：思想、传统、历史遗产和全球视野》G. John Ikenberry, Wang Jisi（王辑思）, Zhu Feng（朱锋）(eds.), *America, China, and the Struggle for World Order: Ideas, Traditions, Historical Legacies, and Global Visions* (Asia Today). Palgrave Macmillan US (2015)

24. 《半路遇中国：如何化解美中产生的对抗》Lyle Goldstein, *Meeting China Halfway: How to Defuse the Emerging US-China Rivalry*. Georgetown University Press (2015)

25. 《不可能的战争：中国、美国和大国冲突的逻辑》Christopher Coker, *The Improbable War: China, The United States and Logic of Great Power Conflict*. Oxford University Press (2015)

26. 《美国对亚洲再平衡战略的起源与演变：外交、军事与经济的层面》Hugo Meijer (eds.), *Origins and Evolution of the US Rebalance toward Asia: Diplomatic, Military, and Economic Dimensions*. Palgrave and Macmillan (2015)

27. 《美中战略竞争：走向新的权力平衡》S. Mahmud Ali, *US-China Strategic Competition: Towards a New Power Equilibrium*. Springer-Verlag Berlin Heidelberg (2015)

28. 《中国幻影：亚洲的美国灾难隐藏史》James Bradley（詹姆斯·布雷德利）, *The China Mirage: The Hidden History of American Disaster in Asia*. Little, Brown and Company (2015)

29. 《中美关系的冲突与合作：变化与连续性、原因与出路》Jean-Marc F. Blanchard, Simon

Shen, *Conflict and Cooperation in Sino-US Relations: Change and Continuity, Causes and Cures*. Routledge (2015)

30. 《长城茶：一位美国女孩在饱受战争蹂躏的中国》Patricia Luce Chapman, *Tea On The Great Wall: An American Girl in War-Torn China*.Earnshaw Books (2015)

31. 《灰烬之宫：中国与美国高等教育的衰落》Mark S. Ferrara, *Palace of Ashes: China and the Decline of American Higher Education*. Johns Hopkins University Press (2015)

32. 《发电厂：美国、中国与电池大战》Steve Levine, *The Powerhouse: America, China and the Great Battery War*.Penguin Viking (2015)

33. 《命中注定的关系：美国关注中国的历史》Gordon H. Chang, *Fateful Ties: A History of America's Preoccupation with China*. Harvard University Press (2015)

34. 《金色贫民窟：广州的美国商业社区与美国对华政策的形成（1784—1844）》Jacques M. Downs, *Golden Ghetto: The American Commercial Community at Canton and the Shaping of American China Policy, 1784—1844*.Hong Kong: Hong Kong University Press (2015)

35. 《澳大利亚—东盟对话：追踪40年的伙伴关系》Sally Percival Wood, Baogang He（何包钢）(eds.), *The Australia-ASEAN Dialogue: Tracing 40 Years of Partnership* (Asia Today). Palgrave Macmillan US (2014)

36. 《美国杂碎：中国食物在美国的故事》Yong Chen, *Chop Suey, USA: The Story of Chinese Food in America*. Columbia University Press (2014)

37. 《不平衡：美国和中国的相互依赖》Stephen Roach, *Unbalanced: The Co-Dependency of America and China*. Yale University Press (2014)

38. 《共同利益：中美视角》P. C. Lo, David Solomon, *The Common Good: Chinese and American Perspectives*. Springer Netherlands (2014)

39. 《论辩中国：十个对话中的美中关系》Nina Hachigian, *Debating China: The U.S.-China Relationship in Ten Conversations*. Oxford University Press, USA (2014)

40. 《1945年的中国：毛泽东的革命与美国的致命选择》Richard Bernstein, *China 1945: Mao's Revolution and America's Fateful Choice*. Knopf (2014)

41. 《鹰与龙：16世纪全球化与欧洲征服中国和美国的梦想》Serge Gruzinski, *The Eagle and the Dragon: Globalization and European Dreams of Conquest in China and America in the Sixteenth Century*. Polity (2014)

42. 《不平衡：美国与中国的相互依赖》Stephen Roach, *Unbalanced: The Co-Dependency of America and China*.Yale University Press (2014)

43. 《水上之火：中国、美国与太平洋未来》Robert Haddick, *Fire on the Water: China, America, and the Future of the Pacific*. Naval Institute Press (2014)

44. 《中国人和美国人共享的历史》Guoqi Xu（徐国琦）, Akira Iriye（入江昭）, *Chinese and Americans: A Shared History*. Cambridge, Massachusetts: Harvard University Press (2014)

45. 《中美关系与国家行动中的情绪作用：理解冷战后的危机相互作用》Taryn Shepperd,

Sino-US Relations and the Role of Emotion in State Action: Understanding Post-Cold War Crisis Interactions. Palgrave Macmillan UK (2013)

46. 《中国选择：我们为什么要分享权力》Hugh White（休·怀特），*The China Choice: Why We Should Share Power.* Oxford University Press, USA (2013)

47. 《美国在中国的第一次冒险：贸易、条约、鸦片和救赎》John R Haddad, *America's First Adventure in China: Trade, Treaties, Opium, and Salvation.* Temple University Press (2013)

48. 《关于中国的谬误：美国如何受益于中国崛起以及避免再次冷战》Donald Gross, *The China Fallacy: How the U.S. Can Benefit from China's Rise and Avoid another Cold War.* Bloomsbury Academic (2013)

49. 《李光耀：大师对中国、美国和世界的见解》Graham Allison, Robert D. Blackwill, Ali Wyne, *Lee Kuan Yew: The Grand Master's Insights on China, the United States, and the World* (Belfer Center Studies in International Security). The MIT Press (2013)

50. 《无尽的危机：垄断金融资本如何从美国到中国制造停滞和动荡》John Bellamy Foster and Robert W. W. McChesney, *The Endless Crisis: How Monopoly-Finance Capital Produces Stagnation and Upheaval from the USA to China.* Monthly Review Press (2012)

51. 《寻求安全感的中国》Andrew J. Nathan（黎安友），Andrew Scobell（施道安），*China's Search for Security.* Columbia University Press (2012)

52. 《美国可向中国学习什么：把最大竞争对手视为最好老师的开明指南》Ann Lee, Ian Bremmer, *What the U.S. Can Learn from China: An Open-Minded Guide to Treating Our Greatest Competitor as Our Greatest Teacher.* Berrett-Koehler Publishers (2012)

53. 《以美国存托凭证与中国市场做交易：如何在大中华区赢得优势》Voon, Alan, *Trading The China Market With American Depository Receipts: How To Play Greater China With A Winning Edge.* J. Wiley & Sons Singapore (2012)

54. 《寻求平衡：中国、美国和东亚的权力平衡》Steve Chan, *Looking for Balance: China, the United States, and Power Balancing in East Asia* (Studies in Asian Security). Stanford University Press (2012)

55. 《当美国首次相遇中国：大航海时代茶叶、药物、金钱的异国情调史》Eric Jay Dolin, *When America First Met China: An Exotic History of Tea, Drugs, and Money in the Age of Sail.* Liveright (2012)

56. 《美中贸易争端：事实、数字和神话》Imad Moosa, *US-China Trade Dispute: Facts, Figures and Myths.* Edward Elgar Publishing (2012)

57. 《自由交易：美国与中国贸易的政治学（1784—1862）》（博士论文）Dael A. Norwood, *Trading in Liberty: The Politics of the American China Trade, c. 1784—1862.* Ph. D. Dissertation, Princeton University (2012)

58. 《勇敢的龙：中国篮球队、美国教练与两种文化冲突》Jim Yardley, *Brave Dragons: A Chinese Basketball Team, an American Coach, and Two Cultures Clashing.* Knopf (2012)

59. 《飞虎队：陈纳德将军和美国第十四航空队在中国的真实故事》Claire Lee Chennault, Jack Samson, *The Flying Tiger: The True Story of General Claire Chennault and the U.S. 14th Air Force in China*. Lyons Press (2012)

60. 《东亚经济、安全和国际关系的联结点》Avery Goldstein（金骏远），Edward D. Mansfield (eds.), *The Nexus of Economics, Securtiy, and International Relations in East Asia*. Stanford University Press (2012)

61. 《纠结的巨人：美国和中国》David Shambaugh（沈大伟），*Tangled Titans: The United States and China*. Rowman & Littlefield (2012)

62. 《中美战略互疑：解析与应对》（智库报告）Kenneth Lieberthal（李侃如），Wang Jisi（王辑思），*Addressing U.S.-China Strategic Distrust*. Brookings (2012)

63. 《皮毛、财富和帝国：美国皮毛交易的史诗》Eric Jay Dolin, *Fur, Fortune, and Empire: The Epic History of the Fur Trade in America*. W. W. Norton & Company (2011)

64. 《卡尔·克劳：洋鬼子在中国》Carl Crow, *Foreign Devils in the Flowery Kingdom*. Earnshaw Books (1940, 2011)

65. 《美国医生在广州：中国的现代化（1835—1935）》Guangqiu Xu, *American Doctors in Canton: Modernization in China, 1835—1935*. Transaction Publishers (2011)

66. 《乒乓外交的起源：被遗忘的中美和解设计师》Mayumi Itoh, *The Origin of Ping-Pong Diplomacy: The Forgotten Architect of Sino-U.S. Rapprochement*. Palgrave Macmillan (2011)

67. 《中国、美国和全球秩序》Rosemary Foot, Andrew Walter, *China, the United States, and Global Order*. Cambridge University Press (2011)

68. 《中国之美国：中国人看美国（1900—2000）》Jing Li, *China's America: The Chinese View the United States, 1900—2000*. State University of New York Press (2011)

69. 《平等条款：重新定义中国与美国和西方的关系》Mingxun Zheng, Thomas S. Robertson, *On Equal Terms: Redefining China's Relationship with America and the West*. Wiley (2011)

70. 《中国人对美国的认知：对中国外交政策动机的探讨》Biwu Zhang, *Chinese Perceptions of the U.S.: An Exploration of China's Foreign Policy Motivations*. Lexington Books (2011)

71. 《幸运儿：来美留学、彻底改变一个古老文明的120个中国幼童》Liel Leibovitz, *Fortunate Sons: The 120 Chinese Boys Who Came to America, Went to School, and Revolutionized an Ancient Civilization*. New York: W.W. Norton (2011)

72. 《权力转型中的美国和中国》David Lai（赖大卫），*The United States and China in Power Transition*. The Strategic Studies Institute (SSI) (2011)

73. 《木兰传奇在中美两国》Lan Dong, *Mulan's Legend and Legacy in China and the United States*. Temple University Press (2011)

74. 《新英格兰商人、中国贸易与加利福尼亚的起源》（博士论文）Michael D. Block, *New England Merchants, the China Trade, and the Origins of California*. Ph. D. Dissertation, University of Southern California (2011)

75. 《一个世界边缘阅读另一个：了解美洲和伊比利亚半岛的"东方"》Ignacio Lopez-Calvo, *One World Periphery Reads the Other: Knowing the "oriental" in the Americas and the Iberian Peninsula*. Newcastle upon Tyne: Cambridge Scholars (2010)

76. 《美国对中国的反应：中美关系史》Warren I. Cohen（孔华润）, *America's Response to China: A History of Sino-American Relations*. Columbia University Press (2010, 2019)

77. 《美中货币争端：政治、经济和法律的新见解》Simon J Evenett, *The US-Sino Currency Dispute: New Insights from Politics, Economics and Law*. Centre for Economic Policy Research (2010)

78. 《中国和美国：全球影响比较》Thomas Lum, Christopher M. Blanchard, Nicolas Cook, Kerry Dumbaugh, Susan B. Epstein, *China and the U.S.: Comparing Global Influence*. Nova Science Pub Inc. (2010)

79. 《中国与美国的质押：经济依存与国内政治》Helen Thompson, *China and the Mortgaging of America: Economic Interdependence and Domestic Politics*. Palgrave Macmillan (2010)

80. 《中美关系：在巴基斯坦寻求战略趋同》（智库报告）Bruce Riedel, Pavneet Singh, *US-China Relations: Seeking Strategic Convergence in Pakistan*. Foreign Policy at Brookings (2010)

81. 《中美国：将改变世界的不安全伙伴关系》Handel Jones, *ChinAmerica: The Uneasy Partnership that Will Change the World*. McGraw-Hill (2010)

82. 《中美新的太空竞赛》Erik Seedhouse, *The New Space Race: China vs. USA*. Praxis Publishing (2010)

83. 《美中关系：危机四伏的过去，务实的现在》Robert G. Sutter（罗伯特.萨特）, *U.S.-Chinese Relations: Perilous Past, Pragmatic Present*. Rowman & Littlefield Publishers (2010)

84. 《飞虎队：陈纳德的美国航空志愿队在中国》Braxton Eisel, *The Flying Tigers: Chennault's American Volunteer Group in China*. Air Force History and Museums Program (U.S.) (2009)

85. 《权力与约束：美中关系的共同愿景》Richard Rosecrance, Gu Guoliang, *Power and Restraint: A Shared Vision for the U.S.-China Relationship*. Public Affairs (2009)

86. 《中美关系巧实力》（智库报告）William Cohen, Hank Greenberg, *Smart Power in US-China Relations*. Center for Strategic and International Studies (CSIS) (2009)

87. 《中国软实力及其对美国的影响：世界发展中的竞争与合作》Carola McGiffert, *Chinese Soft Power and Its Implications for the United States: Competition and Cooperation in the Developing World*. Center for Strategic & International Studies (CSIS) (2009)

88. 《美国军队在中国（1856—1941）》John Langellier, Mike Chappell, *US Armed Forces in China 1856—1941*. Osprey Publishing (2009)

89. 《超级融合：中美如何成为一个经济体，为什么世界的繁荣依赖于它》Zachary Karabell, *Superfusion: How China and America Became One Economy and Why the Worlds Prosperity Depends on It*. Simon & Schuster (2009)

90. 《太遥远的桥？中美之间的共性与差异》Robert Grafstein, Fan Wen (eds.), *A Bridge Too*

Far? Commonalities and Differences between China and the United States. Lexington Books (2009)

91. 《跨太平洋互动：美国和中国（1880—1950）》Vanessa Künnemann, Ruth Mayer (eds.), *Trans-Pacific Interactions: The United States and China, 1880—1950.* New York: Palgrave Macmillan US (2009)

92. 《美国在亚洲》Robert G. Sutter（罗伯特.萨特）, *The United States in Asia.* Rowman & Littlefield Publishers (2008)

93. 《美中关系：国会对华政策》Tao Xie, *US-China Relations: China policy on Capitol Hill.* Routledge (2008)

94. 《尼克松和毛泽东：改变世界的一周》Margaret MacMillan, *Nixon and Mao: The Week That Changed the World.* Random House (2008)

95. 《乔治·布什的中国日记：一个全球总统的形成》Jeffrey A. Engel (editor), *The China Diary of George H. W. Bush: The Making of a Global President.* Princeton University Press (2008)

96. 《小布什与中国：政策、问题和伙伴关系》Chi Wang, *George W. Bush and China: Policies, Problems, and Partnerships.* Lexington Books (2008)

97. 《中国与美国在东北亚的合作与竞争》Suisheng Zhao（赵穗生）, *China and the United States: Cooperation and Competition in Northeast Asia.* Palgrave Macmillan (2008)

98. 《中美关系转型：视角与战略互动》Suisheng Zhao（赵穗生）, *China-US Relations: Transformed Perspectives & Strategic Interactions.* Routledge (2008)

99. 《中国、美国和东南亚：关于政治、安全和经济的争论性视角》Evelyn Goh, Sheldon W. Simon, *China, the United States, and Southeast Asia: Contending Perspectives on Politics, Security, and Economics.* Routledge (2008)

100. 《中国、太空武器与美国安全》Bruce W. Macdonald, *China, Space Weapons, and U.S. Security.* Council on Foreign Relations (CSR) (2008)

101. 《"亚太"世纪的美中关系》S. Mahmud Ali, *U.S.-China Relations in the "Asia-Pacific" Century.* Palgrave Macmillan US (2008)

102. 《中国追求地位的斗争：国际关系的调整》Yong Deng（邓勇）, *China's Struggle for Status: The Realignment of International Relations.* Cambridge University Press (2008)

103. 《不可避免的中国革命：美国失去中国的再反思》Thomas Lutze（罗其韬）, *China's Inevitable Revolution: Rethinking America's Loss to the Communists.* Palgrave Macmillan (2007)

104. 《中国、美国与权力转移理论批判》Steve Chan, *China, the US and the Power-Transition Theory: A Critique.* Routledge (2007)

105. 《重审中国现代民族主义：中美关系与21世纪中国公共舆论的兴起》Simon Shen, *Redefining Nationalism in Modern China: Sino-American Relations and the Emergence of Chinese Public Opinion in the 21st Century.* Palgrave Macmillan (2007)

106. 《美国少林：飞踢、僧侣、铁侠传奇—新中国的奥德赛》Matthew Polly, *American*

Shaolin: Flying Kicks, Buddhist Monks, and the Legend of Iron Crotch: An Odyssey in the New China. Gotham (2007)

107.《进入龙穴：中国的反接近战略及其对美国的影响》Roger Cliff, *Entering the Dragons Lair: Chinese Antiaccess Strategies and Their Implications for the United States*. RAND (2007)

108.《亚洲、美洲与地缘政治转型》William H. Overholt, *Asia, America, and the Transformation of Geopolitics*. Cambridge University Press (2007)

109.《中国浪漫：1776至1876年美国文化中的中国之旅》（中译本《中国传奇：美国人眼里的中国》）John Rogers Haddad（约翰·海达德）, *The Romance of China: Excursions to China in U.S. Culture, 1776 to 1876*. Columbia University Press (2006)

110.《美国在华生意指南：合同协议谈判，文化风俗了解，产品服务营销》Mike Saxon, *An American's Guide to Doing Business in China: Negotiating Contracts and Agreements, Understanding Culture and Customs, Marketing Products and Services*. Adams Media (2006)

111.《老牌中国通卡尔·克劳：一个美国人在上海的生活、时代和冒险》Paul French, *Carl Crow: A Tough Old China Hand-The Life, Times, and Adventures of an American in Shanghai*. Hong Kong University Press (2006)

112.《美国的外交关系（1969—1976），第十七卷：中国（1969—1972）》Steven E. Phillips, Edward C. Keefer, *Foreign Relations of the United States, 1969—1976, Volume XVII, China, 1969—1972*. Department of State, US (2006)

113.《美中贸易争端：愈演愈烈与上升的风险》Gary Clyde Hufbauer, Yee Wong, and Ketki Sheth, *US-China Trade Disputes: Rising Tide, Rising Stakes*. Institute for International Economics (2006)

114.《21世纪的美国与中国：权力转移与和平》Zhiqun Zhu, *US-China In The 21 Century: Power Transition And Peace* (Politics in Asia Series). Routledge (2006)

115.《建立双边国际关系模式：以美中相互作用为例》Xinsheng Liu, *Modeling Bilateral International Relations: The Case of U.S.-China Interactions* (Advances in Foreign Policy Analysis). Palgrave Macmillan US (2006)

116.《21世纪的美国与中国：权力转型与和平》Zhiqun Zhu（朱志群）, *US-China in the 21 Century: Power Transition and Peace* (Politics in Asia Series). Routledge (2006)

117.《美中关系历史辞典》Robert Sutter（罗伯特.萨特）, *Historical Dictionary of United States-China Relations*. The Scarecrow Press, Inc. (2005)

118.《美国与中国和解的构建（1961—1974）：从"红色威胁"到"默契的盟友"》Evelyn Goh, *Constructing the U.S. Rapprochement with China, 1961—1974: from "Red Menace" to "Tacit Ally"*. Cambridge University Press (2004)

119.《美国孤立：新保守主义与全球秩序》Stefan Halper, Jonathan Clarke, *America Alone: The Neo-Conservatives and the Global Order*. Cambridge University Press (2004)

120.《美国对华直接投资》K.C. Fung, *U.S. Direct Investment in China*. The AEI Press (2004)

121. 《美国政治想象中的中国》Carola McGiffert, *China in the American Political Imagination*. Washington, D.C.: Center for Strategic and International Studies (2003)
122. 《中美关系：互相猜疑》Radha Sinha, *Sino-American Relations: Mutual Paranoia*. Palgrave Macmillan UK (2003)
123. 《美国、中国和东南亚安全：轮班换岗》Wayne Bert, *The United States, China and Southeast Asian Security: A Changing of the Guard*. Palgrave Macmillan UK (2003)
124. 《牛仔与龙：粉碎文化深化推进中美商业发展》Charles Lee, *Cowboys and Dragons: Shattering Cultural Myths to Advance Chinese-American Business*. Kaplan Business (2003)
125. 《埃兹拉·庞德与中国》Zhaoming Qian, *Ezra Pound and China*. University of Michigan Press (2003)
126. 《威尔逊与中国：山东问题的修订史》Bruce A. Elleman, *Wilson and China: A Revised History of the Shandong Question*. Routledge (2002)
127. 《以中国之名追寻现代性：中国学生在美国（1900—1927）》Weili Ye（叶维丽）, *Seeking Modernity in China's Name: Chinese Students in the United States, 1900—1927*. Stanford University Press (2001)
128. 《与远方国家的交涉：中国通商口岸的美国公民（1844—1942）》Eileen P. Scully, *Bargaining with the State from Afar: American Citizenship in Treaty Port China, 1844—1942*. Columbia University Press (2001)
129. 《中国外交秘辛：美国外交官与1945年以来的中美关系》Nancy Bernkopf Tucker（唐耐心）, *China Confidential: American Diplomats and Sino-American Relations since 1945*. Columbia University Press (2001)
130. 《中美友谊的传统与挑战：Ailie Gale博士在中国（1908—1950）》Maria Cristina Zaccarini, *The Sino-American Friendship as Tradition and Challenge: Dr. Ailie Gale in China, 1908—1950*. Lehigh University Press (2001)
131. 《同床异梦：经营美中关系（1989—2000）》David M. Lampton（蓝普顿）, *Same Bed, Different Dreams: Managing U.S.-China Relations, 1989—2000* (A Philip E. Lilienthal Book). University of California Press (2001)
132. 《双刃剑：美国和中国不平等的核外交冲突（1950—1958）》Appu K. Soman, *Double-Edged Sword: Nuclear Diplomacy in Unequal Conflicts The United States and China, 1950—1958*. Praeger (2000)
133. 《长城：六任总统与中国》Patrick Tyler, *A Great Wall: Six Presidents and China*. PublicAffairs (2000)
134. 《美国与中国崛起：战略和军事意义》Zalmay Khalilzad, *The United States and a Rising China: Strategic and Military Implications*. Rand Corporation (1999)
135. 《关于面子：从尼克松到克林顿时期美国与中国奇妙的关系史》James Mann, *About Face: A History of America's Curious Relationship with China, from Nixon to Clinton*.

Alfred A. Knopf (1998)

136. 《形象、感知与美中关系的形成》Hongshan Li, Zhaohui Hong (eds.), *Image, Perception, and the Making of U.S.-China Relations* (Sacred Literature). University Press of America (1998)

137. 《即将到来的美中冲突》Richard Bernstein, Ross H. Munro, *The Coming Conflict with China*. New York: Alfred A. Knopf (1997)

138. 《拉塞尔公司（1818—1891）：美国与19世纪中国的贸易和外交》（博士论文）Sibing He（何思兵）, *Russell and Company, 1818—1891: America's Trade and Diplomacy in Nineteenth-Century China*. Ph. D. Dissertation, Miami University (1997)

139. 《失序的伙伴关系：中美及其战后的日本帝国处置政策（1941—1945）》Xiaoyuan Liu, *A Partnership for Disorder: China, the United States, and their Policies for the Postwar Disposition of the Japanese Empire, 1941—1945*. Cambridge University Press (1996)

140. 《寻求平等：中国人在19世纪美国反对歧视的斗争》Charles J. McClain, *In Search of Equality: The Chinese Struggle against Discrimination in Nineteenth-Century America*. University of California Press (1996)

141. 《美国与中国的文化战争（1915—1960）》（硕士论文）Christopher L. Battle, *America and the Chinese Culture Wars, 1915—1960*. Thesis for the Degree of Master of History, University of Arkansas (1995)

142. 《中美交流中的相声与文化》Linda W. L. Young, *Crosstalk and Culture in Sino-American Communication* (Studies in Interactional Sociolinguistics). Cambridge University Press (1994)

143. 《龙、狮和鹰：1949—1958年中—英—美关系》Qiang Zhai, *The Dragon, the Lion, & the Eagle: Chinese-British-American Relations, 1949—1958* (American Diplomatic History). Kent State Univ Pr. (1994)

144. 《龙与鹰：美国启蒙运动中的中国存在》A. Owen Aldridge, *The Dragon and Eagle: The Presence of China in the American Enlightenment*. Detroit: Wayne State University Press (1993)

145. 《无鬼魂之地：从19世纪中叶至今中国人对美国的印象》R. David Arkush, *Land without Ghosts: Chinese Impressions of America from the Mid-Nineteenth Century to the Present*. University of California Press (1993)

146. 《水獭皮、波士顿船和中国货：1785—1841年西北海岸的海上毛皮贸易》James R. Gibson, *Otter Skins, Boston Ships, and China Goods: The Maritime Fur Trade of the Northwest Coast, 1785—1841*. Montreal: McGill-Queen's University Press (1992)

147. 《善行与炮舰：美国和中国两个世纪的遭遇》Hugh Deane, *Good Deeds & Gunboats: Two Centuries of American-Chinese Encounters*. San Francisco: China Books & Periodicals (1990)

148. 《中美关系（1945—1955）：对关键十年的联合评估》Harry Harding（何汉理）, Ming Yüan, *Sino-American Relations, 1945—1955: A Joint Reassessment of a Critical Decade*. SR Books (1989)

149. 《倔强的大地：1898—1937年美国农学家在中国土地上》Randall E. Stross, *The*

Stubborn Earth: American Agriculturalists on Chinese Soil, 1898—1937. University of California Press (1989)

150. 《中国通的遗产：伦理与外交》Paul Gordon Lauren, *The China Hand's Legacy: Ethics and Diplomacy*. Boulder: Westview Press (1987)

151. 《美国对华贸易：衔接历史专业与社会研究课程的框架》（博士论文）Elizabeth Bateman Bond, *America's China Trade: A Framework for Linking the History Profession with Social Studies Curriculum*. Ph. D. Dissertation, The University of North Carolina at Greensboro (1987)

152. 《美中贸易（1784—1844）之中产阶级产品》（博士论文）Nancy Ellen Davis, *The American China Trade, 1784—1844: Products for the Middle Class* (Philadelphia, New York City, Boston). Ph. D. Dissertation, The George Washington University (1987)

153. 《历史视角下的美中贸易：中美两国表现》Ernest R. May, John King Fairbank（费正清）, *America's China Trade in Historical Perspective: The Chinese and American Performance*. Harvard University Press (1986)

154. 《顽固的泥土：中国大地上的美国农学家（1898—1937）》Randall E. Stross, *The Stubborn Earth: American Agriculturalists on Chinese Soil, 1898—1937*. Berkeley: University of California Press (1986)

155. 《野蛮人天堂：中国的美国观（1784—1911）》（博士论文）Chang-Fange Hen, *Barbarian Paradise: Chinese Views of the United States, 1784—1911*. Ph. D. Dissertation, Indiana University (1985)

156. 《帝国主义和理想主义：美国驻华外交官（1861—1898）》David L. Anderson, *Imperialism and Idealism: American Diplomats in China, 1861—1898*. Bloomington: Indiana University Press (1985)

157. 《冒险的追求：美国人与中国贸易（1784—1844）》Margaret C. S. Christman, *Adventurous Pursuits: Americans and the China Trade, 1784—1844*. Washington: Published for the National Portrait Gallery by the Smithsonian Institution Press (1984)

158. 《中国皇后号》Philip Chadwick Foster Smith, *The Empress of China*. Philadelphia Maritime Museum (1984)

159. 《费城人与中国贸易（1784—1844）》Jean Gordon Lee, *Philadelphians and the China Trade, 1784—1844*. Philadelphia Museum of Art (1984)

160. 《美国与中国》（第四版）John King Fairbank（费正清）, *The United States and China*. Fourth Edition. Harvard University Press (1983)

161. 《特殊关系的形成：美国和中国至1914年》Michael H. Hunt, *The Making of a Special Relationship: The United States and China to 1914*. New York: Columbia University Press (1983)

162. 《与中国沟通》Robert A. Kapp, *Communicating with China*. Chicago: Intercultural Press (1983)

163. 《美国与自由中国：美国如何卖掉盟友》James C. H. Shen, Robert Myers (eds.), *The U.S and Free China: How the U.S. Sold Out Its Ally*. Acropolis Books Inc (1983)

164. 《美中贸易谈判》Rosalie L. Tung, *U.S.–China Trade Negotiations* (Pergamon policy studies on business and economics). Elsevier Inc, Pergamon Press (1982)

165. 《庚子赔款：中美纠纷五十年》（博士论文）Terence Eldon Brockhausen, *The Boxer Indemnity: Five Decades of Sino-Amerian Dissension*. Ph. D. Dissertation, Texas Christian University (1981)

166. 《中国官员在美国：中国早期驻美公使（1878—1907）》（博士论文）Kim Man Chan, *Mandarins in America: The Early Chinese Ministers to the United States, 1878—1907*. Ph. D. Dissertation, University of Hawai'i at Manoa (1981)

167. 《有组织的商业与中国市场的神话：美国亚洲协会（1898—1937）》James J. Lorence, *Organized Business and the Myth of the China Market: The American Asiatic Association, 1898—1937*. The American Philosophical Society (1981)

168. 《美国在华安全利益：超越"中国牌"》（硕士论文）Joseph Frederick Bouchard, *United States Security Interests in China: Beyond the "China Card"*. Thesis for the Degree of Master of Arts, Naval Postgraduate School (1981)

169. 《1784年以来中美关系的各个方面》Thomas H. Etzold (ed.), *Aspects of Sino-American Relations since 1784*. New York: New Viewpoints (1978)

170. 《龙与鹰：美中关系的过去与未来》Robert B. Oxnam, *Dragon and Eagle: United States-China Relations: Past and Future*. New York: Basic Books (1978)

171. 《情报的日子：二战时期飞虎队——第14航空大队在中国的摄影记录》Malcolm Leviatt Rosholt, *Days of the Ching Pao: A Photographic Record of the Flying Tigers-14th Air Force in China in World War II*. Rosholt House II (1978)

172. 《华工与美国第一条洲际铁路》（博士论文）Tzu-Kuei Yen, *Chinese Workers and the First Transcontinental Railroad of the United States of America*. Ph. D. Dissertation, St. John's University (New York) (1977)

173. 《18—19世纪中国对美国文化的影响》Henry Trubner, William Jay Rathbun, Yin-wah Ashton, *China's Influence on American Culture in the 18th and 19th Centuries*. China Institute in America; China House Gallery (1976)

174. 《美国在中国的文化实验（1942—1949）》Wilma Fairbank（费慰梅）, *America's Cultural Experiment in China, 1942—1949* (Cultural Relations Programs of the U.S. Department of State: Historical Studies, Number 1). Bureau of Educational and Cultural Affairs (Dept. of State), Washington, D. C. (1976)

175. 《中国通：美国外交官员及其遭遇》E. J. (Ely Jacques) Kahn, *The China Hands: America's Foreign Service Officers and What Befell Them*. New York: Viking (1975)

176. 《中美关系的历史回顾》John King Fairbank（费正清）, *Chinese-American Interactions:*

A Historical Summary. New Brunswick, N. J.: Rutgers University Press (1975)

177. 《美国政治中的中国游说》Ross Y. Koen, *The China Lobby in American Politics*. New York: Harper & Row (1974)

178. 《干预政治：美国在中国内战中的作用》（博士论文）Chi Jen Feng, *The Politics of Intervention: America's Role in the Chinese Civil War*. Ph. D. Dissertation, New York University (1973)

179. 《费城的中国贸易（1682—1846）：跨区域商业与文化互动研究》（博士论文）Jonathan Goldstein, *The China Trade From Philadelphia, 1682—1846: A Study of Interregional Commerce and Cultural Interaction*. Ph. D. Dissertation, University of Pennsylvania (1973)

180. 《史迪威与美国在中国的经验（1911—1945）》Barbara W. Tuchman, *Stilwell and the American Experience in China, 1911—1945*. New York: The MacMillan Company (1971)

181. 《留美学生对中国革命的影响（1911—1949）》Tsung I. Dow, *The Impact of Chinese Students Returned from America: With Emphasis on the Chinese Revolution, 1911—1949*. Florida Atlantic University, Boca Raton (1971)

182. 《中国和我们自己：新一代的探索与修正》Bruce Douglass, Ross Terrill, *China and Ourselves: Explorations and Revisions by a New Generation*. Boston: Beacon Press (1970)

183. 《迪克西使团：1944年在延安的美国陆军观察组》David D. Barrett, *Dixie Mission: The United States Army Observer Group in Yenan, 1944*. Berkeley: Center for Chinese Studies, University of California (1970)

184. 《美国对中国的回应（1784—1844）：共识政策与东印度中队的起源》（博士论文）James Benjamin Wood, *The American Response to China, 1784—1844: Consensus Policy and the Origin of the East India Squadron*. Ph. D. Dissertation. Duke University (1969)

185. 《中国和美国：1784以来两国关系的故事》Foster Rhea Dulles, *China and America: The Story of Their Relations since 1784*. Port Washington, N.Y.: Kennikat Press (1967)

186. 《美国与1933—1938年远东危机：从满洲事变到未宣战的中日战争初期》Dorothy Borg, *The United States and the Far Eastern Crisis of 1933—1938: From the Manchurian Incident through the Initial Stage of the Undeclared Sino-Japanese War*. Cambridge: Harvard University Press (1964)

187. 《中美关系史书目》Robert L. Irick, *American-Chinese Relations, 1784—1941: A Survey of Chinese-language Materials at Harvard = Chung Mei kuan hsi shih chu mu*. Harvard University Press (1960)

188. 《共产党中国与美国远东政策》John M. H. Lindbeck, *Communist China and American Far Eastern Policy*. Washington: U.S. Department of State (1955)

189. 《史迪威中国使命》Charles F Romanus, Riley Sunderland, *Stilwell's Mission to China*. Center of Military History, US Army (1953, 1987)

190. 《中国纠结：从珍珠港事件到马歇尔使团美国在中国的努力》Herbert Feis, *The*

China Tangle: The American Effort in China from Pearl Harbor to the Marshall Mission. Princeton University Press (1953, 1972)

191. 《美国报刊与最近的中国政策（1941—1949）》（硕士论文）Morton Gordon, *The American Press and Recent China Policy, 1941—1949*. Thesis for the Degree of Master of Arts, University of Chicago (1950)

192. 《亚洲遗产与美国人的生活》Arthur E. Christy, *The Asian Legacy and American Life*. The John Day Company (1945)

193. 《中国与美国》Earl Browder, *China and the U.S.A.* New York: Workers Library Publishers (1937)

194. 《美国与中国的文化交往：1784—1844年中美文化的最早接触》George H. Danton, *The Culture Contacts of the United States and China: The Earliest Sino-American Culture Contacts, 1784—1844*. New York: Columbia University Press (1931)

195. 《美国在华投资》C. F. (Charles Frederick) Remer, *American Investments in China*. The Institute of Pacific Relations, Honolulu (1929)

196. 《真正的美国华人：努力让美国公众更全面地了解美国华人》Julius Su Tow, *The Real Chinese in America: Being An Attempt to Give the General American Public a Fuller Knowledge and a Better Understanding of the Chinese People in the United States*. New York city: The Academy Press (1923)

197. 《美国人在东亚：对19世纪美国关于中国、日本和朝鲜政策的批判性研究》Tyler Dennett, *Americans in Eastern Asia: A Critical Study of the Policy of the United States with Reference to China, Japan and Korea in the l9th Century*. New York: Macmillan (1922)

198. 《一位美国驻华外交官》Paul Samuel Reinsch（芮恩施）, *An American Diplomat in China*. Garden City, N.Y., Toronto, Doubleday, Page & Co. (1922)

199. 《美国与中国早期关系史（1784—1844）》Kenneth Scott Latourette（赖德烈）, *The History of Early Relations between the United States and China, 1784—1844*. New Haven, Conn., Yale University Press (1917)

200. 《美国商船的故事》John Randolph Spears, *The Story of the American Merchant Marine*. New York: The Macmillan Company (1915)

201. 《一位东方外交家看美国》T'ing-fang Wu（伍廷芳）, *America: Through the Spectacles of an Oriental Diplomat*. Frederick A. Stokes Company (1914)

202. 《美国之华人问题参考书目》Robert Ernest Cowan, Boutwell Dunlap, *Bibliography of the Chinese Question in the United States*. A. M. Robertson, San Francisco (1909)

203. 《华人与日本人在美国：美国政治社会科学院编年》Emory R. Johnson, *Chinese and Japanese in America: The Annals of the American Academy of Political and Social Science*. Philadelphia: American Academy of Political and Social Science (1909)

204. 《中国留学生入读美国大学》John Fryer, *Admission of Chinese Students to American*

Colleges. Washington: Government Printinh Officce (1909)

205. 《今日中国和美国：条件与关系研究》Arthur H. Smith（明恩溥），*China and America To-day: A Study of Conditions and Relations*. Fleming H.Revell Company (1907)

206. 《东方的美国巡洋舰：远东旅行与研究》John Donaldson Ford, *An American Cruiser in the East: Travels and Studies in the Far East. The Aleutian Islands, Behring's Sea Eastern Siberia, Japan, Korea, China, Formosa, Hong Kong, and the Philippine Islands*. New York: A. S. Barnes (1905)

207. 《中国人如何看我们：摘自写给国内朋友的信件段落》Henry Pearson Gratton, *As a Chinaman Saw Us: Passages from His Letters to a Friend at Home*. New York: D. Appleton and Company (1904)

208. 《美国的东方外交》John Watson Foster, *American Diplomacy in the Orient*. Boston, New York: Houghton, Mifflin and Company (1903)

209. 《美国与太平洋和远东关系（1784—1900）》James Morton Callahan, *American Relations in the Pacific and the Far East, 1784—1900*. Baltimore: Johns Hopkins Press (1901)

210. 《美国在东方：我们的历史、前景与问题一瞥》William Elliot Griffis, *America in the East: A Glance at Our History, Prospects, Problems*. A.S. Barnes and Company (1899)

211. 《美国之中国：美国东部城市中国人社会生活研究》Stewart Culin, American Association for the Advancement of Science, *China in America: A Study in the Social Life of the Chinese in the Eastern Cities of the United States*. Philadelphia: S. N. (1887)

212. 《美国和中国的鸦片吸食：其流行及对个人和国家、即时和长远影响研究》H. H. (Harry Hubbell) Kane, *Opium-smoking in America and China: A Study of Its Prevalence, and Effects, Immediate and Remote, on the Individual and the Nation*. New York: G. P. Putnam's Sons (1882)

213. 《纪念顾盛》By Newburyport (Mass.), City Council; George Bailey Loring, *A Memorial of Caleb Cushing. From the City of Newburyport*. Newburyport: Published by Order of the City Council (1879)

214. 《中华帝国海关收藏目录：1876年费城美国国际展览会》*Catalogue of the Chinese Imperial Maritime Customs Collection, at the United States International Exhibition, Philadelphia, 1876*. Shanghai: Inspector General of Chinese Maritime Customs (1876)

215. 《最古老与最新帝国：中国和美国》William Speer, *The Oldest and the Newest Empire: China and the United States*. Hartford, Conn., Scranton (1870)

216. 《纽约老商人》Walter Barrett, *The Old Merchants of New York City*. New York: Carleton (1864)

217. 《一位美国商人在欧洲、亚洲和澳大利亚：一系列来自爪哇、新加坡、中国、孟加拉国、埃及和荷兰的信件》George Francis Train, *An American Merchant in Europe, Asia, and Australia: A Series of Letters from Java, Singapore, China, Bengal, Egypt, and the*

Holy Land ... etc. New York: G. P. Putnam & Co. (1857)

218.《中国与加利福尼亚：其关系、过去和现在》William Speer, *China and California: Their Relations, Past and Present*. Marvin & Hitchcock, San Francisco (1853)

219.《广州华人：美国人在天朝帝国的旅居》Osmond Tiffany, *The Canton Chinese: Or, The American's Sojourn in the Celestial Empire*. Boston and Cambridge: James Munroe and Company (1849)

8.3.2　中国与苏联/俄罗斯

1.《1917—1991年中苏关系简史》(China Connections) Zhihua Shen（沈志华）, *A Short History of Sino-Soviet Relations, 1917—1991*. Springer Singapore: Palgrave Macmillan (2020)

2.《21世纪的中俄关系》Jo Inge Bekkevold, Bobo Lo, *Sino-Russian Relations in the 21st Century*. Springer International Publishing: Palgrave Macmillan (2019)

3.《镜地：俄罗斯、中国和其间的旅程》Ed Pulford, *Mirrorlands: Russia, China, and Journeys in Between*. Hurst (2019)

4.《中国与俄罗斯：新和解》Alexander Lukin, *China and Russia: The New Rapprochement*. Polity Press (2018)

5.《累犯：俄罗斯与中国革命的比较》Lucien Bianco, *Recidivism: A Comparison of the Russian and Chinese Revolutions*. Chinese University Press (2018)

6.《毛泽东与1959—1973年中苏分裂：一部新历史》Danhui Li（李丹慧）, Yafeng Xia, *Mao and the Sino-Soviet Split, 1959—1973: A New History*. Lexington Books (2018)

7.《中俄边境经济的信任与不信任》Caroline Humphrey, *Trust and Mistrust in the Economies of the China-Russia Borderlands* (Asian Borderlands). Amsterdam University Press (2018)

8.《中国、俄罗斯与21世纪全球地缘政治》Paul J. Bolt, Sharyl Cross, *China, Russia, And Twenty-First Century Global Geopolitics*. Oxford University Press (2018)

9.《中国的苏联梦：宣传、文化和大众想象》Yan Li, *China's Soviet Dream: Propaganda, Culture, and Popular Imagination* (Routledge Contemporary China Series). Routledge (2017)

10.《十月：俄罗斯革命的故事》China Miéville, *October: The Story of the Russian Revolution*. Verso (2017)

11.《权力政治：中国和俄罗斯如何重塑世界》Rob de Wijk, *Power Politics: How China and Russia Reshape the World*. Amsterdam University Press (2015)

12.《后危机时代国际秩序中的俄中关系》Marcin Kaczmarski, *Russia-China Relations in the Post-Crisis International Order* (BASEES: Routledge Series on Russian and East European Studies). Routledge (2015)

13.《中俄关系在中亚：能源政策、北京的新自信和21世纪地缘政治》Thomas Stephan Eder, *China-Russia Relations in Central Asia: Energy Policy, Beijing's New Assertiveness and 21st Century Geopolitics*. Springer Fachmedien Wiesbaden (2014)

14.《后共产主义现代化的十字路口：俄罗斯和中国的比较视角》Christer Pursiainen (eds.),

At the Crossroads of Post-Communist Modernisation: Russia and China in Comparative Perspective. Palgrave Macmillan UK (2012)

15. 《俄罗斯与中国的宗教和国家：压制、生存与复兴》Christopher Marsh, *Religion and the State in Russia and China: Suppression, Survival, and Revival*. Continuum (2011)

16. 《附带损害：中苏对抗与中越联盟的终止》Nicholas Khoo, *Collateral Damage: Sino-Soviet Rivalry and the Termination of the Sino-Vietnamese Alliance*. Columbia University Press (2011)

17. 《中国与俄罗斯关系的未来》James A. Bellacqua, *The Future of China-Russia Relations*. The University Press of Kentucky (2010)

18. 《中国学习苏联：从1949年到现在》Thomas P. Bernstein（白思鼎）, Hua-yu Li（李华钰）(eds.), *China Learns from the Soviet Union, 1949-Present* (The Harvard Cold War Studies). Lexington Books (2010)

19. 《俄罗斯和挑战者：单极时代俄罗斯与中国、伊朗和伊拉克的结盟》Helen Belopolsky, *Russia and the Challengers: Russian Alignment with China, Iran, and Iraq in the Unipolar Era*. Palgrave Macmillan UK (2009)

20. 《便利的轴心：莫斯科、北京和新地缘政治学》Bobo Lo, *Axis of Convenience: Moscow, Beijing, and the New Geopolitics*. Brookings Institution Press (2008)

21. 《俄罗斯与中国的革命和人民比较史》S. A. Smith, *Revolution and the People in Russia and China: A Comparative History*. Cambridge University Press (2008)

22. 《俄罗斯对华和对日政策：叶利钦和普京时期》Natasha Kuhrt, *Russian Policy towards China and Japan: The Yeltsin and Putin Periods*. Routledge (2008)

23. 《苏越关系和中国角色1949—64：变化的联盟》Mari Olsen, *Soviet-Vietnam Relations and the Role of China 1949—64: Changing Alliances*. Routledge (2006)

24. 《斯大林主义的政治经济学》Paul R. Gregory, *The Political Economy of Stalinism: Evidence from the Soviet Secret Archives*. Cambridge University Press (2004)

25. 《1945至1950年的苏联和共产党中国：艰难的联盟道路》Dieter Heinzig, *The Soviet Union and Communist China 1945—1950: The Arduous Road to the Alliance*. Routledge (2003)

26. 《毛泽东、马克思和市场：俄罗斯和中国资本主义的冒险》Dean LeBaron, *Mao, Marx, and the Market: Capitalist Adventures in Russia and China*. Wiley (2001)

27. 《跨越国界的种族挑战：中国和俄罗斯对中亚难题的看法》Yongjin Zhang, Rouben Azizian (eds.), *Ethnic Challenges beyond Borders: Chinese and Russian Perspectives of the Central Asian Conundrum* (St Antony's Series). Palgrave Macmillan UK (1998)

28. 《从改良到革命：苏联和中国共产主义体制的终结》Minxin Pei（裴敏欣）, *From Reform to Revolution: The Demise of Communism in China and the Soviet Union*. Harvard University Press (1998)

29. 《亲密兄弟：中苏同盟的兴衰（1945—1963）》Odd Arne Westad（文安立）, *Brothers in Arms: The Rise and Fall of the Sino-Soviet Alliance, 1945—1963*. Woodrow Wilson Center

Press (1998)

30. 《斯大林、冷战和中国部》Brian Murray, *Stalin, the Cold War, and the Division of China: A Multi-Archival Mystery.* Woodrow Wilson International Center for Scholars (1995)

31. 《红色工厂之梦：斯大林主义兴盛期的中国遗产》Deborah A. Kaple, *Dream of a Red Factory: The Legacy of High Stalinism in China.* Oxford University Press (1994)

32. 《后社会主义世界秩序：俄罗斯、中国和联合国体制》Robert Boardman, *Post-Socialist World Orders: Russia, China and the UN System* (International Political Economy Series). Palgrave Macmillan UK (1994)

33. 《中苏关系（1937—1945）：中国的民族主义外交》John W. Garver（高龙江）, *Chinese-Soviet Relations, 1937—1945: The Diplomacy of Chinese Nationalism.* Oxford University Press (1988)

34. 《中苏稳定与工业精英》Constance Squires Meaney, *Stability and the Industrial Elite in China and the Soviet Union.* Insitute of East Asian Studies, University of Califonia, Berkeley (1988)

35. 《中国关于苏联社会主义的争论（1978—1985）》Gilbert Rozman（饶济凡）, *The Chinese Debate about Soviet Socialism, 1978—1985.* Princeton University Press (1987)

36. 《苏联、东欧和中国的领导人与继承》Martin McCauley, Stephen Carter (eds.), *Leadership and Succession in the Soviet Union, Eastern Europe and China.* Palgrave Macmillan UK (1986)

37. 《满洲的革命斗争：中国共产主义与苏联利益（1922—1945）》Chong-Sik Lee, *Revolutionary Struggle in Manchuria: Chinese Communism and Soviet Interest, 1922—1945.* University of California Press (1984)

38. 《1970年代的中苏冲突：战略三角的演变与启示》Kenneth Lieberthal（李侃如）, *Sino-Soviet Conflict in the 1970s: Its Evolution and Implications for the Strategic Triangle.* RAND (1978)

39. 《苏联与中华人民共和国的贸易法律框架》George Ginsburgs, *The Legal Framework of Trade between the USSR and the People's Republic of China.* Springer Netherlands (1976)

40. 《俄罗斯与中国革命的根源（1896—1911）》Don C. Price, *Russia and the Roots of the Chinese Revolution, 1896—1911* (East Asian). Harvard University Press (1974)

41. 《中苏关于战争问题的对话》John Yin, *Sino-Soviet Dialogue on the Problem of War.* Springer Netherlands (1971)

42. 《17世纪中俄关系》Vincent Chen, *Sino-Russian Relations in the Seventeenth Century.* Springer Netherlands (1966)

43. 《十字路口的共产主义国家：莫斯科与北京之间》Adam Bromke (ed.), with an Introduction by Philip E. Mosely, *Communist States at the Crossroads: Between Moscow and Peking.* New York, Washington, and London: Praeger (1965)

44. 《苏俄与东方（1920—1927）：文献考察》(The Hoover Library on War, Revolution and Peace, Publication No. 25) Xenia Joukoff Eudin, Robert C. North, *Soviet Russia and the East, 1920—1927: A Documentary Survey.* Stanford University Press (1957)

45. 《斯大林时代》Anna Louise Strong, *The Stalin Era*. Today's Press (1956)
46. 《征服西伯利亚：中俄交往、战争、贸易通史》Gerhard Friedrich Muller, Peter Simon Pallas, *Conquest Of Siberia, And The History of the Transactions, Wars, Commerce, Etc.: Carried On between Russia and China, From the Earliest Period*. London: Smith, Elder and Co. (1842)

8.3.3　中国与日本

1. 《中国和日本：面对历史》（中译名《中国和日本：一千五百年的交流史》）Ezra F. Vogel（傅高义）, *China and Japan: Facing History*. Belknap Press: An Imprint of Harvard University Press (2019)
2. 《日本对华"新政"：珍珠港事件前针对美国人的宣传》(Routledge Studies in the Modern History of Asia) June Grasso, *Japan's "New Deal" for China: Propaganda Aimed at Americans Before Pearl Harbor*. Routledge (2019)
3. 《清代中国与德川幕府时期日本的贸易关系：1685—1859》(Studies in Economic History) Hao Peng, *Trade Relations between Qing China and Tokugawa Japan. 1685—1859*. Springer Singapore (2019)
4. 《日本作为全球大国的艰难复兴：民主韧性与美中挑战》Victor Teo, *Japan's Arduous Rejuvenation as a Global Power: Democratic Resilience and the US-China Challenge*. Springer Verlag (2019)
5. 《中国和日本的通商口岸生活》Donna Brunero, Stephanie Villalta Puig, *Life in Treaty Port China and Japan*. Palgrave Macmillan (2018)
6. 《中国和日本拥抱"亚洲"：亚洲主义话语与霸权竞赛（1912—1933）》Torsten Weber, *Embracing "Asia" in China and Japan: Asianism Discourse and the Contest for Hegemony, 1912—1933* (Palgrave Macmillan Transnational History Series). Palgrave Macmillan (2018)
7. 《中国和日本的宗教、文化与公共领域》Albert Welter, Jeffrey Newmark (eds.), Religion, Culture, and the Public Sphere in China and Japan (Religion and Society in Asia Pacific). Springer Singapore (2017)
8. 《三边背景下的中日关系：误解的起源》Yun Zhang, *Sino-Japanese Relations in a Trilateral Context: Origins of Misperception*. Palgrave Macmillan US (2017)
9. 《中日权力政治：力量、金钱和思想》Giulio Pugliese, Aurelio Insisa, *Sino-Japanese Power Politics: Might, Money and Minds*. Palgrave Macmillan UK (2017)
10. 《21世纪中日关系：相互依存的对抗》Lam Peng Er, *China-Japan Relations in the 21st Century: Antagonism Despite Interdependency*. Springer Singapore (2017)
11. 《炮火攻击下的新闻：英文报刊里的中国反日宣传（1928—1941）》Shuge Wei, *News under Fire: China's Propaganda against Japan in the English-Language Press, 1928—1941*. Hong Kong University Press (2017)
12. 《理解日中关系：理论与问题》Ming Wan, *Understanding Japan-China Relations:*

Theories and Issues. World Scientifc (2016)

13. 《中国与旭日帝国：中日关系，过去与现在》June Teufel Dreyer, *Middle Kingdom And Empire Of The Rising Sun: Sino-Japanese Relations, Past And Present*. Oxford University Press (2016)

14. 《被困长春的日本女孩：我如何幸存于中国的战时》Homare Endo, Michael Brase, *Japanese Girl at the Siege of Changchun: How I Survived China's Wartime Atrocity*. Stone Bridge Press (2016)

15. 《暴力冲突中生存：1931—1945年第二次中日战争中的中国翻译》Ting Guo, *Surviving in Violent Conflicts: Chinese Interpreters in the Second Sino-Japanese War 1931—1945*. Palgrave Macmillan UK (2016)

16. 《损失的继承：中国、日本与后帝国时代救赎的政治经济学》Yukiko Koga, *Inheritance of Loss: China, Japan, and the Political Economy of Redemption after Empire* (Studies of the Weatherhead East Asian Institute). University of Chicago Press (2016)

17. 《亲密的对手：日本国内政治和崛起的中国》Sheila A. Smith, *Intimate Rivals: Japanese Domestic Politics and a Rising China*. Columbia University Press (2015)

18. 《日本战后的中国问题：日本的国家认同与中日关系》Robert Hoppens, Christopher Gerteis, *The China Problem in Postwar Japan: Japanese National Identity and Sino-Japanese Relations*. Bloomsbury Academic (2015)

19. 《1930—1940年代日本战时经济规划和动员：国家竞争力》Yoshiro Miwa, *Japan's Economic Planning and Mobilization in Wartime, 1930s—1940s: The Competence of the State*. Cambridge University Press (2015)

20. 《情感言语的编码与解码：中文和日语的跨文化、多模态研究》Aijun Li, *Encoding and Decoding of Emotional Speech: A Cross-Cultural and Multimodal Study between Chinese and Japanese*. Springer-Verlag Berlin Heidelberg (2015)

21. 《尚古主义、语言和医学语文学：从现代早期到现代的中日医学话语》Benjamin A. Elman（艾尔曼）(ed.), *Antiquarianism, Language, and Medical Philology: From Early Modern to Modern Sino-Japanese Medical Discourses*. Brill Academic Publishers (2015)

22. 《现代中日词汇的兴起：七项研究》Joshua A. Fogel（傅佛果）, *The Emergence of the Modern Sino-Japanese Lexicon: Seven Studies* (East Asian Comparative Literature and Culture). Brill Academic Pub. (2015)

23. 《中日之间：傅佛果著作集》Joshua Fogel（傅佛果）, *Between China and Japan: The Writings of Joshua Fogel*. Brill Academic Pub. (2015)

24. 《近代早期中日贸易中的铜》(Monies, Markets, and Finance in East Asia, 1600—1900) Keiko Nagase-Reimer, *Copper in the Early Modern Sino-Japanese Trade*. Brill Academic Publishing (2015)

25. 《理性与情感：法德与中日和解的比较研究》Lin Ren, *Rationality and Emotion:*

Comparative Studies of the Franco-German and Sino-Japanese Reconciliations. VS Verlag für Sozialwissenschaften (2014)

26. 《中日海战（1894—1895）》Piotr Olender, *Sino-Japanese Naval War 1894—1895* (Maritime Series 3105). Mushroom Model Publications (2014)

27. 《首航：千岁丸与近代中日关系的创立》Joshua A. Fogel（傅佛果）, *Maiden Voyage: The Senzaimaru and the Creation of Modern Sino-Japanese Relations* (Philip E. Lilienthal Asian Studies Imprint). University of California Press (2014)

28. 《日本和中国现代经济发展：发展主义、资本主义与世界经济体系》Xiaoming Huang (eds.), *Modern Economic Development in Japan and China: Developmentalism, Capitalism, and the World Economic System* (International Political Economy Series). Palgrave Macmillan UK (2013)

29. 《裁判的理由：19世纪中国和日本的治外法权与皇权》Pär Kristoffer Cassel, *Grounds of Judgment: Extraterritoriality and Imperial Power in Nineteenth-Century China and Japan.* Oxford University Press (2012)

30. 《中日关系的先驱：廖承志和高崎》Mayumi Itoh, *Pioneers of Sino-Japanese Relations: Liao and Takasaki.* Palgrave Macmillan US (2012)

31. 《中日文明简史（第4版）》Conrad Schirokauer, Miranda Brown, David Lurie, Suzanne Gay, *A Brief History of Chinese and Japanese Civilizations* (4 edition). Wadsworth Publishing (2012)

32. 《二战后满洲里的日本遗孤》Yeeshan Chan, *Abandoned Japanese in Postwar Manchuria: The Lives of War Orphans and Wives in Two Countries.* Routledge (2011)

33. 《日本、中国与东亚网络化的地域性》Joel Rathus, *Japan, China and Networked Regionalism in East Asia.* Palgrave Macmillan (2011)

34. 《苦海求生：抗战时期的中国难民》R. Keith Schoppa（萧邦奇）, *In a Sea of Bitterness: Refugees during the Sino-Japanese War.* Harvard University Press (2011)

35. 《中国和日本在亚洲的新的动力：如何从过去创造未来》Guy Faure, *New Dynamics Between China and Japan in Asia: How to Build the Future from the Past.* World Scientific Publishing Company (2010)

36. 《亲近的危险：中日安全关系》Richard C. Bush（卜睿哲）, *The Perils of Proximity: China-Japan Security Relations.* Brookings Institution Press (2010)

37. 《记忆地图：战后的日本和满洲里》Mariko Asano Tamanoi, *Memory Maps: The State and Manchuria in Postwar Japan.* University of Hawai'i Press (2009)

38. 《明治末期的中国与日本：中国政策与日本的民族身份话语（1895—1904）》Urs Matthias Zachmann, *China and Japan in the Late Meiji Period: China Policy and the Japanese Discourse on National Identity, 1895—1904.* Routledge (2009)

39. 《文明与帝国：中国、日本与欧洲国际社会的遭遇》Shogo Suzuki, *Civilization and*

Empire: China and Japan's Encounter with European International Society. Routledge (2009)

40. 《寻求和解：二战以来的中日和德波关系》Yinan He, *The Search for Reconciliation: Sino-Japanese and German-Polish Relations since World War II*. Cambridge University Press (2009)

41. 《阐明汉字文化圈：空间和时间中的中日关系》Joshua A. Fogel（傅佛果）, *Articulating the Sinosphere: Sino-Japanese Relations in Space and Time* (Edwin O. Reischauer Lectures). Harvard University Press (2009)

42. 《中日与东亚地区领导权》Christopher M. Dent, *China, Japan and Regional Leadership in East Asia*. Edward Elgar Pub (2008)

43. 《改变中国和日本公司的治理实践：英美实践的改编》Masao Nakamura (eds.), *Changing Corporate Governance Practices in China and Japan: Adaptations of Anglo-American Practices*. Palgrave Macmillan UK (2008)

44. 《中日争执：破译永恒的冲突》James C. Hsiung, *China and Japan at Odds: Deciphering the Perpetual Conflict*. Palgrave Macmillan (2007)

45. 《东亚与全球经济：日本崛起对中国未来的影响》Stephen G. Bunker, Paul S. Ciccantell, *East Asia and the Global Economy: Japan's Ascent, with Implications for China's Future*. The Johns Hopkins University Press (2007)

46. 《亚洲：中日经济发展》C.D. Cowan, *Asia: Economic Development of China and Japan* (School of Oriental & African Studies). Routledge (2006)

47. 《日本与中国关系：面对一个崛起的大国》Peng Er Lam, *Japan's Relations With China: Facing a Rising Power* (Sheffield Centre for Japanese Studies Routledgecurzon). Routledge (2006)

48. 《日本统治下的朝鲜：话语与权力》Alexis Dudden, *Japan's Colonization of Korea: Discourse and Power*. University of Hawai'i Press (2005)

49. 《中日关系：面向未来的外交》Caroline Rose, *Sino-Japanese Relations: Towards a Future-Oriented Diplomacy* (Routledgecurzon Advances in Asia-Pacific Studies). Routledgecurzon (2005)

50. 《日本、中国和亚洲国际经济的增长（1850—1949）》Kaoru Sugihara, *Japan, China, and the Growth of the Asian International Economy, 1850—1949* (Japanese Studies in Economic and Social History v. 1). Oxford University Press (2005)

51. 《世界经济中的日本和中国》Kellee S. Tsai（蔡欣怡）, Saadia Pekkanen, *Japan and China in the World Economy* (Politics in Asia Series).Routledge (2005)

52. 《日本的中国政策：关系力分析》Linus Hagstrom, *Japan's China Policy: A Relational Power Analysis*. Routledge (2005)

53. 《单一庞大组织阴影下的日本和中苏同盟（1950—1964）》C. W. Braddick, *Japan and the Sino-Soviet Alliance, 1950—1964: In the Shadow of the Monolith*.Palgrave Macmillan UK (2004)

54. 《中国与日本的学术民族主义：以自然、文化和普遍性的概念为框架》Margar Sleeboom, *Academic Nationalism in China and Japan: Framed in Concepts of Nature, Culture and the*

Universal. RoutledgeCurzon (2003)

55. 《亚洲男性：中国和日本男子气概的含义与实践》Kam Louie, Morris Low, *Asian Masculinities: The Meaning and Practice of Manhood in China and Japan*. Routledge (2003)

56. 《日本与中国：合作、竞争与冲突》Hanns Günther Hilpert and René Haak, *Japan and China: Cooperation, Competition and Conflict*. Palgrave Macmillan (2002)

57. 《1932—1945年中国人与日本的合作：调和的限度》David Barrett, Larry Shyu, *Chinese Collaboration with Japan, 1932—1945: The Limits of Accommodation*. Stanford University Press (2002)

58. 《21世纪中日关系：互补与冲突》M. Soderberg, *Chinese Japanese Relations in the 21st Century: Complementarity and Conflict* (European Institute of Japanese Studies East Asian Economics & Business Series, Number 2). Routledge (2002)

59. 《1894—1895年中日战争：认知、权力与主导权》S. C. M. Paine, *The Sino-Japanese War of 1894—1895: Perceptions, Power, and Primacy*. Cambridge University Press (2002)

60. 《日本对华直接投资的区位决定因素与特征》John F. Cassicy, *Japanese Direct Investment in China: Locational Determinants and Characteristics* (East Asia Series). Routledge (2002)

61. 《七世纪与八世纪早期日本学生僧侣传记词典：他们在华旅行及在佛教传播中的作用》Marcus Bingenheimer, *A Biographical Dictionary of the Japanese Student-Monks of the Seventh and Early Eighth Centuries: Their Travels to China and their Role in the Transmission of Buddhism*. Iudicium Verlag (2001)

62. 《满蒙游记：一位日本女权诗人与遭遇战前中国》Yosano Akiko, Joshua A. Fogel（傅佛果）, *Travels in Manchuria and Mongolia: A Feminist Poet From Japan Encounters Prewar China*. Columbia University Press (2001)

63. 《日本帝国外交：1895—1938年领事、条约港口和中国战争》Barbara J. Brooks, *Japan's Imperial Diplomacy: Consuls, Treaty Ports, and War in China, 1895—1938*. University of Hawaii Press (2000)

64. 《日本的整个帝国：满洲与战时帝国主义文化》Louise Young, *Japan's Total Empire: Manchuria and the Culture of Wartime Imperialism* (Twentieth Century Japan: The Emergence of a World Power). University of California Press (1999)

65. 《19世纪日本对中国的认知：福泽谕吉的影响》Sushila Narsimhan, *Japanese Perceptions of China in the Nineteenth Century: Influence of Fukuzawa Yukichi*. Phoenix Publishing House (1999)

66. 《日本在华非正式帝国（1895—1937）》Peter Duus, Ramon H. Myers, Mark R. Peattie (eds.), *The Japanese Informal Empire in China, 1895—1937*. Princeton University Press (1989)

67. 《解读中日关系史：政治决策案例研究》Caroline Rose, *Interpreting History in Sino-Japanese Relations: A Case Study in Political Decision Making* (Nissan Institute Routledge Japanese Studies Series). Routledge (1998)

68. 《日本茶道：从中国起源到千利休》Sen XV Soshitsu, *The Japanese Way of Tea: From Its Origin in China to Sen Rikyu*. University of Hawaii Press (1998)

69. 《工业竞赛中的日本与中国》Wei-Bin Zhang, *Japan versus China in the Industrial Race*. Palgrave Macmillan UK (1998)

70. 《中国和日本种族身份的建构》Frank Dikötter（冯客）(ed.), *The Construction of Racial Identities in China and Japan*. Hong Kong University Press (1997)

71. 《日本与中国的安全关系：从平衡到搭车》Reinhard Drifte, *Japan's Security Relations With China: From Balancing to Bandwagoning* (Nissan Institute Routledge Japanese Studies Series). Palgrave Macmillan UK (1996)

72. 《大中华与日本：东亚经济合作前景展望》Robert Taylor, *Greater China and Japan: Prospects for an Economic Partnership in East Asia*. Routledge (1996)

73. 《1894—1895年日本与中国冲突中的第一次现代战争军队与社会》Stewart Lone, *Japan's First Modern War Army and Society in the Conflict with China, 1894—95*. Palgrave Macmillan Ltd (1994)

74. 《德川世界的中国》Marius B. Jansen, *China in the Tokugawa World*. Harvard University Press (1992)

75. 《中日：政治与文化互动论文集》Akira Iriye, *The Chinese and the Japanese: Essays in Political and Cultural Interactions* (Princeton Legacy Library). Princeton University Press (1980)

76. 《日本对华政策中的问题》Wolf Mendl, *Issues in Japan's China Policy*. Palgrave Macmillan UK (1978)

77. 《日本外交（1894—1922），第一卷：中日战争与三重干预》Morinosuke Kajima, *The Diplomacy of Japan 1894—1922, Volume I: Sino-Japanese War and Triple Intervention*. Kajima Institute of International Peace (1976)

78. 《16世纪明代中国的日本盗版》Kwan-wai So, *Japanese Piracy in Ming China During the 16th Century*. Michigan State University Press (1975)

79. 《中日官方关系（1368—1549）》Yi-T'ung Wang, *Official Relations Between China and Japan, 1368—1549* (Harvard-Yenching Institute Studies). Harvard University Press (1953)

80. 《中日冲突之中方说法》Chih Meng（孟治）, *China Speaks: On the Conflict Between China and Japan*. Macmillan Company (1932)

81. 《中国、日本和美国：远东现状及其对华盛顿会议的态度》John Dewey, *China, Japan and the U.S.A.: Present-Day Conditions in the Far East and Their Bearing on the Washington Conference*. Republic Publishing Co. Inc. (1921)

82. 《中日甲午战争写真图》Kazumasa Ogawa（小川一真）, Rikuchi Sokuryōbu (eds.), *A photographic-album of the Japan-China War*. Tōkyō: Hakubundō (1894)

8.3.4 中国与英国

1. 《争夺英国的华人文化》Ashley Thorpe, Diana Yeh, *Contesting British Chinese Culture*.

Springer International Publishing: Palgrave Macmillan (2018)

2. 《英帝国从中国的撤退（1900—1931）》Phoebe Chow, *Britain's Imperial Retreat from China, 1900—1931* (Routledge Studies in the Modern History of Asia). Routledge (2017)

3. 《战争与和平的商人：鸦片战争中英国对中国的认识》Song-Chuan Chen, *Merchants of War and Peace: British Knowledge of China in the Making of the Opium War*. Hong Kong University Press (2017)

4. 《英国、中国与澳大利亚殖民地》Benjamin Mountford, *Britain, China, and colonial Australia* (Oxford historical monographs). Oxford University Press (2016)

5. 《英国、法国、西德与中华人民共和国（1969—1982）：中国伟大转型的欧洲维度》Martin Albers, *Britain, France, West Germany and the Peoples Republic of China, 1969—1982: The European Dimension of China's Great Transition*. Palgrave Macmillan UK (2016)

6. 《中国对英国文艺复兴时期的文学影响：为多恩和密尔顿提供一种全球化、自由主义国际化的方法》Lu Mingjun, *The Chinese Impact upon English Renaissance Literature: A Globalization and Liberal Cosmopolitan Approach to Donne and Milton*. Ashgate Pub Co (2015)

7. 《国家、经济与大分流：1680年代至1850年代的英国和中国》Peer Vries, *State, Economy and the Great Divergence: Great Britain and China, 1680s—1850s*. Bloomsbury Academic (2015)

8. 《长江摊牌：中国与"紫石英"号考验》Brian Izzard, *Yangtze Showdown: China and the Ordeal of the HMS Amethyst*. Seaforth Publishing; Naval Institute Press (2015)

9. 《浪漫中国的生成：中英文化交流（1760—1840）》Peter J. Kitson, *Forging Romantic China: Sino-British Cultural Exchange, 1760—1840*. Cambridge; New York: Cambridge University Press (2013)

10. 《东风：中国与英国左派（1925—1976）》Tom Buchanan, *East Wind: China and the British Left, 1925—1976*. Oxford University Press (2012)

11. 《帝国的安全政府：英国在亚洲的殖民知识和帝国建设》James Hevia（何伟亚）, *The Imperial Security State: British Colonial Knowledge and Empire-Building in Asia*. Cambridge University Press (2012)

12. 《中国清代的英国博物学家：科学、帝国与文化遭遇》Fa-ti Fan, *British Naturalists in Qing China: Science, Empire, and Cultural Encounter*. Harvard University Press (2009)

13. 《中国和英国：全球化与身份困境》Joseph Lo Bianco, Jane Orton, GAo Yihong, *China and English: Globalisation and the Dilemmas of Identity*. MultiLingual Matters (2009)

14. 《亚洲帝国与英国知识：中国与英帝国的扩张网络》Ulrike Hillemann, *Asian Empire and British Knowledge: China and the Networks of British Imperial Expansion* (Cambridge Imperial and Post-Colonial Studies). Palgrave Macmillan (2009)

15. 《为了所有中国茶叶：英国如何窃取世界最受欢迎的饮料并改变历史》Sarah Rose, *For All the Tea in China: How England Stole the World's Favorite Drink and Changed History*.

Viking (2009)

16. 《中国问题：大国竞争和英国疏离（1894—1905）》T. G. Otte, *The China Question: Great Power Rivalry and British Isolation, 1894—1905*. Oxford University Press (2007)

17. 《英帝国在华势力的基石：海关业务》Donna Brunero, *Britain's Imperial Cornerstone in China: The Chinese Maritime Customs Service, 1854—1949*. Routledge (2006)

18. 《中国事物、英国身份与漫长的18世纪东方主义史前史》（博士论文）Eugenia Zuroski, *Chinese Things, British Identity, and the Pre-history of Orientalism in the Long Eighteenth Century*. Ph. D. Dissertation, Brown University (2006)

19. 《帝国财富：英国与中国的浪漫（1750—1850）》（博士论文）Joanne Tong, *Imperial Fortunes: Britain and the Romance of China, 1750—1850*. Ph. D. Dissertation, University of California, Los Angeles (2006)

20. 《英国博物学家在清代中国：科学、帝国与文化相遇》Fa-ti Fan, *British Naturalists in Qing China: Science, Empire, and Cultural Encounter*. Harvard University Press (2004)

21. 《何伟亚：英国的课业——19世纪中国的帝国主义教程》James Hevia（何伟亚）, *English Lessons: The Pedagogy of Imperialism in Nineteenth Century China*. Durham: Duke University Press and Hong Kong University Press (2003)

22. 《1800年来的中英遭际：战争、贸易、科学与统治》Wang Gungwu（王赓武）, *Anglo-Chinese Encounters since 1800: War, Trade, Science and Governance*. Cambridge University Press (2003)

23. 《中英商业冲突与合作（1860—1911）：上海亲英商业网络的影响》Eiichi Motono, *Conflict and Cooperation in Sino-British Business, 1860—1911: The Impact of the Pro-British Commercial Network in Shanghai*. Palgrave Macmillan UK (2000)

24. 《鸦片政权：中国、英国和日本（1839—1952）》Timothy Brook（卜正民）, Bob Tadashi Wakabayashi, *Opium Regimes: China, Britain, and Japan, 1839—1952*. University of California Press (2000)

25. 《帝国主义回顾：英国与中国的政治经济关系（1950—54）》David Clayton, *Imperialism Revisited: Political and Economic Relations between Britain and China, 1950–54*. Palgrave Macmillan UK (1997)

26. 《跨文化对话：18世纪英国关于中国的表述》（博士论文）Lianhong Chen, *A Cross-Cultural Dialogue: Eighteenth-Century British Representations of China*. Ph. D. Dissertation, University of Illinois at Urbana-Champaign (1996)

27. 《怀柔远人：马嘎尔尼使华的中英礼仪冲突》James L. Hevia（何伟亚）, *Cherishing Men from Afar: Qing Guest Ritual and the Macartney Embassy of 1793*. Duke University Press Books (1995)

28. 《英国与革命中国的遭遇（1949—1954）》James Tuck-Hong Tang, *Britain's Encounter with Revolutionary China, 1949—1954*. Palgrave Macmillan UK (1992)

29. 《中国、英国与商人政治和商业关系（1949—1957）》Wenguang Shao, *China, Britain and Businessmen Political and Commercial Relations, 1949—1957*. Palgrave Macmillan UK (1991)

30. 《英国与中国（1941—1947）：帝国的动力》Aron Shai, *Britain and China, 1941—1947: Imperial Momentum*.Palgrave Macmillan UK (1984)

31. 《我在新中国十五年（要扫除一切害人虫：一个英国外科医生在中华人民共和国，1954至1969年）》Joshua S. Horn（洪若诗）, *Away with All Pests: An English Surgeon in People's China, 1954—1969*. With an introduction by Edgar Snow. Monthly Review Press, U.S. (1971)

32. 《英国贸易与中国开放（1800—1842）》Michael Greenberg, *British Trade and the Opening of China 1800—42*. Cambridge University Press (1970)

33. 《英国对华外交（1880—1885年）》E. V. G. Kiernan（季南）, *British Diplomacy in China, 1880—1885*. The Cambridge University Press (1939)

34. 《英国如何拯救中国》（反缠足、溺婴等）John MacGowan（麦嘉温）, *How England Saved China*. London: T. Fisher Unwin (1913)

35. 《英中商务与外交（主要在19世纪）》A. J. (Arthur John) Sargent, *Anglo-Chinese Commerce and Diplomacy (Mainly in the Nineteenth Century)*. Oxford, The Clarendon press (1907)

36. 《中国与英国》C. C Lu, *China & England*. Sheffield Independent Press (1904)

37. 《巴夏礼在中国》Stanley Lane-Poole, *Sir Harry Parks in China*. London: Methues (1901)

38. 《英国人在华生活》Henry Knollys, *English life in China*. London: Smith, Elder, & Co. (1885)

39. 《英国对华贸易的当前处境与展望》James Matheson（马地臣，又名马德生）, *The Present Position and Prospects of the British Trade With China*.London, Smith (1836)

40. 《中国和英国人：抑或中国人的性格和举止，正如他们与外国人交往的历史所示》Jacob Abbott, *China and the English: or, The Character and Manners of the Chinese. As illustrated in the History of Their Intercourse with Foreigners*.New York, Leavitt, Lord & Co.; Boston, Crocker & Brewster (1835)

41. 《1832年英国与中华帝国关系：英美两国对印度和广州贸易的比较声明》Robert Montgomery Martin, *British Relations with the Chinese Empire in 1832: Comparative Statement of the English and American Trade with India and Canton*. London, Parbury, Allen & Co. (1832)

42. 《大不列颠国王派往中国皇帝的大使的可靠报告》（第一至三卷）George Staunton, *An Authentic Account of an Embassy from the King of Great Britain to the Emperor of China*. Vols1, 2, 3. London: Printed by W. Bulmer and Co. for G. Nicol (1797)

8.3.5 中国与印度

1. 《印度与中国创新、经济发展和知识产权：六个经济部门比较》(Arciala Series on Intellectual Assets and Law in Asia) Kung-Chung Liu, Uday S. Racherla, *Innovation, Economic Development, and Intellectual Property in India and China: Comparing Six Economic Sector.*

Springer (2019)

2. 《佛教喜马拉雅山脉大赛：印度和中国对战略优势的追求》Phunchok Stobdan, *The Great Game in the Buddhist Himalayas: India and China's Quest for Strategic Dominance*. Penguin Books (24 Oct. 2019)

3. 《饥渴的城市：中印社会契约与公共物品供给》Selina Ho, *Thirsty Cities: Social Contracts and Public Goods Provision in China and India*. Cambridge University Press (2019)

4. 《中印之往昔：可能塑造全球未来的过去》Sheldon Pollock, Benjamin Elman (eds.), *What China and India Once Were: The Pasts That May Shape the Global Future*. Columbia University Press (2018)

5. 《中国与印度在非洲的发展合作》Philani Mthembu, *China and India's Development Cooperation in Africa* (International Political Economy Series). Springer International Publishing: Palgrave Macmillan (2018)

6. 《中国和印度的奢侈品牌》Glyn Atwal, Douglas Bryson, *Luxury Brands in China and India*. Palgrave Macmillan UK (2017)

7. 《影子国家：印度、中国和喜马拉雅山（1910—1962）》Bérénice Guyot-Réchard, *Shadow States: India, China and the Himalayas, 1910—1962*. Cambridge University Press (2017)

8. 《中国对印度的教训：发展的政治经济学》Sangaralingam Ramesh, *China's Lessons for India: The Political Economy of Development*. Springer International Publishing (2017)

9. 《中国和印度的创新与知识产权：神话、现实与机遇》Kung-Chung Liu, Uday S. Racherla (eds.), *Innovation and IPRs in China and India: Myths, Realities and Opportunities*. Springer Singapore (2016)

10. 《印度和中国的"他者"政治：非西方语境中的西方观念》(Routledge contemporary Asia series 55) Lion König, Bidisha Chaudhuri, *Politics of the "Other" in India and China: Western Concepts in Non-Western Contexts*. Routledge (2016)

11. 《东亚新兴动力中的印度和中国》G. V. C. Naidu, Mumin Chen, Raviprasad Narayanan (eds.), *India and China in the Emerging Dynamics of East Asia*. Springer India (2015)

12. 《喜马拉雅的召唤：中国和印度的起源》Chung Tan, *Himalaya Calling: The Origins of China and India*. World Century Publishing Corporation (2015)

13. 《中国和印度会议室的玻璃天花板：中印上市企业的女性董事》Alice de Jonge, *The Glass Ceiling in Chinese and Indian Boardrooms: Women Directors in Listed Firms in China and India*. Chandos Publishing (2015)

14. 《跨太平洋伙伴关系，中国和印度：经济和政治影响》Amitendu Palit, *The Trans-Pacific Partnership, China and India: Economic and Political Implications*. Routledge (2014)

15. 《中国和印度的海外移民与外商直接投资》Min Ye, *Diasporas and Foreign Direct Investment in China and India*. Cambridge University Press (2014)

16. 《中国想象中的印度：神话、宗教与思想》John Kieschnick (ed.), Meir Shahar (ed.),

India in the Chinese Imagination: Myth, Religion, and Thought. University of Pennsylvania Press (2013)

17. 《被帝国伤害：印度和中国的后帝国意识形态与外交政策》Manjari Miller, *Wronged by Empire: Post-Imperial Ideology and Foreign Policy in India and China.* Stanford University Press (2013)
18. 《火药的花园：穿越印度和中国寻找茶叶》Jason Goodwin, *The Gunpowder Gardens: Travels through India and China in search of Tea.* Argonaut Books (2013)
19. 《从边境政策到外交政策：清代中国的印度问题与地缘政治转型》Matthew Mosca, *From Frontier Policy to Foreign Policy: The Question of India and the Transformation of Geopolitics in Qing China.* Stanford University Press (2013)
20. 《亚洲的现代精神：中国和印度的精神与世俗》Peter van der Veer, *The Modern Spirit of Asia: The Spiritual and the Secular in China and India.* Princeton University Press (2013)
21. 《中国和印度工业化：其对世界经济的影响》Nobuharu Yokokawa, Jayati Ghosh, Robert Rowthorn, *Industrialization of China and India: Their Impacts on the World Economy.* Routledge (2013)
22. 《中印战略行为：增长的力量和警报》George J. Gilboy, Eric Heginbotham, *Chinese and Indian Strategic Behavior: Growing Power and Alarm.* Cambridge University Press (2012)
23. 《中印国际谈判：新兴商业巨人比较》Rajesh Kumar, Verner Worm, *International Negotiation in China and India: A Comparison of the Emerging Business Giants.* Palgrave Macmillan (2012)
24. 《中国崛起对印度的影响》Harsh V.Pant, *The Rise of China: Implications for India.* Foundation Books (2012)
25. 《中印相遇之地：缅甸与亚洲的新十字路口》Thant Myint-U, *Where China Meets India: Burma and the New Crossroads of Asia.* Farrar, Straus and Giroux (2011)
26. 《中印工业动力：企业、集群与不同增长路径》Moriki Ohara, M. Vijayabaskar, Hong Lin (eds.), *Industrial Dynamics in China and India: Firms, Clusters, and Different Growth Paths.* Palgrave Macmillan UK (2011)
27. 《从东向西：印度、中国和亚洲在中东地区日益增长的影响力》Geoffrey Kemp, *The East Moves West: India, China, and Asia's Growing Presence in the Middle East.* Brookings Institution Press (2010)
28. 《中国和印度：和平前景》Jonathan Holslag, *China and India: Prospects for Peace.* Columbia University Press (2010)
29. 《中印在中亚：新的大国博弈？》Marléne Laruelle, Jean-François Huchet, Sébastien Peyrouse, *China and India in Central Asia: A New Great Game?* Palgrave Macmil (2010)
30. 《中国、印度和国际经济秩序》Muthucumaraswamy Sornarajah, Jiangyu Wang, *China, India and the International Economic Order.* Cambridge University Press (2010)

31.《中国和印度崛起：影响、前景和启示》Amelia U. Santos-Paulino, Guanghua Wan (eds.), *The Rise of China and India: Impacts, Prospects and Implications*. Palgrave Macmillan UK (2010)

32.《中国和印度在非洲的崛起：挑战、机遇和关键干预措施》Fantu Cheru, Cyril Obi, *The Rise of China and India in Africa: Challenges, Opportunities and Critical Interventions*. Zed Books (2010)

33.《中国和印度在中亚：新的"大博弈"》Marlène Laruelle, Jean-François Huchet, Sébastien Peyrouse, Bayram Balci (eds.), *China and India in Central Asia: A New "Great Game"*. Palgrave Macmillan (2010)

34.《新兴巨人：世界经济中的中国和印度》Barry Eichengreen, Poonam Gupta, Rajiv Kumar, *Emerging Giants: China and India in the World Economy*. Oxford University Press (2010)

35.《中国和印度在中亚：新的大博弈？》Bayram Balci, et al, *China and India in Central Asia: A new great game?* Basingstoke, Palgrave Macmillan (2010)

36.《改变亚洲工业地理：中国和印度的影响》Shahid Yusuf, Kaoru Nabeshima, *Changing the Industrial Geography in Asia: The Impact of China and India*. World Bank Publications (2010)

37.《龙与大象：理解中印两国创新能力的发展》Stephen Merrill, David Nelson, Robert Poole, *The Dragon and the Elephant: Understanding the Development of Innovation Capacity in China and India* (Summary of a Conference). National Academy of Sciences (2010)

38.《全球化时代的中国与印度》Shalendra D. Sharma, *China and India in the Age of Globalization*. Cambridge University Press (2009)

39.《让中印相互了解：促进全球增长最快经济体的战略》Anil K. Gupta, Haiyan Wang, *Getting China and India Right: Strategies for Leveraging the World's Fastest Growing Economies for Global Advantage*. Jossey-Bass (2009)

40.《中国和印度崛起：亚洲新戏剧》Lam Peng Er, *The Rise of China and India: A New Asian Drama*. World Scientific (2009)

41.《强化中印与中东和北非的贸易投资联系》Miria Pigato, *Strengthening China's Trade and India's Trade and Investments Ties to the Middle East and North Africa* (Orientations in Development). The World Bank (2009)

42.《大象和龙：印度和中国崛起及其对我们所有人的含义》Robyn Meredith, *The Elephant and the Dragon: The Rise of India and China and What It Means for All of Us*. W. W. Norton & Company (2008)

43.《印度和中国中产阶级消费模式》Christophe Jaffrelot, Peter van der Veer, *Patterns of Middle Class Consumption in India and China*. Sage Publications Pvt. Ltd (2008)

44.《印度银行业的自由化：对中国改革与比较视角的评估》Christian Roland, *Banking Sector Liberalization in India: Evaluation of Reforms and Comparative Perspectives on China*. Physica-Verlag Heidelberg (2008)

45. 《中印对拉丁美洲的挑战：机遇还是威胁》(Latin American Development Forums) Daniel Lederman, Marcelo Olarreaga, Guillermo E. Perry, *China's and India's Challenge to Latin America: Opportunity or Threat*. World Bank Publications (2008)
46. 《非洲的丝绸之路：中国与印度经济新前沿》Harry G. Broadman, *Africa's Silk Road: China and India's New Economic Frontier*. World Bank Publications (2007)
47. 《与巨人共舞：中国、印度及全球经济》L. Alan Winters, L. Alan Winters, Shahid Yusuf, *Dancing with Giants: China, India, And the Global Economy*. World Bank Publications (2007)
48. 《中国—印度关系：当代动力》Amardeep Athwal, *China-India Relations: Contemporary Dynamics*. Routledge (2007)
49. 《中国、印度的经济和战略崛起：1997年金融危机后的亚洲重新组合》David B.H. Denoon, *The Economic and Strategic Rise of China and India: Asian Realignments after the 1997 Financial Crisis*. Palgrave Macmillan (2007)
50. 《中国和印度：全球软件产业的机遇与威胁》John T. McManus, Mingzhi Li and Deependra Moitra, *China and India: Opportunities and Threats for the Global Software Industry* (Chandos Asian Studies Series). Chandos Publishing (2007)
51. 《印度、中国与全球化：新兴超级大国与经济发展的未来》Piya Mahtaney, *India, China and Globalization: The Emerging Superpowers and the Future of Economic Development*. Palgrave Macmillan UK (2007)
52. 《印度和中国的基层民主：参与权》Manoranjan Mohanty, George Mathew, Richard Baum（包瑞嘉）, Rong Ma (eds.), *Grass-roots Democracy in India and China: The Right to Participate*. Sage Publications (2007)
53. 《中国与印度：相互学习，持续增长的改革与政策》Jahangir Aziz, Steven Vincent Dunaway, Eswar Prasad, *China and India: Learning from each other. Reforms and Policies for Sustained Growth*. International Monetary Fund (2006)
54. 《中国和印度：两国经济故事》Dilip Das, *China and India: A Tale of Two Economies*. Routledge (2006)
55. 《中国和印度崛起：为非洲带来什么》Organization for Economic Cooperation & Development, *The Rise of China And India: What's in It for Africa*. OECD (2006)
56. 《管理全球化：中国和印度的教训》David A. Kelly, Ramkishen S. Rajan, Gillian H. L. Goh, *Managing Globalisation: Lessons from China and India*. World Scientific (2006)
57. 《中印经济改革：比较视角下的发展经验》Joseph C. H. Chai, Kartik C. Roy, *Economic Reform In China And India: Development Experience In a Comparative Perspective*. Edward Elgar Publishing (2006)
58. 《了解中国和印度：对美国和世界安全的影响》Rollie Lal, *Understanding China and India: Security Implications for the United States and the World*. Praeger Security International (2006)
59. 《亚洲巨人：中印比较》Edward Friedman（傅礼门）, Bruce Gilley（布鲁斯·吉利）,

Asia's Giants: Comparing China and India. Palgrave Macmillan (2005)

60.《印度和中国近年来的改革发展经验》Wanda S. Tseng, David G. Cowen, *India's and China's Recent Experience with Reform and Growth.* Palgrave Macmillan UK (2005)

61.《佛教、外交和贸易：中印关系的重新调整（600—1400）》Tansen Sen, *Buddhism, Diplomacy and Trade: The Realignment of Sino-Indian Relations, 600—1400.* University of Hawaii Press (2003)

62.《旷日持久的竞赛：20世纪的中印竞争》John W. Garver, *Protracted Contest: Sino-Indian Rivalry in the Twentieth Century.* University of Washington Press (2001)

63.《中国与印度：20世纪90年代中期企业经济绩效和经营策略》Sam Dzever, Jacques Jaussaud (eds.), *China and India: Economic Performance and Business Strategies of Firms in the Mid 1990s.* Palgrave Macmillan UK (1999)

64.《第三世界的不平衡发展：中国与印度研究》A. S. Bhalla, *Uneven Development in the Third World: A Study of China and India.* Antony Rowe Ltd (1992, 1995)

65.《印度与中国的早期中观学派》Richard H. Robinson, *Early Madhyamika in India and China.* Motilal Banarsidass (1976)

66.《印度和中国：1944年5月在中国的演讲》S. Radhakrishnan, *India and China: Lectures Delivered in China in May 1944.* Bombay: Hind Kitabs, Ltd. (1944)

67.《中国和印度的智慧》Lin Yutang（林语堂）, *The Wisdom of China and India.* Random House (1942, 1955)

68.《中国、西班牙和战争》（印度独立后第一任总理尼赫鲁文集）Jawaharlal Nehru, *China, Spain and the War.* Allahabad and London: Kitabistan (1940)

69.《印度论中国》Lohia Rammanohar, *India on China.* Pubhshed by J. B. Kripalani, General Secretary of All India Congress Committee, Allahabad (1938)

70.《印度文学在中国和远东》Probhat Kumar Mukherji, *Indian Literature in China and the Far East.* Greater India Society (1931)

71.《泰戈尔的中国讲演》Rabindranath Tagore（泰戈尔）, *Talks in China. Lectures Delivered in April and May, 1924.* Calcutta: Visva-Bharati (1925)

72.《印度教师在中国》Phanindra Nath Bose, *The Indian Teachers in China.* S. Ganesan (1923)

8.3.6 中国与欧洲

1.《中国的西方视野：北京与欧亚大陆的新地缘政治》Daniel S. Markey, *China's Western Horizon: Beijing and the New Geopolitics of Eurasia.* Oxford University Press (2020)

2.《意中贸易关系的历史透视》(Studies in Economic History) D. Strangio, *Italy-China Trade Relations: A Historical Perspective.* Springer International Publishing (2020)

3.《中国与欧盟监管消费者合同比较分析》Jiangqiu Ge, *A Comparative Analysis of Policing Consumer Contracts in China and the EU.* Springer Singapore (2019)

4.《中国在德国的并购：融合导向和价值提升的故事》(Management for Professionals) Jan

Y. Yang, Lei Chen, Zheng Tang, *Chinese M&As in Germany. An Integration Oriented and Value Enhancing Story*. Springer International Publishing (2019)

5. 《冷战中的欧洲与中国：超越集团逻辑的交流与中苏分裂》Janick Marina Schaufelbuehl, Marco Wyss, Valeria Zanier, *Europe and China in the Cold War: Exchanges Beyond the Bloc Logic and the Sino-Soviet Split*. Brill (2018)

6. 《欧盟和中国在非洲威权体制中的地位》Christine Hackenesch, *The EU and China in African Authoritarian Regimes* (Governance and Limited Statehood). Springer International Publishing: Palgrave Macmillan (2018)

7. 《欧亚事务：中国、欧洲和跨文化对象（1600—1800）》Anna Grasskamp, Monica Juneja, *EurAsian Matters: China, Europe, and the Transcultural Object, 1600—1800*. Springer International Publishing (2018)

8. 《多极世界中的欧盟—中国—非洲三边关系：海德龙（这里就是龙）》Anna Katharina Stahl, *EU-China-Africa Trilateral Relations in a Multipolar World: Hic Sunt Dracones* (The European Union in International Affairs). Palgrave Macmillan UK (2018)

9. 《21世纪的民主与增长：中意分歧案例》Francesco Grillo, Raffaella Y. Nanetti, *Democracy and Growth in the Twenty-first Century: The Diverging Cases of China and Italy*. Springer International Publishing: Palgrave Macmillan (2018)

10. 《中国与欧盟关系：重新评估中国与欧盟全面战略伙伴关系》Hong Zhou (eds.), *China-EU Relations: Reassessing the China-EU Comprehensive Strategic Partnership* (Research Series on the Chinese Dream and China's Development Path). Springer Singapore (2017)

11. 《国际风险投资中的文化距离：探索欧洲与中国管理者的认知》Christoph Lattemann, Francesca Spigarelli, Ernesto Tavoletti, Katiuscia Vaccarini, *Cultural Distance in International Ventures: Exploring Perceptions of European and Chinese Managers*. Springer International Publishing (2017)

12. 《不太可能的合作伙伴：中国、欧盟与战略伙伴关系的形成》Anna Michalski, Zhongqi Pan, *Unlikely Partners: China, the European Union and the Forging of a Strategic Partnership*. Palgrave (2017)

13. 《国际货物买卖：中欧关系的国际私法比较与前瞻性分析》(China-EU Law Series 5) Nicolas Nord, Gustavo Cerqueira (eds.), *International Sale of Goods: A Private International Law Comparative and Prospective Analysis of Sino-European Relations*. Springer Inter (2017)

14. 《中国、欧盟和全球治理的国际政治》Jianwei Wang, Weiqing Song (eds.), *China, the European Union, and the International Politics of Global Governance* Palgrave Macmillan US (2016)

15. 《欧盟与中国经济关系的政治学：不安宁的伙伴关系》John Farnell, Paul Irwin Crookes, *The Politics of EU-China Economic Relations: An Uneasy Partnership*. Palgrave Macmillan UK (2016)

16. 《管理全球挑战：欧盟、中国与欧盟外交网》Stephan Mergenthaler, *Managing Global Challenges: The European Union, China and EU Network Diplomacy*. Springer VS (2015)

17. 《纵观全局中的中国和欧盟：为企业和投资者提供见解》Kerry Brown（凯瑞·布朗）, *China and the EU in Context: Insights for Business and Investors*. Palgrave Macmillan UK (2014)

18. 《主权方面：中瑞关系的思考》Per Sevastik, *Aspects of Sovereignty: Sino-Swedish Reflections*. Martinus Nijhoff (2013)

19. 《归属边界转移与欧洲—中国新移民动力》Ludger Pries, *Shifting Boundaries of Belonging and New Migration Dynamics in Europe and China*. Palgrave Macmillan UK (2013)

20. 《中国、欧盟和全球治理》Jan Wouters, Tanguy de Wilde, Pierre Defraigne, Jean-Christophe Defraigne, *China, the Europe Union and Global Governance*. Edward Elgar Publishing Limited (2012)

21. 《中国、欧盟和全球治理结构调整》Jan Wouters, Tanguy de Wilde, Pierre Defraigne, Jean-Christophe Defraigne, *China, the European Union and the restructuring of global governance*. Edward Elgar Pub (2012)

22. 《中国与欧盟关系的观念差异：全球治理、人权和战略伙伴关系》Zhongqi Pan (eds.), *Conceptual Gaps in China-EU Relations: Global Governance, Human Rights and Strategic Partnerships*. Palgrave Macmillan UK (2012)

23. 《欧洲与中国的尚古主义和精神生活（1500—1800）》Peter N. Miller, Francois Louis, *Antiquarianism and Intellectual Life in Europe and China, 1500—1800* (The Bard Graduate Center: Cultural Histories of the Material World). University of Michigan Press (2012)

24. 《欧洲百科全书中的中国（1700—1850）》Georg Lehner, *China in European Encyclopaedias, 1700—1850*. Brill (2011)

25. 《中国与欧洲航运（1500—1800）：贸易、结算、外交和使命》John E. Wills Jr., John Cranmer-Byng, Willard J. Peterson Jr, John W. Witek, *China and Maritime Europe, 1500—1800: Trade, Settlement, Diplomacy, and Missions*. Cambridge University Press (2010)

26. 《欧盟和中国（1949—2008）：基本文件与评论》Francis G. Snyder (ed.), *The European Union and China, 1949—2008: Basic Documents and Commentary* (China and International Economic Law, Volume 3). Hart Publishing (2009)

27. 《重塑全球秩序：欧洲—中国关系演变及其对东亚和美国的影响》Nicola Casarini, *Remaking Global Order: The Evolution of Europe-China Relations and its Implications for East Asia and the United States*. Oxford University Press, USA (2009)

28. 《欧盟与中国：利益和困境》Georg Wiessala, John Wilson, Pradeep Taneja, *The European Union and China: Interests and Dilemmas* (European Studies). Rodopi B.V., Amsterdam-New York, NY (2009)

29. 《欧盟在亚洲的作用：作为战略伙伴的中国和印度》Bart Gaens, Juha Jokela, Eija Limnell, *The Role of the European Union in Asia: China and India as Strategic Partners*.

Ashgate (2009)

30. 《中国—欧洲关系：影响和美国政策反应》Bates Gill（季北慈）, Melissa Murphy（墨菲）, *China-Europe Relations: Implications and Policy Responses for the United States*. Center for Strategic and International Studies (2008)

31. 《中国、欧盟和世界：和谐地生长？》Frederic Lerais, Mattias Levin, Myriam Sochacki, Reinhilde Veugelers, *China, the Eu and the World: Growing in Harmony?* European Communities (2007)

32. 《中欧关系：认知、政策和前景》David Shambaugh（沈大伟）, Eberhard Sandschneider, Zhou Hong (eds.), *China-Europe Relations: Perceptions, Policies and Prospects*. Routledge (2008)

33. 《OECD报告：中国治理》OECD, *Governance in China*. Organisation for Economic Co-operation and Development (2005)

34. 《中国与丹麦：1674年以来的关系》Kjeld Erik Brødsgaard, Mads Kirkebæk, *China And Denmark: Relations since 1674*. Nordic Institute of Asian Studies (2003)

35. 《欧洲、中国与两个特别行政区：走向新时代》Miguel Santos Neves, Brian Bridges (eds.), *Europe, China and the Two SARs: Towards a New Era*. Miguel Santos Neves and Brian (2000)

36. 《地缘战略三角：与中国、欧洲和俄罗斯共存》Zbigniew Brzezinski（布热津斯基）, *The Geostrategic Triad: Living with China, Europe and Russia*. Center for Strategic & International Studies (2000)

37. 《英法公司在中国的命运（1949—54）：帝国主义被监禁》Aron Shai, *The Fate of British and French Firms in China, 1949—54: Imperialism Imprisoned*. Palgrave Macmillan UK (1996)

38. 《中国与欧洲：18世纪的知识与艺术接触》Adolf Reichwein, *China and Europe: Intellectual and Artistic Contacts in the Eighteenth Century*. London: K. Paul, Trench, Trubner & Co., ltd.; New York: A. A. Knopf (1925)

8.3.7 中国与非洲

1. 《友谊至上：中国援助乌干达卫生发展个案研究》(China And Globalization 2.0) Zeqi Qiu, *When Friendship Comes First: A Case Study of Chinese Development Aid For Health In Uganda*. Palgrave Macmillan (2020)

2. 《中国在非洲的力量：全球新秩序》(Politics and Development of Contemporary China) Olayiwola Abegunrin, Charity Manyeruke, *China's Power in Africa: A New Global Order*. Palgrave Macmillan (2020)

3. 《官方发展援助之外：中国发展合作与非洲农业》(Governing China in the 21st Century) Lu Jiang, *Beyond Official Development Assistance: Chinese Development Cooperation and African Agriculture*. Springer Singapore: Palgrave Macmillan (2020)

4. 《中国如何重塑全球经济：非洲和拉丁美洲的发展影响》Rhys Owen Jenkins, *How China Is Reshaping the Global Economy: Development Impacts in Africa and Latin America*. Oxford University Press (2019)

5. 《管理中非商务往来：提高组织的跨文化能力》(Palgrave Studies in African Leadership) Claude-Hélène Mayer, Lynette Louw, Christian Martin Boness, *Managing Chinese-African Business Interactions: Growing Intercultural Competence in Organizations*. Springer International Publishing; Palgrave Macmillan (2019)

6. 《中国与非洲：在大陆构建和平与安全合作》Chris Alden, Abiodun Alao, Zhang Chun, Laura Barber (eds.), *China and Africa: Building Peace and Security Cooperation on the Continent*. Palgrave Macmillan (2018)

7. 《中国在非洲的外交和经济活动：进步中的关系》Anja Lahtinen, *China's Diplomacy and Economic Activities in Africa: Relations on the Move*. Palgrave Macmillan (2018)

8. 《以后国家主义为中心的中非关系分析：中国资本国际化与埃塞俄比亚的国家与社会关系》Edson Ziso, *A Post State-Centric Analysis of China-Africa Relations: Internationalisation of Chinese Capital and State-Society Relations in Ethiopia* (Critical Studies of the Asia-Pacific). Palgrave Macmillan (2018)

9. 《中国对非洲文艺复兴的影响》Kobus Jonker, Bryan Robinson, *China's Impact on the African Renaissance*. Springer Singapore: Palgrave Macmillan (2018)

10. 《全球的中国幽灵：非洲的政治、劳工和外国投资》Ching Kwan Lee, *The Specter of Global China: Politics, Labor, and Foreign Investment in Africa*. University of Chicago Press (2017)

11. 《中国与非洲：全球业务新范式》Young-Chan Kim (ed.), *China and Africa: A New Paradigm of Global Business* (The Palgrave Macmillan Asian Business Series). Palgrave Macmillan (2017)

12. 《媒体化的中非关系：媒体话语如何协调全球秩序的转移》Shubo Li, *Mediatized China-Africa Relations: How Media Discourses Negotiate the Shifting of Global Order* (Palgrave Series in Asia and Pacific Studies). Palgrave Macmillan (2017)

13. 《中国国有企业在西非：嵌入式全球化》Katy N. Lam, *Chinese State-Owned Enterprises in West Africa: Triple-Embedded Globalization* (Routledge Studies on Asia in the World). Routledge (2017)

14. 《非洲新移民在中国的图谱：种族与归属的文化政治》(Routledge Research in Race and Ethnicity) Shanshan Lan, *Mapping the New African Diaspora in China: Race and the Cultural Politics of Belonging*. Routledge (2017)

15. 《广州的全球化世界：在华南做生意的非洲和外籍商人》Gordon Mathews（麦高登）, Linessa Dan Lin（林丹）, Yang Yang（杨旸）, *The World in Guangzhou: Africans and Other Foreigners in South China's Global Marketplace*. University of Chicago Press (2017)

16. 《下一个世界工厂：中国投资如何重塑非洲》Irene Yuan Sun, *The Next Factory of the World: How Chinese Investment is Reshaping Africa*. Harvard Business Review Press (2017)
17. 《中国在非洲的媒体与软实力：促进与认知》Xiaoling Zhang, Herman Wasserman, Winston Mano (eds.), *China's Media and Soft Power in Africa: Promotion and Perceptions* (Palgrave Series in Asia and Pacific Studies).Palgrave Macmillan US (2016)
18. 《推动撒哈拉以南非洲地区的电力行业：中国的参与》OECD, *Boosting the Power Sector in Sub-Saharan Africa: China's Involvement* (Partner country series). IEA Publications (2016)
19. 《中国龙的力量：对非洲发展与经济增长启示》Spencer Henson, O. Fiona Yap (eds.), *The Power of the Chinese Dragon: Implications for African Development and Economic Growth*. Palgrave Macmillan UK (2016)
20. 《龙、狮和票箱：评估中国对非洲民主的影响》Cameron Silverberg, *The Dragon, the Lion, and the Ballot Box: Evaluating China's Impact on Democracy in Africa*.UC Berkeley Library (2016)
21. 《中国媒体和软实力在非洲：提升与认知》Xiaoling Zhang, Herman Wasserman, Winston Mano (eds.), *China's Media and Soft Power in Africa: Promotion and Perceptions*. Palgrave Macmillan US (2016)
22. 《非洲发展援助与经济可持续增长：中西方接触的限度》Simone Raudino, *Development Aid and Sustainable Economic Growth in Africa: The Limits of Western and Chinese Engagements* (International Political Economy Series). Palgrave Macmillan (2016)
23. 《非洲将养活中国吗？》Deborah Brautigam, *Will Africa Feed China?* Oxford University Press (2015)
24. 《开拓非洲：毛泽东时代中国在阿尔及利亚、加纳和坦桑尼亚的影响》Donovan C. Chau, *Exploiting Africa: The Influence of Maoist China in Algeria, Ghana, and Tanzania*. Naval Institute Press (2014)
25. 《超越中国联系：当代亚非文化生产》Crystal S. Anderson, *Beyond the Chinese Connection: Contemporary Afro-Asian Cultural Production*. University Press of Mississippi (2013)
26. 《中国和欧盟在非洲：合作伙伴或竞争对手》Jing Men, Benjamin Barton, *China and the European Union in Africa: Partners or Competitors*. Ashgate Pub. Co (2011)
27. 《中国和非洲：对中国在非洲的看法》Axel Harneit-Sievers, Stephen Marks, Sanusha Naidu, *Chinese and African Perspectives on China in Africa*. Pambazuka Press (2010)
28. 《中国和非洲关系的发展》Christopher M. Dent, *China and Africa Development Relations*. Routledge (2010)
29. 《造桥：作为非洲基础设施金融家中国日益增长的作用》Vivien Foster, William Butterfield, Chuan Chen, Nataliya Pushak, *Building Bridges: China's Growing Role As Infrastructure Financier for Africa*. World Bank Publications (2009)
30. 《龙的礼物：中国在非洲的真实故事》Deborah Brautigam, *The Dragon's Gift: The Real*

Story of China in Africa. Oxford University Press (2009)

31. 《算盘与麻将：中国人在毛里求斯》Marina Carter and James Ng Foong Kwong, *Abacus and Mahjong: Sino-Mauritian Settlement and Economic Consolidation*. Brill (2009)

32. 《非洲的自由铁路：中国发展项目如何改变坦桑尼亚生活和生计》Jamie Monson, *Africa's Freedom Railway: How a Chinese Development Project Changed Lives and Livelihoods in Tanzania*. Indiana University Press (2009)

33. 《中国在非洲的新存在》Meine Pieter van Dijk, *The New Presence of China in Africa*. Amsterdam University Press (2009)

34. 《中国在非洲及南部的新角色：寻找新视角》Dorothy-Grace Guerrero, Firoze Manji, *China's New Role in Africa and the South: A Search for a New Perspective*. Fahamu and Focus on the Global (2008)

35. 《中国进入非洲：贸易、援助和影响力》Robert I. Rotberg, *China into Africa: Trade, Aid, and Influence*. Brookings Institution Press (2008)

36. 《非洲视角：中国在非洲》Firoze Madatally Manji, Stephen Marks, *African Perspectives on China in Africa*. Fahamu: Pambazuka (2007)

37. 《中国观察专刊：南非的中国社区》*The Chinese Community in South Africa*. China Monitor August (2007)

38. 《中国与非洲：参与和妥协》Ian Taylor, *China and Africa: Engagement and Compromise*. Routledge (2006)

39. 《中国援助与非洲发展：输出绿色革命》Deborah Brautigam, *Chinese Aid and African Development: Exporting Green Revolution*. Palgrave Macmillan UK (1998)

40. 《非洲和中国发展道路》Ukandi G. Damachi, Guy Routh, Abdel-Rahman E. Ali Taha (eds.), *Development Paths in Africa and China*. Palgrave Macmillan UK (1976)

8.3.8 中国与越南

1. 《建设胡志明的军队：中国对北越的军事援助》Xiaobing Li, *Building Ho's Army: Chinese Military Assistance to North Vietnam*. University Press of Kentucky (2019)

2. 《明代中国与越南：近代早期亚洲的边界谈判》Kathlene Baldanza, *Ming China and Vietnam: Negotiating Borders in Early Modern Asia* (Studies of the Weatherhead East Asian Institute). Cambridge University Press (2016)

3. 《中越公民社会网络：健康和环境的非正式开拓者》Andrew Wells-Dang, *Civil Society Networks in China and Vietnam: Informal Pathbreakers in Health and the Environment*. Palgrave Macmillan UK (2012)

4. 《中国和越南的法律改革：亚洲共产党政权比较》John Gillespie, Albert H.Y. Chen, *Legal Reforms in China and Vietnam: A Comparison of Asian Communist Regimes*. Routledge (2010)

5. 《北京与越南和平谈判（1965—1968）：来自中国的新证据》Qiang Zhai, *Beijing and the Vietnam Peace Talks, 1965—68: New Evidence from Chinese Sources*. Woodrow Wilson International

Center for Scholars (2010)

6. 《中国和越南：不对称的政治》Brantly Womack（沃马克），*China and Vietnam: The Politics of Asymmetry*. Cambridge University Press (2006)

7. 《亚洲社会主义与法律变革：越南与中国改革动力学》John Gillespie, Penelope Nicholson, *Asian Socialism And Legal Change: The Dynamics Of Vietnamese And Chinese Reform*. Asia Pacific Press (2005)

8. 《中国和越南的私人企业家》Thomas Heberer, *Private entrepreneurs in China and Vietnam*. Brill (2003)

9. 《越南与中国模式：19世纪上半叶越中两国政府比较研究》Alexander Woodside, *Vietnam and the Chinese Model: A Comparative Study of Vietnamese and Chinese Government in the First Half of the Nineteenth Century* (Harvard East Asian Series). Harvard University Press (1971)

10. 《越南和中国（1938—1954）》King C. Chen, *Vietnam and China, 1938—1954*. Princeton University Press (1969)

8.3.9　中国与东盟

1. 《中国—东盟：建立新伙伴关系》Lu Jianren, Lee Lai To, Bui Truong Giang, Yunling Zhang, *China-ASEAN: Making New Partnership*. Social Science Academic Press (China) (2013)

2. 《东盟产业与中国的挑战》Darryl Jarvis, *ASEAN Industries and the Challenge from China*. Palgrave Macmillan (2011)

3. 《中国与东盟：自由化的经济和社会影响》Zhang Yunling, *China and Asean: Economic and Social Impact of Liberalization*. Social Sciences Academic Press (China) (2009)

4. 《和谐与发展：中国与东盟关系》Hongyi Lai, Tin Seng Lim, *Harmony and Development: ASEAN-China Relations*. World Scientific (2007)

5. 《中国—东盟关系：经济和法律层面》John Wong（黄朝翰），Keyuan Zou, Huaqun Zeng, *China-ASEAN Relations: Economic and Legal Dimensions*. World Scientific (2006)

8.3.10　中国与亚洲

1. 《中国与中东：冒险进入大漩涡》James M. Dorsey, *China and the Middle East: Venturing into the Maelstrom* (Global Political Transitions). Springer International Publishing: Palgrave Macmillan (2019)

2. 《中国与朝鲜的经济交往》(Palgrave Series in Asia and Pacific Studies) Bo Gao, *China's Economic Engagement in North Korea*. Springer Singapore: Palgrave Macmillan (2019)

3. 《习近平时代的中国与东南亚》Alvin Cheng-Hin Lim, Frank Cibulka, *China and Southeast Asia in the Xi Jinping Era*. Lexington Books (2018)

4. 《印尼与中国关系60年：印度尼西亚视角》Lidya Christin Sinaga, *Six Decades of Indonesia-China Relations: An Indonesian Perspective*. Springer (2018)

5. 《红星与新月：中国与中东》James Reardon-Anderson, *The Red Star and the Crescent: China and the Middle East*. Oxford University Press (2018)

6. 《韩中关系的历史与当代意义》Robert Kong Chan, *Korea-China Relations in History and Contemporary Implications* (Critical Studies of the Asia-Pacific). Palgrave Macmillan (2018)

7. 《中国资本主义在东南亚的社会学：挑战与前景》Yos Santasombat, *The Sociology of Chinese Capitalism in Southeast Asia: Challenges and Prospects*. Palgrave MacMillan (2018)

8. 《国际关系与亚洲北部：中俄、朝鲜、蒙古关系》(Asan-Palgrave Macmillan Series) Gilbert Rozman, Sergey Radchenko (eds.), *International Relations and Asia's Northern Tier: Sino-Russia Relations, North Korea, and Mongolia*. Palgrave (2018)

9. 《东南亚与中国：一场相互社会化的较量》Lowell Dittmer（罗德明）, Chow Bing Ngeow, *Southeast Asia and China: A Contest in Mutual Socialization*. World Scientific (2017)

10. 《泰国：在中美间摇摆》(Asian Arguments) Benjamin Zawacki, *Thailand: Shifting Ground Between the US and a Rising China*. Zed Books Ltd (2017)

11. 《亚洲推算：中国、日本和美国在太平洋世纪的命运》Richard McGregor, *Asia's Reckoning: China, Japan, and the Fate of U.S. Power in the Pacific Century*. Viking (2017)

12. 《中国的亚洲梦：新丝绸之路的帝国构建》Tom Miller, *China's Asian Dream: Empire Building along the New Silk Road*. Zed Books (2017)

13. 《东南亚的中国资本主义：文化与实践》Yos Santasombat (eds.), *Chinese Capitalism in Southeast Asia: Cultures and Practices*. Palgrave Macmillan (2017)

14. 《新的大博弈：改革时代中国与南亚和中亚》Thomas Fingar, *The New Great Game: China and South and Central Asia in the Era of Reform* (Studies of the Walter H. Shorenstein Asia-Pacific Research Center). Stanford University Press (2016)

15. 《趋向良好关系：阿拉伯之春后中国在中东的存在》Niv Horesh eds. *Toward Well-Oiled Relations: China's Presence in the Middle East Following the Arab Spring*. Palgrave Macmillan (2016)

16. 《现代中国早期和东北亚：跨国视角》Evelyn S. Rawski（罗友枝）, *Early Modern China and Northeast Asia: Cross-Border Perspectives*. Cambridge University Press (2015)

17. 《中国和朝鲜：中国变化中的战略和政策观点》Carla P. Freeman, *China and North Korea: Strategic and Policy Perspectives from a Changing China*. Carla P. Freeman (2015)

18. 《构建东亚信心：海上冲突、相互依存和亚洲认同思维》Kazuhiko Togo, G. V. C. Naidu (eds.), *Building Confidence in East Asia: Maritime Conflicts, Interdependence and Asian Identity Thinking*. Palgrave Macmillan US (2015)

19. 《中国—巴基斯坦轴心：亚洲新地缘政治》Andrew Small, *The China-Pakistan Axis: Asia's New Geopolitics*. Oxford University Press (2015)

20. 《亚洲对中国不断变化的国际关系的看法》Niv Horesh, Emilian Kavalski (eds.), *Asian Thought on China's Changing International Relations*. Palgrave Macmillan UK (2014)

21. 《中国对外援助研究：亚洲视角》Yasutami Shimomura, Hideo Ohashi (eds.), *A Study of China's Foreign Aid: An Asian Perspective*. Palgrave Macmillan UK (2013)

22. 《云南——中国与亚洲的桥头堡：中国与邻国政治经济关系的案例研究》Tim Summers, *Yunnan-A Chinese Bridgehead to Asia: A Case Study of China's Political and Economic Relations with its Neighbours*. Chandos Publishing (2013)
23. 《国际关系的中国：东亚属下的自我、文明和知识政治》Chih-yu Shih（石之瑜）, *Sinicizing International Relations: Self, Civilization, and Intellectual Politics in Subaltern East Asia*. Palgrave Macmillan US (2013)
24. 《中国的邻国：在新兴的亚洲谁影响中国以及中国影响谁》Asia Briefing Ltd., *China's Neighbors: Who is Influencing China and Who China is Influencing in the New Emerging Asia*. Springer Berlin Heidelberg (2012)
25. 《B-24解放者与Ki-43奥斯卡：中国和缅甸（1943）》Edward M. Young, *B-24 Liberator vs Ki-43 Oscar: China and Burma 1943* (Osprey Duel 41). Osprey Publishing (2012)
26. 《北京政权与中国边界：亚洲20个邻国》Bruce A. Elleman, Stephen Kotkin, Clive Schofield, *Beijing's Power and China's Borders: Twenty Neighbors in Asia*. M. E. Sharpe (2012)
27. 《1948年以来缅甸的中国政策》Maung Aung Myoe, *In the Name of Pauk-Phaw: Myanmar's China Policy Since 1948*. Institute of Southeast Asian Studies (2011)
28. 《中国与亚洲区域主义》Yunling Zhang, *China and Asian Regionalism*. World Scientific (2010)
29. 《中国和亚洲地区主义》Yunling Zhang, *China and Asian Regionalism*. World Scientific (2010)
30. 《亚洲发展之路：韩国、越南、中国和印度尼西亚》Tuong Vu, *Paths to Development in Asia: South Korea, Vietnam, China, and Indonesia*. Cambridge University Press (2010)
31. 《中国—中亚国家：建立新伙伴关系》Vladimir Portyakov, Zheng Yu, Venera Galyamova, Zhang Yunling, *China-Central Asia Countries: Making New Partnership*. Paths International (2010)
32. 《中国的亚洲战略思想》Gilbert Rozman（饶济凡）, *Chinese Strategic Thought Toward Asia*. Palgrave Macmillan (2010)
33. 《中国与亚洲：经济与金融的相互作用》Yin-Wong Cheung, Kar-Yiu Wong, *China and Asia: Economic and Financial Interactions*. Routledge (2009)
34. 《亚洲力量新组合：中国、印度和美国》Alyssa Ayres, C. Raja Mohan, *Power Realignments in Asia: China, India and the United States*. SAGE Publications (2009)
35. 《中国—亚洲关系与国际法》Zou Keyuan (Eds.), *China-Asian Relations and International Law*. Chandos Publishing (2009)
36. 《新亚洲半球：势不可挡的全球权力东移》Kishore Mahbubani, *The New Asian Hemisphere: The Irresistible Shift of Global Power to the East*. Public Affairs (2008)
37. 《中国、亚洲与新世界经济》Barry J. Eichengreen, Yŏng-chʻŏl Pak, Yung Chul Park, Charles Wyplosz, *China, Asia, and the New World Economy*. Oxford University Press (2008)
38. 《中国、东亚与全球经济：区域与历史视角》Takeshi Hamashita, Mark Selden（赛尔登）, Linda Grove (eds.), *China, East Asia and the Global Economy: Regional and Historical Perspectives* (Asia's Transformations: Critical Asian Scholarship). Routledge (2008)

39. 《中亚：华盛顿、莫斯科和北京的观点》Eugene Rumer, Dmitri Trenin, Huasheng Zhao, *Central Asia: Views from Washington, Moscow, and Beijing*. M. E. Sharpe (2007)

40. 《新亚洲中的韩国：东亚一体化与中国因素》Franc¸oise Nicolas, *Korea in the New Asia: East Asian Integration and the China Factor* (Routledge Advances in Korean Studies). Routledge (2007)

41. 《东亚复兴：经济增长理念》Indermit Gill, Homi Kharas, Deepak Bhattasali, Milan Brahmbhatt, Gaurav Datt, *An East Asian Renaissance: Ideas for Economic Growth*. World Bank Publications (2007)

42. 《中国对印度尼西亚政策（1949—1967）》David Mozingo, *Chinese Policy toward Indonesia, 1949—1967*. Equinox Publishing (2007)

43. 《联邦制在亚洲》Baogang He（何包钢）, Brian Galligan, Takashi Inoguchi, *Federalism in Asia*. Edward Elgar Publishing Limited (2007)

44. 《权力转移：中国和亚洲的新动力》David Shambaugh（沈大伟）, *Power Shift: China and Asia's New Dynamics*. University of California Press (2006)

45. 《中国与伊朗：后帝国世界的古代伙伴》John W. Garver（高龙江）, *China and Iran: Ancient Partners in a Post-imperial World*. University of Washington Press (2006)

46. 《盟友与伙伴之间：中韩关系和美国》Jae Ho Chung, *Between Ally and Partner: Korea-China Relations and the United States*. Columbia University Press (2006)

47. 《中国之竞争：东亚的西方列强》Matthew J. Flynn, *China Contested: Western Powers in East Asia*. Chelsea House Publications (2006)

48. 《中国与东南亚简史：朝贡、贸易和影响》Martin Stuart-Fox, *A Short History of China and Southeast Asia Tribute, Trade and Influence*. Allen & Unwin (2003)

49. 《东亚复兴：500年、150年与50年展望》Giovanni Arrighi, Takeshi Hamashita, Mark Selden（赛尔登）(eds.), *The Resurgence of East Asia: 500, 150 and 50 Year Perspectives* (Asia's Transformations). RoutledgeCurzon (2003)

50. 《中国在亚洲和世界经济中的作用：促进稳定与增长》Jan Joost Teunissen, FONDAD Center, *China's Role in Asia and the World Economy: Fostering Stability and growth*. Forum on Debt and Development (FONDAD) (2003)

51. 《1882—1941年马来建国中的华人企业：吉打和槟城》Wu Xiao An（吴小安）, *Chinese Business in the Making of a Malay State, 1882—1941: Kedah and Penang* (Chinese Worlds). RoutledgeCurzon (2003)

52. 《中国与阿拉伯半岛和海湾国家关系（1949—1999）》Mohamed Bin Huwaidin, Mohamed Bin Huwaidin, *China's Relations with Arabia and the Gulf 1949—1999*. Routledge (2002)

53. 《印度尼西亚与中国：存有问题的政治关系》Rizal Sukma, *Indonesia and China: The Politics of a Troubled Relationship*. Routledge (1999)

54. 《东亚增长背后：繁荣的政治和社会基础》Henry S. Rowen, *Behind East Asian Growth:*

The Political and Social Foundations of Prosperity. Routledge (1998)

55. 《中国、韩国、日本：东亚文明的兴起》Gina Lee Barnes, *China, Korea and Japan: The Rise of Civilization in East Asia*. Thames & Hudson (1993)

56. 《泰国对华政策（1949—1954）》Anuson Chinvanno, *Thailand's Policies towards China, 1949—1954*. Palgrave Macmillan UK (1992)

57. 《东风吹彻阿拉伯：中沙导弹交易的起源和影响》Yitzhak Shichor, *East Wind over Arabia: Origins and Implications of the Sino-Saudi Missile Deal*. Institute of East Asian Studies and Center for Chinese Studies, University of California (1989)

58. 《东亚世界秩序的最后阶段：韩国、日本和中华帝国（1860—1882）》Key-Hiuk Kim, *The Last Phase of the East Asian World Order: Korea, Japan, and the Chinese Empire, 1860—1882*. University of California Press (1980)

59. 《中国与巴基斯坦：政府间友善的谅解外交》Anwar Hussain Syed, *China & Pakistan: Diplomacy of an Entente Cordiale*. University of Massachusetts Press (1974)

60. 《暹罗与中国》Salvatore Besso, translated from the Italian by C. Mathews, *Siam and China*. London: Simpkin, Marshall, Hamilton, Kent & Co. Ltd (1914)

61. 《中国与远东》George Hubbard Blakeslee, *China and the Far East* NewYork: Thomas Y. Crowell & Co (1910)

8.3.10.1 亚洲研究

1. 《亚洲文化传统》Carolyn Brown Heinz, Jeremy A. Murray, *Asian Cultural Traditions*. Waveland Press, Inc. (2018)

2. 《天下：成吉思汗以来的亚洲国际关系》(Silk Roads) Timothy Brook（卜正民）, Michael van Walt van Praag, Miek Boltjes (eds.), *Sacred Mandates: Asian International Relations since Chinggis Khan*. University of Chicago Press (2018)

3. 《东亚的殖民统治与土地改革》Sui-Wai Cheung, *Colonial Administration and Land Reform in East Asia* (The Historical Anthropology of Chinese Society Series). Routledge (2017)

4. 《东亚资本主义商业网络：持久趋势与新兴模式》Jane Nolan, Chris Rowley, Malcolm Warner, *Business Networks in East Asian Capitalisms: Enduring Trends, Emerging Patterns*. Elsevier (2015)

5. 《亚洲里里外外：通联之处》Eric Tagliacozzo, Helen F. Siu, Peter C. Perdue（濮德培）, *Asia inside out: Connected Places*. Harvard University Press (2015)

6. 《亚洲国际关系牛津手册》Saadia M. Pekkanen, John Ravenhill, Rosemary Foot, *The Oxford Handbook of the International Relations of Asia*. Oxford University Press (2014)

7. 《现代亚洲的创造者》Ramachandra Guha, Jay Taylor, Rana Mitter（米德）, Odd Arne Westad（文安立）, Srinath Raghavan, Farzana Shaikh, James Rush, Michael D. Barr, Jian Chen（陈兼）, Sophie Quinn-Judge, *Makers of Modern Asia*. The Belknap Press (2014)

8. 《亚洲政治比较：印度、中国和日本》Sue Ellen M. Charlton, *Comparing Asian Politics:*

India, China, and Japan. Westview Press (2014)

9. 《亚洲复兴：为我们的时代概念化一个地区》Prasenjit Duara（杜赞奇）, *Asia Redux: Conceptualizing a Region for Our Times.* Institute of South east Asian Studies (2013)

10. 《秩序之争：冷战后东亚的霸权、等级制度与转型》Evelyn Goh, *The Struggle for Order: Hegemony, Hierarchy, and Transition in Post-Cold War East Asia.* Oxford University Press (2013)

11. 《东亚资本主义：多样性、连续性与变迁》Andrew Walter, Xiaoke Zhang (eds.), *East Asian Capitalism: Diversity, Continuity, and Change.* Oxford University Press (2012)

12. 《中亚调查：战略分析》Biznin Veten, Alâeddin Yalçinkay, Paul B. Henze, June Teufel Dreyer, Linda Benson, Ingvar Svanberg, Witt Raczka, *Central Asian Survey: Strategic Analysis.* Routledge (2012)

13. 《21世纪亚洲的崛起》Scott B. MacDonald, Jonathan Lemco, *Asia's Rise in the 21st Century.* Praeger (2011)

14. 《美国在新亚洲》Evan A. Feigenbaum, Robert A. Manning, *The United States in the New Asia* (Council Special Report). Council on Foreign Relations (2009)

15. 《亚洲转向海洋：大国与海洋战略》Toshi Yoshihara, James R. Holmes, *Asia Looks Seaward: Power and Maritime Strategy.* Greenwood Publishing Group (2008)

16. 《亚洲的国际关系》David Shambaugh（沈大伟）, Michael Yahuda（亚胡达）, *International Relations of Asia* (Asia in World Politics). Rowman & Littlefield Publishers, Inc. (2008)

17. 《东亚文化、社会和政治史》Patricia Buckley Ebrey（伊沛霞）, Anne Walthall, James Palais, *East Asia: A Cultural, Social, and Political History.* Cengage Learning (2008)

18. 《前现代东亚的文化、社会和政治史：至1800年》（第一卷）Patricia Buckley Ebrey（伊沛霞）, Anne Walthall, James Palais, *Pre-Modern East Asia: A Cultural, Social, and Political History, Volume I: To 1800.* Cengage Learning (2008)

19. 《东亚复兴：经济增长的理念》Indermit Gill, Homi Kharas, Deepak Bhattasali, Milan Brahmbhatt, Gaurav Datt, *An East Asian Renaissance: Ideas for Economic Growth.* World Bank Publications (2007)

20. 《登上政治舞台：亚洲和非洲的权力与表现》Julia C. Strauss, Donal Cruise O'Brien, *Staging Politics: Power and Performance in Asia and Africa* (International Library of Political Studies). I. B.Tauris (2007)

21. 《东亚愿景：经济发展的视角》Indermit Singh Gill, Yukon Huang, Homi J. Kharas, *East Asian Visions: Perspectives on Economic Development.* The World Bank and The Institute of Policy Studies (2007)

22. 《超越自由民主：东亚语境下的政治思考》Daniel A. Bell（淡贝宁）, *Beyond Liberal Democracy: Political Thinking for An East Asian Context.* Princeton University Press (2006)

23. 《合法性：东亚和东南亚政治成败的歧义》Lynn T. White（白霖）, *Legitimacy: Ambiguities of Political Success or Failure in East and Southeast Asia*. World Scientific Publishing (2005)
24. 《亚洲多元文化》Will Kymlicka, Baogang He（何包钢）, *Multiculturalism in Asia*. Oxford University Press, USA (2005)
25. 《亚洲安全手册：恐怖主义和新安全环境》James R. Lilley, William M. Carpenter, David G. Wiencek, *Asian Security Handbook: Terrorism and the New Security Environment* (East Gate Book). M E Sharpe Inc (2005)
26. 《国家建构：东南亚的五种历史》Wang Gungwu（王赓武）(ed.), *Nation Building: Five Southeast Asian Histories*. Institute of Southeast Asian Studies (2005)
27. 《高贵与文明：亚洲人对领导力与公共利益的理想》Wm. Theodore de Bary（狄百瑞）, *Nobility and Civility: Asian Ideals of Leadership and the Common Good*. Harvard University Press (2004)
28. 《了解澳大利亚的邻国：东亚和东南亚导论》Nick Knight（尼克·奈特）, *Understanding Australia's Neighbours: An Introduction to East and Southeast Asia*. Cambridge University Press (2004)
29. 《亚洲的种族》Colin Mackerras（马克林）, *Ethnicity in Asia*. RoutledgeCurzon (2003)
30. 《亚洲政治发展：戈登·怀特纪念文集》Robert Benewick, Marc Blecher, Sarah Cook, *Asian Politics in Development: Essays in Honour of Gordon White*. Routledge (2003)
31. 《东亚和东南亚的集体财产与集体前景》Sally Sargeson, *Collective Goods, Collective Futures in East and South-East Asia* (Asian Capitalisms). Routledge (2002)
32. 《构建现代东亚国家》Kai-wing Chow, Kevin M. Doak, Poshek Fu（傅葆石）, *Constructing Nationhood in Modern East Asia*. University of Michigan Press (2001)
33. 《东亚的人权政治》Kenneth Christie, Denny Roy, *The Politics of Human Rights in East Asia*. Pluto Press (2001)
34. 《21世纪的世界秩序与亚太：价值变化、紧急状态与权力重组》James C. Hsiung, *Twenty-First Century World Order and the Asia Pacific: Value Change, Exigencies, and Power Realignment*. Palgrave Macmillan US (2001)
35. 《东亚非正式政治》Lowell Dittmer（罗德明）, Haruhiro Fukui, Peter N. S. Lee, *Informal Politics in East Asia*. Cambridge University Press (2000)
36. 《国家工作：亚洲精英与国家认同》Timothy Brook（卜正民）, André Schmid, *Nation Work: Asian Elites and National Identities*. University of Michigan Press (2000)
37. 《东亚在中心：与世界接触的4000年》Warren I. Cohen（孔华润）, *East Asia at the Center: Four Thousand Years of Engagement with the World*. Columbia University Press (2000)
38. 《促进亚太经济合作：东亚的视角》Yong Deng（邓勇）, *Promoting Asia-Pacific Economic Cooperation: Perspectives from East Asia*. Palgrave Macmillan (1997)

39. 《跨国公司与东亚一体化》Wendy Dobson, Siow Yue Chia (eds.), *Multinationals and East Asian integration*. International Development Research Centre (Canada), Institute of Southeast Asian Studies (Singapore) (1997)
40. 《亚太国际关系（1945—1995）》Michael Yahuda（亚胡达）, *The International Politics of the Asia Pacific, 1945—1995* (Routledge in Asia). RoutledgeCurzon (1996, 2004)
41. 《四小龙：东亚工业化的蔓延传播》Ezra F. Vogel, *The Four Little Dragons: The Spread of Industrialization in East Asia*. Harvard University Press (1991)
42. 《东亚发展中国家》Gordon White (eds.), *Developmental States in East Asia*. Palgrave Macmillan UK (1988)
43. 《亚洲权力与政治：权力的文化维度》Lucian W. Pye（白鲁恂）, *Asian Power and Politics: The Cultural Dimensions of Authority*. The Belknap Press of Harvard University Press (1985)
44. 《欧洲形成过程中的亚洲，第二卷，百年奇观。第三册：学术学科》Donald F. Lach, *Asia in the Making of Europe, Volume II: A Century of Wonder. Book 3: The Scholarly Disciplines*. University of Chicago Press (1977)
45. 《欧洲形成过程中的亚洲，第二卷，百年奇观。第二册：文学艺术》Donald F. Lach, *Asia in the Making of Europe, Volume II: A Century of Wonder. Book 2: The Literary Arts*. The University of Chicago Press (1977)
46. 《亚洲和前面的道路》Robert A. Scalapino（斯卡拉皮诺）, *Asia and the Road Ahead*. University of California Press (1975)
47. 《欧洲形成过程中的亚洲，第二卷，百年奇观。第一册：视觉艺术》Donald F. Lach, *Asia in the Making of Europe, Volume II: A Century of Wonder. Book 1: The Visual Arts*. University of Chicago Press (1970, 1994)
48. 《亚洲：基本书籍指南》Ainslie T. Embree, *Asia: A Guide to Basic Books*. Distributed by ERIC (1966)
49. 《欧洲形成过程中的亚洲，第一卷，世纪发现。第二册》Donald F. Lach, *Asia in the Making of Europe. Volume I. The Century of Discovery. Book 2*. University Of Chicago Press (1965)
50. 《欧洲形成过程中的亚洲，第一卷，世纪发现。第一册》Donald F. Lach, *Asia in the Making of Europe. Volume I. The Century of Discovery. Book 1*. University Of Chicago Press (1965, 1971)
51. 《遥远的亚洲：附轶事和众多插图》Favell Lee Mortimer, *Far off; or, Asia Described, with Anecdotes and Numerous Illustrations*. London: Hatchards, Piccadilly (1879)

8.3.11 中国与世界/其他国家和地区

1. 《国际发展援助与金砖国家》(Governing China in the 21st Century) Jose A. Puppim de Oliveira, Yijia Jing, *International Development Assistance and the BRICS*. Palgrave MacMillan (2020)

2. 《大国：中国与世界》Timothy Brook（卜正民）, *Great State: China and the World*. Profile Books (19 Sept 2019)

3. 《印度洋区域发展年度报告（2018）印太的概念定义与战略实施》 (Research Series on the Chinese Dream and China's Development Path) Cuiping Zhu, *Annual Report on the Development of the Indian Ocean Region (2018)：Indo-Pacific: Concept Definition and Strategic Implementation*. Social Sciences Academic Press and Springer Nature Singapore Pte Ltd. (2019)

4. 《中拉经贸关系》 (Research Series on the Chinese Dream and China's Development Path) Yu Chai, Yunxia Yue, *Sino-Latin American Economic and Trade Relations*. Springer Singapore (2019)

5. 《中国如何看待世界：中国国际关系学者的见解》Huiyun Feng, Kai He, Xiaojun Li, *How China Sees The World: Insights From China's International Relations Scholars*. Palgrave Macmillan (2019)

6. 《与中国共处：一个中等大国的出路》（中国与加拿大）Wendy Dobson, *Living with China: A Middle Power Finds Its Way*. Rotman-Utp Publishing (2019)

7. 《南南合作与中国对外援助》Xiaojing Mao, Xiuli Xu, Meibo Huang, *South-south Cooperation and Chinese Foreign Aid*. Springer Singapore (2019)

8. 《中国对自由准则的挑战：国际秩序的持久性》Catherine Jones, *China's Challenge to Liberal Norms: The Durability of International Order*. Palgrave Macmillan UK (2018)

9. 《上古晚期的地缘政治：从中国到罗马的超级大国命运》 (Routledge Studies in Ancient History) Hyun Jin Kim, *Geopolitics in Late Antiquity: The Fate of Superpowers from China to Rome*. Routledge (2018)

10. 《缩短距离：最近中国、日本和韩国在拉丁美洲积极参与的益处和紧张局势》Nobuaki Hamaguchi, Jie Guo, Chong-Sup Kim, *Cutting the Distance: Benefits and Tensions from the Recent Active Engagement of China, Japan, and Korea in Latin America*. Springer Nature Singapore Pte Ltd. (2018)

11. 《金砖国家创新竞争力2017年报告》 (Research Series on the Chinese Dream and China's Development Path) Xinli Zhao, Minrong Li, Maoxing Huang, Alexander Sokolov, *BRICS Innovative Competitiveness Report 2017*. Springer Singapore (2018)

12. 《中国—拉美轴心：新兴市场及其在日益全球化世界中的作用》Gaston Fornes, Alvaro Mendez, *The China-Latin America Axis: Emerging Markets and their Role in an Increasingly Globalised World*. Palgrave Macmillan (2018)

13. 《不太可能的合作伙伴：中国改革者、西方经济学家和全球中国的形成》Julian Gewirtz, *Unlikely Partners: Chinese Reformers, Western Economists, and the Making of Global China*. Harvard University Press (2017)

14. 《中墨贸易关系：挑战与机遇》(SpringerBriefs in Economics) Yi Liu, Laixun Zhao, *Sino-Mexican Trade Relations: Challenges and Opportunities*. Springer Singapore (2017)

15. 《中国的世界秩序观：天下、文化与世界政治》Ban Wang（王斑）(ed.), *Chinese*

Visions of World Order: Tianxia, Culture, and World Politics. Duke University Press (2017)

16. 《中国与拉丁美洲的转型：政策动态、经济承诺和社会影响》Shoujun Cui, Manuel Pérez García (eds.), *China and Latin America in Transition: Policy Dynamics, Economic Commitments, and Social Impacts.* Palgrave Macmillan US (2016)

17. 《中国在拉丁美洲的战略伙伴关系：1991—2015年中国在阿根廷、巴西、墨西哥和委内瑞拉的石油外交案例研究》Yanran Xu, *China's Strategic Partnerships in Latin America: Case Studies of China's Oil Diplomacy in Argentina, Brazil, Mexico, and Venezuela, 1991—2015.* Lexington Books (2016)

18. 《后西方国际关系的反思：公孙龙的前现代政治》Chih-yu Shih（石之瑜）, Po-tsan Yu, *Post-Western International Relations Reconsidered: The Pre-Modern Politics of Gongsun Long* (Global Political Thinkers). Palgrave Macmillan (2015)

19. 《吸引中国：加拿大政策的神话、愿望和策略，从特鲁多到哈珀》Paul Evans, *Engaging China. Myth, Aspiration, and Strategy in Canadian Policy from Trudeau to Harper.* University of Toronto Press (2015)

20. 《国际经济秩序中的中国：新方向和范式变化》Lisa Toohey, Colin Picker, Jonathan Greenacre, *China in the International Economic Order: New Directions and Changing Paradigms.* Cambridge University Press (2015)

21. 《中国在拉丁美洲：中国挑战和地区影响》R. Evan Ellis, *China on the Ground in Latin America: Challenges for the Chinese and Impacts on the Region.* Palgrave Macmillan US (2014)

22. 《中国与国际社会：适应与自我意识》Jinjun Zhao, Zhirui Chen, *China and the International Society: Adaptation and Self-Consciousness.* World Century Publishing Company (2014)

23. 《中等实力国家与中国崛起》Bruce Gilley, Andrew O'Neil (eds.), *Middle Powers and the Rise of China.* Georgetown University Press (2014)

24. 《1949年后的澳中关系：贸易和政治60年》Yi Wang, *Australia-China Relations post 1949: Sixty Years of Trade and Politics.* Routledge (2012)

25. 《全球趋势2030：非传统世界》National Intelligence Council, *Global Trends 2030: Alternative Worlds.* Center for the Study of Intelligence (2012)

26. 《1945年以来的中国与世界：国际史》Chi-kwan Mark, *China and the World since 1945: An International History.* Routledge (2011)

27. 《中国里里外外：10大不可逆转趋势重塑中国与世界关系》Bill Dodson, *China Inside Out: 10 Irreversible Trends Reshaping China and its Relationship with the World.* Wiley (2011)

28. 《中国：国家故事及其与澳大利亚关系》Elizabeth Onslow, *China: The Story of the Nation And Its Relationship with Australia.* Trocadero Publishing (2011)

29. 《中国大战略中的太平洋岛屿：小国家，大博弈》Jian Yang, *The Pacific Islands in China's Grand Strategy: Small States, Big Games.* Palgrave Macmillan US (2011)

30. 《投资金砖国家：评估巴西、俄罗斯、印度和中国的风险与治理》Svetlana Borodina,

Oleg Shvyrkov, *Investing in BRIC Countries: Evaluating Risk and Governance in Brazil, Russia, India, and China*. McGraw-Hill, Inc. (2010)

31. 《西方为何至今统治世界：历史模式及其揭示的未来》Ian Morris, *Why the West Rules for Now: The Patterns of History, and What They Reveal About the Future*. Profile Books (2010)

32. 《中国与区域化的全球政治》Emilian Kavalski, *China and the Global Politics of Regionalization*. Ashgate Publishing limited (2009)

33. 《中国在世界危机中的新地位：经济、地缘政治和环境维度》Ross Garnaut, Ligang Song and Wing Thye Woo (editors), *China's New Place in a World in Crisis: Economic, Geopolitical and Environmental Dimensions*. ANU E Press (2009)

34. 《想象的帝国：中国和罗马比较》Fritz-Heiner Mutschler, Achim Mittag, *Conceiving the Empire: China and Rome Compared*. Oxford University Press, USA (2009)

35. 《与中国共生：经历危机和转折点的区域国家与中国》Shiping Tang, Mingjiang Li, Amitav Acharya, *Living with China: Regional States and China through Crises and Turning Points*. Palgrave Macmillan (2009)

36. 《中国到来：全球关系的战略框架》Abraham Denmark & Nirav Patel (eds.), *China's Arrival: A Strategic Framework for a Global Relationship*. Center for a New American Security (2009)

37. 《中国站起来：中国与国际体系》David Scott, *China Stands Up: The PRC and the International System*. Routledge (2007)

38. 《中国与发展中的世界：北京的21世纪战略》Joshua Eisenman, Eric Heginbotham, Derek Mitchell, *China and the Developing World: Beijing's Strategy for the Twenty-First Century*. M. E. Sharpe (2007)

39. 《中国与国际机构：全球权力的替代路径》Marc Lanteigne, *China and International Institutions: Alternate Paths to Global Power*. Routledge (2005)

40. 《转型中的权力：国际秩序的和平变革》Charles A. Kupchan, Emanuel Adler, Jean-Marc Coicaud, Yuen Foong Khong, *Power in Transition: The Peaceful Change of International Order*. United Nations (2001)

41. 《中国人对国际关系的看法：一个分析框架》Gerald Chan, *Chinese Perspectives on International Relations: A Framework for Analysis*. Palgrave Macmillan UK (1999)

42. 《1949年以来国际社会中的中国：异化与超越》Yongjin Zhang, *China in International Society since 1949: Alienation and Beyond*. Palgrave Macmillan UK (1998)

43. 《中国和外国领导人之间的对话》Odd Arne Westad（文安立）, Chen Jian（陈兼）et al., *Conversations between Chinese and Foreign Leaders*. Cold War International History Project (1998)

44. 《市场经济和政治变革：中国和墨西哥比较》Juan D. Lindau, Timothy Cheek（齐慕实）, Gaye Christoffersen, Jorge I. Dominguez, David D. Finley, David Hendrickson (eds.),

Market Economics and Political Change: Comparing China and Mexico. Rowman & Littlefield Publishers (1998)

45. 《美国、俄罗斯和中国在新世界秩序中的作用》Hafeez Malik, *The Roles of the United States, Russia and China in the New World Order*. Palgrave Macmillan UK (1997)

46. 《1918—1920年国际体系中的中国：在边缘的中国》Zhang Yongjin, *China in the International System, 1918–20: The Middle Kingdom at the Periphery*. Palgrave Macmillan UK (1991)

47. 《1949以来的中国与世界：独立、现代性与革命的影响》Wang Gungwu（王赓武）, *China and the World since 1949: The Impact of Independence, Modernity and Revolution*. Macmillan Education UK (1977)

48. 《中华帝国对外关系史（第三卷）》Hosea Ballou Morse, *The International Relations of the Chinese Empire*. Vol. 3. London Longmans, Green (1918)

49. 《中华帝国对外关系史（第二卷》Hosea Ballou Morse, *The International Relations of the Chinese Empire*. Vol. 2. London Longmans, Green (1918)

50. 《中华帝国对外关系史（第一卷）》Hosea Ballou Morse, *The International Relations of the Chinese Empire*. Vol. 1. New York: Paragon Book Gallery (1910)

51. 《中国与列强：中国与西方国家交往史篇章》Alleyne Ireland, *China and the Powers: Chapters in the History of Chinese Intercourse with Western Nations*. Boston: Privately printed for Laurens Maynard (1902)

9. 中国法律与军事

9.1 法律与法治

1. 《中国宪政发展（1982—2012）》(Research Series On The Chinese Dream And China's Development Path) Lin Li, Jihong Mo, Guoqiang Zhai, *Constitutional Development In China, 1982—2012*. Springer (2020)
2. 《中华人民共和国最高人民法院精选案例》（第一卷）(Library of Selected Cases from the Chinese Court) China Institute of Applied Jurisprudence (ed.), *Selected Cases from the Supreme People's Court of the People's Republic of China*. Volume 1. Springer Singapore (2020)
3. 《中国商法》(The Palgrave Series on Chinese Law) Danling Yu, *Chinese Business Law*. Springer Singapore, Palgrave Macmillan (2019)
4. 《中国法治十年回顾（2002—2012）》(Research Series on the Chinese Dream and China's Development Path) Lin Li, He Tian, Yanbin Lv, *Rule of Law in China: A Ten-year Review (2002—2012)*. Springer Singapore (2019)
5. 《中国非法证据的排除规则：理论、案例与应用》(Masterpieces of Contemporary Jurisprudents in China) Jingkun Liu, *The Exclusionary Rule of Illegal Evidence in China: Theory, Case, Application*. Springer Singapore (2019)
6. 《中国知识产权创新制度：对企业和国家发展的风险》Dan Prud'homme, Taolue Zhang, *China's Intellectual Property Regime for Innovation: Risks to Business and National Development*. Springer International Publishing (2019)
7. 《中国军事法基本知识》Jian Zhou, *Fundamentals of Military Law: A Chinese Perspective*. Springer Singapore (2019)
8. 《权力与正义：华北乡村的纠纷解决》(China Academic Library) Xudong Zhao, *Power and Justice: Disputes Resolution in a North China Village*. Springer Berlin Heidelberg (2019)
9. 《故意问题：清代和民国时期的凶杀法与刑事司法》Jennifer M. Neighbors（胡宗绮）, *A Question of Intent: Homicide Law and Criminal Justice in Qing and Republican China*. Brill (2018)
10. 《中国、德国、欧盟农业食品法手册：粮食安全、食品安全与农业资源可持续利用》Ines Härtel (eds.), *Handbook of Agri-Food Law in China, Germany, European Union: Food Security, Food Safety, Sustainable Use of Resources in Agriculture*. Springer International Publishing (2018)
11. 《治在法前：中国与印尼的法制政治》(Cambridge Studies in Law and Society) William Hurst, *Ruling Before The Law: The Politics of Legal Regimes in China and Indonesia*.

Cambridge University Press (2018)

12. 《走向可交易的水权：中国水法与政策改革》Jiang, Min, *Towards Tradable Water Rights: Water Law and Policy Reform in China* (Global issues in water policy 18).Springer (2018)

13. 《中国和南非版权例外的概念化：发展中国家的发展观点》Jia Wang, *Conceptualizing Copyright Exceptions in China and South Africa: A Developing View from the Developing Countries* (China-EU Law Series 6).Springer International Publishing (2018)

14. 《中国的走私战争：法律、经济生活与现代国家建构（1842—1965）》Philip Thai, *China's War on Smuggling: Law, Economic Life, and the Making of the Modern State, 1842—1965* (Studies of the Weatherhead East Asian Institute, Columbia University). Columbia University Press (2018)

15. 《中国与国际刑事法院》Dan Zhu, *China and the International Criminal Court* (Governing China in the 21st Century). Palgrave (2018)

16. 《司法证明与推定方法论》Jiahong He, *Methodology of Judicial Proof and Presumption* (Masterpieces of Contemporary Jurisprudents in China). Springer Singapore (2018)

17. 《中国法治之路》Lin Li, *The Chinese Road of the Rule of Law* (China Insights). Springer Singapore (2018)

18. 《中国侵权责任法的立法》Xinbao Zhang, *Legislation of Tort Liability Law in China*. Springer Singapore (2018)

19. 《处于效率与合法性之间的中国实验立法》Madeleine Martinek, *Experimental Legislation in China between Efficiency and Legality*. Springer International Publishing (2018)

20. 《中国法治指数（2017）》(Research Series on the Chinese Dream and China's Development Path) Lin Li（李林）, He Tian（田禾）, Yanbin Lv（吕艳滨）(eds.), *China's Rule of Law Index 2017*. Springer Singapore (2018)

21. 《中国反对走私的战争：法律、经济生活与近代国家的建立（1842—1965）》Philip Thai, *China's War on Smuggling: Law, Economic Life, and the Making of the Modern State, 1842—1965*. Columbia University Press (2018)

22. 《中国古代宪法》Su Li, *The Constitution of Ancient China*. Princeton University Press (2018)

23. 《中国民事诉讼听证中利益冲突的解决：话语信息理论的视角》Yunfeng Ge, *Resolution of Conflict of Interest in Chinese Civil Court Hearings: A Perspective of Discourse Information Theory*. Peter Lang Gmbh, Internationaler Verlag Der Wissenschaften (2018)

24. 《当代中国女法官：性别、审判与生活》Anqi Shen, *Women Judges in Contemporary China: Gender, Judging and Living* (Palgrave Advances in Criminology and Criminal Justice in Asia). Palgrave Macmillan (2017)

25. 《农药法与合规决策：中国农民个案研究》Huiqi Yan, *Pesticide Law and Compliance Decision Making: A Case Study of Chinese Farmers*. Springer (2017)

26. 《中国的版权与粉丝生产力：跨辖区视角》Tianxiang He, *Copyright and Fan Productivity*

in China: A Cross-jurisdictional Perspective. Springer Singapore (2017)

27. 《中国修复式正义：理论与实践比较》Xiaoyu Yuan, *Restorative Justice in China: Comparing Theory and Practice* (Springer Series on Asian Criminology and Criminal Justice Research). Springer International Publishing (2017)

28. 《评估当代中国知识产权合规性：世界贸易组织TRIPS协议》Kristie Thomas, *Assessing Intellectual Property Compliance in Contemporary China: The World Trade Organisation TRIPS Agreement*. Palgrave Macmillan (2017)

29. 《转型期中国最高法院与西方：服务公共目标的裁决》Cornelis Hendrik (Remco) van Rhee, Yulin Fu (eds.), *Supreme Courts in Transition in China and the West: Adjudication at the Service of Public Goals*.Springer International Publishing AG (2017)

30. 《近代中国的版权法与实践》Yimeei Guo, *Modern China's Copyright Law and Practice*. Springer Nature Singapore Pte Ltd (2017)

31. 《中国的威权合法性：法律、工人与国家》Mary E. Gallagher（高敏）, *Authoritarian Legality in China: Law, Workers, and the State*. Cambridge University Press (2017)

32. 《专利维护时间与行业发展：中国实证研究》Yongzhong Qiao (eds.), *Maintenance Time and the Industry Development of Patents: Empirical Research with Evidence from China*. Springer Singapore (2017)

33. 《中国的不当定罪：比较与经验视角》Na Jiang, *Wrongful Convictions in China: Comparative and Empirical Perspectives*. Springer-Verlag Berlin Heidelberg (2016)

34. 《变动中的中国法律体系：律师与法官论民法和刑法》Chuan Feng, Leyton P. Nelson, Thomas W. Simon, *China's Changing Legal System: Lawyers & Judges on Civil & Criminal Law*. Palgrave Macmillan (2016)

35. 《习近平时代的中国社会主义法治改革》John Garrick, Yan Chang Bennett, *China's Socialist Rule of Law Reforms Under Xi Jinping*. Routledge (2016)

36. 《中国的非法定罪：比较和实证和观点》Na Jiang, *Wrongful Convictions in China: Comparative and Empirical Perspectives*. Springer-Verlag Berlin Heidelberg (2016)

37. 《欧盟和中国的竞争法程序权》Caroline Cauffman, Qian Hao (eds.), *Procedural Rights in Competition Law in the EU and China*.Springer-Verlag Berlin Heidelberg (2016)

38. 《中国仲裁：规则与展望》Giovanni Pisacane, Lea Murphy, Calvin Zhang, *Arbitration in China: Rules & Perspectives*. Springer Singapore (2016)

39. 《中国国际私法》Guangjian Tu, *Private International Law in China*. Springer Singapore (2016)

40. 《中国海员权益：2006年海事劳工公约立法与实践重组》Pengfei Zhang, *Seafarers' Rights in China: Restructuring in Legislation and Practice Under the Maritime Labour Convention 2006*. Springer International Publishing (2016)

41. 《送法下乡：中国基层司法制度研究》Suli Zhu, *Sending Law to the Countryside: Research on China's Basic-level Judicial System*.Springer Singapore (2016)

42. 《中国基本劳工权益：法律执行与文化逻辑》Ulla Liukkunen, Yifeng Chen (eds.), *Fundamental Labour Rights in China: Legal Implementation and Cultural Logic*. Springer International Publishing (2016)

43. 《中国刑事辩护：工作中的律师政治学》Sida Liu, Terence C. Halliday, *Criminal Defense in China: The Politics of Lawyers at Work* (Cambridge Studies in Law and Society). Cambridge University Press (2016)

44. 《不羁之民：帝制晚期华南的犯罪、社会与国家》Robert J. Antony, *Unruly People: Crime, Community, and State in Late Imperial South China*. Hong Kong University Press (2016)

45. 《中国电子商务法律问题研究》Yimeei Guo (eds.), *Research on Selected China's Legal Issues of E-Business*. Springer-Verlag Berlin Heidelberg (2015)

46. 《现代中国法治之路》Quanxi Gao, Wei Zhang, Feilong Tian, *The Road to the Rule of Law in Modern China*. Springer Berlin Heidelberg (2015)

47. 《赤脚律师：一个为正义和自由而战的盲人》Chen guangcheng（陈光诚）, *The Barefoot Lawyer: A Blind Man's Fight for Justice and Freedom*. Allen Lane (2015)

48. 《稳定的必要性：中国的人权与法律》Sarah Biddulph, *The Stability Imperative: Human Rights and Law in China*. University of Washington Press (2015)

49. 《中国法治：比较的视角》Katrin Blasek, *Rule of Law in China: A Comparative Approach*. Springer-Verlag Berlin Heidelberg (2015)

50. 《中国劳动法：进展与挑战》Zengyi Xie, *Labor Law in China: Progress and Challenges*. Springer-Verlag Berlin Heidelberg (2015)

51. 《中国法律：知识、实践与变革（1530年代至1950年代）》Li Chen, Madeleine Zelin（曾小萍）, *Chinese Law: Knowledge, Practice and Transformation, 1530s to 1950s* (Brill's Series on Modern East Asia in a Global Historical Perspective). Brill Academic Pub. (2015)

52. 《中国人权律师的维权与抗争》(Routledge research in human rights law.) Eva Pils, *China's Human Rights Lawyers: Advocacy and Resistance*. Routledge (2015)

53. 《帝王眼中的中国法律：主权、正义与跨文化政治》Li Chen, *Chinese Law in Imperial Eyes: Sovereignty, Justice, and Transcultural Politics*. Columbia University Press (2015)

54. 《中国法律的传统与现代转型》Jinfan Zhang, *The Tradition and Modern Transition of Chinese Law*. Springer-Verlag Berlin Heidelberg (2014)

55. 《中国立法：从非交际到交际》Peng He, *Chinese Lawmaking: From Non-communicative to Communicative*. Springer Berlin Heidelberg (2014)

56. 《法律与政治在中国发展中的作用》Guanghua Yu, *The Roles of Law and Politics in China's Development*. Springer Singapore (2014)

57. 《中国刑事审判：一个全面实证研究》Ni He, *Chinese Criminal Trials: A Comprehensive Empirical Inquiry*. Springer-Verlag New York (2014)

58. 《缚住独裁者之手：法治中国的崛起》Yuhua Wang, *Tying the Autocrat's Hands: The Rise*

59. 《简明中国侵权法》Xiang Li, Jigang Jin, *Concise Chinese Tort Laws*. Springer-Verlag Berlin Heidelberg (2014)
60. 《中国和欧洲的民事诉讼：关于法官和当事人作用的文章》C.H. Remco van Rhee, Fu Yulin (eds.), *Civil Litigation in China and Europe: Essays on the Role of the Judge and the Parties*. Springer Science+Business Media Dordrecht (2014)
61. 《电子商务交易法：欧盟、美国和中国的当代问题》Faye Fangfei Wang, *Law of Electronic Commercial Transactions: Contemporary Issues in the EU, US and China*. Routledge (2014)
62. 《中国审判委员会诉讼中的司法裁决：有限理性分析》Li Li, *Judicial Discretion within Adjudicative Committee Proceedings in China: A Bounded Rationality Analysis*. Springer-Verlag Berlin Heidelberg (2014)
63. 《传统文化表现形式的知识产权保护：中国民俗》Luo Li, *Intellectual Property Protection of Traditional Cultural Expressions: Folklore in China*. Springer International Publishing (2014)
64. 《20世纪初中国法律移植：民国时期的北京执业（1910—1940年）》Michael H. K. Ng, *Legal Transplantation in Early Twentieth-Century China: Practicing law in Republican Beijing (1910s—1930s)*. Routledge (2014)
65. 《中国与国际投资法：ICSID成员20年》Wenhua Shan, Jinyuan Su, *China and International Investment Law: Twenty Years of ICSID Membership*. Brill–Nijhoff (2014)
66. 《知识产权理论与实践：对中国TRIPS合规性及其他的重大考验》Wenwei Guan, *Intellectual Property Theory and Practice: A Critical Examination of China's TRIPS Compliance and Beyond*. Springer-Verlag Berlin Heidelberg (2014)
67. 《中国法律实践的历史与理论：走向历史—社会的法理学》Philip C. C. Huang（黄宗智）, Kathryn Bernhardt, *The History and Theory of Legal Practice in China: Toward a Historical-Social Jurisprudence* (The Social Sciences of Practice). Brill Academic Pub. (2014)
68. 《中国法律制度》Pitman Potter, *China's Legal System*. Wiley (2014)
69. 《中国特色法律与经济学：促进21世纪发展的制度》David Kennedy, Joseph E. Stiglitz, *Law and Economics with Chinese Characteristics: Institutions for Promoting Development in the Twenty-First Century* (The Initiative for Policy Dialogue). Oxford University Press (2013)
70. 《中国税法和国际条约》Lorenzo Riccardi, *Chinese Tax Law and International Treaties*. Springer International Publishing (2013)
71. 《中国法律制度内幕》Chang Wang and Nathan Madson, *Inside China's Legal System*. Chandos Publishing (2013)
72. 《来自中国的声音：An CHEN论国际经济法》An CHEN, *The Voice from China: An CHEN on International Economic Law*. Springer-Verlag Berlin Heidelberg (2013)
73. 《中国环境诉讼：政治矛盾研究》Rachel E. Stern, *Environmental Litigation in China: A Study in Political Ambivalence*. Cambridge University Press (2013)

74. 《中国实施清洁发展机制的法律问题》Xiaoyi Jiang, *Legal Issues for Implementing the Clean Development Mechanism in China*. Springer-Verlag Berlin Heidelberg (2013)

75. 《中国法律制度的发展：变革与挑战》Guanghua Yu, *The Development of the Chinese Legal System: Change and Challenges*. Taylor & Francis (2012)

76. 《中国民法典：比较与历史的视角》Lei Chen, C. H. van Rhee, *Towards a Chinese Civil Code: Comparative and Historical Perspectives*. Martinus Nijhoff Publishers (2012)

77. 《当代中国的死刑》Susan Trevaskes, *The Death Penalty in Contemporary China*. Palgrave Macmillan US (2012)

78. 《中国互联网法》Guosong Shao, *Internet Law in China*. Chandos Publishing (2012)

79. 《中国保护隐私：关于中国隐私标准和制定隐私权可能性的研究》Hao Wang, *Protecting Privacy in China: A Research on China's Privacy Standards and the Possibility of Establishing the Right to Privacy*. Springer-Verlag Berlin Heidelberg (2011)

80. 《中国的反垄断法与实践》H. Stephen Harris, Peter J. Wang, Mark A. Cohen, Yizhe Zhang, Sebastien J. Evrard, *Anti-Monopoly Law and Practice in China*. Oxford University Press (2011)

81. 《中国司法：当代中国的民事纠纷解决》Margaret Y. K. Woo, Mary E. Gallagher, *Chinese Justice: Civil Dispute Resolution in Contemporary China*. Cambridge University Press (2011)

82. 《法律、政策与中国周边的实践：选择性适应与制度能力》Pitman B. Potter, *Law, Policy, and Practice on China's Periphery: Selective Adaptation and Institutional Capacity*. Routledge (2011)

83. 《中国环境法：降低风险与确保合规》Charles McElwee, *Environmental Law in China: Mitigating Risk and Ensuring Compliance*. Oxford University Press (2011)

84. 《中国知识产权》Chris Devonshire-Ellis, Andy Scott, Sam Woollard (eds.), *Intellectual Property Rights In China*. Springer-Verlag Berlin Heidelberg (2011)

85. 《中华人民共和国企业所得税法与实务》Fuli Cao, *Corporate Income Tax Law and Practice in the Peoples Republic of China*. Oxford University Press, USA (2011)

86. 《日本、奥斯曼帝国和中国的法律帝国主义主权和治外法权》Kayaoglu Turan, *Legal Imperialism Sovereignty and Extraterritoriality in Japan, the Ottoman Empire, and China*. Cambridge University Press (2010)

87. 《中国内地和中国香港担保金融法》Mark Williams, Haitian Lu, Chin Aun Ong, *Secured Finance Law in China and Hong Kong*. Cambridge University Press (2010)

88. 《了解中国劳动就业法》Ronald C. Brown, *Understanding Labor and Employment Law in China*. Cambridge University Press (2010)

89. 《中国知识产权经济学：专利、贸易与外商直接投资》Johannes Liegsalz, *The Economics of Intellectual Property Rights in China: Patents, Trade, and Foreign Direct Investment*. Gabler Verlag (2010)

90. 《中国宪政建设》Stéphanie Balme, Michael W. Dowdle, *Building Constitutionalism in China*. Palgrave Macmillan (2009)

91. 《18世纪中国的真实犯罪：20个案例》Robert E. Hegel, *True Crimes in Eighteenth-Century China: Twenty Case Histories*. University of Washington Press (2009)
92. 《中国知识产权：盗版、贸易和保护的政治》Gordon C.K Cheung, *Intellectual Property Rights in China: Politics of Piracy, Trade and Protection*. Routledge (2009)
93. 《大赦国际与美国外交政策：危地马拉、美国和中国的人权运动》Maria T Baldwin, *Amnesty International and U.S. Foreign Policy: Human Rights Campaigns in Guatemala, the United States, and China*. LFB Scholarly Pub. (2009)
94. 《盗版与国家：中国知识产权的政治学》Martin Dimitrov, *Piracy and the State: The Politics of Intellectual Property Rights in China*. Cambridge University Press (2009)
95. 《中国司法独立：全球法治推广的教训》Randall Peerenboom, *Judicial Independence in China: Lessons for Global Rule of Law Promotion*. Cambridge University Press (2009)
96. 《中国外商投资法》Vai Io Lo, Xiaowen Tian, *Law for Foreign Business and Investment in China*. Taylor & Francis (2009)
97. 《自杀与正义：中国视角》Fei Wu, *Suicide and Justice: A Chinese Perspective* (Routledge Contemporary China Series). Routledge (2009)
98. 《中国刑事司法史》Klaus Mühlhahn（余凯思）, *Criminal Justice in China: A History*. Harvard University Press (2009)
99. 《中国民事司法之过去与现在》Philip C. C. Huang（黄宗智）, *Chinese Civil Justice, Past and Present* (Asia Pacific Perspectives). Rowman & Littlefield Publishers, Inc. (2009)
100. 《中国法律改革与行政拘留权》Sarah Biddulph, *Legal Reform and Administrative Detention Powers in China*. Cambridge University Press (2008)
101. 《全球贸易体系中的知识产权：欧盟—中国观点》Wei Shi, *Intellectual Property in the Global Trading System: EU-China Perspective*. Springer-Verlag Berlin Heidelberg (2008)
102. 《1978年至今变化中的中国法律体系：权力集中与法律制度的合理化》Bin Liang, *The Changing Chinese Legal System, 1978-Present: Centralization of Power and Rationalization of the Legal System* (East Asia: History, Politics, Sociology, Culture). Routledge (2008)
103. 《大中华区的跨境犯罪政治：中国大陆、香港、澳门案例研究》Sonny Shiu-hing Lo, *The Politics of Cross-Border Crime in Greater China: Case Studies of Mainland China, Hong Kong, and Macao* (Hong Kong Becoming China). M. E. Sharpe (2008)
104. 《违法：中国衰退地区和阳光地带的劳工抗议》Ching Kwan Lee, *Against the Law: Labor Protests in China's Rustbelt and Sunbelt*. University of California Press (2007)
105. 《中国死刑：历史、法律和当代实践》Hong Lu and Terance D. Miethe, *China's Death Penalty-History, Law, and Contemporary Practices*. Routledge (2007)
106. 《中国知识产权与TRIPS合规：中欧视角》Paul Torremans, Hailing Shan, Johan Erauw, *Intellectual Property and TRIPS Compliance in China: Chinese and European Perspectives* (New Horizons in Intellectual Property). Edward Elgar Pub (2007)

107. 《作为中华帝国晚期世界秩序的国际法》R. Svarverud, *International Law as World Order in Late Imperial China* (Sinica Leidensia). Brill (2007)

108. 《中国法律的经济分析》Thomas Eger, Michael Faure, Zhang Naigen, *Economic Analysis of Law in China*. Edward Elgar Publishing Limited (2007)

109. 《中华帝国晚期的写作与法律：犯罪、冲突与判决》Robert E. Hegel, Katherine Carlitz, *Writing and Law in Late Imperial China: Crime, Conflict, and Judgment* (Asian Law Series). University of Washington Press (2007)

110. 《中国法律改革：走向法治》Zou Keyuan, Keyuan Zou, *China's Legal Reform: Towards the Rule of Law*. Martinus Nijhoff (2006)

111. 《中国土地与污染管理：立法、守法和执法；理论与案例》Benjamin, van Rooij, *Regulating Land and Pollution in China: Lawmaking, Compliance and Enforcement; Theory and Cases*. Leiden University Press (2006)

112. 《海洋法与中国近期发展》Myron H. Nordquist, John Norton Moore, Kuen-chen Fu, *Recent Developments in the Law of the Sea and China* (Center for Oceans Law and Policy). Martinus Nijhoff Publishers (2006)

113. 《中国法院延期执法：民事诉讼和经济视角》Qing-Yun Jiang, *Court Delay and Law Enforcement in China: Civil Process and Economic Perspective*. Deutscher Universitats-Verlag (2006)

114. 《中国新的犯罪：公共秩序与人权》Ron Keith, *New Crime in China: Public Order and Human Rights* (Routledgecurzon Contemporary China Series). Routledge (2006)

115. 《中国国际贸易法规：法律与政策》Zhang Xin, *International Trade Regulation in China: Law And Policy*. Hart Publishing (UK) (2006)

116. 《中国、香港和台湾地区的竞争政策与法律》Mark Williams, *Competition Policy and Law in China, Hong Kong and Taiwan*. Cambridge University Press (2005)

117. 《中国法律与投资：中国入世后的法律和商业环境》Vai Io Lo, *Law and Investment in China: The Legal and Business Environments after China's WTO Accession*. Routledge Curzon (2005)

118. 《中欧投资关系法律框架：批判性评估中国与国际经济法》Wenhua Shan, *The Legal Framework of Eu-China Investment Relations: A Critical Appraisal China and International Economic Law*. Hart Publishing (2005)

119. 《中国的海洋法律体系和海洋法》Zou Keyuan, *China's Marine Legal System and the Law of the Sea* (Publications on Ocean Development). Brill Academic Publishers (2005)

120. 《中国法律的语言视角》Deborah Cao, *Chinese Law: A Language Perspective*. Routledge (2004)

121. 《近代中国早期的契约与财产》Madeleine Zelin（曾小萍）, Jonathan K. Ocko, Robert Gardella, *Contract and Property in Early Modern China*. Stanford University Press (2004)

122. 《理解中国的法律制度：孔杰荣教授纪念论文集》C. Stephen Hsu, *Understanding China's Legal System: Essays in Honor of Jerome A. Cohen*. New York University Press (2003)

123. 《中国走向法治的长征》Randall Peerenboom, *China's Long March toward Rule of Law*. Cambridge University Press (2002)

124. 《中国海商法与政策》KX Li and CWM Ingram, *Maritime Law and Policy in China*. Cavendish Publishing Limited (2002)

125. 《中国关于隐私的概念》Bonnie S. McDougall, Anders Hansson, *Chinese Concepts of Privacy*. Brill (2002)

126. 《中国法制：全球化与地方法律文化》Pitman B. Potter, *The Chinese Legal System: Globalization and Local Legal Culture*. Routledge (2001)

127. 《中国变动中的犯罪与社会控制》Jianhong Liu, Lening Zhang, Steven F. Messner, *Crime and Social Control in a Changing China*. Praeger (2001)

128. 《中国新市场上的法律与正义》Ronald C. Keith, Zhiqiu Lin, *Law and Justice in China's New Marketplace*. Palgrave Macmillan UK (2001)

129. 《过失杀人、市场与道德经济：十八世纪中国财产权的暴力纠纷》Thomas M. Buoye（步德茂）, *Manslaughter, Markets, and Moral Economy: Violent Disputes over Property Rights in Eighteenth-Century China*. Cambridge University Press (2000)

130. 《宋本名公书判清明集》Brian E. McKnight（马伯良）, James T. C. Liu, *The Enlightened Judgments: Ching-Ming Chi. The Sung Dynasty Collection* (SUNY Series in Chinese Philosophy and Culture). State University of New York Press (1999)

131. 《窃书是一种优雅的罪行：中国文明中的知识产权法》William P. Alford（安守廉）, *To Steal a Book Is an Elegant Offense: Intellectual Property Law in Chinese Civilization*. Stanford University Press (1997)

132. 《法律传统与传统法律：中国法律、国家和社会控制》Xin Ren, *Tradition of the Law and Law of the Tradition: Law, State, and Social Control in China* (Contributions in Criminology and Penology). Greenwood Press (1997)

133. 《中国法家：早期极权主义者》Zhengyuan Fu, *China's Legalists: The Early Totalitarians* (New Studies in Asian Culture). Routledge (1996)

134. 《宋朝的法律与秩序》Brian E. McKnight（马伯良）, *Law and Order in Sung China*. Cambridge University Press (1992)

135. 《东海海床划界之法律问题》Ying-jeou Ma（马英九）, *Legal Problems of Seabed Boundary Delimitation in the East China Sea* (Maryland studies in East Asian law and politics series). Baltimore: Occasional Papers/Reprints Series in Contemporary Asian Studies, Inc. (1984)

136. 《当代中国法律：研究问题与前景》Jerome Alan Cohen, *Contemporary Chinese Law: Research Problems and Perspectives*. Harvard University Press (1970)

137.《中华人民共和国刑事诉讼程序导论（1949—1963）》Jerome Alan Cohen, *The Criminal Process in the People's Republic of China, 1949—1963: An Introduction*. Harvard University Press (1968)

138.《中华帝国的法律》(Harvard Studies in East Asian Law 1) Derk Bodde（卜德）, Clarence Morris, *Law in Imperial China: Exemplified by 190 Ch'ing Dynasty Cases (Translated from the Hsing-an hui-lan), With Historical, Social, and Juridical Commentaries*.Harvard University Press (1967, 2014)

139.《满州国的法律制度》Sybille van der Sprenkel, *Legal Institutions in Manchu China: A Sociological Analysis*. The Athlone Press, London (1962)

140.《美国法院在中国》Charles Sumner Lobingier（罗炳吉）, *American Courts in China*. Bar Association Publications (1919)

141.《中国刑罚》George Henry Mason, *The Punishments of China*. London: William Miller (1801)

9.2 军事与战争

9.2.1 抗日战争

1.《打倒汉奸：战时中国的正义与民族主义》Yun Xia, *Down with Traitors: Justice and Nationalism in Wartime China*. University of Washington Press (2018)

2.《中国士兵对日本士兵：1937—1938年的中国》Benjamin Lai, Johnny Shumate, *Chinese Soldier vs Japanese Soldier: China 1937—38*. Osprey Publishing (2018)

3.《战时中国国际医疗救援队（1937—1945）》Robert Mamlok, *The International Medical Relief Corps in Wartime China, 1937—1945*. McFarland & Company (2018)

4.《飞往中国的数架飞机：飞虎队的诞生》Eugenie Buchan, *A Few Planes for China: The Birth of the Flying Tigers*. ForeEdge (2017)

5.《从人到鬼，从鬼到人：日本战犯与中国的审判》Barak Kushner（顾若鹏）, *Men to Devils, Devils to Men: Japanese War Crimes and Chinese Justice*.Harvard University Press (2015)

6.《中国的战地记者：抗日战争的遗产》Parks M. Coble, *China's War Reporters: The Legacy of Resistance against Japan*. Harvard University Press (2015)

7.《抗日战争和太平洋战争时期的日本慰安妇与性奴》Caroline Norma, *The Japanese Comfort Women and Sexual Slavery during the China and Pacific Wars*. Bloomsbury Academic (2015)

8.《中国慰安妇：日本帝国的性奴证言》Peipei Qiu, Su Zhiliang, Chen Lifei, *Chinese Comfort Women: Testimonies from Imperial Japan's Sex Slaves*. Oxford University Press (2014)

9.《繁荣的困境：战时中国农村的认同、改革与阻力》Isabel Brown Crook, *Prosperity's Predicament: Identity, Reform, and Resistance in Rural Wartime China*. Rowman & Littlefield (2013)

10.《被遗忘的盟友：中国的二战（1937—1945）》Rana Mitter（米德）, *Forgotten Ally: China's World War II, 1937—1945*. Houghton Mifflin Harcourt (2013)

11. 《中国的抗日战争：为生存而战》Rana Mitter（米德），*China's War with Japan, 1937—1945: The Struggle for Survival*. Allen Lane (2013)
12. 《中国的翅膀：中国飞行黄金时期的战争、阴谋、爱情和冒险》Gregory Crouch, *China's Wings: War, Intrigue, Romance, and Adventure in the Middle Kingdom during the Golden Age of Flight*. Random House Publishing Group: Bantam Books (2012)
13. 《华南的帝国冲突：盟国与日本的代理战争（1935—1941）》Franco David Macri, *Clash of Empires in South China: The Allied Nations' Proxy War with Japan, 1935—1941* (Modern war studies). University Press of Kansas (2012)
14. 《战后满洲被遗弃的日本人：两国战争孤儿和遗孀的生活》Yeeshan Chan, *Abandoned Japanese in Postwar Manchuria: The Lives of War Orphans and Wives in Two Countries*. Routledge (2011)
15. 《战争中的中国人民：人类苦难与社会转型（1937—1945）》Diana Lary（戴安娜·拉里）, *The Chinese People at War: Human Suffering and Social Transformation, 1937—1945*. Cambridge University Press (2010)
16. 《日本战争孤儿在满洲：被遗忘的二战受害者》Mayumi Itoh, *Japanese War Orphans in Manchuria: Forgotten Victims of World War II*. Palgrave Macmillan (2010)
17. 《日本战时医疗暴行：科学、历史与伦理的比较研究》Jing Bao Nie, Nanyan Guo, Mark Selden（赛尔登）, Arthur Kleinman, *Japan's Wartime Medical Atrocities: Comparative Inquiries in Science, History, and Ethics* (Asia's Transformations). Routledge (2010)
18. 《满铁与中国开放：国际史》Bruce A. Elleman, Stephen Kotkin, *Manchurian Railways and the Opening of China: An International History*. M. E. Sharpe (2009)
19. 《P-40战鹰对Ki-43奥斯卡：中国（1944—45）》(Duel 8) Carl Molesworth, *P-40 Warhawk vs Ki-43 Oscar: China 1944—45*. Osprey Publishing (2008)
20. 《战争中的农村中国：抗日战争的影响（1937—1945）》Dagfinn Gatu, *Village China at War: The Impact of Resistance to Japan, 1937—1945* (NIAS Monographs). NIAS Press (2006)
21. 《通敌：战时中国的日本代理与地方精英》Timothy Brook（卜正民）, *Collaboration: Japanese Agents and Local Elites in Wartime China*. Harvard University Press (2005)
22. 《旭日之光：日本的亚洲盟军武装（1931—1945）。第一卷：中国与满洲》Philip S. Jowett, *Rays of the Rising Sun: Armed Forces of Japan's Asian Allies 1931—1945, Vol.1 China and Manchukou*. Helion & Company (2004)
23. 《日本新秩序下的中国资本家：被占领的长江下游（1937—1945）》Parks M. Coble, *Chinese Capitalists in Japan's New Order: The Occupied Lower Yangzi, 1937—1945*. University of California Press (2003)
24. 《满洲危机与日本社会（1931—1933）》Sandra Wilson, *The Manchurian Crisis and Japanese Society, 1931—33*. Routledge (2001)
25. 《中国天空的老虎：飞虎队之飞机》Thomas A. Tullis, *Tigers over China. The Aircraft of*

the A.V.G. Eagle Editions Ltd (2001)

26. 《中国—缅甸—印度战役（1931—1945）：史学和注释书目》Eugene L. Rasor, *The China-Burma-India Campaign, 1931—1945: Historiography and Annotated Bibliography*. Greenwood (1998)

27. 《一位在华敌后海空军情报官员》Byron R. Winborn, *Wen Bon: A Naval Air Intelligence Officer Behind Japanese Lines in China*. University of North Texas Press (1994)

28. 《战争与大众文化：现代中国的抵抗（1937—1945）》Chang-tai Hung, *War and Popular Culture: Resistance in Modern China, 1937—1945*. University of California Press (1994)

29. 《美国、中国、日本论战时亚洲（1931—1949）》Akira Iriye, Warren I. Cohen（孔华润）, *American, Chinese, and Japanese Perspectives on Wartime Asia, 1931—1949*. SR Books (1990)

30. 《中国的反抗与革命：共产党人与第二统一战线》Tetsuya Kataoka, *Resistance and Revolution in China: The Communists and the Second United Front*. University of California Press (1974)

31. 《和平的阴谋：汪精卫与中国战争（1937—1941）》Gerald E. Bunker, *The Peace Conspiracy: Wang Ching-wei and the China War, 1937—1941*. Harvard University Press (1972)

32. 《亚洲陆战：盟军在中国和缅甸的胜利》Trevor Nevitt Dupuy, *Asiatic Land Battles: Allied Victories in China and Burma*. Franklin Watts (1963)

33. 《中国与援手（1937—1945）》Arthur N. Young, *China and the Helping Hand, 1937—1945*. Harvard University Press (1963)

34. 《我为中国人说话》Crow Carl, *I Speak for The Chinese*. Hamish Hamilton (1938)

35. 《中国为世界而战》J. Gunnar Anderson, *China Fights for the World*. Kegan Paul, Trench & Co. Ltd (1938)

36. 《中国在反击》Agnes Smedley（史沫特莱）, *China Fights Back*. Victor Gollancz Ltd. (1938)

9.2.2 南京大屠杀

1. 《南京暴行：二战中被遗忘的大屠杀》Iris Chang（张纯如）, *The Rape of Nanking: The Forgotten Holocaust of World War II*. Basic Books (2012)

2. 《无畏的南京女性：战时日记》Edited and translated by Hua-ling Hu, Zhang Lian-hong, *The Undaunted Women of Nanking: The Wartime Diaries of Minnie Vautrin and Tsen Shui-fang*. Southern Illinois University Press (2010)

3. 《"南京暴行"的形成：日本、中国和美国的历史与记忆》Takashi Yoshida, *The Making of the "Rape of Nanking": History and Memory in Japan, China, and the United States*. Oxford University Press (2006)

4. 《他们在南京：美英国民见证南美大屠杀》Suping Lu, *They Were in Nanjing: The Nanjing Massacre Witnessed by American and British Nationals*. Hong Kong University Press (2004)

5. 《南京1937：记忆和愈合》Feifei Li, Robert Sabella, David Liu (eds.), Perry Link（林培瑞）(foreword), *Nanking 1937: Memory and Healing* (Studies of the East Asian Institute). M. E. Sharpe Inc. (2001)

6. 《历史编纂中的南京大屠杀》Joshua A. Fogel（傅佛果）, *The Nanjing Massacre in History*

and Historiography. University of California Press (2000)

7. 《目睹屠杀：美国传教士在南京见证日本暴行》Kai-Yuan Chang（章开沅）, Eyewitnesses to Massacre: American Missionaries Bear Witness to Japanese Atrocities in Nanjing. M. E. Sharpe Inc. (2000)

8. 《关于南京大屠杀的文件》Timothy Brook（卜正民）, Documents on the Rape of Nanking. University of Michigan Press (1999)

9. 《美国传教士对南京大屠杀的目击证人（1937—1938）》Martha Lund Smalley (ed.), American Missionary Eyewitnesses to the Nanking Massacre, 1937—1938. New Haven, Conn.: Yale Divinity School Library Occasional Publication No. 9 (1997)

9.2.3 朝鲜战争

1. 《中国的朝鲜战争：战略文化与地缘政治》 (New Directions in East Asian History) Xiaobing Li, China's War in Korea: Strategic Culture and Geopolitics. Springer Singapore: Palgrave Macmillan (2019)

2. 《我们为和平而战：朝鲜战争中的23名美国士兵、战俘和叛徒》Brian D. McKnight, We Fight For Peace: Twenty-three American Soldiers, Prisoners of War and Turncoats in the Korean War The Kent State University Press (2014)

3. 《剑桥冷战史：朝鲜战争之僵持岁月》Melvyn P. Leffler, Odd Arne Westad（文安立）, The Cambridge History of the Cold War. Cambridge University Press (2010)

4. 《朝鲜战争历史词典》（第二版）Paul M. Edwards, Historical Dictionary of Korean War (2nd ed.). Scarecrow Press (2010)

5. 《朝鲜战争史》Bruce Cumings, The Korean War: A History (Modern Library Chronicles). Modern Library (2010)

6. 《韩战实录：1951年1月至2月》William T. Bowers, The Line Combat in Korea, January-February 1951. The University Press of Kentucky (2008)

7. 《最寒冷的冬天：美国人眼中的朝鲜战争》David Halberstam, Coldest Winter American and Korean War. Hyperion Books (2007)

8. 《鸭绿江上空的红翼：中国、苏联与韩战中的空中战斗》Xiaoming Zhang, Red wings over the Yalu: China, the Soviet Union, and the air war in Korea. Texas A & M University Press (2002)

9. 《奇人出局：杜鲁门、斯大林、毛泽东与朝鲜战争的起源》Richard C Thornton, Odd Man Out: Truman, Stalin, Mao, and the Origins of the Korean War. Potomac Books (2001)

10. 《中国的朝鲜战争之路：中美对抗的形成》Jian Chen（陈兼）, China's Road to the Korean War: The making of the Sino-American confrontation. Columbia University Press (1996)

11. 《朝鲜战争国际史》William Stueck, The Korean War: An International History. Princeton University Press (1995)

12. 《不确定的伙伴：斯大林、毛泽东和朝鲜战争》Sergi N. Goncharov, John W. Lewis and Xue Lital, Uncertain Partners: Stalin, Mao, and the Korean War. Stanford University Press (1993)

13. 《韩国的灾难：中国人对抗麦克阿瑟》(Williams-Ford Texas A&M University Military History Series) Roy E. Appleman, *Disaster in Korea: The Chinese Confront MacArthur*. Texas A&M University Press (1989)

9.2.4 冷战

1. 《密码战的开端：美国对抗俄国、中国以及全球网络威胁的兴起》John P. Carlin, Garrett M. Graff, *Dawn of the Code War: America's Battle Against Russia, China, and the Rising Global Cyber Threat*. PublicAffairs (2018)
2. 《冷战世界史》Odd Arne Westad（文安立）, *The Cold War: A World History*. Basic Books (2017)
3. 《文化宣传与全球冷战：文化自由联盟主办的期刊》Giles Scott-Smith, Charlotte A. Lerg (eds.), *Campaigning Culture and the Global Cold War: The Journals of the Congress for Cultural Freedom*. Palgrave Macmillan UK (2017)
4. 《东亚冷战》Xiaobing Li, *The Cold War in East Asia*. Routledge (2017)
5. 《冷战初期的中情局和文化自由联盟：奇怪的伙伴》Sarah Miller Harris, *The CIA and the Congress for Cultural Freedom in the Early Cold War: Strange Bedfellows*. Routledge (2016)
6. 《冷战现代主义者：1946至1959年的艺术、文学和美国文化外交》Greg Barnhisel, *Cold War modernists: Art, Literature, And American Cultural Diplomacy, 1946—1959*. Columbia University Press (2015)
7. 《回到冬季：俄罗斯、中国与对美国的新冷战》Douglas E. Schoen, Melik Kaylan, *Return to Winter: Russia, China, and the New Cold War against America*. Encounter Books (2015)
8. 《影子冷战：中苏争夺第三世界》(The New Cold War History) Jeremy Friedman, *Shadow Cold War: The Sino-Soviet Competition for the Third World*. The University of North Carolina Press (2015)
9. 《不受欢迎的远见者：冷战结束时苏联在亚洲的失败》(Oxford Studies in International History) Sergey Radchenko, *Unwanted Visionaries: The Soviet Failure in Asia at the End of the Cold War*. Oxford University Press (2014)
10. 《美国国会、中国和冷战：国内政治、中美和解和正常化（1969—1980）》（博士论文）Paul Coyer, *Congress, China and the Cold War: Domestic Politics and Sino-American Rapprochement and Normalisation, 1969—1980*. Ph. D. Dissertation, The London School of Economics and Political Science (2013)
11. 《文化冷战：中情局与文艺世界》(1999版重印，新增说明) Frances Stonor Saunders, *The Cultural Cold War: The CIA and the World of Arts and Letters*. The New Press (2013)
12. 《去中心的冷战史：局部和全球变化》Jadwiga E. Pieper Mooney, Fabio Lanza, *De-Centering Cold War History: Local and Global Change*. Routledge (2013)
13. 《冷战转折点：尼克松与中国（1969—1972）》Chris Tudda, *A Cold War Turning Point: Nixon and China, 1969—1972*. Louisiana State University Press (2012)
14. 《分裂的梦幻世界：东西方文化冷战》Giles Scott-Smith, *Divided Dreamworlds: The*

Cultural Cold War in East and West (Studies of the Netherlands Institute for War Documentation). Amsterdam University Press (2012)

15. 《中苏分裂、"第三世界"与左派的命运》（博士论文）Jeremy Scott Friedman, *The Sino-Soviet Split, The "Third World," and the Fate of the Left*. Ph. D. Dissertation, Princeton University (2011)

16. 《冷战终结与第三世界：区域冲突新视角》(Cold War History) Artemy Kalinovsky, Sergey Radchenko, *The End of the Cold War and The Third World: New Perspectives on Regional Conflict* (Cold War History). Routledge (2011)

17. 《在冷战前沿：从中国内战到古巴导弹危机和越南的美国通讯杂志》Seymour Topping, *On the Front Lines of the Cold War: An American Correspondents Journal from the Chinese Civil War to the Cuban Missile Crisis and Vietnam*. Louisiana State University Press (2010)

18. 《使冷战相形见绌：美国的意见分歧与文化外交（1940—1960）》Andrew J. Falk, *Upstaging the Cold War: American Dissent and Cultural Diplomacy, 1940—1960* (Culture, Politics, and the Cold War).University of Massachusetts Press (2010)

19. 《剑桥冷战史：结束》（第三卷）Melvyn P. Leffler, Odd Arne Westad（文安立）, *The Cambridge History of the Cold War: Volume 3, Endings*. Cambridge University Press (2010)

20. 《剑桥冷战史：危机与缓和》（第二卷）Melvyn P. Leffler, Odd Arne Westad（文安立）, *The Cambridge History of the Cold War: Volume 2, Crises and Detente*. Cambridge University Press (2010)

21. 《剑桥冷战史：起源》（第一卷）Melvyn P. Leffler, Odd Arne Westad（文安立）, *The Cambridge History of the Cold War: Volume 1, Origins*. Cambridge University Press (2010)

22. 《中苏分裂：共产主义世界的冷战》Lorenz M. Lüthi, *The Sino-Soviet Split: Cold War in the Communist World*. Princeton University Press (2008)

23. 《原子弹与冷战的起源》Campbell Craig, Sergey S Radchenko, *The Atomic Bomb and the Origins of the Cold War*. Yale University Press (2008)

24. 《他们让你做什么：满洲候选人与冷战时期美国》Matthew Frye Jacobson, Gaspar Gonzalez, *What Have They Built You to Do: The Manchurian Candidate and Cold War America*. Univ. of Minnesota Press (2006)

25. 《与敌人谈判：冷战期间美—中会谈（1949—1972）》Yafeng Xia, *Negotiating with the Enemy: U.S.-China Talks during the Cold War, 1949—1972*. Indiana University Press (2006)

26. 《美国和中国的冷战合作（1971—1989）》S. Mahmud Ali, *US-China Cold War Collaboration: 1971—1989*. Routledge (2005)

27. 《跨越阵营：探索比较冷战时期的文化和社会历史》Rana Mitter, Patrick Major (eds.), *Across the Blocs: Exploring Comparative Cold War Cultural and Social History* (Cold War History). Frank Cass and Company Limited (2004)

28. 《中情局、英国左派和冷战：呼唤主旋律》Hugh Wilford, *The CIA, the British Left and*

the Cold War: Calling the Tune. Routledge (2003)

29. 《未来的普通话：冷战时期美国的现代化理论》Nils Gilman, *Mandarins of the Future: Modernization Theory in Cold War America* (New Studies in American Intellectual and Cultural History). The Johns Hopkins University Press (2003)

30. 《文化交流与冷战：揭开铁幕》Yale Richmond, *Cultural Exchange & The Cold War: Raising The Iron Curtain*. Penn State University Press (2003)

31. 《非政治化的文化政治：文化自由联盟、中情局与战后美国霸权》Gil Scott-Smith, *The Politics of Apolitical Culture: The Congress for Cultural Freedom, the CIA & Post-War American Hegemony* (Routledge Psa Political Studies Series, 2). Routledge (2001)

32. 《经济冷战：美国、英国与东西方贸易（1948—1963）》(Cold War History) Ian Jackson, *The Economic Cold War: America, Britain and East-West Trade, 1948—1963*. Palgrave Macmillan (2001)

33. 《引领自由世界：美国民族主义与冷战的文化根源》John Fousek, *To Lead the Free World: American Nationalism and the Cultural Roots of the Cold War*. University of North Carolina Press (2000)

34. 《文化冷战：中情局与文艺世界》Frances Stonor Saunders, *The Cultural Cold War: The CIA and the World of Arts and Letters*. The New Press (1999)

35. 《舞蹈输出：文化外交与冷战》Naima Prevots, *Dance for Export: Cultural Diplomacy and the Cold War*. Wesleyan University Press (1998)

36. 《绘图本冷战史（1945—1991）》Jeremy Isaacs, Taylor Downing, *Cold War: An Illustrated History, 1945—1991*. Little, Brown and Company (1998)

37. 《中国情报部门》Nicholas Eftimiades, *Chinese Intelligence Operations*. Espionage Damage Assessment Branch, US Defence Intelligence Agency（美国国防情报局间谍伤害评估处）. Frank Cass & Co. Ltd (1994)

38. 《搜索"满洲候选人"：中情局与精神控制：行为科学秘史》John D. Marks, *The Search for the: "Manchurian Candidate": The CIA and Mind Control: The Secret History of the Behavioral Sciences*. W. W. Norton & Company (1991)

39. 《纽约知识分子：20世纪30年代至80年代反斯大林主义者左派的兴衰》Alan M. Wald, *The New York Intellectuals: The Rise and Decline of the Anti-Stalinist Left from the 1930s to the 1980s*. The University of North Carolina Press (1987)

40. 《肮脏的工作2：中情局在非洲》Ellen Ray, *Dirty work 2: The CIA in Africa*. Zed Press (1980)

41. 《情报服务的起源：古代近东、波斯、希腊、罗马、拜占庭、阿拉伯穆斯林帝国、蒙古帝国、中国、莫斯科》Francis Dvornik, *Origins of Intelligence Services: The Ancient Near East, Persia, Greece, Rome, Byzantium, the Arab Muslim Empires, the Mongol Empire, China, Muscovy*. Rutgers University Press (1974)

9.2.5 鸦片战争

1. 《帝国暮光：鸦片战争与中国最后黄金时代的终结》Stephen R. Platt（裴士锋）, *Imperial Twilight: The Opium War and the End of China's Last Golden Age*. Knopf (2018)
2. 《关于鸦片的真相：驳斥反对鸦片社会的谬误，为印度—中国鸦片贸易辩护》William H.Brereton, *The Truth about Opium: Being a Refutation of the Fallacies of the Anti-Opium Society and a Defence of the Indo-China Opium Trade*.The Floating Press (2014)
3. 《鸦片战争：毒品、梦想和中国的塑造》Julia Lovell（蓝诗玲）, *The Opium War: Drugs, Dreams and the Making of China*. Picador USA (2011)
4. 《第一次鸦片战争：1839—1842年英中战争》Peter C. Perdue（濮德培）, *The First Opium War: The Anglo-Chinese War of 1839—1842*. Visualizing Cultures at the Massachusetts Institute of Technology (2010)
5. 《毒害一个国家：中国和鸦片诅咒的故事》Samuel Merwin, *Drugging a Nation: The Story of China and the Opium Curse*. Forgotten Books (2010)
6. 《19世纪美国西部的鸦片论争与排华法》Diana L. Ahmad, *The Opium Debate And Chinese Exclusion Laws In The Nineteenth-Century American West*. University of Nevada Press (2007)
7. 《民国时期的中国人与鸦片：坏于洪水猛兽》Alan Baumler, *The Chinese and Opium Under the Republic: Worse Than Floods and Wild Beasts*. State University of New York Press (2007)
8. 《致命之梦：鸦片、帝国主义与中国鸦片战争（1856—1860）》J. Y. Wong, *Deadly Dreams: Opium, Imperialism and the Arrow War (1856—1860) in China* (Cambridge Studies in Chinese History, Literature and Institutions). Cambridge University Press (1998)
9. 《鸦片战争（1840–1842）：19世纪早期野蛮人在天朝上国以及通过战争强迫他们打开大门》Peter Ward Fay, *The Opium War, 1840–1842: Barbarians in the Celestial Empire in the Early Part of the Nineteenth Century and the War by Which They Forced Her Gates Ajar*. The University of North Carolina Press (1975)
10. 《中国人眼中的鸦片战争》Arthur Waley（阿瑟·韦利）, *The Opium War through Chinese Eyes* (China: History, Philosophy, Economics).George Allen and Unwin (1958)；Routledge (2005)
11. 《中国人鸦片战争记述》Edward H. Parker, *Chinese Account of the Opium War*. Shanghai Kelly & Walsh, ltd. (1888)
12. 《中国：一篇出自"天"的修订版文章，附前言及补充》（为鸦片战争辩护）Thomas De Quincey（昆西）, *China: A Revised Reprint of Articles From "Titan", With Preface and Additions*. Edinburgh: James Hogg (1857)
13. 《中国与中国人：他们的宗教、性格、习俗与制造业；鸦片贸易所带来的罪恶；我们的宗教、道德、政治以及与该国商业往来之浏览。》（第一卷；第二卷）Henry Charles Sirr, *China and the Chinese: Their Religion, Character, Customs, and Manufactures:*

the Evils Arising from the Opium Trade: with a Glance at Our Religious, Moral, Political, and Commercial Intercouse with the Country (Reprint Series-Chinese Materials Center, no. 80) Chinese Materials Center, vol. 1; vol. 2 (1849, 1978)

14.《中国战争：从1840年4月中国远征军组建到1842年8月和平条约签订的记述》Duncan Mcpherson, *The War in China: Narrative of the Chinese Expedition from its formation in April, 1840, to the treaty of peace in August, 1842.* London: Saunders and Otley (1843)

9.2.6 中外战争

1.《丛林中的龙：越南战争中的中国军队》Xiaobing Li, *The Dragon in the Jungle: The Chinese Army in the Vietnam War.* Oxford University Press (2020)

2.《中国铁甲舰vs日本巡洋舰：鸭绿江1894》(Duel Ser.) Alan Gilliland, Benjamin Lai, Paul Wright, *Chinese Ironclad Battleship vs Japanese Protected Cruiser: Yalu River 1894.* Osprey (2019)

3.《暗战：俄罗斯和中国击败美国的秘密行动》Jim Sciutto, *The Shadow War: Inside Russia's and China's Secret Operations to Defeat America.* HarperCollins (2019)

4.《约翰·哈特·考伊上校书信日记（1944—1945）：与魏德迈在二战时的中国》Roger B. Jeans (ed.), *Letters and Diaries of Colonel John Hart Caughey, 1944—1945: With Wedemeyer in World War II China.* Lexington Books (2018)

5.《中国海防：明朝将军戚继光及其后》Y.H. Teddy Sim (eds.), *The Maritime Defence of China: Ming General Qi Jiguang and Beyond.* Springer Singapore (2017)

6.《亚洲与一战：共同的历史》(The greater war) Xu, Guoqi（徐国琦）, *Asia and the Great War: A Shared History.* Oxford University Press (2017)

7.《中国历史上的决战》Morgan Deane, *Decisive Battles in Chinese History.* Westholme Publishing (2017)

8.《背叛的盟友：中国在大战中》Christopher Arnander, Frances Wood, *Betrayed Ally: China in the Great War.* Pen & Sword Military (2016)

9.《邓小平的漫长战争：1979—1991年中越军事冲突》Xiaoming Zhang, *Deng Xiaoping's Long War: The Military Conflict between China and Vietnam, 1979—1991* (New Cold War history). The University of North Carolina Press (2015)

10.《1937年的南京：一个注定失败的城市的战斗》Peter Harmsen（何铭生）, *Nanjing 1937: Battle for a Doomed City.* Casemate Publishers (2015)

11.《下一场大战：第一次世界大战的根源与美中冲突的风险》Richard N. Rosecrance, Steven E. Miller, *The Next Great War: The Roots of World War I and the Risk of U.S.-China Conflict* (Belfer Center Studies in International Security). MIT Press (2014)

12.《壬辰战争：日本16世纪入侵韩国并企图征服中国》Samuel Hawley, *The Imjin War: Japans Sixteenth-Century Invasion of Korea and Attempt to Conquer China.* Conquistador Press (2014)

13. 《卫天：中国的蒙古战争（1209—1370）》James Waterson, *Defending Heaven: China's Mongol Wars, 1209—1370*. Frontline Books (2014)
14. 《1937年的上海：长江上的伏尔加格勒》Peter Harmsen（何铭生）, *Shanghai 1937: Stalingrad on the Yangtze*. Casemate Publishers (2013)
15. 《亚洲未知的起义（第二卷）：1947—2009年菲律宾、缅甸、中国西藏、中国大陆、中国台湾、孟加拉国、尼泊尔、泰国和印度尼西亚的人民力量》George Katsiaficas, *Asia's Unknown Uprisings Volume 2: People Power in the Philippines, Burma, Tibet, China, Taiwan, Bangladesh, Nepal, Thailand, and Indonesia, 1947—2009*. PM Press (2013)
16. 《美国战利品：华盛顿"愤世嫉俗的态度"如何使美国战俘向北朝鲜、中国和俄罗斯投降》Mark Sauter, John Zimmerlee, Sydney Schanberg, *American Trophies: How US POWs Were Surrendered to North Korea, China, and Russia by Washington's "Cynical Attitude"*. CreateSpace Independent Publishing Platform (2013)
17. 《凉战：全球竞争的未来》Noah Feldman, *Cool War: The Future of Global Competition*. Random House (2013)
18. 《长征的幸存者：五年战俘生涯（1940—1945）》Dee La Vardera, Charles Waite, *Survivor of the Long March: Five Years as a POW 1940—1945*. The History Press (2012)
19. 《西线上的陌生人：华工与一战》Guoqi Xu（徐国琦）, *Strangers on the Western Front: Chinese Workers in the Great War*. Harvard University Press (2011)
20. 《秘密军队：蒋介石和金三角的毒品军阀》Richard Michael Gibson, Wen H. Chen, *The Secret Army: Chiang Kai-shek and the Drug Warlords of the Golden Triangle*. Wiley (2011)
21. 《失落的殖民地：中国对西方的第一次伟大胜利》（中译本：《1661，决战热兰遮：中国对西方的第一次胜利》）Tonio Andrade（欧阳泰）, *Lost Colony: The Untold Story of China's First Great Victory over the West*. Princeton University Press (2011)
22. 《龙头蛇尾：明代中国与第一次大东亚战争（1592—1593）》Kenneth M. Swope, *A Dragon's Head and a Serpent's Tail: Ming China and the First Great East Asian War, 1592–1598*. University of Oklahoma Press (2009)
23. 《亚洲军事革命：从火药到炸弹》Peter A. Lorge, *The Asian Military Revolution: From Gunpowder to the Bomb* (New Approaches to Asian History). Cambridge University Press (2008)
24. 《被遗忘的战争：英国亚洲帝国的终结》Christopher Alan Bayly, *Forgotten Wars: The End of Britain's Asian Empire*. Penguin Group (CA) (2008)
25. 《战时亚洲平民的日常生活：从太平天国起义到越南战争》Stewart Lone, *Daily Lives of Civilians in Wartime Asia: From the Taiping Rebellion to the Vietnam War* (The Greenwood Press Daily Life Through History Series: Daily Lives of Civilians during Wartime). Greenwood Press (2007)
26. 《战争和国家恐怖主义：漫长20世纪中的美国、日本和亚太地区》Mark Selden（赛尔登），Alvin Y. So, *War and State Terrorism: The United States, Japan, and the Asia-Pacific in the Long Twentieth Century* (War and Peace Library). Rowman & Littlefield Publishers (2003)

27. 《英国与越南战争的起源：英国在印度支那的政策，1943—1950年》Timothy Smith, *Britain and the Origin of the Vietnam War: UK Policy in Indo-China, 1943—50*. Palgrave Macmillan (2007)

28. 《Avia BH-33：捷克斯洛伐克、波兰、比利时、南斯拉夫、希腊、西班牙、日本和中国的战斗机》Jiri Vrany, *Avia BH-33: Fighter in Czechoslovakia, Poland, Belgium, Yugoslavia, Greece, Spain, Japan and China*. Jakab (2006)

29. 《想象中的敌人：中国为不确定的战争做准备》John Wilson Lewis, Xue Litai, *Imagined Enemies: China Prepares for Uncertain War*. Stanford University Press (2006)

30. 《山姆大叔的小战争：美西战争、菲律宾暴动和义和团叛乱（1898—1902）》(G.I. Series 15) John Langellier, *Uncle Sam's Little Wars: The Spanish-American War, Philippine Insurrection, and Boxer Rebellion, 1898—1902*. Greenhill (2006)

31. 《早期近代中国的战争、政治与社会（900—1795）》Peter Lorge, *War, Politics and Society in Early Modern China, 900—1795*. Routledge (2005)

32. 《中国古代和现代早期欧洲的战争与国家形成》Victoria Tin-bor Hui, *War and State Formation in Ancient China and Early Modern Europe*. Cambridge University Press (2005)

33. 《强权带来的民主：美国在冷战后世界的军事干预》Karin von Hippel, *Democracy by Force: US Military Intervention in the Post-Cold War World*. Cambridge University Press (2004)

34. 《鸦片、士兵与福音派：1840—42年英国与中国的战争及其后果》Harry G. Gelber, *Opium, Soldiers and Evangelicals: England's 1840—42 War with China and its Aftermath*. Palgrave Macmillan UK (2004)

35. 《远东战舰（1）：中国与东南亚（公元前202—公元1419）》Wayne Reynolds, Stephen R. Turnbull, *Fighting Ships of the Far East (1): China & Southeast Asia 202 BC-AD 1419*. Osprey Publishing (2002)

36. 《中国现代战争（1795—1989）》Bruce A. Elleman, *Modern Chinese Warfare, 1795—1989*. Routledge (2001)

37. 《1979中越战争：问题、决策和影响》King C. Chen, *China's War with Vietnam 1979: Issues, Decisions and Implications*. Hoover Institution Press (1987)

38. 《中印边界战争》James B. Calvin, *The China-India Border War (1962)*. Marine Corps Command and Staff College (1984)

39. 《印度的中国战争》Neville Maxwell, *India's China War*. Jonathan Cape (1970)

40. 《喜马拉雅的失策：1962年中印边界战争的启幕人》Brig J. P. Dalvi, *Himalayan Blunder: The Curtain-Raiser to the Sino-Indian War of 1962*. Thacker & Company Limited

(1969, 2010)

41. 《中国的战争与政治》John T. Pratt, *War and Politics in China*. Jonathan Cape, Thirty Bedford Square, London (1943)

42. 《1914：青岛的陷落》Jefferson Jones, *The Fall of Tsingtau: With A Study of Japan's Ambitions in China*. Boston and New York: Houghton Mifflin (1915)

43. 《中国与联军》（第一、二卷）Arnold Henry Savage Landor, *China and the allies vols. 1 and 2*. Adamant Media Corporation (1901)

44. 《中日甲午战争简史》Jukichi Inouye, *A Concise History of the War between Japan and China*. Osaka: Z. Mayekawa (1895)

9.2.7 战争文化与生态

1. 《中国早期军事思想》Christopher C. Rand, *Military Thought in Early China*. State University of New York Press (2017)

2. 《中国的战争生态：1938—1950年的河南省、黄河及其他》Micah S. Muscolino, *The Ecology of War in China: Henan Province, the Yellow River, and Beyond, 1938—1950*. Cambridge University Press (2015)

3. 《中国从其他民族战争中吸取的教训》Andrew Scobell（施道安）, David Lai（赖大卫）, and Roy Kamphausen（甘浩森）(eds.), *Chinese Lessons from other Peoples' Wars*. Strategic Studies Institute, U.S. Army War College (2011)

4. 《古代中国之后现代战争：来自中国战略传统的持久思想》Thomas M. Kane, *Ancient China on Postmodern War: Enduring Ideas from the Chinese Strategic Tradition*. Routledge (2007)

5. 《欺骗之道：中国历史与现代的非正统战争》Ralph D. Sawyer, Mei-Chun Lee Sawyer, *The Tao of Deception: Unorthodox Warfare in Historic and Modern China*. Basic Books (2007)

6. 《中国的军事文化哲学：势与力》William H. Mott IV and Jae Chang Kim, *The Philosophy of Chinese Military Culture: Shih vs Li*. Palgrave Macmillan (2006)

7. 《中国战争文化：清代帝国与军队》Joanna Waley-Cohen（卫周安）, *The Culture of War in China: Empire and the Military under the Qing Dynasty*. I. B. Tauris (2006)

8. 《早期近代中国的战争、政治与社会（900—1795）》Peter Lorge, *War, Politics and Society in Early Modern China, 900—1795*. Routledge (2005)

9. 《掌握中国战略理念：势》David Lai（赖大卫）, *Learning from the Stones: A Go Approach to Mastering China's Strategic Concept, Shi*. Strategic Studies Institute (2004)

10. 《美国的亚洲战争：历史与记忆的文化视角》Philip West, Steven I. Levine, Jackie Hiltz, *America's Wars in Asia: A Cultural Approach to History and Memory*. M.E. Sharpe (1998)

11. 《中国古代七部军事名著》Ralph D. Sawyer, *The Seven Military Classics of Ancient China*. Westview Press (1993)

12. 《中国兵法》Edited by Frank A. Kierman, Jr., and John K. Fairbank（费正清）; with contributions by Edward L. Dreyer, etc., *Chinese Ways in Warfare*. Harvard University Press (1974)

9.2.8 内战与军史

1. 《战争中的中国：新中国出现的胜利与悲剧》Hans van de Ven（方德万）, *China at War: Triumph and Tragedy in the Emergence of the New China*. Harvard University Press (2018)

2. 《追踪黄虎：明清之际西南地区的战争、创伤与社会动荡》Kenneth M. Swope, *On the Trail of the Yellow Tiger: War, Trauma, and Social Dislocation in Southwest China during the Ming-Qing Transition*. University of Nebraska Press (2018)

3. 《中华帝国的军队（1840—1911）》Philip Jowett, *Imperial Chinese Armies, 1840—1911* (Osprey Men-at-Arms 505). Osprey Publishing (2016)

4. 《蒋介石何处失去中国：1948年辽沈战役》Harold Miles Tanner, *Where Chiang Kai-Shek lost China: The Liao-Shen Campaign, 1948* (Twentieth-century battles). Indiana University Press (2015)

5. 《中国统一：宋代以战求和》Peter Lorge, *The Reunification of China: Peace through War under the Song Dynasty*. Cambridge University Press (2015)

6. 《中国历史上的战争辩论》Peter A. Lorge, *Debating War in Chinese History*. Brill Academic Publishers (2013)

7. 《剩下的还有什么：适应19世纪中国内战》Tobie Meyer-Fong, *What Remains: Coming to Terms with Civil War in 19th Century China*. Stanford University Press (2013)

8. 《中华帝国晚期的战争财政与后勤：第二次金川战役研究（1771—1776）》Ulrich Theobald, *War Finance and Logistics in Late Imperial China: A Study of the Second Jinchuan Campaign (1771—1776)* (Monies, Markets, and Finance in East Asia, 1600—1900). Brill (2013)

9. 《中国古代的战役》Chris Peers, *Battles of Ancient China*. Pen & Sword Military (2013)

10. 《中国战争：龙的唤醒（1894—1949）》Philip Jowett, *China's Wars: Rousing the Dragon, 1894—1949* (Osprey General Military). Osprey Publishing (2013)

11. 《中国军事史》David A. Graff, Robin Higham, *A Military History of China*. The University Press of Kentucky (2012)

12. 《中国维和的演化途径》Marc Lanteigne, Miwa Hirono, *China's Evolving Approach to Peacekeeping*. Routledge (2012)

13. 《战争中的中国：百科全书》Xiaobing Li, *China at War: An Encyclopedia*. ABC-CLIO (2012)

14. 《中国古代战争》Ralph D. Sawyer, *Ancient Chinese Warfare*. Basic Books (2011)

15. 《中国内战1945—1949》Michael Lynch, *The Chinese Civil War 1945—1949*. Osprey Publishing (2010)

16. 《中国中世纪的赞助与社区：襄阳驻军（公元400—600年）》Andrew Chittick, *Patronage and Community in Medieval China: The Xiangyang Garrison, 400—600 CE*. State University of New York Press (2010)

17. 《战争前线：中国中古时期真实与想象中的战争、边境和身份》Don J. Wyatt (eds.), *Battlefronts: Real and Imagined War, Border, and Identity in the Chinese Middle Period*. Palgrave Macmillan US (2008)

18. 《间谍王：戴笠与中国特工》Frederic Wakeman, Jr.（魏斐德）, *Spymaster: Dai Li and the Chinese Secret Service* (A Philip E. Lilienthal Book in Asian Studies). University of California Press (2003)

19. 《决定性的遭遇：1946至1950年的中国内战》Odd Arne Westad（文安立）, *Decisive Encounters: The Chinese Civil War, 1946—1950*. Stanford University Press (2003)

20. 《战争创伤：战争对现代中国的影响》Diana Lary（戴安娜·拉里）, Stephen MacKinnon, *Scars of War: The Impact of Warfare on Modern China*. UBC Press (2001)

21. 《中国内战中的军队（1911—1949）：共产党士兵（1946）》Collective, *Chinese Civil War Armies 1911—49: Communist Soldier, 1946* (Men at War 78). Osprey Delprado (2000)

22. 《当代中国军事史词典》Larry Wortzel, *Dictionary of Contemporary Chinese Military History*. Greenwood Press (1999)

23. 《中国内战中的军队（1911—1949）》Philip Jowett, Stephen Andrew, *Chinese Civil War Armies 1911—49*. Osprey Publishing (1997)

24. 《百种非正统战略：中国战争的战役与策略》Ralph D. Sawyer, *One Hundred Unorthodox Strategies: Battle and Tactics of Chinese Warfare*. Westview Press (1996)

25. 《中国早期的暴力制裁》Mark Edward Lewis, *Sanctioned Violence in Early China*. State University of New York Press (1990)

26. 《中国古代的军队和敌人（公元前1027年至公元1286年）》John P. Greer, *The Armies and Enemies of Ancient China, 1027 B.C.-1286 A.D.* Wargames Research Group (1975)

9.2.9 军事与军力

1. 《积极防御：1949年以来中国的军事战略》(Princeton Studies in International History and Politics Book 167) M. Taylor Fravel, *Active Defense: China's Military Strategy since 1949*. Princeton University Press (2019)

2. 《中国军事现代化、日本正常化与南海领土争端》Zenel Garcia, *China's Military Modernization, Japan's Normalization and the South China Sea Territorial Disputes*. Springer International Publishing: Palgrave Pivot (2019)

3. 《中国私人军队：保护新丝绸之路》Alessandro Arduino, *China's Private Army: Protecting the New Silk Road*. Palgrave Pivot (2018)

4. 《重塑中国军队：习近平时代解放军的角色与使命》(Asian Security Studies) Richard A. Bitzinger, James Char, *Reshaping the Chinese Military: The PLA's Roles and Missions in the*

Xi Jinping Era. Routledge (2018)

5. 《马卡洛夫手枪：中国、保加利亚与开伯尔通道复制品》Henry C. Brown, Cameron S. White, Edwin H. Lowe, *The Makarov Pistol: China, Bulgaria & Khyber Pass Copies*. Vol. 2. Edwin H. Lowe Publishing, Sydney (2018)

6. 《解放军对中国国家安全政策制定的影响》Phillip Saunders, Andrew Scobell（施道安）, *PLA Influence on China's National Security Policymaking*. Stanford Security Studies (2015)

7. 《评估中国海军力量：技术创新、经济制约和战略意义》Sarah Kirchberger, *Assessing China's Naval Power: Technological Innovation, Economic Constraints, and Strategic Implications*. Springer-Verlag Berlin Heidelberg (2015)

8. 《授权中国武警在社会服务中发挥作用》Xiaohai Wang, *Empowerment on Chinese Police Force's Role in Social Service*. Springer-Verlag Berlin Heidelberg (2015)

9. 《美中军事记分卡：军力、地理和不断变化的力量平衡（1996—2017）》Eric Heginbotham (ed.), ... and thirteen others, *The US-China Military Scorecard: Forces, Geography, and the Evolving Balance of Power, 1996—2017*. RAND Corporation (2015)

10. 《中国大战略与海洋强国》Thomas M. Kane, *Chinese Grand Strategy and Maritime Power* (Cass Series: Naval Policy and History). Routledge (2014)

11. 《评估胡锦涛时代的解放军》Roy Kamphausen, David Lai, Travis Tanner, *Assessing the People's Liberation Army in the Hu Jintao Era*. The Strategic Studies Institute and U.S. Army War (2014)

12. 《缅中边界儿童兵比较研究：演变、挑战与对策》Kai Chen, *Comparative Study of Child Soldiering on Myanmar-China Border: Evolutions, Challenges and Countermeasures*. Springer-Verlag Singapur (2014)

13. 《射道：1637年中国军事训练手册》（明代.高颖《武经射学正宗》英译）Jie Tian, Justin Ma, *The Way of Archery: A 1637 Chinese Military Training Manual*. Schiffer Publishing, Ltd (2014)

14. 《1618—1644年中国明朝的军事崩溃》(Asian States and Empires) Kenneth M. Swope, *The Military Collapse of China's Ming Dynasty, 1618—44*. Routledge (2014)

15. 《中国空降兵》James Fallows, *China Airborne*. Pantheon (2012)

16. 《中国空军：概念、角色和能力的演变》Richard P. Hallion, Roger Cliff, and Phillip C. Saunders, *The Chinese Air Force: Evolving Concepts, Roles, and Capabilities*. National Defense University (2012)

17. 《1949年以来的中国人民解放军：地面部队》Benjamin Lai, *The Chinese People's Liberation Army since 1949: Ground Forces* (Elite 194). Osprey Publihing Limited (2012)

18. 《撼天裂地：21世纪中国空军的职业概念》Roger Cliff, *Shaking the Heavens and Splitting the Earth: Chinese Air Force Employment Concepts in the 21st Century*. Rand Corp (2011)

19. 《中国国防》Peng Guangqian, Zhao Zhiyin, Luo Yong, *China's National Defense*. Cengage Learning Asia Pte Ltd (2010)
20. 《中国军阀（1911—1930）》Philip Jowett, *Chinese Warlord Armies 1911—30* (Men-at-Arms). Osprey Publishing (2010)
21. 《国内外的人民解放军：对中国军队作战能力的评估》（美国陆军战争学院研究报告）Roy Kamphausen（甘浩森）, David Lai（赖大卫）, Andrew Scobell（施道安）, *The PLA at Home and Abroad: Assessing the Operational Capabilities of China's Military*. Strategic Studies Institute (2010)
22. 《军事挑战的全面准备与训练：来自中国、法国、英国、印度和以色列的经验见解》David E. Johnson, Jennifer D. P. Moroney, *Preparing and Training for the Full Spectrum of Military Challenges: Insights from the Experiences of China, France, the United Kingdom, India, and Israel*. RAND Corporation (2010)
23. 《中国回归：权力的长征—人民解放军新的历史使命》Kim Nødskov, *The Return of China: The Long March to Power; The New Historic Mission of the People's Liberation Army*. Royal Danish Defence College Publishing House (2009)
24. 《各种军事挑战的准备和训练：来自中、法、英、印和以色列的经验启示》David E. Johnson, *Preparing and Training for the Full Spectrum of Military Challenges: Insights from the Experiences of China, France, the United Kingdom, India, and Israel*. RAND (2009)
25. 《中国军事现代化：构建区域和全球影响力》Richard D. Fisher Jr., *China's Military Modernization: Building for Regional and Global Reach*. Praeger (2008)
26. 《违反信任：对中国TOMS-kype平台监控与安全实践的分析》Nart Villeneuve, *Breaching Trust: An Analysis of Surveillance & Security Practices on China's TOMS-kype Platform*. The Information Warfare Monitor (2008)
27. 《中国力量的三面：军力、财力和智力》David M. Lampton（蓝普顿）, *The Three Faces of Chinese Power: Might, Money, and Minds*. University of California Press (2008)
28. 《现代中国军队史》Xiaobing Li, *A History of the Modern Chinese Army*. The University Press of Kentucky (2007)
29. 《中国海军2007》United States Office of Naval Intelligence, *China's Navy 2007*. Office of Naval Intelligence (2007)
30. 《中华人民共和国的军事力量》U. S. Department of Defense, *Military Power of the Peoples Republic of China*. Office of the Secretary of Defense (2006)
31. 《今日中国军队：21世纪的传统与变革》Dennis J. Blasko, *The Chinese Army Today: Tradition and Transformation for the 21st Century* (Asian Security Studies Series). Routledge (2006)
32. 《中国军队（1937—1949）：二战和内战》Philip Jowett, Stephen Walsh, *The Chinese Army 1937—49: World War II and Civil War*. Osprey Publishing (2005)

33. 《中国军事现代化：机遇与制约》Keith Crane, *Modernizing China's Military: Opportunities and Constraints*. RAND Corporation (2005)

34. 《中国军事现代化：机遇与制约》Crane Keith, Cliff Roger, Medeiros Evan (eds.), *Modernizing China's Military: Opportunities and Constraints*.Rand (2005)

35. 《解读中国军力》Ka Po Ng, *Interpreting China's Military Power: Doctrine Makes Readiness*. Frank Cass (2004)

36. 《富裕者的贫困：解放军研究的新挑战与新机遇》James C. Mulvenon（毛文杰），Andrew Yang, *A Poverty of Riches: New Challenges and Opportunities in PLA Research*. RAND Corporation (2004)

37. 《中国军力：独立工作组报告》Harold Brown, Joseph W. Prueher, Adam Segal, *Chinese Military Power: Report of an Independent Task Force*. Council on Foreign Relations Press (2003)

38. 《中国军事力量的使用：超越长城和长征》Andrew Scobell（施道安），*China's Use of Military Force: Beyond the Great Wall and the Long March*. Cambridge University Press (2003)

39. 《中国军事现代化：进展、问题和前景》David Shambaugh（沈大伟），*Modernizing China's Military: Progress, Problems, and Prospects*. University of California Press (2002)

40. 《作为组织的人民解放军》James C. Mulvenon（毛文杰），*People's Liberation Army as Organization* (Reference Volume v1.0). RAND (2002)

41. 《中国人的未来战争观》Michael Pillsbury（白邦瑞），*Chinese Views of Future Warfare*. University Press of the Pacific (2002)

42. 《幸运之兵：1978—1998年中国军事商业团体的兴衰》James C. Mulvenon（毛文杰），*Soldiers of fortune: The Rise and Fall of the Chinese Military-Business Complex, 1978—1998*. M.E. Sharpe (2001)

43. 《中国商业技术的军事潜力》Roger Cliff, *The Military Potential of China's Commercial Technology*.Rand Publishing (2001)

44. 《实事求是：后毛泽东时代中国军事研究回顾》James C. Mulvenon（毛文杰），Andrew N. D. Yang (eds.), *Seeking Truth from Facts: A Restrospective on Chinese Military Studies in the Post-Mao Era*. RAND (2001)

45. 《蒸汽时代的中国海军》Richard N. J. Wright, *The Chinese Steam Navy, 1862—1945*. Chatham Publishing (2000)

46. 《中国内战军队（1911—1949）：共产主义士兵（1946）》(Men at War 78) Collective, *Chinese Civil War Armies 1911—1949: Communist Soldier, 1946*. Osprey Delprado (2000)

47. 《中国和中国人民解放军：大国还是挣扎中的发展中国家》Solomon M. Karmel, *China and the People's Liberation Army: Great Power or Struggling Developing State*. Palgrave Macmillan US (2000)

48. 《枪的威力：现代中国军阀的兴起》Edward A. McCord, *The Power of the Gun: The Emergence of Modern Chinese Warlordism*.University of California Press (1993)
49. 《危机中的中国：军事的角色》Beaver Paul (ed.), *China in Crisis. The Role of the Military*. Jane's Information Group Limited (1989)
50. 《军阀士兵：中国普通士兵（1911—1937）》Diana Lary（戴安娜·拉里）, *Warlord Soldiers: Chinese Common Soldiers, 1911—1937*.Cambridge Univ. Press (1985)
51. 《中国国防政策》Gerald Segal, William T. Tow (eds.), *Chinese Defence Policy*. Palgrave Macmillan UK (1984)
52. 《中国战争机器：中华人民共和国战略与武器的技术分析》Ray Bonds, *The Chinese War Machine: A Technical Analysis of the Strategy and Weapons of the People's Republic of China*. Salamander Book (1979)
53. 《中国进入机器时代：中国军事工业中的劳力研究》Kuo-Heng Shih, *China Enters the Machine Age: A Study of Labor in Chinese War Industry*. Harvard University Press (1944)

9.2.10 核力量

1. 《新古典现实主义与中国核学说的不发达》Paolo Rosa, *Neoclassical Realism and the Underdevelopment of China's Nuclear Doctrine*. Palgrave Pivot, Cham (2018)
2. 《中国和全球核秩序：从陌生到积极参与》Nicola Horsburgh, *China and Global Nuclear Order: From Estrangement to Active Engagement*. Oxford University Press (2015)
3. 《中国核能源政策》Xu Yi-chong, *The Politics of Nuclear Energy in China*. Palgrave Macmillan UK (2010)
4. 《关于中美战略核问题的观点》Christopher P. Twomey (eds.), *Perspectives on Sino-American Strategic Nuclear Issues*.Palgrave Macmillan (2008)
5. 《报复的最低限度：中国在核时代的安全探索》Jeffrey G. Lewis, *The Minimum Means of Reprisal. China's Search for Security in the Nuclear Age* (American Academy Studies in Global Security).American Academy of Arts and Sciences (2007)
6. 《南亚核威慑：中国、印度和巴基斯坦》Arpit Rajain, *Nuclear Deterrence in Southern Asia: China, India and Pakistan*. AGE Publications Pvt. Ltd (2005)
7. 《中国作为世界政治中的核大国》Leo Yueh-Yun Liu, *China as a Nuclear Power in World Politics*. Palgrave Macmillan UK (1972)

9.2.11 美军在中国

1. 《长江巡逻：美国海军在中国》Kemp Tolley, *Yangtze Patrol: The U.S. Navy in China*. Naval Institute Press (2013)
2. 《稻田海军：美国水手卧底中国》Linda Kush, *The Rice Paddy Navy: U.S. Sailors Undercover in China*. Osprey Publishing (2012)
3. 《强力带来的民主：美国在冷战后世界的军事干预》Karin von Hippel, *Democracy by Force: US Military Intervention in the Post-Cold War World*. Cambridge (2004)

4.《轻轻踏足：美国海军陆战队在中国，1819—1949》George B. Clark, *Treading Softly: U.S. Marines in China, 1819—1949*. Praeger (2001)

5.《恶魔战士：成为中国上帝的美国士兵》Caleb Carr, *The Devil Soldier: The American Soldier of Fortune Who Became a God in China*. Random House (1995)

6.《美国陆军特种部队服务部：中国袖珍指南》United States, Army Service Forces, Special Service Division, *Pocket Guide to China*. Washington, War and Navy Depts. (1943)

10. 中国经济与自然

10.1 经济增长与发展

1. 《中国经济到来：解读颠覆性增长》Damien Ma, *China's Economic Arrival: Decoding a Disruptive Rise*. Palgrave Macmillan (2020)
2. 《理解中国GDP》Xuguang Song, *Understanding Chinese GDP*. Springer Singapore: Palgrave Macmillan (2020)
3. 《中国基础设施建设40年》(Research Series on the Chinese Dream and China's Development Path) Xin Qiu, *China 40 Years Infrastructure Construction*. Springer Singapore (2020)
4. 《国际商务与新兴经济体企业：第一卷——国际问题与中国视角》(Palgrave Studies of Internationalization in Emerging Markets) Marin A. Marinov, Svetla T. Marinova, Jorma A. Larimo, Tiia Leposky (eds.), *International Business and Emerging Economy Firms: Volume I: Universal Issues and the Chinese Perspective*. Springer International Publishing; Palgrave Macmillan (2020)
5. 《解读浙江发展：文化与社会视角》(WSPC-ZJUP Series on China's Regional Development vol. 1) Lixu Chen, *Interpreting Zhejiang's Development: Cultural and Social Perspectives*. Hackensack (2020)
6. 《改革开放后中国的经济增长与内生威权制度》(Politics and Development of Contemporary China) Hans H. Tung, *Economic Growth and Endogenous Authoritarian Institutions in Post-Reform China*. Springer International Publishing: Palgrave Macmillan (2019)
7. 《国家的反击：中国经济改革是否终了？》Nicholas Lardy, *The State Strikes Back: The End of Economic Reform in China*. Peterson Institute for International Economics (2019)
8. 《中国宏观经济展望：季度预测和分析报告（2019年2月）》(Current Chinese Economic Report Series) Center for Macroeconomic Research at Xiamen University, *China's Macroeconomic Outlook: Quarterly Forecast and Analysis Report, February 2019*. Springer Singapor (2019)
9. 《中国宏观经济展望：季度预测和分析报告（2018年10月）》(Current Chinese Economic Report Series) Center for Macroeconomic Research of Xiamen University, *China's Macroeconomic Outlook: Quarterly Forecast and Analysis Report, October 2018*. Springer Singapore (2019)
10. 《理解琼·罗宾逊的中国》（英国经济学家论中国）(Palgrave Studies in the History of Economic Thought) Pervez Tahir, *Making Sense of Joan Robinson on China*. Springer

International Publishing: Palgrave Macmillan (2019)

11. 《赢在转折点：中国经济转型大趋势》(The Great Transformation of China) Fulin Chi（迟福林）, *Winning at the Turning Point: The Great Trend of China's Economic Transformation*. Springer Singapore: Palgrave Macmillan (2019)

12. 《新常态下中国区域经济的重大变化》(The Great Transformation of China) Xiaowu Song, Shiguo Wu, Xin Xu, *The Great Change in the Regional Economy of China under the New Normal*. Springer Singapore: Palgrave Macmillan (2019)

13. 《转变经济增长方式与中国产业升级》(Research Series on the Chinese Dream and China's Development Path) Qizi Zhang (ed.), *Transforming Economic Growth and China's Industrial Upgrading*-Springer Singapore (2018)

14. 《中国外商投资与经济发展（1979—1996）》Haishun Sun, *Foreign Investment and Economic Development in China: 1979—1996*. Routledge (2018)

15. 《中国宏观经济展望：季度预测和分析报告（2017年10月）》Center for Macroeconomic Research of Xiamen University, *China's Macroeconomic Outlook: Quarterly Forecast and Analysis Report, October 2017* (Current Chinese Economic Report Series). Springer Singapore (2018)

16. 《经济增长协同理论：中国与发达国家的比较研究》Jianhua Liu, Zhaohua Jiang, *The Synergy Theory on Economic Growth: Comparative Study Between China and Developed Countries*. Springer Singapore (2018)

17. 《"十三五"期间中国省级经济竞争力和政策展望（2016—2020）》Jianping Li, Minrong Li, Yanjing Gao, Jianjian Li, Hongwen Su, Maoxing Huang, *China's Provincial Economic Competitiveness and Policy Outlook for the 13th Five-year Plan Period (2016—2020)*. Springer Singapore (2018)

18. 《恶性通货膨胀的世界史》Liping He, *Hyperinflation: A World History* (China perspectives series). Routledge (2018)

19. 《中国宏观经济展望》Center for Macroeconomic Research at Xiamen University, *China's Macroeconomic Outlook* (Current Chinese Economic Report Series). Springer Singapore (2018)

20. 《东南亚、中国和印度经济展望（2018）：通过数字化促进增长》Coll., *Economic Outlook for Southeast Asia, China and India 2018: Fostering Growth through Digitalisation*. OECD Publishing (2018)

21. 《破解中国难题：传统经济智慧为何失误》Yukon Huang, *Cracking the China Conundrum: Why Conventional Economic Wisdom Is Wrong*. Oxford University Press (2017)

22. 《中国经济如何运作》Rongxing Guo, *How the Chinese Economy Works*. Palgrave Macmillan (2017)

23. 《与魔鬼共舞：中国民营化的政治经济学》Yi-min Lin, *Dancing with the Devil: The Political Economy of Privatization in China*. Oxford University Press (2017)

24. 《破解中国难题：为什么传统经济智慧是错误的》Yukon Huang（黄育川），*Cracking the China Conundrum: Why Conventional Economic Wisdom Is Wrong*. Oxford University Press (22 Jun 2017)

25. 《来自中国内部：经济学家来信》Liam Brunt, *China from the Inside: Letters from an Economist*. Palgrave Macmillan (2017)

26. 《从加速积累到社会主义市场经济：1953年至今的经济话语与发展》Kjeld Erik Brdsgaard, Koen Rutten, *From Accelerated Accumulation to Socialist Market Economy in China: Economic Discourse and Development from 1953 to the Present*. Brill (2017)

27. 《中国经济增长：走向可持续经济发展和社会正义——国内和国际经济政策》（第一卷）John Joshua, *China's Economic Growth: Towards Sustainable Economic Development and Social Justice. Volume I: Domestic and International Economic Policies*. Palgrave Macmillan UK (2017)

28. 《中国经济增长：走向可持续经济发展和社会正义——经济政策对生活质量的影响》（第二卷）John Joshua, *China's Economic Growth: Towards Sustainable Economic Development and Social Justice. Volume II: The Impact of Economic Policies on the Quality of Life*. Palgrave Macmillan UK (2017)

29. 《中国宏观经济展望：季度预测和分析报告（2017年2月）》Center for Macroeconomic Research of Xiamen University, *China's Macroeconomic Outlook: Quarterly Forecast and Analysis Report, February 2017* (Current Chinese Economic Report Series). Springer Singapore (2017)

30. 《中国宏观经济展望：季度预测与分析报告（2016年9月）》Center for Macroeconomic Research of Xiamen University, *China's Macroeconomic Outlook: Quarterly Forecast and Analysis Report,* September 2016 (Current Chinese Economic Report Series). Springer Singapore (2017)

31. 《中国手机经济：最大、最快信息消费热潮中的机遇》Winston Ma, Xiaodong Lee, Dominic Barton, *China's Mobile Economy: Opportunities in the Largest and Fastest Information Consumption Boom*.Wiley (2017)

32. 《中国经济分析与预测（2015）》Ping Li, Xuesong Li, Yang Li, Ping Zhang, *Economic Analysis and Forecast of China (2015)* (Research series on the Chinese dream and China's development path). Springer Verlag (2017)

33. 《中国经济史：从古代到十九世纪》Richard von Glahn, *The Economic History of China: From Antiquity to the Nineteenth Century*. Cambridge University Press (2016)

34. 《中国经济：每人都需知晓》Arthur R. Kroeber, *China's Economy: What Everyone Needs to Know* (What Everyone Needs to Know). Oxford University Press (2016)

35. 《中国经济增长前景：从人口红利到改革红利》Cai Fang, *China's Economic Growth Prospects: From Demographic Dividend to Reform Dividend* (In Association with the Social

Sciences Academic Press). Edward Elgar Publishing (2016)

36. 《中国经济改革的逻辑》Xiaojing Zhang, Xin Chang, *The Logic of Economic Reform in China*. Springer-Verlag Berlin Heidelberg (2016)

37. 《经济转型与发展的中国路径》Yinxing Hong, *The China Path to Economic Transition and Development*. Springer Singapore (2016)

38. 《走向均衡增长与经济集聚：中国域乡和地区间发展实证研究》Zhao Chen, Ming Lu, *Toward Balanced Growth with Economic Agglomeration: Empirical Studies of China's Urban-Rural and Interregional Development*. Springer-Verlag Berlin Heidelberg (2016)

39. 《中国循环经济的发展》Jianguo Qi, Jingxing Zhao, Wenjun Li, Xushu Peng, Bin Wu, Hong Wang, *Development of Circular Economy in China*. Springer Singapore (2016)

40. 《中国高速增长的终结》Jun Zhang, *End of Hyper Growth in China*. Palgrave Macmillan US (2016)

41. 《国家试验：中国（上海）自由贸易试验区的制度设计》Lin Xiao, *National Test: System Design of China (Shanghai) Pilot Free Trade Zone*. Springer Singapore (2016)

42. 《中国经济增长年度报告：宏观经济走势》Ping Zhang, Xiahui Liu, Fuhua Yuan, Ziran Zhang (eds.), *Annual Report on China's Economic Growth: Macroeconomic Trend* (Research Series on the Chinese Dream and China's Development Path). Springer-Verlag Berlin Heidelberg (2016)

43. 《中国古代至19世纪经济史》Richard von Glahn, *The Economic History of China from Antiquity to the Nineteenth Century*. Cambridge University Press (2016)

44. 《通过纵向专业化实现中国包容性增长》Wei Wang, *Achieving Inclusive Growth in China: Through Vertical Specialization* (Elsevier Asian studies series). Elsevier, Chandos Publishing (2016)

45. 《中国经济特区发展年度报告（2016）》Yitao Tao, Yiming Yuan (eds.), *Annual Report on the Development of China's Special Economic Zones (2016)* (Current Chinese Economic Report Series). Blue Book of China's Special Economic (2016)

46. 《服务经济的发展：中国经济转型的大趋势》Zhenhua Zhou, *The Development of Service Economy: A General Trend of the Changing Economy in China*. Springer-Verlag Singapur (2016)

47. 《与中国打交道：亲历一个新经济大国的崛起》Henry M. Paulson Jr., *Dealing With China: An Insider Unmasks the New Economic Superpower*. Hachette Group (2015)

48. 《揭秘中国经济发展》Fang Cai（蔡昉）, *Demystifying China's Economy Development* (China Insights). Springer-Verlag Berlin Heidelberg (2015)

49. 《毁灭中国：中国经济奇迹背后的真相》Jeremy R. Haft, *Unmade in China: The Hidden Truth about China's Economic Miracle*. Polity (2015)

50. 《中国经济：调查论集》Iris Claus, Les Oxley, *China's Economy: A Collection of Surveys*.

Wiley-Blackwell (2015)

51. 《中国区域经济发展的前瞻性重要理论思考与实践》Yunxian Chen, *Foresighted Leading Theoretical Thinking and Practice of China's Regional Economic Development*. Springer-Verlag Berlin Heidelberg (2014)

52. 《开放、经济增长与区域差异：中国案例》Yanqing Jiang, *Openness, Economic Growth and Regional Disparities: The Case of China*. Springer-Verlag Berlin Heidelberg (2014)

53. 《混合财富：中国、俄罗斯和西方经济史》Vladimir Popov, *Mixed Fortunes: An Economic History of China, Russia, and the West*. Oxford University Press (2014)

54. 《中国经济发展》Josef C. Brada, Paul Wachtel, Dennis Yang, *China's Economic Development* (Past and Present). Palgrave Macmillan (2014)

55. 《中国经济动态：正在形成中的北京共识？》Jun Li, Liming Wang, *China's Economic Dynamics: A Beijing Consensus in the making?* Routledge (2014)

56. 《失衡的中国经济》Yining Li, *Chinese Economy in Disequilibrium* (China Academic Library). Springer Berlin Heidelberg (2014)

57. 《劳特利奇中国经济手册》Gregory C. Chow, Dwight H. Perkins（珀金斯）, *Routledge Handbook of the Chinese Economy*. Routledge (2014)

58. 《中国：超越奇迹》Yiping Huang, Jian Chang, Steven Lingxiu Yang, *China: Beyond the Miracle* (Emerging Markets Research: The Complete Series). Barclays (2013)

59. 《中国多元文化经济：社会经济指标》Rongxing Guo, *China's Multicultural Economies: Social and Economic Indicators*. Springer US (2013)

60. 《中华人民共和国：避免中等收入陷阱—持续包容增长的政策》OECD, *The People's Republic of China: Avoiding the Middle-Income Trap: Policies for Sustained and Inclusive Growth* (Better Policies). OECD Publishing (2013)

61. 《中国增长：超级经济大国的形成》Linda Yueh, *China's Growth: The Making of an Economic Superpower*. Oxford University Press (2013)

62. 《避免跌落：中国经济重构》Michael Pettis, *Avoiding the Fall: China's Economic Restructuring*. Carnegie Endowment for Int'l Peace (2013)

63. 《中国纵向专业化与贸易顺差》Wang Wei, *Vertical Specialization and Trade Surplus in China*. Chandos Publishing (2013)

64. 《中国区域经济合作决策》Yang Jiang, *China's Policymaking for Regional Economic Cooperation*. Palgrave Macmillan UK (2013)

65. 《中国经济新转型》Masahiko Aoki, Jinglian Wu (eds.), *The Chinese Economy: A New Transition*. Palgrave Macmillan UK (2012)

66. 《中国非凡的经济增长》John Knight, Sai Ding, *China's Remarkable Economic Growth*. Oxford University Press (2012)

67. 《解密中国经济》Justin Yifu Lin, *Demystifying the Chinese Economy*. Cambridge

University Press (2012)

68. 《新中国经济：向未来的动态转变》Elias C. Grivoyannis (eds.), *The New Chinese Economy: Dynamic Transitions into the Future.* Palgrave Macmillan US (2012)

69. 《中国结构经济学：平衡增长的三维框架》Xiang Junbo, *Structural Economics in China: A Three-Dimensional Framework for Balanced Growth.* Enrich Professional Publishing (2012)

70. 《黯然失色：生活在中国经济统治的阴影下》Arvind Subramanian, *Eclipse: Living in the Shadow of China's Economic Dominance.* Institute of International Economics (2011)

71. 《毛式经济学：为何中国共产党人比我们资本家做得更好》Loretta Napoleoni, Stephen Twilley, *Maonomics: Why Chinese Communists Make Better Capitalists than We Do.* Seven Stories Press (2011)

72. 《中国体制转型的政治经济学研究：1979年至今》Raphael Shen, Victoria Mantzopoulos, *The Political Economy of China's Systemic Transformation: 1979 to the Present.* Palgrave Macmillan (2011)

73. 《中国新政：国际金融危机下的经济发展》Xiaoxi Li, Biliang Hu, *China's New Deal: Economic Development Under International Financial Crisis.* Nova Science Publishers Inc. (2011)

74. 《中国经济》Linda Yueh, *Economy of China.* Edward Elgar (2010)

75. 《中国与世界经济》David Greenaway, Chris Milner, Shujie Yao (eds.), *China and the World Economy.* Palgrave Macmillan UK (2010)

76. 《中国的经济开放与地域政治》Yumin Sheng, *Economic Openness and Territorial Politics in China.* Cambridge University Press (2010)

77. 《次贷危机后的中国：新经济格局中的机会》Chi Lo, *China after the Subprime Crisis: Opportunities in The New Economic Landscape.* Palgrave Macmillan (2010)

78. 《解读中国经济》Gregory C. Chow, *Interpreting China's Economy.* World Scientific (2010)

79. 《中国经济》Wu Li, Sui Fumin, *China's Economy.* Cengage Learning (2010)

80. 《中国经济导论：今日现代中国背后的驱动力》Rongxing Guo, *An Introduction to the Chinese Economy: The Driving Forces Behind Modern Day China.* Wiley (2010)

81. 《巴西、中国、印度、印度尼西亚、南非的增长与可持续发展》OECD, *Growth and Sustainability in Brazil, China, India, Indonesia and South Africa.* OECD Publishing (2010)

82. 《中国经济发展》Chris Bramall（克里斯·布拉莫尔）, *Chinese Economic Development.* Routledge (2009)

83. 《中国经济、政治和社会问题》Jack M. Phillips, Logan J. Moore, *China: Economic, Political and Social Issues.* Nova Science Publishers, Inc. (2009)

84. 《旧中国的新经济：十亿贫民的征服》T. K. Bhaumik, *Old China's New Economy: The Conquest by a Billion Paupers.* Sage Publications (2009)

85. 《伟大的中国经济转型》Loren Brandt, Thomas G. Rawski（罗斯基）, *China's Great Economic Transformation.* Cambridge University Press (2008)

86. 《中国经济政策对美国的影响》Mary Jo Devaland, *China's Economic Policy Impact on the United States*.Nova Science Pub Inc. (2008)
87. 《亚洲金融危机之后的中国》Wang Mengkui, *China in the Wake of Asia's Financial Crisis* (Routledge Studies on the Chinese Economy). Routledge (2008)
88. 《中国生产力、效率和经济增长》Yanrui Wu, *Productivity, Efficiency and Economic Growth in China*.Palgrave Macmillan UK (2008)
89. 《蓬勃的中国经济：调整更加均衡的发展》John Wong（黄朝翰）, Wei Liu, *China's Surging Economy: Adjusting for More Balanced Development*. World Scientific (2007)
90. 《中国经济增长面临的挑战》Dwight H. Perkins（珀金斯）, *The Challenges of China's Growth* (Henry Wendt Lecture). The AEI Press (2007)
91. 《中国经济转型与增长》Barry Naughton, *The Chinese Economy: Transitions and Growth*. MIT Press (2007)
92. 《了解中国的增长：推动中国经济未来的力量》Chi Lo, *Understanding China's Growth: Forces that Drive China's Economic Future*. Palgrave Macmillan UK (2007)
93. Chi Lo, *Understanding China's Growth: Forces that Drive China's Economic Future*. Palgrave Macmillan (2007)
94. 《中国改革后的经济：实现和谐，持续增长》Richard Sanders, *China's Post-Reform Economy: Achieving Harmony, Sustaining Growth*. Routledge (2007)
95. 《中国与全球政治经济》Shaun Breslin, *China and the Global Political Economy* (International Political Economy). Palgrave Macmillan UK (2007)
96. 《中国经济长期表现》(Development Centre Studies) Angus Maddison, *Chinese Economic Performance in the Long Run*.OECD Publishing (2007)
97. 《中国经济发展的转折点》Ross Garnaut, Ligang Song (eds.), *The Turning Point in Chinas Economic Development*. Asia Pacific Press (2006)
98. 《中国经济威胁的幻影：下一次亚洲危机的阴影》Chi Lo, *Phantom of the China Economic Threat: Shadow of the Next Asian Crisis*. Palgrave Macmillan (2006)
99. 《从马克思、毛泽东到市场：农业转型的经济学与政治学》Johan Swinnen, Scott Rozelle, *From Marx and Mao to the Market: The Economics and Politics of Agricultural Transition*. Oxford University Press, USA (2006)
100. 《加入WTO后的中国经济》Shuming Bao（鲍曙明）, Shuanglin Lin, Changwen Zhao, *The Chinese Economy After WTO Accession* (The Chinese Economy Series). Ashgate Publishing Limited (2006)
101. 《大中华区的出现：中国大陆、中国台湾和中国香港经济一体化》Yun-Wing Sung, *The Emergence of Greater China: The Economic Integration of Mainland China, Taiwan and Hong Kong* (Studies on the Chinese Economy). Palgrave Macmillan UK (2005)
102. 《中国与西方和日本的经济关系（1949—1979）：粮食、贸易和外交》Chad

Mitcham, *China's Economic Relations with the West and Japan, 1949—1979: Grain, Trade and Diplomacy* (Routledge Studies on the Chinese Economy). Routledge (2005)

103. 《凯洛格论中国：成功策略》（对外经济）Mark Finn, *Kellogg on China: Strategies for Success*. Northwestern University Press (2004)

104. 《新千年亚洲经济合作：中国经济表现（第一卷）》Calla Wiemer, Heping Cao, *Asian Economic Cooperation in the New Millennium: China's Economic Presence* (Advanced Research in Asian Economic Studies, v. 1). World Scientific Publishing (2004)

105. 《当代中国的经济增长、收入分配与减贫》Shujie Yao, *Economic Growth, Income Distribution and Poverty Reduction in Contemporary China* (Routledge Studies on the Chinese Economy). Routledge (2004)

106. 《中国经济增长：中国特色的奇迹》Yanrui Wu, *China's Economic Growth: A Miracle with Chinese Characteristics*. RoutledgeCurzon (2004)

107. 《21世纪保持中国经济增长》Shijie Yao, *Sustaining China's Economic Growth in the 21st Century*. Routledgecurzon (2003)

108. 《中国经济领域的断层线》Charles Wolf, *Fault Lines in China's Economic Terrain*. RAND (2003)

109. 《中国向全球经济转型》Michael Webber, Mark Wang, Zhu Ying, *China's Transition to a Global Economy*. Palgrave Macmillan UK (2002)

110. 《中国与全球经济：国家冠军企业、产业政策和大企业革命》Peter Nolan, *China and the Global Economy: National Champions, Industrial Policy and the Big Business Revolution*. Palgrave Macmillan (2001)

111. 《中美与全球经济》Shuxun Chen, Charles Wolf, Jr. (eds.), *China, the United States, and the Global Economy*. RAND (2001)

112. 《中国经济转型中的当代发展与问题》Charles Harvie, *Contemporary Developments and Issues in China's Economic Transition*. Palgrave Macmillan (2000)

113. 《中国经济增长的来源（1978—1996）》Chris Bramall（克里斯·布拉莫尔）, *Sources of Chinese Economic Growth, 1978—1996* (Studies on Contemporary China). Oxford University Press (2000)

114. 《20世纪90年代的中国经济》Jun Ma, *The Chinese Economy in the 1990s* (Studies on the Chinese Economy). Palgrave Macmillan UK (2000)

115. 《中国经济中工作场所关系的变化》Malcolm Warner (eds.), *Changing Workplace Relations in the Chinese Economy* (Studies on the Chinese Economy). Palgrave Macmillan UK (2000)

116. 《中国经济增长对地区、移民和环境的影响》Terry Cannon (eds.), *China's Economic Growth: The Impact on Regions, Migration and the Environment*. Palgrave Macmillan UK (2000)

117. 《中国未完成的经济革命》Nicholas R. Lardy（尼古拉斯·拉迪）, *China's Unfinished Economic Revolution*. Brookings Institue Press (1998)

118. 《中国经济崛起：中央王国的出现》Greg Mastel, *The Rise of the Chinese Economy: The Middle Kingdom Emerges*. M.E. Sharpe (1997)

119. 《中国经济：从革命到改革》David J. Pyle, *China's Economy: From Revolution to Reform*. Palgrave Macmillan UK (1997)

120. 《中国：分散经济中的宏观经济稳定》World Bank, *China: Macroeconomic Stability in a Decentralized Economy*. World Bank Publications (1995)

121. 《中国经济发展：与日本经验的比较》Ryōshin Minami, *The Economic Development of China. A Comparison with the Japanese Experience* (Studies on the Chinese Economy). Palgrave Macmillan UK (1994)

122. 《中国经济中的国家与市场：有关争议问题论文集》Peter Nolan, *State and Market in the Chinese Economy: Essays on Controversial Issues*. Palgrave Macmillan (1993)

123. 《20世纪初的中国经济：中国近期研究》Tim Wright (eds.), *The Chinese Economy in the Early Twentieth Century: Recent Chinese Studies* (Studies on the Chinese Economy). Palgrave Macmillan UK (1992)

124. 《中国语境下的经济发展：政策问题与分析》Clement Tisdell, *Economic Development in the Context of China: Policy Issues and Analysis*. Palgrave Macmillan (1992)

125. 《中国计划经济的基础：文献调查（1953—1965）》Christopher Howe, Kenneth R. Walker, *The Foundations of the Chinese Planned Economy: A Documentary Survey, 1953—1965*. Palgrave Macmillan UK (1989)

126. 《中华人民共和国的经济发展和社会变革》Willy Kraus, *Economic Development and Social Change in the People's Republic of China*. Springer-Verlag New York (1982)

127. 《中国经济政策与价格稳定》Tong-eng Wang, *Economic Policies and Price Stability in China*. Berkeley: Center for Chinese Studies, Institute of East Asian Studies, University of California (1980)

128. 《中国经济增长与分配》Nicholas R. Lardy（尼古拉斯·拉迪）, *Economic Growth and Distribution in China*. Cambridge University Press (1978)

129. 《中国经济学读物：精选材料及解释性介绍》Charles Frederick Remer, *Readings in Economics for China, Selected Materials with Explanatory Introductions*. Shanghai, Commercial Press, Limited (1922)

10.2 经济管理与改革

1. 《中国矿山废物管理的新进展》Di Wu, *Mine Waste Management in China: Recent Development*. Springer Singapore (2020)

2. 《中国经济特区研究3》(Research Series on the Chinese Dream and China's Development Path) Yiming Yuan (ed.), *Studies on China's Special Economic Zones 3*. Springer Singapore (2020)

3. 《中国经济特区年度发展报告（2018）：中国经济特区蓝皮书》(Research Series on

the Chinese Dream and China's Development Path) Yitao Tao, Yiming Yuan (eds.), *Annual Report on the Development of China's Special Economic Zones (2018) : Blue Book of China's Special Economic Zones*. Springer Singapore (2019)

4. 《中国经济特区年度发展报告（2017）中国经济特区蓝皮书》(Research Series on the Chinese Dream and China's Development Path) Yitao Tao, Yiming Yuan (eds.), *Annual Report on the Development of China's Special Economic Zones (2017) : Blue Book of China's Special Economic Zones*. Springer Singapore (2019)

5. 《公司治理中的制度能动性：在中国的合格境外机构投资者》Wenge Wang, *Institutional Activism in Corporate Governance: Qualified Foreign Institutional Investors in China*. Springer International Publishing: Palgrave Macmillan (2019)

6. 《中国国有经济与国际秩序》Luyao Che, *China's State-Directed Economy and the International Order*. Springer Singapore (2019)

7. 《近代早期经济中的公共物品供给：日本、中国和欧洲的比较视角》Masayuki Tanimoto, R. Bin Wong, *Public Goods Provision in the Early Modern Economy: Comparative Perspectives from Japan, China, and Europe*. University of California Press (2019)

8. 《中国社会经济五年计划中空间要素的变化：从项目布局到空间规划》(Springer Geography) Lei Wang, *Changing Spatial Elements in Chinese Socio-economic Five-year Plan: from Project Layout to Spatial Planning*. Springer Singapore (2019)

9. 《治理企业税收管理：中国国家所有制、机构和市场的作用》Chen Zhang, Rajah Rasiah, Kee Cheok Cheong, *Governing Corporate Tax Management: The Role of State Ownership, Institutions and Markets in China*. Springer Singapore: Palgrave Macmillan (2019)

10. 《中国基本经济制度》(China Governance System Research Series) Changhong Pei, Chunxue Yang, Xinming Yang, *The Basic Economic System of China*. Springer Singapore (2019)

11. 《中国的转让定价：概念、控制、实践和审计评估》Jian Li, Alan Paisey, *Transfer Pricing in China: Concepts, Controls, Practices, and Audit Assessment*. Springer Singapore: Palgrave Macmillan (2019)

12. 《中国经济特区研究2》(Research Series on the Chinese Dream and China's Development Path) Yiming Yuan (ed.), *Studies on China's Special Economic Zones 2*. Springer Singapore (2019)

13. 《管理思想的多样性》Check Teck Foo, *Diversity of Managerial Ideology* (The Chinese Management Book-of-Readings Series). Springer Singapore (2018)

14. 《中国经济改革与发展40年》Xinli Zheng, *China's 40 Years of Economic Reform and Development*. Springer Singapore (2018)

15. 《中国品牌管理研究进展》John M. T. Balmer, Weifeng Chen (eds.), *Advances in Chinese Brand Management* (Journal of Brand Management: Advanced Collections). Palgrave Macmillan UK (2017)

16. 《中国悖论：经济转型前沿》Paul G. Clifford, *The China Paradox: At the Front Line of Economic Transformation*. De Gruyter (2017)

17. 《中国特色社会主义审计理论研究》（修订本）Jiayi Liu, *Study on the Auditing Theory of Socialism with Chinese Characteristics* (Revised Edition). Wiley (2017)

18. 《曾仕强与中国式管理》Li Guoqing（李国庆）, Zhang Yue, Luan Weixia, Zhou Peihong, Mai Xiaoxin, Zhao Rongchen, *Zeng Shiqiang and the Chinese Style of Management*. Cambridge Scholars Publishing (2017)

19. 《中国会计准则：中国新企业会计准则的出台和效应》Lorenzo Riccardi, *China Accounting Standards: Introduction and Effects of New Chinese Accounting Standards for Business Enterprises*. Springer Singapore (2016)

20. 《市场一体化：欧盟对中国监管改革的经验与启示》Niels Philipsen, Stefan E. Weishaar, Guangdong Xu (eds.), *Market Integration: The EU Experience and Implications for Regulatory Reform in China* (China-EU Law Series 2). Springer-Verlag Berlin Heidelberg (2016)

21. 《亚洲经济改革：中国、印度和日本》Sara Hsu, *Economic Reform in Asia: China, India, and Japan*. Edward Elgar Pub. (2016)

22. 《中国内部管理视角的多元化》Check Teck Foo (eds.), *Diversity of Managerial Perspectives from Inside China*. Springer-Verlag Singapur (2015)

23. 《时代变迁中的中国灾害管理》Yi Kang, *Disaster Management in China in a Changing Era*. Springer-Verlag Berlin Heidelberg (2015)

24. 《中国地区间经济发展》Rongxing Guo, Hao Gui, Luc Changlei Guo, *Multiregional Economic Development in China*. Springer-Verlag Berlin Heidelberg (2015)

25. 《中国房产税：历史、试点和前景》Yilin Hou, Qiang Ren, Ping Zhang, *The Property Tax in China: History, Pilots, and Prospects* (Development and Governance 1). Springer International Publishing (2015)

26. 《市场逻辑：中国经济改革的内部观点》Weiying Zhang, Matthew Dale (transl.), *The Logic of the Market: An Insider's View of Chinese Economic Reform*. Cato Institute (2015)

27. 《超越市场与政府：伦理因素对经济的影响》Yining Li, *Beyond Market and Government: Influence of Ethical Factors on Economy*. Springer-Verlag Berlin Heidelberg (2015)

28. 《打破中国数字神话：理解和运用中国统计数据》Matthew Crabbe, *Myth-Busting China's Numbers: Understanding and Using China's Statistics*. Palgrave Macmillan UK (2014)

29. 《中国通货膨胀管理：当前趋势与新策略（第一卷）》Liu Yuanchun, *Managing Inflation in China: Current Trends and New Strategies* (Volume 1) (Enrich Series on Managing Inflation in China). Enrich Professional Publishing (2014)

30. 《管理中国自由裁量权及表现：解决中国企业与跨国公司自由裁量权难题》Hagen Wülferth, *Managerial Discretion and Performance in China: Towards Resolving the Discretion Puzzle for Chinese Companies and Multinationals*. Springer-Verlag Berlin Heidelberg (2013)

31. 《中国知识密集型商务服务业创新管理》Shunzhong Liu, *Innovation Management in Knowledge Intensive Business Services in China*. Springer-Verlag Berlin Heidelberg (2013)

32. 《理解中国管理之过去、现在与未来》Malcolm Warner, *Understanding Management in China: Past, Present and Future*. Routledge (2013)

33. 《中国经济与监管》Michael Faure, Guangdong Xu, *Economics and Regulation in China*. Routledge (2013)

34. 《中国组织危机管理：从变化中受益》Ruth Alas, Junhong Gao (eds.), *Crisis Management in Chinese Organizations: Benefiting from the Changes*. Palgrave Macmillan UK (2012)

35. 《模拟中国资源环境风险管理》Lili Bian, Min Zhou, Aibin Li, Shitong Ge (auth.), Desheng Dash Wu, Yong Zhou (eds.), *Modeling Risk Management for Resources and Environment in China* (Computational Risk Management). Springer-Verlag Berlin Heidelberg (2011)

36. 《经济改革、区域主义和出口：中国和印度比较》Ganeshan Wignaraja, *Economic Reforms, Regionalism, and Exports: Comparing China and India*. East-West Center (2011)

37. 《大分流之前及其后：中欧经济变革的政治》Jean-Laurent Rosenthal, Roy Bin Wong, *Before and Beyond Divergence: The Politics of Economic Change in China and Europe*. Harvard University Press (2011)

38. 《中国税收指南》Chris Devonshire-Ellis, Andy Scott, Sam Woollard (auth.), Chris Devonshire-Ellis, Andy Scott, Sam Woollard (eds.), *The China Tax Guide*. Springer-Verlag Berlin Heidelberg (2011)

39. 《中国未来20年的改革与发展》Ross Garnaut, Jane Golley and Ligang Song (eds.), *China: The Next Twenty Years of Reform and Development*. ANU E Press, Co-published with Social Sciences Academic Press (China) (2010)

40. 《中国股份制改革：摸着石头过河的私有化》Shu-yun Ma, *Shareholding System Reform in China: Privatizing by Groping for Stones*. Edward Elgar Publishing Limited (2010)

41. 《中国管理革命：精神、土地与能源》Roland Berger, *China's Management Revolution: Spirit, Land, Energy*. Palgrave Macmillan (2010)

42. 《中国战略：利用世界增长最快经济体的力量》Edward Tse, *The China Strategy: Harnessing the Power of the World's Fastest-Growing Economy*. Basic Books (AZ) (2010)

43. 《管控中国快速增长：公平和制度》Ravi Kanbur, Xiaobo Zhang, *Governing Rapid Growth in China: Equity and Institutions* (Routledge Studies in the Modern World Economy). Routledge (2009)

44. 《中国组织变革的实施：在黑暗中摸索前进》Ruth Alas (Eds.), *Implementation of Changes in Chinese Organizations: Groping a Way through the Darkness* (Chandos Asian Studies Series). Chandos Publishing (2009)

45. 《中国管理》Birgit Zinzius, *China Management*. Springer (2007)

46. 《管理中国国际业务》Xiaowen Tian, *Managing International Business in China*. Cambridge

University Press (2007)

47. 《中国冲突管理的新方法：朝鲜与"台湾"的案例》Zhao Quansheng, *China's New Approach to Conflict Management: The Cases of North Korea and Taiwan*. Central Asia-Caucasus Institute and Silk Road Studies Program (2006)

48. 《中国改革与非国有经济：自由化战略的政治经济学》Hongyi Lai, *Reform and the Non-State Economy in China: The Political Economy of Liberalization Strategies*. Palgrave Macmillan (2006)

49. 《评估中国市场化程度》Xiaoxi Li, *Assessing the Extent of China's Marketization* (The Chinese Trade and Industry Series). Ashgate Publishing Company (2006)

50. 《中国：开放兼并和收购政策》OECD Investment Policy Reviews. *China: Open Policies towards Mergers and Acquisitions*. OECD Publishing (2006)

51. 《中国所有制：转型过程、结果与前景》Ligang Song, Ross Garnaut, Stoyan Tenev, Yang Yeo, *China's Ownership: Transformation Process, Outcomes, Prospects*. World Bank Publications (2005)

52. 《发展困境：中国土地改革与制度变迁》Peter Ho, *Developmental Dilemmas: Land Reform and Institutional Change in China*. Routledge (2005)

53. 《转型经济中的管理：从柏林墙到中国长城》Malcolm Warner, Vincent Edwards, Gennadij Polonsky, Danijel Pučko, Ying Zhu, *Management in Transitional Economies: From the Berlin Wall to the Great Wall of China*. RoutledgeCurzon (2005)

54. 《中国管理者和官员：国际企业联盟的建立》Jie Tang, *Managers and Mandarins in China: The Building of an International Business Alliance*. Routledge (2005)

55. 《中国管理手册：全球最重要的新兴市场综合问答指南》Engelbert Boos, Christine Boos, Frank Sieren, *The China Management Handbook: A Comprehensive Question and Answer Guide to the World's Most Important Emerging Market*. Palgrave Macmillan (2003)

56. 《中国管理的未来：亚太商业研究》Malcolm Warner, *The Future of Chinese Management: Studies in Asia Pacific Business*. Routledge (2003)

57. 《今日中国经济改革、社会凝聚力和集体认同》Taciana Fisac, Leila Fernandez-Stembridge, *China Today: Economic Reforms, Social Cohesion and Collective Identities*. RoutledgeCurzon (2003)

58. 《中国经济的动力源泉：广东省经济改革》Tung X. Bui, David C. Yang, Wayne D. Jones, Joanna Z. Li, *China's Economic Powerhouse: Economic Reform in Guangdong Province*. Palgrave Macmillan (2003)

59. 《中国国民核算：来源与方法》OECD, *National Accounts for China: Sources and Methods* (China in the Global Economy; Statistics: Emerging Economies Transition). Organisation for Economic Co-operation and Development (2000)

60. 《中国语境中的管理与组织》J. T. Li, Anne S. Tsui, Elizabeth Weldon (eds.), *Management and*

Organizations in the Chinese Context. Palgrave Macmillan UK (2000)

61. 《中国资源会计》Henry M. Peskin, Alessandro Lanza (eds.), *Resources Accounting in China.* Springer Netherlands (1999)

62. 《中国国际管理的跨文化问题》Jan Selmer, *International Management in China: Cross-Cultural Issues* (Routledge Advances in Asia-Pacific Business). Routledge (1998)

63. 《非国家权力：中国经济改革的地方原因（第一卷）》Lynn T. White（白霖）, *Unstately Power, Local Causes of China's Economic Reforms* (Volume 1). M. E. Sharpe (1998)

64. 《中国向社会主义市场经济转变》Osman Suliman, *China's Transition to a Socialist Market Economy.* Praeger (1998)

65. 《中国经济改革》Shangquan Gao, *China's Economic Reform* (Studies on the Chinese Economy). Palgrave Macmillan UK (1996)

66. 《中国的功能分析》Shihsen Chang, Bingren Li, Shengwang Wang, Shaozong Yan, Chung-Chun Yang (eds.), *Functional Analysis in China.* Kluwer (1996)

67. 《走出计划：中国经济改革（1978—1993）》Barry Naughton, *Growing Out of the Plan: Chinese Economic Reform, 1978—1993.* Cambridge University Press (1995)

68. 《中国内部市场发展与调控》Anjali Kumar, *China: Internal Market Development and Regulation.* World Bank Publications (1994)

69. 《能否解读一个煎蛋卷？中国经济改革的理论与实践》Yuan-li Wu, Richard Y. C. Yin, *Can One Unscramble an Omelet? China's Economic Reform in Theory and Practice.* University of Maryland School of Law (1993)

70. 《中国经济改革与政治尝试（1979—1989）》Barna Tálas, *Economic Reforms and Political Attempts in China 1979—1989.* Springer-Verlag Berlin Heidelberg (1991)

71. 《湖南与华南经济转型》A. S. Bhalla, *Economic Transition in Hunan and Southern China.* Palgrave Macmillan UK (1984)

72. 《增长、分配与社会变迁：民国经济论文》Yuan-Li Wu, Kung-Chia Yeh, *Growth, Distribution, and Social Change: Essays on the Economy of the Republic of China.* School of Law, University of Maryland (1978)

73. 《中国经济革命》Alexander Eckstein, *China's Economic Revolution.* Cambridge University Press (1977)

74. 《中华帝国的土地税（1750—1911）》Yeh-Chien Wang, *Land Taxation in Imperial China, 1750—1911.* Harvard University Press (1974)

75. 《中国近代经济简史（1840—1961）》Frank Henry Haviland King, *A Concise Economic History of Modern China (1840—1961).* Praeger, Pall Mall (1969)

76. 《清代中国税收制度（1644—1911）》（博士论文）Shao-Kwan Chen, A. M., *The System of Taxation in China in the Tsing Dynasty 1644—1911.* Ph. D. Dissertation, Columbia University (1914)

10.3 财政与金融、投资

1. 《中国金融市场中的数字媒体与风险文化》Zhifei Mao, *Digital Media and Risk Culture in China's Financial Markets*. Routledge (2019)
2. 《重塑中国货币政策：市场与控制（1998—2008）》Michael Beggs, Luke Deer, *Remaking Monetary Policy in China: Markets and Controls, 1998—2008*. Springer Singapore: Palgrave Pivot (2019)
3. 《中国经济放缓背景下管理金融风险》(Research Series on the Chinese Dream and China's Development Path) Yang Li (ed.), *Managing Financial Risks Amid China's Economic Slowdown*. Springer Singapore (2019)
4. 《中华人民共和国的国际投资战略》(Routledge Revivals) Yadong Luo, *International Investment Strategies in the People's Republic of China*. Routledge (2019)
5. 《中国众筹：一种新的制度经济学方法》(Contributions to Management Science) Andrea S. Funk, *Crowdfunding in China: A New Institutional Economics Approach*. Springer International Publishing (2019)
6. 《中国国际投资战略：双边，区域和全球》Julien Chaisse, *China's International Investment Strategy: Bilateral, Regional, and Global*. Oxford University Press (2019)
7. 《中国在欧盟和美国的对外直接投资：动荡时期的简单规则》Tim Wenniges, Walter Lohman (eds.), *Chinese FDI in the EU and the US: Simple Rules for Turbulent Times*. Springer Singapore: Palgrave Macmillan (2019)
8. 《中国银行业的公司治理》(CSR, Sustainability, Ethics & Governance) Weikang Zou, *Corporate Governance in the Banking Sector in China*. Springer Singapore (2019)
9. 《中国金融与战略》(The Chinese Management Book-of-Readings Series) Check-Teck Foo, *Finance and Strategy Inside China*. Springer Singapore (2019)
10. 《揭秘中国股市：谜团背后的隐藏逻辑》Eric Girardin, Zhenya Liu, *Demystifying China's Stock Market: The Hidden Logic behind the Puzzles*. Springer International Publishing: Palgrave Pivot (2019)
11. 《人民币国际化战略》(Research Series on the Chinese Dream and China's Development Path) Yuanzheng Cao, *Strategies for Internationalizing the Renminbi*. Springer Singapore (2018)
12. 《中央银行的独立性、监管与货币政策：从德国、希腊到中国、美国》Ranajoy Ray Chaudhuri, *Central Bank Independence, Regulations, and Monetary Policy: From Germany and Greece to China and the United States*. Palgrave Macmillan (2018)
13. 《劳特利奇中国会计读本》(Routledge Companions in Business Management and Accounting) Haiyan Zhou (ed.), *The Routledge Companion to Accounting in China*. Routledge (2018)
14. 《中国的金融开放：联盟政治与政策变化》Yu-Wai Vic Li, *China's Financial Opening:*

Coalition Politics and Policy Changes. Routledge (2018)

15. 《中国收购世界：中国海外投资分析》Andrew Collier, *China Buys the World: Analyzing China's Overseas Investments*. Palgrave Pivot (2018)

16. 《中国可持续发展的财政基础：广东再平衡》Ehtisham Ahmad, Meili Niu, Kezhou Xiao (eds.), *Fiscal Underpinnings for Sustainable Development in China: Rebalancing in Guangdong*. Springer Singapore (2018)

17. 《大众融资：中国众筹》Jiazhuo G. Wang et al. (eds.), *Financing from Masses: Crowdfunding in China*. Springer Singapore (2018)

18. 《为中国钱包而战：从世界新秩序中获利》Shaun Rein, *The War for China's Wallet: Profiting from the New World Order*. Walter de Gruyter (2018)

19. 《双中心全球金融体系：中国崛起的视角》Tao Yuan, *The Dual-Center Global Financial System: The Perspective of China's Rise*. Springer Singapore (2018)

20. 《中国证券市场监管》Weiping He, *The Regulation of Securities Markets in China*. Palgrave Macmillan US (2018)

21. 《追求存在与卓越：中国银行业全球扩张的前景及其基准》Shenglin Ben, Jiefang Yu, Yue Gu, Jiamin Lv, Lijun Zhang, Huichao Gong, Hanting Gu, Qi Shuai, *In Pursuit of Presence or Prominence: The Prospect of Chinese Banks' Global Expansion and Their Benchmarks* (Current Chinese Economic Report Series). Springer Singapore (2018)

22. 《中国财政体制概论》Lorenzo Riccardi, *Introduction to Chinese Fiscal System*. Springer Singapore (2018)

23. 《中国债务拐点研究》Xiaohuang Zhu, Song Lin, Lin Wang, Wenqi Wu, Quanli Qin, *A Study of the Turning Point of China's Debt*. Springer Singapore (2018)

24. 《中国资本市场交易与投资策略》Xiaojiang Zhang, *Capital Markets Trading and Investment Strategies in China*. Springer Singapore (2018)

25. 《投资中国与中国海外投资》Xiuping Zhang, Bruce P. Corrie, *Investing in China and Chinese Investment Abroad*. Springer Singapore (2018)

26. 《中国国家资产负债表（2015年）：杠杆调整和风险管理》Yang Li, Xiaojing Zhang, Xin Chang, *China's National Balance Sheet (2015): Leverage Adjustment and Risk Management*. China Social Sciences Press and Springer Nature Singapore Pte Ltd. (2018)

27. 《中国银行在新浪微博上对企业形象的讨论性构建：一种社会语言学综合方法》Wei Feng, *Discursive Constructions of Corporate Identities by Chinese Banks on Sina Weibo: An Integrated Sociolinguistics Approach*. Springer Singapore (2017)

28. 《发展中国：外商直接投资的显著影响》Michael J. Enright, *Developing China: The Remarkable Impact of Foreign Direct Investment*. Routledge (2017)

29. 《中国金融体系：增长与低效》Dominique De Rambures, Felipe Escobar Duenas, *China's Financial System: Growth and Inefficiency*. Palgrave Macmillan (2017)

30. 《影子银行与中国资本主义的兴起》Andrew Collier, *Shadow Banking and the Rise of Capitalism in China*. Palgrave Macmillan (2017)

31. 《中国信托财产的所有权：比较与社会资本视角》Zhen Meng, *Ownership of Trust Property in China: A Comparative and Social Capital Perspective* (Perspectives in Law Business and Innovation). Springer (2017)

32. 《中国公共财政建设指标体系研究》Peiyong Gao, Bin Zhang, Ning Wang, *Research on China's Public Finance Construction Index System* (Research Series on the Chinese Dream and China's Development Path). Springer Singapore (2017)

33. 《中国银行业改革：从入世前到金融危机及其后》Chunxia Jiang, Shujie Yao, *Chinese Banking Reform: From the Pre-WTO Period to the Financial Crisis and Beyond* (The Nottingham China Policy Institute Series). Palgrave Macmillan (2017)

34. 《中国走向全球：中国海外投资如何转变企业》Huiyao Wang, Lu Miao, *China Goes Global: How China's Overseas Investment is Transforming its Business Enterprises* (Palgrave Macmillan Asian Business Series). Palgrave Macmillan UK (2016)

35. 《稳健而有效的中国投资政策》OECD, *Policies for Sound and Effective Investment in China* (Better Policies). OECD Publishing (2016)

36. 《人民币崛起：一个全球货币新体系》William H. Overholt, Guonan Ma, Cheung Kwok Law, *Renminbi Rising: A New Global Monetary System Emerges*. John Wiley & Sons (2016)

37. 《赢得货币：人民币的崛起》Eswar S. Prasad, *Gaining Currency: The Rise of the Renminbi*. Oxford University Press (2016)

38. 《中国金融监管的发展》Bin Hu, Zhentao Yin, Liansheng Zheng (eds.), *Development of China's Financial Supervision and Regulation*. Palgrave Macmillan US (2016)

39. 《中国金融安全：现状分析与制度设计》Dexu He, *Financial Security in China: Situation Analysis and System Design*. Springer Singapore (2016)

40. 《中国金融犯罪：腐败的发展、制裁与系统性传播》Hongming Cheng, *Financial Crime in China: Developments, Sanctions, and the Systemic Spread of Corruption*. Palgrave Macmillan US (2016)

41. 《中国银行转型：不为人知的故事》James Stent, *China's Banking Transformation: The Untold Story*. Oxford University Press (2016)

42. 《无银行贷款融资：中国中小企业融资的新选择》Jiazhuo G. Wang, Juan Yang, *Financing without Bank Loans: New Alternatives for Funding SMEs in China*. Springer Singapore (2016)

43. 《通过自由贸易区投资中国》Lorenzo Riccardi, *Investing in China through Free Trade Zones*. Springer-Verlag Berlin Heidelberg (2016)

44. 《中国影子银行：金融改革的机遇》Chow Soon Ng, Andrew Sheng, *Shadow Banking in China: An Opportunity for Financial Reform*. Wiley (2016)

45. 《中国对外直接投资促进体系》Changhong Pei, Wen Zheng, *China's Outbound Foreign*

Direct Investment Promotion System (Research Series on the Chinese Dream and China's Development Path). Springer-Verlag Berlin Heidelberg (2015)

46. 《中国经济发展的代价：权力、资本和权利贫困》Zhaohui Hong, *The Price of China's Economic Development: Power, Capital, and the Poverty of Rights* (Asian In The New Millennium). University Press of Kentucky (2015)

47. 《中国货币政策调控与金融风险防范：有效性与适度性研究》Hui Zhou, *China's Monetary Policy Regulation and Financial Risk Prevention: The Study of Effectiveness and Appropriateness*. Springer Berlin Heidelberg (2015)

48. 《环球财经本地化：西式私募股权基金在中国的崛起》Justin Robertson, *Localizing Global Finance: The Rise of Western-Style Private Equity in China*. Palgrave Macmillan US (2015)

49. 《融资资金：中国在线贷款》Jiazhuo G. Wang, Hongwei Xu, Jun Ma (eds.), *Financing the Underfinanced: Online Lending in China*. Springer-Verlag Berlin Heidelberg (2015)

50. 《中国风险投资市场：当前法律问题与未来改革》Lin Zhang, *China's Venture Capital Market: Current Legal Problems and Prospective Reforms*. Elsevier (2015)

51. 《现代中国金融改革：前台议员的视角》Sun Guofeng, *Financial Reforms in Modern China: A Frontbencher's Perspective*. Palgrave Macmillan US (2015)

52. 《中国对外直接投资及对世界经济的影响》Shujie Yao, Pan Wang, *China's Outward Foreign Direct Investments and Impact on the World Economy*. Palgrave Macmillan UK (2014)

53. 《中国的公共股权私募》Pengcheng Song, *Private Placement of Public Equity in China*. Springer-Verlag Berlin Heidelberg (2014)

54. 《中国金融市场：问题与机遇》Ming Wang, Kin Keung Lai, Jerome Yen, *China's Financial Markets: Issues and Opportunities*. Routledge (2014)

55. 《中国投资和就业机会》Jeffrey Yi-Lin Forrest, Tao Lixin, *Investment and Employment Opportunities in China*. CRC, Taylor and Francis (2014)

56. 《中国银行业监管：公共部门和私营部门角色》He Wei Ping, *Banking Regulation in China: The Role of Public and Private Sectors*. Palgrave Macmillan UK (2014)

57. 《中国证券市场：走向有效监管》Jing Bian, *China's Securities Market: Towards Efficient Regulation*. Routledge (2014)

58. 《故意的脆弱：银行危机与信贷稀缺的政治根源》Charles W. Calomiris, Stephen H. Haber, *Fragile by Design: The Political Origins of Banking Crises and Scarce Credit*. Princeton University Press (2014)

59. 《中国现代银行业的基石：广州担保体系与银行存款保险的起源（1780—1933）》Frederick Delano Grant, *The Chinese Cornerstone of Modern Banking: The Canton Guaranty System and the Origins of Bank Deposit Insurance 1780—1933*. Brill Nijhoff (2014)

60. 《中国人民银行的崛起：制度变迁的政治学》Stephen Bell, Hui Feng, *The Rise of the People's Bank of China: The Politics of Institutional Change*. Harvard University Press (2013)

61. 《中国资本市场》Yong Zhen, *China's Capital Markets* (Chandos Asian Studies Series). Chandos Publishing (2013)

62. 《共产主义中国的资本家》Keming Yang, *Capitalists in Communist China*. Palgrave Macmillan (2013)

63. 《中国私募股权基金：20年概述（第一卷）》Bin Xia, *Private Equity Funds in China: A 20-Year Overview (Volume 1)*. Enrich Professional Publishing (2013)

64. 《巴西、俄罗斯、印度、中国、韩国和南非的国家智力资本与金融危机》Carol Yeh-Yun Lin, Leif Edvinsson, Jeffrey Chen, Tord Beding, *National Intellectual Capital and the Financial Crisis in Brazil, Russia, India, China, Korea, and South Africa*. Springer-Verlag New York (2013)

65. 《中国证券投资机遇》David M. Darst, *Portfolio Investment Opportunities in China*. Wiley (2013)

66. 《中国超级银行债务、石油和影响：国家开发银行如何重写财务规则》Henry Sanderson, Michael Forsythe, *China's Superbank Debt, Oil and Influence: How China Development Bank is Rewriting the Rules of Finance*. John Wiley & Sons (2013)

67. 《金融如何塑造中国、日本和韩国经济》Yung Chul Park, Hugh Patrick, *How Finance Is Shaping the Economies of China, Japan, and Korea*. Columbia University Press (2013)

68. 《公司治理实施与金融发展的中国经验》Ding Chen, *Corporate Governance Enforcement and Financial Development: The Chinese Experience*. Edward Elgar Pub (2013)

69. 《中国资本市场发展的经验和挑战》Douglas Cumming J. D., Alessandra Guariglia, Wenxuan Hou, Edward Lee, *Developing China's Capital Market: Experiences and Challenges* Palgrave Macmillan UK (2013)

70. 《通向现代财政国家之路：英国、日本、中国》Wenkai He, *Paths toward the Modern Fiscal State. England, Japan, and China*. Harvard University Press (2013)

71. 《财富忧虑：中国新富人的金钱和道德》John Osburg, *Anxious Wealth: Money and Morality Among China's New Rich*. Stanford University Press (2013)

72. 《中国私募股权：挑战与机遇》Kwek Ping Yong, *Private Equity in China: Challenges and Opportunities*. Wiley (2012)

73. 《中国银行业》（第二版）Violaine Cousin, *Banking in China*. Second edition. Palgrave Macmillan (2011)

74. 《中国人民币：国际化与中国金融产品》Peter G. Zhang, Thomas Chan, *The Chinese Yuan: Internationalization and Financial Products in China*. Wiley (2011)

75. 《不情愿的监管者：西方如何创造以及中国如何幸免于全球金融危机》Leo F. Goodstadt, *Reluctant Regulators: How the West Created and How China Survived the Global Financial Crisis*. Hong Kong University Press (2011)

76. 《心连心：中国在国际金融和商业中的作用》Wang Jun, *Accounting With Heart: China's*

Role in International Finance and Business. John Wiley & Sons (Asia) Pte Ltd (2010)

77. 《信用宇宙学：跨国流动与中国目的地政治》Julie Y. Chu, *Cosmologies of Credit: Transnational Mobility and the Politics of Destination in China*. Duke University Press (2010)

78. 《跨国银行在中国：理论与实践》Chen Meng, *Multinational Banking in China: Theory and Practice* (New Horizons in International Business Series).Edward Elgar Publishing Limited (2009)

79. 《中国新兴金融市场：挑战与机遇》James R. Barth, John A. Tatom, Glenn Yago (eds.), *China's Emerging Financial Markets: Challenges and Opportunities*. Springer US (2009)

80. 《后社会主义中国的财富与贫困》Deborah Davis, Wang Feng, *Creating Wealth and Poverty in Postsocialist China*. Stanford University Press (2009)

81. 《中国证券纠纷的解决》Sanzhu Zhu, *Securities Dispute Resolution in China*. Routledge (2008)

82. 《中国金融市场的国际化》Svenja Schlichting, *Internationalising China's Financial Markets*. Palgrave (2008)

83. 《成为你自己的中国股票大师：从中国经济繁荣中获利之终极投资者指南》J. Trippon, *Becoming Your Own China Stock Guru: The Ultimate Investors Guide to Profiting from China's Economic Boom*. John Wiley & Sons (2008)

84. 《中国货币的挑战：过去经验和未来前景》Richard C. K. Burdekin, *China's Monetary Challenges: Past Experiences and Future Prospects*. Cambridge University Press (2008)

85. 《中国汇率政策争论》Morris Goldstein, Nicholas R. Lardy（尼古拉斯·拉迪）, *Debating China's Exchange Rate Policy*. Peterson Institute for International Economcis (2008)

86. 《从华尔街到长城：如何投资中国》Jonathan Worrall, Peter O'shea, *From Wall Street to the Great Wall: How to Invest in China*. John Wiley & Sons (2007)

87. 《中国银行业与金融市场：中国政府内部研究报告》Li Yang, Robert Lawrence Kuhn, *China's Banking and Financial Markets: The Internal Research Report of the Chinese Government*. John Wiley (2007)

88. 《中国的派系与金融：精英冲突与通货膨胀》Victor C. Shih（史宗瀚）, *Factions and Finance in China: Elite Conflict and Inflation*.Cambridge University Press (2007)

89. 《长期承诺、信托与外资银行在中国的崛起》Qing Lu, *Long-Term Commitment, Trust and the Rise of Foreign Banking in China*.Chandos Publishing (2007)

90. 《中国资本市场：加入WTO的挑战》Kam C. Chan, Hung-Gay Fung, Qingfeng Wilson Liu, *China's Capital Market: Challenges from WTO Membership* (Advances in Chinese Economic Studies). Edward Elgar Publishing Limited (2007)

91. 《中国投资银行与投资机遇：财务专业人士综合指南》K. Thomas Liaw, *Investment Banking and Investment Opportunities in China: A Comprehensive Guide for Finance Professionals*. John Wiley & Sons, Inc. (2007)

92. 《中国银行业》Violaine Cousin, *Banking in China*.Palgrave Macmillan (2007)

93. 《国际金融机构对华援助贷款成就评估（1981—2002）》Angang Hu（胡鞍钢）, Guangyu Hu (eds.), *Achievement Evaluation of IFI Assistance Loans to China (1981—2002)*. Springer-Verlag Berlin Heidelberg (2007)

94. 《中国牛市：在全球最大市场中投资有利可图》Jim Rogers, *A Bull in China: Investing Profitably in the World's Greatest Market*. Random House (2007)

95. 《中国外商投资的法律环境与风险》Shoushuang Li, *The Legal Environment and Risks for Foreign Investment in China*. Springer-Verlag Berlin Heidelberg (2007)

96. 《中国金融市场》Salih N. Neftci, Michelle Yuan Menager-Xu, *China's Financial Markets*. Academic Press (2006)

97. 《中国私有化：中国股票市场内幕（第二版）》Carl E. Walter, Fraser J. T. Howie, *Privatizing China: Inside China's Stock Markets*. 2nd Edition. John Wiley & Sons (2006)

98. 《改革中国国有企业和银行》Becky Chiu, Mervyn K. Lewis, *Reforming China's State-Owned Enterprises and Banks* (New Horizons in Money and Finance). Edward Elgar Publishing Limited (2006)

99. 《金融系统恢复：中国和亚洲经济转型》Mariko Watanabe (eds.), *Recovering Financial Systems: China and Asian Transition Economies*. Palgrave Macmillan UK (2006)

100. 《投资中国：新兴风险投资业》Jonsson Yinya Li, *Investing in China: The Emerging Venture Capital Industry*. GMB Publishing (2005)

101. 《印度和中国银行业改革》Lawrence Sáez, *Banking Reform in India and China*. Palgrave Macmillan (2004)

102. 《中国股市发展（1984—2002）：股市政治与市场制度》Stephen Green, *The Development of China's Stockmarket, 1984—2002: Equity Politics and Market Institutions* (Routledge Studies on China in Transition). Routledge (2004)

103. 《中国股市：进展、参与者和前景指南》Stephen Green, *China's Stockmarket: A Guide to Its Progress, Players and Prospects*. Bloomberg Press (2003)

104. 《中国金融改革与经济发展》James Laurenceson, Joseph C. H. Chai, *Financial Reform and Economic Development in China*. Edward Elgar Publishing (2003)

105. 《中华人民共和国银行卡支付系统》Michelle H. W. Fong, *Bankcard Payment System in the Peoples Republic of China*. Idea Group Inc (2003)

106. 《中国银行业改革与货币政策：中国央行准备好加入世贸组织吗？》Yong Guo, *Banking Reforms and Monetary Policy in the People's Republic of China: Is the Chinese Central Banking System Ready for Joining the WTO?* Palgrave Macmillan UK (2002)

107. 《"致富光荣"：20世纪80年代和90年代的中国股市》Carl E. Walter, Fraser T. J. Howie, *'To Get Rich Is Glorious!': China's Stock Markets in the '80s and '90s* (Studies on the Chinese Economy). Palgrave (2001)

108. 《中国外资与社会经济发展：以东莞为例》Godfrey Yeung, *Foreign Investment and*

Socio-Economic Development in China: The Case of Dongguan (Studies on the Chinese Economy). Palgrave Macmillan (2001)

109.《1953—1996年中国投资总量行为：投资荒与波动分析》Laixiang Sun, *Aggregate Behaviour of Investment in China, 1953—1996: An Analysis of Investment Hunger and Fluctuation* (Institute of Social Studies, The Hague). Palgrave Macmillan UK (2001)

110.《珠算银行在日本和中国的兴衰》Yuko Arayama, Panos Mourdoukoutas, *The Rise and Fall of Abacus Banking in Japan and China*. Quorum Books (2000)

111.《中国的信托投资公司》Anjali Kumar, *China's Non-bank Financial Institutions: Trust and Investment Companies* (World Bank Discussion Papers 358). World Bank Publications (1997)

112.《财富之源：中国货币与货币政策（1000—1700）》Richard von Glahn, *Fountain of Fortune: Money and Monetary Policy in China, 1000—1700*. University of California Press (1996)

113116.g, Bingren Li, Shengwang Wang, Shaozong Yan, Chung-Chun Yang (eds.), *Functional Analysis in China*. Kluwer (1996)

114.《中国货币政策与金融机构设计（1978—90）》Leroy Jin, *Monetary Policy and the Design of Financeial Institutions in China 1978—90* (St Antony's/Macmillan Series). Palgrave Macmillan (1994)

115.《中国金融和贸易政策读本》Gordon Bennett (eds.), *China's Finance and Trade: A Policy Reader*. Palgrave Macmillan UK (1978)

116.《中国人民币：世界最稳定货币之一》Che-mao Ts-ai, Yin-hang Hung, *China's Renminbi: One of the Few Most Stable Currencies in the World*. Foreign Languages Press (1969)

117.《1845—1895年中国货币与货币政策》Frank H. H. King, *Money and Monetary Policy in China, 1845—1895* (Harvard East Asian Series). Harvard University Press (1965)

10.4　工业与产业

1.《中国石油企业在拉美》(Latin American Political Economy) Wenyuan Wu, *Chinese Oil Enterprises in Latin America*. Springer International Publishing: Palgrave Macmillan (2019)

2.《车轮上的社会发展：理解中国对汽车依赖性的兴起》(Research Series on the Chinese Dream and China's Development Path) Junxiu Wang (ed.), *Development of a Society on Wheels: Understanding the Rise of Automobile-dependency in China*. Springer Singapore (2019)

3.《铁路与中国转型》Elisabeth Köll, *Railroads and the Transformation of China*. Harvard University Press (2019)

4.《电力系统优化的数学模型与算法》Mingtian Fan, Zuping Zhang, Chengmin Wang, *Mathematical Models and Algorithms for Power System Optimization*. China Electric Power Press (2019)

5.《中国白领浪潮：服务业趋势》(The Great Transformation of China) Changyun Jiang, Qun Lian Hong, Ling Qiu, *China's White-Collar Wave: Service Industry Trends*. Palgrave

Macmillan (2019)

6. 《中国制造 中国商业图标的成功策略》Christian Nothhaft, *Made for China: Success Strategies From China's Business Icons*. Springer International Publishing (2018)

7. 《中国工业化进程》Qunhui Huang, *China's Industrialization Process* (Research Series on the Chinese Dream and China's Development Path). Springer Singapore (2018)

8. 《理解中国的产能过剩》Dianqing Xu, Ying Liu, *Understanding China's Overcapacity*. Springer Singapore (2018)

9. 《中国的烟草控制》Gonghuan Yang, *Tobacco Control in China*. Springer, Singapore (2018)

10. 《有毒的熊猫：历史批判视角下的中国卷烟制造》Matthew Kohrman, Gan Quan, Liu Wennan, Robert N. Proctor, *Poisonous Pandas: Chinese Cigarette Manufacturing in Critical Historical Perspectives*. Stanford University Press (2018)

11. 《中国电力部门》Leo Lester, Mike Thomas (eds.), *China's Electricity Sector*. Palgrave Pivot (2018)

12. 《中国制造业发展研究报告（2016年）》Lianshui Li, Zhanyuan Du (eds.), *A Research Report on the Development of China's Manufacturing Sector (2016)* (Current Chinese Economic Report Series). Springer Singapore (2017)

13. 《中国产能过剩：党的改革议程的障碍》European Chamber, *Overcapacity in China: An Impediment to the Party's Reform Agenda*. The European Union Chamber of Commerce in China (2016)

14. 《解读生产率差异：日本、美国、泰国和中国汽车工厂比较分析》Hiromichi Shibata, *Explaining Productivity Differences: Comparative Analysis of Automotive Plants in Japan, the United States, Thailand and China*. Springer Singapore (2016)

15. 《影响中国民航政策的当代问题：平衡国际与国内优先权》A. Williams, *Contemporary Issues Shaping China's Civil Aviation Policy: Balancing International with Domestic Priorities*. Taylor & Francis (2016)

16. 《中国智能电网发展的监管途径》Gert Brunekreeft, Till Luhmann, Tobias Menz, Sven-Uwe Müller, Paul Recknagel (eds.), *Regulatory Pathways For Smart Grid Development in China*. Springer Vieweg (2015)

17. 《走向动态区域创新体系：珠江三角洲电子产业调查》Wenying Fu, *Towards a Dynamic Regional Innovation System: Investigation into the Electronics Industry in the Pearl River Delta, China*. Springer-Verlag Berlin Heidelberg (2015)

18. 《中国经济基因突变：通过电力经济学和多智能体》Zhaoguang Hu, Jian Zhang, Ning Zhang, *China's Economic Gene Mutations: By Electricity Economics and Multi-agent*. Springer-Verlag Berlin Heidelberg (2015)

19. 《高速时代的中国铁路》Zhenhua Chen, Kingsley E. Haynes, *Chinese Railways in the Era of High-Speed*. Emerald Group Publishing Limited (2015)

20. 《煤炭帝国：推动中国加入现代世界秩序（1860—1920）》Shellen Wu, *Empires of Coal: Fueling China's Entry into the Modern World Order, 1860—1920*. Stanford University Press (2015)

21. 《关于中国经济发展和到2050年电力需求的探讨》Zhaoguang Hu, Xiandong Tan and Zhaoyuan Xu, *An Exploration Into China's Economic Development and Electricity Demand by the Year 2050*. Elsevier (2014)

22. 《中国生产效率的变化：识别与测量》Bing Xu, Juying Zeng, Junzo Watada, *Changes in Production Efficiency in China: Identification and Measuring*. Springer (2014)

23. 《中国石油工业：历史与未来》Lianyong Feng, Yan Hu, Charles A. S. Hall, Jianliang Wang, *The Chinese Oil Industry: History and Future* (SpringerBriefs in Energy). Springer-Verlag New York (2013)

24. 《中国工业间谍：技术获取与军事现代化》William C. Hannas, James Mulvenon（毛文杰）, Anna B. Puglisi, *Chinese Industrial Espionage: Technology Acquisition and Military Modernisation* (Asian Security Studies). Routledge (2013)

25. 《中国电力与能源》Zhenya Liu, *Electric Power and Energy in China*. Wiley (2013)

26. 《分权谈判：中国电力行业碳交易案例研究》Ming Yang, Fan Yang, *Negotiation in Decentralization: Case Study of China's Carbon Trading in the Power Sector*. Springer-Verlag London (2012)

27. 《代驾司机：中国如何计划支配全球汽车产业》G. E. Anderson, *Designated Drivers: How China Plans to Dominate the Global Auto Industry*. John Wiley & Sons (2012)

28. 《可再生能源发电：中国—美国的机遇和挑战》Committee on U.S.-China Cooperation on Electricity from Renewable Resources, *The Power of Renewables: Opportunities and Challenges for China and the United States*. The National Academies Press (2010)

29. 《中国汽车现代化：党—国与跨国公司》Gregory T. Chin, *China's Automotive Modernization: The Party-State and Multinational Corporations*. Palgrave Macmillan UK (2010)

30. 《中国再制造：中国的外商投资者与制度变迁》Scott Wilson, *Remade in China: Foreign Investors and Institutional Change in China*. Oxford University Press (2009)

31. 《中国制造：中国企业家活力的秘密》Winter Nie, Katherine Xin, Lily Zhang, *Made in China: Secrets of China's Dynamic Entrepreneurs*. Wiley (2009)

32. 《中国不良制造：中国制造业博弈内幕（修订更新版）》Paul Midler, *Poorly Made in China: An Insider's Account of the China Production Game*. Revised and Updated. Wiley (2009, 2011)

33. 《新兴产业：中国和印度硬件与软件产业的兴起》Neil Gregory, Stanley Nollen, Stoyan Tenev, *New Industries from New Places: The Emergence of the Hardware and Software Industries in China and India* (World Bank: East Asia). Stanford Economics and Finance (2009)

34. 《中国产业集群分析》Zhu Yingming, *Analysis of Industrial Clusters in China*. CRC Press and Science Press (2009)

35. 《影响中国民航政策的当下问题》Alan Williams, *Contemporary Issues Shaping China's*

Civil Aviation Policy. Ashgate (2009)

36. 《中国烟草控制政策分析》Teh-Wei Hu, *Tobacco Control Policy Analysis In China* (Series on Contemporary China). World Scientific Publishing Company (2008)

37. 《中国在全球污染产业转移中的作用》Haitian Lu, *The Role of China in Global Dirty Industry Migration.* Chandos Publishing (2008)

38. 《没有"中国制造"的一年：一个家庭在全球经济中的真实生活冒险》Sara Bongiorni, *A Year without "Made in China": One Family's True Life Adventure in the Global Economy.* John Wiley & Sons (2007)

39. 《作为世界工厂的中国》Kevin Zhang, *China as a World Factory* (Routledge Studies in the Growth Economies of Asia). Routledge (2006)

40. 《中国换道：外商直接投资、地方政府和汽车行业的发展》Eric Thun, *Changing Lanes in China: Foreign Direct Investment, Local Governments, and Auto Sector Development.* Cambridge University Press (2006)

41. 《中国换挡：汽车制造商、石油、污染与发展》Kelly Sims Gallagher, *China Shifts Gears: Automakers, Oil, Pollution, and Development* (Urban and Industrial Environments). The MIT Press (2006)

42. 《中国工业革命与经济表现》Manoranjan Dutta, *China's Industrial Revolution and Economic Presence* (Advanced Research in Asian Economic Studies). World Scientific (2006)

43. 《中国电力部门：改革何去何从？》Organization for Economic Cooperation & Development, *China's Power Sector: Reforms Where to Next?* OECD and IEA (2006)

44. 《中国化学与制药工业：外国公司的机遇与威胁》Gunter Festel (auth.), Gunter Festel, Udo Oels, Andreas Kreimeyer, Max von Zedtwitz (eds.), *The Chemical and Pharmaceutical Industry in China: Opportunities and Threats for Foreign Companies.* Springer-Verlag Berlin Heidelberg (2005)

45. 《中国工业国有企业：处于盈利与破产之间》Carsten Holz, *China's Industrial State-Owned Enterprises: Between Profitability and Bankruptcy.* World Scientific (2003)

46. 《中国在世界市场：后毛泽东时代的中国工业与国际改革的来源》Thomas G Moore, *China in the World Market: Chinese Industry and International Sources of Reform in the Post-Mao Era* (Cambridge Modern China Series). Cambridge University Press (2002)

47. 《华北工艺生产与社会变迁》Anne P. Underhill, *Craft Production and Social Change in Northern China.* Springer US (2002)

48. 《中国工业生产场所的形成：国家、革命和劳动管理》Mark W. Frazier, *The Making of the Chinese Industrial Workplace: State, Revolution, and Labor Management* (Cambridge Modern China Series). Cambridge University Press (2002)

49. 《中国在世界市场中：毛泽东时代后的中国工业和国际资源改革》Thomas G Moore, *China in the World Market: Chinese Industry and International Sources of Reform in the Post-*

Mao Era. Cambridge University Press (2002)

50. 《中国石油工业和市场》Haijiang Henry Wang, *China's Oil Industry and Market* (Elsevier Global Energy Policy and Economics Series). Elsevier Science Ltd (1999)

51. 《社会主义市场经济条件下的中国电力行业监管》Shiwei Shao, *China Power Sector Regulation in a Socialist Market Economy*. World Bank (1997)

52. 《1949年至今的中国工业革命：政治、计划和管理》Stephen Andors, *China's Industrial Revolution: Politics, Planning, and Management, 1949 to the Present*. The Pantheon Books (1977)

53. 《共产党中国的工业社会：中国经济发展与管理的第一手研究，与印度、苏联、日本和美国工业的显著比较》Barry M. Richman, *Industrial Society in Communist China: A Firsthand Study of Chinese Economic Development and Management, with Significant Comparisons with Industry in India, the U.S.S.R., Japan, and the United States*. Random House (1969)

54. 《中国纺织品：历史、来源、技术、象征和用途研究导论》Alan Priest, Pauline Simmons, *Chinese Textiles: An Introduction to the Study of their History, Sources, Technique, Symbolism, and Use*. The Metropolitan Museum of Art, New York (1934)

55. 《中国蚕业的发展》*Sericultural development in China*. Silk Association of America (1928)

56. 《中国铁路业》Percy Horace Kent, *Railway Enterprise in China*. Edward Arnold (1907)

10.4.1 物流运输

1. 《当代中国物流：互联渠道与协作共享》(Current Chinese Economic Report Series) Xiang Li, Shao-ju Lee, Bing-lian Liu, Ling Wang, *Contemporary Logistics in China: Interconnective Channels and Collaborative Sharing*. Springer Singapore (2019)

2. 《中国当代物流》Jian-hua Xiao, Shao-ju Lee, Bing-lian Liu, Jun Liu, *Contemporary Logistics in China* (Current Chinese Economic Report Series). Springer Singapore (2018)

3. 《当代中国物流：改革与延续》Zhi-lun Jiao, Shao-ju Lee, Ling Wang, Bing-lian Liu (eds.), *Contemporary Logistics in China: Reformation and Perpetuation* (Current Chinese Economic Report Series). Springer Singapore (2017)

4. 《当代中国物流：扩张与国际化》Bing-lian Liu, Ling Wang, Shao-ju Lee, Jun Liu, Fan Qin, Zhi-lun Jiao (eds.), *Contemporary Logistics in China: Proliferation and Internationalization*. Springer-Verlag Berlin Heidelberg (2016)

5. 《中国当代物流：新视野与新蓝图》Ling Wang, Shao-ju Lee, Ping Chen, Xiao-mei Jiang, Bing-lian Liu (eds.), *Contemporary Logistics in China: New Horizon and New Blueprint*. Springer Singapore (2016)

6. 《当代中国物流：同化与创新》Bing-lian Liu, Shao-ju Lee, Ling Wang, Ya Xu, Xiang Li (eds.), *Contemporary Logistics in China: Assimilation and Innovation*. Springer-Verlag Berlin Heidelberg (2014)

7. 《当代中国物流：转型与振兴》Ling Wang (auth.), Bing-lian Liu, Shao-ju Lee, Jian-hua Xiao, Ling Wang, Zhi-lun Jiao (eds.), *Contemporary Logistics in China: Transformation and*

Revitalization. Springer-Verlag Berlin Heidelberg (2013)

8. 《中国船运》Tae-Woo Lee, *Shipping in China* (Plymouth studies in contemporary shipping and logistics). Routledge (2002)

10.5 商业与贸易

1. 《中国在发达国家的并购：经营挑战与机遇》(Measuring Operations Performance) Alessandra Vecchi (ed.), *Chinese Acquisitions in Developed Countries: Operational Challenges and Opportunities*. Springer International Publishing (2019)

2. 《中国消费者：探索全球最大人群》Ashok Sethi, *Chinese Consumers: Exploring the World's Largest Demographic*. Springer Singapore: Palgrave Macmillan (2019)

3. 《利润均衡化的新视角：来自中国的经验证据》Domitilla Magni, *New Perspectives of Profit Smoothing: Empirical Evidence from China*. Springer International Publishing: Palgrave Macmillan (2019)

4. 《中国购物中心的虚拟公共空间：兴起、公共性与后果》Yiming Wang, *Pseudo-Public Spaces in Chinese Shopping Malls: Rise, Publicness and Consequences*. Routledge (2019)

5. 《中国品牌：来自浙江的案例》Martin J. Liu, Jun Luo, *China Branding: Cases from Zhejiang*. Springer Singapore: Palgrave Macmillan (2019)

6. 《重塑中国品牌：全球秩序变化中争夺地位的信号》Xiaoyu Pu, *Rebranding China: Contested Status Signaling in the Changing Global Order*. Stanford University Press (2019)

7. 《中国商业、政府和经济机构》Xiaoke Zhang, Tianbiao Zhu (eds.), *Business, Government and Economic Institutions in China* (International Political Economy Series). Palgrave Macmillan (2018)

8. 《中国商业数字化》(Palgrave Macmillan Asian Business Series) Young-Chan Kim, Pi-Chi Chen, *The Digitization of Business in China*. Springer International Publishing: Palgrave Macmillan (2018)

9. 《东南亚、中国和印度经济展望（2018）：促进电子商务的最新机遇》Coll., *Economic Outlook for Southeast Asia, China and India 2018: Update Promoting Opportunities in E-commerce*. OECD Publishing (2018)

10. 《中国商业模式：独创性与限制》Elisabeth Paulet, Chris Rowley, *The China Business Model: Originality and Limits*. Chandos Publishing (2017)

11. 《作为经济增长因素的外贸：俄中外贸合作》Elena G. Popkova, Yakov A. Sukhodolov, *Foreign Trade as a Factor of Economic Growth: Russian-Chinese Foreign Trade Cooperation*. Springer International Publishing (2017)

12. 《在中国和印度开展业务的比较和背景分析》Deepak Sardana, Ying Zhu, *Conducting Business in China and India: A Comparative and Contextual Analysis* (Palgrave Macmillan Asian Business Series). Palgrave Macmillan UK (2017)

13. 《中国全球采购与供应卓越管理：供应专家采购指南》Marc Helmold, Brian Terry, *Global Sourcing and Supply Management Excellence in China: Procurement Guide for Supply Experts*. Springer Singapore (2017)

14. 《中国市场准入：战略、营销和品牌案例研究》Christiane Prange (eds.), *Market Entry in China: Case Studies on Strategy, Marketing, and Branding* (Management for Professionals). Springer International Publishing (2016)

15. 《通过售后服务实现中国品牌忠诚：特别关注文化因素影响》Alexander Fraß, *Achieving Brand Loyalty in China through After-Sales Services: With a Particular Focus on the Influences of Cultural Determinants* (Business Analytics). Gabler Verlag (2016)

16. 《中国商人在东南亚的经济成功：认同、族群合作与冲突》Janet Tai Landa, *Economic Success of Chinese Merchants in Southeast Asia: Identity, Ethnic Cooperation and Conflict*. Springer-Verlag Berlin Heidelberg (2016)

17. 《现代中国的购物中心与公共空间》Nicholas Jewell, *Shopping Malls and Public Space in Modern China*. Routledge (2016)

18. 《国际商业道德：以中国为中心》Stephan Rothlin, Dennis McCann, *International Business Ethics: Focus on China*. Springer-Verlag Berlin Heidelberg (2016)

19. 《中国造假：民族品牌、假冒文化与全球化》Fan Yang, *Faked in China: Nation Branding, Counterfeit Culture, and Globalization*. Indiana University Press (2016)

20. 《中国：贸易、外商直接投资和发展战略》Yanqing Jiang, *China: Trade, Foreign Direct Investment, and Development Strategies* (Chandos Asian Studies Series, 63). OXford Elsevier Science & Technology, Chandos Publishing (2015)

21. 《中国与拉美国家贸易争端的解决》Dan Wei (eds.), *Settlements of Trade Disputes between China and Latin American Countries* (Laws in Emerging Economies 1). Springer-Verlag Berlin Heidelberg (2015)

22. 《中国商务2.0：分析经济、了解社会并有效地管理》Henk R. Randau, Olga Medinskaya, *China Business 2.0: Analyze the Economy, Understand the Society, and Manage Effectively* (Management for Professionals). Springer International Publishing (2015)

23. 《亚洲商会（1600—1980）》Lin yu-ju, Madeleine Zelin（曾小萍）, *Merchant communities in Asia, 1600—1980*. Pickering & Chatto (2015)

24. 《德中商务网络：利用组织网络与中国开展业务》Alexander Häntzschel, *German-Sino Business Networks: Using Organized Networks to Develop Business with China*. Springer International Publishing (2015)

25. 《中国公共关系：在中国建立和维护您的品牌》David Wolf, *Public Relations in China: Building and Defending your Brand in the PRC*. Palgrave Macmillan UK (2015)

26. 《中国颠覆者：阿里巴巴、小米、腾讯等公司如何改变商业规则》Edward Tse, *China's Disruptors: How Alibaba, Xiaomi, Tencent, and Other Companies are Changing the Rules

of Business. Portfolio (2015)

27. 《商业游说与贸易治理：以中欧关系为例》Jappe Eckhardt, *Business Lobbying and Trade Governance: The Case of EU-China Relations*. Palgrave Macmillan UK (2015)

28. 《新兴关键市场品牌建设和营销：中国、印度、俄罗斯和巴西成功品牌增长的从业者指南》Niklas Schaffmeister, *Brand Building and Marketing in Key Emerging Markets: A Practitioner's Guide to Successful Brand Growth in China, India, Russia and Brazil*. Springer (2015)

29. 《论中国贸易顺差》Tao Yuan, *On China's Trade Surplus*. Springer-Verlag Berlin Heidelberg (2014)

30. 《中国进口影响与评估》Song Hong, Evan Villarrubia, *China's Imports Impact and Evaluation*. Paths International Ltd. (2014)

31. 《中国超级消费者：十亿客户需要什么以及如何向他们出售》Savio Chan, Michael Zakkour, *China's Super Consumers: What 1 Billion Customers Want and How to Sell it to Them*. Wiley (2014)

32. 《关于中国商务、旅游和文化的108条提示》Eddie Flores Jr., Elisia Flores, Jon Murakami, *108 Tips on Business, Travel and Culture in China*. L&L Franchise, Incorporated (2014)

33. 《关于中国商务、旅游和文化的108条提示》Eddie Flores Jr., Elisia Flores, Jon Murakami, *108 Tips on Business, Travel and Culture in China*. L&L Franchise, Incorporated (2014)

34. 《中国消费主义变化的景观》Alison Hulme, *The Changing Landscape of China's Consumerism*. Elsevier, Chandos Publishing (2014)

35. 《中国消费者与个体：彰显个性与适应融入》Michael B. Griffiths, *Consumers and Individuals in China: Standing out, Fitting in*. Routledge (2013)

36. 《中国催化剂：通过全球增长最快的消费市场推动全球经济增长》David M. Holloman, *China Catalyst: Powering Global Growth by Reaching the Fastest Growing Consumer Markets in the World*. Wiley (2013)

37. 《新兴国家的零售国际化：全球零售品牌在中国的定位》Karin Pernemann, *Retail Internationalization in Emerging Countries: The Positioning of Global Retail Brands in China*. Gabler Verlag (2013)

38. 《区域中国：商业和经济手册》Rongxing Guo, *Regional China: A Business and Economic Handbook*. Palgrave Macmillan UK (2013)

39. 《中国正在购买世界吗》Peter Nolan, *Is China Buying the World?* Polity (2012)

40. 《帝制晚期的江南经济：货币、市场和制度的联结》Billy Kee Long So（苏基朗，ed.），*The Economy of Lower Yangzi Delta in Late Imperial China: Connecting Money, Markets, and Institutions*. Routledge (2012)

41. 《中国人要什么：文化、共产主义与现代消费者》Tom Doctoroff（唐锐涛）, *What Chinese Want: Culture, Communism and the Modern Chinese Consumer*. Palgrave Macmillan (2012)

42. 《在中国做生意》Stuart C. Strother, *China: Doing Business in the Middle Kingdom*. Business Expert Press (2012)

43. 《与中国做生意：避免陷阱》Stewart Hamilton, Jinxuan Ann Zhang, *Doing Business with China: Avoiding the Pitfalls*. Palgrave Macmillan (2012)

44. 《营销死亡：中国文化与人寿保险市场的形成》Cheris Shun-ching Chan, *Marketing Death: Culture and the Making of a Life Insurance Market in China*. Oxford University Press, USA (2012)

45. 《中国在全球经济复苏中的作用》(Routledge Studies in the Chinese Economy 44) Xiaolan Fu, *China's Role in Global Economic Recovery*. Routledge (2012)

46. 《中国商业与犯罪风险：2005—2006年中国国际商业犯罪调查》Roderic G. Broadhurst, John Bacon-Shone, Brigitte Bouhours, Thierry Bouhours, *Business and the Risk of Crime in China: The 2005—2006 China international Crime Against Business Survey*. ANU E Press (2011)

47. 《中国商业领袖：西方实践如何与中国智慧最佳交融》Frank T. Gallo, *Business Leadership in China: How to Blend Best Western Practices with Chinese Wisdom*. Wiley (2011)

48. 《在中国成功开展业务》Mona Chung, *Doing Business Successfully in China*. Chandos Publishing (2011)

49. 《在中国设立代表处》Chris Devonshire-Ellis, Andy Scott (auth.), Chris Devonshire-Ellis, Andy Scott, Sam Woollard (eds.), *Setting Up Representative Offices in China*. Springer-Verlag Berlin Heidelberg (2011)

50. 《不只是中国：全球化时代商务召回的兴起》Hari Bapuji, *Not Just China: The Rise of Recalls in the Age of Global Business*. Palgrave Macmillan (2011)

51. 《在华跨国零售商与消费者：从英国和日本转移的组织实践》Jos Gamble, *Multinational Retailers and Consumers in China: Transferring Organizational Practices from the United Kingdom and Japan*. Palgrave Macmillan UK (2011)

52. 《创业中国：1979年以来商业、经济和法律的发展》Linda Yueh, *Enterprising China: Business, Economic, and Legal Developments since 1979*. Oxford University Press (2011)

53. 《中国零售业国际化：外资零售企业的扩张》Lisa Qixun Siebers, *Retail Internationalization in China: Expansion of Foreign Retailers*. Palgrave Macmillan (2011)

54. 《中国对外直接投资的决定因素》(New Horizons in International Business) Hinrich Voss, *The Determinants of Chinese Outward Direct Investment*. Edward Elgar (2011)

55. 《中国在世界贸易中不断增长的作用》Robert C. Feenstra, Shang-Jin Wei, *China's Growing Role in World Trade* (National Bureau of Economic Research Conference Report). The University of Chicago Press (2010)

56. 《如何在中国成功经营》Johan Bjorksten, Anders Hagglund, *How to Manage a Successful Business in China*. World Scientific Publishing Company (2010)

57. 《奢侈中国：市场机遇与潜力》Michel Chevalier, Pierre Xiao Lu, *Luxury China: Market*

Opportunities and Potential. John Wiley & Sons (Asia) (2010)

58. 《向中国大举销售：世界最大市场的谈判原则》Morry Morgan, *Selling Big to China: Negotiating Principles for the World's Largest Market*. John Wiley & Sons (Asia) Pte. Ltd (2010)

59. 《巧克力财富：为中国消费者的情感、思想和钱包而战》Lawrence L. Allen, *Chocolate Fortunes: The Battle for the Hearts, Minds, and Wallets of China's Consumers*. AMACOM (2009)

60. 《中国采购和制造的42个规则》Rosemary Coates, *42 Rules for Sourcing and Manufacturing in China*. Super Star Press (2009)

61. 《商业洞察中国：进入战略和参与的实践建议》Jonathan Reuvid, *Business Insights China: Practical Advice on Entry Strategy and Engagement*. Kogan Page (2008)

62. 《在中国做生意》Tim Ambler, Morgen Witzel, Chao Xi, *Doing Business in China*. Routledge (2008)

63. 《关系与商业：战略理论及其对在华跨国公司的启示》Eike A. Langenberg, *Guanxi and Business: Strategy Theory and Implications for Multinational Companies in China*. Physica-Verlag Heidelberg (2007)

64. 《在中国做生意的傻瓜指南》Robert Collins, Carson Block, *Doing Business in China for Dummies*. Wiley Publishing (2007)

65. 《中国外贸政策：新支持者》Ka Zeng, *China's Foreign Trade Policy: The New Constituencies*. Routledge (2007)

66. 《中国连接市场增长》Ross Garnaut, Ligang Song (eds.), *China. Linking Markets for Growth*. ANU E Press and Asia Pacific Press (2007)

67. 《十亿消费者：第一手中国经商经验》James McGregor（麦健陆）, *One Billion Customers: Lessons from the Front Lines of Doing Business in China*. Free Press (2007)

68. 《"关系"在中国买卖中的作用：江苏省蔬菜供应链调查》Hualiang Lu, *The Role of "guanxi" in Buyer-seller Relationships in China: A Survey of Vegetable Supply Chains in Jiangsu Province*. Wageningen Academic Publishers (2007)

69. 《中国商业红宝书》Sheila Melvin, *The Little Red Book of China Business*. Sourcebooks Inc. (2007)

70. 《中国市场营销能力与战略灵活性》Yonggui Wang, Richard Li-Hua, *Marketing Competences and Strategic Flexibility in China*. Palgrave Macmillan (2007)

71. 《中国茶叶：如何在大陆买卖与赚钱》Jeremy Haft, *All the Tea in China: How to Buy, Sell, and Make Money on the Mainland*. Portfolio Hardcover (2007)

72. 《开发中国商业道德》Xiaohe Lu, Georges Enderle, *Developing Business Ethics in China*. Palgrave Macmillan (2006)

73. 《中国新消费者：社会发展与内需》Elisabeth Croll, *China's New Consumers: Social Development and Domestic Demand*. Routledge (2006)

74. 《中国的商业成功》Markus B. Hofer, Bernhard Ebel, *Business Success in China*. Springer (2006)

75. 《时下中国：在全球最具活力的市场做生意》N. Mark Lam, John Graham, *China Now: Doing Business in the Worlds Most Dynamic Market*.McGraw-Hill (2006)

76. 《中国采购：战略、方法和经验》Guido Nassimbeni, Marco Sartor, *Sourcing in China: Strategies, Methods and Experiences*. Palgrave Macmillan UK (2006)

77. 《中国的游说业务》Scott Kennedy, *The Business of Lobbying in China*. Harvard University Press (2005, 2008)

78. 《中国产业政策与全球商业革命：以家电产业为例》Ling Liu, *China's Industrial Policies and the Global Business Revolution: The Case of the Domestic Appliance Industry*. Routledge (2005)

79. 《中国出口、外商直接投资与经济发展》Xiaolan Fu, *Exports, Foreign Direct Investment and Economic Development in China*. Palgrave Macmillan UK (2004)

80. 《在中国做生意的神话》Harold Chee, Chris West, *Myths about Doing Business in China*. Palgrave Macmillan UK (2004)

81. 《与中国做生意》Li Yong, Jonathan Reuvid, *Doing Business with China*.GMB Publishing (2003)

82. 《中国贸易与投资：欧洲经验》Jim Slater, Roger Strange, Limin Wang, *Trade and Investment in China: The European Experience* (Routledge Studies in the Growth Economies of Asia). Routledge (2003)

83. 《出售中国：改革时期的外商直接投资》Yasheng Huang（黄亚生）, *Selling China: Foreign Direct Investment During the Reform Era* (Cambridge Modern China Series). Cambridge University Press (2003)

84. 《中国与全球商业革命》Peter Nolan, *China and the Global Business Revolution*. Palgrave Macmillan UK (2001)

85. 《中国商业游戏规则》Carolyn Blackman, *China Business: The Rules of the Game*.Allen & Unwin Academic (2001)

86. 《中国城市的消费革命》Deborah S. Davis, *The Consumer Revolution in Urban China* (Studies on China, 22). University of California Press (2000)

87. 《中国贸易方式与国际比较优势》Xiao-guang Zhang, *China's Trade Patterns and International Comparative Advantage* (Studies on the Chinese Economy). Palgrave MD (2000)

88. 《中国商务礼仪：中华人民共和国协议、礼仪和文化指南》Scott D. Seligman, *Chinese Business Etiquette: A Guide to Protocol, Manners, and Culture in the People's Republic of China* (A Revised and Updated Edition). Grand Central Publishing (1999)

89. 《中国出口奇迹：起源、结果和前景》Thomas Chan, Noel Tracy, Zhu Wenhui, *China's Export Miracle: Origins, Results and Prospects*. Palgrave Macmillan UK (1999)

90. 《中国商业环境与机遇：上海及其周边地区》Li Choy Chong, *Business Environment and Opportunities in China: Shanghai and its Surrounding Region*. Deutscher Universitätsverlag (1998)

91. 《北京吉普：西方商业在中国个案研究》Jim Mann, *Beijing Jeep: A Case Study of*

Western Business In China. Westview Press (1997)

92. 《现代中国商业指南》Jon P. Alston, Stephen Yongxin He, Business Guide to Modern China. Michigan State University Press (1997)
93. 《中国新商业精英：经济改革的政治后果》Margaret M. Pearson, China's New Business Elite: The Political Consequences of Economic Reform. Berkeley: University of California Press (1997)
94. 《中国对外贸易改革》World Bank, China: Foreign Trade Reform. World Bank Publications (1994)
95. 《中国如何打开大门：中国对外贸易和投资改革的政治成功》Susan L. Shirk（谢淑丽）, How China Opened Its Door: The Political Success of the PRC's Foreign Trade and Investment Reforms. Brookings Institution Press (1994)
96. 《收获之山：福建与中国的茶贸易（1757—1937）》Robert Gardella（加德拉）, Harvesting Mountains: Fujian and the China Tea Trade, 1757—1937. University of California Press (1994-11-29)
97. 《1979年以来的中国出口》Hong Wang, China's Exports since 1979. Palgrave Macmillan UK (1993)
98. 《中国对外贸易和经济改革（1978—1990）》Nicholas R. Lardy（尼古拉斯·拉迪）, Foreign Trade and Economic Reform in China, 1978—1990. Cambridge University Press (1993)
99. 《茶叶贸易和18世纪的中西商务关系（1740—1840）》Guotu Zhuang（庄国土）, Tea, Silver, Opium and War: The International Tea Trade and Western Commercial Expansion into China in 1740—1840. Xiamen University Press (1993)
100. 《中国外贸改革：对经济增长和稳定的影响》John C. Hsu, China's Foreign Trade Reforms: Impact on Growth and Stability. Cambridge University Press (1989)
101. 《中国经济帝国主义：丝绸生产和出口（1861—1932）》Robert Y. Eng, Economic Imperialism in China: Silk Production and Exports, 1861—1932. Institute of East Asian Studies, University of California (1986)
102. 《中国对外贸易》C. F. Remer, The Foreign Trade in China. The Commercial Press, Shanghai (1926)
103. 《中国对外贸易》Chong Su See, The Foreign Trade of China. New York: Columbia University Press (1919)
104. 《关于中国和中国贸易的评论》R. B. Forbes, Remarks on China and the China Trade. Boston: Samuel N. Dickinson (1844)

10.6 企业与创业

1. 《中国国有企业：经济快速转型中的角色转变》Kee Cheok Cheong, Ran Li, China's State Enterprises: Changing Role in a Rapidly Transforming Economy. Palgrave Macmillan (2019)
2. 《中国企业、组织和技术》Philip Scranton, Enterprise, Organization, and Technology in

China. Springer International Publishing, Palgrave Macmillan (2019)

3.《中国企业转型升级》Yunshi Mao, *Transformation and Upgrading of Chinese Enterprises*. Springer Singapore (2019)

4.《国有企业如何拖累经济增长：中国的理论和证据》Ruiming Liu, *How State-owned Enterprises Drag on Economic Growth: Theory and Evidence from China*. Springer Berlin Heidelberg (2019)

5.《跨国公司、地方能力建设与发展：中国和欧洲跨国公司的作用》Xiaolan Fu, Owusu Essegbey, Godfred K Frempong, *Multinationals, Local Capacity Building and Development: The Role of Chinese and European MNEs*. Edward Elgar Publishing (2019)

6.《中国企业社会责任：文化与所有权对感知与实践的影响》Dashi Zhang, *Corporate Social Responsibility in China: Cultural and Ownership Influences on Perceptions and Practices*. Springer Singapore (2017)

7.《中国公司治理：中国法律下外商投资企业的结构与管理》Giovanni Pisacane, *Corporate Governance in China: The Structure and Management of Foreign-Invested Enterprises under Chinese Law*. Springer Singapore (2017)

8.《中国地理动态与企业空间战略》Shengjun Zhu, John Pickles, Canfei He, *Geographical Dynamics and Firm Spatial Strategy in China*. Springer-Verlag Berlin Heidelberg (2017)

9.《对中国民营企业发展的新解读》Yingqiu Liu (eds.), *New Interpretations on the Development of China's Non-Governmental Enterprises* (Research Series on the Chinese Dream and China's Development Path). Springer Singapore (2017)

10.《中国乡镇企业兴衰的经济学分析》Cheng Jin, *An Economic Analysis of the Rise and Decline of Chinese Township and Village Enterprises* (Palgrave Studies in Economic History). Palgrave Macmillan (2017)

11.《百度SEO：中国市场的挑战与错综复杂》Véronique Duong, *Baidu SEO: Challenges and Intricacies of Marketing in China* (Focus series). ISTE; John Wiley & Sons (2017)

12.《中国民营企业领导力：洞察与访谈》Anne S. Tsui, Yingying Zhang, Chen Xiao-Ping, *Leadership of Chinese Private Enterprises: Insights and Interviews*. Palgrave Macmillan UK (2017)

13.《中国外资企业知识冲突的微妙逻辑》Constanze Wang, *The Subtle Logics of Knowledge Conflicts in China's Foreign Enterprises*. VS Verlag für Sozialwissenschaften (2016)

14.《企业中国2.0：大震动》Qiao Liu, *Corporate China 2.0: The Great Shakeup*. Palgrave Macmillan US (2016)

15.《小米：智能手机与中国梦》Clay Shirky, *Little Rice: Smartphones, Xiaomi, and the Chinese Dream*. Columbia Global Reports (2015)

16.《中国企业社会责任研究报告》Jiagui Chen, Qunhui Huang, Huagang Peng, Hongwu Zhong, *Research Report on Corporate Social Responsibility of China*. Springer-Verlag

Berlin Heidelberg (2015)

17. 《中国可持续发展与企业社会责任：多元视角》René Schmidpeter, Hualiang Lu, Christopher Stehr, Haifeng Huang (eds.), *Sustainable Development and CSR in China: A Multi-Perspective Approach*. Springer In. (2015)

18. 《中国公司治理入门》Jean Jinghan Chen, *A Primer on Corporate Governance: China* (Corporate governance collection). Business Expert Press (2015)

19. 《中国可持续创业：道德、公司治理和制度改革》Douglas Cumming, Michael Firth, Wenxuan Hou, Edward Lee (eds.), *Sustainable Entrepreneurship in China: Ethics, Corporate Governance, and Institutional Reforms*. Palgrave Macmillan US (2015)

20. 《中国私营部门发展和城市化：广泛增长战略》Zhikai Wang, *Private Sector Development and Urbanization in China: Strategies for Widespread Growth*. Palgrave Macmillan US (2015)

21. 《中国私营企业复兴、合法化与发展：国家资本主义赋权》Zongshi Chen, *The Revival, Legitimization, and Development of Private Enterprise in China: Empowering State Capitalism*. Palgrave Macmillan US (2015)

22. 《中国企业管理控制系统》Xianzhi Zhang, *Enterprise Management Control Systems in China*. Springer-Verlag Berlin Heidelberg (2014)

23. 《企业社会信息披露：中国和日本的批评视角》Carlos Noronha, *Corporate Social Disclosure: Critical Perspectives in China and Japan*. Palgrave Macmillan (2014)

24. 《中国企业社会责任报告》Kwang-Yong Shin, *Corporate Social Responsibility Reporting in China*. Springer-Verlag Berlin Heidelberg (2014)

25. 《中国的风险企业：尽职调查指南》Jeremy Gordon, *Risky Business in China: A Guide to Due Diligence*. Palgrave Macmillan UK (2014)

26. 《家族企业创业：中国案例》Henry X Shi, *Entrepreneurship in Family Business: Cases from China*. Springer International Publishing (2014)

27. 《中国企业：反思中国商业网络中的关系和信任》Chee-Kiong Tong (eds.), *Chinese Business: Rethinking Guanxi and Trust in Chinese Business Networks*. Springer Singapore (2014)

28. 《中国绿色领导力：中国最具责任感企业的管理战略》Sam Yoonsuk Lee, Ambigaibalan Ramasamy, Jay Hyuk Rhee, *Green Leadership in China: Management Strategies from China's Most Responsible Companies*. Spring (2014)

29. 《中国企业全球化研究手册》Craig C. Julian, Zafar U. Ahmed, Junqian Xu, *Research Handbook on Globalisation of Chinese Firms* (Research Handbooks in Business and Management Series). Edward Elgar (2014)

30. 《中国和印度国有企业的政治经济》Xu Yi-chong (eds.), *The Political Economy of State-owned Enterprises in China and India*. Palgrave Macmillan UK (2012)

31. 《跨国公司在华子公司：增长与发展战略实证研究》Jinghua Zhao, Jifu Wang, Vipin Gupta and Tim Hudson, *Multinational Corporation Subsidiaries in China: An Empirical*

Study of Growth and Development Strategy. Chandos Publishing (2012)

32. 《跨国公司在中国：经营战略、技术和经济发展》Si Zhang, Robert Pearce, *Multinationals in China: Business Strategy, Technology and Economic Development.* Palgrave Macmillan UK (2012)

33. 《在中国设立外商独资企业》Chris Devonshire-Ellis, Andy Scott (auth.), Chris Devonshire-Ellis, Andy Scott, Sam Woollard (eds.), *Setting Up Wholly Foreign Owned Enterprises in China*. Springer-Verlag Berlin Heidelberg (2011)

34. 《在中国成立合资企业》Chris Devonshire-Ellis, Andy Scott, Sam Woollard (auth.), Chris Devonshire-Ellis, Andy Scott, Sam Woollard (eds.), *Setting Up Joint Ventures in China*. Springer-Verlag Berlin Heidelberg (2011)

35. 《中国企业领导力：如何将西方最佳实践与中国智慧融合》Frank T. Gallo, *Business Leadership in China: How to Blend Best Western Practices with Chinese Wisdom*. Wiley (2011)

36. 《应对中国挑战：在中华人民共和国如何实现企业成功》Kenneth G. Lieberthal（李侃如）, *Managing the China Challenge: How to Achieve Corporate Success in the People's Republic.* Brookings Institution Press (2011)

37. 《创业倡议比较：中国、日本和美国研究》Chikako Usui (eds.), *Comparative Entrepreneurship Initiatives: Studies in China, Japan and the USA*. Palgrave Macmillan UK (2011)

38. 《中国企业治理与资源安全：中国全球资源公司的转型》Xinting Jia, Roman Tomasic, *Corporate Governance and Resource Security in China: The Transformation of Chinas Global Resources Companies*. Routledge (2009)

39. 《中国公司控制与企业改革：分块交易的计量经济学分析》Christian Büchelhofer, *Corporate Control and Enterprise Reform in China: An Econometric Analysis of Block Share Trades*. Physica-Verlag HD (2008)

40. 《中国合资企业：形成、演进与运作》Yue Wang, *Contractual Joint Ventures in China: Formation, Evolution and Operation*. Nova Science Publishers, Inc. (2008)

41. 《私营部门与中国市场发展》Zhikai Wang, *The Private Sector and China's Market Development*. Chandos Publishing (2008)

42. 《国际合资企业的合作与技术禀赋：德国在华企业》(Edition KWV) Michael Hoeck, *Cooperation and Technological Endowment in International Joint Ventures: German Firms in China*. Springer Fachmedien Wiesbaden: Springer Gabler (2008)

43. 《中国国有企业改革：工业和CEO方法》Leila Fernandez-Stembridge, Juan Antonio Fernandez, *China's State Owned Enterprise Reform: An Industrial and CEO Approach*. Routledge (2007)

44. 《中国国有企业改革：从马克思到市场》John Hassard, *China's State Enterprise Reform:*

From Marx to the Market. Routledge (2007)

45. 《中国私营企业的复兴》Shuanglin Lin, Shunfeng Song, *The Revival of Private Enterprise in China* (The Chinese Trade and Industry Series). Ashgate Pub Co. (2007)

46. 《东盟国家和华南地区中小企业电子商务发展服务》United Nations, *E-Business Development Services for SMEs in Selected ASEAN Countries and Southern China*. United Nations (2007)

47. 《中国民族企业：全球与本土视角》(Chinese Worlds) Eric Fong, Chiu Luk (eds.), *Chinese Ethnic Business: Global and Local Perspectives*. Routledge (2007)

48. 《中国创业》Keming Yang, *Entrepreneurship in China*. Ashgate Pub Co. (2007)

49. 《冲突与创新：中国合资企业》Kwok B. Chan, Chan Kwok-bun, *Conflict and Innovation: Joint Ventures in China* (International Comparative Social Studies). Koninklijke Brill NV, Leiden, The Netherlands (2006)

50. 《在华跨国公司：控制利益》Stephen Todd Rudman, *The Multinational Corporation in China: Controlling Interests* (Organization and Strategy). Blackwell Publishing (2006)

51. 《中国民营企业：管理和绩效的多学科视角》Anne S. Tsui, Anne S. Tsui, Yanjie Bian（边燕杰）, Leonard Cheng, *China's Domestic Private Firms: Multidisciplinary Perspectives on Management and Performance*. M. E. Sharpe (2006)

52. 《中国公司治理》Jian Chen, *Corporate Governance in China* (RoutledgeCurzon Studies on the Chinese Economy, 9). RoutledgeCurzon (2005)

53. 《中国外商投资与企业治理》Yanni Yan, *Foreign Investment and Corporate Governance in China*. Palgrave Macmillan UK (2005)

54. 《现代中国国有企业制度的形成：制度变迁动力》Morris L. Bian, *The Making of the State Enterprise System in Modern China: The Dynamics of Institutional Change*. Harvard University Press (2005)

55. 《中国的企业改革：经济全球化过程中的制度挑战》Russell Smyth, *China's Business Reforms: Institutional Challenges in a Globalised Economy*. Routledgecurzon (2004)

56. 《中国理性企业家：新型私营部门的发展》Barbara Krug, *China's Rational Entrepreneurs: The Development of the New Private Sector*. Routledgecurzon (2004)

57. 《奇异与不同：中国企业的过去、现在与未来》Ian Rae, Morgan Witzel, *Singular and Different: Businesss in China Past, Present and Future*. Palgrave Macmillan UK (2004)

58. 《中国赶超与竞争力：以石油大企业为例》Jin Zhang, *Catch-up and Competitiveness in China: The Case of Large Firms in the Oil Industry*. RoutledgeCurzon (2004)

59. 《后街金融：中国的私营企业主》Kellee S. Tsai（蔡欣怡）, *Back-Alley Banking: Private Entrepreneurs in China*. Cornell University Press (2004)

60. 《中国企业ABC：中国市场生存工具包》Martin Krott, Kent Williamsson, *China Business ABC: The China Market Survival Kit*. Copenhagen Business School Press (2003)

61. 《中国新兴全球企业：政治经济与制度调查》Yongjin Zhang, *China's Emerging Global Businesses: Political Economy and Institutional Investigations*. Palgrave Macmillan (2003)

62. 《中国大企业与后工业化挑战》Dyla Sutherland, *China's Large Enterprises and the Challenge of Late Industrialisation*. Routledgecurzon (2003)

63. 《欧洲和亚洲新企业家：俄罗斯、东欧和中国业务发展模式》Victoria E. Bonnell, Thomas B. Gold, *The New Entrepreneurs of Europe and Asia: Patterns of Business Development in Russia, Eastern Europe, and China*. M. E. Sharpe, Inc. (2002)

64. 《中华人民共和国企业管理》Anne S. Tsui, Chung-Ming Lau (eds.), *The Management of Enterprises in the People's Republic of China*. Springer US (2002)

65. 《中国公司治理与企业改革：建立现代市场制度》Stoyan Tenev, Chunlin Zhang, Loup Brefort, *Corporate Governance and Enterprise Reform in China: Building the Institutions of Modern Markets*. The World Bank and the International Finance Corporation (2002)

66. 《政治与市场之间：毛泽东时代后的中国企业、竞争和制度变迁》Yi-min Lin, *Between Politics and Markets: Firms, Competition, and Institutional Change in Post-Mao China* (Structural Analysis in the Social Sciences). Cambridge University Press (2001)

67. 《中国跨国公司战略、结构与绩效》Yadong Luo, *Strategy, Structure, and Performance of MNCs in China*. Greenwood Publishing Group (2001)

68. 《中国企业全球化》Henry Wai-chung Yeung, Kris Olds (eds.), *Globalization of Chinese Business Firms*. Palgrave Macmillan UK (2000)

69. 《中国国际合资企业：所有权、控制和绩效》Yanni Yan, *International Joint Ventures in China: Ownership, Control and Performance*. Palgrave Macmillan UK (2000)

70. 《改革中国企业》OECD, *Reforming China's Enterprises* (Economics: China in the global economy). OECD (2000)

71. 《中国企业改革：毛泽东时代后国家社会关系的变化》You Ji, *China's Enterprise Reform: Changing State Society Relations after Mao* (Routledge Studies in China in Transition, 3). Routledge (1998)

72. 《中国企业改革：毛泽东时代后变化的国家与社会关系》You Ji, *China's Enterprise Reform: Changing State Society Relations after Mao* (Routledge Studies in China in Transition, 3). Routledge (1998)

73. 《处于等级制度与市场之间的中国企业：中国承包经营责任制》Derong Chen, *Chinese Firms Between Hierarchy and Market: The Contract Management Responsibility System in China*. Palgrave Macmillan (1994)

74. 《中华人民共和国的合资企业》Margaret M. Pearson, *Joint Ventures in the People's Republic of China*. Princeton University Press (1992)

75. 《中国乡镇企业：结构、发展与改革》William A. Byrd, Ling Qingsong（林青松）, *China's Rural Industry: Structure, Development, and Reform*. Oxford University Press (1990)

10.7 城市

1. 《变化中的中国城市更新政策：多层等级结构下的政策转移与政策学习》Giulia C. Romano, *Changing Urban Renewal Policies in China: Policy Transfer and Policy Learning Under Multiple Hierarchies*. Palgrave Macmillan (2020)
2. 《差异化城市化模式下的中国发展》(Research Series on the Chinese Dream and China's Development Path) Qiang Li, *China's Development Under a Differential Urbanization Model*. Springer Singapore (2020)
3. 《中国城市建设用地开发：行动中的国家、市场与农民》Tao Liu, *China's Urban Construction Land Development: The State, Market, and Peasantry in Action*. Springer Singapore (2020)
4. 《中国城市化》Houkai Wei, *Urbanization in China* (Research Series on the Chinese Dream and China's Development Path). Springer Singapore (2019)
5. 《中国城市史》(China Connections) Chonglan Fu, Wenming Cao, *An Urban History of China*. Springer Singapore: Palgrave Macmillan (2019)
6. 《中国城市史导论》(China Connections) Chonglan Fu, Wenming Cao, *Introduction to the Urban History of China*. Springer Singapore: Palgrave Macmillan (2019)
7. 《当代中国的城市化及其影响》(Research Series on the Chinese Dream and China's Development Path) Peilin Li（李培林）, *Urbanization and Its Impact in Contemporary China*. Springer Singapore (2019)
8. 《中国高铁新城规划与发展研究》Lan Wang, Hao Gu, *Studies on China's High-Speed Rail New Town Planning and Development*. Springer Singapore (2019)
9. 《在线城市化：中国农村转型中的在线服务》(Advances in 21st Century Human Settlements) Li Zi, *Online Urbanization: Online Services in China's Rural Transformation*. Springer Singapore (2019)
10. 《中国城市萎缩：城市化的另一面》(The Urban Book Series) Ying Long, Shuqi Gao, *Shrinking Cities in China: The Other Facet of Urbanization*. Springer Singapore (2019)
11. 《大剧院都市主义：21世纪的中国城市》Charlie Qiuli Xue, *Grand Theater Urbanism: Chinese Cities in the 21st Century*. Springer Singapore (2019)
12. 《中国及其他东亚国家的城市规划与发展》Guanzeng Zhang, Lan Wang, *Urban Planning and Development in China and Other East Asian Countries*. Springer Singapore (2019)
13. 《中国城市主义的批判性视角》Mark Jayne, *Chinese Urbanism: Critical Perspectives*. Routledge (2018)
14. 《城市规划与管理的大数据支持：中国经验》Miaoyi Li, Zhenjiang Shen, *Big Data Support of Urban Planning and Management: The Experience in China* (Advances in geographic information science). Springer (2018)
15. 《现代中国城市流动：电动自行车的成长》Dennis Zuev, *Urban Mobility in Modern*

China: The Growth of the E-bike. Palgrave Macmillan (2018)

16. 《中国城市的历史地理学》Yannan Ding, Maurizio Marinelli, Xiaohong Zhang (eds.), *China: A Historical Geography of the Urban*. Palgrave Macmillan (2018)

17. 《中国城市化与城市治理：问题、挑战与发展》Lin Ye (eds.), *Urbanization and Urban Governance in China: Issues, Challenges, and Development* (Governing China in the 21st Century). Palgrave Macmillan US (2018)

18. 《走向绿色城市：中德城市生物多样性与生态系统服务》Karsten Grunewald, Lennart Kümper-Schlake, Junxiang Li, Gaodi Xie, *Towards Green Cities: Urban Biodiversity and Ecosystem Services in China and Germany* (Cities and nature). Springer (2018)

19. 《中国中小城市的绿色发展模式》Xuefeng Li, Xuke Liu, *Green Development Model of China's Small and Medium-sized Cities* (Research Series on the Chinese Dream and China's Development Path). Springer Singapore (2018)

20. 《中国智慧城市建设与提升战略研究》Yunhe Pan, *Strategic Research on Construction and Promotion of China's Intelligent Cities*. Springer Singapore (2018)

21. 《智能城市评价系统》Zhiqiang Wu, *Intelligent City Evaluation System* (Strategic Research on Construction and Promotion of China's Intelligent Cities). Springer Singapore (2018)

22. 《现代中国城市流动：电动自行车的发展》Dennis Zuev, *Urban Mobility in Modern China: The Growth of the E-bike*. Palgrave Macmillan (2018)

23. 《中国城市模式》(Springer Geography) Chuanglin Fang, Danlin Yu, Hanying Mao, Chao Bao, Jinchuan Huang, *China's Urban Pattern*. Springer Singapore (2018)

24. 《学习深圳：后毛泽东时代从特区到模范城市的中国实验》Mary Ann O'Donnell, Winnie Won Yin Wong, Jonathan Bach, *Learning from Shenzhen: China's Post-Mao Experiment from Special Zone to Model City*. University of Chicago Press (2017)

25. 《中国城市革命：解读中国生态城市》Austin Williams, *Chin's Urban Revolution: Understanding Chinese Eco-Cities*. Bloomsbury (2017)

26. 《中国南部和东部七大沿海城市的发展和规划》Jianfa Shen, Gordon Kee, *Development and Planning in Seven Major Coastal Cities in Southern and Eastern China*. Springer International Publishing (2017)

27. 《中国城市化与社会经济影响》Zongli Tang (eds.), *China's Urbanization and Socioeconomic Impact*. Springer Singapore (2017)

28. 《中国宜居城市：20世纪城市历史》Toby Lincoln, Xu Tao (eds.), *The Habitable City in China: Urban History in the Twentieth Century*. Palgrave Macmillan US (2017)

29. 《中国生态城市发展》Juke Liu, Weiping Sun, Wenzhen Hu (eds.), *The Development of Eco Cities in China*. Springer Singapore (2017)

30. 《2014年欧洲和中国智能城市比较研究》China Academy of Information and Communications Technology, EU-China Policy Dialogues Support Facility II, *Comparative Study of Smart*

Cities in Europe and China 2014. The Commercial Press China and Springer-Verlag Berlin (2016)

31. 《中国新型城市化发展道路、蓝图与格局》Chuanglin Fang, Danlin Yu, *China's New Urbanization Developmental: Paths, Blueprints and Patterns*.Springer-Verlag Berlin Heidelberg and Science Press Ltd. (2016)

32. 《新中国城中村：深圳的案例》Da Wei David Wang, *Urban Villages in the New China: Case of Shenzhen*. Palgrave Macmillan US (2016)

33. 《中国本土创业状态与新的城市空间：宁波市区重建》Han Zhang, *China's Local Entrepreneurial State and New Urban Spaces: Downtown Redevelopment in Ningbo* (New Perspectives on Chinese Politics and Society). Palgrave Macmillan US (2016)

34. 《中国城市棚户区的创新和升级：转变发展规则》Pengfei Ni, Banji Oyeyinka, Fei Chen (auth.), *Urban Innovation and Upgrading in China Shanty Towns: Changing the Rules of Development-Springer*. Verlag Berlin Heidelberg (2015)

35. 《中国早期与中世纪的城市化：苏州市地名录》Olivia Milburn, *Urbanization in Early and Medieval China: Gazetteers for the City of Suzhou*.University of Washington Press (2015)

36. 《新城区发展：中国案例研究》Zisheng Shao, *The New Urban Area Development: A Case Study in China*.Springer-Verlag Berlin Heidelberg (2015)

37. 《中国城市发展年度报告（2013）》Jiahua Pan, Houkai Wei (eds.), *Annual Report on Urban Development of China 2013* (Current Chinese Economic Report Series). Springer-Verlag Berlin Heidelberg (2015)

38. 《国家政策制度化：中国城市住房改革的演变》Miao Zhang, Rajah Rasiah, *Institutionalization of State Policy: Evolving Urban Housing Reforms in China* (Dynamics of Asian Development). Springer-Verlag Singapur (2015)

39. 《城市创新与中国棚户区改造升级：转变发展规则》Pengfei Ni, Banji Oyeyinka, Fei Chen, *Urban Innovation and Upgrading in China Shanty Towns: Changing the Rules of Development*. Springer-Verlag Berlin Heidelberg (2015)

40. 《中国鬼城：世界人口最多国家的空城故事》Wade Shepard, *Ghost Cities of China: The Story of Cities without People in the World's Most Populated Country* (Zed Books-Asian Arguments). Zed Books (2015)

41. 《规划增长：中国城市和区域规划》Fulong Wu, *Planning for Growth: Urban and Regional Planning in China*.Routledge (2015)

42. 《城市与稳定：中国的城市化、再分配与体制存活》Jeremy Wallace, *Cities and Stability: Urbanization, Redistribution, & Regime Survival in China*. Oxford University Press (2014)

43. 《新时期的中国城市：市场改革、现状与前进道路》Zhiming Cheng, Mark Wang, Junhua Chen (eds.), *Urban China in the New Era: Market Reforms, Current State, and the Road Forward*. Springer Berlin Heidelberg (2014)

44. 《中国新型城镇化战略》China Development Research Foundation, *China's New Urbanization*

Strategy.Routledge (2013)

45. 《民国城市空间新叙事：新兴社会、法律和治理秩序》Madeleine Zelin（曾小萍），*New Narratives of Urban Space in Republican Chinese Cities: Emerging Social, Legal and Governance Orders*. Brill (2013)

46. 《中国城市化：上海、香港、广州》Gregory Bracken, *Aspects of Urbanization in China: Shanghai, Hong Kong, Guangzhou*. Amsterdam University Press (2012)

47. 《中国城市社区建设的政治》Thomas Heberer, Christian Göbel, *The Politics of Community Building in Urban China*. Routledge (2011)

48. 《迈向中国可持续城市：2008年部分中国城市分析与评估》Jingzhu Zhao, *Towards Sustainable Cities in China: Analysis and Assessment of Some Chinese Cities in 2008*. Springer-Verlag New York (2011)

49. 《中国城市大转型：政治和财产》You-tien Hsing（邢幼田），*The Great Urban Transformation: Politics and Property in China*. Oxford University Press (2010)

50. 《有形的龙：中国城市革命及其世界影响》Thomas J. Campanella, *The Concrete Dragon: China's Urban Revolution and What It Means for the World*. Princeton Architectural Press (2008)

51. 《中国城市的边缘化：比较的视角》Fulong Wu, Chris Webster, *Marginalization in Urban China: Comparative Perspectives*. Palgrave Macmillan (2010)

52. 《转型中的中国城市：城市与社会变迁研究》John Logan, *Urban China in Transition: Studies in Urban and Social Change*. Wiley-Blackwell (2008)

53. 《中国都市化：后果、战略和政策》Shahid Yusuf, Tony Saich（托尼·赛奇），*China Urbanizes: Consequences, Strategies, and Policies*. The International Bank for Reconstruction and Development / The World Bank (2007)

54. 《中国的新兴城市：新都市主义的形成》Fulong Wu, *China's Emerging Cities: The Making of New Urbanism*. Routledge (2007)

55. 《改革开放后的中国城市发展：国家、市场与空间》Fulong Wu, Jiang Xu, and Anthony Gar-On Yeh, *Urban Development in Post-Reform China: State, Market, Space*. Routledge (2007)

56. 《融资城市：巴西、中国、印度、波兰和南非的财政责任与城市基础设施》George J. Peterson, *Financing Cities: Fiscal Responsibility and Urban Infrastructure in Brazil, China, India, Poland and South Africa*. Sage Publications Pvt. Ltd (2007)

57. 《市场社会主义条件下的中国城市空间发展》Terry McGee, *China's Urban Space Development Under Market Socialism*. Routledge Studies on China in Transition. Routledge (2007)

58. 《全球化与中国城市》Fulong Wu, *Globalisation and the Chinese City*. Routledge (2006)

59. 《中国可持续性城市住宅：低能耗设计的原则和案例研究》Leon Glicksman, Juintow Lin, *Sustainable Urban Housing in China: Principles and Case Studies for Low-Energy Design*. Springer (2006)

60. 《中国城市化、能源和空气污染：未来挑战》Chinese Academy of Engineering, Chinese

Academy of Sciences, National Academy of Engineering, *Urbanization, Energy, and Air Pollution in China: The Challenges Ahead.* National Academies Press (2005)

61. 《中国城市转型》John Friedmann, *China's Urban Transition.* University of Minnesota Press (2005)

62. 《中国城市的社会空间与治理：单位的前世今生》David Bray, *Social Space and Governance in Urban China: The Danwei System from Origins to Reform.* Stanford University Press (2005)

63. 《中国城市：当代文化的民族志》Nancy Chen, Constance Clark, Suzanne Gottschang, Lyn Jeffery, *China Urban: Ethnographies of Contemporary Culture.* Duke University Press (2001)

64. 《时空中的中国城市：苏州城市形态的发展》Yinong Xu, *The Chinese City in Space and Time: The Development of Urban Form in Suzhou.* Honolulu: University of Hawai'i Press (2000)

65. 《中国城市：改革时代经济发展的秘诀》Jae Ho Chung, *Cities in China: Recipes for Economic Development in the Reform Era* (Routledge Studies-China in Transition, 7). Routledge (1999)

66. 《中国城市土地改革》Li Ling Hin, *Urban Land Reform in China.* Palgrave Macmillan UK (1999)

67. 《中国城市公民竞争：农民工、国家与市场逻辑》Dorothy J. Solinger（苏道锐）, *Contesting Citizenship in Urban China: Peasant Migrants, the State, and the Logic of the Market.* University of California Press (1999)

68. 《创业国家：改革时代天津房地产和商业部门》Jane Duckett, *The Entrepreneurial State in China: Real Estate and Commerce Departments in Reform Era Tianjin.* Routledge (1998)

69. 《中国：新兴市场经济中的城市土地管理》World Bank, *China: Urban Land Management in an Emerging Market Economy.* World Bank Publications (1993)

70. 《中国沿海城市：现代化的催化剂》Yue-Man Yeung, *China's Coastal Cities: Catalysts for Modernization.* University of Hawaii Press (1991)

71. 《中华帝国晚期的城市》G. William Skinner（施坚雅）, *The City in Late Imperial China* (Reith Lectures). Stanford University Press (1977)

10.8 农业与农村

1. 《中国农村家庭经济》Wenrong Qian, *The Economy of Chinese Rural Households.* Springer Singapore: Palgrave Macmillan (2020)

2. 《1930年代中国农业：对卜凯（John Lossing Buck）重新发现的"中国土地利用"微数据的调查》Hao Hu, Funing Zhong, Calum G. Turvey, *Chinese Agriculture in the 1930s: Investigations into John Lossing Buck's Rediscovered 'Land Utilization in China' Microdata.* Springer International Publishing (2019)

3. 《示范农业：当代中国的有机独立农业》Sacha Cody, *Exemplary Agriculture: Independent Organic Farming in Contemporary China.* Springer Singapore: Palgrave Macmillan (2019)

4. 《中国农村社会发展》Wenrong Qian, *Societal Development in Rural China.* Springer

Singapore: Palgrave Macmillan (2019)

5. 《中国的制造业城镇》Yue Gong, *Manufacturing Towns in China*. Springer Singapore, Palgrave Macmillan (2019)

6. 《建立中国适当的土地污染管理体制：美国和英国的经验教训》Xiaobo Zhao, *Developing an Appropriate Contaminated Land Regime in China: Lessons Learned from the US and UK*. Springer Berlin Heidelberg (2019)

7. 《从公社到资本主义：中国农民如何失去集体农业变成城市贫民》Zhun Xu, *From Commune to Capitalism: How China's Peasants Lost Collective Farming and Gained Urban Poverty*. Monthly Review Press (2018)

8. 《农民的新命运》Shukai Zhao, *The New Fate of Peasants*. Jointly published with The Commercial Press, Ltd. and Springer Singapore (2018)

9. 《1661—1980年中国历史上的农田：重建与时空特征》Xiaobin Jin, Yinkang Zhou, Xuhong Yang, Yinong Cheng, *Historical Farmland in China during 1661—1980: Reconstruction and Spatiotemporal Characteristics* (Historical Geography and Geosciences). Springer International Publishing AG (2018)

10. 《中国农业转型》Jun Du, *Agricultural Transition in China* (Palgrave Studies in Economic History). Springer International Publishing: Palgrave Macmillan (2018)

11. 《变化中的中国干旱区碳循环》Xiujun Wang, Zhitong Yu, Jiaping Wang, Juan Zhang, *Carbon Cycle in the Changing Arid Land of China* (Springer Earth System Sciences). Springer Singapore (2018)

12. 《民国时期农业信贷的演变（1912—1949）》Hong Fu, Calum G. Turvey, *The Evolution of Agricultural Credit during China's Republican Era, 1912—1949*. Springer International Publishing: Palgrave Macmillan (2018)

13. 《中国农村发展道路》Xiaoshan Zhang, Zhou Li, *China's Rural Development Road* (Research Series on the Chinese Dream and China's Development Path). Springer Singapore (2018)

14. 《中国农村的城乡不平等》Yan Gao, Shailaja Fennell, *China's Rural-Urban Inequality in the Countryside*. Springer Singapore (2018)

15. 《对中国农业的见解》Yunhua Zhang, *Insights into Chinese Agriculture*. Springer Singapore (2018)

16. 《粮食安全与中国现代化道路：走向可持续农业》Marie-Hélène Schwoob, *Food Security and the Modernisation Pathway in China: Towards Sustainable Agriculture* (Critical Studies of the Asia-Pacific). Palgrave Macmillan (2018)

17. 《中国转基因生物（GMO）：全球争论如何改变中国农业生物技术政策》Cong Cao, *GMO China: How Global Debates Transformed China's Agricultural Biotechnology Policies*. Columbia University Press (2018)

18. 《苦与甜：中国农村食物、意义与现代性》Ellen Oxfeld, *Bitter and Sweet: Food, Meaning,*

and Modernity in Rural China. University of California Press (2017)

19. 《农民的再生》Shukai Zhao, Regeneration of Peasants. Jointly published with The Commercial Press, Ltd. and Springer Singapore (2017)
20. 《革命前夕的农村中国：1949—1950年的四川田野笔记》G. William Skinner, Stevan Harrell, William Lavely (eds.), Rural China on the Eve of Revolution: Sichuan Fieldnotes, 1949—1950. University of Washington Press (2017)
21. 《中国农村福利》Yi Pan, Rural Welfare in China (International Perspectives on Social Policy, Administration, and Practice).Springer International Publishing (2017)
22. 《农民政治》Shukai Zhao, The Politics of Peasants. Springer Nature Singapore Pte Ltd. and The Commercial Press, Ltd. 2017)
23. 《以我名字命名的村庄：一部中国对外开放的家族史》Scott Tong, A Village with My Name: A Family History of China's Opening to the World. University of Chicago Press (2017)
24. 《中国农业改革与发展》Zhou Li, Reform and Development of Agriculture in China (Research Series on the Chinese Dream and China's Development Path). Springer Singapore (2017)
25. 《现代乡村：民国时期的自我与国家重建》Kate Merkel-Hess, The Rural Modern: Reconstructing the Self and State in Republican China. University of Chicago Press (2016)
26. 《红色革命与绿色革命：社会主义中国的"科学种田"》Sigrid Schmalzer（舒喜乐）, Red Revolution, Green Revolution: Scientific Farming in Socialist China. University of Chicago Press (2016)
27. 《1949年以来中国农业改革与农村转型》Thomas Dubois, Huaiyin Li（李怀印）, Agricultural Reform and Rural Transformation in China since 1949 (Historical Studies of Contemporary China). Brill Academic Publishing (2016)
28. 《当代中国农村改革》Xiang Wu, Contemporary Chinese Rural Reform. Springer Singapore (2016)
29. 《2014年中国农村家庭金融发展报告》Li Gan, Zhichao Yin, Jijun Tan, Report on the Development of Household Finance in Rural China 2014. Springer Singapore (2016)
30. 《中国农村治理、社会组织和改革：以安徽省为例》Hongguang He, Governance, Social Organisation and Reform in Rural China: Case Studies from Anhui Province. Palgrave Macmillan UK (2015)
31. 《中国农村可持续发展：野外调查与中日比较分析》Bingtao Qin, Sustainable Development in Rural China: Field Survey and Sino-Japan Comparative Analysis. Springer-Verlag Berlin Heidelberg (2015)
32. 《中国农村社区改造及其他：社区创业与企业、基础设施开发和投资模式》Ying Zhu, Hong Lan, David A. Ness, Ke Xing, Kris Schneider, Seung-Hee Lee, Jing Ge, Transforming Rural Communities in China and Beyond: Community Entrepreneurship and Enterprises, Infrastructure Development and Investment Modes. Springer International Publishing (2015)

33.《中国农村生计：转型期政治经济学》Heather Xiaoquan Zhang, *Rural Livelihoods in China: Political Economy in Transition*. Routledge (2015)

34.《满洲里：一个叫作荒原的乡村与中国农村转型》Michael J. Meyer, *In Manchuria: A Village Called Wasteland and the Transformation of Rural China*. Bloomsbury Press (2015)

35.《中国绿色粮食计划：世界最大生态恢复与农村发展项目回顾》Claudio O. Delang, Zhen Yuan, *China's Grain for Green Program: A Review of the Largest Ecological Restoration and Rural Development Program in the World*. Springer International Publishing (2015)

36.《中国农村发展：创新机构与市场的崛起（第一卷）》Lu Yilong, *Rural Development in China: The Rise of Innovative Institutions and Markets* (Volume 1). Enrich Professional Publishing (2014)

37.《中国社会主义新农村：现代性来到怒江河谷》Russell Harwood, *China's New Socialist Countryside: Modernity Arrives in the Nu River Valley*. University of Washington Press (2014)

38.《驯服的村庄"民主"：一个当代中国村庄的选举、治理和庇护》Guohui Wang, *Tamed Village "Democracy": Elections, Governance and Clientelism in a Contemporary Chinese Village*. Berlin Springer (2014)

39.《中国农村经商：凉山的新型民族企业家》Thomas Heberer, *Doing Business in Rural China: Liangshan's New Ethnic Entrepreneurs*. University of Washington Press (2014)

40.《中国农村税费改革：收入、阻力和威权统治》Hiroki Takeuchi, *Tax Reform in Rural China: Revenue, Resistance, and Authoritarian Rule*. Cambridge University Press (2014)

41.《中国农产品市场的政治经济学：全球化时代市场的社会建构》Louis Augustin-Jean, Björn Alpermann (eds.), *The Political Economy of Agro-Food Markets in China: The Social Construction of the Markets in an Era of Globalization*. Palgrave Macmillan UK (2014)

42.《当代中国农村社会稳定问题研究》Xing Ying, *A Study of the Stability of Contemporary Rural Chinese Society*. Springer Berlin Heidelberg (2013)

43.《同谋社区：中国农村的日常伦理》Hans Steinmüller, *Communities of Complicity: Everyday Ethics in Rural China*. Berghahn (2013)

44.《中国粮食安全与农田保护》Xiaojing Yang, Nong Zhao, Yushi Mao, *Food Security and Farm Land Protection in China* (Series on Chinese economics research 2.). World Scientific Pub. (2013)

45.《中国乡村与全球市场：新集体与农村发展》Tony Saich（托尼·赛奇）, Biliang Hu, *Chinese Village, Global Market: New Collectives and Rural Development*. Palgrave Macmillan US (2012)

46.《中国的巧妙手段：中国工厂化养殖遭遇的挑战》Mia MacDonald, Sangamithra Iyer, *China Skillful Means: The Challenges of China's Encounter with Factory Farming*. Brighter Green (2011)

47.《中国东部土壤流失控制的理论与实践》J. C. Zhang, D. L. DeAngelis, J. Y. Zhuang, *Theory and Practice of Soil Loss Control in Eastern China*. Springer-Verlag New York (2011)

48. 《中国农村改革的政治：21世纪初的国家政策和乡村困境》Christian Göbel, *The Politics of Rural Reform in China: State Policy and Village Predicament in the Early 2000s*. Routledge (2010)

49. 《中国背景下的农村转型与发展：政策与人民日常生活》Norman Long, Ye Jingzhong, Wang Yihuan, *Rural Transformations and Development-China in Context: The Everyday Lives of Policies and People*. Edward Elgar Publishing (2010)

50. 《市场的反应：尼加拉瓜、古巴、俄罗斯和中国经济转型中的小农》(Rural Studies) Laura J. Enríquez, *Reactions to the Market: Small Farmers in the Economic Reshaping of Nicaragua, Cuba, Russia, and China*. Pennsylvania State University Press (2010)

51. 《中国农村社会主义与改革的微观历史（1948—2008）》Huaiyin Li（李怀印）, *Village China Under Socialism and Reform: A Micro-History, 1948—2008*. Stanford University Press (2009)

52. 《以竹为生：一个四川手工造纸村的20世纪社会史》Jacob Eyferth（艾约博）, *Eating Rice from Bamboo Roots: The Social History of a Community of Handicraft Papermakers in Rural Sichuan, 1920—2000*. Harvard University Asia Center (2009)

53. 《当代中国农村没有代表的税收》Thomas P. Bernstein（白思鼎）, Xiaobo Lu, *Taxation without Representation in Contemporary Rural China* (Cambridge Modern China Series). Cambridge University Press (2008)

54. 《中国农业与粮食安全：加入世贸组织和区域贸易协定有什么影响？》Chunlai Chen and Ron Duncan, *Agriculture and Food Security in China: What Effect WTO Accession and Regional Trade Agreements?* Canberra: Asia Pacifc Press (2008)

55. 《中国农村的产业化》Chris Bramall（克里斯·布拉莫尔）, *The Industrialization of Rural China*. Cambridge University Press (2007)

56. 《中国农村的农民与革命：华北平原和长江三角洲的农村政治变革（1850—1949）》Chang Liu（刘昶）, *Peasants and Revolution in Rural China: Rural Political Change in the North China Plain and the Yangzi Delta, 1850—1949* (Routledge Studies on the Chinese Economy). Routledge (2007)

57. 《中国非正式制度与农村发展》Biliang Hu, *Informal Institutions and Rural Development in China* (Routledge Studies on the Chinese Economy).Routledge (2007)

58. 《高家村：现代中国的农村生活》Mobo C. F. Gao（高默波）, *Gao Village: Rural Life in Modern China*. University of Hawai'i Press (2007)

59. 《资源利用与农业可持续发展：中国集约化作物的风险与后果》Lin Zhen, Michael Zoebisch, *Resource Use and Agricultural Sustainability: Risks and Consequences of Intensive Cropping in China*. Kassel University Press (2006)

60. 《中国农村：20世纪末经济和社会变革》Jie Fan, Thomas Heberer, Wolfgang Taubmann, *Rural China: Economic and Social Change in the Late Twentieth Century*. M.E. Sharpe, Inc. (2006)

61. 《中国农村的权力和财富：制度变迁的政治经济学》Susan H. Whiting, *Power and Wealth in Rural China: The Political Economy of Institutional Change* (Cambridge Modern China Series). Cambridge University Press (2006)

62. 《中国农村工业化：1949年以来的奉命政策生成》Shi Cheng, *China's Rural Industrialization: Policy Growing under Orders since 1949*. Palgrave Macmillan (2006)

63. 《加入WTO后的中国农村经济：问题与对策》Shunfeng Song, Aimin Chen, *China's Rural Economy after WTO: Problems and Strategies*. Ashgate Publishing Limited (2006)

64. 《黄河沿线之中国：对农村社会的反思》Cao Jinqing, *China Along the Yellow River: Reflections on Rural Society* (Routledgecurzon Studies on the Chinese Economy). Routledgecurzon (2005)

65. 《神圣的村庄：华北农村的社会变迁与宗教活动》Thomas David DuBois, *The Sacred Village: Social Change and Religious LIfe in Rural North China*. University of Hawaii Press (2005)

66. 《农村中国转型：中国地方制度如何塑造产权》Chih-jou Jay Chen, *Transforming Rural China: How Local Institutions Shape Property Rights in China*. RoutledgeCurzon (2004)

67. 《竞争力的根源：中国农业利益的演变》Daniel H. Rosen, *Roots of Competitiveness: China's Evolving Agriculture Interests* (Policy Analyses in International Economics). Washington, DC: Institute for International Economics (2004)

68. 《中国转型期的农村发展：新农业》Peter Ho, Jacob Eyferth, Eduard B. Vermeer (eds.), *Rural Development in Transitional China: The New Agriculture* (The Library of Peasant Studies). Frank Cass & Co. Ltd (2004)

69. 《中国红土的性质、管理和利用》M. J. Wilson, Zhenli He, Xiaoe Yang (auth.), M. J. Wilson, Zhenli He, Xiaoe Yang (eds.), *The Red Soils of China: Their Nature, Management and Utilization*. Springer Netherlands (2004)

70. 《阳邑公社的头几年》David Crook（戴维·柯鲁克）, Isabel Crook（伊莎白·柯鲁克）, *First Years of Yangyi Commune*. Routledge (1966) ; Taylor & Francis e-Library (2003)

71. 《中国农村可持续发展：边缘地区的农民创新与自我组织》Bin Wu, *Sustainable Development in Rural China: Farmer Innovation and Self-Organisation in Marginal Areas*. Routledge (2003)

72. 《改革后中国农村市场关系的发展：对农民、移民和农民企业家的微观分析》Hiroshi Sato, *The Growth of Market Relations in Post-Reform Rural China: A Micro-Analysis of Peasants, Migrants and Peasant Entrepeneurs*. Routledge (2003)

73. 《中国农村企业融资》Jun Li, *Financing China's Rural Enterprises*. Routledge (2002)

74. 《模范造反：中国首富村的兴衰》Bruce Gilley（布鲁斯·吉利）, *Model Rebels: The Rise and Fall of China's Richest Village*. University of California Press (2001)

75. 《中国农村的市场和社会结构》G. William Skinner（施坚雅）, *Marketing and Social Structure in Rural China*. Association for Asian Studies (2001)

76. 《移地：中国和印尼的农业土壤变化》Peter H. Lindert, *Shifting Ground: The Changing*

Agricultural Soils of China and Indonesia. The MIT Press (2000)

77. 《十字路口的中国农业》Yongzheng Yang, Weiming Tian (eds.), China's Agriculture at the Crossroads. Palgrave Macmillan UK (2000)

78. 《在自己的阴影里：改革后中国农村生存条件的田野报告》Xin Liu（流心）, In One's Own Shadow: An Ethnographic Account of the Condition of Post-reform Rural China. University of California Press (2000)

79. 《加快中国农村转型》Albert Nyberg, Scott Rozelle, World Bank, Accelerating China's Rural Transformation. World Bank Publications (1999)

80. 《中国农业改革：获得制度权力》Yiping Huang, Agricultural Reform in China: Getting Institutions Right (Trade and Development). Cambridge University Press (1998)

81. 《干部和亲属：中国西部地区一个社会主义村庄的形成（1921—1991）》Gregory A. Ruf, Cadres and Kin: Making a Socialist Village in West China, 1921—1991. Stanford University Press (1998)

82. 《乡土中国：云南农村经济研究》Chih-I Chang, Hsiao Tung-Fei, Earthbound China: A Study of the Rural Economy of Yunnan (The Sociology of East Asia). Routledge (1998)

83. 《广东农村经济（1870—1937）：中国最南端的农业危机及其起源研究》Alfred H. Y. Lin, Rural Economy of Guangdong 1870—1937: A Study of the Agrarian Crisis and its Origins in Southernmost China (Studies in the Chinese Economy). Palgrave Macmillan (1997)

84. 《解放中国农民：改革时代的农村改革》David Zweig（崔大伟）, Freeing China's Farmers: Rural Restructuring in the Reform Era (Socialism and Social Movements). M. E. Sharpe (1997)

85. 《中国农村第三次革命》Ross Garnaut, Shutian Guo, Guonan Ma, The third Revolution in the Chinese Countryside. Cambridge University Press (1996)

86. 《中国农村的改革与发展》Runsheng Du (auth.), Thomas R. Gottschang (eds.), Reform and Development in Rural China (Studies on the Chinese Economy). Palgrave Macmillan UK (1995)

87. 《中国农业的不稳定性（1931—1990）：气候、技术、制度》Y. Y. Kueh（郭益耀）, Agricultural Instability in China, 1931—1990: Weather, Technology, and Institutions. Clarendon Press (1995)

88. 《中国农业改革与粮食生产》Shujie Yao, Agricultural Reforms and Grain Production in China (Studies on the Chinese Economy). Palgrave Macmillan UK (1994)

89. 《透视中国农村发展的连续性与变化：集体与改革时代》Louis Putterman, Continuity and Change in China's Rural Development: Collective and Reform Eras in Perspective. Oxford University Press, USA (1993)

90. 《中国农村起飞：经济改革的制度基础》Jean C. Oi（戴慕珍）, Rural China Takes off: Institutional Foundations of Economic Reform. Berkeley: University of California Press (1999)

91. 《工业化与中国农村现代化》Dong Fureng, Industrialization and China's Rural

Modernization (Studies on the Chinese Economy). Palgrave Macmillan UK (1992)

92.《中国农村社会转型：以太湖地区为例（1368—1800）》James C. Shih, *Chinese Rural Society in Transition: A Case Study of the Lake Tai Area, 1368—1800*. Institute of East Asian Studies, University of California, Berkeley, Center for Chinese Studies (1992)

93.《中国农村改革与农民收入：毛泽东时代后中国选定区域农村改革的影响》Ling Zhu, *Rural Reform and Peasant Income in China: The Impact of China's Post-Mao Rural Reforms in Selected Regions*. Palgrave Macmillan UK (1991)

94.《当代中国的国家与农民：乡村政府的政治经济》Jean C. Oi（戴慕珍）, *State and Peasant in Contemporary China: The Political Economy of Village Government* (Center for Chinese Studies, University of Michigan). University of California Press (1991)

95.《文化、权力与国家：1900—1942年的华北农村》Prasenjit Duara（杜赞奇）, *Culture, Power, and the State: Rural North China, 1900—1942*. Stanford University Press (1991)

96.《中国农民：一场革命的人类学研究》Sulamith Heins Potter, Jack M. Potter, *China's Peasants: The Anthropology of a Revolution*. Cambridge University Press (1990)

97.《长江三角洲的小农家庭与乡村发展（1350—1988）》Philip C. C. Huang（黄宗智）, *The Peasant Family and Rural Development in Yangzi Delta: 1350—1988*. Stanford University Press (1990)

98.《中国的土地激进主义（1968—1981）》David Zweig（崔大伟）, *Agrarian Radicalism in China, 1968—1981* (Harvard East Asian Series). Harvard University Press (1989)

99.《耗尽地球：湖南的国家和农民（1500—1850）》Peter C. Perdue, *Exhausting the Earth: State and Peasant in Hunan, 1500—1850* (Harvard East Asian Monographs).Harvard University Asia Center (1987)

100.《华北的小农经济与社会变迁》Philip C. C. Huang（黄宗智）, *The Peasant Economy and Social Change in North China*. Stanford, Calif.: Stanford University Press (1985)

101.《中国农村制度变迁与经济发展》Keith Griffin, *Institutional Reform and Economic Development in the Chinese Countryside*. Palgrave Macmillan UK (1984)

102.《中国现代经济发展中的农业》Nicholas R. Lardy（尼古拉斯·拉迪）, *Agriculture in China's Modern Economic Development*. Cambridge University Press (1983)

103.《破碎的地球：中国农村人》Steven W. Mosher, *Broken Earth: The Rural Chinese*. The Free Press (1983)

104.《转型期的农民中国：走向社会主义的发展动力（1949—1956）》Vivienne Shue（许慧文）, *Peasant China in Transition: The Dynamics of Development Toward Socialism, 1949—1956*. University of California Press (1981)

105.《汉代农业：早期中国农业经济的形成（公元前206—公元220年）》(Han Dynasty China) Cho-Yun Hsu（许倬云）, Zhuoyun Xu, Jack L. Dull, *Han Agriculture: The Formation of Early Chinese Agrarian Economy, 206 B.C.-A.D. 220*. University of

Washington Press (1980)

106. 《农民中国的转型：1949—1956年社会主义发展的动力》Vivienne Shue（许慧文），*Peasant China in Transition: The Dynamics of Development Toward Socialism, 1949—1956*. University of California Press (1980)

107. 《中国和印度巴基斯坦（原文如此）的农村地方政府与农村发展》G. Shabbir Cheema, *Rural Local Government and Rural Development in China, India Pakistan*. South Asian Institute, University of the Panjab (1977)

108. 《农业变迁与华南农民经济》Evelyn Sakakida Rawski（罗友枝），*Agricultural Change and the Peasant Economy of South China* (Harvard East Asian series). Harvard University Press (1972)

109. 《共产党中国的农民生活》W. R. Geddes, *Peasant life in Communist China*. Society for Applied Anthropology (1963)

110. 《中国乡村：十九世纪的帝国控制》Kung-Chuan Hsiao（萧公权），*Rural China: Imperial Control in the Nineteenth Century* (University of Washington Publications on Asia). University of Washington Press (1960)

111. 《当前中国农业发展与问题：中国共产党土地政策调查》Guojun Zhao, *Agricultural Development and Problems in China Today: A Survey of Chinese Communist Agrarian Policies*. New Delhi, Indian Council of World Affairs; New York, Institute of Pacific Relations (1958)

10.9　科技与自然

10.9.1　科学技术

1. 《中国电子科学蓝皮书（2018）》Chinese Academy of Sciences, etc., (eds.), *China's e-Science Blue Book 2018*. Springer Singapore (2020)

2. 《人工智能超级大国：中国、硅谷和新的世界秩序》Kai-Fu Lee（李开复），*AI Superpowers: China, Silicon Valley, and the New World Order*. Houghton Mifflin Harcourt (2018)

3. 《解读中国人工智能梦：中国人工智能引领世界战略的背景、要素、能力与后果》Jeffrey Ding, *Deciphering China's AI Dream: The Context, Components, Capabilities, and Consequences of China's Strategy to Lead the World in AI*. University of Oxford (2018)

4. 《国际视野下的中国高速铁路技术》Youtong Fang, Yuehong (Helen) Zhang (eds.), *China's High-Speed Rail Technology: An International Perspective* (Advances in High-speed Rail Technology). Springer Singapore (2018)

5. 《数字时代的管理：中国将超越硅谷？》Annika Steiber, *Management in the Digital Age: Will China Surpass Silicon Valley?* (SpringerBriefs in Business). Springer International Publishing (2018)

6. 《人工智能超级大国：中国、硅谷与世界新秩序》Kai-Fu Lee, *AI Superpowers: China, Silicon Valley, and the New World Order*. Houghton Mifflin Harcourt (2018)

7.《中国的技术创新者：创造并保持领先于商业趋势的典型案例》Xiaoming Zhu, *China's Technology Innovators: Selected Cases on Creating and Staying Ahead of Business Trends* (Management for professionals). Springer (2017)

8.《中国的沼气系统》Bin Chen, Tasawar Hayat, Ahmed Alsaedi, *Biogas Systems in China*. Springer-Verlag (2017)

9.《关于中国技术问题：宇宙工艺学随笔》Yuk Hui, *The Question Concerning Technology in China: An Essay in Cosmotechnics*. Urbanomic (2016)

10.《中国技术追赶战略：工业发展、能源效率与二氧化碳排放》Michael T. Rock, Michael A. Toman, *China's Technological Catch-Up Strategy: Industrial Development, Energy Efficiency, and CO2 Emissions*. Oxford University Press (2015)

11.《中国科技史》（第二卷）Yongxiang Lu（卢涌祥）(eds.), *A History of Chinese Science and Technology: Volume 2*. Springer Berlin Heidelberg (2015)

12.《欧盟和中国的纳米技术与伦理治理：科技的全球方法》Sally Dalton-Brown, *Nanotechnology and Ethical Governance in the European Union and China: Towards a Global Approach for Science and Technology*. Springer International Publishing (2015)

13.《科技治理与伦理：来自欧洲、印度和中国的全球视野》Miltos Ladikas, Sachin Chaturvedi, Yandong Zhao, Dirk Stemerding (eds.), *Science and Technology Governance and Ethics: A Global Perspective from Europe, India and China*.Springer International Publishing (2015)

14.《中国科学技术的传播与普及》Fujun Ren, Jiequan Zhai, *Communication and Popularization of Science and Technology in China*. Springer Berlin Heidelberg (2014)

15.《中国云计算兴起：中国走向科技至上的历程》Jinzy Zhu, *China Cloud Rising: China's Journey Towards Technology Supremacy*.Springer-Verlag Berlin Heidelberg (2014)

16.《现代中国科学技术：19世纪80年代至20世纪40年代》Jing Tsu, Benjamin A. Elman（艾尔曼）(eds.), *Science and Technology in Modern China, 1880s-1940s*. Brill (2014)

17.《技术、性别、历史：重新审视帝制中国的大转型》Francesca Bray（白馥兰）, *Technology, Gender and History in Imperial China: Great Transformations Reconsidered*. Routledge (2013)

18.《从文化透镜看科学形象：中国关于科学本质的研究》Hongming Ma, *The Images of Science Through Cuplattltural Lenses: A Chinese Study on the Nature of Science*.SensePublishers (2012)

19.《（德）薛凤：工开万物：17世纪中国的知识与技术》Dagmar Schäfer, *The Crafting of the 10,000 Things: Knowledge and Technology in Seventeenth-Century China*. University Of Chicago Press (2011)

20.《中国农业科技：2050年的路线图》Qiguo Zhao, Jikun Huang, *Agricultural Science & Technology in China: A Roadmap to 2050*. Springer (2011)

21.《中国信息科技：2050年路线图》Guojie Li, *Information Science & Technology in China: A Roadmap to 2050*.Springer (2011)

22. 《中国大型研究基础设施发展：2050年路线图》Hesheng Chen, *Large Research Infrastructures Development in China: A Roadmap to 2050*.Springer (2011)
23. 《东方之光：中世纪伊斯兰科学如何帮助塑造西方世界》John Freely, *Light From the East: How the Science of Medieval Islam Helped to Shape the Western World*. I. B. Tauris (2011)
24. 《通过信息技术寻求转型：巴西、中国、加拿大和斯里兰卡的战略》Nagy K. Hanna (auth.), Nagy K. Hanna, Peter T. Knight (eds.), *Seeking Transformation through Information Technology: Strategies for Brazil, China, Canada and Sri Lanka*. Springer-Verlag New York (2011)
25. 《中国商业与技术》Jing Luo, *Business and Technology in China*. ABC-CLIO (2010)
26. 《中国公共卫生科技：2050年路线图》Kaixian Chen, Qishui Lin, Jiarui Wu (eds.), *Science & Technology on Public Health in China: A Roadmap to 2050*. Springer-Verlag Berlin Heidelberg (2010)
27. 《流动、迁移与中国科学研究体系》Koen Jonkers, *Mobility, Migration and the Chinese Scientific Research System* (Routledge Contemporary China Series). Routledge (2010)
28. 《中国科技：2050年路线图。中国科学院战略总报告》Yongxiang Lu (eds.), *Science & Technology in China: A Roadmap to 2050. Strategic General Report of the Chinese Academy of Sciences*.Springer Berlin Heidelberg (2010)
29. 《遗产技术和应用的数字化保存》Dongming Lu, Yunhe Pan, *Digital Preservation for Heritages Technologies and Applications*. Springer Berlin Heidelberg (2010)
30. 《技术史：中国科技》（第二十九卷）Ian Inkster, *History of Technology, Volume 29: Technology in China*.Continuum International Publishing Group (2009)
31. 《中国信息技术手册》Miltiadis D. Lytras (auth.), Patricia Ordóñez de Pablos, Miltiadis D. Lytras (eds.), *The China Information Technology Handbook*.Springer US (2009)
32. 《全球科技革命之中国深入分析：天津滨海新区和天津经济技术开发区的新兴技术机遇》Richard Silberglitt, Anny Wong, *The Global Technology Revolution, China, in Depth Analyses: Emerging Technology Opportunities for the Tianjin Binhai New Area & The Tianjin Economic-Technological Development Area*. Rand Publishing (2009)
33. 《中国新兴技术优势：评估高端人才的作用》Denis Fred Simon, Cong Cao, *China's Emerging Technological Edge: Assessing the Role of High-End Talent*. Cambridge University Press (2009)
34. 《中国农业生物技术的起源与前景》Valerie J. Karplus, Xing Wang Deng, *Agricultural Biotechnology in China: Origins and Prospects*. Springer-Verlag New York (2008)
35. 《硅龙：中国如何赢得技术竞赛》Rebecca Fannin, *Silicon Dragon: How China Is Winning the Tech Race*. McGraw-Hill (2008)
36. 《中国技术知识生产中的图形与文本》Francesca Bray（白馥兰），Vera Dorofeeva-Lichtmann, Georges Métailié (ed.), *Graphics and Text in the Production of Technical Knowledge in China: The Warp and the Weft* (Sinica Leidensia).Koninklijke Brill NV, Leiden: The

Netherlands (2007)

37. 《中国特色创新：中国高科技研究》Linda Jakobson (eds.), *Innovation with Chinese Characteristics: High-Tech Research in China*.Palgrave Macmillan UK (2007)

38. 《中国信息技术（IT）培训服务：2006战略参考》Philip M. Parker, *Information Technology (IT) Training Services in China: A Strategic Reference, 2006*. Icon Group International (2007)

39. 《中国天才：3000年科学、发现和发明》Robert Temple, *The Genius of China: 3, 000 Years of Science, Discovery, and Invention*.Inner Traditions (2007)

40. 《中国科学进步》Lu Yongxiang, *Science Progress in China*.Elsevier Science (2006)

41. 《中国近代科学文化史》Benjamin A. Elman（艾尔曼）, *A Cultural History of Modern Science in China* (New Histories of Science, Technology, and Medicine 15). Harvard University Press (2006)

42. 《中国：技术超级大国》Jon Sigurdson, Jiang Jiang, Xinxin Kong, *Technological Superpower China*.Edward Elgar (2005)

43. 《自有主张：1550到1900年的中国科学》Benjamin A. Elman（艾尔曼）, *On Their Own Terms: Science in China, 1550—1900*. Harvard University Press (2005)

44. 《中国金盾：中华人民共和国企业与监控技术的发展》Greg Walton, *China's Golden Shield: Corporations and the Development of surveillance Technology in the Peoples Republic of China*. International Centre for Human Rights and Democratic Development (2001)

45. 《中国工业技术：市场改革与组织变化》Gu Shulin, *China's Industrial Technology: Market Reform and Organizational Change*. Routledge (1999)

46. 《十载革新：中国的科技政策》International Development Research Centre, *A Decade of Reform: Science & Technology Policy in China*. IDRC (International Development Research Cent (1998)

47. 《中国科学技术哲学史研究》Yu Guangyuan (auth.), Fan Dainian, Robert S. Cohen (eds.), *Chinese Studies in the History and Philosophy of Science and Technology*. Springer Netherlands (1996)

48. 《早期现代科学的兴起：伊斯兰教、中国和西方》Toby E. Huff, *The Rise of Early Modern Science: Islam, China and the West*. Cambridge University Press (1993)

49. 《非殖民化的历史：1492年至今印度、中国和西方的技术与文化》Claude Alvares, *Decolonising History: Technology and Culture in India, China, and the West from 1492 to the Present Day*. Other India Press (1991, 1993, 1997)

50. 《中国、印度和日本的技术发展：跨文化视角》Erik Baark, Andrew Jamison (eds.), *Technological Development in China, India and Japan: Cross-Cultural Perspectives*.Palgrave Macmillan UK (1986)

51. 《向中国转移技术：日意格与自强运动》Steven A. Leibo, *Transferring Technology to China:*

Prosper Giquel and the Self-strengthening Movement. University of California, Berkeley, Center for Chinese Studies (1985)

52. 《中国、日本和西方的学术与科学传统》Shigeru Nakayama, *Academic and scientific traditions in China, Japan, and the West*. University of Tokyo Press (1984)

53. 《中国科学与社会主义建设》Liang-Ying Hsu, Xu Liangying, Dainian Fan, Pierre M. Perrolle, John C. S. Hsu, Fan Dianian, *Science and Socialist Construction in China* (The China Book Project).M E Sharpe Inc (1982)

54. 《中华人民共和国技术与科学导论》Jon Sigurdson, *Technology and Science in the People's Republic of China: An Introduction*.Pergamon Press (1980)

55. 《当代中国科学》Leo A. Orleans, *Science in Contemporary China*.Stanford University Press (1980)

56. 《中国科学：古代传统的探索》Shigeru Nakayama, Nathan Sivin, *Chinese Science: Explorations of an Ancient Tradition* (M.I.T. East Asian science series). The MIT Press (1973)

57. 《中国大陆的科研开发组织与支持》Yuan-li Wu（吴元黎）, Robert Sheeks, *The Organization and Support of Scientific Research and Development in Mainland China*. Praeger Publishers (1970)

58. 《长江之帆船与舢板：中国航海研究》G. R. G. Worcester, *The Junks and Sampans of the Yangtze: A Study in Chinese Nautical Research*.2Vols. Shanghai: The Statistical Department of the Inspectorate General of Customs (1947—1948)

10.9.2　创新

1. 《人工智能超级大国：中国、硅谷和新的世界秩序》Kai-Fu Lee（李开复）, *AI Superpowers: China, Silicon Valley, and the New World Order*. Houghton Mifflin Harcourt (2018)

2. 《中国创新：挑战全球科学技术体系》Richard P. Appelbaum, Denis Simon, Cong Cao, Xueying Han, Rachel Parker, *Innovation in China: Challenging the Global Science and Technology System*. Polity Press (2018)

3. 《红色中国的绿色革命：公社体制下的技术创新、制度变迁与经济发展》Joshua Eisenman, *Red China's Green Revolution: Technological Innovation, Institutional Change, and Economic Development Under the Commune*. Columbia University Press (2018)

4. 《中国区域创新指数（2017）》Xielin Liu, Taishan Gao, Xi Wang, *Regional Innovation Index of China: 2017*. Springer Singapore (2018)

5. 《中国公共服务创新》Yijia Jing, Stephen P. Osborne (eds.), *Public Service Innovations in China*. Palgrave (2017)

6. 《掌握中国创新：中国创新之路的历史见解》Joachim Jan Thraen, *Mastering Innovation in China: Insights from History on China's Journey towards Innovation*. Gabler Verlag (2016)

7. 《中国下一个战略优势：从模仿到创新》George S. Yip, Bruce McKern, *China's Next Strategic Advantage: From Imitation to Innovation*. The MIT Press (2016)

8. 《中国创新：龙之尾》William H. Johnson, *Innovation in China: The Tail of the Dragon*. Business Expert Press (2015)

9. 《中国创新之源：体制高度创新》Yingying Zhang, Yu Zhou, *The Source of Innovation in China: Highly Innovative Systems*. Palgrave Macmillan UK (2015)

10. 《中国创新之路》Xiaolan Fu, *China's Path to Innovation*. Cambridge University Press (2015)

11. 《中国创新激励：建设创新型经济》Xuedong Ding, Jun Li, *Incentives for Innovation in China: Building an Innovative Economy*. Routledge (2015)

12. 《美国、中国和印度的创新、创业与经济：历史展望和未来趋势》Rajiv Shah, Zhijie Gao, Harini Mittal, *Innovation, Entrepreneurship, and the Economy in the US, China, and India: Historical Perspectives and Future Trends*. Elsevier Science, Academic Press (2015)

13. 《中西方合作创新》Caroline Gijselinckx, Li Zhao, Sonja Novkovic (eds.), *Co-operative Innovations in China and the West*. Palgrave Macmillan UK (2014)

14. 《外包服务价值网络的合作、学习与创新：中国软件服务外包》Pamela Abbott, Yingqin Zheng, Rong Du, *Collaboration, Learning and Innovation Across Outsourced Services Value Networks: Software Services Outsourcing in China*. Springer International Publishing (2014)

15. 《山寨中国的终结：亚洲创造力、创新和个人主义的兴起》Shaun Rein, *The End of Copycat China: The Rise of Creativity, Innovation, and Individualism in Asia*. Wiley (2014)

16. 《中国从创新中获益》Oliver Gassmann, Angela Beckenbauer, Sascha Friesike, *Profiting from Innovation in China*. Springer-Verlag Berlin Heidelberg (2012)

17. 《中国创新：中国软件产业》Shang-Ling Jui, *Innovation in China: The Chinese Software Industry*. Routledge (2010)

18. 《中国建设创新型经济》Celeste Varum, Can Huang, Joaquim Borges Gouveia, *China: Building an Innovative Economy*. Chandos Publishing (2008)

19. 《中国创造：新的大跃进》Michael Keane, *Created in China: The Great New Leap Forward* (Routledge Media, Culture and Social Change in Asia). Routledge (2007)

20. 《中国创新：和谐转型？》Shulin Gu, Mark Dodgson, *Innovation in China: Harmonious Transformation?* eContent Management (2006)

21. 《创造的歧路：古代中国的变革与技艺之辩》Michael Puett, *The Ambivalence of Creation: Debates Concerning Innovation and Artifice in Early China*. Stanford University Press (2001)

10.9.3 动植物

1. 《中国野生动物非法贸易：对分销网络的认识》(Palgrave Studies in Green Criminology) Rebecca W. Y. Wong, *The Illegal Wildlife Trade in China: Understanding The Distribution Networks*. Springer International Publishing: Palgrave Macmillan (2019)

2. 《纤毛虫图谱：中国南海发现的物种》Xiaozhong Hu, Xiaofeng Lin, Weibo Song, *Ciliate Atlas: Species Found in the South China Sea*. Springer Singapore (2019)

3. 《丛林宝石：一位博物学家的故事，穿越海南丛林寻找中国最难捉摸甲虫的探险之旅》

Yikai Zhang, *Jungle Gems: A Naturalist's Tale. An Illustrated Adventure through the Jungles of Hainan in Search of the Most Elusive Beetle in China*. Unbound (2019)

4. 《熊猫国家：中国现代偶像的建设与保护》E. Elena Songster, *Panda Nation: The Construction and Conservation of China's Modern Icon*. Oxford University Press (2018)

5. 《中国水产养殖：成功案例与现代趋势》Jian-Fang Gui et al. (eds.), *Aquaculture in China: Success Stories and Modern Trends*. Wiley Blackwell (2018)

6. 《中国历史上的动物：从最初至1911年》Dagmar Schafer, Martina Siebert, Roel Sterckx（胡司德）, *Animals Through Chinese History: Earliest Times to 1911*. Cambridge University Press (2018)

7. 《当代中国生物物理史》Christine Yi Lai Luk, *A History of Biophysics in Contemporary China* (SpringerBriefs in History of Science and Technology). Springer International Publishing (2015)

8. 《中国动物：法律与社会》Deborah Cao, *Animals in China: Law and Society*. Palgrave Macmillan UK (2015)

9. 《中国哺乳动物》Andrew T. Smith, Yan Xie, *Mammals of China* (Princeton Pocket Guides). Princeton University Press (2013)

10. 《中国鄱阳湖无鳍长江海豚之条件性评估》Yanyan Dong, *Contingent Valuation of Yangtze Finless Porpoises in Poyang Lake, China*. Springer Netherlands (2013)

11. 《大熊猫之路：中国政治动物的奇妙历史》Henry Nicholls, *The Way of the Panda: The Curious History of China's Political Animal*. Pegasus Books (2011)

12. 《纸路：中国西部和西藏植物学考察的档案与经验》Erik Mueggler, *The Paper Road: Archive and Experience in the Botanical Exploration of West China and Tibet*. University of California Press (2011)

13. 《与华南及海外世界有关的中文文本和贸易讲座中的禽兽》(Maritime Asia, 22) Roderich Ptak, *Birds and Beasts in Chinese Texts and Trade Lectures Related to South China and the Overseas World*. Otto Harrassowitz (2011)

14. 《猴子与墨盒：现代中国早期的自然史及其转变》Carla Nappi, *The Monkey and the Inkpot: Natural History and Its Transformations in Early Modern China*. Harvard University Press (2009)

15. 《中国生物伦理学、信任与市场挑战》Julia Tao, *China: Bioethics, Trust, and the Challenge of the Market* (Philosophy and Medicine: Asian Studies in Bioethics and the Philosophy of Medicine). Springer Science+Business Media B.V. (2008)

16. 《中国野生动物保护：保护西部野生动物栖息地》(East Gate Books) Richard B. Harris, George B. Schaller, *Wildlife Conservation in China: Preserving the Habitat of China's Wild West*. M. E. Sharpe (2007)

17. 《淑女与熊猫：首位从中国带回其最富异国情调动物的美国女探险家的真实经历》Vicki Croke, *The Lady and the Panda: The True Adventures of the First American Explorer to Bring Back China's Most Exotic Animal*. Random House Publishing Group (2005)

18. 《中国植物的多样性与分布》Geoffrey P. Chapman, Yin-Zheng Wang, *The Plant Life of China: Diversity and Distribution*.Springer-Verlag Berlin Heidelberg (2002)
19. 《中国云南的花卉》Zeng, Xiao-Lian, *Flowers in Yunnan China*.Yunnan Artist Press (2002)
20. 《在中国探寻植物：中国植物探索史和西藏游历》E. H. M. (Euan Hillhouse Methven) Cox, *Plant-hunting in China: A History of Botanical Exploration in China and the Tibetan Marches*. London Collins (1945)
21. 《荔枝与龙眼》George Weidman Groff, *The Lychee and Lungan*. Orange Judd Company (1921)
22. 《中国昆虫自然史》Edward Donovan, *An Epitome of the Natural History of the Insects of China*.London, Bensley (1798)

10.9.4 天文太空

1. 《当地球是平的：古希腊和中国宇宙学研究》(Historical & Cultural Astronomy) Dirk L. Couprie, *When the Earth Was Flat: Studies in Ancient Greek and Chinese Cosmology*. Springer (2018)
2. 《呼唤太空：中国未来空间科学任务战略报告与研究》Ji Wu, *Calling Taikong: A Strategy Report and Study of China's Future Space Science Missions* (Science Policy Reports). Springer Singapore (2017)
3. 《天体计算的基础：三个中国古代天文系统》Christopher Cullen, *The Foundations of Celestial Reckoning: Three Ancient Chinese Astronomical Systems* (Scientific Writings from the Ancient and Medieval World). Routledge (2017)
4. 《当中国走向月球》Marco Aliberti, *When China Goes to the Moon...* Springer International Publishing (2015)
5. 《中国早期占星学和宇宙学：顺天应地》David W. Pankenier, *Astrology and Cosmology in Early China: Conforming Earth to Heaven*.Cambridge University Press (2013)
6. 《中国在太空的大跃进》Brian Harvey, *China in Space: The Great Leap Forward*. Springer (2013)
7. 《中国空间战略》Stacey Solomone, *China's Strategy in Space*.Springer-Verlag New York (2013)
8. 《授时历丛考》(Sources and Studies in the History of Mathematics and Physical Sciences) Nathan Sivin（席文）, *Granting the Seasons: The Chinese Astronomical Reform of 1280, With a Study of Its Many Dimensions and a Translation of Its Records*. Springer (2009)
9. 《伟大的中国古代工程》Lance Kramer, *Great Ancient China Projects: You Can Build Yourself* (Build It Yourself series).Nomad Press (2008)
10. 《中国早期的空间建构》Mark Edward Lewis, *The Construction Of Space In Early China* (SUNY Series in Chinese Philosophy and Culture).State University of New York Press (2005)
11. 《踱步太空：唐代接近星辰》Edward H. Schafer, *Pacing the Void: T'ang Approaches to the Stars*.Floating World Editions (2005)
12. 《中国占星术：现代生活的古老秘密》Sabrina Liao, *Chinese Astrology: Ancient Secrets for Modern Life*. Grand Central Publishing, Oxmoor House (2001)

13. 《中国老住宅》Ronald G. Knapp, *China's old Dwellings*. Honolulu: University of Hawai'i Press (2000)
14. 《中国宇宙论的发展与衰退》John B. Henderson, *The Development and Decline of Chinese Cosmology*. Columbia University Press (1984)
15. 《日本天文学史：中国背景与西方影响》(Harvard-Yenching Institute Monograph Series, 18) Nakayama Shigeru, *A History of Japanese Astronomy: Chinese Background and Western Impact*. Harvard University Press (1969)

10.9.5 数理化

1. 《论数学现代性九章：中国数学的全球史纠葛随笔》Andrea Bréard, *Nine Chapters on Mathematical Modernity: Essays on the Global Historical Entanglements of the Science of Numbers in China*. Springer International Publishing (2019)
2. 《雁栖湖代数讲座》（第三卷）Wen-Wei Li, *Yanqi Lake Lectures on Algebra*. Vol. 3. University of Chinese Academy of Sciences (2019)
3. 《21世纪中国数学教育》Yiming Cao, Frederick K.S. Leung (eds.), *The 21st Century Mathematics Education in China* (New Frontiers of Educational Research). Springer-Verlag (2018)
4. 《中国数学奥林匹克（2011—2014）：问题与对策》Bin Xiong, Peng Yee Lee (eds.), *Mathematical Olympiad in China (2011—2014) : Problems and Solutions* (Mathematical Olympiad Series). World Scientific Publishing Company (2018)
5. 《通过变量教授学习数学：儒家传统与西方理论的融合》Rongjin Huang, Yeping Li (eds.), *Teaching and Learning Mathematics through Variation: Confucian Heritage Meets Western Theories*.SensePublishers (2017)
6. 《雁栖湖代数讲座》（第一卷）Wen-Wei Li, *Yanqi Lake Lectures on Algebra*. Vol. 1.University of Chinese Academy of Sciences (2016)
7. 《复兴中国古代数学：吴文俊著作中的数学、历史与政治》Jiri Hudecek, *Reviving Ancient Chinese Mathematics: Mathematics, History and Politics in the Work of Wu Wen-Tsun* (Needham Research Institute Series).Routledge (2014)
8. 《中国人如何教数学：来自内部人士的观点》Lianghuo Fan, Ngai-Ying Wong, Jinfa Cai, Shiqi Li (eds.), *How Chinese Teach Mathematics: Perspectives from Insiders* (Series on Mathematics Education 6). World Scientific Publishing Company (2014)
9. 《中国人如何教授数学以及改进教学》Yeping Li, Rongjin Huang, *How Chinese Teach Mathematics and Improve Teaching* (Studies in Mathematical Thinking and Learning Series). Routledge (2013)
10. 《线性代数的中国根源》Roger Hart, *The Chinese Roots of Linear Algebra*. The Johns Hopkins University Press (2011)
11. 《转瞬即逝的脚步：追溯中国古代算术与代数概念》Lam Lay Yong, Ang Tian Se, *Fleeting Footsteps: Tracing the Conception of Arithmetic and Algebra in Ancient China*.World Scientific

Publishing Company (2008)

12. 《埃及、美索不达米亚、中国、印度和伊斯兰数学：资料手册》Victor J. Katz (ed.), *The Mathematics of Egypt, Mesopotamia, China, India, and Islam: A Sourcebook*. Princeton University Press (2007)

13. 《中国与爱因斯坦：物理学家及其理论在中国的接受（1917—1979）》Danian Hu, *China and Albert Einstein: The Reception of the Physicist and His Theory in China, 1917—1979*. Harvard University Press (2005)

14. 《算数书英译》Christopher Cullen, *The Suan Shu Shu: A Translation of a Chinese Mathematical Collection of the Second Century BC, with Explanatory Commentary*. Needham Research Institute, Cambridge (2004)

15. 《中国数学占星术：走向星球》Ho Peng Yoke, *Chinese Mathematical Astrology: Reaching out to the Stars*. RoutledgeCurzon (2003)

16. 《翻译科学：1840—1900年西方化学传入晚清中国》David Wright, *Translating Science: The Transmission of Western Chemistry into Late Imperial China, 1840—1900*. Brill Academic Publishers (2000)

17. 《中国数学史》Jean-Claude Martzloff, *A History of Chinese Mathematics*. Springer-Verlag Berlin Heidelberg (1997, 2006)

18. 《中国古代的天文和数学：周髀算经》Christopher Cullen, *Astronomy and Mathematics in Ancient China: The Zhou Bi Suan Jing* (Needham Research Institute Studies). Cambridge University Press (1996)

19. 《杨辉算法的批判性研究：中国13世纪的数学著作》LAM Lay Yong, *A Critical Study of the Yan Hui Suan Fa: A Thirteenth-Century Chinese mathematical Treatise*. Singapore University Press (1977)

20. 《毕达哥拉斯是中国人吗？中国古代直角三角形理论考》(Pennsylvania State University Studies) T. I. Kao, Frank J. Swetz, *Was Pythagoras Chinese? An Examination of Right Triangle Theory in Ancient China*. Pennsylvania State University Press (1977)

21. 《13世纪的中国数学：秦九韶的〈数书九章〉》Ulrich Libbrecht, *Chinese Mathematics in the Thirteenth Century: The Shu-shu chiu-chang of Ch'in Chiu-shao*. MIT Press (1973)

10.10 水利、环保、能源

10.10.1 气候水利

1. 《解决水量和水质禀赋分布不均问题：中国境内的物理和虚拟水输送》(Springer Briefs in Water Science and Technology) Yiping Li, Harold Lyonel Feukam Nzudie, Xu Zhao, Hua Wang, *Addressing the Uneven Distribution of Water Quantity and Quality Endowment: Physical and Virtual Water Transfer within China*. Springer Singapore (2020)

2. 《中国应对气候变化年度报告》(Research Series on the Chinese Dream and China's

Development Path) Weiguang Wang, Yaming Liu, *Annual Report on China's Response to Climate Change*. Social Sciences Academic Press and Springer Nature Singapore (2020)

3. 《中国水污染防治的政治与治理》(Politics and Development of Contemporary China) Liping Dai, *Politics and Governance in Water Pollution Prevention in China*. Springer International Publishing, Palgrave Pivot (2019)

4. 《定格风景：中国三峡的技术诗史》Corey Byrnes, *Fixing Landscape. A Techno-Poetic History of China's Three Gorges*. Columbia University Press (2019)

5. 《中国水资源与水利工程的可持续发展》(Environmental Earth Sciences) Wei Dong, Yanqing Lian, Yong Zhang (eds.), *Sustainable Development of Water Resources and Hydraulic Engineering in China*. Springer International Publishing (2019)

6. 《中国水系统：第三卷，鄱阳湖流域》(Terrestrial Environmental Sciences) TianXiang Yue, Erik Nixdorf, Chengzi Zhou, Bing Xu, Na Zhao, Zhewen Fan, Xiaolan Huang, Cui Chen, Olaf Kolditz, *Chinese Water Systems: Volume 3: Poyang Lake Basin*. Springer International Publishing (2019)

7. 《中国水系统：第二卷，城市集水区水资源管理：巢湖》(Terrestrial Environmental Sciences) Agnes Sachse, Zhenliang Liao, Weiping Hu, Xiaohu Dai, Olaf Kolditz, *Chinese Water Systems: Volume 2: Managing Water Resources for Urban Catchments: Chaohu*. Springer International Publishing (2019)

8. 《联合国气候变化框架公约下技术转移的法律障碍：以中国为例》Chen Zhou, *The Legal Barriers to Technology Transfer under the UN Framework Convention on Climate Change: The Example of China*. Springer Singapore (2019)

9. 《中国碳排放交易体系试点概述：广东温室气体排放交易机制的解构与评估》Daiqing Zhao, Wenjun Wang, Zhigang Luo, *A Brief Overview of China's ETS Pilots: Deconstruction and Assessment of Guangdong's Greenhouse Gas Emission Trading Mechanism*. Springer Singapore (2019)

10. 《人类世界的中国冲击：气候变化时代的图像、音乐和文本》Kwai-Cheung Lo, Jessica Yeung, *Chinese Shock of the Anthropocene: Image, Music and Text in the Age of Climate Change*. Springer Singapore: Palgrave Macmillan (2019)

11. 《走向可交易水权：中国水法与政策改革》Min Jiang, *Towards Tradable Water Rights: Water Law and Policy Reform in China* (Global issues in water policy 18). Springer (2018)

12. 《评估中国水权》Yahua Wang, *Assessing Water Rights in China* (Water Resources Development and Management). Springer Singapore (2018)

13. 《中国灾害的性质：1931年长江洪水》Chris Courtney, *The Nature of Disaster in China: The 1931 Yangzi River Flood*. Cambridge University Press (2018)

14. 《煤层底板地下水爆破风险评价方法研究及华北煤田应用》Yifan Zeng, *Research on Risk Evaluation Methods of Groundwater Bursting from Aquifers Underlying Coal Seams*

and Applications to Coalfields of North China (Springer Theses). Springer International Publishing (2018)

15.《中国水利系统》Yonghui Song, Beidou Xi, Yuan Zhang, Kun Lei, Richard Williams, Mengheng Zhang, Weijing Kong, Olaf Kolditz, *Chinese Water Systems* (Terrestrial Environmental Sciences). Springer International Publishing (2018)

16.《中国空气污染经济学：实现更好、更清洁的增长》Ma Jun, *The Economics of Air Pollution in China: Achieving Better and Cleaner Growth*. Columbia University Press (2017)

17.《河流、平原与国家：北宋的戏剧性环境事件（1048—1128）》Ling Zhang, *The River, the Plain, and the State: An Environmental Drama in Northern Song China, 1048—1128* (Studies in Environment and History). Cambridge University Press (2016)

18.《水之王国：中国秘史》Philip Ball, *The Water Kingdom: A Secret History of China*. The Bodley Head (2016)

19.《中国气候与环境变化（1951—2012）》Dahe Qin, Yongjian Ding, Mu Mu (eds.), *Climate and Environmental Change in China: 1951—2012*. Springer-Verlag Berlin Heidelberg (2016)

20.《中国农场水源管理：机构、政策和资源稀缺条件下的灌溉改造》Jikun Huang, Qiuqiong Huang, Scott Rozelle, Jinxia Wang, *Managing Water on China's Farms: Institutions, Policies and the Transformation of Irrigation Under Scarcity*. Elsevier, Academic Press (2016)

21.《中国水库流域的水污染与水质控制》Tinglin Huang (eds.), *Water Pollution and Water Quality Control of Selected Chinese Reservoir Basins*. Springer International Publishing (2016)

22.《中国低碳健康城市技术评估与实践》Weiguang Huang, Mingquan Wang, Jun Wang, Kun Gao, Song Li, Chen Liu (eds.), *China Low-Carbon Healthy City, Technology Assessment and Practice*. Springer-Verlag Berlin Heidelberg (2016)

23.《中国碳排放》Zhu Liu, *Carbon Emissions in China*. Springer-Verlag Berlin Heidelberg (2016)

24.《黄河：现代中国的水利问题》David A. Pietz, *The Yellow River: The Problem of Water in Modern China*. Harvard University Press (2015)

25.《中国有毒污染物：水质标准研究》Zhenguang Yan, Zhengtao Liu (eds.), *Toxic Pollutants in China: Study of Water Quality Criteria*. Springer Netherlands (2015)

26.《从长江流域到东海大陆边缘的生态连续性》Jing Zhang (eds.), *Ecological Continuum from the Changjiang (Yangtze River) Watersheds to the East China Sea Continental Margin*. Springer International Publishing (2015)

27.《中国西南地区气候变化研究》Zongxing Li, *Study on Climate Change in Southwestern China*. Springer-Verlag Berlin Heidelberg (2015)

28.《水坝与中国发展：水电的道德经济》Bryan Tilt, *Dams and Development in China: The Moral Economy of Water and Power* (Contemporary Asia in the World). Columbia University Press (2015)

29.《大坝的困境：中国水利水电工程对环境影响的探索》Pu Wang, Shikui Dong, James

Lassoie, *The Large Dam Dilemma: An Exploration of the Impacts of Hydro Projects on People and the Environment in China*. Springer Netherlands (2014)

30. 《气候变化、土地利用转型与社会经济发展条件下水资源供需分析与建模：中国西北乌鲁木齐地区的水资源挑战与适应对策》Katharina Fricke, *Analysis and Modelling of Water Supply and Demand Under Climate Change, Land Use Transformation and Socio-Economic Development: The Water Resource Challenge and Adaptation Measures for Urumqi Region, Northwest China*. Springer International Publishing (2014)

31. 《调节市政供水优惠：中国转型期责任》Yan Wei, *Regulating Municipal Water Supply Concessions: Accountability in Transitional China*. Springer-Verlag Berlin Heidelberg (2014)

32. 《大型湖泊和水库营养物质的富营养化分布与转化：以三峡库区为例》Zhenyao Shen, Junfeng Niu, Ying Wang, *Distribution and Transformation of Nutrients and Eutrophication in Large-scale Lakes and Reservoirs: The Three Gorges Reservoir*. Springer-Verlag Berlin Heidelberg (2013)

33. 《中国地方气候治理：混合动力与市场机制》Miriam Schröder, *Local Climate Governance in China: Hybrid Actors and Market Mechanisms*. Palgrave Macmillan UK (2012)

34. 《可持续城市水管理的经济学：以北京为例》Xiao Liang, *The Economics of Sustainable Urban Water Management: The Case of Beijing*. CRC Press: Balkema (2011)

35. 《龙遇到怒河：中华人民共和国的自然与权力》R. Edward Grumbine, *Where the Dragon Meets the Angry River: Nature and Power in the People's Republic of China*. Island Pr (2010)

36. 《长江：中国壮丽的河流》Molly Aloian, *The Yangtze: China's Majestic River*. Crabtree Publishing (2010)

37. 《中国三峡水库滑坡减灾》Chuanzheng Liu, Yanhui Liu, Mingsheng Wen, Tiefeng Li, Jianfa Lian, Shengwu Qin (auth.), Fawu Wang, Tonglu Li (eds.), *Landslide Disaster Mitigation in Three Gorges Reservoir, China*. Springer-Verlag Berlin Heidelberg (2009)

38. 《中国水勇士：公民行动和政策变化》Andrew C. Mertha, *China's Water Warriors: Citizen Action and Policy Change*. Cornell University Press (2008)

39. 《太湖、中国动力与环境变化》Boqiang Qin, *Lake Taihu, China Dynamics and Environmental Change* (Monographiae Biologicae). Springer (2008)

40. 《浅水湖泊的富营养化（特别提及中国太湖）》Boqiang Qin, Zhengwen Liu, Karl Havens (eds.), *Eutrophication of Shallow Lakes with Special Reference to Lake Taihu, China*. Springer Netherlands (2007)

41. 《逐步增加：提升中国城市供水设施绩效》Greg Browder, Shiqing Xie, Yoonee Kim, *Stepping Up: Improving the Performance of China's Urban Water Utilities*. The World Bank (2007)

42. 《控制巨龙：中国帝制晚期的儒家工程师与黄河》Randall A. Dodgen, *Controlling the Dragon: Confucian Engineers and the Yellow River in the Late Imperial China*. University

of Hawaii Press (2001)

43. 《中国温室气体排放控制中的问题与选择》Todd Johnson, *China Issues and Options in Greenhouse Gas Emissions Control*. Parts 63-330.World Bank (1996)

44. 《中国与全球变化：合作机遇》Panel on Global Climate Change Sciences in China（中国全球气候变化科学小组）, Committee on Scholarly Communication with the People's Republic of China, Office of International Affairs, National Research Council, *China and Global Change: Opportunities for Collaboration*. National Academies Press (1992)

10.10.2 环保生态

1. 《中华人民共和国环境保护部2017年新闻发布会记录》Ministry of Environmental Protection of the People's Republic of China, *2017 Press Conference Records of Ministry of Environmental Protection, the People's Republic of China*. Springer Singapore (2020)

2. 《中国退化草地的遥感监测与评估：草地碳源和碳汇的核算》(Springer Geography) Wei Zhou, Jianlong Li, Tianxiang Yue, *Remote Sensing Monitoring and Evaluation of Degraded Grassland in China: Accounting of Grassland Carbon Source and Carbon Sink*. Springer Singapore (2020)

3. 《烟气污染物的光催化控制技术》(Energy and Environment Research in China) Jiang Wu, Jianxing Ren, Weiguo Pan, Ping Lu, Yongfeng Qi, *Photo-catalytic Control Technologies of Flue Gas Pollutants*. Springer Singapore (2019)

4. 《中国环境人文：边缘环境的实践》(Chinese Literature and Culture in the World) Chia-ju Chang, *Chinese Environmental Humanities: Practices of Environing at the Margins*. Springer International Publishing: Palgrave Macmillan (2019)

5. 《中国西部工业固体废物的回收利用》Fenglan Han, Lan'er Wu, *Industrial Solid Waste Recycling in Western China*. Springer Singapore (2019)

6. 《中国森林碳实践与低碳发展》Zhi Lu, Xiaoquan Zhang, Jian Ma, Caifu Tang, *Forest Carbon Practices and Low Carbon Development in China*. Springer Singapore (2019)

7. 《中国生态可持续性面临的挑战：跨学科视角》Xiaojun Yang, Shijun Jiang (eds.), *Challenges Towards Ecological Sustainability in China: An Interdisciplinary Perspective*. Springer International Publishing (2019)

8. 《走向绿色城市：中德城市生物多样性与生态系统服务》Karsten Grunewald, Lennart Kümper-Schlake, Junxiang Li, Gaodi Xie, *Towards Green Cities: Urban Biodiversity and Ecosystem Services in China and Germany* (Cities and nature). Springer (2018)

9. 《中国的生态发展》Wu Deng, Ali Cheshmehzangi, *Eco-development in China* (Palgrave Series in Asia and Pacific Studies). Springer Singapore: Palgrave Macmillan (2018)

10. 《中国环境污染：每人都需要了解的内容》Daniel K. Gardner, *Environmental Pollution in China: What Everyone Needs to Know*. Oxford University Press (2018)

11. 《中国土壤污染与修复研究开发20年》Yongming Luo, Chen Tu (eds.), *Twenty Years of Research*

and Development on Soil Pollution and Remediation in China. Springer Singapore (2018)

12. 《生态时代和经典中国自然主义：陶渊明个案研究》Shuyuan Lu, *The Ecological Era and Classical Chinese Naturalism: A Case Study of Tao Yuanming*. Springer Singapore (2017)

13. 《中国环境政策与治理》Hideki Kitagawa (eds.), *Environmental Policy and Governance in China*. Springer Japan (2017)

14. 《环境保护等离子体修复技术》ChangMing Du, JianHua Yan, *Plasma Remediation Technology for Environmental Protection*. Springer Singapore (2017)

15. 《从喜马拉雅山到海洋的环境可持续发展：中国和印度的斗争与创新》Shikui Dong, Jayanta Bandyopadhyay, Sanjay Chaturvedi (eds.), *Environmental Sustainability from the Himalayas to the Oceans: Struggles and Innovations in China and India*. Springer International Publishing (2017)

16. 《中国环境空气污染与健康影响》Guang-Hui Dong (eds.), *Ambient Air Pollution and Health Impact in China* (Advances in Experimental Medicine and Biology 1017). Springer Singapore (2017)

17. 《满洲形成过程中的帝国与环境》Norman Smith (ed.), *Empire and Environment in the Making of Manchuria* (Contemporary Chinese Studies). UBC Press (2017)

18. 《中国—东盟环境展望：实现绿色发展》China-ASEAN Environmental Cooperation Center, *China-ASEAN Environment Outlook 1 (CAEO-1): Towards Green Development*. Springer (2017)

19. 《中国的自然灾害》Peijun Shi (eds.), *Natural Disasters in China*. Springer-Verlag Berlin Heidelberg (2016)

20. 《中国碳交易：环境话语与政治》Alex Lo, *Carbon Trading in China: Environmental Discourse and Politics*. Palgrave Macmillan UK (2016)

21. 《生态经济与和谐社会》Futian Qu, Ruomei Sun, Zhongxing Guo, Fawen Yu (eds.), *Ecological Economics and Harmonious Society*. Springer Singapore (2016)

22. 《中国环境治理与生态文明》Jiahua Pan, *China's Environmental Governing and Ecological Civilization*. Springer-Verlag Berlin Heidelberg (2016)

23. 《中国生态城市建设》Jingyuan Li, Tongjin Yang (eds.), *China's Eco-city Construction*. Springer-Verlag Berlin Heidelberg (2016)

24. 《中国农业生态学：科学、实践与可持续管理》Stephen R. Gliessman, Luo Shiming, *Agroecology in China: Science, Practice, and Sustainable Management* (Advances in agroecology). CRC Press (2016)

25. 《当代中国生态研究》Wenhua Li (eds.), *Contemporary Ecology Research in China*. Springer-Verlag Berlin Heidelberg (2015)

26. 《中国绿色发展指数报告2012：区域比较》Xiaoxi Li, Jiancheng Pan (eds.), *China Green Development Index Report 2012: Regional Comparison*. Springer-Verlag Berlin Heidelberg

(2015)

27. 《中国的环境危机：国家发展局限性的探讨》Vaclav Smil, *China's Environmental Crisis: An Inquiry into the Limits of National Development.* Routledge (2015)

28. 《基于林业方法的中国滨海盐碱地复垦与利用》Jianfeng Zhang, *Coastal Saline Soil Rehabilitation and Utilization Based on Forestry Approaches in China.* Springer-Verlag Berlin Heidelberg (2014)

29. 《中国黄土高原的退化恢复与发展》Mei-Jie Yan, Qiu-Yue He, Norikazu Yamanaka, Sheng Du (auth.), Atsushi Tsunekawa, Guobin Liu, Norikazu Yamanaka, Sheng Du (eds.), *Restoration and Development of the Degraded Loess Plateau, China.* Springer Japan (2014)

30. 《中国生态系统服务与管理战略》Yiyu Chen, Beate Jessel, Bojie Fu, Xiubo Yu, Jamie Pittock (eds.), *Ecosystem Services and Management Strategy in China.* Springer-Verlag Berlin Heidelberg (2014)

31. 《中国环境治理：变化社会中的动力、挑战与前景》Bingqiang Ren, Huisheng Shou (eds.), *Chinese Environmental Governance: Dynamics, Challenges, and Prospects in a Changing Society.* Palgrave Macmillan US (2013)

32. 《今日中国环境问题：日本看法》Hidefumi Imura, *Environmental Issues in China Today: A View from Japan.* Springer Japan (2013)

33. 《中国绿色低碳发展》Jinjun Xue, Zhongxiu Zhao, Yande Dai, Bo Wang (eds.), *Green Low-Carbon Development in China.* Springer International Publishing (2013)

34. 《环保之风：打造全球的中国西南》Michael J. Hathaway, *Environmental Winds: Making the Global in Southwest China.* University of California Press (2013)

35. 《建立中国适当的土地污染制度：来自美国和英国的经验教训》Xiaobo Zhao, *Developing an Appropriate Contaminated Land Regime in China: Lessons Learned from the US and UK.* Springer-Verlag Berlin Heidelberg (2013)

36. 《中国绿色发展指数报告：2011》Xiaoxi Li, Jiancheng Pan (eds.), *China Green Development Index Report 2011.* Springer-Verlag Berlin Heidelberg (2013)

37. 《中国森林生态系统服务支付计划：政策、实践与绩效》Dan Liang, *Payment Schemes for Forest Ecosystem Services in China: Policy, Practices and Performance.* Wageningen Pers (2012)

38. 《绿色中国：东西方的可持续增长》Taco C.R. van Someren, Shuhua van Someren-Wang, *Green China: Sustainable Growth in East and West.* Springer-Verlag Berlin Heidelberg (2012)

39. 《绿色经济及其在中国的实施》David Ness, Huang Haifeng, Manhong Mannie Liu, *The Green Economy and Its Implementation in China.* Enrich Professional Publishing (2011)

40. 《中国生态环境科学技术：2050路线图》Jingzhu Zhao, *Ecological and Environmental Science & Technology in China: A Roadmap to 2050.* Springer (2011)

41. 《绿色中国：贸易和外商直接投资的益处》Ka Zeng, Joshua Eastin, *Greening China: The Benefits of Trade and Foreign Direct Investment* (Michigan Studies in International Political

Economy). University of Michigan Press (2011)
42. 《中国污染》Michael I. Chang, *Pollution in China*. Nova Science Pub Inc (2011)
43. 《中国的环境与历史》Robert B. Marks, *China: Its Environment and History* (World Social Change). Rowman & Littlefield Publishers (2011)
44. 《中国环境危机：国内和全球政治影响与反应》Joel Jay Kassiola, Sujian Guo（郭苏建）, *China's Environmental Crisis: Domestic and Global Political Impacts and Responses (Environmental Politics and Theory)*. Palgrave Macmillan (2010)
45. 《经济增长与环境监管：中国走向更加光明的未来之路》Tim Swanson, Tun Lin, *Economic Growth and Environmental Regulation: China's Path to a Brighter Future*. Routledge (2010)
46. 《中国环境与中国环境新闻记者研究》Hugo de Burgh, Zeng Rong, *China's Environment and China's Environment Journalists: A Study*. Intellect Ltd (2010)
47. 《中国环境变化与粮食安全》Jenifer Huang McBeath, Jerry McBeath, *Environmental Change and Food Security in China*. Springer Netherlands (2010)
48. 《中国环境》Liu Junhui, Wang Jia, *China's Environment*. Cengage Learning Asia (2010)
49. 《中国荒漠化及其控制》Longjun Ci, Xiaohui Yang, *Desertification and Its Control in China*. Springer (2010)
50. 《中国西北地区牧场的可持续利用》Victor Squires, Hua Limin auth., Victor Squires, Limin Hua, Guolin Li, Degang Zhang (eds.), *Towards Sustainable Use of Rangelands in North-West China*. Springer Netherlands (2010)
51. 《嵌入式行动主义在中国：社会运动的机遇和约束》Peter Ho, Richard Louis Edmonds (eds.), *China's Embedded Activism: Opportunities and Constraints of a Social Movement*. Routledge (2008)
52. 《中国与国际环境责任：跨界污染的法律救济》Michael Faure, Song Ying, *China And International Environmental Liability: Legal Remedies for Transboundary Pollution* (New Horizons in Environmental Law). Edward Elgar Publishing Limited (2008)
53. 《中国空气污染控制的设备与服务：战略参考（2007）》Philip M. Parker, *Air Pollution Control Equipment and Services in China: A Strategic Reference, 2007*. ICON Group International, Inc. (2007)
54. 《污染的负担在中国：实物损害的经济评估》World Bank, *The Cost of Pollution in China: Economic Estimates of Physical Damage*. The World Bank (2007)
55. 《国际援助和中国环境：驯服黄龙》Katherine Morton, *International Aid And China's Environment: Taming the Yellow Dragon*. Routledge (2006)
56. 《满足中国木浆增长需求：对人工林发展、纤维供应和天然林影响的诊断评估》Jean-Marc Roda & Santosh Rathi, *Feeding China's Expanding Demand for Wood Pulp: A Diagnostic Assessment of Plantation Development, Fiber Supply, and Impacts on Natural Forests*. Center for International Forestry Research (2006)

57. 《大象的撤退：中国环境史》Mark Elvin, *The Retreat of the Elephants: An Environmental History of China*. Yale University Press (2006)

58. 《中国环境与可持续发展的挑战》Day K.A. (ed.), *China's Environment and The Challenge of Sustainable Development*. M. E. Sharpe (2005)

59. 《老虎和穿山甲：中国的自然、文化和水土保持》Chris Coggins, *The Tiger and the Pangolin: Nature, Culture, and Conservation in China*. University of Hawai'i Press (2003)

60. 《无尽的边疆：近代早期世界环境史》John F. Richards, *The Unending Frontier: An Environmental History of the Early Modern World*. University of California Press (2003)

61. 《绿色中国：寻求生态替代品》Ian G. Cook, *Green China: Seeking Ecological Alternatives*. RoutledgeCurzon (2002)

62. 《中国之气、土、水：新千年环境优先事项》Robert T. Livernash, *China: Air, Land, and Water. Environmental Priorities for a New Millennium*. World Bank Publications (2001)

63. 《中国造林扶贫和天然林管理评估》Scott Rozelle, Jikun Huang, Syed Arif Husain, Aaron Zazueta, *China: From Afforestation to Poverty Alleviation and Natural Forest Management Evaluation* (Country Case Study Series). World Bank Publications (2000)

64. 《动态土壤结构的相互作用：中国和瑞士最新研究》Zhang Chuhan and John P. Wolf (Eds.), *Dynamic Soil-Structure Interaction: Current Research in China and Switzerland*. Elsevier, Academic Press (1998)

65. 《老虎、大米、丝绸和淤泥：帝国晚期华南的环境与经济》Robert Marks, *Tigers, Rice, Silk, and Silt: Environment and Economy in Late Imperial South China*. Cambridge University Press (1998)

66. 《清水蓝天：新世纪中国环境》Todd Johnson, Feng Liu, Richard S. Newfarmer, World Bank, *Clear Water, Blue Skies: China's Environment in the New Century*. World Bank Publications (1997)

67. 《中国植树造林：永久预防饥荒与消除饥荒》John H. Reisner, *Reforesting China: Permanent Famine Prevention versus Famine Relief*. China Society of America, New York City: Thirteen Astor Place (1921)

10.10.3 能源

1. 《国家能源转型：德美现实与中国选择》(The Great Transformation Of China) Tong Zhu, Lei Wang, *State Energy Transition: German and American Realities and Chinese Choices*. Palgrave Macmillan (2020)

2. 《中国成为全球清洁能源冠军：揭开面纱》(Palgrave Series in Asia and Pacific Studies) Philip Andrews-Speed, Sufang Zhang, *China as a Global Clean Energy Champion: Lifting the Veil*. Springer Singapore: Palgrave Macmillan (2019)

3. 《中国家庭能源消费2016年报告》Xinye Zheng, Chu Wei, *Household Energy Consumption in China: 2016 Report*. Springer Singapore (2019)

4. 《通过全球化实现现代化：中国为何对全球外国能源项目提供资金》Bo Kong, *Modernization

Through Globalization: Why China Finances Foreign Energy Projects Worldwide. Springer Singapore: Palgrave Pivot (2019)

5. 《中国大型风能电力系统的集成》Zongxiang Lu, Shuangxi Zhou, *Integration of Large Scale Wind Energy with Electrical Power System in China.* John Wiley & Sons (2018)

6. 《中国能源、环境与转型绿色增长》Ruizhi Pang, Xuejie Bai, Knox Lovell, *Energy, Environment and Transitional Green Growth in China.* Springer Singapore (2018)

7. 《日本和中国能源转型：关闭矿井、铁路发展与能源叙事》Tai Wei Lim, *Energy Transitions in Japan and China: Mine Closures, Rail Developments, and Energy Narratives.* Palgrave Macmillan (2017)

8. 《中国能源效率与节约：家庭行为、立法、区域分析与影响》Bin Su, Elspeth Thomson (eds.), *China's Energy Efficiency and Conservation: Household Behaviour, Legislation, Regional Analysis and Impacts.* Springer Singapore (2016)

9. 《能源经济学：中国的能源效率》Yi-Ming Wei, Hua Liao, *Energy Economics: Energy Efficiency in China.* Springer International Publishing (2016)

10. 《了解克服中国能源挑战的选择》Zheng Li, Angelo Amorelli, Pei Liu, *Informing Choices for Meeting China's Energy Challenges.* Springer Singapore (2016)

11. 《中国可持续能源治理》Geoffrey Chun-fung Chen, *Governing Sustainable Energies in China* (Politics and Development of Contemporary China). Palgrave Macmillan (2016)

12. 《中国可再生能源革命》John A. Mathews, Hao Tan, *China's Renewable Energy Revolution.* Palgrave Macmillan UK (2015)

13. 《可再生能源与能源安全的政治经济：日本、中国和北欧的共同挑战与国家应对》Espen Moe, Paul Midford (eds.), *The Political Economy of Renewable Energy and Energy Security: Common Challenges and National Responses in Japan, China and Northern Europe.* Palgrave Macmillan UK (2014)

14. 《中国能源安全与经济可持续增长》Shujie Yao, Maria Jesus Herrerias (eds.), *Energy Security and Sustainable Economic Growth in China.* Palgrave Macmillan UK (2014)

15. 《利用一切必要手段：中国对资源的索求如何改变世界》Elizabeth C. Economy（易明）, Michael Levi, *By All Means Necessary: How China's Resource Quest is Changing the World.* Oxford University Press (2014)

16. 《中国能源战略：对北京海运政策的影响》Gabriel B.Collins, Andew S.Erickson, Lyle J. Goldstein, William S.Murray, *China's Energy Strategy: The Impact on Bejing's Maritime Policies.* Naval Institute Press (2012)

17. 《安全的石油与可替代能源：中国和欧盟能源路径的地缘政治》M. Parvizi Amineh, Yang Guang, *Secure Oil and Alternative Energy: The Geopolitics of Energy Paths of China and the European Union.* Brill Academic Pub (2012)

18. 《中国能源经济：形势、改革、行为和能源强度》Hengyun Ma, Les Oxley, *China's*

Energy Economy: Situation, Reforms, Behavior, and Energy Intensity. Springer-Verlag Berlin Heidelberg (2012)

19. 《赢家通吃：中国对资源的渴求及其世界含义》Dambisa Moyo, *Winner Take All: China's Race for Resources and What It Means for the World*. Basic Books (2012)

20. 《中国能源治理：向低碳经济转型》Philip Andrews-Speed, *The Governance of Energy in China: Transition to a Low-Carbon Economy*. Palgrave Macmillan UK (2012)

21. 《中国能源与环境政策：走向低碳经济》Zhang, ZhongXiang, *Energy and Environmental Policy in China: Towards a Low-Carbon Economy*. Edward Elgar Publishing (2011)

22. 《能源经济学：中国的二氧化碳排放》Yiming Wei, Lancui Liu, Gang Wu, Lele Zou, *Energy Economics: CO2 Emissions in China*. Springer (2011)

23. 《中国经济与社会中的煤矿开采（1895—1937）》Tim Wright, *Coal Mining in China's Economy and Society 1895—1937* (Cambridge Studies in Chinese History, Literature and Institutions). Cambridge University Press (2009)

24. 《融资节能：来自巴西、中国、印度及其他地区的经验教训》Robert P. Taylor, Chandrasekar Govindarajalu, Jeremy Levin, Anke S. Meyer, William A. Ward, *Financing Energy Efficiency: Lessons from Brazil, China, India, and Beyond*. The World Bank (2008)

25. 《能源未来与城市空气污染：中国与美国的挑战》Committee on Energy Futures and Air Pollution in Urban China and the United States, *Energy Futures and Urban Air Pollution: Challenges for China and the United States*. National Academy of Sciences (2008)

26. 《中国和全球能源危机：中国石油和天然气开发与展望》Tatsu Kambara, Christopher Howe, *China and the Global Energy Crisis: Development and Prospects for China's Oil and Natural Gas*. Edward Elgar Publishing Limited (2007)

27. 《中国能源市场：商品和可再生能源的交易与风险管理》Armelle Guizot, *Chinese Energy Markets: Trading and Risk Management of Commodities and Renewables*. Palgrave Macmillan (2007)

28. 《中国技术—能源—环境—健康链（TEEH）炼焦个案研究》Karen Polenske, *The Technology-Energy-Environment-Health (TEEH) Chain In China: A Case Study of Cokemaking*. Springer (2006)

29. 《中国环境服务：2006战略参考》Philip M. Parker, *Environmental Services in China: A Strategic Reference, 2006*. Icon Group International, Inc. (2006)

30. 《中国对能源安全的追求》Erica Strecker Downs, *China's Quest for Energy Security*. RAND (2006)

31. 《中国的过去与未来：能源、食品、环境》Vaclav Smil, *China's Past, China's Future: Energy, Food, Environment*. Routledge (2004)

32. 《中国能源、食品、环境之过去与未来》Vaclav Smil, *China's Past, China's Future: Energy, Food, Environment*. RoutledgeCurzon (2003)

33. 《开发中国天然气市场：能源政策的挑战》OECD, *Developing China's Natural Gas Market: The Energy Policy Challenges*. Organization for Economic Cooperation & Development (Dec. 2002)

34. 《中国西北农村地区可再生能源市场评估》Tuntivate Voravate, Douglas F. Barnes, V. Susan Bogach, *Assessing Markets for Renewable Energy in Rural Areas of Northwestern China*. World Bank Technical Paper (2000)

35. 《中国能源供应中的煤炭：CIAB亚洲委员会报告》OECD, *Coal in the Energy Supply of China: Report of the CIAB Asia Committee*. Organization for Economic (1999)

36. 《中国：加快可再生能源发展的国际援助战略》Robert Prescott Taylor, V. Susan Bogach, *China: A Strategy for International Assistance to Accelerate Renewable Energy Development*. World Bank Publications (1998)

10.11 人力资源

1. 《进入壁垒：中国职场的挑战与突破》（外国人在中国企业工作）Paul Ross, *Barriers to Entry: Overcoming Challenges and Achieving Breakthroughs in a Chinese Workplace*.Springer Singapore: Palgrave Macmillan (2020)

2. 《组织转型与系统治理：企业劳动关系》Jingdong Qu, Chunhui Fu, Xiang Wen, *Organizational Transition and Systematic Governance: Labor Relations in Enterprises* (Social Development Experiences in China). Springer Singapore (2018)

3. 《中国经济转型与劳动力市场改革》Xinxin Ma, *Economic Transition and Labor Market Reform in China*. Springer Singapore: Palgrave Macmillan (2018)

4. 《新兴经济中的劳动力转移：基于中国现实与理论的视角》Xiaochun Li (eds.), *Labor Transfer in Emerging Economies: A Perspective from China's Reality to Theories* (New Frontiers in Regional Science: Asian Perspectives 12). Springer Singapore (2017)

5. 《外籍经理的适应与知识获取：中国跨国公司的个人发展》Yan Li, *Expatriate Manager's Adaption and Knowledge Acquisition: Personal Development in Multi-National Companies in China*.Springer-Verlag Singapur (2016)

6. 《政企关系：中国企业家与民营企业发展》Ming Lu, Hui Pan, *Government-Enterprise Connection: Entrepreneur and Private Enterprise Development in China*.Springer-Verlag Singapur (2016)

7. 《人力资本对中国经济增长的贡献》John Joshua, *The Contribution of Human Capital towards Economic Growth in China*. Palgrave Macmillan UK (2015)

8. 《中国人力资源和薪资》Chris Devonshire-Ellis, Christian Fleming, Eunice Ku (eds.), *Human Resources and Payroll in China*. Springer-Verlag Berlin Heidelberg (2014)

9. 《外籍人士在中国：经验、机遇与挑战》Ilaria Boncori, *Expatriates in China: Experiences, Opportunities and Challenges*. Palgrave Macmillan UK (2013)

10. 《关于人力资源管理实践的中国传统思维》Li Yuan, *Traditional Chinese Thinking on*

HRM Practices (Heritage and Transformation in China). Palgrave Macmillan UK (2013)

11. 《人力资源尽职调查：中国兼并与收购》ChyeKok Ho, ChinSeng Koh, *HR Due Diligence: Mergers and Acquisitions in China*. Chandos Publishing (2012)

12. 《中国人力资源管理：人力资源实践案例》Doug Davies, Liang Wei (Eds.), *Human Resources Management in China: Cases in HR Practice*. Chandos Publishing (2011)

13. 《中国人力资源》Chris Devonshire-Ellis, Andy Scott, Sam Woollard auth., Chris Devonshire-Ellis, Andy Scott, Sam Woollard (eds.), *Human Resources in China*.Springer-Verlag Berlin Heidelberg (2011)

14. 《中国职场变化：活力、多样性与差异》Peter Sheldon, Sunghoon Kim, Yiqiong Li, Malcolm Warner, *China's Changing Workplace: Dynamism, Diversity and Disparity* (Routledge Contemporary China Series). Routledge (2011)

15. 《中国失业：经济、人力资源与劳动力市场》Lee Warner, *Unemployment in China: Economy, Human Reources and Labour Markets* (Routledge Contemporary China Series). Routledge (2007)

16. 《中国跨国公司人力资源管理》Edwards & Shen, *Human Resource Management in Chinese Multinationals* (Routledge Contemporary China). Routledge (2006)

17. 《中国人力资源管理、工作和就业》Fang Lee Cooke, *HRM, Work and Employment in China*. Routledge (2005)

18. 《走向中国劳动力市场》John Knight, Lina Song, *Towards a Labour Market in China* (Studies on Contemporary China). Oxford University Press (2005)

19. 《入世对中国就业的影响》A. S. Bhalla, Shufang Qiu, *Employment Impact of China's WTO Accession* (Routledgecurzon Studies on the Chinese Economy). Routledgecurzon (2004)

20. 《中国劳动力市场改革》Xin Meng, *Labour Market Reform in China* (Trade and Development). Cambridge University Press (2000)

21. 《中国人才流向美国：20世纪90年代海外留学生与学者的观点》David Zweig, Chen Changgui, *China's Brain Drain to the United States: Views of Overseas Chinese Students and Scholars in the 1990s*. University of California, Berkeley (1995)

22. 《中国工业人力资源管理》Malcolm Warner, *The Management of Human Resources in Chinese Industry* (Studies on the Chinese Economy). Palgrave Macmillan UK (1995)

23. 《中国经理人如何学习：中国的管理和产业培训》Malcolm Warner, *How Chinese Managers Learn: Management and Industrial Training in China* (Studies on the Chinese Economy). Palgrave Macmillan UK (1992)

24. 《后革命时期中国工资政策的政治学分析》Akio Takahara, *The Politics of Wage Policy in Post-Revolutionary China* (Studies on the Chinese Economy). Palgrave Macmillan UK (1992)

11. 中西交通

11.1 总论

1. 《古代欧亚晚期的帝国与交往：罗马、中国、伊朗和草原（约250—750）》Nicola Di Cosmo（狄宇宙），Michael Maas, *Empires and Exchanges in Eurasian Late Antiquity: Rome, China, Iran. and the Steppe, ca. 250—750*. Cambridge University Press (2018)
2. 《与中国的跨文化交流：超越（逆向）本质主义和文化主义》Fred Dervin, Regis Machart (eds.), *Intercultural Communication with China: Beyond (Reverse) Essentialism and Culturalism*. Springer Singapore (2017)
3. 《古代和中世纪早期的欧亚帝国：古罗马世界、中亚和中国的接触与交流》Hyun Jin Kim, Frederik Juliaan Vervaet, Selim Ferruh Adal (eds.), *Eurasian Empires in Antiquity and the Early Middle Ages: Contact and Exchange between the Graeco-Roman World, Inner Asia and China*. Cambridge Univers (2017)
4. 《西方的终结与其他警示故事》Sean Meighoo, *The End of the West and Other Cautionary Tales*. Columbia University Press (2016)
5. 《火药时代：世界史上的中国、军事创新与西方兴起》Tonio Andrade（欧阳泰）, *The Gunpowder Age: China, Military Innovation, and the Rise of the West in World History*. Princeton University Press (2016)
6. 《古代中国和罗马的国家权力》Walter Scheidel, *State Power in Ancient China and Rome*. Oxford University Press (2015)
7. 《西班牙、中国和日本在马尼拉（1571—1644）：本地比较与全球联系》Birgit Tremml-Werner, *Spain, China and Japan in Manila, 1571—1644: Local Comparisons and Global Connections*. Amsterdam University Press (2015)
8. 《改变参照对象：中西跨越时空学习》Leigh K. Jenco, *Changing Referents: Learning across Space and Time in China and the West*. Oxford University Press (2015)
9. 《在爪哇的荷兰商业与中国商人：贸易和金融中的殖民关系》Alexander Claver, *Dutch Commerce and Chinese Merchants in Java: Colonial Relationships in Trade and Finance, 1800—1942*. Brill (2014)
10. 《郑和海上航行（1405—1433）与中国和印度洋世界的关系：多语种书目》Ying Liu, Zhongping Chen, Gregory Blue, *Zheng He's Maritime Voyages (1405—1433) and China's Relations with the Indian Ocean World: A Multilingual Bibliography*. Brill Academic Publishers (2014)

11. 《英国、印度和中国间的知识流通：从早期现代世界到20世纪》Bernard Lightman, Gordon McOuat, Larry Stewart, *The Circulation of Knowledge Between Britain, India and China: The Early-Modern World to the Twentieth Century*. Brill (2013)

12. 《宝藏舰队的冒险：中国发现世界》Ann Martin Bowler, L. K. Tay-Audouard, *Adventures of the Treasure Fleet: China Discovers the World*. Perseus Books Group: Tuttle Publishing (2013)

13. 《塞尔登先生的中国地图：解密消失的制图师》Timothy Brook（卜正民）, *Mr. Selden's Map of China: Decoding the Secrets of a Vanished Cartographer*. Bloomsbury Press (2013)

14. 《马可波罗在中国：来自货币、盐类和收入的新证据》Hans Ulrich Vogel, *Marco Polo Was in China: New Evidence from Currencies, Salts and Revenues* (Monies, Markets, and Finance in East Asia, 1600—1900). Brill (2012)

15. 《中国学者论西方思维、领导力、改革和发展思想》Sylvester Chen, Michael Kompf (eds.), *Chinese Scholars on Western Ideas about Thinking, Leadership, Reform and Development*. Sense Publishers (2012)

16. 《中国与伊斯兰世界拼图：前现代亚洲的跨文化交流》Professor Hyunhee Park, *Mapping the Chinese and Islamic Worlds: Cross-Cultural Exchange in Pre-Modern Asia*. Cambridge University Press (2012)

17. 《哲学与文化思想中的怀疑、时间和暴力：中西解读与分析》Artur K. Wardega, Artur K. Wardega, *Doubt, Time and Violence in Philosophical and Cultural Thought: Sino-Western Interpretations and Analysis*. Cambridge Scholars Publishing (2012)

18. 《跨太平洋时代西方的远东愿景（1522—1657）》Christina H. Lee, *Western Visions of the Far East in a Transpacific Age, 1522—1657*. Ashgate Pub Co (2012)

19. 《欧洲与中国：十七至十八世纪的科学与艺术》Luis Saraiva (ed.), *Europe and China: Science and the Arts in the 17th and 18th Centuries*. World Scientific Publishing Company (2012)

20. 《晚清西学东渐》Xiong Yuezhi, *Eastward Dissemination of Western Learning in the Late Qing Dynasty*. 3-Enrich Professional Publishing (2012)

21. 《跨文化史与他者的归化》Michal Jan Rozbicki, George O. Ndege, *Cross-Cultural History and the Domestication of Otherness*. Palgrave Macmillan (2012)

22. 《大秦：考古学、文献学与中西关系史研究》Gosciwit Malinowski, Aleksander Parori, Bartlomiej Sz. Szmoniewski (eds.), *Serica: Da Qin. Studies in Archaeology, Philology and History of Sino-Western Relations*. Wroclaw (2012)

23. 《中国风暴之眼：东西方的生活》Paul T. K. Lin and Eileen Chen Lin, *In the Eye of the China Storm: A Life between East and West*. McGill-Queen's University Press (2011)

24. 《中国与航海时代的欧洲（1500—1800）：贸易、结算、外交和使命》John E. Wills Jr, John Cranmer-Byng, Willard J. Peterson Jr, John W. Witek, *China and Maritime Europe, 1500—1800: Trade, Settlement, Diplomacy, and Missions*. Cambridge University Press (2011)

25. 《人应该如何生活：中国古代伦理与希腊罗马古代风俗比较》R. A. H. King, Dennis

Schilling, *How Should One Live: Comparing Ethics in Ancient China and Greco-roman Antiquity*. Walter de Gruyter (2011)

26. 《遭遇中国：现代国家、古老的文化》Hu Wenzhong（胡文仲）, Cornelius N. Grove, and Zhuang Enping., *Encountering the Chinese: A Modern Country, an Ancient Culture*. 3rd ed. Nicholas Brealey Publishing (2010)

27. 《塞缪尔·福尔摩斯日记（马戛尔尼卫兵之一）》Samuel Holmes, *The Journal of Mr Samuel Holmes, One of the Guard on Lord Macartney's Embassy to China and Tartary*. Cambridge University Press (2010)

28. 《西方到来之前的东亚：五个世纪的贸易与朝贡》David C. Kang, *East Asia before the West: Five Centuries of Trade and Tribute*. Columbia University Press (2010)

29. 《荷兰人1594、1595和1596年从东北向中国三次航行的真实描述》Gerrit de Veer, Charles T. Beke (editor), William Phillip (translator), *A True Description of Three Voyages by the North-East towards Cathay and China, Undertaken by the Dutch in the Years 1594, 1595 and 1596*. Cambridge University Press (2010)

30. 《世外桃源的旅行者：拉班·索玛与从中国到西方的第一次旅程》Morris Rossabi（罗茂锐）, *Voyager from Xanadu: Rabban Sauma and the first Journey from China to the West*. University of California Press (2010)

31. 《罗马与中国：古代世界帝国的比较视角》Walter Scheidel, *Rome and China: Comparative Perspectives on Ancient World Empires*. Oxford University Press, USA (2009)

32. 《西方列强在亚洲：缓慢上升与迅速衰落，1415—1999》Arthur Cotterell, *Western Power in Asia: Its Slow Rise and Swift Fall, 1415—1999*. Wiley (2009)

33. 《中西方的伟大相遇：1500—1800》D. E. Mungello（孟德卫）, *The Great Encounter of China and the West, 1500D1800*. Rowman & Littlefield Publishers, Inc. (2009)

34. 《中国的莎士比亚：两个世纪的文化交流》Alexander C. Y. Huang, *Chinese Shakespeares: Two Centuries of Cultural Exchange*. Columbia University Press (2009)

35. 《1434：一支庞大的中国舰队抵达意大利并点燃文艺复兴之火》Gavin Menzies（孟席斯）, *1434: The Year a Magnificent Chinese Fleet Sailed to Italy and Ignited the Renaissance*. Harper Collins Publishers (2008)

36. 《迷失在中国：一个人试图了解世界上最神秘国家的奇怪而真实故事，或他如何舒适地生吃鱿鱼》J. Maarten Troost, *Lost on Planet China: The Strange and True Story of One Man's Attempt to Understand the World's Most Mystifying Nation, or How He Became Comfortable Eating Live Squid*. Broadway Book (2008)

37. 《纸上中国：16世纪末至19世纪初的欧洲和中国作品》Marcia Reed, Paola Dematte, *China on Paper: European and Chinese Works from the Late Sixteenth to the Early Nineteenth Century*. Getty Research Institute (2007)

38. 《东方之光：现代西方的东方智慧》Harry Oldmeadow, *Light from the East: Eastern*

Wisdom for the Modern West (Perennial Philosophy Series). World Wisdom (2007)

39. 《东方遇上西方：文明遭遇与东亚资本主义精神》Kyong-dong Kim, Hyun-Chin Lim (ed.), *East Meets West: Civilizational Encounters and the Spirit of Capitalism in East Asia*. Brill (2007)

40. 《东西方之外的欧洲和亚洲》Gerard Delanty, *Europe and Asia Beyond East and West* (Routledge ESA/European Sociological Association Studies in European Societies). Routledge (2006)

41. 《马可·波罗在中国：忽必烈国度的威尼斯人》Stephen Haw, *Marco Polo in China: A Venetian in the Realm of Khubilai Khan*. Routledge (2006)

42. 《映射意义：晚清中国的新学领域》Michael Lackner and Natascha Vittinghoff, *Mapping Meanings: The Field of New Learning in Late Qing China (Sinica Leidensia)*. Brill (2004)

43. 《中国的上帝与恺撒：政教关系紧张的政策含义》Jason Kindopp, Carol Lee Hamrin, *God and Caesar in China: Policy Implications of Church-State Tensions*. The Brookings Institution (2004)

44. 《帝国的冲突：现代世界形成中的中国发明》Lydia H. Liu（刘禾）, *The Clash of Empires: The Invention of China in Modern World Making*. Harvard University Press (2004)

45. 《西方论中国》Arthur Hacker, *China Illustrated: Western Views of the Middle Kingdom*. Tuttle Publishing (2004)

46. 《西方文明的东方起源》John M. Hobson（约翰·霍布森）, *The Eastern Origins of Western Civilisation*. Cambridge University Press (2004)

47. 《中国：插图本之西方中国观》Arthur Hacker, *China: Illustrated Western Views of the Middle Kingdom*. Tuttle Publishing (2004)

48. 《数学史：葡萄牙与东亚》Luis Saraiva, Conference History of Mathematical Sciences, *History Of Mathematical Sciences: Portugal And East Asia II* (Universtiy of Macau, China 10-12 October 1998). World Scientific Publishing Company (2004)

49. 《1421：中国发现世界》Gavin Menzies（孟席斯）, *1421: The Year China Discovered the World*. William Morrow Paperbacks (2003)

50. 《马可·波罗游记》Marco Polo, Manuel Komroff, *The Travels of Marco Polo*. W. W. Norton & Company (2002)

51. 《1500年以来的西方和中国》John S. Gregory, *The West and China since 1500*. Palgrave Macmillan UK (2002)

52. 《从中国到巴黎：2000年数学思想传播》Benno van Dalen, Joseph W. Dauben, Yvonne Dold-Samplonius, Menso Folkerts, *From China to Paris: 2000 Years Transmission of Mathematical Ideas*. Franz Steiner Verlag (2002)

53. 《"东方辉煌和欧洲智慧"：帝国晚期中国的钟表》Catherine Pagani, *"Eastern magnificence and European ingenuity": Clocks of Late Imperial China*. The University of Michigan Press (2001)

54. 《晚明中国的治国方略和知识更新：徐光启的跨文化集成》Catherine Jami, Peter Engelfriet, Gregory Blue (eds), *Statecraft and Intellectual Renewal in Late Ming China: The*

Cross-cultural Synthesis of Xu Guangqi (1562—1633). Brill (2001)

55. 《东方遇到西方：东亚的人权与民主》Daniel A. Bell（淡贝宁）, *East Meets West: Human Rights and Democracy in East Asia*. Princeton University Press (2000)

56. 《妖妇与圣人：古代希腊与古代中国的知识与智慧》Steven Shankman, Stephen Durrant, *The Siren and the Sage: Knowledge and Wisdom in Ancient Greece and China*. Continuum (2000)

57. 《北京六分仪：中国历史上的全球潮流》Joanna Waley-Cohen（卫周安）, *The Sextants of Beijing: Global Currents in Chinese History*. W. W. Norton & Company (2000)

58. 《从近期考古发现看公元前第二个千年中西文化接触与交流》Li Shuicheng, *A Discussion of Sino-Western Cultural Contacts and Exchange in the Second Millennium B. C. Based on Recent Archaeological Discoveries*. Sino-Platonic Papers (1999)

59. 《马可·波罗去过中国吗》Frances Wood, *Did Marco Polo Go To China*. Westview Press (1998)

60. 《差点成英雄：约翰·梅亚雷斯到中国、夏威夷和西北海岸的旅程》J. Richard Nokes, *Almost A Hero: The Voyages of John Meares, R.N., to China, Hawaii and the Northwest Coast*. Washington State University (1998)

61. 《西方史和世界史中的亚洲：教学指南》Ainslee Thomas Embree, Carol Gluck, *Asia in Western and World History: A Guide for Teaching*. M. E. Sharpe Inc. (1997)

62. 《解构殖民史：1492年至今印度、中国和西方的技术与文化》Claude Alvares, *Decolonising History: Technology and Culture in India, China, and the West from 1492 to the Present Day*. Other India Press (1997)

63. 《欧洲和中国的物质文化（1400—1800）：消费主义的兴起》S. A. M. Adshead, *Material Culture in Europe and China, 1400—1800: The Rise of Consumerism*. Palgrave Macmillan UK (1997)

64. 《当中国称霸海上》Louise Levathes（李露晔）, *When China Ruled the Seas: The Treasure Fleet of the Dragon Throne, 1405—1433*. Oxford University Press (1994)

65. 《西方科学传入中国（1840—1900）》（博士论文）David Frank Aston Wright, *The Transmission of Western Science into China (1840—1900)*. Ph. D. Dissertation, London University (1995)

66. 《当中国统治海洋：龙船宝座舰队（1405—1433）》Louise Levathes, *When China Ruled the Seas: The Treasure Fleet of the Dragon Throne 1405—1433*. Simon & Schuster (1994)

67. 《龙、东方与西方研究》Qiguang Zhao, *A Study of Dragons, East and West*. Peter Lang Publishing Inc. (1993)

68. 《距离的扩散：中西诗学对话》Wai-Lim Yip, *Diffusion of Distances: Dialogues Between Chinese and Western Poetics*. University of California Press (1993)

69. 《阿拉伯古典叙述中的印度和中国》Ibn Khurradādhbih, Sulaymān al-Tājir, trans. S. Maqbūl Aḥmad, *Arabic classical accounts of India and China*. Indian Institute of Advanced

Study in association with Rddhi-India, Calcutta (1989)

70. 《使馆与幻想：荷兰和葡萄牙使节致康熙（1666—1687）》John E. Wills, Jr., *Embassies and Illusions: Dutch and Portuguese Envoys to K'ang-hsi, 1666—1687*. Council on East Asian Studies, Harvard University (1984)

71. 《欧洲形成时期的亚洲，第二卷，百年奇观，第三册学术学科》Donald F. Lach, *Asia in the Making of Europe, Volume II: A Century of Wonder. Book 3: The Scholarly Disciplines*. University of Chicago Press (1977, 1994)

72. 《欧洲形成时期的亚洲，第二卷，百年奇观，第二册文学艺术》Donald F. Lach, *Asia in the Making of Europe, Volume II: A Century of Wonder. Book 2: The Literary Arts*. University of Chicago Press (1977, 1994)

73. 《欧洲形成时期的亚洲，第二卷，百年奇观，第一册视觉艺术》Donald F. Lach, *Asia in the Making of Europe, Volume II: A Century of Wonder. Book 1: The Visual Arts*. University of Chicago Press (1970, 1994)

74. 《欧洲形成时期的亚洲，第一卷，百年发现，第二册》Donald F. Lach, *Asia in the Making of Europe, Volume I: A Century of Wonder. Book 2*. University of Chicago Press (1965, 1971, 1994)

75. 《欧洲形成时期的亚洲，第一卷，百年发现，第一册》Donald F. Lach, *Asia in the Making of Europe, Volume I: A Century of Wonder. Book 1*. University of Chicago Press (1965, 1971, 1994)

76. 《局外人：西方在印度和中国的经验》Rhoads Murphey, *The Outsiders: The Western Experience in India and China*. University of Michigan Press (1977)

77. 《寻求富强：严复与西方》Benjamin I. Schwartz（史华慈，）*In Search of Wealth and Power: Yen Fu and the West*. Belknap Press (1964)

78. 《中国对西方的反应：文献通考（1839—1923）》Ssu-yü Teng（邓嗣禹），John K. Fairbank（费正清），*China's Response to the West: A Documentary Survey, 1839—1923*. Cambridge: Harvard University Press (1954)

79. 《西方世界对中国的入侵》E. R. (Ernest Richard) Hughes（修中诚），*The Invasion of China by the Western World*. Adam & Charles Black (1937)

80. 《中西交往概述》W. E. Soothill（苏慧廉），*China and the West: A Sketch of Their Intercourse*. Oxford University Press (1925)

81. 《中国与伊朗：中国对伊朗古代文明史的贡献，特别参照植物栽培和产品史》Berthold Laufer, *Sino-Iranica: Chinese Contributions to the History of Civilization in Ancient Iran. With Special Reference to the History of Cultivated Plants and Products*.Field Museum of Natural History Chicago (1919)

82. 《我的回忆》（第一、二卷）Raphael Pumpelly, *My Reminiscences*. Vols. 1, 2. New York: Henry Holt and Company (1918)

83. 《波斯和中国》Josiah Conder, *Persia and China: A Popular Description, Geographical, Historical, and Topographical.* Vol. II. London, James Duncan, Paternoster Row (1914)

84. 《外国人在华之地位》V. K. Wellington Koo, *The Status of Aliens in China.* New York: Columbia University (1912)

85. 《蒲安臣与中国第一次派赴外国的使团》Frederick Wells Williams, *Anson Burlingame and the First Chinese Mission to Foreign Powers.* New York: Charles Scribner's Sons (1912)

86. 《鲁布鲁克东行记（1253—1255）》Willem van Ruysbroeck, da Pian del Carpine Giovanni, William Woodville Rockhill（柔克义）, *The Journey of William of Rubruck to the Eastern Parts of the World, 1253—1255.* London: Printed for the Hakluyt Society (1900)

87. 《中国与罗马东方》Friedrich Hirth（夏德）, *China and the Roman Orient. Researches into their Ancient and Mediæval Relations as Represented in Old Chinese Records.* Leipsic & Munich Georg Hirth (1885)

88. 《我们的中国男孩：两个年轻美国人斯科特和保罗·克莱顿在中国海中遇难及其中国奇遇的惊险故事》Harry W. French, *Our Boys in China: The Thrilling Story of Two Young Americans, Scott and Paul Clayton Wrecked in the China Sea, with Their Strange Adventures in China.* New York: Charles Dillingham (1883)

89. 《外国人在中国》L. N. Wheeler, *The Foreigner in China.* Chicago: S. C. Geiggs and Company (1881)

90. 《15世纪中国与中亚和西亚国家的交往》E. Bretschneider, *Chinese Intercourse with the Countries of Central and Western Asia during the Fifteenth Century.* Printed at the China Mail Office (1877)

91. 《太平洋之旅：由陛下指挥，为发现北半球而进行》James Cook, James King, *A Voyage to the Pacific Ocean: Undertaken by Command of His Majesty for Making Discoveries in the Northern Hemisphere: Performed under the Direction of Captains Cook, Clerke and Gore, in the years 1776, 1777, 1778, 1779 and 1780, Being a Copious, Comprehensive and Satisfactory Abridgment of the Voyage.* 4 Vols. London: Printed for John Stockdale, Scatcherd and Whitaker, John Fielding, and John Hardy (1874)

92. 《我在中国的生命之晨：从1833年东印度公司体制的最后一年至1839年监禁外国社团的对外交往史纲要》Gideon Nye, *The Morning of My Life in China: Comprising an Outline of the History of Foreign Intercourse from the Last Year of the Regime of Honorable East India Company, 1833, to the Imprisonment of the Foreign Community in 1839.* Canton (1873)

93. 《在遥远中国的外国人》Walter Henry Medhurst, *The Foreigner in Far Cathay* (Cambridge Library Collection-Travel and Exploration).Cambridge University Press (1872, 2010)

94. 《中国大使馆的接待和娱乐》By the City of Boston, *Reception and Entertainment of the Chinese Embassy.* Boston: Alfred Mudge & Son, City Printers (1868)

95. 《法国首任驻华大使馆日记（1698—1700），据Saxe Bannister未刊手稿翻译》Saxe

Bannister, *A Journal of the First French Embassy to China, 1698—1700. Tr. from an unpublished manuscript by Saxe Bannister*. London, T. Cautley (1859)

96. 《番鬼：圣哈辛托在印度、中国和日本海域》William Maxwell Wood, *Fankwei; or, The San Jacinto in the Seas of India, China, and Japan*. New York: Harper & Brothers (1859)

97. 《美国远征队赴中国海和日本记事》Matthew Calbraith Perry, Francis Lister Hawks, *Narrative of the Expedition of an American Squadron to the China Seas and Japan*. New York: D. Appleton and Company (1857)

98. 《中国商业指南：包含一系列细则和规定》Samuel Wells Williams（卫三畏）, *A Chinese Commercial Guide: Consisting of a Collection of Details and Regulations Respecting Foreign Trade with China, Sailing Directions, Tables, etc*. 4th ed., rev. and enl. Canton: Printed at the Office of the Chinese Repository (1856)

99. 《东亚漫游：包括中国和马尼拉，数年居住地》Benjamin Lincoln Ball, *Rambles in Eastern Asia: Including China and Manila, During Several Years' Residence*. Boston: James French (1856)

100. 《中国和东印度群岛旅行记》（全二卷）Peter Osbeck, *A Voyage to China and the East Indies. Together with a Voyage to Suratte, by Olof Toreen and an Account of the Chinese Husbandry, by Captain Charles Gustavus Eckeberg. Tr. from the German, by John Reinhold Forster, F. A. S*. In 2 Vols. London: Printed for Benjamin White, at Horace's Head, in Fleet-Sreet (1771)

101. 《美国驻广州第一任领事山茂召少校日记》Samuel Shaw, Josiah Quincy, *The Journals of Major Samuel Shaw, the First American Consul at Canton*, with a Life of the Author by Josiah Quincy. Edited by Josiah Quincy. Boston: Wm. Crosby and H. P. Nichols (1847)

102. 《环球航行：1740, 1741, 1742, 1743, 1744年》George Anson, *A Voyage Round the World: In the Years 1740, 1741, 1742, 1743, 1744*. London: Printed for the Society for Promoting Christian Knowledge (1845, 1749)

103. 《1838—40年访问之美国笔记》〔共两卷〕George Combe, *Notes on the United States of North America, during a Phrenological Visit in 1838-39-40. In 2 Vols*. Philadelphia: Carey and Hart (1841)

104. 《印度斯坦和中国游记》Howard Malcolm, *Travels in Hindustan and China*. Edinburgh: William and Robert Chambers (1840)

105. 《番鬼在中国》（第一卷至第三卷）C. Toogood Downing, The Fan-qui in China. In 3 vols. London: Henry Colburn Publisher (1838)

106. 《彼得·帕利关于亚洲的故事：有地图和众多雕刻》Samuel G. Goodrich, *Peter Parley's Tales About Asia: With a Map and Numerous Engravings*. Boston: Gray & Bowen and Carter & Hendee (1830)

107. 《东方商业》William Milburn, *Oriental Commerce*. London: Printed for Kingsbury, Parbury, and Allen (1825)

108. 《中国海航行史》John White, *History of a Voyage to the China Sea*. Boston: Wells and Lilly (1823)

109. 《英国使团来华航海见闻录》Henry Ellis, *Journal of the Proceedings of the Late Embassy*. Philadelphia: Printed and Published by A. Small (1818)

110. 《阿尔塞斯特号黄海之行叙事》John McCleod, *Narrative of a Voyage, in His Majesty's late Ship Alceste, to the Yellow Sea, along the Coast of Corea ... to the Island of Lewchew*. Philadelphia: Published by M. Carey and Son (1818)

111. 《南北半球航行与旅行的叙述：包括三次环球航行》Amasa Delano, *A Narrative of Voyages and Travels in the Northern and Southern Hemispheres: Comprising Three Voyages around the World*. E.G. House (1817)

112. 《詹姆斯·沙兰历险记》James Sharan, *The Adventures of James Sharan: Compiled from the Journal, Written during his Voyages and Travels in the Four Quarters of the globe*. Baltimore: Printed by G. Dobbin & Murphy, 10 Baltimore-street for James Sharan (1808)

113. 《最著名航程的历史记载（含有关中国的内容）》（第八卷）William Fordyce Mavor, *An Historical Account of the Most Celebrated Voyages*. 13 vols. Philadelphia: M. and J. Conrad. Vol. 8, pp. 237–287 contains "Travels in China by the Jesuits Le Compte and Du Halde." (1802)

114. 《最著名航程的历史记载（含有关中国的内容）》（第十一卷）William Fordyce Mavor, *An Historical Account of the Most Celebrated Voyages*. 14 vols. Philadelphia: S. F. Bradford. Vol. 11, pp. 237–287 contains the text of "Travels in China" as that in the M. and J. Conrad edition (1802)

115. 《1794年和1795年荷兰东印度公司驻中华帝国朝廷使节纪实》（第一、二卷）André Everard Van Braam Houckgeest, Moreau de Saint-Méry, *An Authentic Account of the Embassy of the Dutch East-India Company, to the Court of the Emperor of China, in the Years 1794 and 1795*. In 2 vols. London: Printed for R. Phillips (1798)

116. 《环球旅行记》（第六卷含中国内容）Christopher Smart, Oliver Goldsmith, Samuel Johnson, *The World Displayed: or, A Curious Collection of Voyages and Travels, Selected from the Writers of All Nations*. Vol. 6, pp. 184–247 contains "A Description of China. By Louis Le Compte and P. Du Halde" (1795)

117. 《太平洋之旅》（第一卷至第四卷）James Cook, *A Voyage to the Pacific Ocean ... in the Years 1776, 1777, 1778, 1779 and 1790....* Written by Captain James Cook, F. R. S., and Captain James King, L. L. D. and F. R. S. In 4 vols. London: W. & A. Strahan (1793)

118. 《前往马达加斯加和东印度群岛的航行》Alexis M. Rochin, *A Voyage to Madagascar and the East Indies ... Translated from the French ... To Which Is Added a Memoir on the Chinese Trade* (by M. Brunei). London: G. G. J. & J. Robinson (1792)

119. 《关于鸦片的就职论文》（博士论文）Hast Handy, *An Inaugural Dissertation on Opium*:

Submitted to the Examination of John Ewing, S. T. P. Provost; and to the Trustees and Medical Professors of the College of Philadelphia; for the Degree of Doctor of Medicine: on the Second Day of June, A. D. 1791. Philadelphia: T. Lang (1791)

120.《关于从美国引种胭脂虫、从中国引入清漆和牛油树……等的通信》James Anderson, *Correspondence for the Introduction of Cochineal Insects from America, the Varnish and Tallow Trees from China, the Discovery and Culture of White Lac, the Culture of Red Lac…*. Madras (1791)

121.《欧洲人在东西印度群岛殖民和贸易的哲学及政治历史》（第一至八卷）Guillaume Thomas Francois Raynal, *A Philosophical and Political History of the Settlements and Trade of the Europeans in the East and West Indies*. Published, in Ten Volumes, by the ABBE Raynal. Newly Translated from the French, by J. O. Justamond, in 8 vols. London: Printed for T. Cadell, in the Strand (1788)

122.《哲学家的旅行：对非洲和亚洲不同国家礼仪和艺术的观察》Pierre Poivre, *The Travels of a Philosopher: or Observations on the Manners and Arts of Various Nations in Africa and Asia*. London: Printed for J. Davidson (1769)

123.《从俄罗斯圣彼得堡到亚洲不同地区的游记》（第一、二卷）John Bell, Lorenz Lange, *Travels from St. Petersburg, in Russia, to Diverse Parts of Asia*. Volumes 1, 2. Glasgow: Printed for the Author by R. and A. Foulis (1763)

124.《安森勋爵环球航行补录》Abbé Coyer, *A Supplement to Lord Anson's Voyage round the World. Containing a Discovery and Description of the Island of Frivola*. London: Printed for A. Millar ... and J. Whiston and B. White... (1752)

125.《中国台湾历史与地理描述》George Psalmanazar, *An Historical and Geographical Description of Formosa: An Island Subject to the Emperor of Japan. Giving an Account of the Religion, Customs, Manners, &c., of the Inhabitants*. London: Printed for M. Wotton, Abel. Roper and B. Lintott...; Fr (1705)

11.2 丝绸之路/一带一路

1.《一带一路倡议之中巴经济走廊：概念、背景与评估》(Contemporary South Asian Studies) Siegfried O. Wolf, *The China-Pakistan Economic Corridor of the Belt and Road Initiative: Concept, Context and Assessment*. Springer International Publishing (2020)

2.《中国全球化与"一带一路"倡议》(Politics and Development of Contemporary China) Jean A. Berlie, *China's Globalization and the Belt and Road Initiative*. Palgrave Macmillan (2020)

3.《全球背景下的中国"一带一路"倡议：第二卷，中巴经济走廊及其商业影响》(Palgrave Macmillan Asian Business Series) Jawad Syed, Yung-Hsiang Ying, *China's Belt and Road Initiative in a Global Context: Volume II: The China Pakistan Economic Corridor and its Implications for Business*. Springer International Publishing; Palgrave Macmillan (2020)

4.《全球背景下的中国"一带一路"倡议：第一卷，商业与管理视角》(Palgrave

Macmillan Asian Business Series) Jawad Syed, Yung-Hsiang Ying, *China's Belt and Road Initiative in a Global Context: Volume I: A Business and Management Perspective*. Springer International Publishing; Palgrave Macmillan (2019)

5. 《中国海上丝绸之路倡议与东南亚：困境、疑虑与决心》(Palgrave Studies in Asia-Pacific Political Economy) Jean-Marc F. Blanchard, *China's Maritime Silk Road Initiative and Southeast Asia: Dilemmas, Doubts, and Determination*. Springer Singapore Palgrave (2019)

6. 《绘制中国"一带一路"倡议》(International Political Economy Series) Li Xing, *Mapping China's 'One Belt One Road' Initiative*. Springer International Publishing: Palgrave Macmillan (2019)

7. 《一带一路：中国的世界秩序》Bruno Maçães, *Belt and Road: A Chinese World Order*. Hurst (2019)

8. 《中国的阿喀琉斯之踵："一带一路"倡议与印度的不满》Srikanth Thaliyakkattil, *China's Achilles' Heel: The Belt and Road Initiative and Its Indian Discontents*. Springer Singapore: Palgrave Macmillan (2019)

9. 《中国"一带一路"倡议对金融的影响：经济可持续增长的途径》Piotr Łasak, René W. H. van der Linden, *The Financial Implications of China's Belt and Road Initiative: A Route to More Sustainable Economic Growth*. Springer International Publishing: Palgrave Pivot (2019)

10. 《"一带一路"：中国力量之关键》Bruno Maçães, *Belt and Road: The Sinews of Chinese Power*. Hurst & Company (2018)

11. 《新丝绸之路：世界的现在和未来》Peter Frankopan, *The New Silk Roads: The Present and Future of the World*. Bloomsbury Publishing (2018)

12. 《确保一带一路：中国境外投资新浪潮下的风险评估、私人担保和特殊保险》Alessandro Arduino, Xue Gong (eds.), *Securing the Belt and Road Initiative: Risk Assessment, Private Security and Special Insurances Along the New Wave of Chinese Outbound Investments*. Palgrave (2018)

13. 《中国全球经济再平衡与新丝绸之路》B. R. Deepak (eds.), *China's Global Rebalancing and the New Silk Road*. Springer Singapore (2018)

14. 《丝绸之路再思考：中国"一带一路"倡议与新兴欧亚关系》Maximilian Mayer (eds.), *Rethinking the Silk Road: China's Belt and Road Initiative and Emerging Eurasian Relations*. Palgrave Macmillan (2018)

15. 《全球舞台上的"一带一路"倡议：中国与欧洲视角》Yu Cheng, Lilei Song, Lihe Huang (eds.), *The Belt & Road Initiative in the Global Arena: Chinese and European Perspectives*. Palgrave Macmillan (2018)

16. 《中国在中东的存在："一带一路"的启示》Anoushiravan Ehteshami, Niv Horesh (eds.), *China's Presence in the Middle East: The Implications of the One Belt, One Road Initiative* (Durham Modern Middle East and Islamic World Series). Routledge (2018)

17. 《中国"一带一路"倡议》Wenxian Zhang, Ilan Alon, Christoph Lattemann, *China's Belt and Road Initiative* (Palgrave Studies of Internationalization in Emerging Markets). Springer International Publishing: Palgrave Macmillan (2018)

18. 《中国"一带一路"倡议：一场权力的游戏？》（硕士论文）Alexander Ross Billington, *China's Belt & Road Initiative: A Game of Thrones?* Thesis for the Degree of Master of Arts, Long Island University, C. W. Post Center (2018)

19. 《中国"一带一路"倡议》Wei Liu, *China's Belt and Road Initiatives*. Springer Singapore (2018)

20. 《印度洋区域发展年度报告（2017）："一带一路"倡议与南亚》(Research Series on the Chinese Dream and China's Development Path) Wang Rong, Cuiping Zhu, *Annual Report on the Development of the Indian Ocean Region (2017)：The Belt and Road Initiative and South Asia*. Springer Singapore (2018)

21. 《中国"一带一路"倡议的政治经济学》(Series on China's Belt and Road Initiative vol. 1) Lei Zou, *The Political Economy of China's Belt and Road Initiative*. World Scientific Publishing Co. Pte. Ltd (2018)

22. 《中国的亚洲梦：帝国筑起新丝绸之路》Tom Miller, *China's Asian Dream: Empire Building along the New Silk Road*. Zed Books (2017, 2019)

23. 《欧洲和中国的新丝绸之路》Frans-Paul van der Putten, John Seaman, *Europe and China's New Silk Roads*. ETNC-report (2016)

24. 《罗马帝国与丝绸之路：古代世界经济与帕提亚、中亚和汉代帝国》Raoul McLaughlin, *The Roman Empire and the Silk Routes: The Ancient World Economy and the Empires of Parthia, Central Asia and Han China*. Pen and Sword History (2016)

25. 《印度洋地区年度发展报告（2015）》Rong Wang, Cuiping Zhu (eds.), *Annual Report on the Development of the Indian Ocean Region (2015)：21st Century Maritime Silk Road*. Springer Singapore (2016)

26. 《丝绸之路：一部全新的世界史》Peter Frankopan, *The Silk Roads: A New History of the World*. Bloomsbury Publishing (2015)

27. 《丝绸之路》Eileen Ormsby, *Silk Road*. Macmillan Australia (2014)

28. 《顺应丝绸之路：跨学科、跨文化的变革》Laurence Raw, *The Silk Road of Adaptation: Transformations Across Disciplines and Cultures*. Cambridge Scholars Publishing (2013)

29. 《丝绸之路简介》James A. Millward, *The Silk Road: A Very Short Introduction*. Oxford University Press (2013)

30. 《丝绸之路旅行：沙漠探险、佛的秘密图书馆和新出土世上最古老印刷书籍》Joyce Morgan, Conrad Walters, *Journeys on the Silk Road: A Desert Explorer, Buddha's Secret Library, and the Unearthing of the World's Oldest Printed Book*. Lyons Press (2012)

31. 《丝绸之路新史》Valerie Hansen, *The Silk Road: A New History*. Oxford University Press (2012)

32. 《汉代丝绸之路：从西安到浩罕》Donna Kurtz, *The Silk Road: from Xi'an to Kokand during the Han Dynasty* (The World of Ancient Art). University of Oxford (2012)

33. 《丝绸之路研究基金会：文化遗产和身份政治》Roel During, *Cultural Heritage and Identity Politics*. Silk Road Research Foundation (2011)

34. 《世界历史中的丝绸之路》Xinru Liu, *The Silk Road in World History*. Oxford University Press (2010)

35. 《丝绸之路的秘密：教师研究指南与背景信息》Bowers Museum, *Secrets of the Silk Road: Study Guide & Background Information for Teachers*.Gread 6 and Up.Bowers Museum Education Department (2010)

36. 《丝绸之路的宗教信仰：全球化的前现代模式》Richard Foltz, *Religions of the Silk Road: Premodern Patterns of Globalization*. Palgrave Macmillan (2010)

37. 《中亚—高加索分析师》Svante E. Cornell (Ed.), *Central Asia-Caucasus Analyst*. Central Asia-Caucasus Institute & Silk Road Studies Program (2010)

38. 《丝绸之路帝国：从青铜时代至今的中欧亚历史》Christopher I. Beckwith, *Empires of the Silk Road: A History of Central Eurasia from the Bronze Age to the Present*. Princeton University Press (2009)

39. 《丝绸之路沿线古玻璃研究》Gan Fuxi, *Ancient Glass Research Along the Silk Road*. World Scientific Publishing Company (2009)

40. 《新丝绸之路：东亚与世界纺织品市场》Kym Anderson, *The New Silk Roads: East Asia and World Textile Markets*. Cambridge University Press (2009)

41. 《新丝绸之路：崛起的阿拉伯世界如何远离西方并重新发现中国》Ben Simpfendorfer, *The New Silk Road: How a Rising Arab World is Turning Away from the West and Rediscovering China*. Palgrave Macmillan (2009)

42. 《丝绸之路上的地图和形象之旅》Phillipe Foret, Andreas Kaplony, *The Journey of Maps and Images on the Silk Road* (Brill's Inner Asian library). Brill (2008)

43. 《丝绸之路沿线贸易与当代社会：拉达克民族史》Jacqueline Fewkes, *Trade and Contemporary Society along the Silk Road: An Ethno-history of Ladakh*. Routledge (2008)

44. 《非洲的丝绸之路：中国与印度新经济前沿》Harry G. Broadman, *Africa's Silk Road: China and India's New Economic Frontier*. World Bank Publications (2007)

45. 《国际经济法与数字鸿沟：新丝绸之路》Rohan Kariyawasam, *International Economic Law And Digital Divide: New Silk Road*. Edward Elgar Publishing (2007)

46. 《世界旅游组织：丝绸之路》UNWTO, *The Silk Road*.Graforama (Madrid) (2007)

47. 《丝绸之路：从西安到喀什》Judy Bonavia, *The Silk Road: Xi'an to Kashgar* (8th edition). Odyssey Publications (2007)

48. 《丝绸之路史前史》E. E. Kuzmina, *The Prehistory of the Silk Road*. University of Pennsylvania Press (2007)

49. 《丝绸之路的阴影》Colin Thubron, *Shadow of the Silk Road*. Harper Perennial (2007)
50. 《世界旅游组织：丝绸之路上的旅游明珠》UNWTO, *Tourism Pearls of the Silk Road*. Madrid (2006)
51. 《致富丝绸之路：如何通过投资亚洲新发现的繁荣之地获益》Yiannis G. Mostrous, Elliott H. Gue, Ivan D. Martchev, *The Silk Road to Riches: How You Can Profit by Investing in Asia's Newfound Prosperity*. Pearson Education (2006)
52. 《维吾尔的敦煌赞助：10世纪北方丝绸之路的区域艺术中心》Lilla Russell-Smith（毕丽兰）, *Uygur Patronage in Dunhuang: Regional Art Centres on the Northern Silk Road in the Tenth Century.* Brill Academic Pub (2005)
53. 《玄奘的丝路之旅》Sally Hovey Wriggins, *The Silk Road Journey With Xuanzang.* Westview Press (2004)
54. 《马来半岛：海上丝绸之路十字路口（公元前100—公元1300年）》Michel Jacq-Hergoualc'H, Victoria Hobson, *The Malay Peninsula: Crossroads of the Maritime Silk Road (100 BC—1300 AD)*. Brill Academic Publishers (2001)
55. 《乌兹别克斯坦：过渡到丝绸之路上的威权主义》Neil J. Melvin, *Uzbekistan: Transition to Authoritarianism on the Silk Road*. Harwood Academic Publishers (2000)
56. 《丝绸之路古遗址保护》Neville Agnew, *Conservation of Ancient Sites on the Silk Road*. Getty Publications (1997)
57. 《当丝绸等价黄金：中亚与中国纺织》James C. Y. Watt, *When Silk Was Gold: Central Asian and Chinese Textiles*. Metropolitan Museum (1997)
58. 《华南丝绸区：地方历史转型与世界制度理论》Alvin Y. So, *South China Silk District: Local Historical Transformation and World-System Theory*. State University of New York Press (1986)
59. 《丝绸之路上的外国恶魔：寻找中亚失落的城市和宝藏》Peter Hopkirk, *Foreign Devils on the Silk Road: The Search for Lost Cities and Treasures of Chinese Central Asia*. John Murray (1980)

11.3 全球化

1. 《中国重联：连接根深蒂固的过去与新世界秩序》Gungwu Wang（王赓武）, *China Reconnects: Joining a Deep-Rooted Past to a New World Order.* World Scientific Publishing Company (2019)
2. 《跨印度洋世界的早期全球互连（第一卷）：商业结构和交换》Angela Schottenhammer, *Early Global Interconnectivity across the Indian Ocean World, Volume I: Commercial Structures and Exchanges*. Palgrave Macmillan (2019)
3. 《跨印度洋世界的早期全球互连（第二卷）：思想、宗教和技术交流》Angela Schottenhammer, *Early Global Interconnectivity across the Indian Ocean World, Volume II: Exchange of Ideas, Religions, and Technologies*. Palgrave Macmillan (2019)
4. 《全球史与新的多中心方法：世界网络系统中的欧洲、亚洲和美洲》Manuel Perez

Garcia, Lucio De Sousa, *Global History and New Polycentric Approaches: Europe, Asia and the Americas in a World Network System*. Palgrave (2018)

5. 《中国、日本和韩国公共资助的交通研究：政策、治理与外部合作前景》George A. Giannopoulos (eds.), *Publicly Funded Transport Research in the P. R. China, Japan, and Korea: Policies, Governance and Prospects for Cooperation with the Outside* (Lecture Notes in Mobility). Springer (2018)

6. 《中国国际移民：移民全球化的现状、政策与社会反应》Lu Miao, Huiyao Wang（王辉耀）, *International Migration of China: Status, Policy and Social Responses to the Globalization of Migration*. Springer (2017)

7. 《严峻的新世界：全球化终结与历史的回归》Stephen D. King, *Grave New World: The End of Globalization, the Return of History*. Yale University Press (2017)

8. 《在茶叶中联系亚洲跨区域贸易：1920—1960年福建—新加坡贸易中的海外华商》Jason Lim, *Linking an Asian Transregional Commerce in Tea: Overseas Chinese Merchants in the Fujian-Singapore Trade, 1920—1960* (Chinese Overseas-History, Literature, and Society). Brill (2017)

9. 《海上流浪者、白银和武士：全球史中的东亚海事（1550—1700）》(Perspectives on the Global Past) Tonio Andrade（欧阳泰）, Xing Hang (eds.), *Sea Rovers, Silver, and Samurai: Maritime East Asia in Global History, 1550—1700*. University of Hawaii Press (2016)

10. 《中国在东盟的全球生产网络》Young-Chan Kim (eds.), *Chinese Global Production Networks in ASEAN*. Springer International Publishing (2016)

11. 《中国参与全球能源治理》OECD, *China's Engagement in Global Energy Governance* (IEA Partner Country Series). IEA (2016)

12. 《领导力发展的全球化：对德国和中国经理人影响的实证研究》Jingjing Wang, *Globalization of Leadership Development: An Empirical Study of Impact on German and Chinese Managers* (Internationale Wirtschaftspartner). Gabler Verlag (2015)

13. 《东亚海上冲突与商业：郑氏家族与近代世界的形成（约1620—1720年）》(Studies in Weatherhead East Asian Institute, Columbia University) Xing Hang, *Conflict and Commerce in Maritime East Asia: The Zheng Family and the Shaping of the Modern World, c.1620—1720*. Cambridge University Press (2015)

14. 《中国与21世纪危机》Minqi Li, *China and the Twenty-first-Century Crisis*. Pluto Press (2015)

15. 《重新评估中国加入WTO》Wang Luolin, *China's WTO Accession Reassessed* (Routledge Studies on the Chinese Economy). Routledge (2015)

16. 《中国企业全球化：对跨国投资者的启示》Robert Taylor, *Globalisation of Chinese Business: Implications for Multinational Investor* (Chandos Asian studies series). Chandos Publishing, Elsevier Ltd (2014)

17. 《中国走向西方：中国企业走向全球需要了解的一切》Joel Backaler, *China Goes West:*

Everything You Need to Know About Chinese Companies Going Global. Palgrave Macmillan UK (2014)

18.《中国在全球金融中：国内金融抑制和国际金融实力》Sandra Heep, *China in Global Finance: Domestic Financial Repression and International Financial Power*. Springer International Publishing (2014)

19.《全球史学思想指南》Prasenjit Duara（杜赞奇）, Viren Murthy, Andrew Sartori (eds.), *A Companion to Global Historical Thought*. Wiley-Blackwell (2014)

20.《文献、世界历史和中国国力：中国人眼中的全球崛起》（德）Gotelind Müller（顾德琳）, *Documentary, World History, and National Power in the PRC: Global Rise in Chinese Eyes*. Routledge (2013)

21.《塑造中国的全球想象力：在世博会展示国家品牌》Jian Wang, *Shaping China's Global Imagination: Branding Nations at the World Expo*. Palgrave Macmillan US (2013)

22.《全球茶叶育种：成就、挑战与展望》Liang Chen, Zeno Apostolides, Zong-Mao Chen, *Global Tea Breeding: Achievements, Challenges and Perspectives* (Advanced Topics in Science and Technology in China). Springer-Verlag Berlin Heidelberg (2012)

23.《贸易创造的世界：1400年至今的社会、文化和世界经济》Kenneth Pomeranz（彭慕兰）, *The World That Trade Created: Society, Culture, and the World Economy, 1400 to the Present*. Routledge (2012)

24.《中国—拉美轴心：新兴市场与全球化未来》Gastón Fornés, Alan Butt Philip, *The China-Latin America Axis: Emerging Markets and the Future of Globalisation*. Palgrave Macmillan UK (2012)

25.《金丝烟：中国烟草史（1550—2010）》Carol Benedict, *Golden-Silk Smoke: A History of Tobacco in China, 1550—2010*. University of California Press (2011)

26.《大分流之前及其超越：中欧经济变化的政治学》Jean-Laurent Rosenthal, R. Bin Wong（王国斌）, *Before and Beyond Divergence: The Politics of Economic Change in China and Europe*. Harvard University Press (2011)

27.《罗马与远东：古代阿拉伯、印度和中国的陆路贸易路线》Raoul McLaughlin, *Rome and the Distant East: Trade Routes to the ancient lands of Arabia, India and China*. Continuum (2010)

28.《16世纪末的菲律宾群岛、摩鹿加群岛、暹罗、柬埔寨、日本和中国》Antonio de Morga, Henry E. J. Stanley (translator), *The Philippine Islands, Moluccas, Siam, Cambodia, Japan, and China, at the Close of the Sixteenth Century*. Cambridge University Press (2010)

29.《新兴房地产投资市场：投资中国、印度和巴西》David J Lynn; Tim Wang, *Emerging Market Real Estate Investment: Investing in China, India, and Brazil*. John Wiley (2010)

30.《中国和印度的全球化与劳工：影响与反应》Paul Bowles, John Harriss (eds.), *Globalization and Labour in China and India: Impacts and Responses*. Palgrave Macmillan UK (2010)

31.《地球及其人民：全球史》Richard Bulliet, Pamela Kyle Crossley, Daniel Headrick,

Steven Hirsch, Lyman Johnson, David Northup, *The Earth and Its Peoples: A Global History*. Cengage Learning (2010)

32. 《1450—1700年的世界》John E. Wills Jr., *The World from 1450 to 1700*. Oxford University Press, USA (2009)

33. 《地球及其人民：全球史简介，第一卷，至1550年》Richard Bulliet, Pamela Crossley, Daniel Headrick, Steven Hirsch, Lyman Johnson, *The Earth and Its Peoples: A Global History, Brief Edition, Volume I: To 1550*. Wadsworth Publishing (2009)

34. 《地球及其人民：全球史简介，第二卷，自1500年》Richard Bulliet, Pamela Crossley, Daniel Headrick, Steven Hirsch, Lyman Johnson, *The Earth and Its Peoples: A Global History, Brief Edition, Volume II: Since 1500*. Wadsworth Publishing (2009)

35. 《中国与全球化：中国社会、经济与政治转型》Doug Guthrie, *China and Globalization: The Social, Economic and Political Transformation of Chinese Society*. Routledge (2009)

36. 《全球化：担心中国人夺走工作的非理性恐惧》Bruce C. N. Greenwald, Judd Kahn, *Globalization: The Irrational Fear That Someone in China Will Take Your Job*. John Wiley & Sons, Inc., Hoboken, New Jersey (2009)

37. 《中国与全球经济一体化：加入世贸组织、外商直接投资和国际贸易》Chunlai Chen, *China's Integration With the Global Economy: WTO Accession, Foreign Direct Investment and International Trade*. Edward Elgar Pub (2009)

38. 《奇怪的相似：全球背景下的东南亚（800—1830）。第二卷，大陆的映照：欧洲、日本、中国、南亚与群岛》Lieberman Victor, *Strange Parallels: Southeast Asia in Global Context, c.800—1830.Volume 2, Mainland Mirrors: Europe, Japan, China, South Asia, and the Islands* (Studies in Comparative World History). Cambridge University Press (2009)

39. 《世界经济中的中国》Zhongmin Wu, *China in the World Economy* (Routledge Studies on the Chinese Economy). Routledge (2009)

40. 《2050年的世界：超越金砖国家，更广泛地看待新兴市场的增长前景》（智库报告）Hawksworth, John and Gordon Cookson, *The world in 2050: Beyond the BRICs: A Broader Look at Emerging MarketGrowth Prospects*. Pricewaterhouse Cooper (2008)

41. 《中国召唤：一只脚迈进全球大门》Alex Mackinnon, Barnaby Powell, *China Calling: A Foot in the Global Door*. Palgrave Macmillan (2008)

42. 《六大热门市场：如何从巴西、俄罗斯、印度、中国、韩国和墨西哥投资获利》Pran Tiku, *Six Sizzling Markets: How to Profit from Investing in Brazil, Russia, India, China, South Korea, and Mexico*. Wiley (2008)

43. 《荷兰东印度公司与中国的茶叶贸易（1757—1781）》Yong Liu, *The Dutch East India Company's Tea Trade with China, 1757—1781*. Brill (2007)

44. 《中国边缘化：转型和全球化视角》Heather Xioquan Zhang, Bin Wu, Richard Sanders, *Marginalisation in China: Perspectives on Transition and Globalisation*. Ashgate (2007)

45. 《新兴经济体与国际商业转型：巴西、俄罗斯、印度和中国》Subhash C. Jain, *Emerging Economies and the Transformation of International Buisness: Brazil, Russia, India and China.* Edward Elgar Publishing (2007)

46. 《维梅尔的帽子：从一幅画看17世纪全球贸易》Timothy Brook（卜正民）, *Vermeer's Hat: The Seventeenth Century and the Dawn of the Global World.* Bloomsbury Press (2007)

47. 《帝国的生意：东印度公司与英帝国（1756—1833）》H. V. Bowen, *The Business of Empire: The East India Company and Imperial Britain, 1756—1833.* Cambridge University Press (2006)

48. 《全球化、竞争与中国的增长》Jian Chen（陈兼）, Shujie Yao (eds.), *Globalization, Competition, and Growth in China.* Routledge (2006)

49. 《广州贸易：1700—1845年中国沿海的生活与企业》Paul A. Van Dyke, *The Canton Trade: Life and Enterprise on the China Coast, 1700—1845.* Hong Kong University Press (2005)

50. 《中国全球化与经济增长》Yang Yao, Linda Yueh, *Globalisation And Economic Growth in China* (Series on Economic Development and Growth). World Scientific Publishing Co. Pte. Ltd. (2006)

51. 《中国的世界交往与贸易》[瑞典]Hans Bielenstein（毕汉思）, *Diplomacy And Trade In The Chinese World, 589—1276.* Brill Academic Pub. (2005)

52. 《中国在全球经济中：中国治理》OECD, *China in the Global Economy: Governance in China.* OECD Publishing (2005)

53. 《全球化与中国国家转型》Yongnian Zheng（郑永年）, *Globalization and State Transformation in China* (Cambridge Asia-Pacific Studies). Cambridge University Press (2004)

54. 《帝国的生存：葡萄牙贸易、中国社会和中国南海（1630—1754）》G. B. Souza, *The Survival of Empire: Portuguese Trade and Society in China and the South China Sea 1630—1754.* Cambridge University Press (2004)

55. 《世界贸易：从古代至今》（四卷本）Cynthia Clark Northrup, Jerry H. Bentley, Alfred E. Eckes Jr., Patrick Manning, Kenneth Pomeranz（彭慕兰）, Steven Topik, *World Trade: From Ancient Times to the Present* (4 Volumes Set). Routledge (2004)

56. 《中国加入世贸组织手册及其影响》Ching Cheong, Ching Hung-Yee, *Handbook on China's WTO Accession and Its Impacts.* World Scientific Publishing Co Pte Ltd (2003)

57. 《中国全球化与文化潮流》Liu Kang, *Globalization and Cultural Trends in China.* University of Hawaii Press (2003)

58. 《奇怪的相似：全球背景下的东南亚（800—1830）。第一卷，大陆一体化》Victor Lieberman, *Strange Parallels: Southeast Asia in Global Context, c. 800—1830. Volume 1, Integration on the Mainland* (Studies in Comparative World History). Cambridge University Press (2003)

59. 《1421：中国发现世界》Gavin Menzies（加文·孟席斯）, *1421: The Year China*

Discovered the World. Bantam Press (2002)

60. 《中国在世界市场：后毛泽东时代的中国工业与改革的国际资源》Thomas G. Moore, *China in the World Market: Chinese Industry and International Sources of Reform in the Post-Mao Era* (Cambridge Modern China Series). Cambridge University Press (2002)

61. 《华南的全球化》Carolyn Cartier, *Globalizing South China* (RGS-IBG Book Series). Blackwell Publishers Ltd (2001)

62. 《遭遇中国网络：1880—1937年在华之西方、日本和中国公司》Sherman Cochran, *Encountering Chinese Networks: Western, Japanese, and Chinese Corporations in China, 1880—1937.* University of California Press (2000)

63. 《大分流：欧洲、中国及现代世界经济的发展》Kenneth Pomeranz（彭慕兰），*The Great Divergence: China, Europe, and the Making of the Modern World Economy.* Princeton University Press (2000)

64. 《1840年以来的中国与全球经济》Lu Aiguo, *China and the Global Economy since 1840.* Palgrave Macmillan (1999)

65. 《白银资本：重视经济全球化中的东方》Andre Gunder Frank（弗兰克），ReORIENT: *Global Economy in the Asian Age.* University of California Press (1998)

66. 《中国参与全球经济一体化》Dipak Das Gupta, World Bank, *China Engaged: Integration with the Global Economy.* World Bank Publications (1997)

67. 《奇怪的公司：中国移民、混血女人和巴达维亚荷兰人》Leonard Blussé, *Strange Company: Chinese settlers, Mestizo Women and the Dutch in Voc Batavia.* Foris Publications (1986)

68. 《茶叶：东印度茶叶公司1773年向美洲殖民地运送茶叶的信件和文件合集》Francis S. Drake, *Tea Leaves: Being a Collection of Letters and Documents Relating to the Shipment of Tea to the American Colonies in the Year 1773, by the East India Tea Company.* Boston: A. O. Crane (1884)

69. 《由东北向中国三次航行的真实描述》Gerrit de Veer, Charles T. Beke (editor), *A True Description of Three Voyages by the North-East towards Cathay and China, Undertaken by the Dutch in the Years 1594—96.* Cambridge University Press (1853, 2009)

11.4 华侨与移民

1. 《在加拿大做华人：身份、补偿和归属的斗争》William Ging Wee Dere, *Being Chinese in Canada: The Struggle for Identity, Redress and Belonging.* Douglas & McIntyre (2019)

2. 《目的地中国：后改革时代向中国移居》Angela Lehmann, Pauline Leonard, *Destination China: Immigration to China in the Post-Reform Era.* Palgrave Macmillan US (2019)

3. 《皇冠与资本家：华人与泰民族的建立》(Critical dialogues in Southeast Asian Studies) Wasana Wongsurawat, *The Crown and the Capitalists: The Ethnic Chinese and the Founding of the Thai Nation.* University of Washington Press (2019)

4. 《在华外籍人士管理：语言和身份视角》Ling Eleanor Zhang, Anne-Wil Harzing, Shea

Xuejiao Fan, *Managing Expatriates in China: A Language and Identity Perspective* (Palgrave Studies in Chinese Management).Palgrave Macmillan UK (2018)

5. 《全球城市中的跨国生活：新加坡华人移民的多方位研究》Caroline Plüss, *Transnational Lives in Global Cities: A Multi-Sited Study of Chinese Singaporean Migrants*. Springer International Publishing, Palgrave Macmillan (2018)

6. 《回迁的决策：在日高技能华人研究》Ruth Achenbach, *Return Migration Decisions: A Study on Highly Skilled Chinese in Japan*.VS Verlag für Sozialwissenschaften (2017)

7. 《缅甸殖民地时期的中国人：多民族国家的移民社区》Yi Li, *Chinese in Colonial Burma: A Migrant Community in A Multiethnic State*.Palgrave Macmillan US (2017)

8. 《城市形成与全球劳工制度：中国移民与意大利的快速时尚产业》Antonella Ceccagno, *City Making and Global Labor Regimes: Chinese Immigrants and Italy's Fast Fashion Industry*. Springer International Publishing (2017)

9. 《当代中国侨民》Min Zhou, *Contemporary Chinese Diasporas*. Palgrave Macmillan (2017)

10. 《东南亚的中国创制：知识、身份与移民的中国性》Zhiyu Shi（石之瑜）, *Producing China in Southeast Asia: Knowledge, Identity, and Migrant Chineseness*. Springer Nature Singapore Pte Ltd. (2017)

11. 《迁移中的福建人：现代早期海事世界中的民族、家庭和性别身份》Guotong Li, *Migrating Fujianese: Ethnic, Family, and Gender Identities in an Early Modern Maritime World*. Brill (2016)

12. 《华裔美国人：一个民族的历史与文化》Jonathan H. X. Lee, *Chinese Americans: The History and Culture of a People*. ABC-CLIO (2016)

13. 《难以捉摸的避难所：冷战时期的中国移民》Laura Madokoro, *Elusive Refuge: Chinese Migrants in the Cold War*. Harvard University Press (2016)

14. 《堂战：纽约唐人街中的罪恶、金钱和谋杀的不为人知的故事》Scott D. Seligman, *Tong Wars: The Untold Story of Vice, Money, and Murder in New York's Chinatown*. Viking (2016)

15. 《当代中国的反向移民：海归、创业与中国经济》Huiyao Wang（王辉耀）, Yue Bao, *Reverse Migration in Contemporary China: Returnees, Entrepreneurship and the Chinese Economy*. Palgrave Macmillan UK (2015)

16. 《20世纪90年代以来澳大利亚的华人移民创业：中澳关系成功案例研究》Jia Gao, *Chinese Migrant Entrepreneurship in Australia from the 1990s: Case-Studies of Success in Sino-Australian relations*.Elsevier Chandos Publishing (2015)

17. 《欧洲的中国移民：意大利普拉托及其他地方》Loretta Baldassar, Graeme Johanson, Narelle McAuliffe, Massimo Bressan (eds.), *Chinese Migration to Europe: Prato, Italy, and Beyond*.Palgrave Macmillan UK (2015)

18. 《从农场到运河街：唐人街在全球市场上的替代食品网络》Valerie Imbruce, *From Farm to Canal Street: Chinatown's Alternative Food Network in the Global Marketplace*. Cornell

University Press (2015)

19. 《全球华人侨民的多语言现象：跨国联系与当地社会现实》Li Wei (ed.), *Multilingualism in the Chinese Diaspora Worldwide: Transnational Connections and Local Social Realities* (Routledge Critical Studies in Multilingualism). Routledge (2015)

20. 《异族：从"苦力"时代至二战的美国华人移民》Elliott Young, *Alien Nation: Chinese Migration in the Americas from the Coolie Era through World War II*. The University of North Carolina Press (2014)

21. 《中亚的华人构成：国际关系中的地区与相互交织的行动者》Nadine Godehardt, *The Chinese Constitution of Central Asia: Regions and Intertwined Actors in International Relations*. Palgrave Macmillan (2014)

22. 《中国第二大陆：百万移民在非洲如何建立新帝国》Howard W. French, *China's Second Continent. How a Million Migrants Are Building a New Empire in Africa*. Knopf (2014)

23. 《记住三水的红头巾：新加坡和中国的移民与社会记忆》Kelvin Low, *Remembering the Samsui Women: Migration and Social Memory in Singapore and China*. University of Washington Press (2014)

24. 《在中国的跨国生活：全球化城市中的外籍人士》Angela Lehmann, *Transnational Lives in China: Expatriates in a Globalizing City*. Palgrave Macmillan UK (2014)

25. 《侨务：海外华人的域外政策》James Jiann Hua To, *Qiaowu: Extra-Territorial Policies for the Overseas Chinese* (Chinese Overseas). Brill Academic Pub (2014)

26. 《中国移民与非洲发展：新帝国主义者抑或变革推动者》Giles Mohan, *Chinese Migrants and Africa's Development: New Imperialists or Agents of Change*. Zed Books (2014)

27. 《跨越边界：缅甸的云南华人移民故事》Wen-Chin Chang, *Beyond Borders: Stories of Yunnanese Chinese Migrants of Burma*. Cornell University Press (2014)

28. 《排华之路：丹佛暴动、1880年大选与西方崛起》Liping Zhu, *The Road to Chinese Exclusion: The Denver Riot, 1880 Election, and Rise of the West*. University Press of Kansas (15 Aug 2014)

29. 《印尼华人再评估：历史、宗教与归属》Siew-Min Sai, Chang-Yau Hoon, *Chinese Indonesians Reassessed: History, Religion and Belonging* (Routledge Contemporary Southeast Asia Series). Routledge (2013)

30. 《世界花园：亚洲移民与加州圣克拉拉谷的农业发展》Cecilia M. Tsu, *Garden of the World: Asian Immigrants and the Making of Agriculture in California's Santa Clara Valley*. Oxford University Press (2013)

31. 《第一位华裔美国人：王清福的非凡人生》Scott D. Seligman, *The first Chinese American: The Remarkable Life of Wong Chin Foo*. Hong Kong: Hong Kong University Press (2013)

32. 《陈嘉庚：海外华人传奇》Ching-Fatt Yong, *Tan Kah-Kee: The Making of an Overseas Chinese Legend (Revised Edition)*. World Scientific Publishing Company (2013)

33. 《世界唐人街：镀金贫民区、科技城市、文化散居地》Bernard P. Wong and Tan Chee-Beng, *Chinatowns around the world: gilded ghetto, ethnopolis, and cultural diaspora*. Brill (2013)
34. 《世界各地的唐人街：镀金贫民区、民族聚居地和文化的散居》Edited by Bernard P. Wong and Tan Chee-Beng, *Chinatowns around the world: Gilded Ghetto, Ethnopolis, and Cultural Diaspora*. Brill (2013)
35. 《另一种华人激进主义：争取留在澳大利亚的中国学生运动》Gao Jia, *Chinese Activism of a Different Kind: The Chinese Students Campaign to Stay in Australia*. Brill (2013)
36. 《中国社区和文化生产崛起后的移民社群中国性》Julia Kuehn, *Diasporic Chineseness after the Rise of China Communities and Cultural Production*. UBC Press (2013)
37. 《中国劳工在南非（1902—1910）：种族、暴力与全球奇观》Rachel K. Bright, *Chinese Labour in South Africa, 1902–10: Race, Violence, and Global Spectacle*. Palgrave Macmillan UK (2013)
38. 《欧亚人：美国、中国内地和中国香港的混合身份（1842—1943）》Emma Jinhua Teng, *Eurasian: Mixed Identities in the United States, China, and Hong Kong, 1842—1943*. University of California Press (2013)
39. 《芝加哥华人：1870年来的种族、跨国移民和社区》Huping Ling, *Chinese Chicago: Race, Transnational Migration, and Community Since 1870*. Stanford University Press (2012)
40. 《澳大利亚的中国面孔：澳大利亚出生的华人多代族群》Lucille Lok-Sun Ngan, Chan Kwok-bun, *The Chinese Face in Australia: Multi-generational Ethnicity among Australian-born Chinese*. Springer-Verlag New York (2012)
41. 《旧金山唐人街：历史与建筑指南》Philip P. Choy, *San Francisco Chinatown: A Guide to its History and its Architecture*. City Lights Publishers (2012)
42. 《中国墨西哥人：跨太平洋迁徙与寻找家园（1910—1960）》Julia María Schiavone Camacho, *Chinese Mexicans: Transpacific Migration and the Search for a Homeland, 1910—1960*. The University of North Carolina Press (2012)
43. 《物质文化、社会网络与科罗拉多乌雷华人（1880—1920）》（硕士论文）Alexis Ryan Knee, *Material Culture, Social Networks and the Chinese of Ouray, Colorado, 1880—1920*. Thesis for the Degree of Master of Arts, Colorado State University, Fort Collins, Colorado (2012)
44. 《纸上儿女：在南非成长的中国人》Ufrieda Ho, *Paper Sons and Daughters: Growing up Chinese in South Africa* (Modern African Writing Series). Ohio University Press (2011)
45. 《重建祖村：在中国的新加坡人》Khun Eng Kuaah-Pearce, *Rebuilding the Ancestral Village: Singaporeans in China*. Hong Kong University Press (2011)
46. 《1878年以来在多伦多的中国人》Arlene Chan, *The Chinese in Toronto from 1878*. Dundurn (2011)
47. 《连接海洋与大洋边缘：19世纪30年代至20世纪30年代印度洋、大西洋、太平洋与中国海的移民》Donna R. Gabaccia, Dirk Hoerder, *Connecting Seas and Connected Ocean Rims: Indian, Atlantic, and Pacific Oceans and China Seas Migrations from the 1830s to the 1930s*. Brill (2011)

48. 《中华人民共和国的华侨》Glen Peterson, *Overseas Chinese in the People's Republic of China*. Routledge (2011)

49. 《在中国和新加坡的广东社团：性别、宗教、医药和金钱》Marjorie Topley, Jean Debernardi, *Cantonese Society in China and Singapore: Gender, Religion, Medicine and Money*. Hong Kong University Press (2011)

50. 《淘金：美国西部的华裔矿工和商人》Sue Fawn Chung, *In Pursuit of Gold: Chinese American Miners and Merchants in the American West*. University of Illinois Press (2011)

51. 《跨国世界中的唐人街：城市现象的神话与现实》Vanessa Künnemann, Ruth Mayer, *Chinatowns in a Transnational World: Myths and Realities of an Urban Phenomenon*. Routledge (2011)

52. 《东南亚的身份与族群关系：中国性的种族化》Chee Kiong Tong, *Identity and Ethnic Relations in Southeast Asia: Racializing Chineseness*. Springer Netherlands (2011)

53. 《天使岛：移民美国的门户》Erika Lee, Judy Yung, *Angel Island: Immigrant Gateway to America*. Oxford University Press (2010)

54. 《声称侨民：亚裔/华裔美国的音乐、跨国主义和文化政治》Su Zheng, *Claiming Diaspora: Music, Transnationalism, and Cultural Politics in Asian/Chinese America* (American musicspheres). Oxford University Press (2010)

55. 《当下亚裔美国人研究：批评性读本》Jean Yu-wen Shen Wu, Thomas C. Chen, *Asian American Studies Now: A Critical Reader*. New Brunswick, N.J. Rutgers: University Press (2010)

56. 《印尼华人和政权更迭》Marleen Dieleman, Juliette Koning, Peter Post, *Chinese Indonesians and Regime Change*. Brill Academic Pub (2010)

57. 《经纪人的归属：加拿大排外时代的华人（1885—1945）》Lisa Rose Mar, *Brokering Belonging: Chinese in Canada's Exclusion Era, 1885—1945*. Oxford University Press (2010)

58. 《马尼拉的华人与华人混血儿：家庭、身份与文化（19世纪60年代—20世纪30年代）》Richard T. Chu, *Chinese and Chinese Mestizos of Manila: Family, Identity, and Culture, 1860s–1930s* (Chinese Overseas). Brill (2010)

59. 《拉丁美洲和加勒比地区的中国人》Walton Look Lai, Tan Chee-Beng, *The Chinese in Latin America and the Caribbean*. Brill (2010)

60. 《宇宙信用：跨国流动和目的地中国的政治》Julie Y. Chu, *Cosmologies of Credit: Transnational Mobility and the Politics of Destination in China*. Duke University Press (2010)

61. 《当代美国华人：移民、种族和社区改造》Min Zhou, *Contemporary Chinese America: Immigration, Ethnicity, and Community Transformation* (Asian American History & Culture). Temple University Press (2009)

62. 《华人在印度尼西亚的国家地位（1900—1958）》Donald E. Willmott, *The National Status of the Chinese in Indonesia: 1900—1958*.Equinox Publishing (2009)

63. 《捆绑的纽带：近代新加坡的华人代际关系》Kristina Goransson, *The Binding Tie: Chinese Intergenerational Relations In Modern Singapore*.University of Hawaii Press (2009)

64. 《蛇头：唐人街的地下世界与美国梦的史诗故事》Patrick Radden Keefe, *The Snakehead: An Epic Tale of the Chinatown Underworld and the American Dream*.Doubleday (2009)

65. 《唐人街的儿童：1850至1920年在旧金山成长的华裔美国人》Wendy Rouse Jorae, *The Children of Chinatown: Growing Up Chinese American in San Francisco, 1850—1920*.The University of North Carolina Press (2009)

66. 《在中国侨民家中：记忆、身份与财产》Kuah-Pearce Khun Eng, Andrew P. Davidson (eds.), *At Home in the Chinese Diaspora: Memories, Identities and Belongings*. Palgrave Macmillan UK (2008)

67. 《东南亚华侨华人：历史、文化与商业》Ian Rae, Morgen Witzel, *Overseas Chinese of South East Asia: History, Culture, Business*. Palgrave Macmillan (2008)

68. 《东南亚及更远之地的中国人：社会经济与政治层面》Ching-Hwang Yen, *The Chinese In Southeast Asia And Beyond: Socioeconomic and Political Dimensions*.World Scientific Publishing Company (2008)

69. 《华人必须走：暴力、排斥与在美外国人的形成》Beth Lew-Williams, *The Chinese Must Go: Violence, Exclusion, and the Making of the Alien in America*. Harvard University Press (2018)

70. 《苦力诉说：在古巴的中国契约劳工与非洲奴隶》Lisa Yun, *The Coolie Speaks: Chinese Indentured Laborers and African Slaves in Cuba* (Asian American History & Cultue). Temple University Press (2008)

71. 《1800年至今在英国的中国人：经济、跨国与身份》Gregor Benton（班国瑞）, Edmund Terence Gomez, *The Chinese in Britain, 1800-present: Economy, Transnationalism, Identity*. Palgrave Macmillan (2008)

72. 《他者中的华人：中国近现代移民史》Philip A. Kuhn（孔飞力）, *Chinese Among Others: Emigration in Modern Times* (State & Society in East Asia). Rowman & Littlefield Publishers (2008)

73. 《棉花地的筷子：密西西比三角洲中国杂货商的生活》John Jung（劳思源）, *Chopsticks in the Land of Cotton: Lives of Mississippi Delta Chinese Grocers*. Yin & Yang Press (2008)

74. 《南方的炒饭：在深入南方的中国洗衣店生活》John Jung（劳思源）, *Southern Fried Rice: Life in a Chinese Laundry in the Deep South*. Yin & Yang Press (2008)

75. 《超越唐人街：中国新移民与全球扩张》Mette Thuno, *Beyond Chinatown: New Chinese Migration And the Global Expansion of China* (Nias Studies in Asian Topics).Nordic Inst of Asian Studies (2007)

76. 《中国移民与国际主义》Gregor Benton（班国瑞）, *Chinese Migrants and Internationalism*.

Routledge (2007)

77. 《弥天大谎：白色澳洲的华裔澳大利亚人》John Fitzgerald（费约翰）, *Big White Lie: Chinese Australians in White Australia*. University of New South Wales Press (2007)

78. 《在美国出生的中国人》（漫画书）Gene Luen Yang, *American Born Chinese*. First Second (2006)

79. 《美国华人之声：从淘金热至今》Judy Yung, Gordon Chang, Him Mark Lai (Editors), *Chinese American Voices: From the Gold Rush to the Present*. University of California Press (2006)

80. 《苦力与甘蔗：解放时代的种族、劳力和食糖》Moon-Ho Jung, *Coolies and Cane: Race, Labor, and Sugar in the Age of Emancipation*. The Johns Hopkins University Press (2006)

81. 《中国文化的全球空间：美国和德国的流散华人社区》Sylvia Van Ziegert, *Global Spaces of Chinese Culture: Diasporic Chinese Communities in the United States and Germany* (Asian Americans: Reconceptualizing Culture, History, Politics). Routledge (2006)

82. 《美国华人跨国主义：排华时期中美两国间的人员、资源和思想流动》Sucheng Chan, *Chinese American Transnationalism: The Flow of People, Resources, and Ideas between China and America During the Exclusion Era*. Temple University Press (2005)

83. 《美国人优先：美国华人和二战》K. Scott Wong, *Americans First: Chinese Americans and the Second World War*. Harvard University Press (2005)

84. 《亚裔美国人研究指南》Kent A. Ono, *A companion to Asian American studies*. Blackwell Publishing (2005)

85. 《中国移民》Michael Teitelbaum, *Chinese Immigrants (to the US)*. Facts On File (2005)

86. 《一个中国家庭的跨国史：移民信件、家族企业和反向移民》Haiming Liu, *The Transnational History of a Chinese Family: Immigrant Letters, Family Business, And Reverse Migration*. Rutgers University Press (2005)

87. 《祝好运：美国华人庆典和文化基本指南》Rosemary Gong, *Good Luck Life: The Essential Guide to Chinese American Celebrations and Culture*. Harper Paperbacks (2005)

88. 《中国移民》Michael Teitelbaum, Robert Asher, *Chinese Immigrants (Immigration to the United States)*. Facts On File, Inc. (2005)

89. 《瘟疫与火焰：对抗黑死病与1900年焚烧檀香山唐人街》James C. Mohr, *Plague and Fire: Battling Black Death and the 1900 Burning of Honolulus Chinatown*. Oxford University Press, USA (2004)

90. 《美国华人史》Iris Chang（张纯如）, *The Chinese in America: A Narrative History*. Viking Adult (2003)

91. 《欧洲唐人街：20世纪90年代海外华人身份探析》Flemming Christiansen, *Chinatown, Europe: An Exploration of Overseas Chinese Identity in the 1990s*. Routledge (2003)

92. 《新世界里的新文化：五四运动与新加坡的中国侨民（1919—1932）》David Kenley, *New Culture in a New World: The May Fourth Movement and the Chinese Diaspora in*

Singapore, 1919—1932. Routledge (2003)

93. 《唐人街的上帝：纽约移民社区演进中的宗教与生存》Kenneth Guest, *God in Chinatown: Religion and Survival in New Yorks Evolving Immigrant Community* (Religion, Race, and Ethnicity).New York University Press (2003)

94. 《中国海外移民：华人移民的文化、教育和社会维度》Michael W. Charney, Tong Chee Kiong, Brenda S. A. Yeoh, *Chinese Migrants Abroad: Cultural, Educational, and Social Dimensions of the Chinese Diaspora*.World Scientific Publishing Co Pte Ltd (2003)

95. 《亚洲移民与教育：移民社会和移民群体之间的教育紧张关系》Wang GungWu（王赓武）(auth.), Michael W. Charney, Brenda S. A. Yeoh, Tong Chee Kiong (eds.), *Asian Migrants and Education: The Tensions of Education in Immigrant Societies and among Migrant Groups*. Springer Science+Business Media Dordrecht (2003)

96. 《温哥华的中国人（1945—1980）：身份和权力的追求》Wing Chung Ng, *The Chinese in Vancouver, 1945—80: The Pursuit of Identity and Power*.UBC Press (2000)

97. 《非洲裔美国人遭遇日本和中国：亚洲的黑色国际主义（1895—1945）》Marc S. Gallicchio, *The African American Encounter with Japan and China: Black Internationalism in Asia, 1895—1945*. UNC Press Books (2000)

98. 《全球民族聚集：美国社会的唐人街、日本城和马尼拉城》Michel S. Laguerre, *Global Ethnopolis: Chinatown, Japantown and Manilatown in American Society*.Palgrave Macmillan UK (2000)

99. 《孤儿与勇士：创立华裔美国文化与身份》Gloria Heyung Chun, *Of Orphans and Warriors: Inventing Chinese American Culture and Identity*. Rutgers University Press (2000)

100. 《海外华人：从乡土中国到寻求自治》Wang Gungwu（王赓武）, *The Chinese Overseas: From Earthbound China to the Quest for Autonomy* (The Edwin O. Reischauer Lectures). Harvard University Press (2000)

101. 《东方人：流行文化中的亚裔美国人》Robert Lee, *Orientals: Asian Americans in Popular Culture*. Philadelphia Temple University Press (1999)

102. 《我们需要两个世界：西方社会的中国移民协会》Minghuan Li, *We Need Two Worlds: Chinese Immigrant Associations in a Western Society*.Amsterdam University Press (1999)

103. 《解缚的声音：旧金山中国妇女历史纪录片》Judy Yung, *Unbound Voices: A Documentary History of Chinese Women in San Francisco*. University of California Press (1999)

104. 《在美国大门口：排外时代的中国移民（1882—1943）》Erika Lee（李艾轲）, *At America's Gates: Chinese Immigration during the Exclusion Era, 1882—1943*.University of California, Berkeley (1998); The University of North Carolina Press (2003)

105. 《海外华人的半个世纪》Elizabeth Sinn, *The Last Half Century of Chinese Overseas*. Hong Kong University Press (1998)

106. 《重建唐人街：少数民族飞地与全球变迁》Jan Lin, *Reconstructing Chinatown: Ethnic

Enclave, Global Change. University of Minnesota Press (1998)

107. 《自称美国：排斥时代的华裔身份建构》Kevin Scott Wong, *Claiming America: Constructing Chinese American Identities During the Exclusion Era.* Temple University Press (1998)

108. 《西印度群岛的中国人（1806—1995）：文献史》Walton Look Lai, Walton Look Lai, *The Chinese in the West Indies, 1806—1995: A Documentary History.* The Press University of the West Indies (1998)

109. 《中国人在欧洲》Gregor Benton（班国瑞）, Frank N. Pieke（彭轲）(eds.), *The Chinese in Europe.* Palgrave Macmillan UK (1998)

110. 《一个中国人的机遇：在洛基山矿业一线的华人》Liping Zhu, *A Chinaman's Chance: The Chinese on the Rocky Mountain Mining Frontier.* University Press of Colorado (1997)

111. 《作为东南亚人的华人》Leo Suryadinata (eds.), *Ethnic Chinese as Southeast Asians.* Palgrave Macmillan US (1997)

112. 《中国移民与中国大陆：新兴经济合作体》Constance Lever-Tracy, David Ip, Noel Tracy, *The Chinese Diaspora and Mainland China: An Emerging Economic Synergy.* Palgrave Macmillan UK (1996)

113. 《唐人街帮派：勒索、企业以及犯罪和公共政策中的种族研究》Ko-lin Chin, *Chinatown Gangs: Extortion, Enterprise, and Ethnicity Studies in Crime and Public Policy.* Oxford University Press (1995)

114. 《金山上：我的华裔美国家庭百年之旅》Lisa See, *On Gold Mountain: The One-Hundred-Year Odyssey of My Chinese-American Family.* Vintage (1996)

115. 《法严于虎：中国移民与现代移民法的形成》Lucy E. Salyer, *Laws Harsh As Tigers: Chinese Immigrants and the Shaping of Modern Immigration Law* (Studies in Legal History). University of North Carolina Press (1995)

116. 《第一郊区唐人街：加利福尼亚州蒙特利公园的重建》Timothy Fong, *The First Suburban Chinatown: The Remaking of Monterey Park, California.* Temple University Press (1994)

117. 《古巴委员会报告：华人在古巴不为人知的历史（1876年英文原文）》Denise Helly, *The Cuba Commission Report: A Hidden History of the Chinese in Cuba. The Original English-Language Text of 1876.* The Johns Hopkins University Press (1993)

118. 《东南亚侨汇（1910—1940）》George L. Hicks, *Overseas Chinese Remittances from Southeast Asia, 1910—1940.* Select Books Pte Ltd (1993)

119. 《唐人街：城市飞地的社会经济潜力》Min Zhou, *Chinatown: The Socioeconomic Potential of an Urban Enclave.* Temple University Press (1992)

120. 《拯救中国，拯救自己：纽约华人手工洗衣联盟》Renqiu Yu, *To Save China, to Save Ourselves: The Chinese Hand Laundry Alliance of New York.* Temple University Press (1992)

121. 《美国的排华运动（1863—1892）》（硕士论文）Frank Pinon Barajas, *Chinese Exclusion in the United States, 1868—1892.* Thesis for the Degree of Master of Arts in

History, California State University, Fresno (1991)

122.《白人的省份：1858至1914年不列颠哥伦比亚省的政治家与中国、日本移民》Patricia Roy, *A White Man's Province: British Columbia Politicians and Chinese and Japanese Immigrants, 1858—1914*. University of British Columbia Press (1989)

123.《慷慨的面容：巴布亚新几内亚华人的人格与贸易观念》Margaret Willson, *The Generous Face: Concepts of Personhood and Trade among the Papua New Guinea Chinese*. London School of Economics and Political Science (1989)

124.《华女阿五》（此书曾出版于1945, 1948, 1950, 1978）Jade Snow Wong（黄玉雪）, Kathryn Uhl, *Fifth Chinese Daughter*. University of Washington Press (1989)

125.《唐人街：加拿大的城中城》David Chuenyan Lai, *Chinatowns: Towns Within Cities in Canada*. University of British Columbia Press (1988)

126.《第二次世界大战以来东南亚华人身份的变化》Jennifer W. Cushman, Wang Gungwu（王赓武）(eds.), *Changing Identities of the Southeast Asian Chinese since World War II*. Hong Kong University Press (1988)

127.《南加州华裔的娱乐与体育》Lynne Emery, *Games and Sport of Southern California's Chinese-Americans*. Paper Presented at the Annual Convention of the American Alliance for Health, Physical Education, Recreation and Dance (1984)

128.《北京、河内与华侨》Pao-min Chang, *Beijing, Hanoi, and the overseas Chinese*. University of California, Berkeley, Center for Chinese Studies (1982)

129.《德兰士瓦的中国矿工》Peter Richardson, *Chinese Mine Labour in the Transvaal*. Palgrave Macmillan UK (1982)

130.《木兰花中的莲花：密西西比华人》Robert Seto Quan, Julian B. Roebuck, *Lotus Among the Magnolias: The Mississippi Chinese*. University Press of Mississippi (1982)

131.《南洋来的中国资本家：中国近代海外华人企业（1893—1911）》Michael R. Godley, *The Mandarin-Capitalists from Nanyang: Overseas Chinese Enterprise in the Modernisation of China 1893—1911*. Cambridge University Press (1981, 2002)

132.《儿童书中的亚裔美国人》Council on Interracial Books for Children, *Asian Americans in Children's Books*. Interracial Books for Children Bulletin (1976)

133.《亚裔美国人的过去、现在与未来》Natalie Isser, *Asian Americans: Then, Now, and Tomorrow*. Paper presented at World Educators Conference on Multicultural Education (Honolulu, Hawaii) (1976)

134.《亚洲人在美国：精选参考文献注释书目》T. K. Tong, Robert Wu, *Asians in America: An Annotated Bibliography of Selected Reference Works* (Bibliography prepared by the Curriculum Development Program in Comparative Ethnicity Project). City Coll. Research Foundation, New York, NY (1975)

135.《华人在美生活及其影响（1776—1960）》Chinese Historical SoCiety of America, San

Francisco, Calif., *The Life, Influence and the Role of the Chinese in the United States, 1776—1960. Proceedings of the National Conference Held at the University of San Francisco July 10, 11, 12, 1975*. Department of Health, Education, and Welfare, Washington, D.C. (1975)

136. 《美国华人故事》Mel Jue, San Francisco Unified School District, CA. Chinese Bilingual Pilot Program, *The Story of the Chinese in America*. ERIC Clearinghouse (1974)

137. 《关于美国亚洲人的专题论文/学位论文：附其他海外亚洲人的选择参考》Paul M. Ong, William Wong Lum, *Theses and Dissertations on Asians in the United States: With Selection References to Other Overseas Asians*. Asian American Studies, Department of Applied Behavioral Sciences, University of California, Davis, California (1974)

138. 《美国的亚洲人：精选书目》Isao Fujimoto, Michiyo Yamaguchi Swift and Rosalie Zucker, *Asians in America: A Selected Annotated Bibliography*. University of California, Davis. Asian American Research Project. Working publication; no. 5. (1971)

139. 《美国的亚洲人：社会工作教育中使用的精选书目》Harry H. L. Kitano, *Asians in America: A Selected Bibliography for Use in Social Work Education*. New York: Council on Social Work Education (1971)

140. 《美国黑人、印度裔美国人、墨西哥裔美国人和亚裔美国人对美国历史的贡献》*Contributions of Black Americans, Indian Americans, Mexican Americans and Asian Americans to American History*. Santa Clara County Office of Education, San Jose, Calif. (1970)

141. 《不受欢迎的移民：1785—1882年美国华人形象》Stuart Creighton Miller, *The Unwelcome Immigrant: The American image of the Chinese, 1785—1882*. Berkeley: University of California Press (1969)

142. 《中国人在柬埔寨》William Willmott, *The Chinese in Cambodia* University of British Columbia (1967)

143. 《美国人和中国人：历史文章与参考书目》Kwang-Ching Liu, *Americans and Chinese: A Historical Essay and a Bibliography*. Cambridge: Harvard University Press (1963)

144. 《泰国华人社会史》G. William Skinner（施坚雅）, *Chinese Society in Thailand: An Analytical History*. Cornell University Press (1957)

145. 《美国在远东的记录（1945—1951）》Kenneth Scott Latourette（赖德烈）, *The American Record in the Far East, 1945—1951*. The Macmillan Company (1954)

146. 《国务院对华文化交流的援助》Willys R. Peck, *State Department Aid to Cultural Exchange with China*. Washington, DC; Government Printing Office (1944)

147. 《加州的反华运动》Elmer Clarence Sandmeyer, *The Anti-Chinese Movement in California* University of Illinois Press, Urbana (1939)

148. 《广州"番鬼"录》William C. Hunter, *The 'Fan Kwae' at Canton before Treaty Days, 1825—1844*. Shanghai, China, The Oriental Affairs (1938)

149. 《唐人街：共生与同化研究》（博士论文）Ching Chao Wu, *Chinatowns: A Study of*

Symbiosis and Assimilation. Ph. D. Dissertation, The University of Chicago (1928)

150.《旧中国点滴》（介绍旧金山唐人街）Charles Warren Stoddard, *A Bit of Old China*.H. S. Crocker Company, San Francisco (1925)

151.《唐人街故事》Sax Rohmer, *Tales of Chinatown*. Garden City, N.Y.: Doubleday, Page (1922)

152.《中国移民》Mary Roberts Coolidge, *Chinese Immigration*.H. Holt and Co., New York (1909)

153.《老唐人街照片》Will Irwin, *Pictures of Old Chinatown*.Moffat, Yard and Company, New York (1908)

154.《美国华人豁免阶层的处理》Ng Poon Chew, *The Treatment of the Exempt Classes of Chinese in the United States*. A Statement from the Chinese to America, San Francisco, California (1908)

155.《肉与米：美国男子气概对抗亚洲苦力。哪个能存活？》Samual Compers, Herman Gutstadt, *Meat vs. Rice: American Manhood against Aasitic Coolieism. Which Shall Survive?* American Federation of Labor, Asiatic Exclusion League (1902, 1908)

156.《唐人街素描十图》Ernest C. Peixotto, Robert Howe Fletcher, *Ten Drawings in Chinatown*. A. M. Robertson, San Francisco (1898)

157.《中国移民：社会和经济层面》George Frederick Seward, *Chinese Immigration in its Social and Economic Aspects*. Charles Scribner's Sons, New York (1881)

158.《旧金山的中国人》Willard B. Farwell, John E. Kunkler, *Chinese in San Francisco*. San Francisco Municipal Reports. San Francisco: Published by Order of the Board of Supervisors (1885)

159.《加州华人：旧金山华人生活及其习惯、道德和举止》G. B. Densmore, *The Chinese in California: Description of Chinese Life in San Francisco, Their Habits, Morals and Manners*. Pettit & Russ, San Francisco (1880)

160.《中国移民：1879年9月10日在萨拉托加社会科学协会上宣读的论文》Samuel Wells Williams（卫三畏）, *Chinese Immigration: A Paper Read before the Social Science Association, at Saratoga, September 10, 1879*. New York: Charles Scribner's Sons (1879)

161.《唐人在金山》Otis Gibson, *The Chinese in America*.Cincinnati: Hitchcock & Walden (1877)

162.《加利福尼亚华人问题的另一面：对中国人指控的答复》Augustus Layres, *The Other Side of the Chinese Question in California: or A Reply to the Charges Against the Chinese*. Taylor & Nevin (1876)

163.《中国移民：其社会、道德和政治效应。向加利福尼亚州参议院中国移民特别委员会提交的报告》*Chinese Immigration: Its Social, Moral, and Political Effect. Report to the California State Senate of its Special Committee on Chinese Immigration*. California Legislature and Senate. (1878)

164.《从中国立场看中国问题》Yong Lai, Kay Yang, Yup A., Foon Lai, Leong Chung, *The Chinese Question from a Chinese Standpoint*. Cubery & Co. Printers, San Francisco (1874)

165.《中国人为什么移民，他们为到达美国而采取的手段，以及旅游素描、娱乐事件和社会习俗》Russell H Conwell, *Why the Chinese Emigrate, and the Means they Adopt for the Purpose of Reaching America, with Sketches of Travel, Amusing Incidents, Social Customs*. Boston: Lee, Shepard and Dillingham (1871)

166. 《关于赞成移民的论点：附移民协会建议措施的解释》*Arguments in Favor of Immigration, with an Explanation of the Measures Recommended by the Immigrant Union*. Published by the California Immigrant Union (1870)

167. 《致加州立法机关谦卑的恳求：代表中华帝国来美移民》William Speer, *A Humble Plea, Addressed to the Legislature of California, in Behalf of the Immigrants from the Empire of China to This State*. San Francisco, California: Office of the Oriental (1856)

12. 中国研究参考

12.1 中国学研究

1. 《殖民遗产与当代中国研究及中国性：忘却二元对立，制定自我策略》Chih-Yu Shih（石之瑜），Prapin Manomaivibool（巴萍），Mariko Tanigaki, Swaran Singh (Editor), *Colonial Legacies and Contemporary Studies of China and Chineseness: Unlearning Binaries, Strategizing Self*. World Scientific Pub Co Inc (2020)

2. 《菲律宾的中国研究：知识路径与研究领域的形成》(Routledge Contemporary China) Chih-yu Shih（石之瑜）(editor), Tina S. Clemente (editor), *China Studies in the Philippines: Intellectual Paths and the Formation of a Field*. Routledge (2019)

3. 《SAGE当代中国手册》Weiping Wu, Mark Frazier (eds.), *The SAGE Handbook of Contemporary China*. 2 Volumes. SAGE Publications Ltd (2018)

4. 《重塑当代中国研究方法论："一点"理论再审视》Peter Kien-hong YU, *Reinventing the Methodology of Studying Contemporary China: Retesting the One-dot Theory*. Springer Singapore (2017)

5. 《汉学家日语：词汇与翻译阅读入门》Joshua A. Fogel（傅佛果），Fumiko Joo, *Japanese for Sinologists: A Reading Primer with Glossaries and Translations*. University of California Press (2017)

6. 《北美民国研究档案资源指要》Chengzhi Wang（王成志），Su Chen（陈肃），*Archival Resources of Republican China in North America*. New York: Columbia University Press (2016)

7. 《全球化视角下的中国研究》Xiaohong Zhou, Translated by Zhang Daozhen, *Chinese Studies from the Perspective of Globalization*. Paths International Ltd. (2016)

8. 《荷兰中国学：过去、现在和未来》Wilt Idema, *Chinese Studies in the Netherlands: Past, Present and Future*. Brill (2014)

9. 《卜德中国文明论文集》Derk Bodde（卜德），edited by Charles Leblanc, *Essays on Chinese Civilization*. Princeton University Press (2014)

10. 《北美中国研究综述》Haihui zhang（张海惠），zhaohui Xue, Shuyong Jiang, Gary Lance Lugar (Eds), A Scholarly Review of Chinese Studies in North America. Association for Asian Studies (2013)

11. 《北美中国研究学者英中姓名对照》Haihui Zhang（张海惠），Zhaohui Xue, Shuyong Jiang, and Gary Lance Lugar, *English/Chinese Comparison Table for Names of Chinese Studies Scholars*. In *A Scholarly Review of Chinese Studies in North America*, Association for Asian

Studies (AAS) (2013). The latest version of this item is by 14 Nov 2017.

12. 《中美学术图书馆关于教学、政府文件和外联的比较研究》Hanrong Wang and Bethany Latham, *Academic Libraries in the US and China: Comparative Studies of Instruction, Government Documents, and Outreach*. Chandos (2013)

13. 《现代亚洲研究》Arthur Lewis Rosenbaum, C. Shackle, C. Shackle, Peter Robb, Robert A. Huttenback, Justus M. Van Der Kroef, Mischa Titiev, Alastair Lamb, *Modern Asian Studies* (Assortment). Cambridge University Press (2012)

14. 《未了中国缘：一部自传》John Paton Davies, *China Hand: An Autobiography*. Philadelphia: University of Pennsylvania Press (2012)

15. 《中国观察家：北京汤姆的自白》Richard Baum（包瑞嘉）, *China Watcher: Confessions of A Peking Tom*.University of Washington Press (2010)

16. 《大学的中国研究：澳大利亚与英国的比较案例研究》Chia-Mei JaneCoughlan, *The Study of China in Universities: A Comparative Case Study of Australia and the United Kingdom*. Amherst, N.Y.: Cambria Press (2008)

17. 《中国社会科学院：塑造改革、学术界与中国（1977—2003）》Margaret Sleeboom-Faulkner, *The Chinese Academy of Social Sciences (CASS): Shaping the Reforms, Academia and China (1977—2003)*. Koninklijke Brill NV, Leiden, the Netherlands (2007)

18. 《普林斯顿大学：当代中国书目（2007—2008）》Lubna Malik, Lynn White（白霖）, *Contemporary China: A Book List*. Princeton University (2007—2008)

19. 《中国观察：来自欧洲、日本和美国观点》Robert Ash, David Shambaugh（沈大伟）, Seiichiro Takagi, *China Watching: Perspectives from Europe, Japan and the United States* (Routledge Contemporary China). Routledge (2006)

20. 《在中国做田野调查》Maria Heimer, *Doing Fieldwork in China*.University of Hawaii Press (2006)

21. 《比较研究的可比性问题》（专集）Xudong Zhang, Marilyn Ivy, Michael Dutton, *Problems of Comparability: Possibilities for Comparative Studies*. Special Issue of Boundary 2, Duke University Press (2005)

22. 《焚香膜拜：汉学先驱与中国古典语文学的发展》David B. Honey, *Incense at the Altar: Pioneering Sinologists and the Development of Classical Chinese Philology* (American Oriental Series v. 86) New Haven: American Oriental Society (2001)

23. 《美国国会图书馆亚洲收藏指南》Library of Congress, *Asian Collections: An Illustrated Guide*. Washington (2000)

24. 《中国观察趋势：中华人民共和国50年》*Trends in China Watching: Observing the PRC at 50*. Washington, D.C.: The Sigur Center for Asian Studies, George Washington University (1999)

25. 《中国访问：中国学术生活和工作指南（第二版）》Anne F. Thurston with Karen Turner-Gottschang and Linda A. Reed; Committee on Scholarly Communication with China, American

Council of Learned Societies, National Academy of Sciences, Social Science Research Council, *China Bound, Revised: A Guide to Academic Life and Work in the PRC* (CSCPRC Report). Washington, D.C.: National Academy Press (1994)

26. 《美国当代中国学》David Shambaugh（沈大伟）, *American Studies of Contemporary China*. Woodrow Wilson International Center for Scholars (1993)

27. 《英语世界的中国研究：精选参考书目》Zongxun Na, *Chinese Studies in English: A Selected Bibliography of Books* (AICS bibliographical series; no. 1).American Institute of Chinese Studies (1991)

28. 《中国研究》Stephen Quirke, *Middle Kingdom Studies*. SIA Publishing (1991)

29. 《费正清与美国对现代中国的理解》Paul M. Evans, *John Fairbank and the American Understanding of Modern China*. New York: B. Blackwell (1988)

30. 《中国访问：中国学术生活和工作指南（第一版）》Karen Turner-Gottschang with Linda A. Reed, for the Committee on Scholarly Communication with the People's Republic of China, *China Bound: A Guide to Academic Life and Work in the PRC*. Washington, D.C.: National Academy Press (1987)

31. 《中国社会科学与人文学科的新方向》Michael B. Yahuda（亚胡达）(eds.), *New Directions in the Social Sciences and Humanities in China*. Palgrave Macmillan UK (1987)

32. 《中国修辞学：汉学家著作书目选注》Mary Garrett, *Chinese Rhetoric: A Selected, Annotated Bibliography of Works by Sinologists*. ERIC (1987)

33. 《中国学方法论问题》Amy Auerbacher Wilson, Sidney L. Greenblatt, Richard W. Wilson, *Methodological Issues in Chinese Studies*. New York: Praeger (1983)

34. 《中国社会科学与田野调查：田野观察》Anne F. Thurston, Burton Pasternak (ed.), *The Social Sciences and Fieldwork in China: Views from the Field*. Boulder, Colo.: Published by Westview Press for the American Association for the Advancement of Science (1983)

35. 《理解共产主义中国：美国和"中华民国"的中国学（1949—1978）》Tai-Chūn Kuo（郭岱君）, Ramon Hawley Myers（马若孟）, *Understanding Communist China: Communist China studies in the United States and the Republic of China, 1949—1978* (Hoover Press publication). Stanford, Calif.: Hoover Institution Press, Stanford University (1986)

36. 《中国人：现代中国注释书目》Rosemary Griebel, Alberta Educational Communications Corporation; Cultural Development Division, *The Chinese: An Annotated Bibliography on Modern China*. Alberta Library Services Branch (1986)

37. 《国务院在华职责：麦卡锡时代及以后，1933—1977》（谢伟思口述史）John S. Service, *State Department Duty in China, the McCarthy Era, and after, 1933—1977: Oral History Transcript: And Related Material, 1977—1981*. University of California (1981)

38. 《书里的中国：西方语言基本参考书目》Norman E. Tanis, David Perkins, Justine Pinto, *China in Books: A Basic Bibliography in Western Language* (Foundation in library and

information science; v. 4). Greenwich, Conn.: Jai Press (1979)

39. 《中华人民共和国30年综述》Joyce K. Kallgren (ed.), *The People's Republic of China after Thirty Years: An Overview*. Berkeley: Center for Chinese Studies, Institute of East Asian Studies, University of California (1979)

40. 《中国书目解题汇编》Tsuen-hsuin Tsien（钱存训）, *China: An Annotated Bibliography of Bibliographies*. Boston: G. K. Hall (1978)

41. 《美国高校中国学研究评介（1958—1975）》Paul Kwang Tsien Sih（薛光前）, *An Evaluation of Chinese Studies in American Universities and Colleges: 1958—1975*. Saint John's University, Jamaica, NY. Center of Asian Studies. S.l.: Distributed by ERIC Clearinghouse (1978)

42. 《中国资源与课程指南》ArlenePosner, *China: A Resource and Curriculum Guide*. University of Chicago Press (1973)

43. 《关心亚洲学者委员会：在人民共和国内部》Committee of Concerned Asian Scholars, *China! Inside the People's Republic*. Bantam Books (1972)

44. 《了解中国：对美国学术资源的评估：给福特基金会的报告》John M. H. Lindbeck, *Understanding China: An Assessment of American Scholarly Resources. A Report to the Ford Foundation* (Praeger library of Chinese affairs). Praeger (1971)

45. 《中国学平装书目》David Weitzman, *Chinese Studies in Paperback*. Berkeley, Calif.: McCutchan Pub. Co. (1967)

46. 《当代中国研究指南》Peter Berton, Eugene Wu（吴文津）, *Contemporary China: A Research Guide*.Stanford, California: Hoover Institution on War, Revolution, and Peace (1967)

47. 《西方汉学家作者目录》Donald Leslie and Jeremy Davidson, *Author Catalogues of Western Sinologists*.Canberra, Dept. of Far Eastern History, Research School of Pacific Studies, Australian National University (1966)

48. 《美国大学、学院和研究所中文教学与测试：会议报告（一、二）》*The Teaching and Testing of Chinese in American Colleges, Universites, and Institutes: Conference Reports Numbers I and II*. ERIC Clearinghouse (1959; 1960)

49. 《美国大学课程里的中国和日本》Edward C. Carter, *China And Japan in our University Curricula*. The University of Chicago Press (1930)

50. 《推动中国研究》*The Promotion of Chinese Studies*.Washington, D.C.: American Council of Learned Societies Bulletin, Number 10 (1929)

51. 《七年来的中国历史研究》Kenneth Scott Latourette（赖德烈）, *Chinese Historical Studies during the Past Seven Years*. Reprinted from The American Historical Review, Vol. XXVI, No. 4, July, 1921.

52. 《中国研究》Alexander Wylie（伟烈亚力）, *Chinese Researches*. Shanghai (1897)

53. 《东方研究：1888—1894年费城东方俱乐部论文选》Oriental Club of Philadelphia, *Oriental Studies: A Selection of the Papers Read Before the Oriental Club of Philadelphia 1888—*

1894. Boston: Ginn (1894)

12.1.1 汉学家与中国学家

1. 《对中国开放：1981—1982年（中美关系）正常化回忆录》Charlotte Furth（费侠莉），*Opening to China: A Memoir of Normalization, 1981—1982*. Cambria Press (2017)

2. 《马士：海关税务司与中国历史学家》John King Fairbank（费正清），et al., *H. B. Morse, Customs Commissioner and Historian of China*. University Press of Kentucky (2015)

3. 《知识就是快乐：艾思柯传》Lindsay Shen, *Knowledge Is Pleasure: A Life of Florence Ayscough*. Hong Kong University Press (2012)

4. 《激进主义、革命与近代中国改革：莫里斯·迈斯纳纪念文集》Catherine Lynch, Robert B. Marks, Paul G. Pickowicz（毕克伟），*Radicalism, Revolution, and Reform in Modern China: Essays in Honor of Maurice Meisner* (AsiaWorld). Lexington Books (2011)

5. 《中国与20世纪历史使命：个人回忆录》Frederick W. Mote（牟复礼），*China and the Vocation of History in the Twentieth Century: A Personal Memoir*. Princeton, N.J.: East Asian Library Journal in association with Princeton University Press (2010)

6. 《李约瑟：热爱中国的人——一位揭开中国神秘面纱的古怪科学家的神奇故事》Simon Winchester（文思淼），*The Man Who Loved China: The Fantastic Story of the Eccentric Scientist Who Unlocked the Mysteries of the Middle Kingdom*. HarperCollins Publishers (2008)

7. 《中国通回忆录》Tim Clissold（祈立天），*Mr. China: A Memoir*. HarperBusiness (2006)

8. 《王赓武生平与著作》Gregor Benton（班国瑞），Hong Liu (eds.), *Diasporic Chinese Ventures: The Life and Work of Wang Gungwu*. RoutledgeCurzon (2004)

9. 《我生命中的中国：历史学家自己的历史》C. Martin Wilbur（韦慕庭），*China in My Life: A Historian's Own History*. Armonk, N.Y.: M.E. Sharpe (1996)

10. 《纪念费正清》Paul A. Cohen（柯文），Merle Goldman（梅谷）(eds.), *Fairbank Remembered*. Harvard University Press (1992)

11. 《拉铁摩尔与中国的"丢失"》Robert P. Newman, *Owen Lattimore and the Loss of China*. Berkeley: University of California Press (1992)

12. 《蒋介石的美国顾问：欧文·拉铁摩尔回忆录》Compiled by Fujiko Isono（矶野富士子），*China Memoirs: Chiang Kai-shek and the War against Japan*. Tokyo: University of Tokyo Press (1990)

13. 《中国人对自然与社会的看法：纪念卜德》Charles Le Blanc, Susan Blader (eds.), *Chinese Ideas about Nature and Society: Studies in Honour of Derk Bodde*. Hong Kong University Press (1987)

14. 《与中国的五十年不解之缘》John King Fairbank（费正清），*Chinabound: A Fifty-Year Memoir*. New York: Harper & Row (1982)

15. 《莫扎特式历史学家：列文森纪念文集》Maurice Meisner, Rhoads Murphey, *The Mozartian Historian: Essays on the Works of Joseph R. Levenson*. University of California Press (1976)

12.1.2 区域研究

1. 《比较区域研究：方法理论和跨区域应用》Ariel I. Ahram, Patrick Köllner, Rudra Sil, *Comparative Area Studies: Methodological Rationales and Cross-Regional Applications*. Oxford University Press (2018)
2. 《十字路口的区域研究：流动转向后的知识生产》Katja Mielke, Anna-Katharina Hornidge (eds.), *Area Studies at the Crossroads: Knowledge Production after the Mobility Turn*. Palgrave Macmillan US (2017)
3. 《支持区域研究：高校图书馆指南》Lesley Pitman, *Supporting Research in Area Studies: A Guide for Academic Libraries* (Chandos information professional series). Chandos Publishing (2015)
4. 《重建区域研究：跨越亚太地区的教学与学习》Terence Wesley-Smith, Jon Goss, *Remaking Area Studies: Teaching and Learning Across Asia and the Pacific*. University of Hawai'i Press (2010)
5. 《知识政治：区域研究与学科》David L. Szanton, *The Politics of Knowledge: Area Studies and the Disciplines* (Global, Area, & International Archive). University of California Press (2004)
6. 《人权与多样性：重新审视地区研究》David P. Forsythe, Patrice C. McMahon, *Human Rights and Diversity: Area Studies Revisited* (Human Rights in International Perspective). University of Nebraska Press (2004)

12.2 工具书

1. 《明代职官中英辞典》Ying Zhang, Susan Xue, Zhaohui Xue, Li Ni, *Chinese-English Dictionary of Ming Government Official Titles*. Revised Edition. https://escholarship.org/uc/item/2bz3v185 (2018)
2. 《中国经济史词典》(Historical Dictionaries of Asia, Oceania, and the Middle East) Lawrence R. Sullivan, *Historical Dictionary of the Chinese Economy*. Rowman & Littlefield (2018)
3. 《牛津亚洲国际关系手册》Saadia M. Pekkanen, John Ravenhill, Rosemary Foot, *The Oxford Handbook of the International Relations of Asia*. Oxford University Press (2014)
4. 《东亚研究之写作》Michael Radcha, *Student's Guide to Writing in East Asian Studies*. Harvard University (2014)
5. 《美国和中国的学术图书馆》Hanrong Wang and Bethany Latham, *Academic Libraries in the US and China: Comparative Studies of Instruction, Government Documents, and Outreach*. Chandos Publishing (2013)
6. 《亚裔美国文学与戏剧历史辞典》Wenying Xu, *Historical Dictionary of Asian American Literature and Theater* (Historical Dictionaries of Literature and the Arts). Scarecrow Press (2012)
7. 《中国国际关系手册》Shaun Breslin, *Handbook of China's International Relations* (Routledge International Handbooks). Routledge (2010)
8. 《清代名人传略》（第一卷）Arthur W. Hummel（恒慕义）, *Eminent Chinese of the Ch'ing Period, 1644—1912*. Vol. 1. Global Oriental (2010)
9. 《清代名人传略》（第二卷）Arthur W Hummel（恒慕义）, *Eminent Chinese of the Ch'ing*

Period, 1644—1912. Vol. 2. Global Oriental (2010)

10. 《马礼逊藏书目录》The University of Hong Kong Libraries, *Catalogue of the Morrison Collection*. The University of Hong Kong Libraries (2010)

11. 《近代中国大百科全书》David Pong（庞百腾）, *Encyclopedia of Modern China*. Gale, Cengage Learning (2009)

12. 《近代中国历史辞典（1800—1949）》James Z. Gao, *Historical Dictionary of Modern China (1800—1949)*. The Scarecrow Press, Inc. (2009)

13. 《中国中古历史词典》Victor Xiong, *Historical Dictionary of Medieval China*. Scarecrow Press (2009)

14. 《中华全书：跨越历史和现代，审视最新和最古老的全球大国》（五卷本）Linsun Cheng, Kerry Brown（凯瑞·布朗）, *Berkshire Encyclopedia of China, 5-volume set: Modern and Historic Views of the World's Newest and Oldest Global Power*.Berkshire Publishing Group (2009)

15. 《中国中世纪历史词典》Victor Cunrui Xiong, *Historical Dictionary of Medieval China*. Scarecrow Press (2008)

16. 《普林斯顿中国书目》（在线）Lubna Malik and Lynn White, *Princeton China Bibliography*. Winter 2007—2008 Edition. http://www.princeton.edu/~lynn/chinabib.pdf

17. 《后汉至三国传记词典（公元23—220年）》Rafe de Crespigny（张磊夫）, *A Biographical Dictionary of Later Han to the Three Kingdoms (23—220 AD)*. Brill (2007)

18. 《道教百科全书》Fabrizio Pregadio, *Encyclopedia of Taoism*. Routledge (2007)

19. 《中华人民共和国历史词典》Lawrence R. Sullivan, *Historical Dictionary of the People's Republic of China*. The Scarecrow Press, Inc. (2007)

20. 《中国博物馆》Li Xianyao; Luo Zhewen; Martha Avery, *China's Museum*.China Intercontinental Press (2004)

21. 《中国：全球研究手册》Robert Andre LaFleur, *China: A Global Studies Handbook*. ABC-CLIO (2003)

22. 《现代亚洲百科全书：算盘中国》（第一卷）David Levinson, *Encyclopedia of Modern Asia (Vol. 1): Abacus-China*. Charles Scribners & Sons Publishing (2002)

23. 《中国鸟类野外手册》John Mackinnon & Karen Phillipps, *A Field Guide to the Birds of China* (In Chinese and Latin names index). Hunan Education Press (2000)

24. 《秦、前汉、新代传记辞典（公元前221—公元24年）》Michael Loewe（鲁惟一）, *A Biographical Dictionary of the Qin, Former Han and Xin Periods (221 BC-AD 24)*. Brill (2000)

25. 《亚裔美籍名人传》Dorothy Cordova, Stephen S. Fugita, Franklin Ng（吴兆麟）, Jane Singh, Hyung-chan Kim, *Distinguished Asian Americans: A Biographical Dictionary*. Greenwood Press (1999)

26. 《中国历史手册》Endymion Wlkinson（魏根深）, *Chinese History: A Manual*. Harvard-Yenching Institute (1998)

27. 《中国图书馆与图书馆事业》Sharon Lin, *Libraries and Librarianship in China*. Greenwood (1998)
28. 《中华人民共和国政治词典》Colin Mackerras（马克林）, Donald H. McMillen, Andrew Watson（安德鲁·沃森）, *Dictionary of the Politics of the People's Republic of China*. Routledge (1998)
29. 《中国大百科：历史与文化》Dorothy Perkins, *Encyclopedia of China: History and Culture*. Routledge (1998)
30. 《中华人民共和国历史辞典》Lawrence R. Sullivan（沙利文）& Nancy R. Hearst, *Historical Dictionary of the People's Republic of China*. The Scarecrow Press, Inc. (1997)
31. 《世界文化百科全书：俄罗斯与欧亚大陆/中国》（第六卷）David Levinson, *Encyclopedia of World Cultures: Volume VI: Russia And Eurasia/China*. G.K. Hall & Company (1994)
32. 《中国古代文献书目指南》Michael Loewe（鲁惟一）, *Early Chinese Texts: A Bibliographical Guide*. The society for the study of early China (1993)
33. 《世界文化百科全书：东南亚和东亚》（第五卷）David Levinson, *Encyclopedia of World Cultures: Southeast and East Asia, Vol. 5*. G.K. Hall & Company (1993)
34. 《中国文化象征词典：中国生活与思想中的隐性符号》Wolfram Eberhard（艾伯华）, Translated from the German by G. L. Campbell, *A Dictionary of Chinese Symbols: Hidden Symbols in Chinese Life and Thought*. Routledge (1986)
35. 《中华帝国官职辞典》Charles Hucker, *A Dictionary of Officials Titles in Imperial China*. Stanford: Stanford University Press (1985)
36. 《东汉声训手册》W. South Coblin, *A Handbook of Eastern Han Sound Glosses*. The Chinese University of Hong Kong (1983)
37. 《今日中国百科全书》（修订和扩大版）Fredric M. Kaplan, Julian M. Sobin, *Encyclopedia of China Today, Revised and Expanded*. Eurasia Press, Inc. (1982)
38. 《袁同礼中国艺术及考古西文文献书目》Harrie A. Vanderstappen（范德本）, *The T. L. Yuan Bibliography of Western Writings on Chinese Art and Archaeology*. London Mansell (1975)
39. 《中国佛教术语词典：附梵语和英语对应词，梵文—巴利文索引》William Edward Soothill（苏慧廉）, Lewis Hodous（何乐益）, *A Dictionary of Chinese Buddhist Terms: With Sanskrit and English Equivalents and a Sanskrit-Pali Index*. Routledge (1937, 2004)
40. 《中国名人录：中国领导人传记》*Who's who in China: Biographies of Chinese Leaders*. 5th ed. Shanghai: The China Weekly Review (1936)
41. 《中国名人录：包含中国最知名的政治、金融、商业和专业人士的图片和传记》*Who's Who in China: Containing the Pictures and Biographies of China's Best Known Political, Financial, Business and Professional Men*. Third edition. Shanghai: The China Weekly Review (1925)
42. 《中国百佳图书：英文图书调查清单》Frederick Wells Williams, *The Best Hundred Books on China: A Finding List of Books in English*. New Haven, Conn., Yale University Library (1924)

43. 《纽约华人名录》Warner Montagnie Van Norden, *Who's Who of the Chinese in New York*. New York (1918)
44. 《中文引语手册："成语考"翻译，附中文文本、笔记、解释和方便参考的索引》J. H. Stewart Lockhart, *A manual of Chinese quotations: Being A Translation of the Ch'eng Yu K'Ao*（成語考）*with the Chinese Text, Notes, Explanations and an Index for Easy Reference*. Kelly&Walsh, limited (1903)
45. 《中国政府：分类整理、注释、带附录的中国职位手册》William Frederick Mayers（梅辉立）, *The Chinese government: A Manual of Chinese Titles, Categorically Arranged and Explained, with an Appendix*. Kelly and Walsh, Limited (1897)

12.2.1 传记回忆录

1. 《再评袁世凯》(Contemporary Chinese Studies) Patrick Fuliang Shan, *Yuan Shikai: A Reappraisal*. UBC Press (2018)
2. 《平如美棠：我俩的故事》Rao Pingru (author), Nicky Harman (translator), *Our Story: A Memoir of Love and Life in China*. Pantheon Books (2018)
3. 《我的中国少年生活》(Customs and Cultures of the World) Jim Whiting, Shi Yu Li, *My Teenage Life in China*. Mason Crest Publishers (2017)
4. 《上苍之礼：一个中国西北少年的成长故事》Yang Jialiang（杨佳亮）, *A Gift from the Gods: Boyhood in Northwest China*. Asian Highlands Perspectives (AHP) (2017)
5. 《蒋介石及其时代：新的历史和史学视角》Laura De Giorgi & Guido Samarani, *Chiang Kai-shek and His Time: New Historical and Historiographical Perspectives*. Edizioni Ca' Foscari (2017)
6. 《漂移的中国人：跨越太平洋的幻想与失败》（描述中国知识分子蒋希曾坎坷一生）Hua Hsu, H. T. Tsiang, *A floating Chinaman: Fantasy and Failure across the Pacific*. Harvard University Press (2016)
7. 《中国头号通缉犯：我从科学家到国家公敌的历程》Fang Lizhi（方励之）, Perry Link（林培瑞）, *The Most Wanted Man in China: My Journey from Scientist to Enemy of the State*. Henry Holt and Co. (2016)
8. 《蒋介石传》Emily Hahn（项美丽）, *Chiang Kai-Shek: An Unauthorized Biography*. Open Road Media (2015)
9. 《毕竟是书生：周一良回忆录（1913—2001）》Zhou Yiliang, Joshua A. Fogel（傅佛果）, *Just a Scholar: The Memoirs of Zhou Yiliang (1913—2001)*. Boston: Brill (2014)
10. 《宋氏三姐妹》May-ling Soong Chiang, Emily Hahn（项美丽）, Qingling Song, Ai-ling Soong, *The Soong Sisters*. Open Road Media (2014)
11. 《潘先生》Emily Hahn（项美丽）, *Mr. Pan: A Memoir*. Open Road Media (2014)
12. 《一九二七年底回忆》Zhu Qihua〔朱其华, auth.), translated by Zhu Hong, foreword by John T. Ma, edited with an introduction by Doug Merwin, *China 1927: Memoir of a Debacle*. MerwinAsia (2013)

13. 《唐太宗李世民：使中国成为亚洲最伟大帝国的皇帝》Hing Ming Hung, *Li Shi Min, Emperor Taizong of the Tang Dynasty: The Emperor Who Made China the Greatest Empire in Asia*. Algora Publishing (2013)
14. 《张学良：从未战斗的将军》Aron Shai, *Zhang Xueliang: The General Who Never Fought*. Palgrave Macmillan UK (2012)
15. 《我在中国长大》Savannah Grace, *Sihpromatum: I Grew My Boobs in China*. Sihpromatum Publishing House (2012)
16. 《吴庆瑞论中国文选》Yongnian Zheng（郑永年），John Wong（黄朝翰），*Goh Keng Swee on China: Selected Essays*. World Scientific Publishing Company (2012)
17. 《在中国大受欢迎：我不可思议的冒险——养家庭，玩蓝调，在北京成为明星》Alan Paul, *Big in China: My Unlikely Adventures: Raising a Family, Playing the Blues, and Becoming a Star in Beijing*. Harper Collins Publishers Ltd. (2011)
18. 《蒋介石最后一位驻莫斯科大使：傅秉常战时日记》Yee Wah Foo, *Chiang Kaishek's Last Ambassador to Moscow: The Wartime Diaries of Fu Bingchang*. Palgrave Macmillan, London (2011)
19. 《社会主义好！新中国工人回忆录》Lijia Zhang（张丽佳），*Socialism Is Great! A Worker's Memoir of the New China*. Anchor Books (2011)
20. 《太后与我》Edmund Backhouse, Derek Sandhaus, *Décadence Mandchoue: The China Memoirs of Sir Edmund Trelawny Backhouse*. Earnshaw Books (2011)
21. 《中国末代皇帝溥仪自传》Henry Pu Yi, Paul Kramer, *The Last Manchu: The Autobiography of Henry Pu Yi, Last Emperor of China*. Skyhorse Publishing (2010)
22. 《中国见证人：沉默一代的声音》（口述史）Xinran（薛欣然），*China Witness: Voices from a Silent Generation*. Random House (2010)
23. 《从菩提伽耶到拉萨到北京：舍利弗子的生活和时代（1335—1426），菩提伽耶最后的住持》Arthur Philip McKeown, *From Bodhgaya to Lhasa to Beijing: The Life and Times of Sariputra (c. 1335—1426), last abbot of Bodhgaya* (A dissertation presented). Harvard University (2010)
24. 《帝国军阀：曹操传记（公元155—220年）》(Sinica Leidensia 99) Rafe de Crespigny（张磊夫），*Imperial Warlord: A Biography of Cao Cao, 155—220 AD*. Brill Academic Publishers (2010)
25. 《郑观应：晚清商人改革家及其对经济、政治、社会的影响》Guo Wu, *Zheng Guanying: Merchant Reformer of Late Qing China and His Influence on Economics, Politics, and Society*. Cambria Press (2010)
26. 《苦海：毛泽东之前的中国时代》Charles N. Li, *The Bitter Sea: Coming of Age in a China before Mao*. HarperCollins Publishers (2009)
27. 《历史学家吴晗：中国时代之子》Mary G. Mazur, *Wu Han, Historian: Son of China's Times*. Lexington Books (2009)
28. 《英若诚自传：水流云在》Ying Ruocheng, Claire Conceison, *Voices Carry: Behind Bars and*

Backstage during China's Revolution and Reform. Rowman & Littlefield Publishers (2009)

29. 《从黑乡到红色中国：一个女孩从战争蹂躏的英国到革命中国的故事》Esther Cheo Ying, *Black Country to Red China: One Girl's Story from War-torn England to Revolutionary China*. Vintage Books (2009)

30. 《莫理循中国生活历险记》Peter Thompson, Robert Macklin, *The Life and Adventures of Morrison of China*. Allen & Unwin (2008)

31. 《毛泽东的得力助手：从哈佛校园到天安门广场，我在中国外交部的生涯》Chaozhu Ji（冀朝铸）, *The man on Mao's Right: from Harvard Yard to Tiananmen Square, My Life inside China's Foreign Ministry*. Random House (2008)

32. 《易卜生与现代中国》He Chengzhou, *Ibsen and Modern China*. University of Turin (2007)

33. 《回家记》Yi-Fu Tuan（段义孚）, *Coming Home to China*. University of Minnesota Press (2007)

34. 《中国教训：五位同学与新中国的故事》John Pomfret（潘文）, *Chinese Lessons: Five Classmates and the Story of the New China*. Henry Holt and Co. (2007)

35. 《穿越白色恐怖之旅：女儿回忆录》Kang-i Sun Chang（孙康宜）, Matthew Towns, *Journey Through the White Terror: A Daughter's Memoir*. National Taiwan University Press (2006)

36. 《梦醒子：一位华北乡居者的生平（1857—1942）》Henrietta Harrison（沈艾娣）, *The Man Awakened from Dreams: One Man's Life in a North China Village, 1857—1942*. Stanford University Press (2005)

37. 《成长于人民共和国：两个中国革命女儿的对话》Ye Weili（叶维丽）, Ma Xiaodong（马笑冬）, *Growing Up in The People's Republic: Conversations between Two Daughters of China's Revolution*. Palgrave Macmillan (2005)

38. 《艾格尼丝·史沫特莱生平》Ruth Price, The Lives of Agnes Smedley. Oxford University Press (2005)

39. 《现代中国的先驱：了解神秘的中国》Lee Khoon Choy, *Pioneers of Modern China: Understanding the Inscrutable Chinese*. World Scientific Publishing Company (2005)

40. 《马海德：美国医生在中国的传奇》Sidney Shapiro（沙博理）, *Ma Haide: The Saga of American Doctor George Hatem in China*. Cypress Book Co. (1993)；Foreign Languages Press, China (2004)

41. 《合肥四姐妹》Annping Chin（金安平）, *Four Sisters of Hofei: A History*. Scribner (2004)

42. 《一个人的帮派：红卫兵回忆》Fan Shen, *Gang of One: Memoirs of a Red Guard*. American Lives (2004)

43. 《圆满：一个加拿大学者的中国情怀》Ruth Hayhoe（许美德）, *Full Circle: A Life with Hong Kong & China*. Women's Press, Toronto (2004)

44. 《设计共产主义中国：一个人的故事》You-Li Sun, Dan Ling, *Engineering Communist China: One Man's Story*. Algora Publishing (2003)

45. 《中国之友：路易·艾黎的神话》Anne-Mari Brady, *Friend of China: The Myth of Rewi*

Alley. RoutledgeCurzon (2003)

46. 《华人世界秩序中的权力与身份：王赓武教授纪念文集》Billy K. L. So (ed.), *Power and Identity in the Chinese World Order: Festschrift in Honour of Professor Wang Gungwu*. Hong Kong University Press (2003)

47. 《我方的历史》Chin Peng（陈平）Ian Ward, Norma Miraflor, *My Side of History*. Media Masters (2003)

48. 《艺术流亡：丰子恺的一生（1898—1975）》Geremie R. Barmé, *An Artistic Exile: A Life of Feng Zikai (1898—1975)*. University of California Press (2002)

49. 《幕后之人：李敦白传》Sidney Rittenberg, Amanda Bennett, Mike Wallace, Michael Hunt, *The Man Who Stayed Behind*. Duke University Press (2001)

50. 《中国与我：部分自传》Emily Hahn（项美丽）, *China to Me: A Partial Autobiography*. E-Rights Ltd (1999)

51. 《红屋三十年：共产党中国的童年和青年回忆》Zhu Xiao Di（朱小棣）, *Thirty Years in a Red House: A Memoir of Childhood and Youth in Communist China*. University of Massachusetts Press (1998)

52. 《来自中国的国际象棋冠军：谢军的生活和比赛》Xie Jun, *Chess champion from China: the life and games of Xie Jun*. Gambit (1998)

53. 《蚕丝：钱学森传》Iris Chang（张纯如）, *Thread of the Silkworm*. Basic Books (1996)

54. 《大冒险时期：埃德加·斯诺在中国》S. Bernard Thomas, *Season of High Adventure: Edgar Snow in China*. Berkeley: University of California Press (1996)

55. 《九层天堂与九层地狱：一位中国高尚者的试验史（陈永贵传）》William Hinton（韩丁）, with Qin Huailu and Dusanka Miscevic, *Ninth Heaven to Ninth Hell: The History of a Noble Chinese Experiment*. Barricade Books (1995)

56. 《川岛芳子》Lilian Lee（李碧华）, *The Last Princess of Manchuria*. William Morrow & Co. (1994)

57. 《名望之山：中国历史名人录》John E., Jr. Wills, *Mountain of Fame: Portraits in Chinese History*. Princeton University Press (1994)

58. 《美国医生马海德在中国的传奇》Sidney Shapiro（沙博理）, *Ma Haide: The Saga of American Doctor George Hatem in China*. Cypress Book Co. (1993)

59. 《一滴泪》Ningkun Wu（巫宁坤）, Yikai Li（李怡楷）, *A Single Tear: A Family's Persecution, Suffering, Love and Endurance in Communist China*. Hodder & Stoughton Ltd (1993)

60. 《伍廷芳（1842—1922）：近代中国历史的改革与现代化》Linda Pomerantz, *Wu Tingfang (1842—1922): Reform and Modernization in Modern Chinese History*. Hong Kong University Press (1992)

61. 《寸金：格蕾丝·塞维斯中国回忆录》John S. Service (ed.), *Golden Inches: The China Memoir of Grace Service*. Berkeley: University of California Press (1989)

62. 《艾格尼丝·史沫特莱传》Janice R. Mackinnon, Stephen R. MacKinnon, *Agnes Smedley*. University of California Press (1988)

63. 《上海生死劫》Nien Cheng（郑念）, *Life and Death in Shanghai*. Grove Press (1986)

64. 《浮生六记》(Penquin Classics) Shen Fu, Leonard Pratt, Chiang Su-Hui, *The Recollections of a 17th Century Aimless Drifter & Chronic Philanderer in Qing China: Six Records of a Floating Life*.Penguin Group USA (1983)

65. 《中国学习者：路易·艾黎生平》Willis Airey, *A learner in China: A Life of Rewi Alley*. Caxton Press (1970)

66. 《近代中国的改革家：张謇（1853—1926）》Samuel C. Chu, *Reformer in Modern China: Chang Chien, 1853—1926*. Columbia University Press (1965)

67. 《逃离红色中国》Robert Loh, Humphrey Evans, *Escape from Red China*. Coward-McCann, Inc. New York (1962)

68. 《儿时琐忆》Yee Chiang, *A Chinese Childhood*. John Day Company (1953)

69. 《孔子的女儿：个人历史》Wong Su Ling, Earl Herbert Cressy, *Daughter of Confucius: A Personal History*. Farrar, Straus and Young: New York (1952)

70. 《中国伟人列传》Helena Kuo（郭镜秋）, *Giants of China*. The P. T. I. Book Depot (1947)

71. 《我在中国25年》John B. Powell, *My Twenty Five Years in China*. The Macmillan Company (1945)

72. 《飞离中国》Edna Lee Booker, *Flight From China*. The Macmillan Company (1945)

73. 《我的中国岁月（1926—1941）》Hallett Abend, *My life in China: 1926 to 1941*. Harcourt Brace and Company (1943)

74. 《容闳自传：西学东渐记》Wing Yung, *My Life in China and America*. New York: Henry Holt and Co. (1909)

75. 《一个美国工程师在中国》William Barclay Parsons（柏生士）, *An American Engineer in China*. New York: McClure, Phillips and Co. (1900)

76. 《戈登在中国》E. A. Lyster (ed.), *With Gordon in China: Letters from Thomas Lyster, Lieutenant Royal Engineers*.T. Fisher Unwin (1891)

77. 《约翰·昆西·亚当斯生平回忆录》Josiah Quincy, *Memoir of the Life of John Quincy Adams*. Boston: Crosby, Nichols, Lee and Company (1860)

78. 《中国已故道光皇帝生平》Karl Friedrich August Gützlaff, *The life of Taou-Kwang, late Emperor of China; with memoirs of the court of Peking; including a sketch of the principal events in the history of the Chinese empire*.Smith, Elder and co. (1852)

79. 《最近的中国监禁叙事》John Lee Scott, *Narrative of a Recent Imprisonment in China after the Wreck of the Kite*. Cambridge University Press (1841)

12.2.2 皇后传略

1. 《武曌皇帝与其万神殿》N. Harry Rothschild, *Emperor Wu Zhao and Her Pantheon of*

Devis, Divinities, and Dynastic Mothers (Empress of China Wu hou, Sheng Yen series in Chinese Buddhist studies). Columbia University Press (2015)

2. 《慈禧：开启现代中国的皇太后》Jung Chang（张戎）, *Empress Dowager Cixi: The Concubine Who Launched Modern China*. Knopf (2013)

3. 《西太后统治下的中国：慈禧的生平与时代》J. O. P. Bland, Edmund Trelawny Backhouse, Derek Sandhaus, *China under the Empress Dowager: The History of the Life and Times of Tzu Hsi*. Earnshaw Books (2011)

4. 《慈禧太后》X. L. Woo, *Empress Dowager Cixi: China's Last Dynasty and the Long Reign of a Formidable Concubine: Legends and Lives during the Declining Days of the Qing Dynasty*. Algora Publishing (2003)

5. 《最后的女皇》Keith Laidler, *The Last Empress: The She-Dragon of China*. Wiley (2003)

6. 《慈禧外传/慈禧统治下的中国/慈禧外记》J. O. P. Bland（濮兰德）, E. Backhouse, *China under the Empress Dowager: Being the History of the Life and Times of Tzu Hsi, Compiled from the State Papers and the Private Diary of the Comptroller of Her Household*. London William Heineman (1910)

致　谢

　　本书是作者2017—2018年度受国家留学基金委资助,在美国丹佛大学做访问学者期间,利用美国高校和科研机构所收藏的有关当代中国研究的部分文献资料,进行收集、整理和翻译的一项初步成果。

　　本书得以完成,首先要特别感谢张西平教授、侯且岸教授,是他们的悉心指导,引领我走上海外汉学/中国学研究的道路。还要感谢北京外国语大学国际中国文化研究院的各位领导和同事,尤其是梁燕教授、顾钧教授、任大援教授、黄丽娟教授、李真副教授、孙健副教授、张西艳副教授、谢明光博士、谢辉副研究员、张明明博士、姜丹老师、牟琴老师、周健老师等各位同人的关心支持。感谢北京语言大学阎纯德教授,中国社会科学院何培忠研究员、唐磊研究员,华东师范大学萧延中教授,北京联合大学梁怡教授、刘文忠教授、周文华教授,北京行政学院韦磊副教授、刘汉峰副教授,燕山大学李晔教授,郑州师范学院郭磊教授等师友的大力帮助。

　　感谢美国丹佛大学美中合作中心主任赵穗生教授,美国纽约皇后图书馆劳雷尔顿(Laurelton)分馆馆长王小良教授,美国加州大学洛杉矶分校(UCLA)东亚图书馆馆长陈肃教授,美国哥伦比亚大学东亚图书馆馆长王成志教授,美国卡特中心中国项目主任刘亚伟教授。感谢韩国明知大学姜允玉教授,韩国加图立关东大学李奎泰教授,印度国际大学中国学院院长阿伟杰特教授,西班牙马德里康普顿斯大学罗慧玲博士。

　　感谢我在美国访学期间的诸位好友:薛永基、薛晓斌、周五香、柯文秀、张小庆、刘增明、吕慧娟、程波辉、陶岚、史学斌、熊洁、余一凡、万璐、张德峰、郭子瑜、李玉敏、任会芬……

　　感谢多年来给予我无私帮助和支持的领导和师友,他们是李顺和、李保平、胡国顺、杨天增、高增、程传江、宫新平、宫宏林、刘合存、李淑芬、陈娟、陈发印、肖清志、孙凯、张瑛等。

　　感谢北外国际中国文化研究院的研究生郭玉红、余倩虹、宋逸鸥、刘乐艺、尹丽、侯一菲、耿瑞敏、张天皓、闫畅、司君琪、李乐男等同学，在资料收集和整理方面的付出。

感谢本书的两位责任编辑潘占伟老师和李媛老师，感谢他们的认真严谨态度和出色的编辑工作，为本书的付梓出版付出了大量心血。

最后，还要感谢我的爱人陈菊英女士，在工作之余承担起全部家庭事务，使我能够得以全身心投入学术研究和教学工作中；儿子管梓壮，在美国读书期间帮忙查阅英文资料，补充了本书的部分缺憾。

本书只是一个阶段性的初步成果，资料还不够全面，尤其是一些代表性的著作难免遗漏，分类和翻译一定还有很多不完善之处，敬请专家同人批评指正。

管永前

2021年7月8日